Whitton

Al McNeely '90

R·B·Bennett

Woodsworth

Tim Buck

Steve Brodie
(Bloody Sunday)

The Great Depression

The Great

"The historian of the future, when he writes about Canada and the Great Depression, will comment upon the remarkable ineptitude of Canadian public men when faced with this emergency. He will write of the obstinate refusal of governments to face realities; of their pitiful and tragic tactics of 'passing the buck' to one another; and of their childish expectation that providence, or some power external to themselves, would come to their rescue and save them from the consequences of their refusal to look into the future, foresee events that loomed black in the sky, plain to be seen, and take such steps as were possible to mitigate the fury of the storm. The severity of the condemnation will be measured by the extent of the power which was not used and the responsibility that was denied."

—Winnipeg *Free Press*, March 18, 1933

Depression

1929–1939

By Pierre Berton

Canadian Cataloguing in Publication Data

Berton, Pierre, 1920–
  The Great Depression 1929–1939

ISBN 0-7710-1270-5

1. Depressions – 1929 – Canada. 2. Canada – Economic conditions – 1918-1945.* I. Title.

HC115.B47 1990   330.971′062   C90-093951-6

Endpapers by Tom McNeely
Maps by Jack McMaster

McClelland & Stewart Inc.
The Canadian Publishers
481 University Avenue
Toronto, Ontario
M5G 2E9

Printed and bound in Canada

Books by Pierre Berton

The Royal Family
The Mysterious North (1956), (1989)
Klondike (1958), (1972)
Just Add Water and Stir
Adventures of a Columnist
Fast, Fast, Fast Relief
The Big Sell
The Comfortable Pew
The Cool, Crazy, Committed World of the Sixties
The Smug Minority
The National Dream
The Last Spike
Drifting Home
Hollywood's Canada
My Country
The Dionne Years
The Wild Frontier
The Invasion of Canada
Flames Across the Border
Why We Act Like Canadians
The Promised Land
Vimy
Starting Out
The Arctic Grail
The Great Depression

PICTURE BOOKS
The New City (with Henri Rossier)
Remember Yesterday
The Great Railway
The Klondike Quest

ANTHOLOGIES
Great Canadians
Pierre and Janet Berton's Canadian Food Guide
Historic Headlines

FOR YOUNGER READERS
The Golden Trail
The Secret World of Og

FICTION
Masquerade (pseudonym Lisa Kroniuk)

Contents

Overview
The worst of times

Nobody could tell exactly when it began and nobody could predict when it would end. At the outset, they didn't even call it a depression. At worst it was a recession, a brief slump, a "correction" in the market, a glitch in the rising curve of prosperity. Only when the full import of those heartbreaking years sank in did it become the Great Depression – Great because there had been no other remotely like it and (please God!) there would never be anything like it again.

In retrospect, we see it as a whole – as a neat decade tucked in between the Roaring Twenties and the Second World War, perhaps the most significant ten years in our history, a watershed era that scarred and transformed the nation. But it hasn't been easy for later generations to comprehend its devastating impact. The Depression lies just over the hill of memory; after all, anyone who reached voting age in 1929 is over eighty today. There are not very many left who can remember what it was like to live on water for an entire day, as the Templeton family did in the Parkdale district of Toronto in 1932, or how it felt to own only a single dress – made of flour sacks – as Etha Munro did in the family farmhouse on the drought-ravaged Saskatchewan prairie in 1934.

The statistics of those times are appalling. At the nadir of the Depression, half the wage earners in Canada were on some form of relief. One Canadian in five was a public dependant. Forty per cent of those in the workforce had no skills; the average yearly income was less than five hundred dollars at a time when the poverty line for a family of four was estimated at more than twice that amount.

This army of the deprived was treated shabbily by a government that used words like "fiscal responsibility" and "a sound dollar" as excuses to ignore human despair. Balancing the budget was more important than feeding the hungry. The bogey of the deficit was enlisted to tighten the purse strings.

9

R.B. Bennett, who presided over the five worst years of the Depression, said he was determined to preserve the nation's credit "at whatever sacrifice." But the burden of that sacrifice did not fall on the shoulders of Bennett or his equally parsimonious opponent, Mackenzie King. It fell on those who, in spite of the politicians' assurances to the contrary, were starving and naked – on the little girl in Montreal who fainted one day in school because, as her teacher discovered, it wasn't her turn for breakfast that morning; on another little girl in Alberta who could go to school only on those days when it was her turn to wear "the dress"; on the Ottawa landlord who collapsed in the street from hunger because none of his tenants had been able to pay their rent; on the New Brunswick father who awoke one cold winter night in a house without fuel to check on his three-month-old baby, only to find her frozen to death.

The most shocking statistic of all reveals that the federal government from 1930 to 1936 spent more of the taxpayers' money to service the debt of the Canadian National Railways than it did to provide unemployment relief. That debt was the legacy of the great Canadian boom. The builders of the Canadian Northern and the Grand Trunk Pacific (not to mention the government's own National Transcontinental), revered as audacious and far-seeing captains of industry, left a questionable legacy. The bondholders enjoyed a free ride on the backs of the people. Where was "fiscal responsibility" then? Without that burden of debt the government could have doubled its relief payments to every family in Canada.

Had there been no railway debt, would either Mackenzie King or R.B. Bennett have taken that more generous route? One doubts it. Neither had any co-ordinated plan of relief. Like the business leaders who backed them, they were convinced the Depression couldn't last and so made no long-range plans to deal with the crisis. Planning, after all, was a dirty word in the thirties, a subversive notion that smacked of Soviet Russia.

Both the Liberal and the Conservative governments stumbled from crisis to crisis, adopting band-aid solutions that often became part of the problem. At every level of government the authorities attacked the symptoms and not the cause, trying vainly to hold down the lid on the bubbling kettle of protest. If single transients clog the streets of the big cities – get them out of sight.

10

If radicals demand a better deal for the jobless - jail them. If "foreigners" ask for relief - deport them. If farmers stage hunger strikes - disperse them with police billies. At no time did those in charge consider the practical advantages of allowing the dispossessed to let off steam unmolested.

Every level of government tried to evade its responsibilities for the unemployed. Ottawa washed its hands of the problem, as Ottawa often does, and tried to lay it on the provinces. The provinces tried to lay it on the municipalities. The municipalities tried to lay it on the local taxpayers, who couldn't cope with it because so many were themselves out of work. Then everybody - taxpayers, municipalities, and provinces - turned on Ottawa.

Relief was given grudgingly. The Calvinist work ethic belonged to an earlier century, but it lived on into the thirties. Conventional wisdom dictated that any healthy man could always find a job; that if he was idle, it was deliberate; that to ask for public charity was shameful; that those who got too much wouldn't want to work. Thus, it was held, relief should provide no more than the bare necessities and should never approach the level of "real" wages.

Bennett himself clung to this view and indicated more than once that the current generation of Canadians was "soft," that it lacked the rugged independence and the ability to make sacrifices of its forbears. That sounded incongruous coming from one of the richest men in Canada, who owed much of his wealth to a legacy. By Bennett's standards, anybody who applied for relief was a failure. Rather than endure this humiliation, thousands shunned the relief offices. In 1934, a United Church worker in central Manitoba discovered that many farm families were going without underwear or shoes for their children, who as a result couldn't attend school. All were entitled to relief, but they couldn't bring themselves to apply for it.

Families made do as long as possible before "going on the pogey," as the phrase had it. Houses went without repair, automobiles were allowed to wear out, clothing was patched, re-patched, and patched again before they would endure "the soul-searing shame of applying for relief."

That was the phrase that a Great War veteran, Victor Nelson Swanston, used in 1931 when he finally made the mortifying journey to the Regina relief office. He had no choice: he had been

11

laid off his auto assembly job. He had worked briefly as a harvest hand. But now his resources were spent, there was no food left in the house, and his wife was in tears.

Out came an inspector to make absolutely sure the family was destitute. He searched the empty cupboards, and he even opened the door of the oven to make sure the cunning Swanstons hadn't squirreled away any food. In the end, the family was given enough to eat.

To pay for his weekly groceries, Swanston was put to work digging ditches and cleaning Regina's streets. There were no rest periods because if the men stopped to smoke there was always an angry taxpayer rushing to phone the city works department to ask why these ne'er-do-wells weren't working. At school, the four Swanston children were jeered at. "Reliefers! Reliefers!" their schoolmates shouted. There was no hiding their shame; their daily free half-pint of milk gave their secret away.

The catastrophe that was visited upon the Swanston family fell unevenly across the country. The big cities were the worst off, led by Montreal; by 1932, a third of its people were on relief. The big Ontario cities were almost as badly hit, the rural areas less so. Farm dwellers, except in the drought country, could at least grow their own food. Prince Edward Island, one gigantic farm, had the lowest per capita relief costs in the country. If the Maritimes appeared to suffer less it was partly because they had always been in an economic slump, and, except in Cape Breton, there were fewer industries to close and throw people out of work. But nature devastated the West; by 1937, two-thirds of Saskatchewan's farmland had turned to desert. Outside the drought country, cities such as Winnipeg, Edmonton, and Calgary suffered the most. British Columbia, Canada's fastest-growing province, was almost as badly off, especially in Vancouver where a flourishing building boom quickly collapsed.

The checkerboard pattern of want in the Depression determined the political pattern in the years that followed. The Atlantic provinces remained faithful to the old-line parties while the West shoved them aside. Dissent, which had not flourished in the twenties, sparked half a dozen new political movements. People ceased to trust their traditional leaders, who had misled or even lied to them. In their search for a way out of the economic dilemma, some embraced new ideologies – communism, socialism,

12

fascism. Others were convinced that the country ought to be run by "experts" – a denial of democracy that appealed to those who espoused Howard Scott's Technocracy movement. The quest for a Messiah – scientific in the case of Scott, religious in the case of Frank Buchman, whose Oxford Group (and later Moral Rearmament) became another Depression fad – was a feature of the decade. Three new premiers – Aberhart of Alberta, Hepburn of Ontario, Duplessis of Quebec – were swept into office on populist platforms. All turned out to be authoritarians, perfectly prepared to trample on the rights of those who opposed them.

Canadians have always been a cautious people. The Depression made them more cautious than ever. The longing for security that brought family allowances, medicare, and unemployment insurance is still deep in the subconscious of the Depression generation. The children of those years cling to their jobs as a shipwrecked sailor clings to a raft. Three decades later, the adult world raised in the thirties would be baffled by what it saw as the irresponsibility of a new generation that thought nothing of quitting work, having a good time, and then casually seeking other employment. The Depression, it might be said, helped foster the generation gap of the sixties.

Lara Duffy, a Toronto housewife who was four years old when her father lost his job in 1932, has never been able to come to terms with her eldest daughter's spending sprees. "Money doesn't mean anything to her. I don't think she's looked at a price tag for years." She herself can't abide waste; she can't even bear to discard worn-out clothing, always finding somebody who can use it. "It's just impossible for me to waste things." Yet in some ways she is as unrestrained about spending as her daughter, and that too is a result of the Depression: "Sometimes I have too many of some things. It's a reaction: because you had nothing, now you have to have too much of what you were once deprived of." As a schoolgirl she had one pair of shoes. "Now I have lots of shoes; that seems to be something I have to do for me." To this day Mrs. Duffy cannot abide the taste of plum jam or sausages because that was the kind of cheap relief fare her family lived on during the Depression. For seven years her father was out of work, constantly and vainly seeking a job.

A steady job – that was the supreme goal of those whose youth was scarred and shaped by the thirties. It was something to struggle for, something to cling to. Men like Verdun Clark of Toronto were never afraid of hard work all their lives because they could remember the day when there was no work and no food. Born in 1916 and named for the bloodiest battle of the Great War, Clark was one of a family of five children deserted by their father, as so many were during those hard times. As a result, he was determined that what had happened to his family would never happen to his own children.

Clark could never forget the times when food was so scarce that he would go down to the St. Lawrence Market to shoot pigeons off the rafters so that his mother could make a pigeon pie for dinner. He could never forget the little store at the corner of Queen and Augusta where Cooper the butcher would cock an eye at him and ask: "How's your dog, Vern?" Both knew there was no dog, but Clark would reply with a straight face, "Not too bad." And Cooper would respond with an equally straight face, "I'd better give you a few bones. I'll give you some with a little meat on." There were thousands of Verdun Clarks in the thirties, living on soup made from scraps dispensed by sympathetic tradesmen. That's how people were in the Depression, generous in the midst of want. As Verdun Clark would often remark, years later, "They aren't like the people today. There's no comparison. No comparison."

And so Verdun Clark, who was just thirteen when the Depression began, worked hard all his life and is proud of it. "I have *worked*. I don't think I ever had a job that was only eight hours a day. I worked for fifty-six years. I never lost a day's work in all those years. I was determined that I would never lose my family. I would work twenty hours a day if necessary to overcome it; which I did. The Depression helped me because it gave me that determination that I had to go ahead and work."

The Depression also played havoc with *laissez-faire*. For the first time, Canadians began to realize that government *must* interfere in the private affairs of the nation. The Canadian Wheat Board, the Bank of Canada, the Canadian Broadcasting Corporation, and Trans-Canada Airlines were among the public corporations born of those hungry years. Anyone who advocated today's social services in the pre-Depression era would have been considered a dangerous radical – and, in truth, some were. But the hard times changed people's outlook.

14

Yet for a good many Canadians there were no hard times. For those who held a decent job, the thirties was a wonderful period. Because of deflation, everything got cheaper. A single man making fifty dollars a month wasn't exactly on Easy Street, but he wasn't poor either. He could buy a hamburger for a dime. He could take his girl to dinner and a movie for two dollars; he could buy a tailored suit with two pairs of pants for twenty.

Bruce Hutchison, then a young political reporter for the Vancouver *Province*, married, with two children, lived comfortably even when his wages were cut from fifty-five to fifty dollars a week. His standard of living actually rose as prices fell. "We always had a maid in the house, the best food in our stomachs, two second-hand cars in the garage, and in our minds the smug, bogus security of the fortunate. It never occurred to me that we were well off . . . ."

Thousands of Canadians lived as Hutchison did, breezing through the hard times without a care. For them the Depression was a blur; the shabby men selling shoelaces on the street corners were as foreign as Laplanders, the newspaper headlines about hunger marches and jobless riots as far removed as those from Ethiopia, China, and Spain. They gambolled their way through the decade, fox-trotting to the clarinets of Goodman and Shaw, or speeding down the quiet country lanes in their Packard Straight Eights. For them, the memories of the thirties evoked a different set of symbols – Monopoly games, miniature golf, the "candid camera," Knock-Knock jokes.

One member of this favoured company recalled those times with nostalgia and affection thirty years later in an interview with *Maclean's*. "You could take your girl to a supper dance at the hotel for $10," he remembered, "and that included a bottle and a room for you and your friends to drink it in."

Ten dollars was a great deal of money in 1935 – a year in which department store seamstresses found they had to work evenings to earn the minimum weekly wage of $12.50. But for others it was a pittance.

"I'm glad I grew up then. It was a good time for everybody. People learned what it means to work," said John David Eaton.

1929

1

For most people, the Depression began on that manic morning of *The*
October 29, to be known forever as Black Tuesday, when the easy, *Great*
buoyant era of the twenties – the roaring, turbulent, high-flying *Repression*
twenties – came to a dead stop. Yet those fevered October days
were no more than symptoms of a deeper malady, undiagnosed
and untreated.

The germs were already there in the hot, dry summer of 1929,
when the crops began to fail on the southern prairies and the
boom ran wild and out of hand and the country continued to
overbuild on borrowed funds. The Great Depression was beginning and nobody knew it. The Great Repression was already
under way but nobody cared. One did not need to visit Munich to
see dissidents beaten to the ground. It was happening here.

In the decade that followed – the hungry, the dirty, the sad,
shameful, mean-spirited thirties – the image of a policeman's
truncheon bringing a shabbily dressed man to his knees would
become familiar. Human rights and civil liberties were of no
more concern to the average Canadian, struggling to make ends
meet, than to the average German. It is appalling to recall that
under the vagrancy laws it was a crime to be poor and homeless
in 1929. But scarcely anybody gave that a thought; in those heady
days, anybody who wanted a job could get one. If you didn't work
you were a bum, and if the police caught you and hauled you off a
freight train, you went to jail – and good riddance. But the day
was coming when two million people would be bums, when the
freight trains would be jammed with homeless men, when the
jails would be bursting with "vagrants," and when some who
protested these conditions would be branded dangerous subver-
sives and packed off to the penitentiary.

That day, in fact, had already arrived. The events of August 13
in Toronto – another Black Tuesday, though nobody called it that
– were as much a curtain raiser for the decade to come as the
market crash that followed ten weeks later.

We can glimpse the opening skirmish in this bloody affair
through the shocked eyes of a twenty-two-year-old bystander,
John Morgan Gray, who in the post-war years would become a
major literary figure as president of the Macmillan Company of

Canada. On that balmy summer evening, Gray had decided to stroll over to Queen's Park with a few friends from a nearby University of Toronto fraternity house. The park, a grass-covered, tree-shaded square behind the Parliament Buildings, provided one of the few green spaces in the downtown core and was thus a favourite with Torontonians, who liked to take short cuts across it, or listen to concerts in the bandstand, or take their ease on the park benches to observe the passing show. The passing show that night promised to be special. The communists were planning a rally, and the police had announced that they would break it up. Gray was a graduate of Upper Canada College and the University of Toronto, but in spite of his education and a recent sojourn in Europe, he knew nothing of international politics. He and his friends had walked over out of curiosity, to watch the fun and see "what wild Communists looked like."

The wild communists, it turned out, looked disappointingly commonplace. Gray spotted them at the south end of the park, an unimpressive group of about sixty people, some with children, making their way toward the bandstand. As Gray described them, "they looked both ordinary and harmless, not remotely dangerous to the city or the country as a whole."

Nothing interesting was happening or seemed about to happen. From his vantage point, about a hundred yards away, Gray couldn't tell whether or not anyone was speaking. There was no cheering, only "a kind of irresolute shifting about in the little crowd."

And then suddenly, like an explosion, scores of police, some on horseback, some on motorcycles with sidecars, burst from the bushes that partially screened the Parliament Buildings and drove straight at the little group, oblivious to the crowd of spectators, who scrambled or stumbled out of the way.

What followed shocked and sickened Gray. Near the end of his life, when he wrote his memoirs, the spectacle that he had witnessed remained seared on his mind. The little group tried at first to hold together as though to confront their attackers. That, of course, was impossible, for they had no weapons, not even a stick or a stone. They broke and fled in a dozen directions before the police onslaught, so that the park became the scene of a dozen small skirmishes.

20

One man came racing across the park directly toward Gray. A motorcycle officer saw him and roared after him. He tried desperately to escape, dodging between the trees, but the motorcycle followed every move until the victim tripped and fell. In an instant the policeman in the sidecar was out, kicking his victim brutally as he tried to get up. At last he simply lay on the grass, "trying to cover his head, and crying out as his body recoiled under the heavy boot."

We ask, sometimes, why the German bystanders did not interfere when the Brownshirts beat up the Jews, but deep down we know the answer. As Gray wrote, "I suppose we all had some impulse to intervene, to try to stop this cruel nonsense, but we didn't. We weren't after all on the wretched man's side, except that each of us could feel the boot in his guts. Instead, we turned away sickened as the broken man was stood up and led away for questioning. For a while we were moody and thoughtful, ashamed perhaps that we had not even tried to help a fellow human, shocked at the picture of a hard world beyond our experience. But presently we were playing cards and singing around the piano, and in a day or two this glimpse of *real-politik* remained only as a trace that would surface less and less often as time passed."

The man whom Gray saw being chased and beaten was probably Jack MacDonald, the black-browed leader of the Communist party, who had been billed in advance as the speaker of the evening. The new police chief, Denny Draper, hated all communists and was determined to snuff out the party. When they tried to hire a hall, he stopped them. When they applied for permission to hold an outdoor meeting, he refused. Thus the Queen's Park rally was technically illegal, and MacDonald, who carefully removed his glasses and thrust them into his pocket when the police erupted onto the square, knew exactly what to expect. "I haven't even said a word, boys," he shouted as two officers seized him.

In short, the illegal rally hadn't officially begun. That didn't matter to the police. MacDonald was struck in the face, kicked from behind, knocked down, and kicked again and again. "For God's sake," he cried, the tears running down his cheeks. "Don't kick me!" He broke away twice, and it was probably at this point that Gray saw him zigzagging across the park before his final capture.

From the Estevan riot of 1931 to the Vancouver post office strike of 1938, the grey years of the Depression would be marked by police overkill. The prelude to these bloodier events was the Queen's Park "riot" of August 1929. The Toronto police made no attempt to distinguish between communists, sympathizers, and ordinary bystanders. All were treated as the enemy. One youth was manhandled for daring to question the assault. "Give it to them!" a policeman shouted. "They're all yellow." Others cried, "Get out and stay out! Get back to Russia!"

And so Joe Winkle, strolling through the park to watch a lawn-bowling tournament, was struck in the face by a detective's fist. Edward Smith was told to get out of the park but before he could move was hammered three or four times by a policeman's billy. Montagu Kellaway, a war veteran who, like Smith, didn't move fast enough, suffered a cracked jaw. William Godfrey, who had dined with his sisters, was taking a short cut home when a police-man kicked him from behind. When he tried to protest, the policeman shouted, "Go back to Moscow!" and hit him across the mouth. As for Meyer Klig, who wasn't an innocent bystander and was known to the police as a party member, he received a twenty-minute drubbing with rubber truncheons in the privacy of the Parliament Buildings.

It would be heartening to believe that this nightmarish attack was an inexplicable departure from the accepted rules of law and behaviour, an unexpected burst of pent-up emotion after a long summer's day. It was nothing of the sort. It was planned with cold-blooded precision and carried out in the presence of the chief, Denny Draper, himself. And it was only one of a series of similar incidents that had the approval of the mayor, the police commission, and three of the city's four dailies – the *Toronto Daily Star* being the exception, as it generally was in such atrocities. The usual establishment attitude was summed up in the *Globe*'s approving editorial the following morning: "SEND THE BOLSHEVIKS BACK."

The press insisted on terming the incident a "riot," a peculiar name for an eruption of savagery that was planned and carried out by constituted authority. "Riot" would become the euphemism of the Depression, applied to any parade, demonstration, rally, or work stoppage that brought out the police and threatened the established order. There would be quite literally hundreds of these so-called riots in the turbulent decade that followed. In one year alone – 1934 – forty-three were serious enough to make the pages of the Toronto newspapers.

Labour groups, churches, and ordinary citizens were outraged by the action of the police that August. There were the usual calls for an inquiry and the usual replies that none was needed. And yet, over the months that followed, the feeling began to grow that something was wrong, that the system was out of kilter, that the social order wasn't working. Only the communists were demanding radical change, and they made few converts. It's one of the ironies of those times that the incidents they provoked, as the Depression deepened, did not benefit them politically. What they did do was to arouse the collective conscience of the academic elite. It was the university professors, many of them committed Christians, who would eventually take action against repression and lay the groundwork for the modern welfare state. It was the police who forced them into it.

2

It is easy enough to look back on that buoyant and carefree *The* summer of 1929 and ask why nobody saw trouble ahead. The *legacy* signs were clear The country was heavily overbuilt, the export *of* market was fragile, wheat prices were falling, the stock market *optimism* was impossibly high, and unemployment was rising. No one appeared to notice. The Canadians of those times seem to us to have been dancing blindfold on the lip of a precipice. They lolled in their summer cottages playing cheerful melodies – "Happy Days Are Here Again," "Keep Your Sunny Side Up" – on scratchy gramophones. They flocked to the new talkies to see *Disraeli*, with George Arliss, or the aptly named *Gold Diggers of Broadway.* They listened to "The Goldbergs" on their Atwater-Kents and gobbled up the new murder mysteries by Dashiell Hammett and Ellery Queen. Those who had money – and some who didn't – took a flyer on the stock market and exulted over their paper profits. Some – Lottie Nugent, a thirty-year-old Toronto office worker, was one – invested every cent they had and fully expected to grow rich.

Lottie Nugent, the head bookkeeper at Monarch Brass in Toronto, bought on margin, as most people did. She took her life savings of three thousand dollars and used that to make small down payments on six stocks, expecting to be able to repay the balance out of profits when the stocks rose. Why should she worry? After all, her broker was her boyfriend.

Why should anyone worry? The politicians, the leading businessmen, the journalists, and every reputable banker had been forecasting that the boom would go on. On New Year's Day, the nation was assaulted by an avalanche of predictably optimistic messages from sober business leaders of the stamp of Edward Beatty, president of the CPR, who said he'd never seen the country looking better, or S.J. Moore, president of the Bank of Nova Scotia, who predicted that "an unprecedented period of prosperity" lay ahead. The bankers confined a growing sense of unease to no more than a whisper in the fine print of their annual reports because, as one put it, "the counsels of caution have little honour with the speculative public."

The politicians and the journalists had no qualms, and this was especially true in Western Canada, which would suffer the greatest blows from the Depression. John Brownlee, Premier of Alberta, declared that "at no time since the formation of the provinces have conditions, both in Alberta and Canada, been more auspicious." But Brownlee's party, the United Farmers of Alberta, would be wiped out by the economic disaster that followed. Perhaps the most jubilant editorial appeared in the New Year's edition of the Regina *Leader*: "We believe that there is also a . . . greater measure of brotherhood, also a greater charitableness, than existed in the world a twelvemonth back. The finer things of life are steadily winning new appreciation and new devotion." Charity and brotherhood would soon be in short supply when Regina teetered on the edge of bankruptcy and police bullets wounded jobless protesters in the streets.

To those of us who look back across the twentieth century at 1929 and who have seen later recessions come and go and cycles of drought appear and vanish, this mindless optimism seems incredible. But Canada had just come through some thirty-five

24

years of unparalleled prosperity, interrupted only by the Great War and a mild slump in the early twenties. Laurier's famous remark about Canada's Century was on everybody's lips, and with good reason. From 1896 to 1912 the boom had roared on, fuelled by an unprecedented immigration explosion. During that first heady decade, as one million immigrants poured off the colonist cars to populate the empty prairies, enthusiastic magazine articles and newspaper features had underscored Laurier's prediction.

Canadians were a cocky lot in the twenties. Certainly the Great War had exacted a sobering toll, but the country could not help being intoxicated by the successes of the Canadian Corps, symbolized by the remarkable victory at Vimy Ridge. Now a full-fledged member of the League of Nations, Canada was emerging from colonial status as a result of the Balfour Declaration of 1924, which promised eventual autonomy. We were a *nation*. We had come of age. The Twentieth Century belonged to us.

Oddly, and ironically, the proud process of nation building contributed to the economic disaster that followed. Greed and over-optimism cost Canada dear. The country was a victim of its own ambitions. We were so ecstatic over the triumph and success of the first Pacific railway that we went railway mad. One railway wasn't enough; we had to build *three* – an extravagant and wasteful venture. The new lines often ran parallel to one another even in long stretches of unproductive land. When the railway craze ended and the new railways went broke, the government was forced to take them over. But it was the taxpayers and not the bondholders who were saddled with the crushing debt of the hybrid CNR.

Canada was in hock to strangers. Almost half the public debt and four-fifths of the private debt were in foreign hands. The West was built on borrowed money. Everything from new towns to family farms was mortgaged at interest rates that would remain fixed when wages and prices tumbled. Yet the day was coming when deflation would bump up the real rate of interest from 6 per cent to 10 per cent.

Nobody worried about that. The railway binge was followed by another building binge – railway stations and hotels, skyscrapers and factories. In 1927, to the hosannas of the people of Toronto, the golden-haired heir to the throne had, at last, opened the

Union Station, that granite and marble temple to the age of steel and steam. Now, in 1929, Torontonians were boasting that they had the largest hotel and also the tallest building in the British Empire, which really meant the tallest building in Canada, since the rest of the empire had yet to be seduced by the North American craze for skyscrapers. The changing skylines of Canadian cities hinted at prosperity and progress. A new Hotel Vancouver was rising on the West Coast, while the fashionable Empress in Victoria and the equally fashionable Chateau Laurier in Ottawa had expanded with luxurious new wings. The Royal Bank opened its splendid new head office in Montreal. The Toronto *Star* got itself a skyscraper; Eaton's built a new art-deco store on College Street, just a block from the future site of the new temple to hockey that Conn Smythe was planning.

The building boom went too far. After the stagnant war years manufacturers scrambled to put up new plants to boost productivity through new devices and to build fat inventories. By the summer of 1929 the country was stuck with a surfeit of goods nobody wanted. The boom had distorted the employment situation. When construction stopped, jobs vanished. Even before the crash, Canadian unemployment figures were rising. Investment in an overdeveloped, overstocked country made little sense, and speculative money started to dry up. But spending increased. The automobile had touched off another orgy of expansion. New roads had to be built on borrowed money, new suburban homes financed with mortgage loans. Dazzled by prosperity, people were spending more and saving less, living beyond their means on the instalment plan.

John A. Macdonald's National Policy, which had worked so well in the nineteenth century, was outdated. Build a railway to the Pacific, Macdonald had decided; use it to populate the West, to haul wheat to the seaports, to carry Eastern manufactured goods, protected by high tariffs, to the settlers. But the railways were overbuilt, the good land was gone, the immigration flow was down to a trickle, the Eastern goods cost too much because of the tariff, and the foreign markets were drying up. Every nation was taking the high tariff route, halting the international flow of goods and resources.

Canada lived – thrived – on its exports, chiefly wheat and newsprint and to a lesser extent hydroelectric power and base metals.

26

If foreigners didn't want to buy these natural resources, the country was in jeopardy because there weren't enough Canadians to consume them. The West provided the world with 40 per cent of its wheat, but by 1929 the wheat economy was in trouble, partly because of the drought but also because the wheat pools, which collected and marketed the farmers' grain, refused to believe the signs and portents from abroad. The Europeans had recovered from the war and were growing their own wheat. The price dropped, but the pools held back, hoping for bigger profits, even though the elevators were bursting with unsold grain. Once again greed and optimism were Canada's undoing. Her former customers turned to Australia and Argentina, and Canada, in spite of the poor crop in 1929, was stuck with a glut of grain.

The pulp and paper industry had also been seduced by good times, overexpanding blindly and at a terrifying rate. In the twenties, production doubled but the price tumbled from eighty-two to sixty-two dollars a ton. And there was only one major customer, the United States, which bought 90 per cent of the output. If the U.S. economy faltered, Canada was in trouble.

Though few realized it, the country was in a precarious position. Canada's export trade accounted for a quarter of her gross national product, and so she was at the whim of an international buyer's market. If the Americans stopped buying automobiles, the country would be stuck with unsaleable base metals. And when Spain, Portugal, and Italy put a high tariff on imported dried cod, Atlantic fishermen would suffer.

The impact of the Depression on Canada was compounded by a fickleness of nature that seemed to have been ordained on high. The setting was that vast triangle of land that takes its name from Captain John Palliser, an explorer sent out by the British government in 1857 to assess the agricultural potential of the soil. Palliser turned in a gloomy report. A triangle of arid plains, he wrote, extended from the Waterton Lakes in Alberta to what is now Boissevain, Manitoba, having its apex at the 52nd parallel of latitude, the site of the modern city of Saskatoon. In most of this huge area he considered farming to be impossible. He wrote of short grass that formed no turf, tracts of loose sand and stiff clay baked under "the influence of early spring into a hard cracked surface, that resists germination of seeds." The farmers of the thirties would have reason to sympathize with Palliser, whose

27

expedition had experienced "great inconvenience" in traversing the triangle "from want of wood, water and grass."

Palliser had seen the prairies at their worst. Unfortunately, an amateur botanist, John Macoun, saw them at their best when he visited the area in the 1870s. The triangle, he kept insisting, was "the Garden of the whole country." His bubbling and misplaced enthusiasm helped convince the CPR to change its route and take the line through the very country that Palliser had condemned.

The truth lay somewhere between Palliser's sour indictment and Macoun's rosy vision. The great central plain of North America is never far from desert conditions at any time. A change of two inches of rainfall can cause a crop failure. The wet winds from the Pacific, spilling their moisture on the western slopes of the mountains, sweep hot and dry across the southern prairie. This is really ranching country, but the overflow of immigrants, unable to get better farms farther north, invaded it during the first decade of the century, and broke it with the plough. When the rains dwindled, the light soil was reduced to a fine dust that would eventually blow across the plains in clouds so thick they blackened the sky.

Memories were fickle on the southern prairies. The original settlers, who had exchanged their sod huts for substantial farm houses, tended to remember the early years when the rain was plentiful and crops were good. They dismissed the cycle of drought that had lasted from 1917 to 1921. The rain came back, and for most of the twenties the golden fields brought prosperity. The harvest was so great in 1928 that one hundred million bushels of wheat were still in storage the following year, when the drought returned and the size of the crop was cut by 40 per cent.

Few worried. The pools and the farmers believed that the problem was temporary. Vernon Knowles of the Toronto *Mail and Empire*, after an 1,800-mile trip through the dry belt in August, played down the drought in a seven-part series of articles that stressed the "buoyant confidence of the farmers." The paper summed it up in a cheerful lead paragraph: "The writer has drawn a bright picture of acres of Canadian prairie too firmly started on the road to prosperity to be seriously retarded by one poor harvest."

Clifford Sifton's Manitoba Free Press Company was too shrewd to believe the Eastern financial community would swal-

28

low this hucksterism without the reassurance of the Voice of the West. It took an advertisement in the Montreal *Gazette* that fall to express its optimism over "prevailing good business conditions." The ad insisted that "the farmer will not be the stranded, financially pinched and close-fisted figure that has been pictured to us so many times during this trying year. . . . The crop is in and everybody looks forward to another great year of Western expansion."

In short, the press proclaimed that the dry season of 1929 was an aberration. Had the Westerners studied the rainfall cycle of the Palliser Triangle that optimism might have been muted. Within two years the dry-belt farmers would be more than stranded and financially pinched. They would be down and out.

3

That fall, a kind of smug self-satisfaction had settled over the *Crash!* country. It was fashionable in some circles to look down one's nose at American mores. This was the year of the St. Valentine's Day Massacre in Chicago. It couldn't happen here, people said; Canada would never nurture an Al Capone. As for the vulgar radio programs that were leaking across the border, Canada had an answer to that. The Aird Royal Commission had advocated a nationally owned, un-commercial broadcasting system organized along British lines.

This was the year that the last frontiers were conquered from the air. In 1929 Punch Dickins, the Canadian bush pilot, reached the Arctic in a Fokker Super Universal; Richard Byrd crossed the South Pole in a Ford Tri-motor; the marvellous *Graf Zeppelin* circled the world – feats that seemed to herald a shining future that every Canadian could enjoy, thanks to the wheat glut in the West and the booming stock market in the East.

The stock market was fuelled by borrowed cash. Shares could be bought from brokers for as little as 10 per cent of their value. Brokers, using the shares as collateral, borrowed the purchase money for their clients in the "call market." Nobody minded the high interest rates because the value of the stocks was soaring. If the stock went down, however, and the loans were called, the brokers would demand more margin – more cash – from their clients. Otherwise, the shares would have to be sold so that the brokers could raise enough money to cover the debt they had contracted.

In the first two months of the year, the stock profits were astronomical – on paper. In January you could buy a hundred shares of Home Oil for $350 with a down payment of less than $50 and sell them in March for $1,575. You could buy Royalite at $65 and sell it for $200, Okalta at $30 and sell it for more than $300. But hardly anybody sold, because everybody believed stock prices would continue to rise. And for another six months they did.

Only a minority of Canadians plunged into the market, but those who did became obsessed to the point of mania. R.J. Manion, a future leader of the Tory party, who visited the Toronto exchange that year, was shocked "at the strained and anxious expression on the faces of the crowds . . . as they watched with excited intensity the gyrations of the stock prices." Manion wondered if everybody wasn't in some way intoxicated by the gambling spirit in the air, which was "having a thoroughly demoralizing effect upon the masses of the people." The faces, he noted, were not the habitual poker faces of the professional gamblers but often "worried, frightened . . . the harassed and tortured expressions of men who are driven by the get-rich-quick passion prevalent in such times."

It is easy to look back and ask: why didn't they take their profits out and sell before it was too late? But again, optimism and greed overruled prudence. Why should anybody sell when the supposed experts were urging them to buy? In July, the *Financial Post* took an informal survey of the country's leading brokers and investment bankers that "failed to reveal any person who is pronouncedly pessimistic as to the future." Indeed, how could any of these admit that they doubted the value of the stocks they were busily hustling to the public?

On September 3 two Canadian oil stocks, Imperial and British American, went through the roof to score record highs. The following day the Dow Jones average in New York hit the highest point in its history. Nobody, with the possible exception of the white-goateed Roger Babson, a noted statistician, realized that it had reached an all-time peak. The next day Babson predicted "a stock market crash, which will rival the collapse of the Florida

30

land boom." Hardly anyone agreed, but Babson was right: the great bull market that had roared on without interruption since 1924 was over.

The first wave of selling began on September 6 and for the rest of the month the market was erratic. Prices dipped, rose, faded, and rallied, but the trend was down. The experts didn't want to believe Babson. Lionel Edie, a professor of finance at the University of Chicago, was widely quoted when he called the downward trend "a normal adjustment of values," a phrase he would regret the next day, October 4, when the New York market was hit by a hurricane of selling. The Toronto market followed suit, as it customarily did, recording a paper loss of two hundred millions. On Bay Street, everyone seemed to have a tale of margin holders ruined when they were forced to sell at a loss. One heavy plunger was reported to have dropped two hundred thousand dollars on International Nickel, one of the year's leading blue chips. Another was wiped out when Yellow Cab plunged from 57 to 21. When he bought the stock, he said, with a sense of injury, he had been told that when he woke up the following morning it would be worth a hundred dollars a share!

Even then, most people were convinced that the bottom had been reached and bargains were waiting to be picked up – a false optimism encouraged by the financial press, which had its own ends to serve. The Toronto *Star*'s financial service reported the Bay Street belief that "Canadian stocks had been squeezed of the last drop of moisture and were parched now for buying." A prominent New York broker made headlines the following day, October 5, by announcing that the Canadian mining market would be the bull market of the 1930s. The *Financial Post*, in an ebullient forecast, reported that "the long term outlook for shareholders in sound Canadian companies remains good. . . . The outright owner of shares in leading companies . . . need not worry when stocks sell at below the prices he paid for them, if he has a well diversified list."

But what was a "sound Canadian company"? How many speculators were "outright owners"? Thousands who had bought on margin owed their brokers for well over half – even as much as 90 per cent – of the cost of the stock they'd bought. And what was "a well diversified list"? The office workers and housewives who could least afford losses had been lured into buying the most volatile shares – the ones that promised quick rewards. These would be the first to be swept away when the panic began.

Most were encouraged to hang on to their shaky investments when the market rallied slightly. By October 17 a modest recovery was under way. But on that day the Toronto exchange reeled under a heavy wave of selling, the worst since October 4. It was repeated on Wall Street on October 21. The following day the market rebounded. This uneasy roller coaster ride should have been a warning to the amateur speculators. For many, however, it came too late. They couldn't afford to get out and so hung on, victims of the incurable conceit of the twenties. Things could only get better – that was their justification. Hadn't Irving Fisher, a respected professor of economics at Yale, passed off the new bear market as "a temporary shakedown"? Like his friend and colleague Professor Edie from Chicago, Fisher was unfortunate in his timing. The next day, October 24, would always be known as Black Thursday.

In the first hours of that day, traders who had exhausted their margin began to dump thousands of shares on the market. Prudence gave way to fear and, as prices began to plummet, fear to panic. An unprecedented wave of selling took place everywhere that day. Few who took part in that torrent would ever forget the wall of sound that rose from the exchanges in Montreal, Toronto, New York, Chicago, and Winnipeg. In the Winnipeg Grain Exchange, for six dreadful minutes just after 11 a.m., the babel of noise became so cacophonous that excited traders, lost in the swirl, could not make themselves heard and developed splitting headaches. In those six minutes, wheat plunged from $1.40 to $1.31 a bushel and millions of bushels were dumped on the market.

On Wall Street in New York, the roar of the voices of a thousand brokers, hoarse from shouting, echoed off the high ceiling of the exchange and travelled for blocks. One hundred uniformed police had to be brought in to keep the curiosity seekers from halting traffic. In the visitors' gallery, seven hundred spectators looked down on the turbulent scene below. Many were in tears; some were actually screaming. Among these glum visitors was Winston Churchill, who was visiting America and was himself wiped out. Shortly after noon when the gallery was closed, they were forced to join the jostling mob outside.

32

The prices chalked on the big boards couldn't keep up with the minute-by-minute changes. Brokers toiled blindly, selling, selling, selling to those who thought – often wrongly – that they were picking up bargains. Toronto had no clear idea of the New York situation because the wire services couldn't handle the volume of trading demands made on them. The radio, which broadcast a continuous recital of stock quotations, albeit tardily, was the only reliable source of information.

All the exchanges established new records that day. In Montreal, where a 25,000-share day was usual, an unprecedented 400,000 shares were traded. That was a trifle compared to New York, where nearly thirteen million shares changed hands in the most terrifying stampede the exchange had ever known.

Yet optimism still prevailed, especially when the heads of the three largest banks in the United States were seen, early that afternoon, hastening, singly, up the steps of the good, grey financial House of Morgan at the corner of Wall and Broad streets, kittycorner from the exchange. Shortly after that, the senior Morgan partner, Thomas W. Lamont, met the press and delivered himself of a cheerful assessment. The problem with the market, he said, was technical rather than fundamental and would "result in betterment."

At three, the closing gong sounded in New York to a chorus of boos, groans, and sighs of relief, producing a brief but blessed moment of silence before the wall of noise returned, fading finally from the paper-littered floor of the exchange. Brokers leaned dazed against the posts, their collars torn, their faces gleaming with perspiration. But it was not the end of the day for the thousands of employees of the financial houses, who would have to toil through the night to tabulate the day's transactions.

Neither the bankers and brokers nor the politicians could get it through their heads that their world had stopped turning. A bankers' pool, organized by the House of Morgan, tried to stem the tide by investing more than two hundred million dollars on the New York market. Thirty-five of the leading New York brokerage houses issued a statement insisting that the market was "fundamentally sound." That was the phrase that would be parroted again and again during the turbulent months that followed. Herbert Hoover seized on it immediately. "The fundamental business of the country," the President intoned, " . . . is on a sound and prosperous basis." These soothing phrases, together with the heavy investment by the bankers' pool, helped to steady the market on Friday. But on Monday, October 28, prices resumed their tumble.

In Canada, the bankers followed the cheerful lead of their American colleagues. The man in the street might be pardoned for believing that the bottom had been reached, especially when the general manager of the Royal Bank announced that "fundamental conditions are sound . . . and there is no room for pessimism." But with the total value of shares on the Toronto Stock Exchange dropping at the rate of one million dollars a minute, the financial community could no longer put faith in its own press releases. The brokers worked far into the night sending out margin calls by phone and wire, warning their customers that they could not protect them past ten o'clock on Tuesday morning.

In Toronto it was estimated that between five thousand and ten thousand margin calls went out that night. Early next morning people waited in queues at the brokerage houses, proffering cash and cheques, trying to hold on to their stock before the brokers sold them out. Prices were falling so fast that hundreds lost everything and still owed large sums.

There was no longer any stock that could be called "blue chip." When the Toronto exchange opened – it was not possible to close the doors on the dense crowd – it was discovered that the bluest of the blue, International Nickel and Brazilian Traction, had dropped ten and eleven points respectively overnight – erasing a total of $200 million from the market value of the two companies. Black Tuesday, October 29, 1929, had begun.

It was far more Stygian than Black Thursday. In Montreal early that morning, thousands besieged the brokerage offices – "packed not unlike sheep in a pen," to quote one witness – and waited silently for the ticker to spell out their fate. The market had scarcely opened before the crash was apparent. As the tickers hummed and clicked and the prices were chalked on the big boards, the silence was eerie. People talked in whispers. Then, as the dimensions of the disaster sank in, some women began quietly to sob. In one Toronto brokerage office a man fainted. He was hastily laid out in a back room and left alone to recover as everybody rushed back to the stock board.

34

Thursday's chaotic scenes now appeared mild by comparison. Stocks did not rally briefly or follow an up-and-down sequence as they had the previous week. Prices plunged straight down as the big traders flung great blocks of shares onto the market – five thousand shares, ten thousand shares at a time. The word used most often to describe the pandemonium that day is "terror." Suddenly, tens of thousands who had been seduced into seeing a bright future unhampered by debt or financial care could see nothing ahead but disaster.

The stunned hush in the brokerage offices contrasted sharply with the terrifying sound, animal-like in its intensity, that burst once again from the stone walls of the Montreal exchange. It was not confined to the trading floor. On the street outside, men and women jostled and shouted while hundreds more forced their way into the corridors and the gallery.

It was all but impossible to hear above the noise. Runners in blue and red blazers struggled through the mob on the floor, bringing scribbled instructions from brokerage houses to their men on the scene. Each trader would seize the piece of paper, then raise his voice in a hoarse cry, trying to sell something that nobody wanted to buy. So confused was the selling, so intense the sound, that traders standing within six feet of one another would often be screaming widely different prices for the same stock.

Stocks were sacrificed at almost any price. Runners carrying completed sales slips pushed their way back to the central desk, where clerks were supposed to relay the latest figures to the ticker and to the boys chalking prices on the big board in the gallery above. But the clerks found it impossible to keep up with the mounting piles of paper.

Gordon Bongard, who was thirty years old at the time, remembered that "there was a hell of a roar and it was pretty smoky, so it was awfully hard on your voice." He told Doug Fetherling that "it was hard to find a buyer because everybody wanted to get out fast . . . and a lot of mistakes were made in the rush. At times there might be two or three different prices being quoted in different parts of the room." Traders were supposed to fill out a slip and get the buyer to initial it, after which it went to an exchange employee who put it on the tape. But the confusion was such that many slips were improperly filled out and others were simply lost.

Beneath the big board, exhausted traders occasionally paused to scribble prices in their notebooks – prices that were already outdated. Then, "like cattle milling in a stampede," they returned to the fray. There was scarcely time to draw breath, let alone light a cigarette. One man tried, but as he reached for a match, another order came along. He shouldered his way through the packed group near the centre of the floor with the cigarette dangling from his lips. It was still there, unlit, eleven minutes later.

In the scramble to sell, people were pushed, shoved, even trampled. Human values were forgotten. "There's no more sympathy on that floor than at an abattoir," one Montreal trader exclaimed. "It's the coldest, cruelest thing in the world. Nothing matters but the dollar." So much for the Regina *Leader*'s predictions of "a greater measure of brotherhood" in 1929.

The brokers got no rest again that night, for the records of the day's business – the little slips on which buy and sell orders were recorded – were in chaos and had to be sorted out. St. James Street, that gloomy cavern of brick and stone, took on the deceptive trappings of high carnival as crowds jammed the financial area. Office windows, usually dark after five, glowed with light. Two thousand automobiles, many of them chauffeur driven, were angle-parked against the austere façades. Newsboys dashed about shouting the day's shocking headlines: "WORLD MARKETS NOSEDIVE TO NEW DEPTHS." Taxis sped through streets usually deserted, bringing worried investors to the financial houses. Restaurants stayed open and did a roaring business. Those who had no time for dinner fortified themselves from the lines of peanut and popcorn wagons. Far into the night the spectacle continued, like a tribal rite marking the end of innocence – the final flare-up of a gaudy, get-rich-quick decade, which some future sloganeer would dub the Roaring Twenties.

The legacy of Black Tuesday was disillusionment. "Fundamentally sound!" shouted one man, as he dashed into his broker's office with the afternoon paper. "Fundamentally sound? Look: Tunney and Dempsey are in the ring, and Tunney knocks Dempsey out. There he is, lying on the canvas. Fundamentally sound? Sure he's fundamentally sound. But he's out."

Thousands who had counted their paper profits and found themselves rich now discovered that they were hopelessly in debt,

36

like Tom Gallagher, the manager of Dominion Securities in Montreal. Gallagher had invested everything he had – eight thousand dollars – to buy, on margin, eighty thousand dollars' worth of stock. As the price soared he expected to pay for his shares with the profits and eventually become wealthy. *Eventually* – that was the weasel word that trapped so many. On the evening of Black Tuesday, Gallagher found that events had overtaken him, that his savings had vanished, and that he now *owed* eight thousand dollars.

There were those who took their losses philosophically. According to one story, perhaps apocryphal, a Toronto investor reached home on the evening of Black Tuesday to tell his wife he'd resigned from six clubs, sold their second car, put his garage up for rent, and cancelled all the family's charge accounts. After that he fired the maid and went to bed.

The stories of brokers leaping from tall buildings is one of the myths of the great crash. But there were suicides. There was, for instance, the case of poor Lottie Nugent, the Toronto bookkeeper, who, it will be recalled, had invested all she had – $3,000 – as down payment on six stocks. Her broker friend, with all the optimism of his breed, urged her to hang on, certain that they would go up again. But when the brokerage firm went bankrupt, she was faced with a demand to close out her account and pay $4,421.27 owing on the stocks. She was given six days to pay; it might as well have been six years, for all the hope the creditors had of realizing a debt that was certainly equal to five years of her salary. Unlike Tom Gallagher, she did not have a father who could cover her losses. She went back to her room in a Huron Street boarding house and turned on the gas. When the police found her body, it was still warm.

Others far more prominent than Lottie Nugent were wiped out in the débâcle. These included a future prime minister, Louis St. Laurent, who would still be paying off his debts during the Second World War. R.B. Bennett, the Leader of His Majesty's Opposition, also took a beating, but he could afford it. The cannier Mackenzie King, who ignored the crash in his voluminous diary, lost nothing; his fortune was secure in gilt-edged bonds. King, indeed, seemed oblivious to the implications of the market disaster. On October 30, in a remarkably smug statement, the Prime

Minister declared that "while no doubt a number of people have suffered owing to the sharp decline in stocks, the soundness of Canadian securities generally is not affected."

"Business was never better, nor faith in Canada's future more justified," said Mackenzie King.

4

The world of 1929 Canadians were not prepared for the Depression that followed. The businessmen weren't prepared, the politicians weren't prepared, and the people weren't prepared. The coming disaster would call for bold, imaginative action, but Canada, in the twenties, was not a bold or imaginative country. Unlike the United States, it had yet to find its feet as an independent, united nation. Its semi-colonial status and its narrow regionalism had inhibited original thought and common endeavour.

The country's ten million people were cooped up in scattered population islands that seem, in retrospect, to have been hermetically sealed. The modern communications network we take for granted was almost non-existent. There was no national broadcasting system, no national airline, no Trans-Canada Highway to provide a sense of community – and no unique flag or official national anthem to rally round. The long-distance telephone was expensive and awkward – beyond the reach of most people. And there was little sense of history. Other nations revelled in theirs; Canadians thought theirs dull. Outside Quebec, the majority thought of themselves as British first, Canadian second; to them, Quebec was an unknown country.

The chief unifying force was the railway system, but travel was expensive and denied to all but a select few. Ironically, the Depression changed all that, allowing thousands of young men to burst out of their isolation and, for the first time, gain a sense of country as they scrambled aboard the passing freights and criss-crossed the land.

By western standards, Canada was an old-fashioned country. Almost half the people lived on farms or in small towns, far from the centres of sophistication – such as they were. Except for the Group of Seven or the National Hockey League, there was little indigenous culture. The tiny minority who cared about theatre,

38

ballet, or opera made do with travelling companies from the United States or Great Britain, or staged their own amateur performances. Beer and rye whiskey were the accepted tipples; wine was for winos; and nobody used the word "gourmet" to describe the meat and potatoes fare of those days.

Such phrases as the "Roaring Twenties" or the "Crazy Twenties" give a distorted view of the decade. In Canada, life was tranquil and the pace was slow. Why hustle? The world was perfect as it was. The screech of traffic and the dissonance of the ghetto-blaster belonged to the future. The horse-drawn delivery wagons that clip-clopped through the quiet streets moved at a leisurely trot. Music was not yet part of the culture of the young. It was confined, sweetly, to the Sunday bandstand, the cottage gramophone, or the parlour radio. Radios were battery powered, and when the Depression struck and batteries became a luxury, some would fall silent.

For many the country was still emerging from the frontier. In the isolated prairie villages, people went without running water or electricity. Even in a city like Saint John, New Brunswick, bathrooms were unusual. The boarding house was still popular, hence the appeal of the Major Hoople comic strip. In the cities, one out of six home owners took in lodgers – a word that has long been out of use.

Sophisticated developments that we take for granted weren't known in 1929: sliced bread, frozen food, wall-to-wall broadloom, fluorescent lights, contact lenses, Teflon frying pans, credit cards – the list is endless. People didn't rush to buy "health foods" – there were none – but they worried about diseases that have since become almost unknown. Only a few vitamins had been isolated; there were no antibiotics and few vaccines. Houses were quarantined for as long as a month for a host of childhood afflictions, including the dreaded diphtheria. The real horror for the young was infantile paralysis, as poliomyelitis was called. Tuberculosis was as frightful a scourge then as AIDS today. In most cases it was terminal. Jogging? The word wasn't in the lexicon. Diet? Many were trying to *gain* weight. "YOU SKINNY GIRLS!" the Ironized Yeast ads shouted. "*Hundreds have gained 5 to 15 pounds this easy way.*"

It was a narrower, more rigid society than today's, and those adjectives apply not only to the so-called inflexible laws of economics but also to something as innocent as motherhood. Breast-feeding was supposed to be strictly controlled at precise four-hour intervals no matter how lustily the baby cried for food. Infants were not to be cuddled too much – that would spoil them. Mothers were admonished that "the less a baby is handled the better" and advised to slap them on the buttocks to make them cry because "it keeps the lungs well expanded."

Those women who worked outside the home – and most married women didn't – made about half the wages of their male counterparts. Male chauvinism, which a later generation would decry, was alive and well, even on the nation's campuses, where a more enlightened attitude might have been expected. But the University of British Columbia segregated its classrooms. Dalhousie denied certain scholarships to co-eds. Toronto's prestigious History Club barred women members, explaining, perhaps, the shortage of women historians. And the University of Alberta actually had a Woman Haters' Club, whose president (in 1935) would be elected head of the student council. It was assumed that a woman went to college to find a man, not a job. After that she was supposed to stay home. Jobs were about to become very scarce indeed, prompting the demand that women stay out of the workforce entirely.

Women weren't supposed to like sex, which was talked about (by men) in whispers and usually with sniggers, an attitude that emphasizes the prudery of those times. The subject was publicly taboo, as were all references to abortion, pregnancy, menstruation, and masturbation. Contraception was illegal under the Criminal Code, and a divorce was almost impossible to obtain. In 1929, only 816 couples were divorced in Canada; more than twice that number left the country to get an easier separation elsewhere.

A few bold souls advocated "companionate marriage" and were vilified for it. They suggested that newlyweds should practise birth control for two years to decide whether they were compatible and then, if necessary, consider no-fault divorce while still childless. But when J. Lyle Telford, a left-wing physician and future Vancouver mayor, gave a lecture on the subject at UBC, the Vancouver *Sun* went after him editorially, charging that what Telford was advocating was "a social poison that gratifies the erotic impulse." One angry reader wrote that Telford should be sterilized. Another declared he was "unworthy of Canada."

That was bad enough, but if you sneered at the sovereign, or indeed "any foreign prince," you could be clapped into jail for sedition. In 1928, in Sudbury, one man was. His name was Arvo Vaara, the editor of a Finnish-language newspaper, who went so far as to express indifference as to whether the ailing George V lived or died. For those dangerous views he served eight months of a one-year sentence.

For Canada, as the wretched Vaara learned to his cost, was still very much a British nation. School children didn't learn any American history, but the name of every English monarch from William the Conqueror on was drilled into them. The names of those forgotten British folk heroes Hereward the Wake and Wat Tyler were as familiar to the lower grades as Jacques Cartier and Samuel de Champlain.

No politician yet dared to suggest abandoning the good old Union Jack. Most English-speaking Canadians would have agreed with the Premier of Saskatchewan that "over sixty thousand Canadians died following this flag . . . and say the flag that was good enough for them is good enough for me."

That yearning to cling to Imperial symbols sprang partially from the fear that too many non-British immigrants would alter the traditional ethnic mix. In good times, "foreigners" were welcomed as settlers, at the bottom of the social scale. In hard times they weren't wanted at all, and the fear of the newcomer would soon become a hallmark of Depression life. As for Quebeckers, they were considered a breed apart and certainly inferior by the white Anglo-Celtic Protestants who controlled the country.

Canada in the twenties was a racist country. The vast majority of Canadians, from the Prime Minister down, were at least passively anti-Semitic. Everybody knew what the warning sign RE-STRICTED meant at golf clubs and tourist resorts. It bothered few that banks, insurance companies, department stores, financial firms, and a variety of other institutions, from Procter and Gamble to Maclean Hunter, barred Jews from employment. Jewish doctors couldn't get hospital affiliations. Law firms rarely hired Jews. The universities and professional schools refused to hire Jewish faculty and devised quotas for Jewish students. High offices in the federal government from the Senate to the Supreme Court were barred to Jews. The Privy Council that year agreed that a woman could become a senator, and a woman shortly afterward did; but it was twenty-five years before a Jew was admitted to the upper house and forty before a Jew sat on the Supreme Court. The files of the RCMP hint at the general attitude. The undercover constables who were assigned to keep tabs on anybody they considered left of centre had a habit of classifying their non-WASP quarry as a "Jew" or a "foreigner" or both.

Jews, like communists, were fair game in 1929. An incident that occurred in Toronto that year underscored the racism in that citadel of WASP privilege. The police, backed by their commission, had issued an extraordinary order. No one, they decreed, could make a public speech in any language but English! Today it sounds laughable - the kind of thing a right-wing crank might suggest on an open-line show - but the police were in deadly earnest. When Philip Halpern, editor of the Jewish weekly *Kampf*, tried to address a communist rally in Yiddish, he was immediately arrested. The *Globe*, quick off the mark as usual, endorsed the action in a long editorial entitled "The Police Are Right." And those who protested the action, it said, were indulging in "silly twaddle."

These authoritarian measures were a foretaste of what was to come when the Depression settled in. Within a month of the stock market crash, mounted police were breaking up a demonstration of hundreds of unemployed men in Vancouver. The jobless statistics were mounting - already 10,000 in Toronto, 8,500 in nine prairie cities - but nobody in authority took action. When A.R. Mosher, president of the All-Canadian Congress of Labour, demanded an immediate federal conference to consider the situation, the government turned him down. Mackenzie King's Minister of Labour insisted that the crash hadn't affected Canada as it had the United States. His complacent remarks echoed those of the bankers who, as always, were seeing shafts of sunlight breaking through the dark economic clouds.

Hard as it is to swallow, the same financial seers who had predicted good times at the start of the year ignored the crash and predicted good times on the eve of the next. A heavenly choir of bank executives raised hymns of praise to undimmed prosperity, trotting out the familiar clichés - "undiminished confidence

42

in Canada's continued growth . . . " (White of the Commerce); "constructive optimism" (Moore of the Nova Scotia); " . . . future as promising as any time in her history" (Bogert of the Dominion); and, of course, "fundamental conditions are sound" (Gordon of the Bank of Montreal).

The press, as usual, trailed along, indulging in the familiar boosterism. "There's very little the matter with Canada!" exclaimed Frank Yeigh, editor of *Saturday Night*. "CANADA STANDS UNSHAKEN AFTER MARKET COLLAPSE," headlined the *Ottawa Citizen*. But the prize for the murkiest crystal ball must go to the Vancouver *Sun*, which, with the unfettered conceit that was even then the hallmark of the West Coast press, went so far as to announce that "Vancouver people can create in 1930 the greatest era of activity and prosperity . . . that this continent has ever known."

The Days When a Dollar Was Stretched

This selected list of prices of goods and services in 1933, the nadir of the Depression, shows how far a dollar went in the thirties compared with today. All measurements have been adapted to pre-metric figures.

	1933 price	1990 price
tin of Campbell's tomato soup	approx. 8 cents	59 cents
1 lb. minced beef	8 cents	$4.40
loaf of bread	6 cents	$1.59
milk per quart	9.5 cents	$1.63
dozen eggs	24-26 cents	$1.65
ticket to first-run movie (after 6:30 p.m.)	Loew's, 50 cents	$7.00
rent, 3-bedroom apt. (Toronto)	$40	$1,300
price of 3-bedroom house:		
Toronto (West Annex)	$4,700	$300,000
Victoria (Oak Bay)	$3,000	$135,000
postage stamp	1 cent	39 cents
Toronto *Star* newspaper	2 cents	35 cents
university fees (U. of T.)	$550	$1,610
cup of coffee	5 cents	50 cents
hamburger	10 cents	from 99 cents (McDonald's) up
Coca-Cola	5 cents (6½ ozs.)	75 cents (10 oz. can)
man's white shirt	$1.95	$36
haircut (barber)	50 cents	$6 to $15
Ford car, 5-passenger	$685, 4-cyl., 4-door	Escort LX $9,920
sterling silver - Birks Chantilly, 5-piece set	$12.61	$475
Maclean's magazine	10 cents	$2 plus tax
best-selling novel	30 cents (U.S.) (*Master of Jalna*)	$26.95 (*The Negotiator*)
pack of 25 cigarettes	25 cents	$4.40
bottle of Canadian Club whisky	15 cents per ounce	70 cents per ounce

44

1930

1

As the New Year approached, the Prime Minister of Canada had *"Not a* confided to his diary that all was right with the world. "A good *five cent* year it has been on the whole," he told himself, "a year in which *piece!"* there has been I believe, some improvement in mental and moral strength, some slight growth in wisdom. . . . "

He continued to congratulate himself: "The session of parliament was a good one. I had to carry much of the load myself, but I came out stronger in public regard I believe than I went in. . . . The summer was a good one and a happy one. . . . The fall has been good." For thousands the fall had been very bad, but King didn't mention the market crash. He was still basking in the glow of Ramsay MacDonald's visit to Canada. King, who loved to hobnob with great men, was certain that the British prime minister's brief sojourn was "an important international event which added a little I believe to my prestige in the country. . . . "

He saw no dark clouds on the political horizon. " . . . I believe that with the party & the country I am stronger than any time since I assumed office . . . I thank God with all my heart for protecting me through the year now drawing to a close. . . . "

These smug and self-complacent scribblings seem almost demented in the light of what we now know, but King was not alone in his musings. The business and political world felt the same way.

The exception seemed to be R.B. Bennett, who was demanding a radical change in government policy to ensure prosperity. A radical change was the last thing that Bennett expected from the cautious King and the last thing that he himself contemplated when he took office, unless by radical he meant an increase in the country's protective tariffs. But he *was* Leader of the Opposition, and so his demands were as predictable as the response of John Dafoe's Manitoba *Free Press*. The Liberal voice of Western Canada pointed the finger of scorn at the Tory leader for his "lamentations."

"Whom are we to believe," the paper asked, " . . . the sober financial executives who say that conditions are essentially sound and full of hope for the future, or the politicians who declare that in many respects the country is in a deplorable state . . . ?"

The sober financial executives, of course, were dead wrong. The country *was* in a deplorable state, for which the Honourable Mr. Bennett had no cure and which Mackenzie King simply ignored, in the belief that the trouble would shortly go away. Within a fortnight, with ten thousand jobless men in Winnipeg alone, Dafoe was less sure of himself and was calling for federal action. The mayors of the larger Western cities, from the Lakehead to British Columbia, poured into Winnipeg on January 29 for a conference on unemployment. They wanted the federal government to underwrite a third of all relief costs, to launch a massive program of public works, to appoint a royal commission to investigate the situation, and to stop all immigration to Canada – radical suggestions indeed, by the standards of the day.

The *Free Press* now changed its tune to declare that unemployment was "a social condition . . . which cannot be explained away by soft phrases or met by emergency palliatives."

Nonetheless, when a Western delegation headed by Winnipeg's pugnacious mayor, Ralph Webb, went to Ottawa, it got neither soft phrases nor emergency palliatives but instead tough talk. The Depression had struck the West but was only beginning to be felt in Eastern Canada. Cushioned from reality in the green womb of his Kingsmere estate, Mackenzie King shocked the delegates by refusing to believe there *was* a crisis. "If the situation is so deplorable as you try to picture, why is not eastern Canada represented?" he asked Webb. "The answer is that, generally speaking, the employment situation in Canada is not abnormal. I have a telegram from the government of the province of Quebec that conditions there are quite satisfactory."

Standing on the rock of the British North America Act, the Prime Minister told the delegates they must first go to their provinces for help; the federal government had no duty to assist the municipalities, which, he suggested, were simply being greedy.

Here was the crux of the problem. Canada's unwieldy constitution divided responsibility in such a way that the destitute could not rely on help from anybody. Throughout the decade political leaders would lean on the BNA Act in order to pass the buck. If the provinces wanted help, King told the delegation, let them ask for it; but none had asked. The canny prime minister was well aware that any province that asked for government funds to pay for municipal relief would be forced to shoulder part of the

48

burden. That was why Simon Fraser Tolmie, the Premier of British Columbia, was disclaiming all responsibility for relief, and why Premier Howard Ferguson of Ontario was doing his best to discourage any municipal pleas for aid.

Though relief was traditionally accepted as a municipal problem, the burden was becoming unbearable. In Regina, to cite a typical situation, the weekly relief bill had soared from ten thousand dollars in December 1929 to a staggering forty thousand in January.

Returning empty-handed from Ottawa, Mayor Webb found his city faced on March 6 with a major communist demonstration. The bulk of the Winnipeg police force waded into the crowd with billies and struck down a number of demonstrators. Even the diminutive alderman Bill Kolisnyk, who was haranguing the meeting, was not spared. He was, after all, a Communist.

But policemen's truncheons couldn't crack the problem that Webb and the Western mayors faced. As they had discovered, few politicians or businessmen in the East had grasped the truth that the country was suffering from a depression that wouldn't go away. The Prime Minister continued to think of the problem as seasonal. The only way to deal with it, he had told the delegates, was through a system of unemployment insurance. It was an easy out for King, since under the country's awkward division of powers, unemployment insurance was a provincial responsibility. For the whole of the decade left-wing politicians, labour unions, social workers, some editorial writers, and even R.B. Bennett called for unemployment insurance with no result. It wasn't just the constitutional roadblocks that stood in the way; it was also the knowledge that while some form of jobless insurance might help in a future depression, it wouldn't be of much use in this one.

Predictably, the business community was not enthusiastic about any increase in social services. "Whither are we drifting in this matter of socialistic paternalism?" asked the Montreal *Gazette*, the voice of St. James Street. " . . . While human nature remains as it is . . . it is sheer madness to tell idle and shiftless men and women that the state will step in and save them from the penalties of their violation of fixed social laws."

Edward Beatty, the president of the CPR, which owed its existence to repeated transfusions of public funds, resorted to the age-old argument that too much charity would make the recipient soft. Beatty said he wasn't opposed to unemployment insurance or the dole in principle, he was just worried about "the effects of its application upon the individual."

But the individual was already beginning to feel the effects of the government's apathy. The inane suggestion that government handouts to the jobless (as opposed to handouts to the railways) would somehow sap initiative was on a par with the equally inane theory that the Depression was psychological and not real. That, however, was the opinion of the head of one of the country's leading advertising agencies. Hard times, J.J. Gibbons told the press, were merely a state of mind!

Parliament met on February 20, but the government was so indifferent to the mounting crisis that the House didn't get around to discussing it until March 31. The debate lasted more than a week, and by that time it must have been clear that the country was in serious trouble.

Member after member of the Opposition rose to give evidence. Tommy Church, the former mayor of Toronto, told of counting a line-up of 347 hungry men waiting one morning outside the Yonge Street Mission. Another reported twelve hundred being fed daily at a Montreal soup kitchen. A third told of hundreds sleeping in the CPR station in Calgary. Hugh Guthrie, formerly a Conservative Cabinet minister, rattled off a series of new statistics: four or five thousand men jobless in Vancouver; four hundred families being fed by the city of Edmonton; twenty-five to thirty thousand out of work in Toronto; thousands of mechanics laid off in Windsor. This was all guesswork. Nobody knew how many were unemployed in Canada because there were no verifiable statistics.

The country had been thrust into the Depression blindly and, as the debate that week made obvious, nobody really knew how serious it was or what caused it. Various speakers on both sides of the Commons attributed the unemployment situation to the high tariff, the low tariff, the wheat pool, the wheat crop, immigration, the gold standard, the stock market crash, world conditions, mechanization, the weather, American competition, foreign treaties, the reduction of purchasing power, the lack of technical education, the unprotected shipbuilding industry, and the lack of railway traffic.

The Liberal position was that there was no real unemployment problem; it was merely a seasonal aberration. W.K. Baldwin, the

50

septuagenarian member from Baldwin's Mills, Quebec, went so far as to insist, in the face of overwhelming evidence to the contrary, that there was work in Canada for anyone who wanted it. Those who wouldn't work ought to be deported, Baldwin declared. He went on to invoke the example of Benito Mussolini. "In Italy, the chief ruler makes the people stay on the land," he said. "I would vote for a law to make an able-bodied man work."

With no clear policy on unemployment, the government contented itself with attacking the "blue ruin talkers" as King's Minister of Labour, Peter Heenan, called them. That was too much for H.H. Stevens, who had for years represented the hard-hit riding of Vancouver-Centre. Up he jumped to ask sardonically: "Are the minister and his colleagues aware of *any* unemployment problem which exists in Canada at the present time or which has existed during the past three months?" Heenan carefully stepped around that question. R.J. Manion twisted the knife a little deeper. "It is appalling," he cried, "to think that the government has no policy on this question . . . [or] on any other question except the policy of hanging on to power."

This parliamentary furore was doing nothing for the jobless. In Edmonton, even as Manion was speaking, eight hundred unemployed, led by communist organizers, marched to the city hall asking for work, only to be told by the mayor that their demands were "ridiculous" and "unreasonable."

On April 3, the Prime Minister entered the debate in the House and, in the course of a long speech, managed to dig himself into a hole from which there would be no escape. His position was that the problem was purely local and required no infusion of funds from Ottawa. Why should the taxpayers of wealthy provinces be asked to take money from the federal treasury to help certain provinces and certain municipalities? It was a question that struck at the very underpinnings of the Canadian federal system and chipped away at the cement of national unity, which King himself had always made his cause. The Prime Minister, in short, was suggesting that Central Canada – the hated "East" – should remain aloof from the growing destitution in the West.

A system of federally supported unemployment relief was quite unnecessary, King declared. "I submit that there is no evidence in Canada today of an emergency situation which demands anything of that kind." All the talk about unemployment, he indicated, was no more than a political move by the Opposition "because of a point of view that they intend to take in discussion on the budget."

King was engaging in the kind of obfuscation for which he was well known, spinning cobwebs to mask the real issue, speaking extemporaneously without the security of one of those contrived and cautious speeches over which he often laboured far into the night. For the past three days he had been goaded mercilessly by the Opposition, which wanted him to loosen the federal purse strings and help out the provinces, half of which had Tory governments. The thought of handing money over to the Tories was too much for the Liberal leader.

"So far as giving money from this federal treasury to provincial governments is concerned," King said, "in relation to this question of unemployment as it exists today, I might be prepared to go to a certain length possibly in meeting one or two western provinces that have Progressive premiers at the head of their governments . . . ."

The House broke into an uproar. King had lost control of himself and was provoked into a gaffe that would cost him the election. "But," he continued, "I would not give a single cent to any Tory government!"

"Shame!" shouted Bennett.

"Shame!" cried Stevens.

At that point King should have backtracked, but, uncharacteristically, he failed to scent disaster and plunged on. "My honourable friend is getting very indignant. Something evidently has got under his skin. May I repeat what I have said? With respect to giving moneys out of the federal treasury to any Tory government in this country for these alleged unemployment purposes, with these governments situated as they are today, with policies diametrically opposed to those of this government, I would not give them a five cent piece."

At that the Speaker was forced to call for order. The Opposition could scarcely believe its good luck. The phrase "five cent piece" would haunt the Liberals in the months that followed, but King himself appeared oblivious to the damage he had inflicted on his party. He pooh-poohed the idea of a national conference on unemployment. What was needed, he said, was more foreign investment in Canada. He followed that with the extraordinary statement that if Canada admitted to having an unemployment problem by holding such a conference, that act alone would dry up foreign investment!

After King sat down, Isaac Macdougall, a Nova Scotia Tory, asked if there was anything in the British North America Act to prevent the federal government from helping the provinces meet the unemployment crisis.

"Nothing," King replied.

"Then why don't you do it?" Macdougall asked.

"Because," King answered, "we have other uses for our money, other obligations."

He still didn't understand the full impact of his words about the five-cent piece. The Liberal claque had responded with the usual applause that any major speech by a party leader demanded. King, who was susceptible to the most transparent forms of flattery, thought he'd given a magnificent speech. He didn't get back to his Ottawa residence, Laurier House, until four the following morning, but he took the time to write that "our side of the House was well pleased. . . . I got a splendid reception from the men, as fine an ovation as I have ever received in the Commons. It was a fighting speech and except in two particulars was what was needed."

Those two particulars, however, caused him some unease. "I made a slip I think. . . . It was a slip in that it can be read apart from the context and it is capable of much misrepresentation as applied to unemployment. . . ."

He returned to the matter the following day: ". . . I went perhaps too far. It is not in accord with my gen'l attitude of conciliation etc. - But it has the other purpose of making a definite line of cleavage between the Libs & Cons which our men like. It is, however, not good speaking to lay one's self open to where explanation is necessary. . . ."

By April 8, King realized that he was in trouble. The press had already pounced on the five-cent piece remark. "I feel very sorry about this unnecessary break," King wrote. "I can see wherein the Tories intend to misrepresent it as meaning not a cent for unemployment & not a cent to a Tory province for anything. It may afford a chance on the public platform for me to show how I am seeking to guard expenditure, & I believe will appeal to the people when limited to unemployment, as most persons get nothing therefrom."

These internal musings demonstrate how out of touch the Prime Minister was with the realities of the Depression. In the cities and the small towns, housewives had become accustomed to – and appalled by – the steady stream of shabby young men knocking at their back doors, asking for a handout. Everybody except those in the top echelons of society was affected by unemployment. Few (except the same top echelons) wanted the government to pinch pennies when jobless men were going hungry. The cries for a national conference on unemployment had been so strident that King in his circumlocutory way was forced to back into one.

Since the government didn't want to be seen to reverse its policy, it called for a dominion-provincial conference on immigration at which time the unemployment situation could also be discussed. It never took place because King decided in May to call an election. It was the very worst time to go to the country, but the Prime Minister didn't seem to realize that. The campaign would begin in June. Election Day would be July 30. Mackenzie King was certain he would win.

2

Mother's When he went to the polls in the summer of 1930, William Lyon
boy Mackenzie King had been Prime Minister of Canada for the best part of nine years. He was fifty-six, at the mid-point in his career, and, although he would never admit it, as healthy as a horse. For King was a monumental hypochondriac. To read the despairing comments in his diary about his condition, one would think he was poised on the brink of a breakdown from exhaustion or nervous tension.

"It must be a brain fatigue greater than I imagine" (February 1, 1927). "Too fatigued to do my work properly" (January 23, 1929). "My brain was fagged out . . ." (October 17, 1929). The litany of complaint is unending: "tired and strained" . . . "excessively weak and faint" . . . "fatigued and exhausted."

King portrayed himself, to himself, as a man all but crushed by the burden of office, with no one at his side to help shoulder the load, yet gamely prepared to sacrifice his health and well-being for the good of the Party and the nation. "It is hard not to get discouraged with the load I have to carry so largely alone," he wrote early in 1929, adding, "I am determined to keep up if I can."

Of course he kept up, for there was nothing wrong with him. When he paid his periodical visits to his doctor he was pronounced perfectly sound. We know the truth of that because he methodically listed in his diaries every detail of the examination, from his blood count ("hemoglobin – 90% . . . 12.42 gms.") to his urinalysis ("clear amber colour").

These famous diaries, so voluminous and so intimate, are the keys that unlock the secrets of King's psyche. They strip him to the bone and do so in his own words. Surely no other statesman has been so nakedly revealed as this outwardly bland politician. It is all there – his eccentricities, his complexities, his sexual guilt, his mother fixation, his egotism, his parsimony, his personal furies. To the historian, these diaries, running to thousands of pages, are almost as much a burden as an asset, for we know far more about King than we do about his contemporaries – too much, perhaps, to make fair comparisons. The others did not keep revealing journals.

In poring over the river of words that King bequeathed to the nation one must ask this question: what if others had kept diaries as frank and intimate as King's? How many of his contemporaries would then appear in a new and perhaps less appealing light?

Without the diaries we would know little of King's loneliness, his sexual naïveté, his dislike of pomp and circumstance, his spiritualism, his extraordinary self-esteem, his love of flattery, his hypochondria, and his several petty guilts. In the thirties, he was thought of as a stodgy fussbudget, a colourless politician who made long, boring speeches – a typical Canadian, in short. But it wasn't King who was colourless, and it wasn't the Canadians, either. The fault lay with the journalists who didn't make the effort to understand their countrymen or their Prime Minister. They were seduced by King himself into believing what he wanted them to believe. If he appeared boring it was part of his protective guise, like his habitually funereal attire – black suit, starched white collar and cuffs. One of his speech writers once complained that King had removed all the colourful phrases from his script. King replied, wryly, that it was the colourful phrases that people remembered (and that returned to haunt the speaker).

Only the diaries reveal how desperately lonely this most complex of political bachelors could be. His only close friend was a woman, Mrs. Godfroy Patteson, five years older than himself, his constant companion, sometime hostess, and intimate confidante. He had known her for more than a decade. She and her banker husband had the use of what might be described as a grace-and-favour cottage on King's estate at Kingsmere, about a dozen miles from Ottawa. Though Joan Patteson was a kind of surrogate wife, it was in no sense a *ménage à trois*. The relationship was platonic, though there had, apparently, been one brief period in which it teetered on the verge of physical passion. Godfroy's presence protected the circumspect Prime Minister from wagging tongues. He got on well with the banker, but it was to Joan that he turned for advice, comfort, and conversation; they shared a mutual interest in books, politics, and, of course, the occult.

Only a handful of people knew of King's interest in the spirit world. If any members of the press knew, they kept discreetly silent. In those days one did not invade a prime minister's private life. (Another of King's eccentricities – the collection of fragments of old buildings for his Kingsmere estate – was never referred to until after his death.) Certainly it would not have helped a campaign already in trouble to let it be known that the Prime Minister was consulting a Mrs. Bleaney from Kingston who put him in touch with the ghosts of those he habitually referred to as his "loved ones." These included his mother and father, brother and sisters, and on occasion his political hero, Wilfrid Laurier. To King, these shades from the void seemed more real than the flesh-and-blood politicians he dealt with by day. These were his real companions, who came to him in his dreams and what he called his "visions." Students of the diaries have concluded that far from influencing his political decisions, the apparitions told him no more than he wished to hear. Sometimes their predictions went awry. That baffled and saddened King, but he carried on pluckily, seance after seance, his faith unshaken.

In August of 1927, for example, Mrs. Bleaney had told him he would be married the following year "to someone I already know, younger than myself." Mrs. Bleaney was dead wrong. King would never marry, in spite of his repeated protestation: "I should have a wife of my own." Mrs. Bleaney was forgiven.

A year after the medium's flawed prediction, King was still longing for marriage. It would, he wrote, "make my life infinitely happier. I need a wife, and I pray God that I may yet have one to love who is wholly my own. . . . " It was a cry from the heart that recurs throughout his long years in office.

Yet King made little effort to find a wife, and when a suitable prospect appeared he fled like a startled buck pursued by wolves. There was no lack of eligible women. He corresponded with several, including the granddaughter of General Ulysses S. Grant, Julia Grant, who had married and would later divorce an Italian prince. But he shrank from the ultimate intimacy. It was easier and less distracting to lean, when he needed to, on Joan Patteson.

Nor could any woman hope to compare for beauty, compassion, selflessness, or purity of soul with his sainted mother, who haunted his dreams and his seances, guiding his destinies, consoling him in his darker moments, and leaving precious little time or space for a rival.

It was King's occasional habit, when returning to Laurier House late at night, to press his thin lips against the unyielding marble of his mother's effigy. He not only idolized her, he invented her. The real woman - strong-minded, ambitious, calculating, and manipulative - was far removed from King's fictional creation.

Isabel King had dominated the family, overshadowing her passive and largely inadequate husband, who plays a minor role in King's recorded visions. The child of a famous Canadian rebel, she gave his name to her elder son and never let William forget who his grandfather was, or the humiliation and poverty she had suffered during those desperate days when he was on the run after the Rebellion of 1837 in Upper Canada. The son's task was to support her, to worship and enshrine the memory of his grandfather, and to right the wrongs that the rebellious Mackenzie had sustained at the hands of the establishment, known in those days as the Family Compact.

The irony is that King, the rebel worshipper, was anything but a rebel himself. After a term as Minister of Labour in the Laurier Cabinet and a conciliator in hundreds of strikes, he joined the establishment. John D. Rockefeller, Jr., a man of whom his grandfather would never have approved, hired him to repair his shattered image after one of the bloodiest and most appalling strikes in U.S. history. King's solution was to impose company unions on the Colorado miners, scarcely the act of a committed radical. They were, in the words of the chairman of the congressional committee appointed to investigate the matter, "specious substitutes for trade unions that will deceive, mollify and soothe public opinion while bulwarking the employers' arbitrary control." To King the hero-worshipper, who always basked in the approval of great men, Rockefeller was the greatest of all.

Though he tended to cry poor, King was a rich man. By 1930 he was worth about five hundred thousand dollars, at least four million in 1990 dollars. Half of it had been raised from wealthy Liberal supporters by his friend the Tea King, Peter Larkin. His investments would pay him at least twenty thousand annually, his salary as Leader of the Opposition another ten thousand, and his tax-free sessional indemnity four thousand more. That was an enormous sum in those days of deflation and limited income tax, when the average office employee earned only two thousand dollars a year and the average production worker only half that amount. King's annual take-home pay, calculated in 1990 terms, was in the neighbourhood of a quarter of a million dollars.

He could not and did not spend it all. Yet when he determined to buy some additional property next door to his Kingsmere estate, he boggled at the price of fifteen hundred dollars. "It wasn't worth five hundred to me," he thought, "save to prevent Jews or other undesirable people getting in" – a phrase King used more than once in his diary. Like most of his class, he was an anti-Semite. "The greatest danger and menace," he wrote, "is a sale to Jews, who have a desire to get in at Kingsmere & who would ruin the whole place." It goes a long way to explain King's lack of interest when in the worst days of the Nazis his immigration department turned back to Europe a shipload of Jewish refugees, many to their deaths.

He had convinced himself during a visit to India a few years before the Great War that "it is in every way desirable that Canada should be kept for the white races and India for the black, as Nature appears to have decreed." He was far more at home with men like Signor Mussolini, then the darling of the Canadian right wing, whom he visited in Rome in the fall of 1928. "I have been

58

enthused," he wrote, "about the manner in which this country has been bro't together & is going ahead, the order of it all, the fine discipline, the evident regard for authority & for M.[ussolini] himself." It filled him with admiration to note the way in which Mussolini had offered to clean up an Italy "filled with communists, banished them all to an island, cleared the streets of beggars and the houses of harlots. . . ." Mussolini was a "truly remarkable man of force of genius, fine purpose, a great patriot." So much for the grandson of the rebel who had tried to topple the Family Compact.

The distaste he felt for communism was less political than it was religious. The communists were godless atheists and King was a committed, if quirky, Christian who felt himself unworthy in the sight of his Maker. It was part of his obsession with spiritualism. In his *Industry and Humanity*, a naïve and almost unreadable book that he published in 1918 and of which he was excessively proud, he suggested that the church could solve "the vast problems of Industry and of the State." Brotherly love was all that was needed to come to grips with economic and social questions. "It is from the reverence for life which men get from their mothers, and from the faith which a religion pure and undefiled imparts, that there comes the spirit of mutual aid through which the material interests of the world make way for the nobler aspirations of the soul."

King may have believed that, but as a practical politician he was far more devious, more canny, and more ruthless than his words suggest. Friends, enemies, biographers, and revisionist historians have all agreed on one thing: he was a consummate politician. It was hard to pin him down, to use his own words against him (the "five-cent" remark was an exception) because his speeches were masterpieces of ambiguity. He toiled over them for days at a time, but only his diaries reveal that he approached the task with something akin to terror.

King once gave himself a full week to prepare for a speech in Toronto, but a week, he felt, wasn't nearly long enough. "I shudder," he wrote, "as I think of the little time ahead." Three days later, he still hadn't mastered the speech. Another two days passed; it still wasn't finished, and King was "nearly desperate" – almost in tears. Another day and he was suffering from "brain fatigue greater than I can imagine." Twenty-four hours later he was still struggling away, totally disconsolate. "It lacks punch," he wrote – but then, King's speeches always lacked punch. "I can clearly see that I am not at all up to the mark." He could only hope that God would give him strength to bring it off.

Apparently God did, for King was able to speak for two hours – so long that his deputy, Ernest Lapointe, had to cut his own speech short and the other speakers were forced to cancel theirs. King felt "immensely relieved," but one's sympathies are with the audience and with his fellow Liberals who found their own time gobbled up. That didn't bother King, who felt that a Higher Power was running the affair and had carried him through.

Each time he spoke, he felt himself under nervous strain and tension. Once, when he tried to reply to "an exceedingly poor speech" by Bennett, he felt that he had failed. "Some fiendish influence seems to have taken hold of me . . . and makes it impossible for me to think." Fiendish influences were always at war with King's soul. Was it fatigue, he wondered, or "passions"? That word recurs in the diaries. He wrote of feeling, one evening, a "sort of internal fever, fighting passions." And again: "I have been consumed by a sort of inner fire, partly over-eating I fear, but mostly passions which will not let me rest as I should."

The celibate could not rid himself of guilt. He dared not utter the terrible word "masturbation" even to his secret self, but it is clear that, in common with most men of his time including a good many doctors, he believed the practice to be not only evil but also debilitating. "If I could only get over the feeling that there was something wrong in these desires & realize they are natural & all that is necessary is to control & subdue them I should be much happier." But he could not conquer them or rid himself of the burden they imposed. "To be married would have, of course, be best of all but that will have to come or not as may be ordained. I have given up worrying about it." Yet his worries continued.

The most terrifying occasion of the year for Mackenzie King was the night of the Press Gallery dinner in Ottawa. There, politicians in general and political leaders in particular were supposed to sit still and applaud while the members of the Fourth Estate poked fun at them. Even worse, from King's point of view, they were expected to deliver a witty, self-deprecating address.

King, who had little sense of humour, was not up to that. He resented what he considered the "vulgarity of the affair."

It wasn't dignified, nay, it was downright unworthy. He felt indignant at "the course [*sic*] nature of the references to myself and many others. The whole proceeding was wholly unworthy . . . [of] thoughtful & serious minded men. As a matter of fact it gives to the press an idea of their power to destroy & make reputations such as they should never be permitted to have."

Vulgarity and ostentation disgusted him, especially where the British upper classes were involved. Canada was just beginning to emerge from the long shadow of the mother country, and King was in the forefront of those nationalists who couldn't abide the pomp, circumstance, and out-and-out grovelling that accompanied royal and vice-regal occasions.

Back in 1927, during the country's Diamond Jubilee, he had been irritated by the Governor General's request for five thousand dollars to entertain highly placed visitors from England, including the Prince of Wales and Prime Minister Stanley Baldwin. "I am beginning to be 'fed' up with the English invasion," he wrote. The fawning over high dignitaries in Ottawa social circles disgusted him. At one lavish dinner, at which both he and the Governor General were guests, he was dismayed to find that a marionette show had been hired for their amusement, complete "with cartoons which were lampoons . . . and this in the presence of a lot of foolish young people and empty headed old ones." It was unworthy, King thought, considering the high position of the guests, "a children's party for grown ups." He was very conscious of the dignity of his position as the prime minister of an imperial dominion that would soon become an autonomous member of the new Commonwealth. He disliked being patronized and sometimes unconsciously snubbed by those British peers who reigned but did not rule from Rideau Hall. Once on a drive with the vice-regal party from the Quebec Citadel to luncheon thirty miles distant, he found himself relegated to a little side seat in an ADC capacity. "It shews," King wrote, "what a wrong sense of proportion people come to have."

That led King to muse that the whole business of having a governor general from the old country was getting out of date. "It is perfectly absurd for two people to be surrounded by flunkies,

A.D.C.s getting 'Your Excellency' at every turn & from every breath, salutes, etc. . . . The life indeed disgusts me. I get fed up with it." He returned to the subject more than once: "The truth is I find myself very little in sympathy with the whole social side of Govt. House life. . . . Its patronizing attitude shrivels me completely. . . ."

These words were written a year before the general election. By this time King had a clear idea of the kind of Canada he wanted – one that was in no way subordinate to Great Britain. When Sir William Clark, the British High Commissioner, tried to tell him how Hugh Keenleyside, his new chargé d'affaires in Japan, should act in Tokyo, King "got thoroughly mad & told him that we in Canada did not need to be told how to behave . . . by the Br. Frgn Office, or his office." King went on to declare that this "tranquil consciousness of effortless superiority" on the part of Englishmen was intolerable as far as Canadians were concerned. It was an uncharacteristic outburst from the most circumspect of politicians, and King was surprised himself at the bluntness of his words; but he "could not contain the feeling of indignation at the way the High Comm'rs office has been seeking to 'keep tabs' on us."

How ironic then, in the light of these convictions, that less than a year following the election, the Statute of Westminster would give Canada the autonomy that King craved, but the prime minister who signed it would be Mackenzie King's bitterest antagonist, the staunchest of imperialists, the man who brought back British titles to Canada, himself a future peer of the realm – Richard Bedford Bennett.

3

Mrs. When the campaign began in June, two hundred thousand Cana-
Bleaney's dians were out of work, the price of wheat had plunged by 54 per
clouded cent from the previous year, and the prairies were assaulted by
crystal the worst drought in Canadian history. Cora Hind, the West's first
ball woman journalist, described the situation that summer in the *Free Press*: "One of the truly pathetic things is the number of men looking for work and not finding it, tramping in the broiling heat with their packs on their backs. Not the hobo type, but good,

respectable, capable, keen to earn a living and far too many of them looking as if they and a good meal were strangers."

The seriousness of the situation completely escaped Mackenzie King, who continued to insist that there was no national emergency, but Bennett seized on it, ran with it, and made it *the* issue of the campaign. King was at a disadvantage, though he failed to realize it. Goaded into an early election, he was forced to do battle on his opponent's ground.

Bennett opened his campaign in Winnipeg on June 9 in the skating rink of the cavernous Winnipeg Amphitheatre, where at the party's first convention in 1927 he had been elected Conservative leader. Although the meeting was scheduled for 8:15 that night, hundreds were already waiting outside when the doors opened at 7:10. For the next hour a stream of motor cars and a parade of streetcars disgorged their passengers, most of whom were men. As the building filled up – it would hold seven thousand – the band of the Canadian Legion blared forth above the buzz of the crowd. Banners draped along the walls made it clear that the Tory campaign would be tied to the economy: ELECT A CONSERVATIVE GOVERNMENT AND RELIEVE UNEMPLOYMENT . . . TIME TO CHANGE! VOTE CONSERVATIVE FOR BETTER TIMES . . . and VICTORY FOR THE CONSERVATIVE PARTY MEANS PROSPERITY FOR CANADA.

A gigantic portrait of John A. Macdonald stared down from its gilt frame above the platform at the west side of the auditorium, flanked by enlarged photographs of former Tory stalwarts – John Norquay, one-time premier of Manitoba, and Macdonald's old crony Charles Tupper.

At 8:30 the band struck up "O Canada," and as the faithful roared, clapped, and cheered their approval, Bennett and his party came down the aisles and bounded onto the stage with such vigour that they knocked over a vase of red roses.

Now the ebullient leader – "our beloved chief," as his introducer called him – plunged into a fighting speech that focused on the unemployment issue. Yet Bennett's solutions, cheered to the roof by the crowd, seemed remarkably old-fashioned. "I will make the tariff fight for you," he declaimed, promising to maintain and indeed strengthen the traditional Tory policy of high duties to protect Canadian industries against "overseas competition."

"My concern," he said, "must always be for the unemployed men of Canada, and not for those of Great Britain or any other countries." The words had a nice solid ring, comforting reminders of the old National Policy. But what, really, did this panacea have to do with appalling conditions dictated by a different kind of crisis? Bennett spoke for an hour and a half – a brief speech by the standards of the time – and ended with a pledge that any government he headed would introduce any act necessary to end the Depression "or perish in the attempt." That brought down the house.

This was the first time that radio had been used extensively in an election, and Mackenzie King, listening to his rival on the airwaves, was not impressed. "Such demagoguery, declamation & ranting . . . ," he wrote. "I cannot see how he can hope to win to his side men of any real intelligence."

But Bennett's appeal was undeniable. In Regina, where thousands more heard him, the party made sure that the front seats were occupied by the unemployed, each man identified by a white card on his lapel. King might declare, as he did, that Bennett was exploiting misery for political purposes, that he was exaggerating the problem "out of all proportion," but the Tory leader's speeches were corralling votes.

"I will use tariffs to blast a way into the markets that have been closed to you," he declared in Winnipeg. That bellicose phrase would dog him for the next five years. It was on a par with King's five-cent-piece blunder or Pierre Trudeau's later pledge to wrestle inflation to the ground.

Canadians, Bennett said, didn't want charity; they wanted work. "I will not permit this country with my voice or vote, to ever become committed to the dole system."

"Ever," "never," and "forever" are words that the canny politician learns to avoid. In less than two years, Bennett would be forced to eat his. Both leaders were mired in the past, seeking old-fashioned solutions – a high protective tariff, a balanced budget – for a new set of problems.

But Bennett was more specific than his cautious opponent. Unemployment, he told a Calgary audience, "has now ceased to be a local or Provincial one and . . . has assumed national importance" – a jab at King's position. He promised he would call a special session of Parliament immediately to deal with it. He would inaugurate a system of public works to provide jobs. He would build the St. Lawrence Seaway. He would start construction on the Trans-Canada Highway. He would introduce a national system of old-age pensions. "The bogey of unemployment would be destroyed." There was no excuse for it in Canada "if a Government does its duty."

"The Conservative party," Bennett told a Moncton audience, "is going to find work for all who are willing to work, or perish in the attempt" - another promise that he would live to regret. And then, the clincher: "Mr. King promises consideration of the problem of unemployment. I promise to end unemployment. Which plan do you like best?"

In those days there were no airplanes to speed the candidates from one political rally to the next. The indefatigable Tory leader travelled fourteen thousand miles, all by private rail car. He made seventy speeches, some lasting two hours, and spent sixty thousand dollars of his personal fortune in the seven weeks of the campaign. His solutions may have been old-fashioned, but his style was that of a fervent evangelist, in direct contrast to that of his plodding opponent.

King couldn't fathom it. He thought Bennett was going too far in making unemployment the big issue of the campaign. "Labour is not likely to be deceived, and the men who are working are not going to worry particularly over some of those who are not," he wrote, in a monumental misreading of the mood of the electorate. Those remarks, which he confided to his diary just two days before he opened his own campaign in Brantford, show how far the Prime Minister was removed from the realities of the day. It is a measure of the Liberal myopia that their main newspaper advertisements scarcely mentioned unemployment but emphasized instead taxation and trade.

By the time King reached the West in early July, his speeches were being interrupted by boos and catcalls, demonstrations and humiliating taunts of "five cent piece." He tried to explain what he had really meant during that unfortunate exchange in Parliament, tried sometimes to laugh it off ("A party is in a pretty bad way when it has to adopt a five cent issue"). It didn't work.

The campaign was, to use his own words, "heavy sledding." In Quebec he discovered only at the last minute, and to his dismay, that he was expected to speak out of doors on a damp, cold night to more than five thousand voters. Worse, he realized he was addressing a predominantly French-speaking audience, many members of which couldn't understand a word he said. Just as he began, a spatter of rain came down. There he stood, wearing the light suit he had chosen in expectation of an indoor affair, shivering in the cold, distracted by the ineptitude of his own people, "too weary to speak, let alone think." Somehow he managed to get through the ordeal, but the experience - "a sort of nightmare" - left him profoundly depressed.

Halifax was also hard going. Again the arrangements were terrible: for one thing, the audience was too far from the platform. He managed to hold his temper at the taunts in Calgary but was terrified in Vancouver to discover that there were no loudspeakers. In Edmonton, returning east, he was greeted by the unemployed with jeers and banners. By the time he reached Saskatoon, he wrote, "I really felt as tho I would not be able to hold out."

While the two political leaders criss-crossed the nation, an uglier drama was being enacted on the streets of Toronto. In addition to the various splinter parties that formed the "Ginger Group" in Parliament under J.S. Woodsworth, one other national party had nominated candidates. For the Communist Party of Canada, the Depression was an opportunity for action; it was determined to contest the election.

Its new leader, who had ousted Jack MacDonald, was a diminutive English-born machinist, Tim Buck, who looked more like a shoe salesman than the cartoon stereotype of a bearded, bomb-throwing Bolshevik. Buck was short, wiry, quiet spoken, clean shaven, and well read, though largely self-educated. During his family's days of deepest poverty in England, Buck would recall, their home was the only one in the neighbourhood that had a complete set of the works of Shakespeare.

Buck's Conservative father, a former innkeeper whose hero was Disraeli, believed that "there was absolutely nothing wrong with Britain and her Empire that the Tories couldn't fix." But young Tim, who went to work as a machinist's apprentice, was enthralled by the speeches of Keir Hardie, the Scottish Labour M.P. Later, when he opted for socialism, his father wouldn't speak to him. In 1910 Buck decided to emigrate and chose Canada because the steamship fare was cheaper than it was to Australia. By then he was a radical and a strong union member. He read Marx, joined the Workers' Party of Canada, and in June of 1921, in Fred Farley's barn in Guelph, Ontario, helped form the Communist Party of Canada, which he would lead from 1930 until his death in 1973.

A few days after the election was called, two strapping plain-clothesmen walked into Buck's Toronto office. "Put on your coat, Tim," one of them said, "the Chief wants to see you."

Buck knew both men well enough to call them by their first names – Dan Mann and Bill Nursey, members of Chief Draper's infamous Red Squad, the same group that had precipitated the Queen's Park riot a year earlier. He asked if they had a warrant. They didn't. But Buck had enough experience with the Toronto police to know that nothing was to be gained by refusing them. They would simply drag him down to the squad car, warrant or no warrant, and no citizen would bother to protest.

Since 1927, the average Torontonian had come to the conclusion that the Communist party was an illegal organization because the police treated it that way. It wasn't, of course. It was a legal political entity contesting a democratic election with the same rights and privileges enjoyed by the Liberals and the Conservatives – at least on paper. In practice, the party's street corner meetings were invariably broken up and its members refused the use of meeting halls that were open to the rest of the public. The police commission, three of the city's four newspapers (the *Star* was the exception), a majority of the city fathers, and most citizens saw nothing reprehensible about these violations of civil rights.

At police headquarters, Buck encountered an old comrade, the Reverend A.E. Smith, late of Winnipeg and now chairman of the Canadian Labor Defense League organized by the party to provide free legal aid for those of its members who were haled into court.

"A.E.!" exclaimed Buck, "have you been called, too?"

"I wasn't called," Smith replied. "I was ordered."

After a wait of fifteen minutes they were summoned to the chief's office. Dennis Colburn Draper was even smaller than Buck, but his no-nonsense approach to police work had cowed more than one constable on the Toronto force. A tiny martinet with hard eyes, a bristling black Prussian-style moustache, a firm jaw, and a tense, crouching stride, he was unquestionably brave.

In the Great War he had managed the rare feat of twice winning the Distinguished Service Order, the most coveted decoration after the Victoria Cross. The first was awarded for hauling his mortally wounded commander to safety while he himself was wounded, the second for courage at Passchendaele. By the end of the war he had risen to brigadier-general.

He took a post-war job as timber cruiser and purchasing agent for a paper company, but he'd had no police experience when he was made chief in 1928. There were those who thought the job should have gone to a member of the force, but Draper proved himself quickly. When one of his men was shot, he took command of the hot pursuit that followed. In bowler hat and gaiters, he drove every available officer across the fields of three neighbouring municipalities until his quarry was hunted down.

Denny Draper had all the qualities, good and bad, of a Great War officer. A strict disciplinarian, he believed in direct action and in bending the rules when he considered it necessary. He didn't hold with civil rights where malcontents – or those he considered malcontents – were concerned. Over the objections of the mayor, he authorized the use of the police baton as a means of persuasion. He believed that bookmakers should be given the lash, and he was all for longer penitentiary terms for lawbreakers. His hobbies were predictable: he was a good horseman, a crack shot, and an avid gun collector.

Now the chief pointed a finger at Smith and rapped out a question: "You born in Russia?"

"No, sir. I was born in Canada."

"I didn't ask you if you were born in Canada."

He pointed a finger at Buck.

"You born in Russia?"

"No, sir, I was born in England."

"I didn't ask you if you were born in England. Whether you were born in Russia or not is beyond my power to prove at this moment. But I know you're lying and I want to tell you that you've told your last lie to me. I've been watching you fellows and I know you're in the pay of Russia, and I'm going to tread on you so hard that you'll never be able to raise your heads again in this city. I'm going to clean this city up."

Smith tried to point out that he was a candidate in the forthcoming federal election.

"Don't you lie to me about being candidates," shouted Draper.

"Well, sir," said Buck, "I'm a candidate also."

"I've had enough of this insolence from you fellows," said Draper. He rang a bell. "Take these fellows out. And let me tell you two before you leave, I'm going to have you behind bars, just as sure as my name is Dennis Draper."

Thus it came about that in the election of 1930, a legal political party with nine candidates in the field found it impossible to conduct a campaign. When a gang of toughs disrupted one meeting at Spadina and Dundas streets, three mounted policemen and four uniformed constables stood by smiling. The majority of Torontonians condoned this harassment because the party was unpopular.

The Communists couldn't afford the radio and wouldn't have been given access to the air waves if they had had the money. But on the last night of the campaign, Saturday, July 26, Canadians were treated to a marathon of campaign speeches broadcast by the Liberals and Conservatives. There were now 435,000 radio sets in Canada, an increase of 35 per cent over the previous year. Probably one million people heard all or part of the political addresses that droned on to midnight. Those were the days when a politician could get away with the most long-winded of broadcasts. King and Bennett had very little competition. They carefully avoided clashing with each other, just as they steered away from competing with the "Amos 'n' Andy" show. But apart from that wildly successful fifteen-minute program, radio listeners had a limited choice.

Bennett, in a fighting mood, chose to speak to ten thousand people at a rally in Ottawa. King followed, characteristically alone, hunched before a microphone set up in a dining room of the Chateau Laurier. Beside him in twin gold frames were portraits of his mother and his father. From the far end of the table, two of his heroes, Laurier and Mackenzie, gazed down at him. In the presence of his "loved ones" he took more comfort, drew more security than was possible in an open-air rally where untoward mishaps sometimes conspired to throw him off his stride.

He attacked his opponent with an age-old weapon, as hoary as democracy itself. Bennett, he indicated, was a doomsayer, shedding crocodile tears over the supposed unemployment crisis and crying "blue ruin" around the country. As usual he was pleased with himself, though a little concerned about a certain harshness in his throat - nothing to worry about, though, when contrasted with Bennett's "ranting." The contrast, he was sure, would be to his opponent's disadvantage.

He was convinced he would win. "There may be a real Liberal sweep," he wrote on election day. " . . . I look to the Govt. coming back stronger than it was." After all, hadn't the estimable Mrs. Bleaney predicted that Bennett would never last as leader?

But Mrs. Bleaney was wrong again, overwhelmed, perhaps, by the need to tell her client what he wanted to hear. The Conservatives swept the country, gaining a clear majority with 137 seats to the Liberals' 91. Six splinter parties, mainly on the progressive side, garnered 17.

R.B. Bennett was now Prime Minister-elect and, in spite of Mrs. Bleaney's crystal ball, would remain in power for five full years. There were some who claimed that the entire election was an example of Mackenzie King's much-vaunted canniness - that he had foreseen what was coming and actually wanted to relinquish power and leave his opponent the impossible task of trying to take the country through hard times before being swept aside by a Liberal tidal wave. But King was the very opposite of prescient. The magnitude of the Depression utterly escaped him. He wasn't canny, only lucky: he would not take the blame for the worst five years in Canadian history. Had he remained prime minister in 1930, he could never have survived politically after 1935.

4

"Bonfire Bennett" Richard Bedford Bennett was not the sort of man to keep a diary or, if he had been, to leave it around for posterity. One simply cannot imagine him scribbling away of a night, confiding his most intimate thoughts, passions, and terrors to a daily journal. He tore up his personal correspondence and his private documents. His letters to his mother, whom he venerated as King did his, were burned after his death. Thus we cannot examine Bennett from the inside as we can his opponent. We view him from afar, no doubt unfairly - an austere, forbidding, pugnacious figure with precious little humanity to him, a "bumptious" leader, in his

70

opponent's words, who was "apt to be very unpleasant, and give a nasty tone to public affairs."

To this day no scholarly biography has been published of the man who presided over Canada during its five hungriest years. It is understandable: apart from the daunting absence of primary evidence, few writers really want to deal with failure. When Bennett took office, the hopes of the country were with him. By the time he was ousted, those hopes had turned to ashes.

In retrospect he cuts a slightly comic figure, in his silk hat, his wing collar, his grey double-breasted waistcoat, and his striped pants, a pre-war costume that most of his colleagues had already discarded. Even in the country, it is said, Bennett stuck to that old-fashioned uniform. Arch Dale, the wickedly effective cartoonist of the Manitoba (later Winnipeg) *Free Press*, did not have to caricature him. He simply pictured Bennett as he was, complete with rimless glasses, double chin, and frown.

Bennett not only looked like a bloated capitalist, he *was* a bloated capitalist. When he arrived in Calgary in January of 1897, a gangling twenty-six-year-old from the Bay of Fundy, he was determined to make himself look substantial and so devoured gargantuan breakfasts in the Palliser Hotel until he attained the fashionable girth that was then the hallmark of the successful captain of industry. He had been raised in straitened circumstances after his father's shipbuilding business failed, but by 1930 he was one of the richest men in Canada, having inherited the controlling interest in the Eddy Match Company in the twenties from his friend Jennie Shirreff Eddy, the widow of the match king, and her brother, Joseph T. Shirreff.

The picture of Bennett that emerges from the memories of those who knew him and from his own actions in Parliament and as prime minister is of a human bulldozer, battering his way through the problems that beset him. He had a memorable voice, firm and resonant, and a "blustering, two-fisted way of smashing out words" – words that poured from him in such a torrent that Hansard reporters laid out extra pencils when he rose to speak. He was once clocked at the incredible speed of 220 words a minute – a sharp contrast to King's ponderous delivery. In his younger days, he'd been called "Bonfire Bennett." After listening to him on the radio, one contemporary remarked that "one cannot help but think he looked on the microphone as a public meeting or a mob."

Nonetheless, his oratory had a powerful effect on his listeners, as the 1930 election proved. Tommy Douglas of the CCF, who entered the House in 1935 and observed Bennett when he was Leader of the Opposition, thought he was "probably one of the greatest orators and best parliamentarians the country ever had."

The new prime minister worked fourteen to sixteen hours a day, dictated at top speed to two stenographers, toiling in shifts, and exhausted both. His secretary, Andrew MacLean, described his working through the night before leaving for the Imperial Conference in London. Bennett had to catch the 5:30 a.m. train from Ottawa to Quebec, but at three that morning he was still furiously dictating. One stenographer was trying to keep up with him while MacLean, completely fagged out, snored on a sofa. Two more weary stenographers, their notebooks crammed from cover to cover with shorthand, had fallen asleep in an anteroom, heads on each other's shoulders. At four, Mildred Herridge appeared to urge her brother to pack and perhaps take an hour's rest before boarding the train. Bennett replied that it would take no more than a minute to get his things together; he would need the extra hour to complete his work.

He needed every waking moment because he simply could not delegate. A poor administrator with a minimum of Cabinet experience, he dominated every department of government, invading areas that should have been left to his ministers. He insisted that he himself take care of every detail, no matter how small. A story making the rounds of Ottawa at the time contained more than a little truth. A stranger, seeing the Prime Minister striding down the hill, asked a friend why he kept muttering to himself. Came the reply: "He's holding a Cabinet meeting."

This inability to shuck off the minor burdens of office was carried to extremes. Bennett believed that he should personally answer every letter he received. As a result his desk was piled with documents. He made himself available to everyone who wanted an appointment, so that his office resembled a railway waiting room. He had never had a home of his own. In Calgary, he had occupied a suite in the Palliser Hotel, in Ottawa, in the Chateau Laurier. He lived on the job within a narrow geographical circle – Chateau, Rideau Club, East Block.

He read a great deal – heavy tomes, biographies and histories, nothing frivolous. He had committed a good many hymns and poems to his prodigious memory, but otherwise he had no hobbies – no interest in sport (he wouldn't even enter a bowling alley), very little in art or culture. Musically, he was tone deaf, although Elgar's jingoistic anthem "Land of Hope and Glory" stirred his imperial emotions when it was rendered on the organ. By contrast, Mackenzie King detested the song, especially the phrase "make thee mightier yet."

In private, Bennett was a shy, lonely man with a strong sense of purpose. Like Isabel King, his mother was the dominant figure in the family, firm minded, ambitious for her son, and determined that he would succeed where her husband, an easygoing shipbuilder, had failed. In a household that was not without its tensions, she shaped her boy, and he worshipped her. His strict Methodism came from her (he deplored tobacco, alcohol, cards, and gambling, and read six verses of the Bible every day of his life). So, too, his ambition. In his early twenties he had announced his twin goals: to become prime minister and a millionaire. He achieved both.

He had few social graces, didn't give a hoot about other people's opinions, and was often indifferent to their feelings. Robert Manion, who succeeded him as Tory leader, wrote that "too often his temperamental explosiveness . . . cost him loyal friendships that he should have cherished. . . . At times his apparent contempt for the opinions of others whom he deems less able than himself stirs up antagonisms against him."

Bennett was not popular with the press – he had once sneered at editorial writers who made only a few dollars a day. Like so many self-centred and self-sufficient men, he had little sense of humour. Grattan O'Leary of the Ottawa *Journal*, a strong Tory newspaper, remarked that "when he laughs it is as though he were making a good-natured concession to the weakness of others."

He did not trust the electorate, finding it "almost incomprehensible that the vital issues of death to nations, peace or war, bankruptcy or solvency, should be determined by the counting of heads and knowing as we do that the majority . . . are untrained and unskilled in dealing with that which they have to determine."

His brusqueness masked his inner shyness. Manion wrote that "personally he can be one of the most lovable and attractive leaders when in the mood – which is about half the time." Tommy Douglas, who had thought of Bennett as a blustering bully, grew to admire him after he entered the House in 1935. Douglas wrote that Bennett "had a human side which he kept from the public." He was kind to Douglas and his CCF colleague M.J. Coldwell, congratulated both on their maiden speeches, got Douglas books on parliamentary procedure, and often called him over for a chat. But that was after Bennett was no longer prime minister and had had a change of heart. "I think he was a man who hadn't had close contact with people," Douglas wrote. "Consequently he didn't know people and was shy of them."

Certainly he had difficulty communicating. It rarely occurred to him to praise his colleagues in his public addresses. As the former Tory leader Arthur Meighen put it, drily: "Platitudes of affection do not pertain to him." Meighen went on to say that "on the rough, ruthless battlefields of life, he has triumphed, and he depends, and does not fear to depend upon his achievements for his following and his fame."

Both Manion and Meighen in their memoirs seem to be struggling to say something good about their colleague – something that will mask their own ambivalence. For he was a difficult man to love and an even more difficult man to know – pugnacious, impulsive, sometimes bullying, and subject to outbursts of anger. Unlike Mackenzie King, who wallowed in the praise even of those he knew to be sycophants, Bennett did not seek affection, public or private. His many philanthropies were unpublicized. Few knew that he was putting a good many young men through college, or that in answer to a stream of pleading letters, he was sending out two- and five-dollar bills to people in need.

He remained a bachelor to the end, though he knew many women and enjoyed their company. His boyhood friend Lord Beaverbrook described his attitude to marriage as "quaint." A wife, Bennett had told him, "must while being domestic in her tastes have such large sympathies and mental qualities as to be able to enter into the ambitions and hopes of her husband, whatever they may be. . . . " As Beaverbrook remarked, that was a big order. "Bennett was, it seems, one of those men who liked women but feared that he might be dominated by a wife or, perhaps, brought to unhappiness through some clash in temperament."

Domination, of course, he could not abide. The headstrong prime minister under a woman's thumb? *Unthinkable!* That was Bennett's tragedy, and the country's. The softening influence of a

74

consort might have made R.B. Bennett more tractable. A domestic *mise en scène* could have had a liberating influence on a man who, for all of his career, had nobody to come home to. It is ironic that, in the end, this perplexing and often misunderstood politician should have been thwarted and made over, not by a wife or a mistress or a political opponent, but by the times themselves.

5

The Communists came off very badly in the federal election, *Old-fashioned* especially for a party that was considered strong enough to *nostrums* launch a successful revolution against the entrenched forces of capitalism. In the nine ridings the party contested, it gained a mere 7,601 votes out of a total of 168,540.

In spite of this, the authorities, especially in Ontario, continued to treat the party as a threat to established order. A month after the election, Charlie Sims, a hard-line communist, was sent to Sudbury to try to organize the employees of the International Nickel Company. At a public meeting on a Sunday night, Sims, who had survived previous beatings at the hands of the Toronto police, was hauled off his soapbox, arrested, and charged with unlawful public assembly, even though a permit wasn't required to hold a public meeting in Sudbury. The city council had got around that difficulty by rushing through a new by-law empowering the police to break up *any* meeting of three or more persons. This transparent device could never have survived in court, and Sims and three colleagues were quickly released, but not before the judge had delivered a tongue-lashing in which he declared, "You foreigners should go back to the land you came from. . . ."

From Port Arthur, where the police raided the party's headquarters, seizing files, smashing typewriters and furniture, to Niagara Falls, where a large mob led by Red Hill, the Niagara daredevil, broke up a communist-sponsored meeting, the attacks continued. The charges were often trumped up. In Toronto, two party members were arrested for conducting a raffle in aid of the unemployed. Police tried to plant a bottle of cheap wine in the Toronto headquarters in a vain attempt to arrest some of the comrades on liquor charges. The plant was discovered; but later that month authorities padlocked the Bay Street offices on the grounds they constituted a firetrap. The offices were on the top floor. Tenants on the lower floors, who continued in business unmolested, were apparently considered fireproof.

One of the uglier incidents that autumn took place during a street corner meeting in support of Tim Buck, who was running in the civic election for Board of Control. The city police under Inspector Douglas Marshall broke it up and seized two of Buck's supporters, Oscar Ryan and the veteran Tom Ewen (also known as McEwen), and threw them into the back of a police car.

"We'll fix you sons of bitches," Marshall told them. "We'll drive you off the streets."

When Ryan expostulated that they had every right to hold a street meeting, Marshall cried, "Shut that bastard's mouth!" whereupon a hefty sergeant known as the Terror of No. 2 Station pushed his elbow into Ryan's face.

At the station, according to evidence later sworn to by the pair, Marshall seized Ryan, threw him to the floor, and kicked him so hard that he lost several of his front teeth. In the yard outside, Ewen was felled by a blow to the face, then punched, kicked, and dragged into the station by one leg. There he was "attacked with savage blows on his face and sharp kicks on the body by the Police."

Ewen was so badly injured that he vomited blood and had to be rushed to the hospital. The two comrades who bailed him out the next morning described his face as "a mass of wounds, his left nostril still swollen and clotted with blood and stuffed with gauze and his eye black." He spent a week in bed recovering.

That same fall, the Nazi party in Germany made staggering gains in the federal election. As Hitler rose to power, Canadians became aware of the bullying tactics of his storm troops, who broke up anti-Nazi street corner meetings and beat up the speakers. Later, when Hitler took office and the policy of police suppression became official, it was fashionable in Canada to decry these brutal attacks on freedom of speech or assembly. It occurred to only a few – a small coterie of university professors in Montreal and Toronto and the corporal's guard of progressive politicians under J.S. Woodsworth – that the same thing had been going on in parts of Canada for some time before the Nazi party began to make headlines in Europe.

76

R.B. Bennett, meanwhile, was contemplating more orthodox methods of dealing with the growing Depression. Shortly after the election he assembled his Cabinet, whose senior members with only two exceptions were closely allied with the Eastern financial establishment. These included his predecessor, Arthur Meighen; his deputy, Sir George Perley, a bank director and railway executive; his Minister of National Revenue, E.B. Ryckman, who was forced to shuck off a portfolio of directorships before joining the Cabinet; and his Secretary of State, C.H. Cahan, a wealthy St. James Street lawyer with wide business interests, supposedly backed by Lord Atholstan, publisher of the *Montreal Star*. The two exceptions were his Minister of Railways, R.J. Manion of Port Arthur, and his Minister of Trade and Commerce, H.H. "Harry" Stevens, an accountant and broker from Vancouver.

In the words of one political commentator, "the new government group was dominated by eastern, urban, creditor and capitalist interests to a greater degree than any previous government." This was the Cabinet that Bennett picked to deal with restless Westerners, drought-stricken farmers, and the growing army of jobless men drifting back and forth across the country on freight cars.

True to his promise, Bennett called a fall session of Parliament six weeks after the election to face the burgeoning crisis. He had already, by order-in-council, brought foreign immigration to a virtual halt. Now he introduced two measures designed to soften the economic blows under which the country was reeling and also, no doubt, to maintain the image of the Prime Minister as a man of action.

Both measures were rushed through Parliament without much forethought, study, or planning. The first, the Unemployment Relief Act of 1930, provided twenty million dollars for assistance to the unemployed, a sum then considered enormous because it was ten times the amount spent for the entire decade of the twenties. (The full federal budget for that year was less than five hundred million.) Mackenzie King was predictably appalled at this extravagance. "It is a big price to pay for a Tory victory," he wrote. "It is a sort of wholesale purchase. . . . It makes one cynical to see the little regard for the public money." As events were to prove, however, this was no more than a fraction of the amount required to alleviate the country's misery. Bennett couldn't stomach the idea of handouts to the dispossessed, however. Four-fifths of the money was to be for "work not charity . . . to provide employment for wages, not doles."

Yet Bennett had no idea how the money was to be spent and, apparently, didn't want to know. It was shovelled out to any municipality that could prove it had a project that would create jobs. Ottawa paid a miserly quarter of the cost, the province paid half, and the municipality paid the rest. But when the municipalities controlled the purse strings it was an open invitation to inefficiency, patronage, and graft.

Bennett ignored this because, like King, he didn't believe the Depression would last. Unemployment had always been seasonal; the government thought it would end by spring. The relief act was a mere stopgap, due to expire on March 31, 1931. At that point there were still two million dollars left in the kitty because some towns and cities couldn't afford to spend a nickel on public works, even with provincial and federal help.

Ottawa had reluctantly set aside a fifth of the relief money, four million dollars, for direct relief – the hated dole – in those regions where public works were impracticable. But again the government had no idea how the money was to be spent. Much of it would be handled by private charities, although relief committees were being organized haphazardly across the country. There were then only a few score of trained social workers in Canada, all struggling with immense case loads. In September, one described their dilemma: "One meets some Workers of whom one thinks – 'How old she looks! I never before thought of her as being old' . . . many of us have grown a bit brittle and require 'handling' as to our tempers. Can you see your cherished standards, one by one, go by the board; can your sympathies be torn day after day by tragedies of which most of the rest of the city remain unheeding; can you stand day after day in the position of being the only person to whom these families have to turn and yet be absolutely unable to relieve their anxiety and suffering?"

On September 16, a week after he introduced the relief bill, Bennett made good on his election promise to raise the protective tariff. He went even further than his most protectionist supporters could have hoped for, clamping duties as high as 50 per cent on 180 items ranging from butter, eggs, wheat, and oats to textiles,

78

paper products, and kitchen ware. It was a monumental revision, the most drastic and sweeping since the first customs duties were enacted in 1859. Bennett claimed that the industries thus protected would take on an additional twenty-five thousand employees. But again, nobody had done any homework. There was apparently no time to hold public hearings or to investigate the industries that would be affected. How the government had decided which tariffs to raise, and why, remained a mystery.

As before, these measures were seen as temporary solutions to a short-term problem. What the Prime Minister and his Eastern capitalist supporters failed to realize was that while the new tariffs might help the manufacturers of Central Canada, they did nothing for those Canadians who depended on the export market – the producers of those traditional Canadian staples, wheat, fish, and pulpwood, the farmers and the fishermen who were the hardest hit by the slump. In fact, it could be argued that the tough tariff policy inhibited trade because it made some of Canada's best customers less eager to buy her raw materials.

It was clear by December that it was no longer possible to grow grain for profit on the prairies. In a single year, the price of No. 1 Northern wheat had dropped from $1.43 to 60 cents a bushel. It cost more than that to produce.

By this time some of the nation's leaders had replaced the word "recession" with the stronger "depression." Sir Henry Thornton, president of the CNR, who at the start of the New Year had dismissed the downturn as a "passing phase," used the dreaded word in a conversation with Mackenzie King in August, thus managing to execute a 180-degree turn in six months. "He fears a difficult winter ahead & a world depression lasting some time," King noted.

King took some personal comfort from those words. The CNR president's gloomy forecast, he confided to his diary, "reveals wisdom of not having waited till next year." The former prime minister was already weaving a tissue of myth that he had shrewdly foreseen the accelerating disaster and got out while the going was good. Like so many of his fellow Canadians that fall, the parsimonious King took a careful look at his own finances. Unlike most, he saw that he had "nothing to fear."

Others less fortunate were making their voices heard. In Vancouver, where a crowd of fifteen hundred protesters had been dispersed by police batons, the mayor was forced to declare a state of emergency when he discovered that all the money earmarked for relief had been exhausted. "The situation in Vancouver is beyond our control," the city clerk wired to the Prime Minister on New Year's Eve. The city, he reported, could no longer handle its 25-per-cent share of jobless relief. "There are thousands of people in this city who are hungry and are in need of clothing and shelter." To this cry for help he added a note of genuine bafflement that citizens could be so hard up when "there is in this Dominion enough of all these things that the unemployed need." It was a sentiment that would be voiced again and again: the stores and the factories were full to overflowing; why then were people starving and in rags?

But Bennett remained convinced that the country could not afford to feed and clothe more thousands, that the Depression would melt away with the snows in spring. No amount of evidence appeared to change his view. A few months later, Harry Stevens sent him some revealing photographs showing groups of jobless men crouched against the rain in makeshift shelters on vacant waterfront property in Vancouver.

Bennett shot back an answer by return mail. His smug reply reveals the antiquity of his social philosophy. The Depression by then was almost two years old, and still the Prime Minister of Canada remained unconvinced of its seriousness. On the contrary, he appears to have persuaded himself that his government's hasty measures had solved the crisis and that any man who really wanted work could find it. How else to explain his words to Stevens? "I thank you for the photographs you were good enough to send me showing how the unemployed housed themselves on the waterfront in Vancouver. *Surely our unemployment relief measures will rectify conditions for those who are anxious to obtain work*" (emphasis added).

Harry Stevens's reaction to this extraordinary response can only be guessed at. He didn't bother to reply.

1931

For all of 1931, R.B. Bennett tried to pretend that the Depression *Still* didn't exist. That summer he dispatched his lean, aging Minister *fundamentally* of Labour, Senator Gideon Robertson, on a fact-finding tour *sound* across the West. But in spite of what Robertson saw and what he was told, he remained remarkably obtuse, bolstering the Prime Minister's own view that Western M.P.s were "blackening Canada's character" by talking about hard times.

At fifty-seven, Robertson was not the ideal choice for the labour portfolio. A former trade union leader, he was pilloried as a turncoat by the Left because of his ruthless intervention in the Winnipeg General Strike of 1919. The radicals called him "that skunk Robertson." In the upper house he had thwarted almost single-handed Mackenzie King's attempts to have the infamous Section 98 withdrawn from the Criminal Code. Imposed as a result of the Winnipeg General Strike, the measure gave the authorities the power to jail anybody who attended a meeting of any organization that advocated change by violence of the system of government. It would shortly be used to imprison Canadians for their beliefs.

Robertson began his tour in Vancouver. There he encountered the remarkable Andrew Roddan, minister of First United Church in the heart of the city's rundown East End. Roddan was doing his best to feed the jobless, the numbers in the daily bread lines at his Church of the Open Door running to more than twelve hundred. That year he ministered to the needs of some fifty thousand homeless men.

Roddan told the labour minister that conditions in the East End "jungles" were worse than they had been in Russia. He had been reading about the Soviet Union and "had not seen any picture or read any story that equalled [Vancouver's] conditions as a breeding place for bolshevism." Roddan painted a hideous picture of life that month at the corner of Prior and Campbell. A hundred men were sleeping in shacks made of bits of tin and wood, auto hoods, old car bodies, signs, and scraps of cloth found on a nearby dump. He found men sleeping in the rain among rats "as big as kittens," and foraging alongside them for scraps of discarded food. Water for washing and drinking came from a stagnant pool. But Robertson, in Roddan's view, didn't "seem able to grasp the seriousness of the situation." In fact, the senator announced that conditions weren't as bad as he'd feared – this in spite of his own statistics that twenty thousand jobless men were now congregated in the city, many of them transients.

When he reached Alberta, where the unemployed figure had already hit ten thousand, the senator remained determinedly cheerful. Conditions were improving, he told the Edmonton Canadian Club; Canada, he predicted, would be the first country to recover from the slump.

There was only one problem: the transients. The government was pretending that unemployment relief was a municipal, not a national, responsibility. But the tens of thousands of young Canadians criss-crossing the country on freight trains exploded that fiction: the municipalities couldn't afford to feed the hordes passing through and didn't feel responsible for them. Robertson saw this mass movement as a serious menace to public safety. In spite of the solid middle-class credentials of the occasional transient he encountered – one turned out to be the son of an old friend, another a high school gold medallist – he was convinced that the boxcars were crammed with communists and foreigners. His solution was threefold: get the railways to clamp down on those riding the freights; get the transients out of sight in semi-military work camps; and deport those "aliens who are spreading dissension." If that were done, the municipalities could look after their own – or so the senator believed.

He was brought up short when he travelled south to Regina and Southern Saskatchewan and saw the effects of the two-year-old drought. For the first time he seemed to grasp the magnitude of the country's plight. Robertson, who had lived twenty-five years in Western Canada, could scarcely believe what he saw. A third of all the municipalities in the south of the province had suffered crop failures. Seventy-five were hopelessly in debt. The whole region, stretching for one hundred miles, a shocked Robertson told the Prime Minister, "is a barren drifting desert, with no vegetation in sight and water supply is almost wholly exhausted . . . . This scene of desolation beggars description, and in areas populated by roughly 150,000 persons, it is inevitable that there can be no crops whatever this year, and that feed and fuel will have to be supplied if the people are to be preserved. . . . "

84

The water shortage was devastating. Farmers had to travel as far as twenty miles to haul brackish and muddy water from the expiring sloughs for drinking and washing. Few could afford gas or oil for their trucks, and the underfed horses were often too weak to make many journeys. Thus water had to be hoarded like gold; families were forced to endure the blazing heat of summer without taking a bath, and even the water they used to clean their hands had to be strained and saved, first to wash clothes and finally to scrub floors.

The farm people lived on a monotonous diet of stewed jack rabbit and boiled Russian thistle. They had no potatoes because the crop had failed, no milk because the cows had been sold for lack of feed, no green vegetables because the garden seeds refused to germinate.

And the wind! As a survivor of the drought later told Barry Broadfoot, "The wind blew all the time, from the four corners of the world. . . . I could go about 10 feet beyond the house fence and pick up a clod of dirt, as big as this fist. I'd lay it on my hand and you could see the wind picking at it. Pick, pick, pick. Something awful about it. The dry dust would just float away, like smoke. . . . I used to say the wind would polish your hand shiny if you left it out long enough. You've got to understand, this was no roaring wind. It was just a wind, blowing all the time, steady as a rock.

"That dirt which blew off my hand, that wasn't dirt, mister. That was my land, and it was going south into Montana or north up towards Regina or east or west and it was never coming back. The land just blew away."

Even before Robertson returned to Ottawa, the Canadian Red Cross had organized a national appeal to aid the 125,000 destitute farm people in Southern Saskatchewan. The response, especially from Ontario, was heartwarming and helped bring about a rapprochement between East and West. The farm families would long remember the hundreds of tons of clothing, collected by the churches, that arrived washed, pressed, and packed in 247 freight cars. The children would never forget the first tinned fruit and fresh apples they'd seen in two years. Only the salt cod from the Maritimes baffled the prairie people; much of it was wasted because no one had explained it must be soaked and desalted.

In Winnipeg, Robertson received an eloquent presentation from D.J. Allan, reeve of Kildonan, who insisted that fifteen million dollars would have to be spent on public works in Greater Winnipeg to provide for the jobless. "It is true," the reeve declared, "that it would mean mortgaging our future, but better that than to starve the present generation." He then put into words what a lot of Canadians were thinking – a sentiment that Vancouver's council had voiced on New Year's Eve: "In a country with full elevators and granaries, with its factories and industries suffering from overproduction of goods, with wealth in goods and wealth in money, it is unthinkable that we can let our people go hungry without the comfort of a fire or stay out of school for lack of shoes and clothing, and this is happening and will happen in greater degree unless some immediate relief is given."

Winnipeg's hard-nosed mayor, Ralph Webb, had blunter proposals, which coincided with the senator's own views: put the transients to work building the Trans-Canada Highway, kick out "all foreign agitators and undesirables," and ban the communist newspaper, the *Worker*.

Back in Ottawa in July, Robertson told the Prime Minister that the Depression was only temporary and that "perhaps next year with any kind of luck we may be out of it." More than luck would be needed. Bennett knew he would have to do something about the victims of the drought and also about the transients. Since he had pledged that he would never allow the dole, he would have to find work for the jobless. But, like King before him, he shrank from making any form of public welfare a federal responsibility.

His election rhetoric returned to haunt him. He was conscious that in Calgary he had declared in a ringing voice that relief was no longer a local problem but had become "national in importance." He had chided King for pretending otherwise. Now he was forced into a position where he would have to advance a hefty share of federal money because scores of Canadian municipalities and one entire province – Saskatchewan – were too poor to shoulder the burden. He dodged part of the responsibility by insisting that the provinces should distribute the money through independent relief commissions. Relief camps for single men would also be run by the provinces, again with some federal help. British Columbia jumped at his offer and set up twenty-seven camps to provide for 18,340 men – a scheme marked by ineptitude, blatant patronage, and even fraud.

86

In mid-September, the federal government announced a comprehensive program to deal with unemployment by undertaking "the construction of useful public works." Ottawa had no intention of initiating any of these; again, that would be up to the provinces and municipalities. But because the government would deal only with the provinces, a good deal of red tape would have to be cut before the municipalities could get at the money. They must prove that the works were actually contributing to unemployment relief; no other capital expenditure was eligible for federal grants. That meant that no province, city, or town could put a spade into the ground or turn a wheel and expect Ottawa's help until the project was approved. By the time the programs got under way in November, the hardest-hit provinces were in the grip of winter and little outdoor work could be done until the following spring.

2

Hard times were becoming harsh times. Crime and violence, *Rocking* starvation and despair, repression and brutality were the visible *the boat* signs of the government's reluctance to cope with unemployment. When, in June, Dr. T.F. Donnelly, a Saskatchewan M.P., produced a telegram in the House with the shocking news that fifteen farm families in his drought-ridden constituency were literally starving to death, the Prime Minister replied, as usual, that this was not a federal responsibility. R.C. Vooght, the despondent manager of a Camrose, Alberta, lumberyard, didn't wait to starve. When his business failed, Vooght shot and killed his wife and two daughters, then drowned himself in a nearby lake.

An unprecedented wave of bank holdups swept the country – five in Winnipeg alone in less than a year – and brought brutal penalties. In February, a sixteen-year-old boy who held up a bank at Fort Frances was strapped to an iron rack, lashed twenty times on his back with a cat-o'-nine-tails, and given five years in prison for stealing $540. The sentence provoked no editorial comment but did inspire a protest from J.S. Woodsworth, one of the few politicians who regularly denounced such practices. "Canadians will not stand for this kind of thing," Woodsworth declared, but of course Canadians did. The Great Repression was well under way.

The country that had once invited Eastern Europeans to hew wood and haul water on the Western plains now wanted to send them all home. Elizabeth Penner, who came to Canada in 1925 and later went to the United States to take nurse's training, was one who was held at the border. It took three months and hard lobbying before the immigration department relented and let her back in. A Polish settler who had worked hard to earn a good living was told he couldn't bring his sweetheart to Canada because the government had tightened the law to prevent people from arriving for purposes of marriage.

In Toronto, members of the Communist party – or indeed any organization *thought* to be communist – were still being denied basic civil liberties by the police. In January, the Fellowship of Reconciliation, a new group of Christian pacifists, decided to sponsor a Sunday debate in a local theatre on the resolution "that the Toronto Police Commission is justified in its present attitude in regard to free speech." The head of the commission and the chief, Denny Draper, were invited to take the affirmative. The response to this even-handed invitation was extraordinary. The police not only refused to attend but also labelled the event "a communistic meeting under thin disguise" and threatened the theatre owner with a five-thousand-dollar fine under Section 98 of the Criminal Code if he didn't cancel the fellowship's lease.

Out of such arbitrary actions are great movements born. This was one of several similar acts of repression that led indirectly to the formation of the Co-operative Commonwealth Federation, Canada's first national socialist party. The spark, in Toronto, was Frank Underhill, then a peppery professor of history at the university. Underhill was so enraged by the police commission's action that he immediately composed a letter to the press declaring that "the right of free speech and assembly is in danger of suppression in this city" and deploring the police policy as "short sighted, inexpedient and intolerable." Sixty-eight people, most of them fellow faculty members, signed it.

As a result, the debate the police had tried to smother raged in the press for more than a month. It tells something about the state of the public mind, and also about the state of journalism in Toronto, that three of the four newspapers attacked the letter's signatories as communist sympathizers and insisted that free speech wasn't an issue. The *Globe* demanded that the professors who signed the "ridiculous document" be fired if they didn't recant. The *Evening Telegram* agreed with Sir John Aird, president of the Canadian Bank of Commerce, that the academics should "stick to their knitting." Only the *Star* supported the cause of free speech. The university kept quiet, its president concerned that this hint at radicalism might affect public and corporate support. One member of his board, the millionaire philanthropist Sir Joseph Flavelle, was privately vexed that the professors had "put themselves at variance with other representative bodies. . . ." In short, they had rocked the boat.

That same January in Montreal, the police turned out in force to break up a series of communist meetings demanding relief for the unemployed. In a striking example of overkill, the authorities dispatched 125 constables and 26 detectives to a single meeting in the Prince Albert Hall. As a result of this spate of raids, thirty-eight people were arrested and faced with one of a series of convenient charges: making seditious utterances, unlawful assembly, or simply failing to move on when ordered to do so. One luckless passerby, Izzy Houck, who stopped out of curiosity to watch a phalanx of police hustle eighteen men and one woman into custody, was himself arrested, fined three dollars, and jailed for three days.

When the communists tried to hold a meeting to protest these methods, the police pounced again, broke up the gathering, and arrested the speaker. That was too much for a young McGill law professor, Frank Scott, who wrote indignantly to the Montreal *Gazette* that the action was "clearly high handed and apparently illegal." As Scott pointed out, the only disorder occurred *after* the police made their arrests and started to disperse the audience. Their methods "amounted to a prejudging of the case before any evidence of crime existed."

Scott's voice was a lonely one. As in Toronto, the press and a good section of the general public were on the side of the police. The *Gazette* declared that the action was quite proper. "There is nothing to be gained," the editor wrote, "by a microscopic examination of abstract principles." That was a remarkable statement from a member of the Fourth Estate, an institution always ready to take up the cudgels for the equally abstract principle of press freedom, especially when the authorities tried to apply the child labour laws to newsboys. The police chief was unrepentant. "I cannot allow this sort of thing to take place in Montreal," he said. The principal of McGill, Sir Arthur Currie, told Scott to stop identifying himself as a law professor when writing to the press, even though Scott hadn't mentioned McGill. Currie didn't forbid Scott to protest but made it clear he'd be happier if he desisted.

The leading universities, presided over by boards of solid businessmen, had always been bastions of conservative thought, but now a few embers of resentment, sparked by the Depression, were smouldering. It had been a slow process; after all, eighteen months had elapsed since the shocking battle in Queen's Park. Yet there was movement.

The Depression had nudged both Underhill and Scott farther to the left. Each was at the centre of an informal discussion group whose members were drawn together by a growing concern over what was happening to the country. Each was groping toward some fairer way of organizing society. Though they had not met, both were gripped by a similar sense of mission that had religious overtones, by a hatred of establishment hypocrisy, and by a strong commitment to liberal-democratic values. They both came from strong Christian backgrounds. Scott was the son of Canon F.G. Scott, the most famous padre in the Canadian armed forces during the Great War. Underhill had been raised as a strict Presbyterian. Both had been exposed to Fabian thought at Oxford, Scott as a Rhodes Scholar, Underhill on a Flavelle Travelling Scholarship.

The determined Anglican and the stubborn Calvinist were drawn together by their political and social views although their personalities were markedly different. The lanky Scott, with his long, monklike features, was very much a social animal – personable, witty, outgoing. He belonged to a large and prominent Quebec family and was already recognized for both his poetry and his mastery of constitutional law. The circle of like-minded people whom he gathered around him was known simply as "The Group." Most had also studied at Oxford.

Underhill, by contrast, was a stubby, compact figure with a shy, sometimes waspish personality. He was a small-town cobbler's son – a precocious and often lonely bookworm to whom plays, movies, and all dances were forbidden as ungodly. But his was a questioning nature. By his fourth university year he had become a confirmed agnostic, yet was still unable and probably unwilling to

90

rid himself of the Calvinist streak. As he said, "I was born with this naïve feeling that if you don't keep a tight hold on yourself, you'll never accomplish anything. . . . To waste your energy on what seems to be a dissolute life never attracted me."

He was already a public supporter of the Western Progressives who were, he believed, "the only hope for a civilization in this country in which we won't all be abject slaves to a few vulgar, ignorant money barons from Toronto and Montreal." That was vintage Underhill. He had little use for big business for he said he had discovered through his researches that the country had been built by "grasping, unscrupulous businessmen." Now he saw those views confirmed. His hero, understandably, was J.S. Woodsworth.

Underhill was constantly in hot water with the university authorities. As a contributor to the then radical *Canadian Forum*, he knew he could never achieve "that austere impersonal objectivity which was exemplified by most of [his] academic colleagues who lived blameless lives, cultivated the golden mean and never stuck their necks out."

Clearly, he and Scott were destined to meet. The encounter, which has taken on mythological trappings in left-wing circles, took place in August. Underhill had persuaded John Dafoe to let him cover a world economic planning conference in Williamstown, Massachusetts. There he met Scott, who was attending as secretary to McGill's dean of law, Percy Corbett. The trio decided to take advantage of a free day to drive to the foot of Mount Greylock in the Berkshires and picnic on the slopes.

In that seminal discussion, Scott enthusiastically expounded to Underhill his theory that the Depression would force the establishment of a new political party. But unless the party knew where it was going, Scott went on to say, it would be swallowed by Mackenzie King's Liberals, who had already digested most of the Progressives. He argued that a research group was needed to set goals and provide a socialist underpinning. His model was the British Fabian Society. By the end of the day the two men had agreed to launch just such a group in their separate cities.

It is pleasant to contemplate these men, stretched out on a mountain slope, munching their sandwiches in the August sunshine and planning the future of their country. Did they know that they were making history – that this encounter would lead, within a year, to the launching of a new political movement that would change Canadian society? Probably not, though Underhill the historian may have sensed its significance. Did he ever appreciate the irony that this meeting, which helped to launch the socialist movement in Canada, should have taken place in the United States?

The League for Social Reconstruction, as the new group came to be called, had no American antecedents. Its parentage was entirely British; the men and women who planned it were mostly graduates of Oxford. Canada in those days took its political cues from the old country. Indeed, it's probable that without the Oxford experience of its founders, the League for Social Reconstruction would never have come into being.

In Montreal, Scott's two chief lieutenants were Eugene Forsey and King Gordon, both sons of the manse, both Rhodes Scholars. Like Scott they had been strongly influenced by the Christian socialism of R.H. Tawney of Balliol College, a strong critic of the capitalist system and perhaps the most influential reformer of his day.

The craggy-faced Forsey, aged twenty-seven, a man of dry wit who rarely suffered fools and was a wicked mimic of his contemporaries, was teaching political economy at McGill. Gordon was the son of the Reverend Charles Gordon, whose books (*The Sky Pilot, Glengarry School Days*, and others), written under the pen name of Ralph Connor, were international best-sellers. A friend and colleague of J.S. Woodsworth, the elder Gordon was a convert to the Social Gospel, the activist doctrine that swept the nonconformist Protestant churches before the Great War. King Gordon, aged thirty-one, heavily influenced by his father, and an active layman in the United Church, had just arrived in Montreal as a professor of Christian ethics at the United Theological College. More patient than the excitable Forsey, King Gordon had, in the words of a friend, "a great sense of humour which kept fanaticism in check."

They were joined by twenty-two-year-old David Lewis, who had studied under both Scott and Forsey and, like them, would soon go to Oxford as a Rhodes Scholar. Born in Polish Russia, he had already adopted his father's socialism and would one day become leader of the New Democratic Party. His familiarity with organized labour, especially in the Montreal needle trades, lent a practical tone to the academics' planning.

The idea of a Canadian Fabian society was one whose time had come. Such a group would have been formed even if Scott and Underhill had never met. When Underhill returned to Toronto from Williamstown he found that, quite spontaneously, events were already on the move along the lines he and Scott had discussed. Several professors who had signed his January protest letter had joined the movement, including Harry Cassidy, in whose house Underhill's informal group had been meeting. A tall, slender, tennis-playing social economist, Cassidy was also secretary and research director for the Unemployment Research Committee of Ontario. To that point, no one had made a study of unemployment or unemployment relief. No one, in fact, even knew the extent of the problem. The government apparently didn't care; it had made no effort to compile statistics. But Cassidy, with private funds, was already at work on the subject and would shortly provide the first extensive review in his influential book *Unemployment and Relief in Ontario, 1929-1932*.

This was a yeasty period in Canadian academic and artistic life. The earnest young theorists – Scott, Forsey, Gordon, Cassidy, Lewis, and others – who struggled that autumn to jolt their country out of its economic and social rut were destined to become the elder statesmen of the Left. Prominent all of their lives, they remained activists until their deaths. Their gospel was to be found in the pages of the *Canadian Forum*, a periodical of small circulation but immense influence, to which many of them contributed. Marching out of step on the flanks of this leftward movement were some unlikely characters who seemed to have joined the wrong parade. One was J.S. McLean, the wealthy meat packer, whose political ideas were far to the right but whose bankroll kept the *Forum* alive. Another was William Folger Nickle, a prominent Tory businessman and close friend of R.B. Bennett, who was honorary chairman of the Unemployment Research Committee, the mixed bag of academics and businessmen who had hired Cassidy to produce his monumental study.

Meanwhile, another Rhodes Scholar, Graham Spry, had climbed aboard. Spry was then the head of the Canadian Radio League, lobbying vigorously for a public radio system. Today he is venerated as the father of Canadian radio broadcasting; in 1931 he was concerned about his own future and also about the effects of the Depression on the country.

A former journalist, he wanted to do something to help "the poor bozos" of Canada. He was convinced that if the Liberal party didn't move to the left there would soon be a third party in Canada. He was planning to buy the *Farmer's Sun*, the weekly organ of the United Farmers of Ontario, and put it at the disposal of the new group. The funds came from his wealthy friend Alan Plaunt, who had helped him found the Radio League. Spry himself was so poor he was reluctant to take off his overcoat at meetings because the clothes he wore underneath were so shabby. But the League for Social Reconstruction changed his life in more ways than one. There he encountered a pretty if penniless economist, Irene Biss, the daughter of a British Labourite. Seven years later, when they could at last afford it, the two were married.

All that autumn, the two groups in Toronto and Montreal produced draft after draft – five in all – of a manifesto for the new league. They were grappling with a dilemma that has continued to plague the moderate Left: how radical should their rhetoric be? If it was too tame it would have little effect. If it was too strident it might sound like a communist document and scare off supporters. Montreal had the final draft and opted for caution in the hope (the eternal hope!) of attracting French-Canadian supporters. Finally, as the New Year dawned, the two groups arrived at a meeting of minds. A month later the LSR came into being and the politics of Canada entered a new era.

3

The The Fabians believed in "the inevitability of gradualism," the
Red Marxists in sudden, dramatic, and often violent action. Long
Menace before the LSR was even thought of, the Communist Party of Canada had seized the initiative and was exploiting the Depression for its own purposes. Controlled by dedicated and experienced leaders, it represented the only hope for tens of thousands of hopeless men and women. While the old-line parties clung to the status quo, the Communists promised a better world through radical change.

94

The financial and political establishments were terrified of the Communists. They were, as R.B. Bennett rightly declared, "a threat to the system." At a time of crisis, while the leaders of the major parties babbled on about the need for fiscal responsibility and a balanced budget, the Communists were the only people who seemed to care about the impoverished. They were also superbly organized through a network of grassroots organizations – the Young Communist League, the Young Pioneers, the Canadian Labor Defense League, the Workers' Unity League, the Farmers' Unity League, and the Unemployed Workers' Association.

Most Canadians, however, especially those who weren't on relief, would have tended to agree with Sir William Mulock, the white-bearded Chief Justice of Ontario, who, at a banquet of stock breeders in February, blamed every social malady except measles on the Communists. Communism, he said, was a diabolical force that would suppress religion, destroy marriage, nationalize women [sic!], abolish home life, and turn children into criminals. Communists should be barred from Canadian shores in the interests of British freedom, the Chief Justice declared.

British freedom was continually being invoked in the matter of the Red Menace. As Sam McBride, the mayor of Toronto, put it, "our stopping of Communist meetings shows that we are truly British." Being truly British, in those days, was a step above being truly Canadian. McBride's successor insisted that free discussion must be confined to what was considered compatible with "British institutions, British traditions and British principles" – this from the chief magistrate of a city where the British principles and traditions of free speech and assembly were assaulted and trampled almost daily.

But then, "British" in those days was a euphemism for "not foreign." Although the leaders of the Communist party were almost all British, the rank and file were largely immigrants, mainly Finns and Ukrainians. To the average Canadian, these foreigners were bent on destroying the British way of life in Canada. It was the same attitude that prompted some cities to require that all meetings be addressed in English and that the Union Jack should be the only flag carried in a street parade. The latter ordinance, which neatly outlawed the Red Flag, was just as conveniently overlooked when the Stars and Stripes appeared on July 4 or the Orange banner on July 12.

Mayor Ralph Webb of Winnipeg said that all the Reds should be dumped into the Red River. The old soldier's feeble jest was popular, especially with those members of the Canadian Legion who acted as Webb's storm troopers when the Reds took to the streets to demonstrate on behalf of the unemployed. The inference was that the communists were to blame for unemployment. The chief constable of Vancouver agreed. The unemployment situation, he said, was inspired by communists. Major-General James MacBrien, another old soldier newly appointed Commissioner of the RCMP, felt the same way. "If we were rid of them," said MacBrien, neatly if illogically summing up the entire economic dilemma, "there would be no unemployment."

MacBrien, a spit-and-polish officer, was brought in by Bennett to replace Cortlandt Starnes, the rugged veteran of the Klondike gold rush, who did not take the Red Menace as seriously as the Prime Minister thought he should. Compared to the easy-going Starnes, who had seen enough of the country to know that there were other menaces as grave as communism, MacBrien was close to being as fanatical on the subject as he was about many other things. He was fanatical about his appearance. *Maclean's* called him "one of the three best looking men in Canada . . . no debutante who has seen him in his major general's uniform has ever been quite the same." He was fanatical about his health: he swam daily in the Chateau Laurier pool and pointedly eschewed tobacco. He was equally fanatical about security. Security without peace, he once announced, was better than peace without security. After a term as chief of the general staff, with a chestful of medals for bravery, he had retired from the army to become a civilian air pilot when the government appointed him. Back in uniform, he was just the type of tough, unbending martinet to carry out R.B. Bennett's war on communism.

For MacBrien saw communists everywhere, preaching sedition, plotting revolution, undermining the status quo, boring from within like maggots in a wheel of cheese. That suspicion was shared by many if not most of the constabulary. To the typical Mounted Policeman, anyone slightly to the left of the established political parties was a dangerous agitator – words used by the undercover policemen who trailed the saintly J.S. Woodsworth, reporting on his speeches and his actions until finally ordered in 1925 to desist on the grounds that it was unseemly of the force to be shadowing a man who'd been an elected Member of Parliament for four years.

"This man continues to speak along the most radical lines," wrote the spy assigned to Woodsworth, "probably knowing he has already placed himself in a bad position, and, feeling that he cannot very well be in a worse *thinks he is at liberty to say just what he thinks*" (emphasis added).

MacBrien's men even invaded the sanctity of the first-class mail. Letters addressed to communist organizers were opened and read by the RCMP. Peter Hunter, an organizer for the Young Communist League, was one who was called to the Hamilton post office to have his mail from the World Youth Committee examined. He was required to open it for inspection before it was given to him and was told that if it wasn't in English it would have to be held for translation. Thus were the morals of the nation protected from wicked alien influences.

Early in his term, Bennett was prepared to crush the Communist party under what he would later refer to as "the iron heel of ruthlessness," another remark that would come back to haunt him. In February, a private conference of police chiefs assembled in the office of his Minister of Justice, Hugh Guthrie, painted an alarming picture of dissent and riot in their cities. Egged on by the Communists, the unemployed were staging demonstrations. The police wanted the power to suppress the party, as if by that action alone they could solve the problems the party was exploiting.

The federal government didn't have the machinery to act. It was true that under Section 98 of the Criminal Code, any association that advocated or believed in political or economic change by violence could be declared unlawful. The court case, however, had to be initiated by a province, not by Ottawa. Guthrie would have to put the pressure on Attorney General Colonel William Price, of Ontario, where the party had its national headquarters.

In March, Guthrie sent Colonel Price a sheaf of secret RCMP documents and assured him of the federal government's full co-operation "should [he] conclude that some definite action should be taken. . . ." He promised that more documents would be available and that an undercover Mountie was prepared to testify. In short, an elaborate fiction was being constructed to make a federal prosecution look as if it were provincial.

"I'm under pressure," Price told his staff. He knew a squeeze when he saw one. He wasn't a Red hunter, at least not then. Section 98 had rarely been invoked successfully and had lain dormant through the previous decade. But Ottawa was not easily denied. Price knuckled under and set about preparing a case against the Communist leadership. It would be another four months before he was ready to proceed.

The terror inspired by the Communists was far out of proportion to their real numbers. In late June, Harry Meighen, deputy reeve of York County, caused a one-day sensation by announcing that a thousand men were drilling with rifles and Mills bombs, preparing for an armed invasion to commandeer food from the Eaton and Simpson department stores. This was a total fabrication. At the time there were no more than thirteen hundred dues-paying members in the Communist Party of Canada. To bolster its image the party claimed four thousand. To bolster *its* image, the RCMP estimated five thousand.

The idea that thirteen hundred men and women – or even five thousand – could take over a country of ten million stretching from Victoria to Halifax seems ludicrous today and, indeed, seemed ludicrous then to many party members. Peter Hunter in Hamilton was amused by his local party leader, who had devised plans for a complete takeover of the city, noting the home of every police officer, fire station, hydro substation, and telephone exchange. "We considered him a bit off the beam," Hunter recalled. The dedicated leaders of the party had been to Moscow and were well aware of the revolutionary goals of the Communist International, but their own goals were more modest.

It is true that the Communists were using the unemployed for their own political ends. So, indeed, were the major parties. After his defeat, Mackenzie King viewed the unemployment crisis as a bonus for his own Liberals and a chance to get in a lick at Bennett. Although "sorry for the country's sake," he recorded on March 31 his satisfaction when told by Woodsworth and other Labour M.P.s that things were far worse than they had been the previous year under a Liberal administration.

That the Communists were sincere is beside the point; after all, so was Hitler. The gospel according to Karl Marx made them just as blindly orthodox as their capitalistic opponents, who clung to the dogma of the balanced budget no matter what the cost in human suffering. Yet in the ranks of the Reds and, indeed, among the leadership there was also a sense of genuine outrage not unmixed with human compassion for those who had been felled by economic disaster.

Unlike the members of the business establishment, the Communists rubbed shoulders daily with the underprivileged and knew at first hand what conditions were really like. They were poor themselves. Some, like A.E. Smith, were committed Christians who actually believed in the brotherhood of man and thought that communism was the most practical way to achieve it. Others were attracted by working for a cause, as people have been from time immemorial. Some were bitter, some naïve, some ruthless, all dedicated and dreadfully poor.

Tom Ewen's daughter, Jean, recalled in her memoirs that "there was more RCMP shekels circulating within the party than Moscow gold" - a reference to the undercover Mounties who lived on government salaries. When Ewen quit his job as a blacksmith at the Riddle Carriage Works in Saskatoon to become leader of the Workers' Unity League, his family suffered. "Being a full time functionary of the Communist party sounds like a bloody good job," his daughter wrote, drily. "Actually we became poorer than we had ever dreamed possible." They moved from their handsome brick home with its white columns, front porch, and cosy fireplace to a miserable shack on Flora Avenue in North Winnipeg.

Peter Hunter wrote that the full-time organizers were prepared to spend every waking minute promoting the party. Ewen's family saw little of him; he'd be away weeks at a time, and they never knew when he would go or when he would return. These zealots, in Hunter's words, "worked for . . . nothing more than the same relief voucher upon which so many depended. But they had a cause which needed them, a cause which held out hope for the future." For that they were prepared to suffer eviction, beatings, long jail terms, and, when the Spanish Civil War erupted, even death.

While Attorney General Price, under Ottawa's prodding, worked with his staff to prepare indictments against the leaders of the party, the Communists were making every day count. By

April, Tom Ewen had managed to get one hundred thousand signatures on a petition demanding the government initiate non-contributory unemployment insurance, a thirty-five-hour week, and a minimum wage of twenty-five dollars a week for both sexes. These were standard communist demands throughout the thirties, and it is doubtful that Ewen or anybody else in the party expected them to be met. It was the gesture that counted, not the results, and so he and thirty-five others headed for Ottawa to present their demands to the Prime Minister.

Ewen knew the publicity value of confrontation, especially against a man with Bennett's short fuse. His lively account of their meeting in the Railway Committee Room shows that he got the results he wanted.

Bennett did not greet the delegation. He strode into the room, laid down his walking stick, peeled off his gloves, shrugged out of his topcoat, and placed them with his bowler hat on a nearby chair. Then, with his labour minister, Gideon Robertson, he strode to the platform and uttered his first words: "I want some paper!" Several aides scrambled to obey the order and produced a bundle of some five hundred sheets.

"Now," shouted Bennett, "I want the names and addresses of all of you." He sat down and proceeded to write down all thirty-six names in his own hand. The Reverend A.E. Smith of the Canadian Labor Defense League, who was present (and has also left a lively account), was convinced he was searching for foreigners who, if they were not naturalized, could be deported. But the delegation had been hand picked; almost all were Canadian or British born.

Bennett turned to Smith, who had arranged the meeting. "What have you got to say?" he asked him. Smith indicated Ewen, who put forward the gist of the league's demands in his thick Scots burr.

Bennett rose and, in Ewen's words, "literally exploded." The destitution being felt in Canada, he declared, came from "wasteful living" and "unwise investments." Unemployment insurance would undermine the free institutions of Canada.

"Never," cried Bennett, "will I or any government of which I am a part, put a premium on idleness or put our people on the dole." He pointed a finger at Ewen, " . . . and I have a place where they will take care of you."

100

A covey of Mounties escorted the delegation to the street as the Prime Minister delivered a parting shot, " . . . and don't misrepresent me in what I have said to YOU!" To which Ewen replied, "Have no fear, Mr. Prime Minister, I'll give it to the people straight."

Tom Ewen and his group of squeaky-clean British subjects realized that their demands – modest as they seem today – would be turned down. Nonetheless it was gestures like theirs that attracted thousands of sympathizers. The age of hype had scarcely begun, but the Communists were already masters at grabbing headlines. Although that probably didn't help the party's public image as a group of shrill, self-serving, and dangerous wild men, it did focus the spotlight on the social ills of the time.

The Communists hadn't caused the problem, but they certainly exploited it; most of the mounting turmoil of the early Depression years – the hunger marches, the demonstrations, the confrontations with the police, the mass meetings, the street corner rough and tumble – was the result of their organizing. And the authorities, from the lowliest RCMP constable to the Prime Minister himself, played directly into their hands. It was a battle that Bennett could not win. In the end the much maligned Party would help drive him from office.

In the summer of 1931, however, Red baiting was popular – with the public, with the press, with the mayors of the major cities, with the police, and with most politicians. Undoubtedly there were many who agreed with Commissioner MacBrien that if only the party could be muzzled, the protests would stop and the Depression would go away. At the very least, its members would be prevented from embarrassing the authorities.

By August, Colonel Price's case was prepared and the government was ready to pounce. At six o'clock on the evening of the eleventh, eighteen members of the RCMP, Ontario Provincial Police, and Toronto city police were called into the Queen's Park office of Major-General V.A.S. Williams, the provincial police commissioner. No one had any idea of what was up until Williams spoke.

"Gentlemen," he said, "we are going to strike a death blow at the Communist Party – we hope. We are going to arrest the leaders, we are going to search their headquarters, as well as the homes of the men, and we are going to seize every paper and every document which will link the members with the party and the party in Russia."

The raids that followed were carried out with military precision. Six police cars sped off to the homes of the six party leaders. Simultaneous raids took place at the party's headquarters and the offices of the *Worker* and the Workers' Unity League. Other raids, all carefully timed, were staged by the RCMP in Timmins, Ontario, and Vancouver.

Tim Buck's shabby, red brick semi-detached house at 54 Delaney Crescent was empty when the police forced open the door to be greeted by a scene of lower-middle-class respectability: pet rabbits in cages chewing on grass, a piano in the living room with sheet music for several popular songs, and a Roll of Honour with a daily star against the name of each child who'd eaten his morning porridge – in addition, of course, to the inevitable portraits of Marx and Lenin.

The police tore into the house, ripping pictures from their frames, strewing clothing and bed linen, books, and even the contents of kitchen cupboards on the floor. When they left, with a mountain of documents, they didn't bother to replace the lock torn from the door. The other homes received a similar treatment.

Nine leading Communists were charged on three counts under Section 98: with being members of an unlawful association, with being officers of that association, and also with seditious conspiracy. The Ontario attorney general told the press that the raids had come about as the result of an interview with Hugh Guthrie. Guthrie blandly denied this, claiming the federal government had nothing to do with the raids and maintaining the fiction that the matter was purely provincial. But in the trial that followed, it was the federal police who supplied the bulk of the evidence.

The Toronto press, again with the exception of the *Star*, applauded the raids and proceeded to convict the accused before any evidence was heard. The *Financial Post* declared that "the files of the Mounted Police contain all the evidence needed for the jailing or deportation of many of the chief Soviet agents." The *Evening Telegram* tried to discredit its long-time rival, the *Star*, by describing it as "the Little Brother of the Reds." But in Winnipeg, the *Free Press* took a saner view. "The situation the Government has to meet would still remain though every Communist now in

102

Canada had been deported," the paper wrote. Jailing nine men was not going to solve the problem of a stagnant economy.

4

Two of the deepest pockets of destitution in Canada lay more *Quail* than two thousand miles apart – in the lignite fields of Southern *on* Saskatchewan and the coal and steel villages of Cape Breton, *toast* Nova Scotia. By the summer of 1931, conditions in both these regions were explosive, waiting only for the fuse to be lit. In Saskatchewan, the explosion occurred and bloodshed resulted. In Sydney, it was snuffed out.

With the Sydney steel mill closed and scores of families close to starvation, jobless men were ready to take desperate measures. One night at a meeting of the Unemployed Workers' Association feeling ran so high that an ex-steelworker rose to move that everyone go home, get a gun, and march on city hall to demand an increase in relief. The motion was seconded and passed before the chairman, Dan MacKay, realized what was happening. "Good God!" said MacKay. "Did they know what they were voting for?" A debate followed; parliamentary procedure was invoked, and the motion was finally rescinded.

It would not have been astonishing if it *had* passed, for relief that year did not provide bare subsistence, as George MacEachern, a twenty-six-year-old unemployed steelworker, discovered. MacEachern had been married in 1929. In 1930 he managed to get some pick-and-shovel work out of town, but by May 1931, when his first child was born, his savings were gone. To this moment he had not considered applying for relief – he'd always thought that was something for paupers. But now he swallowed his pride and went on the dole – the direct relief that R.B. Bennett opposed but that more and more communities like Sydney were dispensing in the absence of anything resembling public works. The family of three was given vouchers for just three dollars' worth of groceries a week – nothing for rent, light, telephone, or fuel and, shockingly, nothing for milk. It would take a third of the family's "income" just to provide milk for the new baby.

MacEachern joined the Unemployed Workers' Association and became an active executive, first as recording secretary and eventually as chairman. One of his first tasks was to sit on a committee to try to get milk for the children of the unemployed. One family of ten - the mother had tuberculosis - could afford only a pint of milk a day. They could get no more: the town council refused to help them and the Red Cross was out of funds. Yet because the farmers couldn't afford to bring milk into the town, they were feeding it to the pigs.

MacEachern found some people literally starving. One man who lived in a shack was so sick his friends asked the city health officer to investigate. They were told there was nothing wrong with the invalid that warm clothes and good food wouldn't cure. True enough; on a dollar a week, his main fare was turnips. He died insane in the Dartmouth Mental Hospital.

The death of an old man named Small at the local mission was put down by the superintendent to "malnutrition." MacEachern's friend Harry Morgan put it more bluntly. "He died of starvation and Christian sympathy," he said. "That's what killed him." Others died of what MacEachern called "a wearing away process." With their resistance lowered by malnutrition, they succumbed to the first disease that came along.

When MacEachern became chairman of the union, he decided to canvass the local aldermen privately to try to get an increase in the relief payments. The man who represented MacEachern's ward, Seymour Hines, agreed to sponsor such a motion at the next council meeting. But when Hines arrived and looked down at the front row filled with officials from the steel company, he knew the motion wouldn't pass. "They didn't speak," MacEachern recalled later; "they didn't have to." In the discussion that followed, one alderman, Dan MacDonald, charged that the unemployed wanted "quail on toast." Another declared that if a vote of the taxpayers was taken, *all* relief would dry up. Hines's motion was defeated; only the mover and seconder voted for it.

The union called a mass meeting in the Unemployed Workers' Hall. Only a few council members attended. Alderman Hines again spoke in favour of an increase in relief. The next speaker, an alderman who had voted against the motion, broke down and cried. He admitted that although he was in favour of more relief and had promised to vote for it, his courage had failed when the vote was taken.

104

This confession threw the meeting into such an uproar that MacEachern found he couldn't keep order. MacDonald, the man who'd made the "quail on toast" remark, managed to slip out by a side door, but another councilman, who also tried to flee, had the sleeve of his jacket torn off. The next morning the police picked up some of those who had addressed the meeting and charged them with failure to pay their poll tax. The charges were not pressed; at the station they were simply warned against "stirring up trouble" - a wishful admonition, typical of those dark years, that suggests the gap of understanding between those in authority and those in want.

In Sydney, as elsewhere, the upper classes, such as they were, seemed totally divorced from the conditions of the destitute. MacEachern discovered that in court one day when a member of the union was charged with stealing coal and fined ten dollars. At that, the defence lawyer, George Morrison, cried out in horror. "In Heaven's name," he asked the judge, "where do you think the man is going to get the $10? I should think if he had $10 he wouldn't bother stealing coal. He stole it because he didn't have any money." After some discussion, the magistrate dropped the sum to five dollars. Morrison explained that it would be just about as difficult for the accused to get five dollars as ten. The fine was dropped to three dollars and eventually to a simple payment of costs.

In nearby Glace Bay, conditions were just as grim. Coal mining in the thirties was a form of serfdom. The miners could never move away because they were always in debt to the company store, "a jolly little system of perversion invented to overcome the inconvenience of anti-slavery laws," in the words of Bill McNeil, who grew up there. Half a century after the Depression, McNeil, in a bitter indictment, wrote that the town was built on the cheap by companies that came in to savage the region's natural resources.

The local stores, churches, schools, and town council were all in thrall to "the Company" - Dominion Coal - which built the roads and the cheap houses, kept the miners in debt, and blacklisted those who tried to complain. "The Company's immense influence extended not only to the local governing councils but also to the provincial and federal governments. . . . " McNeil, who was to become a CBC producer, wrote that "many children died during the Depression in Glace Bay. Nobody said they starved to death, but that was actually the reason."

The miners were a proud bunch, unwilling to accept a handout except as a last resort. In desperation some would sneak out to the local relief station, fearful that they would be seen, following a long and circuitous route of back alleys, sometimes hiding in the shadows for hours until they could claim their bit of lard, some sugar, flour, or bread. No one wanted to be seen "carrying the sack," as the local phrase had it – a telltale bag containing relief supplies.

Although there was coal everywhere in Glace Bay – in huge storage bins, in railway cars, and in seams that cropped out on the surface of the ground – people were invariably cold because the company police prevented them from taking it. By the end of the thirties, there wasn't an available stick of wood left in town. Driftwood, picket fences, shingles, and clapboard, even telephone poles disappeared in the dead of night to prevent people from freezing to death. The company houses had no basements and no insulation. The walls were full of cracks. The floors were uncarpeted. The only furniture, other than a kitchen table, consisted of a few chairs and a couple of mattresses upstairs. Newspapers took the place of curtains.

Appalling as conditions were in Cape Breton, those in the Souris coalfields of Southern Saskatchewan were worse. This was lignite country. The soft, dirty coal, mined in the vicinity of Bienfait, nine miles east of Estevan on the U.S. border, was sold domestically. Mining therefore was seasonal. Until the Depression, the miners earned a year-round living by working six months in summer as farm help. But now there was no work on the farms. The big coal companies were themselves teetering on the edge of insolvency, largely because they could not compete with the cheaper strip-mining techniques introduced to the area by the Truax-Traer firm. In the face of this threat, they cut the meagre wages even lower.

The five largest companies, known as the Group, conspired to fix prices, control production limits, and handle labour problems. These were Bienfait Mines Limited, Crescent Collieries Limited, Eastern Collieries of Bienfait Limited, Western Dominion Collieries Limited, and Manitoba and Saskatchewan Coal Limited,

106

better known as M&S. Together with a sixth company, National Mines, where working conditions were better, they were called the Big Six.

Before the Depression the average earnings in the Souris fields were only half those paid elsewhere in Saskatchewan and Alberta. By 1931 they had fallen by an additional 21 per cent. Some miners made as little as nine dollars a week; twenty-five was considered exceptional. Those working on a tonnage basis (twenty-five cents a ton, reduced from fifty-six cents) did better than those on straight hourly wages. But to scrape together a living these men had to work fourteen to sixteen hours a day, cooped up like moles from sunrise to sunset. They rarely saw daylight.

The company's deductions could actually leave a worker in debt. The miners had to buy their own slickers and boots – boots that cost five dollars a pair and lasted barely a month in the ankle-deep water. Each man paid a dollar and a half a month for the company doctor plus an extra fee in cash for a visit to him. They paid for powder, they paid for squibs, they paid for carbon for their lamps, they paid for sharpening their shovels and picks. At the M&S mine, they paid fifty cents to use the bath house and three-quarters of a cent a gallon for water delivery.

These sums added up. An experienced miner, for instance, could make a $3.60 keg of black powder last long enough to mine twenty-five tons, for which he was paid $6.25. A less experienced man, who managed only ten tons, could find himself permanently in debt. All were regularly cheated on their tonnage. When they were paid for mining a ton, it was always a long ton – 2,240 pounds. But when they bought a ton of coal they got only a short ton – 2,000 pounds. The weighing system was crooked and the scales inaccurate. Although most ore cars carried at least three tons of coal, the men were never paid for more than two tons a carload.

Nor were they paid for any work they did apart from the coal they mined. Besides being dangerous, a cave-in cost them, not the company, money. Harry Hesketh, working with his son for Bienfait Mines, lost half a day's work when a cross-piece broke, dumping two and a half feet of clay on the floor of the mine. When he asked for recompense for cleaning it up, he was told, "We don't pay anybody for anything like that."

Pete Gembey, who worked for Western Dominion, toiled for sixty hours and was paid for twenty because he'd spent most of his time fixing a piece of machinery that had broken down. Some men had to work for an hour and a half just getting rid of water before they could start mining coal. They also had to lay track and repair it for no extra pay.

They didn't dare complain. In the five mines of the Group there were no grievance committees. Plenty of hungry men stood ready to take the places of those who had the temerity to question the system. Anyone who complained was told bluntly to pack up his tools and get out.

John Billis, working for Eastern Collieries, had been standing for ten hours in two feet of water when he was told he had to work overtime to fill an order. He'd been loading coal all day and was dead tired, but his boss warned him, "If you go home you don't come back any more." His fellow miner, Wilbur Enmark, who suffered a broken leg after a cave-in, complained about the company's meagre compensation for injury. Ed Pierce, the mine manager, told him to take what he'd been offered or he'd get a damned sight less. When Enmark had the audacity to hire a lawyer, Pierce told him he'd be blacklisted. "I will chase you out of the country!" he said. Enmark had no work for a year.

When its weigh scales broke down, Bienfait Mines took it upon itself to guess at the amounts. The miners objected and refused to go underground. When Harry Hesketh was sent to explain the situation to the mine manager, he was summarily fired.

Working conditions in the mines were ghastly. In the Crescent mine, Martin Day worked continually in water that often rose to the mid-calf. Day was paid not by the ton but at the rate of a dollar a linear foot. Under good conditions he could clear seven dollars a day. But when the water was bad it took two days to make that quota. Naked electrical wires added to the hazard; Day, a Scottish-born miner, had never seen uncovered wires before.

The air was always bad, often heavy with smoke from blasting. The "black damp" – air from an old shaft thick with carbon dioxide – was so dense that in Bienfait Mines the fan was unable to move it. When the men tried to light their lamps, the black damp would snuff them out. In twenty-eight years in that mine

108

Harry Hesketh had never seen any instrument taken down to test the air. The black damp had no odour. It could only be detected when the lamps flickered out. By that time the men could be overcome from lack of oxygen.

The Mine Act was never completely enforced, as one mine inspector told a royal commission that later uncovered these conditions. Yet the deep-seam operators were never prosecuted. John R. Brodie, vice-president of Bienfait Mines, was to swear that he considered the conditions excellent. "I do not think," he said, "there is anything in Western Canada to surpass it. . . . There are very few hazards as compared with other operations in other parts of western Canada."

The working conditions below ground that Brodie described so lyrically were matched by the living conditions on the surface. The transients in the burgeoning urban jungles were no worse off than the families jammed into the tar-paper shacks that the companies constructed among the mountains of slag for their employees. In this grassless and treeless world, there was no comfort. When the district sanitary officer was finally ordered to inspect 113 of these shanties in the late fall, he found 53 cold, 43 leaky, 52 dirty, 25 overcrowded, and all in need of repair. Only two companies provided showers for their miners. Four made no provision whatever for sanitation.

John Harris and his family lived in a two-room shack without a basement built on a slope. The company provided neither furniture nor storm door and windows. Wind blew the snow through the window frames; rain poured down through the roof, which the company refused to repair. During a storm, the family moved their beds up the slope and put out pans and pails to catch the water.

The Baryluk family of eleven lived in a one-bedroom shack protected from the elements by only two inches of wood. Sleeping two or three to a bed in this overcrowded hovel, they found themselves stepping onto a floor thick with snow in the winter mornings. Yet they and others found it better to live in the company shacks because by doing so they were recognized as permanent employees and thus guaranteed work.

The worst off were the foreign workers, some of whom existed in shacks made from empty dynamite boxes. These pig-sties often had only three walls of wood, the fourth being the hillside itself. Pete Gembey's first house was in "shack valley" in Taylorton. "It was in a ravine right up against the big hill. They dug a square hole and they put boards on it and they slapped on a roof. ... The roof was tar paper and partly covered with dirt. ... You couldn't keep it clean. ... The boards ... they would dry up and cracks would form, about half an inch or so. Some boards had knot holes and sometimes a snake would crawl through. ..."

Single men were crammed into bunkhouses, two to a bug-infested bed. For that and electric light they were charged $1.30 a day and had to provide their own bedding. If they didn't use the company bunkhouse, they paid a weekly "fine" of one dollar.

The foremen who lived on the mine property were better housed. The mine managers lived comfortably in Estevan, where they had electric light and running water. The absentee owners lived in luxury in Calgary, Winnipeg, and New York City.

The companies squeezed their workers in every possible way. All put pressure on their employees to use the company store, but M&S went further: it insisted. As Fred Booth, a machinist's helper, explained, he had no choice anyway. "I am always in hole to the company. ... It was Hobson's choice for me. ..." Even if the company had allowed him to go into Bienfait and buy provisions more cheaply, he didn't have a car and he didn't have the cash. He got credit at the company store but paid through the nose. For groceries that would have cost him three dollars in Bienfait he was charged six by the company. As a result, many miners got pay envelopes containing only a note showing an increasing debt.

At the M&S mine, the manager, Alex "Happy" Wilson, went to great lengths to prevent his employees from shopping outside the fenced-in compound. Peter Boruk's mail-order parcel from Eaton's was broken into and the contents hurled at him as the timekeeper chased him from the office. Mrs. Francis Gray was warned: "If you're going to get stuff from Eaton's you will have to leave camp." Her parcels, too, were opened.

Pedlars and farmers were banned from the mine premises, but some of the women would steal across to the briquet plant just outside the compound to bargain with the locals for eggs and meat. When Wilson drove by, they would throw the produce into a nearby ditch to avoid being caught. Others sneaked into Este-

110

van for some illicit shopping to return thirty pounds heavier, their purchases hung from their waists under billowing skirts. M&S even got its pound of flesh when John Slenka's cow wandered off: the company fined him ten dollars. When he tried to buy hay from a farmer at five dollars a load, they stopped him. Company hay went for six dollars and was so rotten the cows wouldn't eat it.

Is it surprising, then, that with these conditions, and with further pay cuts in the offing, the miners in the Souris fields should start to talk about forming a union? It wouldn't be easy; these men and their predecessors had been trying and failing to organize for more than twenty-five years. But now they were more desperate than they had ever been, and thus the stage was set for one of the bloodiest confrontations in Canadian labour history.

5

No labour union wanted to touch the Souris fields. The United *Blood*
Mine Workers of America had tried in 1907. The owners refused *on the*
to negotiate, fired all who joined the union, and formed a protec- *coal*
tive association to dismiss or blacklist all future union militants.
When, in 1915, the UMWA tried again, the owners locked out the miners and had them fined and prosecuted under wartime regulations.

In 1920 the Souris miners applied to the first of the "vertical" unions – the One Big Union, as it was called. Out came an organizer from Calgary, P.M. Christophers. He was immediately kidnapped by a seven-man vigilante committee that included a provincial police corporal, hustled out of town, and warned he'd be tarred and feathered if he returned. All seven vigilantes were acquitted of wrongdoing. The police were then brought in to protect mine properties, three dozen militants lost their jobs, and would-be union men were threatened with rent increases and loss of credit.

Thus when the miners in the summer of 1931 asked for help from the Trades and Labour Congress and the All-Canadian Congress of Labour, they got no response. As a last resort they turned to the Workers' Unity League and its new affiliate, the Mine Workers' Union of Canada, which had broken away from its international parent, the UMWA. (The story was a familiar one: the American-run union had not cared enough about its Alberta branch to give it any help.)

On August 25, the new union's president, James Sloan, a short, grey-eyed Scot, arrived in Estevan and held an organizational meeting. Six hundred miners joined the union, allowing Sloan to boast that he had a "100 per cent sign up of mine employees of the coal fields."

The fact that any union, and a communist-led union at that, could so quickly have signed up a majority of the miners suggests that the limits of despair had been truly reached. The problem of organization was a daunting one. The prospective members were living on company property under the eyes of company security guards. Many couldn't write or speak English. Boatloads of Slavs and Swedes had been imported in the late 1920s to do most of the menial work for the lowest possible wages, making it easy for the companies to cut the miners' pay after 1928. It was in their interests to play up ethnic divisions: the British-born got the best jobs; the bosses were English, Irish, or Scots. As Howard Babcock, a company cook, was later to testify, they "tried to compete with each other, trying to get the most work out of the foreign miner." They did their best, he said, "to keep the animosity between the two groups at fever pitch all the time. . . ."

Most of the men who rushed to join the union in spite of these divide-and-conquer tactics didn't care about political affiliation. They simply wanted a better deal. The mine owners, however, seized on a heaven-sent issue and used it as an excuse to refuse to negotiate with the "Red Union." The Big Six sent a message to Sloan: "We will not meet with you or any representative of an organization such as yours which, by your own statement, boasts a direct connection with the 'entire Workers' Unity League and the Red Internationale of Soviet Russia.' " In response, the union voted to cease work at midnight September 7 unless the mine owners met with their representatives.

In the light of the tragedy that followed, it's important to note that the community remained calm as the deadline approached. Sergeant William Mulhall, the resident Mounted Policeman in the district, reported on September 5 that there was "no immediate cause for alarm." The rugged Mulhall was not a man to panic. He was close to retirement, with twenty-three years' ser-

112

vice in the Police; he had fought in the Boer War with the Royal Scots Fusiliers and had joined the South African Constabulary under the legendary Sam Steele before coming to Canada. He had considerable sympathy for the miners and advised his superiors that "our investigation must be carried out with care and patience. . . ."

It was the mine owners, not the union, who were predicting violence and urging that more police be rushed to Estevan. Mulhall believed they wanted a strike. The ringleader was Charles Morfit, consulting engineer for Western Dominion Collieries at Taylorton. Morfit, an American, had given the company some bad advice that had caused serious losses. As Mulhall pointed out, "if the plant is forced to close down through strike conditions, it will form a loophole of escape . . . without exciting severe criticism from the investors. . . ."

Mulhall reported that most of the miners weren't in favour of communism but thought they'd had unjust treatment and needed a leader to air their grievances. "If these had been adjusted," he wrote, "the present situation would have been avoided." Meanwhile there was no reason to expect any violence or destruction of property.

Two days later, on September 7, a second Mounted Policeman, Detective Constable G.A. Sincennes, arrived from Regina and confirmed Mulhall's appreciation of the situation. He attended a union meeting, "orderly in every manner," in which Sloan counselled against violence in order to retain the sympathy of the community. Sincennes believed the miners would abide by that advice.

At midnight, the miners struck. For a week, the situation remained calm. The mine operators still refused to meet with the union. The RCMP sent reinforcements to Estevan. An attempt by three of the operators to bring in strikebreakers was thwarted when the boarding house cook refused to feed them. These were farmers, not miners, and Mulhall reported that the real object was "to provoke strikers to some act of overt violence thus creating a situation demanding police interference and promoting a crisis." Again, Mulhall put the blame on Morfit of Western Dominion. "Mr. Morfit is an American with extreme views who has had experience in the Pennsylvania USA strikes, when riots occurred and the miners were literally 'mowed down.' His attitude is that the present situation be handled by the police in a similar manner."

The companies now moved to get rid of Sergeant Mulhall. J.W. Spalding, the RCMP's assistant commissioner in Regina, was told that the Mounted Policeman lacked tact and common sense. "His apparent inability to be able to grasp the present situation here, as well as his very indifferent attitude of action, is being attributed, as a cause of the greater part of the trouble." Mulhall, of course, had grasped the situation very well, and Spalding in a blunt reply backed up his man. That assessment was reinforced by Inspector F.W. Schutz, who reported that if Mulhall hadn't handled the affair of the strikebreakers with tact there would have been bloodshed. He too believed that "the operators wish the Police to start something." Some of the Americans had been heard to say that "if this was in the States it would soon be settled that the strikers would be mowed down with machine guns if they carried on the way they do up here."

On September 27, two diametrically opposed reports reached Regina. The RCMP was told by Schutz that "you would not think a strike was in progress at all. . . . There is no Bolshevik or red talk going on as far as I can learn." At the same time the attorney general of Saskatchewan received a wire from the Big Six demanding more reinforcements and charging that "mob law has ruled." Bloodshed, they insisted, was imminent.

Nine smaller mines, meanwhile, had signed with the union while one large company continued to operate. This was the Truax-Traer mine, two miles east of Estevan, whose strip operation had caused such dismay among the deep-seam companies. This mine employed no pick-and-shovel men because all the work was done by machinery; none of its employees were unionized. But on September 24, the union decided to move in. Two hundred strikers massed in front of the company office and tried to get the steam-shovel men to quit work. A dozen Mounted Policemen were rushed to the scene and a truce arranged until the two sides could negotiate.

The strike, by this time, had split the community of Estevan. The ordinary townspeople sympathized with the miners; the establishment - leading merchants, town council, newspaper - tended to favour the owners. The Estevan *Mercury* was strongly opposed to the strike, raising the old cry, blaming "outside inter-
114

ests" for paralysing "the province's most essential industry." It continued to harp on the "introduction of foreign influences and strange leaders" and wrote glibly about "the disruption of good relations that have existed since the opening of the coal fields forty years ago." In one fanciful passage it decried "the state of unpleasantness in that vale of peaceful industry."

There was nothing in the paper to suggest that the conditions in that Elysian vale were vile; but then, there never had been. Reading the *Mercury*, one could only conclude that bosses and workers were all part of a happy family whose cool, sequestered way of life had been brutally disrupted by interlopers.

The explosion came because the town council panicked and then tried to cover up its panic. The union decided to hold a parade on September 29, from Bienfait through Taylorton and into Estevan. Its purpose was to dramatize the plight of the miners and publicize a meeting scheduled for the evening. The star speaker, who had come from Winnipeg, would be the redoubtable Annie Buller, a short, husky woman and a fiery speaker who was the darling of the communist movement. The town council, which had shown where it stood by denying relief to the strikers, met hurriedly that morning and voted to ban the parade and deny the use of the hall to the union.

That decision, more than any other factor, led to bloodshed that afternoon. Some of the local merchants, it was said, feared the parade would get out of hand and their stores would be looted and damaged. No doubt the mine owners' statements about "mob rule" had made them nervous. Yet there had been parades held in and around Bienfait for days without violence. The miners were planning to bring women and children; were they really prepared for a bloody confrontation?

The council later tried to claim they had warned the strikers that the police would confront them. That was a cover-up designed to free the council from blame for what happened later. The copy of the telegram that Dan Moar of the union executive received didn't mention any police action – just that permission to hold a parade and a meeting had been denied. The minutes of the council proceedings for that morning were either destroyed or never recorded. A confirming letter, which *did* mention the police, wasn't mailed until after the fact and was not received until the following day; it appears to have been an attempt to white-

115

wash the council's actions and was written some hours after the trouble began. Moar was later to testify that "had there been any such knowledge of such an order to the police, the miners would never have attempted to hold either a parade or motor-car procession in Estevan."

A convoy of trucks and cars, the miners reasoned (splitting hairs), wasn't actually a parade. It certainly looked like a parade – thirty or forty vehicles, many draped with Union Jacks and banners reading "DOWN WITH COMPANY STORES," "WE WANT HOUSES, NOT PIANO BOXES," "WE WILL NOT WORK FOR STARVATION WAGES." The miners intended to drive into Estevan, confront the mayor, and ask him to rescind the ban on the evening meeting.

The police were apparently not expecting them or they would surely have met the cavalcade on the outskirts of town. Half of the forty-seven members of the RCMP were two miles away at the Truax-Traer strip mine, where the earlier events had suggested the real trouble lay. So much for the pretence that the strikers had been warned that the police would stop them.

Now, as the long line of vehicles came within half a block of the city hall it encountered twenty-two policemen hastily strung out across the road, determined to prevent the cavalcade from proceeding farther. Eyewitness accounts of what happened next are confused, but one thing is clear: Chief Alex McCutcheon of the Estevan police got involved in a struggle with Martin Day, the Scottish-born digger from Crescent Collieries, who struck him a blow that put him out of action. "Come on, boys," Day was shouting. "Come on, give it to them!" The Mounted Police sent at once to the Truax-Traer mine for reinforcements.

Almost immediately the fire truck was called in to disperse the strikers with a jet of water. But while the firemen tried to connect the hoses, they were set upon by the miners. A twenty-five-year-old Taylorton man, Nick Nargan, climbed to the top of the truck and attacked the engine with a crowbar. A shot rang out, and to the horror of the onlookers, Nargan fell dead.

Across the street, a wide-eyed thirteen-year-old, Glenn Petersen, was attracted by the noise. He left the basement washroom of the Hillsdale School, climbed onto an incinerator outside the building, and peered out, watching the mêlée until his father, a garage owner, dashed up and pulled him away. "You wanta get

116

yourself killed?" the elder Petersen asked his son. It wasn't an idle question.

The scene would stay with Petersen all his life. A full-fledged riot was now in progress. The strikers were picking up rocks and other missiles and flinging them at the police; the police were backing slowly away, firing their revolvers into the ground or in the air. By the time RCMP reinforcements from Truax-Traer joined the fray, the situation was out of control. Three strikers were dead or dying, eleven more were injured, four bystanders were wounded, and five policemen were sent to hospital. Although the police tried to suggest that the strikers were armed, no policeman suffered a gunshot wound, but all of the injured strikers were struck with .45-calibre police bullets. A city constable, W.D. MacKay, later estimated that six hundred shots had been fired.

The police also tried to insist that they did not open fire until the strikers forced them back to the wall. In fact, the shooting began when Nick Nargan was killed on top of the fire engine. Many of the police were young and inexperienced. Of the forty-three RCMP constables on duty that day, thirty-four had less than a year's service with the force and twenty-six were under the age of twenty-five.

A good many of the bullets went wide. Clyde Butterworth, an Estevan music teacher walking a block north of the town hall, was shot in the leg. A fifteen-year-old, Tony Martin, who was strolling down the main street, got a bullet in his wrist. His companion, Bernie Hitchcock, had a miraculous escape when a bullet took out one of his front teeth.

The worst case was that of a Mrs. King, a weaver, who had come from England to visit her brother in a neighbouring community. She had chosen that day of all days to visit a doctor in Estevan. Seven bullets from Mounted Police guns pierced the walls of the room in which she was waiting. She was hospitalized for forty days and continued to get treatment as an outpatient until December 17. Neither the federal nor the provincial government would accept responsibility for her injuries.

The police bullets drove the unarmed strikers from town. Most piled into the nearest car or truck and fled back to Bienfait, chased by police who were still firing their weapons.

Two strikers picked up Julian Gryshko, one of their number

117

who had been shot in the abdomen, and drove him to the private hospital run by Dr. James Creighton, who acted as company doctor for all the collieries. Creighton had phoned in to remind the nurses in charge that no one was to be treated unless he had paid a week's fee in advance or was a policeman in uniform "because the Government pays the men in uniform." Gryshko was denied aid and was driven to Weyburn, fifty miles away. He died before his friends could get him to the hospital.

Meanwhile, Pete Gembey and three others brought Peter Markunas, a twenty-seven-year-old miner from Bienfait, into Creighton's hospital on a stretcher only to be turned away by the matron. Gembey remembered her order: "Take him away, we don't treat no Red guys around here." Markunas was also driven to Weyburn. He died there in hospital two days later.

The funeral that followed was the largest the district had ever known. Fifteen hundred people tried to crowd into the Ukrainian Labour Temple in Estevan, which the strikers had used as a headquarters. After the service, most filed in a mile-long cortège to the graveyard.

The strike was still in effect, but the heart had gone out of the strikers. The union leadership was either in jail or in hiding. Thirteen had been arrested immediately after the riot, and more were captured later. The trials that followed were marked by allegations of official bias, stacked evidence, and at least one case of jury tampering. The counsel for the mine owners bought drinks for some of the jurors and confided, "We will have to get the whole bunch of red sons of bitches." The attorney general had already made his position clear when he referred to several of the accused as "radicals," "reds," "Communists," and "agitators."

Of the twenty men and one woman arrested, eleven went to jail for as little as three months and as much as two years. Some served time only because they were too poor to pay the fines. The charges were dropped or dismissed for seven, including James Sloan, the union leader, who hadn't been present at the riot. Oddly, another of these was Martin Day, whose attack on the police chief was generally credited with starting the fracas. But another man got a year in jail for starting the riot and assaulting a police officer.

That curious twist served to point up one of the serious problems faced by the police – the difficulty of identifying the rioters,

118

whom few of them knew by sight. In fact, many of the identifications were open to question, as a local policeman, Constable W.D. MacKay, was to testify. MacKay, who personally knew many of the rioters, could identify only a few, and yet "we had a policeman there who had never seen them before, could identify everybody that came up." MacKay was astonished that the Mounties from out of town were able to identify people they'd never seen before. "I always thought," he said, in a piece of diplomatic understatement, "they were stretching a little bit."

One woman who proved difficult to identify was the indomitable Annie Buller, who had been slated to speak at the banned meeting that night. She should have been an easy person to spot at the riot, for she was unmistakable – a small, stout woman with bright red hair and strong features. In fact, the evidence that she was present at the scene was remarkably flimsy. Several witnesses swore she was in Bienfait at the time of the riot, and this included her boarding-house keeper, who was anything but a communist. At one point the wrong woman, a Miss Carroll, was arrested because the police were confused by the similarity of her clothing. In spite of this, Annie Buller was eventually sentenced to nine months' hard labour in the Battleford jail.

The strike collapsed within ten days of the riot. Several union sympathizers – "agitators from Winnipeg," Inspector W.J. Moorehead called them – turned up to urge the rank and file to vote against returning to work. Moorehead dispatched a sergeant and eight men to arrest them on the catch-all charge of vagrancy. Two days later the strike ended.

The official RCMP attitude can be seen in Moorehead's report of October 15: "The rioters consisted largely of Foreigners as very few English speaking people took an aggressive part. . . . I would strongly recommend discriminate deportation of the radical foreign element. In my opinion and until this method is put into effect, there is sure to be continued trouble. . . . "

The Premier, James Anderson, made his own position clear on October 17 when he urged the miners to sever relations with the union leaders "because of their revolutionary tendencies." The union had no chance. The owners continued to refuse to meet with it.

The royal commission set up to investigate conditions in the mines accepted most of the miners' grievances, but unfortunately its terms of reference did not include an impartial investigation of the riot. Judge Edmund Wylie, the commissioner, recommended a fairer wage scale and better working and living conditions. There was some improvement, but the operators followed few of the recommendations. The blacklist continued. Pete Gembey, for instance, who was blacklisted in 1931, didn't get his job back for ten years.

It didn't pay to take a stand. Late that year, Sergeant J.G. Metcalfe reported to his superiors in Regina that any man "who has nerve enough to approach the Owners on behalf of the workers . . . is immediately branded a Red. . . ."

No one wanted to help the families of the dead and wounded miners rendered destitute by the events of September 29. The union had approached the Estevan town council, which refused to issue any relief. The RCMP was worried that the union would then go after the federal government for assistance. But Ottawa denied all responsibility, insisting that the union look after its own. The union, however, was rapidly falling apart. In the years that followed, no other labour organization was found to replace it. The mine operators flatly refused to recognize any organized group until 1945, when times were better and the now militant United Mine Workers of America under John L. Lewis moved in and successfully organized the coalfields.

Most of the principals are long dead, but in Estevan the strike has never been forgotten. And no one who strolls down Fourth Street from Souris Avenue to Eleventh can miss the small monument that stands in front of the old city hall. Here are engraved the names of the three men who died on that bloody afternoon almost sixty years ago. One line has been carefully erased, but everybody in town is familiar with it and never tires of repeating to the visitor the original obliterated words: "MURDERED BY THE RCMP."

6

Nine on trial The royal commission into the Estevan tragedy was still sitting in Regina on November 2 - Martin Day and Dr. Creighton both gave testimony that day - when another hearing began to make headlines in Toronto. In the wood-panelled No. 3 Courtroom of

120

Toronto's romanesque city hall, the trial of Tim Buck and eight comrades, arrested in the August raids on Communist headquarters, got under way at last.

There they sat, nine ordinary-looking men, the objects of considerable curiosity, some apprehension, and a modicum of sympathy – a mixed bag of party stalwarts and lesser lights. The diminutive Buck and his tall, spare colleague Tom Ewen of the Workers' Unity League were the big game. The grizzled Malcolm Bruce, editor of the *Worker*, was another obvious catch. Others seemed to have been chosen arbitrarily and in one instance by accident. Big John Boychuk and Mathew Popovich, in their blue serge suits – contrasting with the work clothes that Bruce habitually wore – were leaders of the Ukrainian wing of the party. Tom Hill, leader of the Finnish wing, looked almost professorial with his slicked-down hair and steel-rimmed glasses. Three younger men – Buck's protégé Sam Carr, recently returned from the Lenin School in Moscow, Tomo Cacic, a thirty-six-year-old Croatian-born party member who was trying to start a radical Croatian newspaper, and the twenty-two-year-old Mike Gilmore of the Young Communist League – were smaller fry. Cacic had wandered into the WUL headquarters to read some party literature and chat with the secretary when the police scooped him up. Gilmore had been arrested because he was bunking in Ewen's flat when the police arrived. When they couldn't find Ewen, they grabbed Gilmore instead. Since the YCL was not named in the indictment, he was released before the trial ended.

On the third day of the trial the nine men in the dock were startled to see a familiar if incongruous figure walk into the courtroom – a swarthy, stubby Mounted Policeman, only five feet five inches tall, with a solemn poker face and mild brown eyes. In spite of his scarlet tunic and blue breeches he didn't look a bit like a Mountie – at least, the Hollywood version. Even the Stetson seemed too big for him, while his European features belied the stereotype. Nevertheless he was an active member of the force and had been since 1918.

His real name was John Leopold, but the Communists recognized him as Jack Esselwein, a former comrade until his exposure three years before. Once a trusted member of the party (Tom Ewen's children knew him as "Uncle Jack"), he was privy to its darker secrets – the star witness for the Crown.

The government had brought Sergeant Leopold down from the

121

Yukon, where he was stationed, to identify the accused men as Communists and to nail down the party's commitment to violent revolution. No other outsider knew as much about the inner workings of the party as he – but then, he had been a respected insider for seven years. He had emigrated to Canada from Bohemia in 1911, homesteaded on the prairies, and joined the Mounted Police just after the war. Because he was intelligent and spoke four languages, the force waived the rules about stature. By 1920 Leopold was at work under cover, checking into left-wing movements in Regina, posing as Jack Esselwein, a part-time housepainter. He soon became secretary of the Regina Workers' Party, the above-ground name of the then underground Communist party. Thus he was a trusted member of the party from its founding year, 1921, until he was exposed in 1928.

There he sat in the witness box, facing but never looking directly at the men who had once been his closest comrades. Understandably nervous, he stared at the ceiling, moistening his lips from time to time as he discussed his own role in the party's apparatus. It was a role that had once got him arrested and fined for taking part in a demonstration outside the consulate of the United States in Toronto protesting the U.S. government's role in the execution of Nicola Sacco and Bartolomeo Vanzetti, the two most famous anarchists of their day. It was the only case on record in which the Communist party had paid the fine (albeit unwittingly) of a member of the hated RCMP.

Leopold was the icing on the government's cake, a show-piece who garnered columns of newspaper copy. But the prosecution knew that its real case rested on the documents, most of them of Russian origin, the Mounted Police had gathered and hoped would tie the party to the Soviet Union and the Communist International.

The government had been able to find no evidence that the Canadian Communists had advocated violence. What it had to prove was guilt by association. Buck, Ewen, and the others had always been careful in their public pronouncements. On the witness stand, Buck denied that the party advocated overturning the government by force. "We teach the inevitability of the collapse of capitalism, that is all."

The defence, however, was up against Section 98 of the Criminal Code, the notorious legislation that, in Frank Scott's words, "for permanent restriction of the rights of association, freedom

122

of discussion, printing and distribution of literature, and for severity of punishment, is unequalled in the history of Canada and probably of any British country for centuries past."

The section had been drafted at the time of the Winnipeg General Strike of 1919, which terrified the authorities into taking draconian action. It was an example of the kind of over-reaction to an isolated incident of violence that has characterized the so-called "Peaceable Kingdom." Canada, a country that has never known a revolution, has always been fearful that one might explode at any time. When D'Arcy McGee was shot in 1868, scores of innocent people were jailed, and the same pattern would appear a century later in Quebec when Pierre Laporte was strangled. In the face of apprehended insurrection, the government of the day has always been ready to stamp on civil liberties. The phrase "peace, order and good government" is not an empty one. Bennett managed to insert the words into the 1931 relief act. That made it possible to deport undesirables without the nuisance of legal proceedings. King, to his credit, fought this provision, which was removed but would be reinstated by a stubborn Bennett in 1933.

Section 98 was in force for fifteen years. It was the government's big stick against radical thought because it made mere membership in an illegal organization convincing evidence of guilt. If any organization could be shown to advocate a change in the political or economic system by force or violence, then every member was guilty. If you went to even one of its meetings, gave it money, spoke publicly in its favour, distributed its literature, or wore its emblem you were liable to twenty years' imprisonment. And contrary to British legal practice, you were held to be guilty until you could prove your innocence. Anyone who rented a hall to an illegal group was subject to a five-thousand-dollar fine. Anyone who printed its literature advocating violent political change, or who imported similar literature, could also go to jail for twenty years. In fact, *anybody* who advocated violence in this context, whether he belonged to an illegal association or not, could go to jail.

Not deeds but words alone were enough to convict. And those words could be second-hand. No documentary evidence was submitted in the 1931 trial to show that the Communist Party of Canada had ever committed an act of violence or that the arrested men had ever advocated violent overthrow of the government. It was enough that they belonged to an organization that came under the umbrella of another organization, the Communist International, that did appear to advocate it.

It wasn't difficult for the prosecution to prove the international link. Leopold testified to it, and the documents supported him. At its second world conference, the Comintern had declared that a general strike wasn't enough to achieve victory. "The proletariat must resort to an armed uprising . . . an organized political party is absolutely essential . . . hapless labour organizations will not suffice."

If that was the Canadian party's stated goal, there was no evidence to suggest that the men in the dock had the slightest hope of accomplishing it, nor was there any evidence that they had tried. The defence argued that the party had conducted itself legally in Canada and that it wasn't bound to follow the Moscow line; nor did it advocate or teach revolution. As one of the defendants put it, "it is not necessary for us to spread discontent among the Canadian people. It is being done without our assistance."

In the Marxist view of history, revolution was inevitable; the party was merely preparing for the day, which it was certain would come. It would be naïve to believe that the men in the dock might not have harboured wistful hopes for enough power to give the revolution a little shove. But Tim Buck, who was acting as his own counsel, attempted to make the argument of inevitability over and over again in his summing up.

All the testimony had been presented by the end of the afternoon of November 10, and Buck expected to have the evening to prepare for his address to the jury the following day. Instead of adjourning the session, however, Mr. Justice Wright turned to him and said, "Well, Mr. Buck, have you anything to say?"

Buck was taken aback. He had a great deal to say, but he wasn't prepared. He asked for a recess of at least fifteen minutes. The judge allowed him five; he had so little sympathy for the Communist leader that he had not even allowed him to sit at the table reserved for the other lawyers. In spite of this, Buck spoke off the cuff for more than three hours, interrupted constantly by the judge, who was clearly out of patience with his attempts to give not only a history of the Communist Party of

Canada but also the history and theory of Marxism and international communism.

"I do not want to stop you or have the police remove you," the judge said at one point, "but I want you to confine yourself to the evidence. You are making a harangue on things entirely outside of the evidence. Kindly confine yourself to the case here."

Buck tried to hammer home his point that no social system could be overthrown simply because a person or party decided that it should be overthrown, and he insisted that that was the communist belief. Change was effected by economic and historical forces, while "violence has all through history been the result of the fact that the ruling class has fought to maintain its privileged position."

It is doubtful whether anyone on the jury understood that fine distinction. Buck later admitted that much of what was said was over the jury's heads. As he put it, "they just gave up listening." Some were asleep long before he finished. "I think the judge was awake but he was showing very little interest."

Buck, however, was speaking for the record. The twelve good men and true may not have been listening, but the comrades were. The speech a milestone in the history of the Communist Party of Canada - was reprinted in full by the Canadian Labor Defense League. Until this point, Buck's position as party leader had been shaky. His address to the jury confirmed it for life.

When the court adjourned that evening, the party faithful gathered at Buck's house to congratulate him. Buck was elated, but after the gathering broke up, Becky Buhay, an impassioned orator for the movement, reported to him the gloomy opinion of J.L. Cohen, a left-wing lawyer who had often defended party members. "Sommerville is going to have you convicted," Buhay told him, mentioning the name of the Crown prosecutor, "independent of anything you say, on the premise that if the Party is allowed to continue, there will be riots and violence, even if you don't advocate it."

Riots and violence - the Peaceable Kingdom's abiding phobia! Buck realized that she was right. The following day, November 11, in a two-hour address to the jury, Norman Sommerville, K.C., hammered home that point, never forgetting that this was Armistice Day. The aim of the men on trial, he said flatly, was civil war

– not in the far distant future but here and now – and "the men in the box constitute the general staff for that civil war."

"The time to put out the fire is before the conflagration," he said. "These men, professional agitators, have been travelling up and down the country . . . setting class against class . . . stirring up strife."

In his summing up, Mr. Justice Wright took a similar view. The Communist party itself, he indicated, was on trial, and the question was "whether it shall be allowed to grow and flourish on Canadian soil." He believed the testimony of Leopold, who had sworn that the party intended to overthrow the existing system in the country by force. The other witnesses, he indicated, were less objective and therefore less credible. "If you think force and violence a logical, natural result of their teachings," he told the jurors, they must agree that the accused were "advocating, advising and defending force and violence for the overthrow of governmental and industrial institutions." It didn't matter whether the revolution was a long way off. "It is not a question of time but a question of the intent of their teachings. . . ."

As for the controversial Section 98, "whether it is harsh or not it is the law." The judge made it clear where he stood on the controversy. "Is it unreasonable to prohibit force and violence, and does it seem very natural in a free country that changes in government or institutions shall be achieved, not by force and violence, but by pleading and reason and argument?"

Then he turned to the third count against the accused – seditious conspiracy – and bore down on the Criminal Code's definition of sedition, emphasizing one clause that made it seditious to excite "ill will between different classes of the King's subjects." The judge asked, "In a democratic country like this, where the proletarian of today may be the bourgeois of tomorrow . . . is it just and proper to set one of these classes against the other?" The question was, of course, rhetorical.

The conclusion was foregone, as Cohen had predicted. The jury found the eight defendants guilty on all counts with no recommendations or reservations. Thus Canada became the first country with parliamentary institutions, apart from Japan, to outlaw communist organizations and to declare their property, belongings, and facilities subject to confiscation.

The sentences were extraordinarily harsh. Seven of the eight were sentenced to five years at hard labour on the first two counts and two years, to be served concurrently, on the third – seditious conspiracy. One man, Tomo Cacic, was sentenced to two years only. On appeal, the Chief Justice, the same William Mulock who had that year called communism "a treasonable, seditious virus," upheld the first two verdicts against the seven but quashed the third as insufficiently stated. It didn't matter to the prisoners, who would have to serve their five years in Kingston Penitentiary anyway because the sentences were concurrent.

The Prime Minister was determined that the guilty men would serve every day of their sentence with no hope of parole or pardon. No doubt he felt that he had contained the Red Menace and the turbulence that had marred his first year in office would end. If so, it was wishful thinking. The party was hydra-headed, and its front organizations became more active than ever. The jailing of Tim Buck and the others had not in any sense put a damper on the party. It had, instead, given it new life and energy by providing it with a group of martyrs and a rallying point on which to focus.

1932

1

Once again as the New Year dawned, everybody from the mayor *The* of Winnipeg to the vice-president of the CNR announced that the *dole* worst was over. "Canada has survived the crisis," the Prime Minister declared. One might have expected him to bring some new eloquence to his optimistic remarks, but no, he was content to dust off the old saw about economic conditions being "fundamentally sound." He clearly loved that time-worn phrase, loved its solidity, loved its reassuring ring, loved it so much, indeed, that he inserted it in the Throne Speech in February. And why not? Hadn't Roger Babson, the man who had predicted the market crash, announced that "the Depression is in retreat"?

This time the great seer was wrong. Those who had been living on their savings and avoiding relief were coming to the end of their resources, unable to spend a nickel on new clothes and certainly not on repairs to their homes. In Halifax, to take a horrible example, 192 houses had been condemned, yet 370 families who couldn't afford better shelter were crowded into them; and the authorities were loath to throw them out. Another 1,273 houses that should have been condemned were reprieved because the Board of Health optimistically claimed they could be brought up to standard. But who could afford to do it? As many as seven families would save money by crowding into quarters designed for far fewer, using a common sink in the hallway and climbing several flights of stairs to get water. More than 11,000 men, women, and children in that city were exposed to substandard sanitary conditions. But it was cheaper for the municipal governments to wink at health rules than it was to force people out and onto relief. Public charity was seen as a last resort. Few wanted to accept it; no level of government was anxious to pay for it.

The haphazard means of administration of relief in Canada – a patchwork quilt of provincial, municipal, and private charities – was based on the British Poor Laws of the nineteenth century. These were designed to make public aid so unpleasant that only the desperate would resort to it. The conventional Victorian attitude was that idleness was a sin and that those who didn't work (the leisure classes excepted) were morally weak or lazy. R.B. Bennett echoed this obsolete attitude when he declared that year

131

that "the people are not bearing their share of the load. Half a century ago people would work their way out of their difficulties rather than look to a government to take care of them. The fibre of some of our people has grown softer and they are not willing to turn in and save themselves."

The puritanical ethic to which the Prime Minister subscribed decreed that people should be made to work for relief. But the municipal make-work programs were rarely successful because they were so wasteful. To stretch the job, picks and shovels replaced labour-saving machinery – as in an Ontario project where relief applicants were put to work levelling a knoll and filling in a hollow.

Payments for relief work were parsimonious, covering only the barest necessities. An applicant was required to prove his family was close to destitution before he could get help. In many communities, he had to turn in his liquor permit. In some he was forced to sell his car. Even a telephone in the home could make him ineligible.

Because the municipalities were still convinced that the crisis was seasonal, those men lucky enough to get this work were laid off in the summer. Nor was there enough relief work for all. In Toronto, the average relief applicant got only one week's work in eight, hardly enough to support a single man, let alone a family. Some could afford neither boots nor work clothing; others were so undernourished they didn't have the energy to lift a shovel. If they weren't British, their chances of getting relief work were low. In Toronto, no unnaturalized foreigner could even apply for relief. Transients, of course, got nothing because they had no claim on any municipality. If they stayed around for more than a day they were charged with vagrancy and booted out of town. Residence requirements grew tougher; in some towns, a family had to spend a year in the area before its members were designated "residents" and allowed public aid.

Some went to extreme lengths to overcome that problem. In Vancouver, an aging character known as "Happy" Dunning persuaded a friendly policeman to arrest him for vagrancy. In court, he pleaded with the magistrate to send him to jail for thirty days. He needed the extra month, he explained, to establish a year's residence in the city, after which he could apply for relief. "I've seen tough times before," he told the court, "but you could always make out by moving on. Now every place you go is worse than the last one, and there's nothing else but jail and then *pogey*."

In spite of these conditions, no one – and certainly not the government – really knew how many people were out of work or who they were. That failure was underscored by the publication that September of the only comprehensive study to be undertaken until the end of the decade. It was sponsored not by the government but by the private sector and confined to the province of Ontario.

This was the survey that Dr. Harry Cassidy, one of the founding members of the League for Social Reconstruction, had begun in 1931 for the Unemployment Research Committee. Cassidy, at thirty-two, was at the top of his field, a cheerful academic, full of energy and drive. A trained economist, he was also an idealist. He had returned to Canada from a teaching position in the United States because, he said, he wanted to "play some part in the social engineering that is essential to the development . . . of a worthwhile culture." Like most of his colleagues in the LSR – Underhill, Scott, and others – he was a man in search of a new political movement. During the 1930 election campaign he had been sickened by politicians clinging to past glories and ignoring current problems. "Bennett invokes shades of Sir John A. and his National Policy," he wrote to his wife. "I think it is a disgusting performance – with Bennett being inane and silly most of the time and King being dishonest."

In March 1932, W.F. Nickle, the honorary chairman of the committee, sent an outline of Cassidy's report and then the manuscript to his friend the Prime Minister, praising the research and suggesting that it could be of "great value to you by way of giving a lead in public opinion." It's doubtful whether Bennett ever read it. Certainly he ignored it. For Cassidy's findings challenged some widely held myths – those to which Bennett himself subscribed.

Unemployment, Cassidy reported, was a "virulent social disease" that was eating away at the country's morale and undermining the confidence of the people, who were living in "hopeless despair" and had developed a bitter attitude towards established institutions. The problem wasn't seasonal and couldn't be solved by emergency measures. In many ways, Cassidy indicated, the dole was preferable to the wasteful and inefficient system of municipal make-work. Cassidy's statistics on industrial

133

unemployment were the first to be published in Canada after three years of depression, and they were shocking. From a 1929 low of 2 per cent the jobless rate in Ontario had risen to a staggering 36 per cent.

Nor were Cassidy's solutions designed to give Bennett any comfort, for they would cost more money. Cassidy saw the problem as a national one, with Ottawa taking the major share of the responsibility and instituting a comprehensive and generous plan to deal with unemployment. Small wonder that Bennett ignored his report.

Yet it was already apparent, by the spring of 1932, that the government's relief policy wasn't working. The provinces could not afford to subsidize any more public works, and so Bennett, who had roared into power by promising never to adopt the hated dole, was now forced to reverse himself and institute a policy of direct relief. He attempted to blunt the effects of that embarrassment by making the provinces and municipalities responsible for spending the money. Ottawa retained its hands-off policy.

Under municipal management, spending continued to be niggardly, as the Red Cross discovered in Ontario. Those on relief received scrip or vouchers that allowed them to buy groceries – but only certain prescribed items. In one city, relief recipients weren't allowed to buy tomatoes with their scrip; in another, spices and seasonings were excluded. Eggs were generally taboo, and in one city in the heart of the dairy district, milk was denied except to infants and invalids. Another town, using the government scale of relief allowances, preferred to earn a cent a quart on relief milk rather than pass the savings on to the jobless. One stingy community penalized families of more than five by holding them to a weekly spending allowance of twenty-five cents per person. If anyone earned more than a dollar a week, that sum was deducted from the family's food allowance.

Medical aid was almost non-existent. In one Winnipeg area, as James Gray pointed out in *The Winter Years*, one relief doctor served sixteen thousand patients, and there was no dentist. Gray and his family got vouchers for food, fuel, and rent only – nothing for tobacco, cigarette papers, toothpaste, razor blades, lipstick, face powder, aspirin, streetcar fare, or a haircut, let alone movies or newspapers. And, of course, any recipient seen at the racetrack was cut off immediately.

134

With Cassidy's research gathering dust on his desk, Bennett turned to another, more formidable social worker in the person of Charlotte Whitton, the full-time director of the Canadian Council on Child Welfare. He considered her "the most capable woman engaged in social welfare in the Dominion." She was short and stubby, possessed of a caustic wit, a fiery temper, and inexhaustible energy – a "young cyclone," in the description of a friend.

Whitton was a woman with a mission. There was a bulldog set to her features and a bulldog tenaciousness to her character. Social workers were a new presence in Canada, and she was determined to make that presence a powerful one. The best way to achieve the goal was to wrest control of the relief machinery from the bureaucrats and turn it over to professionals like herself. To that end she proposed to the Prime Minister that she take three months off from her job and study unemployment relief in the West. She was convinced that untrained political hacks were costing the government millions through waste and inefficiency and that large numbers of people – long-term indigents, for example – were getting money specifically earmarked for Depression relief that ought to come out of another pocket.

This is what Bennett wanted to hear; it wasn't lack of government money, as Cassidy had suggested, that was causing the problem, it was the way the money was handled. The Prime Minister gave his enthusiastic consent, whereupon Whitton immediately set off on a whirlwind tour that, in three months, covered no fewer than eighty five separate communities with names like Pipestone, Aneroid, Yellow Grass, Blairmore, Sicamous, Comox, Alert Bay, Gimli, and Dauphin. She scarcely stopped to draw breath as she hustled from one community to the next, jaw set, brows knit, fiery red hair trimmed by the barber's scissors, questioning, questioning, questioning in her raspy voice and scratching it all down in her notebooks. Years later, she would bring that same unsparing vigour to her several tempestuous terms as mayor of Ottawa.

Whitton had planned a short holiday in British Columbia but cancelled it because, as she told the Prime Minister, "I found things too upsetting, and demanding too much intensive effort to lose any time." Reading her lengthy letters, written in flowing longhand, Bennett must have had some cause to regret his optimistic New Year's Day remarks, for she wrote: "I do not think that the East, blue as it feels, has any conception of what has happened and is happening financially in these western provinces."

In Winnipeg, she reported, "things are bad and getting constantly worse." Sixty new families a day were applying for relief, bringing the total to 5,670 when she arrived on June 16. The city was also caring for 3,200 homeless men and the "homeless girl problem is growing even worse than normal." The transient problem, she warned Bennett, was "getting out of hand." Whitton estimated that there were more than one hundred thousand roaming about Canada, and it concerned her that "a better class is joining them daily, and giving them leadership and organization." The federal government must take hold, she wrote, "and 'beat' anyone else to organization."

Again and again she hammered home her point – that because local relief spending was handled incompetently and carelessly, money could be saved if the federal government took over. "The more I see . . . of politics in the West the more I think there is danger as great in provincial relief. . . . What is bothering me is that all the West through there is impatience and annoyance that there is no 'federal lead'."

On the boat north from Victoria to Prince Rupert, she used her spare time to butter up the Prime Minister. She had risen at 6:30 on a cold morning, she wrote, to hear him open the Imperial Economic Conference in Ottawa. "Your splendid address came through wonderfully well, your voice was vibrant, strong, and unmistakeably young. . . . I could almost imagine the out thrust chin and frowning intensity which accompanied that delivery. . . . I got great pleasure out of some of those very neat phrases . . . that 'driving clear channels through the stagnant streams' of our trade was particularly happy." It was hard to imagine the conference failing, she told him, "with you in the chair, and all the people through the West hanging suspended to this meeting as the force that will 'bring us round the corner'." Whitton's flattery would prove as unavailing as Mrs. Bleaney's predictions to Mackenzie King.

Obeisance paid, Whitton got down to facts. British Columbia, she reported, was in confusion. The government, knowing it was doomed in the following year's provincial election, had ceased to function and was breaking up. The municipalities were desperate. She forecast riots in Port Alberni where "people were actually without food." Vancouver was facing a serious financial crisis. "The provincial crew . . . are trying to make 'Ottawa' the goat," she told him; but the public wasn't buying that, and "every effort in this direction only enhances your prestige." Again she belaboured her one theme: there was "no central authority, plan or leadership within the provincial group."

She did not tell him then – she saved it for her later report – of the graft and patronage that accompanied the setting up of relief camps for transient men in British Columbia. By shifting its responsibilities onto the shoulders of the province the federal government had invited trouble. British Columbia was fertile ground for boondoggle, corruption, and impropriety, and there was no lack of examples. The relative of one cabinet minister received an annual rent of seven thousand dollars when his property was used for a relief camp. In Mission, 104 carpenters were put on the payroll at four dollars a day each; an investigation revealed that all the work was done by four men. The government bought lumber from "friendly firms" at more than double the going rate. Tools had to be ordered by the dozen when only one or two were needed because "they did not break up the lot." The big logging companies had offered to rent their own well-equipped camps at low rates, but the province refused. One lumber company executive of long experience told Whitton that he had never seen such "graft, extravagence [sic] and exploitation" as existed in the provincial camps. All this disturbing evidence supported her original thesis.

Whitton's two-hundred-page report, written on her return, was predictable. Left in the hands of the provincial and municipal authorities, the relief system was in a mess – "potentially in Western Canada there could be nearly 1100 systems of relief. . . ." The ablest people in public life, she wrote, were at the federal level, the least able at the municipal; yet the most serious problem facing the country had been left to be administered by inexperienced municipal personnel who "would never be considered by even a small business for any responsible position calling for vision, energy and executive ability. . . ."

In one eloquent passage, she provided some insight into the psychological trauma of applying for unemployment relief. She

137

wrote of "the overbearing ignorance, abrupt roughness, discourtesy and general lack of consideration with which the unemployed are received in only too many relief offices; the dark, dingy, ramshackle quarters in old firehalls, basements, ramshackle buildings, etc., into which men and women must crowd and wait, often in long queues, standing against walls, herded indiscriminately; the routine mass treatment accorded the weary, unending, often 'haggard' lines can only darken despair already deep and desolate; can only wear down pride and self respect already endangered; can only lead to bitter, brooding resentment and determination to 'beat the system' that allows such things."

Yet Charlotte Whitton was convinced that thousands were beating the system and getting relief to which they weren't entitled. In her determination to convince Bennett that money could be saved by social workers at the federal level, she over-reached herself. To support her claim that local officials were inept, she estimated that an astonishing 40 per cent of those getting direct unemployment relief either didn't need it or could be helped by other, more conventional means.

In Whitton's remarkably callous view, no one should be given the dole unless it could be proved that his or her needs were a direct result of the Depression. Unemployed women of middle age who had never been steadily employed fitted her standard of ineligibility. "They present a problem at any time that should rest primarily upon local resources." Deserted wives and single girls should be taught housework. Women on mothers' allowances did not "form a justifiable charge." The same was true of seasonal workers – trappers, farmers, and miners, especially in areas such as Cape Breton that had been depressed before the Depression. She conceded that their situation was pitiable but not "justifiably chargeable to direct relief."

Whitton revealed her own Calvinist outlook (or paraphrased Bennett's) when she wrote that there was less need for relief in the small towns and rural villages, where "life is characterized generally by a thrift and resourcefulness that has been a real factor in the sturdiness of Canada generally." Unless it could be proved that a real emergency existed "there is grave danger of undermining the self reliance of what has always been perhaps the sturdiest group in the national character."

138

The drought, she considered, was a different problem, a temporary one that would not be a drag on the public purse for very long. In a remarkably optimistic passage, she wrote that "there is every anticipation of early emergence from dependence on public aid, as soon as uncontrollable circumstances cease. Furniture, home and other resources have not been dissipated, nor faith lost in the possibility of future self-support. There is hope, determination, and full co-operation in regard to the future, and frequently a definite plan for repayment of relief extended. . . ." Those who had moved out of the drought areas were not eligible for relief but might be helped by "colonization aid" in their new communities.

"The Breed" (Whitton's name for the mixed bloods and Métis) had always been a problem, her report noted, "and a menace both to the Indian and white races, with whom they mingle." Since they had already suffered from a low standard of "living, health and morality" they should not be given the dole. Money should come out of another federal pocket and it should be "consistent with their normal needs and habits." It was "inexcusable" to issue supplies such as sugar, coffee, canned goods, bacon, butter, corn syrup, dried or tinned foods and so on if these had never formed part of the staple diet. The implication here was that the dole should not be used to change the status quo. Those who were traditionally deprived must not be given an allowance that would help them escape from the cycle of poverty.

Whitton's attitude to "foreigners" also reflected the general public view. There were too many on relief, she believed, and they were troublesome. "Language difficulties, their tendency to segregate, their corporate loyalties, their susceptibility to seditious propaganda, their known proclivity to hoard money, and the consequent difficulty of ascertaining their need of relief all greatly complicate an already difficult job. . . ."

Her solution to the problem of jobless hordes riding the freights was blunt, though not original: again, the federal government must assume responsibility; the military should take over. Every transient should be forced to register and carry a registration card in the nature of a passport. Homeless boys under eighteen would be placed in homes or given provincial relief along with young men between eighteen and twenty-five, with Ottawa paying half. Those over twenty-five were to be confined in what Whitton called "concentration camps" – a word that Adolf Hitler had yet to redefine. Anyone who left these camps without permission would be denied relief; if he was found "riding the rails," he would be handed over to the police. That was one of the few recommendations of the Whitton report that came into being, though the impetus was from another source.

What Whitton had actually recommended was that Ottawa should pare down the cost of the dole by throwing a good many relief expenditures on the provincial and municipal authorities she appeared to despise. Her report emphasized waste and extravagance at the lower levels of government, but there was precious little in it about human suffering. The effect on the Prime Minister was the very opposite of what she wanted. The report confirmed Bennett's worst fears. The provinces were wasting Ottawa's money, therefore Ottawa would give them less. But Bennett still had no intention of taking responsibility for the distribution of the dole, let alone hiring more social workers. He didn't need *that* burden. Whitton had simply confirmed his own social and political philosophy – that it was time individual Canadians took responsibility for maintaining themselves. A balanced budget and a sound dollar – those were R.B. Bennett's priorities. Massive relief expenditures were not part of his program.

2

Shovelling The squeeze was being felt at every level that year. The federal
out the government squeezed the provinces, the provinces squeezed the
unwanted municipalities, and the municipalities squeezed the people. In January, for instance, Manitoba's Minister of Public Works warned the city of Winnipeg that it must pare down its direct relief spending; if not, the province would start cutting back its share of the expenses to a third. Faced with that threat, the city made all recipients sign a note promising to pay back any funds they'd been given.

In Sudbury, one of several communities that urged the immediate deportation of all "undesirables," civic workers had their wages cut, residence qualifications for relief were increased to a year, couples who had been married for less than six months were

140

cut off, and any person who could be shown to be domiciled elsewhere was denied aid.

Nobody wanted to pay for the rising cost of relief. On the one hand, the provinces were pleading with Bennett to increase Ottawa's share of relief payments. On the other, many of his own supporters were urging him to decrease them. These penny-pinchers resorted to the outworn argument that relief sapped the spirit of enterprise. A special report prepared by a committee of the Canadian Bar Association deplored the encroachment of the state in the sphere of individual activity. The lawyers, meeting in Calgary in September, were told that unemployment was a problem for the private sector and that "the attempt to shift the burden to governments is bound to prove expensive to industry and to the public generally."

The easiest way, and the most popular, to cut relief costs was to get rid of the foreigners and troublemakers. "Bohunks" and "Polacks," to use the common expressions, were seen to be taking food from the mouths of the native born. Red agitators were stirring up trouble and threatening traditional Canadian values.

Bennett lived in terror that peace, order, and good government would be disrupted by a Soviet-style revolution. The extraordinary precautions he took before meeting a delegation of unemployed on March 3 illustrates a distrust bordering on paranoia. The meeting took place not in his office but on the steps of the Parliament Buildings, and, as always, its outcome was foreordained. Bennett, however, treated the encounter as he would have a military invasion. He actually had an armoured car circling Parliament Hill. He had armed policemen everywhere: fifty city police marching up and down Wellington Street in front of the Parliament Buildings, thirty-five more in a state of readiness at the police station, a detachment of the RCMP - a hundred strong - guarding the East and West blocks, another detachment of twenty-six RCMP on horseback held in reserve behind the Centre Block, and dozens of plainclothesmen mingling with the crowd. There he stood at the top of the stairs, a pugnacious figure - Bennett, the champion of law and order - ready to face his enemies and not give an inch. The outcome of this "Chicago-like flaunting of firearms," as the Ottawa *Journal* called it, was anti-climactic. The jobless men presented their demands, Bennett bluntly refused them, and the delegation left peacefully.

141

Bennett's view – that radicals and "foreigners" should be sent back to Russia, or wherever it was they came from – was the view of the majority. In the worst years of the Depression from 1930 to 1935, Canada deported more than twenty-eight thousand men and women either because they were radicals or because they made the mistake of asking for relief. Unless they were naturalized citizens they had no chance; they were hustled aboard steamships leaving for the old country, often secretly and with no right of appeal.

The Communists were the easiest to deport. The party's leaders had been jailed following the 1931 trial, and most Canadians didn't care what happened to the rank and file. A notorious case was that of Arvo Vaara of Sudbury, the Finnish-Canadian editor who had been jailed in 1928 for sedition. Now he was seized by the RCMP, together with his Finnish-born translator, Martin Parker, and driven to Police headquarters on the morning of May 4. Both men were denied phone calls and visitors. To avoid any public demonstration, five plainclothesmen bundled the pair into a car that evening and whisked them to a deserted train station fifteen miles out of town. At midnight the Montreal-bound express made an unscheduled stop to pick them up.

Guarded by two RCMP constables, they were lodged in cells in Montreal and denied all communication with the outside world. They were then transferred to Halifax – to the steel-and-concrete Melville Barracks, an army post turned into a detention centre. They were locked up with several other deportees, denied bail or visitors, and given little or no exercise. There was no trial, only a secret hearing before an immigration board. On December 17, all the detainees were shipped back to Europe – Vaara to Finland, a country he hadn't seen for twenty-three years.

When the press tried to find out what had happened to Vaara, it came up against a blank wall. The RCMP told the *Ottawa Citizen* that the raid was carried out by the provincial police. The provincial police claimed to know nothing about it. When asked if he had any idea where the men were taken, Inspector Alfred Buddy answered, "Not the slightest. We have no report on them."

But the attorney general of Ontario knew. "This man was in trouble three times for statements derogatory to His Majesty," Colonel Price explained. That, apparently, justified his deportation. Vaara was the man who had been jailed for expressing

142

indifference about George V's recovery. It was essential, Price indicated, to protect Canadians from such people.

Vaara was one of ten men swept up by police in six cities following the traditional May Day parades in 1932. Only one – Orton Wade, who had spoken at a May Day demonstration – was able to prove that he was Canadian born, but only when he had already been handcuffed and dispatched to Halifax.

Danny Chomiki had no such excuse. He had come to Canada with his Polish parents as a child in 1913, a time when the country was luring Eastern Europeans with an unprecedented advertising campaign. Now he had a Canadian name, Holmes, a Canadian wife, and a Canadian-born child. That made no difference. He was spirited away to Halifax without his wife's knowing what was happening to him. When his lawyer asked to see the warrant for his arrest, he was refused. When J.S. Woodsworth took up the case with the immigration department, the civil servants fobbed him off on the minister, who claimed to have no knowledge of the matter. In December, Danny Holmes was shipped back to Poland – a country he could scarcely remember. When he had left it two decades before, it was part of Austria.

The government made every attempt to hush up these political deportations. None of these men could afford to bring witnesses in their defence all the way to Halifax, where the ubiquitous Sergeant Leopold was already installed to finger them as members of an illegal party. That, of course, was why Halifax was chosen, although the Minister of Justice, Hugh Guthrie, tried to maintain the fiction that the site was simply a convenient rendezvous with the shipping company. As one Progressive member of the House, Edward Garland, exclaimed, "Who knows that they will get a decent investigation? . . . I have heard people condemn the Russian OGPU . . . for the way they secretly hurry people away to Siberia and give explanations afterwards. That was the way these men were dealt with. . . ."

Officially, there was no such thing as "political deportation" in democratic Canada. It wasn't needed. A variety of categories was used to camouflage the real reasons for shipping unnaturalized Canadians out of the country. One convenient charge was "entry by misrepresentation"; it was used to deport Miolaj Dramuta, who had been brought to Canada in 1926 to do farm work. After an RCMP spy described him as a communist, an immigration

143

official combed through his file to discover that he had once worked in an Edmonton meat-packing plant and also as a teacher. Therefore, he wasn't a farmer and on that basis was thrown out of the country.

An immigrant could be charged with "unlawful assembly," as Askeli Panjata was. Panjata made the mistake of marching in a parade of unemployed workers in Port Arthur. He was jailed and packed off to Halifax before his friends were aware of it.

He could be charged as a vagrant – that useful catch-all that made police work so easy in the thirties – as Sam Langley was. Langley had had a deportation order hanging over him, but not implemented, since 1929, when he'd been arrested under the disorderly conduct section of the vagrancy act during a Toronto free-speech demonstration. Nothing happened for more than two years. Then the order was suddenly reactivated, Langley was picked up in Sudbury, spirited away to Halifax, and deported.

He could be charged with "entry without inspection," as Hans Kist was after he deserted his ship in Vancouver in 1930. Kist, who had been involved in a strike at Fraser Mills, B.C., was said by immigration officials to be "saturated with Communist beliefs and revolutionary ideas of a particularly virulent nature." Hans Kist was deported to his native Germany – an act tantamount to signing his death warrant. The Nazis agreed with the Canadian description of him as "a thorough going troublemaker" and "a dangerous type." They sent him to a concentration camp and tortured him to death.

Kist's fate after leaving Canada is one of the few of which there is record. Another – that of Tomo Cacic – reads like an adventure thriller. Cacic was one of the eight Communists jailed following the 1931 trials and the only one to receive a lighter sentence – two years instead of five. That proved his undoing, because he was released before the Bennett government left office. (Under the Liberals, political deportations came to an end.)

Cacic, who was deported to Yugoslavia, knew that he faced arrest and probable execution in his native country. He determined to avoid that fate. On the train trip across Europe he managed, with the help of the communist underground, to secure a Soviet passport and a new name. He escaped from his guards and made his way to the Soviet Union. He worked there for three years, fought in the war in Spain, survived two years in a French concentration camp, escaped again, and made his way to Yugoslavia, where he fought with Tito's partisans. In spite of various infirmities – he suffered from tuberculosis and lost a leg in battle – he survived in his native country until his death in 1969 at the age of seventy-three, a die-hard communist to the end.

But it was not just die-hard communists who faced deportation from Canada under the Bennett regime. Anyone who had been in the country for less than five years could be deported as a public charge simply by applying for relief. That regulation covered not only the "undesirables" but also thousands of others who had been recruited to come to Canada in the twenties by a business-oriented community looking for cheap labour. The Canadian Manufacturers' Association had lobbied the government to broaden its immigration policy, and in 1926 the two major railways and the Canadian Bankers' Association quietly backed the campaign. In fact, until the Depression, Canada had not only welcomed newcomers, it had also wooed them and subsidized them with low rail fares and free land, especially in the West. The immigrants, in turn, had helped make the country prosperous. Now, with hard times returning, the government was callously prepared to throw them out.

In short, foreigners were wanted only when times were good. Once the economy turned sour, the latent distrust of the stranger, especially the non-British stranger, surfaced. Senator Robertson had echoed the prevailing opinion when he declared that "Russian and other European people who have only been in this country a short time . . . should not be allowed to work . . . while hundreds of Canadians are standing in the breadline."

By 1932, it had become the unpublicized policy of the Department of Immigration to get all unnaturalized foreigners off the relief rolls by one method or another – to "shovel them out," in the apt phrase of Barbara Roberts, a student of immigration policies in the thirties, whose book, *Whence They Came*, recounts many of these horror stories. To soothe public opinion, the department engaged in a hoax. The fiction was that foreigners, including British-born, weren't being kicked out because they applied for relief but because they were "unemployable" or because, in the department's view, they were eager to return home.

Roberts found a concerted effort by the government "to conceal, deny, or justify their practices. Spurious or misleading state-

145

ments were cooked up and purveyed, editors regaled with letters and rationalizations, statements made in Parliament, in public and in private. In some instances the Department representatives misled; in others they lied."

In many cities – Sault Ste Marie was one – immigrants applying for relief had to sign a form requesting voluntary patriation before they could get it. One Manitoba politician actually boasted that "in our town [Winnipeg], when those foreigners from across the tracks apply for relief we just show them a blank application for voluntary deportation. Believe me, they don't come back. It's simple but it has saved the city a lot of money." This practice allowed the department to cook its own statistics so that Canadians weren't made aware of the shovelling out process.

The department shamelessly stretched and distorted its own definition of "unemployable" and "voluntary." An immigrant would be told he'd be deported and then asked if he looked forward to seeing friends and family. If he did, he would be listed as a "voluntary deportee." If he didn't appeal the deportation ruling, he was again put into the voluntary column. He was "unemployable" if he sounded less than enthusiastic for a certain kind of work or discouraged about his inability to find a job. Roberts dug up one case where the department claimed that an immigrant had refused farm work, when the transcript before the board of inquiry showed the exact opposite. In some cases whole families were ordered deported even if the wife was self-supporting or living apart from her husband.

In its eagerness to rid the country of jobless immigrants, the department circumvented its own procedures in the interests of speed and efficiency. Lists of names were telegraphed to Ottawa without any supporting evidence. Ottawa then wired back warrants for deportation without any examination of these cases. The documentation came later after the cases were heard by a board of inquiry and deportation ordered. In short, there were no proper administrative proceedings. The men, women, and children who were sent back across the ocean were denied due process.

They were herded aboard trains, fed cold sandwiches, given unclean blankets, and prevented from moving about freely. At the so-called Montreal Detention Hospital, whole families lived on pork and beans, often slept on the floor because of a shortage of

146

beds, or were crowded together into a large room with nothing more than a curtain to separate the sexes. They were, in truth, in jail; even the fire escapes were locked. There was nothing to do; no arrangements were made for exercise or fresh air, and in winter there was little heat. When the boilers failed for six weeks in 1932, no one could wash properly nor could dishes be sterilized because there was no hot water. Vermin were everywhere, but the department felt it inadvisable "to adopt a policy of delousing every deportee." There was no segregation; the insane, the tubercular, the syphilitic, and the common criminal were mixed with those who had once been given a shining vision of a promised land, only to find the vision distorted and the promise revoked.

3

Boxcar cowboys

By 1932, Canada had become a nation of hoboes. The hordes of transients being shuffled back and forth across the country represented a new and unprecedented phenomenon. Nothing like it had ever been seen before; nor would it be seen again. Between seventy thousand and one hundred thousand men, almost all young and single, were riding the freights along the traditional Canadian east-west axis, using the traditional Canadian mode of travel, the railway. Here was an army of the deprived - undisciplined, ragged, hungry, and often desperate, but an army nonetheless, roughly the size of the Canadian Corps of 1917 whose four divisions had, for the first and last time, fought under a single command to capture Vimy Ridge.

This legion of vagrants has provided us with the enduring images of the Depression: the homeless men begging for food at the back door and then moving on; the panhandlers selling pencils on the streets; the multitudes squatting on the roofs of the CPR freights. These are the wan symbols of hard times, but it must also be remembered that the majority were in their teens and early twenties, that most were single, and that to many riding the rails was a lark. For thousands, the chance to jump aboard a moving freight was also a chance at freedom, at adventure, at excitement and even danger. The Depression gave them the perfect excuse to get away on their own, to escape the drabness of life in some Canadian backwater – a drabness rendered gloomier by economic disaster – and to travel the country from sea to sea. In other circumstances they might have stayed put, married early, and settled down. Now they were off on what used to be called "the open road."

The very fact that they were *moving* helped to temper for them the harshness of those times. For everybody else, except for the very rich, the thirties was a static decade. Who else could cross the country? There was no time and there was no money; for some, a streetcar ticket was a luxury. The jobless families couldn't go anywhere. If they moved, they lost their chance for local relief and had to wait six months to a year (*three* years in Montreal) to qualify for the dole. Those who were lucky enough to have steady work didn't dare move. In the thirties you clung to your job as a drunk clings to a lamp post. You hung on in spite of brutal bosses, long hours, pay cuts, and shortened vacations. Eaton's clerks had their two-week annual holidays reduced to one week and all but two of their statutory holidays cancelled – a deprivation that rendered them even less mobile. Sometimes it was as much as your job was worth even to leave your house briefly. Most five-and-dime clerks were hired on a part-time basis, which meant they had to stay close to home, praying that the phone would ring and summon them back for a few hours. But single young men could take off at any time for anywhere, as long as they stayed a step or two ahead of the railway police. It can be argued, too, that they had fewer worries than those who were tied down by their responsibilities.

Charles Wesley Sherwin, who began riding freights when he was sixteen, would always remember sitting at his ease in the open boxcars, waving at people at the level crossings, as the train pounded through the small prairie towns. The people always waved back. "Maybe we were lucky," Sherwin recalled. "We didn't have to worry about whether the crop was seven bushels to the acre or fifty or whether the cow calved . . . or mortgages and taxes. All we had to worry about was the cops and our immediate welfare."

The freight trains gave thousands of young men a chance to see from coast to coast a land they had experienced only vicariously in the school geography classes. Most were introduced for the first time to the glories of the cloud-draped Selkirks (never
148

mind the cinders in the Connaught Tunnel), to the winding ribbon of the North Saskatchewan River, to the industrial cities of Central Canada, to the apple orchards of the Annapolis and Okanagan valleys, to Fundy's tidal bore and the Fraser's sprawling delta. The boxcars provided an education in the endless diversity of the nation as well as an adventure.

Harry Mavis and his friend Albert Lockwood, both in their early twenties, decided to gamble on just such an adventure in July. They couldn't get work and were tired of loafing around Vancouver. Some of their friends had already been east and told them there was nothing to it – all you needed was a few clothes, blankets, and a little money. Lockwood and Mavis scraped up seventeen dollars between them, mainly by selling a few belongings. On July 31, they hopped a freight out of Coquitlam. On August 16 they were in Nova Scotia and on September 22 back again in Vancouver.

It was a journey that neither man would ever forget, and a fulfilling one. Mavis said that if he ever went east again, that was the way he'd want to travel. They never got over being tired and they were often hungry, but that did not bother them unduly. They ate bananas at ten cents a dozen and stale buns given them by sympathetic counter clerks in bakeries. They picked up the odd meal visiting relatives. They slept in railway waiting rooms, in the boiler room of a roundhouse, on top of a tank car (an arm hooked around a ladder rung), in empty boxcars, in the tall grass by a siding, or flat on their backs, legs astraddle like a child in a crib, roped to the top of a freight car. At the end of their journey, while washing up in the restrooms of the B.C. Electric depot, they recounted their adventures to a group of streetcar workers their own age and told them how they had travelled 8,142 miles on their grubstake of seventeen dollars. "They said they wished they weren't working so they could go on a trip such as ours," Mavis remembered. "Imagine anyone wishing they were not working in the hungry thirties."

Although it was technically illegal to ride the freights, the railway companies took a lenient view until the summer of 1932, when the government announced that the practice was to be stopped. The RCMP began to block harvest workers who had ridden the freights to the west in the early summer from returning east – an action that caused a storm of protest from the

149

prairie towns that now faced the problem of thousands of young men being dumped on their doorsteps.

In fact, the ban had very little effect. A kind of moccasin telegraph swiftly identified the good towns and the bad towns, the mean "bulls," as the railway police were universally called, from the easy-going ones. The mythology of the transient era is rich with tales of bulls beating up young men; but, as Charles Sherwin discovered, some were remarkably understanding. One day in Schreiber, Ontario, when Sherwin stepped off a boxcar to get a breath of fresh air, a CPR policeman nabbed him. But when Sherwin said he'd left his suitcase with his personal effects aboard the vanishing freight, the accommodating bull wired ahead to Nipigon to have it sent back by the next train. In Edmonton, Sherwin asked permission to sleep in the city jail, a common request, especially in winter. A policeman, who learned he'd had nothing to eat, bought him a pound of butter and a loaf of bread, which he devoured on the spot.

Sherwin spent the decade riding the freights. As far as can be determined, he holds the record for boxcar travel in the thirties. By the time the Depression ended for him and he found work as a miner, he had crossed the country no fewer than sixty-five times and knew every town, city, and hobo jungle in Canada.

On his first trip out of his home town of Hillier, Ontario, at age seventeen, he didn't even bother to carry a toothbrush but simply climbed aboard a mixed train heading north to Trenton. Clinging to a pitching flat car, he felt sad and alone – a green kid who'd never been out of his home community; nonetheless, it was something he felt he had to do. At Trenton, the divisional point, he rode the front end of a tank car, protected from the wind and flying cinders by the bulk of the car ahead. The speed terrified him; he had never travelled so fast before, and his knuckles were white from clinging to the rail as the car pitched and jerked beneath him.

By the time he reached Montreal, he was starving. An elderly bachelor took him home, fed him bacon and eggs, and asked him to stay. It was not a homosexual proposition; his host was a war veteran suffering from bleeding hemorrhoids and terrified that, if he were alone, he might bleed to death. Young Sherwin was so naïve he thought the affliction was contagious. He caught a CPR freight back to Belleville.

150

He didn't go home, for he was hooked. Instead, he caught another freight going north. At Peterborough, he stayed in his first jungle, on the Trent Canal, and there he began to learn something of the art of survival on the road. As the new kid, he was sent to the butcher shop to ask for leftovers and bacon ends. Others who had asked once too often picked up wilting vegetables while one man entered a café, ordered a cup of coffee, and left with the salt and pepper. The result was Sherwin's first, but by no means his last, mulligan stew.

Charlie Sherwin learned by picking up tips from older and wiser men on the road – the best way to board a freight, for instance, and the trick of greasing the rails to make the train slow down. With his last quarter he bought a dozen packages of black shoelaces at Woolworth's and began peddling them door to door at whistle stops. He took the advice of his new-found friends and decided to ride the coal-and-water tender of a CNR passenger train west, for that was the preferred spot on a freight, albeit a dangerous one because it exposed the rider to the railway police. When he tried to climb aboard, the fireman saw him and waved him off. When he persisted, the man turned a hose on him. None of this bothered Sherwin, who returned home, elated at his first adventure, laughing at the system, full of new confidence.

He and his friend Mac Hardy decided to head west to see a buddy who was homesteading north of Edmonton. They hopped a freight into Toronto, walked across town to the West Toronto station, and caught the nightly fast freight at eleven. He and Mac were the first to leap into a "reefer" (refrigerator car) followed by twenty-seven others, all of whom fell hungrily on a pile of bananas left behind on the floor.

Sherwin had learned in his first journey that reefer cars were the warmest because they were so well insulated. He also knew enough to tie the door down in such a way that it couldn't be locked from the outside. Men had been known to die, locked in reefers. At Chapleau, he unwired the door, only to step into the beam of a railway bull's flashlight. He, his buddy, and all the others were lodged in jail and charged with trespassing on CPR property. In lieu of a ten-dollar fine, they were sentenced to thirty days and shipped off to Burwash Provincial Jail in chains. Their parents bailed them out, but that was enough for Mac Hardy. Charlie Sherwin, however, had no intention of going home. He

151

was small enough to climb into the toolbox of a passenger tender, and so off he went, heading west, swearing he'd never travel with a mob again.

By this time he was a dyed-in-the-wool boxcar cowboy, an enlisted soldier in the growing army of amateur hoboes who were teaching each other how to beg, steal, outwit the authorities, and go without eating. Bob Drouin, who spent four of his teen years riding the freights, once existed for five and a half days by eating dandelion heads. Bill Mitchell, of Weyburn, Saskatchewan, a future Canadian novelist, found that if necessary he could go without food for three days. Mitchell disciplined himself never to eat more than one meal daily while on the road. In cheap restaurants, where you could get a three-course meal for a quarter, he'd take all the extra bread and pats of butter and save them for the following day. No matter how hungry he was, he never removed the five-dollar bill he kept hidden in his sock. When charged with vagrancy he could produce it to prove that he did have "visible means of support."

These men were not "bums" in the traditional sense, nor did they resemble the stereotypes that appeared in the cartoons of those days. Rosella Diduck, who lived on a farm near Kamsack, northeast of Regina, watched them arrive from the west, leaping off the train before it reached the station to avoid the railway police. In the jungles down by the river they occupied themselves making furniture and baskets out of willow, which they sold. When they asked for food at the Diducks' back door they offered to split wood in return for a meal, and before they ate, Rosella noticed, they'd ask for a bar of soap and go to the well to wash their hands. "Everybody thought very kindly of these men, even though they hadn't had a hair cut . . . they had a dignity about them. As soon as they could they went to the barber's to be trimmed."

They soon became wise in the ways of the road. Joe Zacher, known as the Vermilion Kid because he hailed from Vermilion, Alberta, was taught the art of begging by an old-timer, Paddy the Priest. Paddy was sixty, and he'd been a professional hobo all his life. Joe Zacher was twenty-one, "green as a poplar tree and as hard to burn." To be a good beggar, Paddy told him, you must be kind, grateful, and polite, must choose your words and responses

152

carefully. Joe learned to say, "Pardon me, sir, could you kindly help a fellow out with a small amount of change for a bite to eat?" Whether the answer was yes or no (and it was usually no), he always replied with a polite thank you.

Paddy the Priest taught the Vermilion Kid how to keep the law off his back. Zacher learned to keep a magazine or newspaper under his arm, to walk at a fast snappy pace, and never to look back over his shoulder. In that way he established himself as a man, if not of substance, at least of a fixed address and visible means of support.

"Good afternoon, lady," the Vermilion Kid would say. "I'm sorry to bother you. May I ask if your name is May James?"

It wasn't, of course.

"I'm sorry, lady, that I made this mistake. I thought you were a lady I knew. My bad luck. Lady, I haven't had anything to eat since yesterday." Six times out of ten he was called back and offered some change.

In Winnipeg, young Zacher found he could buy fifteen nickel-sized washers for fifteen cents and use them to beat the illegal slot machines in the Chinese cafés. He learned to buy a loaf of stale bread and then ask if he could have a can of beans to eat with it. Another trick – Sherwin did well with it in Winnipeg, too – was to write a letter home and then beg money for a stamp.

In spite of the common phrase "riding the rods," scarcely anybody dared to use that method of travel except a few old-time hoboes who carried a cleated board which they slid beneath the car above the rods. It was very dangerous and it wasn't necessary.

There were other dangers. If you stuck your feet out of the boxcar door, you stood a chance of having them chopped off at the next bridge; some men suffered unexpected amputation as a result. If you rode "blind baggage" on the couplings between the cars, you could be seriously hurt or even killed if the train jerked to a sudden stop. Men asleep on top of a boxcar sometimes rolled off and were killed when the train swayed around a curve. The smart ones roped themselves on. Bob Drouin and twenty-five others were once locked in a boxcar by a Mounted Policeman for three days and almost starved. On some of the older cars the wheels had become worn down on one side. This couldn't be detected until the train gathered speed. On such cars, sleep was impossible because, as Sherwin noted, "half the time you were in mid air." The continual bucking, however, did keep the riders warm when the weather outside was freezing.

Nonetheless, the cold could be a killer, as Robert Brodie discovered one bitter winter's night when he tried to board a freight in Saskatchewan. Brodie, nicknamed "Steve" after the sporting Irishman who was said to have jumped off Brooklyn Bridge on a bet, was twenty-two years old. He had been hiking all day and now, having reached a railway water tower, waited for the freight to slow down so that he could leap aboard. It was too cold; his hands could not maintain their grip on the railing. He was about to fall when a pair of strong arms reached down and pulled him into the boxcar.

His saviour was quite obviously an ex-soldier.

"Get those damn leather boots off!" he barked. "Make yourself some shoes out of newspaper; tie them with binder twine and start walking or you'll lose your feet!" Steve Brodie obeyed.

The stranger ordered him to trudge up and down the boxcar, but warned him away from the far end, which Brodie assumed was being used as a latrine. Finally Brodie could walk no more. The stranger bullied him, kicked him, told him he'd die in the forty-below weather unless he kept moving.

Brodie was exhausted, but when he tried to lie down he found himself dragged to the forbidden end of the boxcar. The stranger directed the flame of his lighter at a dark bulk on the floor, and there, in the flickering light, Brodie looked in horror upon the forms of three young men, all in their teens, huddled together, frozen to death.

"It saved my life," said Brodie, who was to play a key role in unemployed demonstrations in Vancouver later that decade.

In addition to suffering from cold the transients were plagued by grit, smoke, and cinders. They could easily be identified by their eyelashes. In Drouin's words, "you'd swear it was mascara." In Calgary, the men who leaped from the freights tried to wash off the soot in the Elbow River, knowing that if the police spotted the black rings around their eyes, they were candidates for jail. At the Water Street Mission in Ottawa, it was just the opposite. Because the mission discouraged repeat visitors, the stiffs would blacken their faces at the coal yards to fool the man at the door into thinking they'd just got off the train.

They quickly learned the argot of the road. They were all "stiffs" or "bindle stiffs." A freight was a "drag"; a stiff who asked for a handout at the front door was a "ding dong beggar"; at the back door he was a "lump bandit." A scrounger was a "jungle buzzard," a village policeman a "town clown," a city cop a "harness bull." A "winter Christian" was anyone who took refuge in a Salvation Army hostel for the cold season, professed to give his life to "Jerusalem Slim" (Jesus Christ), and turned agnostic as soon as the weather warmed. A "gay cat" was a happy young innocent; a "scenery hog" was a green transient. A "tap" was a sucker; anybody who rode the boxcars was a "john"; a "McGoof hound" drank fortified wine. A "wolf" was an older man whose male lover was a "gazooney" or a "prushun." A "dino" was a daredevil who took a chance, ordered a three-course meal in a restaurant, and then announced he was broke. The friendliest restaurants were run by Greek and Chinese immigrants; generally, they let the dinos work out the bill washing dishes. Others called the police.

Some of the argot of the road – wino, junkie, punk, canned heat artist – has since entered the language. Sometimes the meaning has changed: a "dingbat" among the stiffs of the thirties was a man who was always dinging people on the street for a nickel for a cup of coffee. Generally he was arrested for vagrancy.

Every town had its jungle, where, as Sherwin learned, the stiffs gathered to cook mulligan and exchange information. James Ealey, a teenager from Toronto's Cabbagetown, had warm memories of the Montreal jungle on a hill near the St. Lawrence where some three hundred men regularly slept. Nuns from a nearby convent arrived each evening with stew, tea, and bread and returned each morning with muffins and porridge. The Toronto jungle was just north of the Prince Edward viaduct on the Danforth – a well-run camp in the charge of a committee of twelve, with whitewashed stones to mark the pathways between the shacks. Strict discipline was enforced, and the youngsters who swam in the Don River not far away were kept out of the area by the transients to protect them from molesters.

The best hobo jungles were remarkably clean, with pails and cans for brewing tea or for washing clothes hanging neatly on the fence. Every jungle had a fireplace made of stones with boxcar brake irons on which to stand pots or perhaps a heavy stick, split

155

from a barn door, with a wire attached to the end for the cooking pail. Canned heat (Sterno) was the universal stimulant, especially for the older hoboes. The pink jelly was strained through a sock and mixed with soda pop and water. Charles Sherwin would never forget the mountain of empty Sterno tins which greeted him when he first entered the Sudbury jungle, right in the heart of town.

It was spectacles like these – homeless men living in shacks in the jungles, swarming aboard rattling freights, begging on the streets of the Western cities – that shocked the Chief of the General Staff, A.G.L. "Andy" McNaughton, when he crossed the country on a tour of military establishments late that summer. McNaughton was a man of considerable imagination and drive. An unconventional gunnery officer in the Great War, he had brought his scientific imagination to the problems of counter-battery work; as a result, his artillery had knocked out 70 per cent of the German guns just before the battle of Vimy Ridge. Now this lean and shaggy general, the best-known military man in the country, proceeded to devote his orderly mind to the problem of the single, unemployed transients.

The waste of manpower galled him. The health and morale of tens of thousands of men – the very men who would have to fight the next war, if it came – were deteriorating to the point where he thought it doubtful if they could or would work again. Worse, they were increasingly susceptible to communist propaganda, and, in the General's view, subversion. If they didn't fight for their country they might easily be the storm troopers in a revolution McNaughton's army would have to suppress. In 1932, the possibility of revolution didn't seem so unreal. Here, the General concluded, was a situation that had all the makings of serious trouble for the future – and probably the near future at that.

On the face of it, his solution was ingenious and sensible. It certainly appealed to R.B. Bennett, who seemed convinced that revolution was a real and present danger. At the opening of Parliament on October 6, Bennett leaned over to whisper to McNaughton that Cabinet was very much interested in his scheme. He asked for a detailed proposal and wanted it on his desk by half-past nine the following morning. To the enthusiastic General, who had planned more than one skirmish in less time,

156

this was an acceptable deadline. He worked all night and produced the document as requested.

McNaughton's solution had two aims. It would get the men off the streets, out of the cities and out of sight, and, at the same time, it would improve their bodies and their minds by providing honest, useful work in a group of camps run by the military but not subject to army discipline. The scheme would be entirely voluntary. Men could enter the camps and leave when they pleased. They would be fed, clothed, and housed and would work on projects of national importance – building airfields and highways that had been postponed because of the Depression. In addition, they would be given twenty cents a day with which to buy cigarettes, toiletries, and other sundries.

The camps, in effect, would be holding units to keep younger men in reasonable physical condition until they could find work. What could be more sensible, more generous, more exciting than a program "to build up morale through work, to proceed by persuasion and not by compulsion, and to do everything possible to facilitate the flow back of men to industry as soon as they should be mentally and physically fit and positions available"?

Press, politicians, and general public exulted. The newspapers went overboard in praising the idea. The Winnipeg *Tribune* burbled that "the camps provide just such an outing as a young man's heart should long for – an outdoor life, as a man among men, plenty of time for sport, and plenty of sport at hand. . . . They are enjoying life to the full; and work more eagerly than wellpaid workmen . . , there has been no evidence of any desire to depart. On the contrary, the boys are writing their unemployed friends to 'come on in.' "

This paean of praise was nation-wide. The British United Press declared that the plan "may be numbered among the most successful social experiments of the fight against depression." The Halifax *Mail* described the program as "a veritable miracle of common sense expediency." Reporters toured the camps and returned to portray them as a paradise on earth compared to the shiftless life previously endured by the occupants. "Life is made as congenial and pleasant as possible," the Kingston *Whig-Standard* reported. "Good companionship is enjoyed . . . everything to provide ordinary comfort for the men is done." The press did not report that their information came from camp officials only, that the men themselves were forbidden to talk to newspaper reporters.

The newspaper emphasis was on the lack of army discipline and the voluntary nature of the scheme. As the Ottawa *Journal* put it, "men at these camps are free to come and go, do not wear a uniform, are fed well and comfortably housed, live under splendid conditions. There are few rules, no rigorous restrictions on their freedom of action, nothing approaching a military atmosphere. There is no punishment for violation of rules. If a man will not do his share of the work he is dismissed from the camp, and a report on his conduct goes to the relief authorities of his home community, but that is all."

What the newspapers left unsaid was that those who left camp for any reason were denied all further relief. Men either stayed or starved. Nor did the press understand that while the camps rejected military discipline, they held to military law, which made it difficult and dangerous to complain.

But one group of men, living in a camp in Riding Mountain park, managed to smuggle out a letter that reached J.S. Woodsworth. He read portions of it to the House: "Picture to yourself a tarpaper shack 79 feet x 24 with no windows, along each side there is a row of double decker bunks, these are spaced off with 8 x 1 board so that there is room for two men in each bunk. The bunks are filled with straw and you crawl into them from the foot end. Along the front of the lower bunk a narrow board is placed upon which the men may sit. The place is very meagrely lighted and ventilation by three skylights. . . . So narrow is the passageway between the bunks that when the men are sitting on the bench there is scarcely room to pass between them. This shack . . . houses 88 men. There is a marked resemblance to a hog pen or a dog pound. At times the place reeks of the foul smell and at night the air is simply fetid. The floor is dirty and the end of the shack where the men wash . . . is caked with black mud. The toilet is thoroughly filthy, unsanitary, and far too small."

Woodsworth asked rhetorically why men would suffer such indignities and then supplied the answer. The camp was isolated – fourteen miles from the nearest railway. Stool-pigeons reported the slightest attempt at organization. There was intermittent surveillance by the RCMP and a general breaking down of morale.

158

The press, which had been so enthusiastic about the camp scheme, played down or ignored Woodsworth's remarks and the Canadian public continued to be lulled into believing that the problem of the homeless single men was on its way to solution. But Bennett, McNaughton, and those who planned the relief camps were not living in the real world. The "gift" of twenty cents a day was "slave wages" to those who had laboured for eight hours. That phrase would soon enter general parlance to bewilder and madden the Prime Minister, who never comprehended its meaning.

The irony was that McNaughton's scheme for staving off revolution had the seeds of revolution inherent in it. Within two years the camps that had been greeted with such applause would be known throughout the country as slave camps. In the end the program would prove another of the Bennett government's disasters.

4

Restructuring the future

In the hot, dry summer of 1932, when the main crop in the Palliser Triangle seemed to be Russian thistle, two significant gatherings caught the attention of the nation. The first, the Imperial Economic Conference held in July, got more coverage but accomplished very little. The second, the founding convention of the Co-operative Commonwealth Federation in Calgary, made fewer headlines but was of greater significance. The Ottawa conference looked back; the Calgary convention tried to chart the future.

On July 18, every steamer in Quebec harbour sounded a welcome and the crowd that blackened the shores cheered hoarsely as the pride of the CPR, the *Empress of Britain*, fastest passenger liner in the world, nosed its white prow into the dockside. A formidable delegation was on board. It included half the members of the British Cabinet, two of whom – Stanley Baldwin and Neville Chamberlain – would be prime ministers later in the decade, and representatives of five of the nine British nations that would be at the conference.

At that moment, Canada was at the centre of the British world – the old Empire and the new Commonwealth – and R.B. Bennett was the centre of the conference that followed. He was convinced that he was about to make good on his election promise to blast his way into the markets of the world. He wanted, if not free trade, at least a freer trade within the British sphere. That, in Bennett's view, was the real path to prosperity.

Press and public seized on the conference with all the yearning and fervour of a castaway who sees a wisp of smoke on the horizon. An American professor told R.J. Manion that he hoped "the conference might break the vicious cycle of the depression." If the Empire led, he said, the rest of the world would follow. That pretty well summed up Bennett's position. Stanley Baldwin, who looked the very image of the cartoonist's John Bull, said the same thing as the ship arrived. "We believe," he announced, "we can set an example to the whole world in breaking down obstacles to commerce . . . and so bring peoples safely through the tragic depression of recent times."

This was wishful thinking. Bennett's own policies underlined the growing concern about American encroachment in the Canadian economy. By strengthening her ties with Great Britain and the Commonwealth, Canada might be able to ward off the American threat. The mercurial Canadian-born press baron Lord Beaverbrook, who would ride the hobby horse of Empire free trade all his life, saw in the conference the fulfilment of a dream, even though he could not attend because of an unfortunate breach with his long-time friend Bennett. ("How I longed to be there," he sighed, in a later memoir.) It was Beaverbrook's conviction that "the day of Empire unity had dawned" – the first step, he was convinced, towards an economic union in the British world.

But the influential John Dafoe, the rumpled sage of Winnipeg, who had been to more than one imperial conference himself, was not going to settle for a narrow British *zollverein* on the Beaverbrook model. He intimated as much in the *Free Press*. Dafoe saw the British position as "a means of extending free trade within the Empire and as a stepping stone to enlarged free trade with the whole world." Failure in Ottawa, he warned, would mean a political crisis in those nations responsible for that failure.

In the crowded lobby of the Chateau Laurier in Ottawa that week, two hundred newspapermen from the British and world press joined the jostling, cosmopolitan throng – turbaned Hindus carrying briefcases; hard-eyed businessmen in eighty-dollar
160

suits; stylish women on the arms of florid politicians; statesmen or would-be statesmen in striped pants and pearl grey vests to match their pearl grey hair. The air crackled with talk about Danish ham, Australian wool, Canadian wheat. As one observer noted, "more economics, statistics and monetary theory are being talked about in Ottawa at this moment than in all the other capitals of the world combined."

At the same time, in the same city, 576 shabbily dressed men and women were congregating in a newly whitewashed garage for the Workers' Economic Conference, clearly sponsored (though clandestinely) by the outlawed Communist party. Most of the delegates, from every corner of Canada, reached the capital by riding boxcars or by hitchhiking, though one group of forty-five actually walked from Montreal. They slept for three days in the conference hall on tarpaulins padded with wood chips, and presented to the Prime Minister a familiar program that included a thirty-five-hour week with no reduction in pay, non-contributory unemployment insurance, the repeal of Section 98, and the release of Tim Buck and his colleagues from prison, all of which, in the briefest of confrontations, the Prime Minister rejected.

The Imperial Conference accomplished very little more. Nobody wanted to make major sacrifices where protective tariffs were concerned. Each country, including Canada, wanted more than it was prepared to give. Twenty leading Canadian manufacturers were holed up in the Chateau, reportedly in a panic because they feared Bennett might give away too much. They needn't have worried. In simple terms, the Canadian government wanted the mother country to continue the preference it was extending to Canadian imports and increase it by taxing all natural and processed foreign products that competed with imports from Canada. Britain was being asked to boost taxes on butter from Denmark and beef from Argentina in favour of Canadian products. Such a "stomach tax," as it was called, was politically impossible.

Canada offered considerably less. Bennett had promised to extend the free list and the Canadian Manufacturers' Association provided a lengthy catalogue of goods that it announced it would be happy to admit from Great Britain without any protective tariff. On the face of it, this was a magnificent gesture of goodwill. But the British had not come unprepared; accompanying that delegation was a formidable group of trade and tariff experts who combed through the CMA's list after Bennett presented it and began to hoot with laughter at such items as "hog de-hairers," "Queen bees," "herring de-boners," and – most hilarious of all – an item described as "Mickey Mouse machines, for making noises of."

The list was a sham. Many of the items were unobtainable in either Canada or Great Britain; others were under patent in the United States and weren't applicable. When the experts translated the impressive-looking array of free goods into dollars and cents, they discovered that the advantage to British exporters would not reach even one hundred thousand dollars.

Another stumbling block to achievement was Bennett's own abrasive personality. By turns intransigent and bombastic, he tried to impose his will on the men who ran the empire. According to Stanley Baldwin, Bennett "had a brainstorm every day which wiped out what he had agreed to the day before." Baldwin then maliciously quoted a former Liberal minister's characterization of Bennett: "He has the manners of a Chicago policeman and the temperament of a Hollywood film star."

The negotiations grew so ugly that, at one point, Bennett asked the Canadian Pacific to have a liner standing by to take the British home. That ultimate breach didn't occur, but there's no doubt that Bennett made a lifelong enemy of Neville Chamberlain, who complained at the outset of "Bennett's very aggressive tone." Chamberlain later declared that "most of our difficulties centred around the personality of Bennett. Full of high Imperial sentiments, he has done little to put them into practice. Instead of guiding the conference in his capacity as Chairman, he has acted merely as the leader of the Canadian delegation. In that capacity he has strained our patience to the limit." The breach between the two men was never healed. Chamberlain's revenge came a few years later after Bennett had retired and was living in England. The name of the former prime minister was advanced as a candidate for a peerage. Chamberlain blocked it, and Bennett had to wait until Churchill was prime minister.

As the bargaining and haggling in Ottawa "tolled the bell for the funeral of Empire solidarity," to quote a disconsolate Beaverbrook, the moderate left wing of the Canadian political spectrum was preparing for a more modest gathering in Calgary. The launching of the new movement, in the words of its leader, J.S. Woodsworth, was "of far greater consequence to the future of Canada than the Imperial Economic Conference now in session in Ottawa; for while the Ottawa Conference is seeking to restore prosperity by adding a few patches to the disintegrating system of capitalism, the object of the Federation is fundamental social reconstruction."

The federation was, of course, the Co-operative Commonwealth Federation, which its founders insisted on calling a "movement" rather than a political party.

The time was ripe. Since the days of the National Policy, few Canadians had seriously questioned the basis of the social and economic order that had seemed to work so well. Now it was apparent, especially in the West, that the government was not prepared to deal with the new crisis in any imaginative way. The country was in a ferment. The illegal Communist party, using a series of front organizations, had seized the initiative on the left, promoting hunger marches, farmers' revolts, and industrial strikes. But the government was still talking as if old panaceas such as the protective tariff would solve the economic crisis. To the old-line parties, the horrors of a deficit were greater than the demoralization of unemployment.

Suddenly the concept of a new political movement gathered momentum, revolving around the spare, goateed figure of J.S. Woodsworth, the one man who had the confidence of all the disparate groups striving to form a new coalition of the Left. Critical mass was reached in less than six months – a remarkably short period in which to form a new party. In February, the League for Social Reconstruction was officially formed in Montreal and Toronto. That same month, the United Farmers of Alberta determined to organize a similar group in the West. In May, members of the Ginger Group of Farmer-Labour M.P.s met in Ottawa with some of the founders of the LSR to plan a "Commonwealth Party," with Woodsworth as temporary president.

On July 1, the UFA set the date and the place for its proposed meeting of left-wing organizations. It was to be August 1 in Calgary. Later that month, in Saskatchewan, provincial farmer and labour groups agreed to form a common front. Finally, the Western Labour Conference – the umbrella organization representing both labour and socialist parties in the four western provinces – switched its annual convention to Calgary to coincide with the UFA meeting.

The West dominated the convention that followed, with the United Farmers of Alberta supplying the greatest number of delegates. The names of the organizations represented in Calgary show how fragmented was the democratic Left in Canada: the Canadian Labour Party, the Dominion Labour Party, the Socialist Party of Canada (British Columbia), the United Farmers of Canada (Saskatchewan), the Independent Labour Party of Manitoba, the Canadian Brotherhood of Railway Engineers, and the newly formed LSR. Individually, these splinter groups had little political clout. Bound together, they hoped to change the social and economic environment of the country.

After a rousing public meeting in Calgary's Labour Temple on Sunday, July 31, the delegates on August 1 got down to work. They represented a cross-section of the Left: fifteen farmers, twenty construction workers, two lawyers, six teachers, one miner, one professor, six housewives, three accountants, six railway workers, three journalists, two steam engineers, one hotel-keeper, one retired minister, one motion-picture operator, three nurses, two union executives, twelve working politicians, and nineteen jobless men and women.

They chose a name and they chose a leader. The first was contentious, the latter foreordained. Of J.S. Woodsworth, an acerbic commentator in *Maclean's* noted that "it can hardly be said that he is a politician, since no politician would handicap a new party with a descriptive label like Co-Operative Commonwealth Federation." As usual, the establishment press failed to understand the significance either of the movement or of its name. As it turned out, the initials CCF fitted as easily into the headlines as "Grit" or "Tory."

The convention's purpose was to form a federation to work for a socialist Canada, but not through violence or agitation in the communist style. Change would be effected through Parliament in the tradition of the British Labour Party. The details of the program would be laid out the following year in Regina in the form of a manifesto to be written with the help of the young intellectuals in the LSR. The human symbol of the movement would be the incorruptible Woodsworth, a man who cared for neither fame nor gain – perhaps the only party leader in Canadian history who was totally selfless.

Woodsworth had been raised as a Methodist activist. His doctrine was the Social Gospel, which had swept the evangelical churches in the early years of the century. His personal credo could be summed up in his own words: "A curse still hangs over inactivity. A severe condemnation still rests upon indifference. . . . Christianity stands for social righteousness as well as personal righteousness. . . . We have tried to provide for the poor. Yet, have we tried to alter the social conditions that lead to poverty?"

The slums of England, where Woodsworth had worked in his youth, and the All People's Mission in the heart of Winnipeg's immigrant district had politicized him. The Winnipeg General Strike made him a national figure. Jailed, tried, and acquitted of sedition, he emerged as the leader of the democratic Left.

A skilled parliamentarian, he it was who had sparked the unemployment debate in the House that helped defeat Mackenzie King's Liberals. He had waged an exhausting but eventually successful battle to establish the first divorce court in Canada – divorce having been as inflammatory a subject then as abortion in the 1980s. He had made an exhaustive study of unemployment insurance and argued vainly year after year for its establishment in Canada. He fought for civil liberties, bombarding the House with case histories of police brutality, suppression of human rights, invasion of privacy, and unwarranted deportation.

They called him a Red, but he had no use for the shrill communists and for all of his life would keep them at arm's length while fighting in and out of Parliament to allow them to state their views without interference. For that he got no gratitude. The communist *Worker* sneered at him as "the pacifist flunky of the ruling class."

He had visited the Soviet Union and had hobnobbed with the British Fabians, but his own brand of socialism was distinctively Canadian. "I believe that we in Canada must work out our salvation in our own way," he was to say. "I am convinced that we may develop in Canada a distinct type of socialism. I refuse to follow slavishly the British model or the American model or the Russian model. We in Canada will solve our problems along our own lines." He was a Canadian through and through. In those days the census takers insisted that all should list their racial origins, no matter how many centuries their forbears might have spent in Canada. Woodsworth stubbornly refused.

He looked ascetic and frail, but he wasn't. He was blessed with the inner toughness that is bestowed on those who refuse to veer one millimetre from the moral principles they set for themselves. "We are starting with not a dollar in the treasury," he wrote that September, " - an immense task ahead." He would not spare himself to meet it. In the year following the Calgary convention he would travel the country to rouse support, sleeping in nothing more luxurious than an upper berth to keep down expenses. Indeed, he sometimes sat up all night in a day coach rather than pay for a sleeping-car. He was prepared to go to any lengths to spread his political gospel, which, to Woodsworth, was the Christian gospel. He talked to brakemen and conductors on the trains and he talked to housewives in their kitchens, often helping them with their chores. As his Marxist son-in-law, the lanky West Coaster Angus MacInnis, once remarked: "If J.S. heard of three Eskimos in the Arctic Circle who wanted a meeting, he'd be off to them on the next train."

In the twelve-month period following the Calgary convention, Woodsworth, in spite of his heavy parliamentary schedule, managed to make two hundred speeches and give innumerable press interviews. In those despairing years, he was the conscience of Canada.

5

An attempt Having exhausted their appeals, Tim Buck and his seven Com-
at political munist comrades began to serve their terms in Kingston Peniten-
murder tiary on February 19, 1932. Buck would always remember that first day. Joined by six hardened criminals including the notorious bank robber Mickey McDonald, they were lined up before the acting warden, Gilbert Smith, who told them: "Having been convicted of a criminal offence you have no rights. You are not a person in the eyes of the law." Smith then read off the penitentiary's list of rules - twenty-two don'ts. "Repression," Buck later wrote, "seeped out of every one of them."

Then Smith asked Buck to identify himself.

"So you're Buck. Now I want you to understand that what I've been saying is only part of what could be said. We have the means here by which to tame lions and you don't look to me very much like a lion."

"I never pretended to be . . . " Buck started to say, but the warden cut him off.

"Silence!" he shouted. A guard seized Buck by the arm and repeated, "Silence!" At length the Communist leader was allowed to speak. He asked for reading material to be sent to him but was told he must first read the prison library's five thousand books. He asked if he could order some biographies; that was refused. He asked if he could subscribe to Hansard, the record of the House of Commons debates; that was turned down because the superintendent of penitentiaries said there were "too many radical speeches in it." Sometime later he was denied permission to buy books in German for language study because "German is the language of your so-called Communist International." When Buck asked permission to study French, he was told, "You don't live in Quebec. The answer is no. . . . You're asking to study French in the hope that you'll be able to use it for agitation and for the fomenting of unrest."

Conditions in Kingston Penitentiary at that time were close to medieval. That was the word William Withrow used to describe the philosophy of those who ran the institution. Withrow, a convicted abortionist, was released late in 1929 after serving three years. By the time Buck and the others were incarcerated, Withrow had embarked on a campaign to change a situation so evil as "to make the very imps in hell weep." His tireless crusade for penal reform helped bring about the famous Archambault Royal Commission that looked into penitentiary conditions later in the decade.

A few months after Buck was imprisoned, Withrow told a United Church men's club, " . . . there are political prisoners in Kingston today, men whose only crime is opposition to those in power. . . . These men are no different from you and me and yet they are kept in dungeons, damp and dirty, that would not be used to hold cattle."

The wretched conditions that Withrow had experienced were exacerbated now by overcrowding – a direct result of the Depression. In 1929, twenty-seven hundred convicts were held in federal

167

penitentiaries. Three years later, a wave of bank robberies, thefts, burglaries, and other acts of violence brought on by poverty and desperation had boosted the population to more than four thousand.

By 1932, Kingston Penitentiary was in a state of tension. In addition to the major complaints – the execrable food, the lack of exercise (only fifteen minutes a day in the "bullpen" and no recreational games), the ban on verbal communication, and the barbarous corporal punishment – there was a host of minor irritants.

It was a misdemeanour, for instance, to be found with a newspaper. Although small quantities of tobacco were issued, cigarette papers were not; the convicts were forced to use toilet paper to roll their own. During their entire prison term, inmates were allowed only one approved visitor. On these occasions a guard was interposed between the two, making private conversation impossible. Correspondence was heavily censored and so were magazines.

If a man made a request to the warden he could be sent to the "Prison of Isolation," which the inmates called the Hole. Here, in a cell situated halfway below ground with the windows painted over, he existed on porridge, bread, and boiled potatoes and was allowed no exercise. Electric light from a naked bulb was turned on for a brief hour or half-hour at meal times only. One convict, John O'Brien, endured these conditions for a year.

Any inmate who stepped out of line could be sentenced to ten or twenty blows with a hideous instrument known, euphemistically, as the Paddle – so called, no doubt, to convince the general public that the punishment was no worse than a mild slap on the bottom of a recalcitrant child. The reality was that the prison authorities were using physical torture as a means of discipline and brutal revenge.

The offender was laid face down on a table, his arms and legs stretched out tightly – as on a rack – and strapped together. Another strap, cinched around his body, made the slightest movement impossible. He was blindfolded so that, in Withrow's words, "he must not see his castigator and besides, things are harder to bear in the darkness."

The Paddle itself was a thick strap, three feet long, with a wooden handle. Diamond-shaped holes were cut in the material,

168

which was sometimes soaked overnight "the more effectively to mutilate the victim." When the Paddle was applied to the naked buttocks, the skin was sucked through the holes. Withrow claimed that only a few of the guards were selected to do this brutal work. "We knew them. They were vicious through and through. It was said they enjoyed this cruel pastime. . . . Oh! The pain and the anguish! Oh! The bruising and the bleeding! Smack! Smack! Smack! Bruises and blood. Ten blows! Fifteen! Twenty! The guard uses all the force of his strong arms."

Withrow estimated that 10 per cent of the prison population was beaten annually in this way. He recounted stories of prisoners who were tortured every few days, carried from the table limp and unconscious, and thrown on the floor of the Hole to recover as best they might.

His description of these conditions differed markedly from that of justice minister Hugh Guthrie. Guthrie later declared in the House, " . . . there is nothing brutal about it. What the prisoners resent is the indignity of it; they will tell you so. . . . They strap children in school. My mother used to strap me at home – yes, and in the same place they strap the prisoners . . . as far as the records of Canadian penitentiaries disclose there is no record of any injury, any skin broken, or any blood flowing. . . . " But then, one might ask, would any prison official have put it on the record?

On October 17, matters came to a head at Kingston as a result of a series of "kites" (clandestine messages) circulated among the prisoners. What was later called a riot was really a sit-down strike. At three that afternoon, the inmates decided to walk out of the shops and engage in a peaceful demonstration to impress the officials with the need for redress of their complaints. In particular, they wanted more recreation and a regular issue of cigarette papers. Warden Smith got wind of their plans and locked them in. A group in the mailbag shop threw a hose out the window, climbed down it, and burned the locks off the doors with an acetylene torch.

In the confused accounts of what happened next, several points stand out. Tim Buck, who had originally opposed the sit-down strike as unproductive, continually urged caution, and warned the strikers against violence. He advised them to stay out of the yard and go instead to the South Dome. When the warden refused to negotiate and brought in a detachment of soldiers, who began shooting, Buck was asked by the strikers to reason with Smith. "No agreement! No agreement!" Smith told him. "These men have committed a crime and you're the one who's responsible, Buck." To which Buck replied, "Well, we can also discuss that later but in the meantime it seems to me the most important thing is to get the soldiers to stop shooting before panic sets in among these men." To that, Smith grudgingly agreed.

That, in effect, ended the "riot" before it became a riot. The men returned peacefully to their cells. Smith promised to recommend a public investigation, adding a pledge that no one would be punished until he received a fair hearing and that the men could return to work the following day. Smith was not allowed to keep his pledge.

Over the next two days, the penitentiary was relatively quiet. But a spirit of revolt was simmering. It was thoughtlessly encouraged by Major-General D.M. Ormond, the superintendent of penitentiaries, who arrived from Ottawa on the morning of October 20 to conduct an inquiry into the disturbance. The Archambault Royal Commission later described Ormond as "arrogant . . . deceitful [and] dictatorial," and on this occasion he certainly lived up to those adjectives. He refused to listen to any delegation of prisoners, insisting on the old army rule that complaints must be made individually. He refused to allow cigarette papers to be distributed. He banned the periods of daily exercise that Smith had promised. He called out the militia to back up the prison guards, who were issued rifles, revolvers, and shotguns. Acting Warden Gilbert Smith would be relieved of his duties two days later.

Work became impossible. Confined to their cells without supper, the men began rattling their tin cups against the cell bars and shouting until the din in Cell Blocks C and E was overpowering. Cell Block D, where Tim Buck was held, was relatively quiet.

Around five in the afternoon, Buck heard more shouting, apparently coming from E and C blocks and the Prison of Isolation. It was later revealed that officers or guards were firing through the peepholes into cells occupied by prisoners, even though there was no danger that these men could escape or cause injury. In the Prison of Isolation, a convict named Price, hit in the shoulder by

170

a bullet, was left in his cell without medical attention or food for twenty-two hours. An inquiry later reported there was no justification for this neglect.

D Block remained quiet. About eight in the evening, Buck could hear more shots being fired. Suddenly, somebody at the north end of the block shouted that the guards were coming over to D.

"Duck, boys, they're going to shoot here."

Buck was making up his bed. Somebody else shouted, "They won't shoot in here, we're not trying to escape."

At that moment, Tim Buck felt a sharp rush of air in his hair and the crack of a bullet overhead. He looked out of the window of his cell and saw, through the drizzling rain, a group of men in penitentiary oilskins on the lawn below. He caught a gleam of light on rifle barrels and immediately ducked for cover. Someone shouted that the guards were only firing blanks, but Buck warned: "Blanks nothing. You should see the inside of my cell."

Even as he spoke, a bullet whizzed past his left ear. Another struck a bar of his cell with a resounding *wang*. A third hit the wall between his cell and the doorway of the adjoining cell. A shotgun charge spattered the back of the cell.

Political murder, officially condoned, had up to that time been unknown in Canada. But there isn't the shadow of a doubt that a deliberate attempt was made on the night of October 20, 1932, to kill Tim Buck and that it was tacitly approved by the prison authorities and, at the very least, condoned by higher-ups in Ottawa. There had been no disturbance in his cell block, no damage to property, no hurling of trays or other objects as had happened elsewhere in the penitentiary. The shooting was not the work of a single, deranged individual but of a group of several guards who knew exactly what they were doing. As Woodsworth was to say many months later in the House, "There are nearly nine hundred prisoners in the penitentiary. How was it that the cell selected for the shooting was the one in which there was a Communist?"

At the time of the shooting, Woodsworth had no knowledge of the incident, nor did the general public or the press. The authorities covered it up. Buck asked Ormond for an investigation; there was none. Ormond was convinced that the October 17 "riot" was a Communist plot. Only Buck was charged with inciting to riot.

His comrades were charged either as participants or with conspiracy. All of them were put in the Hole and kept there until they were tried.

Buck was brought to court in Kingston, a diminutive figure only five feet six inches tall, his wrists shackled to those of two burly guards and his ankles shackled to their ankles. This enforced lock step was clearly staged for the benefit of photographers to make the mild-mannered Buck look like a dangerous criminal, bent on escape. He had come to court before without shackles, and the judge, G.E. De Roche, quickly ordered them removed.

De Roche didn't believe the strike of October 17 amounted to very much. He referred to it as a peaceful disturbance that had developed into a riot and "as riots go I would say this was a very mild riot." Nor did he believe that Buck was the instigator – quite the opposite. "I believe," he told the prisoner, "that you had an honest desire that no harm should come to either person or property." Nonetheless, because Buck had taken part in an unlawful assembly, the judge reluctantly sentenced him to an additional nine months. Under the harsh laws of the time, he might have given him seven years.

Until this time, ten months after the disturbance at Kingston, no member of the public was aware that an attempt had been made to murder Buck. For all of that period, the authorities had managed to keep a lid on the affair. The story broke wide open, however, when Buck was subpoenaed to testify at the trial of another of the rioters, the notorious Mickey McDonald. "Sure they fired at me," Buck stated in answer to a defence question. The Toronto Trades and Labour Council immediately demanded an explanation from the Minister of Justice. Guthrie in turn asked for an explanation from Superintendent Ormond, who replied that there was no substantial evidence to bear out Buck's statement.

A further investigation, later described by the Archambault Commission as "neither comprehensive nor thorough," followed. Guthrie used that flawed and misleading report to tell the House that "Buck is one of those who were encouraging the disorder. At the door of his cell he was making speeches and encouraging the rioters, and for the purpose of frightening him, I suppose, or cowing him, certain guards fired into the ceiling of his cell."

172

None of that was true, and Guthrie must have known it. Certainly he knew that the shooting incident occurred on October 20, three days *after* the so-called riot of October 17. At that point there was no riot. Buck was not haranguing his fellow prisoners (secure in their cells). He wasn't standing at the door of his cell; he was making his bed. The shots weren't fired into the ceiling, as an investigation of the bullet holes made clear; they were fired at Tim Buck. "Certain guards," as Guthrie called them, were not acting independently, as his remarks in the House suggested; they were acting as a team. They pumped at least three bullets and ten shotgun pellets into Buck's cell.

Very little of these revelations filtered down to the general public, who could be pardoned for believing that all the shooting had taken place in the course of a wild mêlée of which Buck was the instigator. "TIM BUCK DESIGNATED PRISON RIOT LEADER," one headline had read, just before Buck's preliminary hearing. "TIM BUCK IS CONVICTED OF RIOTING AT PENITENTIARY" read another, six months later.

The impression left on the public's mind was that the "fiery little orator," as the press called him, had masterminded and personally led an all-out prison riot and escape attempt. It wasn't until the end of the decade when the Archambault Commission made its report that Buck was cleared. After an exhaustive examination of all the evidence the commission declared him innocent of all the charges levelled against him. His only crime had been to leave his prison workbench when the others did because, understandably, he didn't want to be called a "rat."

1933

1

R.B. Bennett's credibility was running out. He had promised to *The* "blast a way into the closed markets of the world," but that *shame* promise had fizzled out with the Imperial Economic Conference. *of* He had pledged that no government of which he was leader *relief* would introduce the dole, but the dole had been a fact for more than six months. He had said repeatedly that the Depression was over when it was quite clearly continuing. Now, in March of 1933, he said it again in the House of Commons. Canada, the Prime Minister declared (carefully employing the past tense), had weathered the Depression better than any other country in the world. The truth was just the opposite. With the possible exception of the United States, Canada had taken the hardest blow. Bennett's remarkable statement scarcely squared with the figures his Minister of Labour would shortly release, which showed that 1,357,262 Canadians were now accepting direct relief. That was more than all who had enlisted for service in the Great War.

His desk was flooded with telegrams, letters, and resolutions from organizations, business leaders, political supporters, and ordinary working people detailing specific cases of need. To all these Bennett had the same answer – the one he had given the previous year to the town clerk of Glace Bay who wrote to ask for immediate aid because municipal relief had broken down and "semi-starvation" existed. Bennett replied personally with what had become a form letter: "Unemployment relief is the primary responsibility of the municipality and secondly that of the province. . . . " Ottawa, in short, could not directly help.

It was an easy out for Bennett – simply dumping the problem on such already overburdened municipalities as Sydney and Glace Bay, whose limited resources could not cope with problems brought on when the mines laid off wage-earners. For example, Sydney had millions of gallons of water available but declined to give any of it away to landlords, who, in turn, couldn't afford to pay the water rates because poor tenants could not afford to pay their rent.

John Dafoe's editorial of January 12, 1933, lit into the government for this shrugging off of responsibility. "Its record has shown a tardiness and half heartedness even in co-operating with

177

the provinces, which has been frequently condemned, even by friends of the Government." One figure – automobile production, a notable economic bellwether – made it clear that Canada had *not* rounded the corner. In 1929, new car sales had outnumbered bicycle sales by a ratio of five to one. But people could no longer afford new cars. By 1933, the ratio had sunk to less than two to one.

From coast to coast, Canada seethed with dissension. Seven jobless men went to jail in Edmonton for taking part in a hunger march. Fourteen farmers received suspended sentences for their part in a riot in Arborg, Manitoba, earlier in the winter – a riot brought on by a forced tax sale. Twenty-two men were jailed for a riot in a Saskatoon relief camp that caused the death of an RCMP inspector. Four more were arrested in Nelson, B.C., for another jobless parade. The call for a national system of non-contributory unemployment insurance reached a crescendo. One thousand men and women marched on the Manitoba legislature demanding it. Two hundred paraded in Calgary. Hundreds mobbed the city hall in Victoria. But unemployment insurance was no panacea; though it might help mitigate a future depression, it was too late for it to be of much use in this one. Besides, Bennett had already made his own position clear: "No government with which I am associated will ever establish a system of non-contributory unemployment insurance."

By May, having used up all their savings, thousands more went on the dole, swelling the relief rolls to a million and a half. They went reluctantly because even when the voucher system was adopted by most municipalities, the stigma of being a "reliefer" was clearly advertised. As Frank Croft remembered, "merchants couldn't see why they should wrap shoe boxes or clothing when the customer was in no condition to complain. When you saw a man with his coat over his arm it was a good bet that he was either on his way to a pawnshop or had just turned in a relief voucher for it."

With their nest-egg gone and nothing more coming in, the newly destitute were forced to make what was to them a shameful, last-ditch decision. One such was a Toronto businessman, Arthur Lendrum, who for the past two years had watched his small company drift into bankruptcy. Borrowed money, together with an income now rapidly dwindling, had for a time helped him make ends meet. But when the holders of the second mortgage on his home fore-

178

closed, he and his family were forced to move to a low-rent district. The day soon came when the Lendrums' entire funds amounted to only fifteen dollars. "It's no use trying to keep up any longer, Arthur," his wife told him. "We'll have to apply for relief."

Lendrum kept putting it off, hoping something would turn up. It never did. At last, on a gloomy Thursday afternoon at the end of January, "goaded by the spectre of want," he asked for help.

The following afternoon an inspector called and took some notes. He asked to see Lendrum's bank passbook, checked over the electrical equipment in the house - washing machine, floor polisher, vacuum cleaner - examined the scanty supply of coal, and departed "knowing more about our private affairs than our relatives did." He told Mrs. Lendrum that her husband should go to the House of Industry (it had been given that name when used as a poor house) where relief supplies and vouchers were dispensed.

Lendrum couldn't bring himself to take this final, irreversible step. That would be an admission that he, who had been a successful small businessman, earning a good independent living, had failed. He vacillated through the weekend. Finally, on Monday he realized he had no choice, for the family was faced with starvation. That afternoon he mustered his courage and walked down to Elm Street, feeling the way a dog does when it puts its tail between its legs.

When he reached the building, he felt lost and disoriented. He had no idea what the procedure was. He spotted a man standing near the doorway. "What do I do now?" he asked.

"Take a seat on the benches there," came the reply.

Lendrum looked inside. The first row of benches was full but there was some room in the second row. He made his way between the rows, feeling horribly mortified but then a little relieved when he realized that a sort of order prevailed and that no one was staring at him.

As he took his seat he looked about him. He felt conspicuously well dressed. If only his overcoat was shabbier, his hat a little slouchier! Yet nobody took any notice. He turned to an elderly man sitting next to him.

"I never thought it would come to this," he said in a low voice.

"Not me neither," came the reply. It was a mild voice, modulated and pleasing, the kind of voice one might expect to hear from a clergyman of ripe experience. In it Lendrum detected a note of gentle resignation. The man was an old-timer, he learned; he'd been coming to the House of Industry for months and knew the ropes.

"How do they run things?" Lendrum asked.

"We wait here till there's room in that other place," his new companion told him, jerking a thumb towards a door at the end of the room. "Your first time, ain't it? Oh, well, there's nothing to be ashamed of."

He explained that they would eventually be sent to a second room "where there's a bunch of gals sitting at tables." You would give them your name and address, he said, "and then stand back until your address is called. Then you goes up to the girl and gets your tickets. I'll show you how it's done."

Lendrum looked about him at men and women presenting tickets to others who stood in front of tall piles of parcels stacked against the walls.

"Them as has families gets the large parcels," his friend told him. "But if there's only two of you, like me and the missus, you gets the small parcel. I come every ten days but if you has a family you come in every week."

Lendrum watched curiously, taking in the faces of the relief recipients. Most, he noted, brightened up when they were given their parcel. Many smiled; some joked a little lamely. Others never changed expression. They had brought shopping bags, suitcases, pieces of luggage, or sacks, which they slung over their shoulders.

The lines moved, row by row, up the stairs to a second waiting room, crowded with benches. Lendrum's row filed in and took seats. At the far end was another door with a man standing in front who called out "next two rows" at ten-minute intervals. As the people in these rows stood up and shuffled forward, their places were taken by others from the downstairs waiting room.

A peculiar scene, Lendrum thought. It reminded him of wartime and refugee queues except that there was no evidence of grief or wounds, no bedlam of chattering tongues. The crowd was largely male, with a few women and one or two children; a good many had foreign accents. There was one black.

Over the whole assembly solid Canadian order reigned supreme. There was a strange quiet. Most of the supplicants had come alone. They knew nobody, nobody knew them; and so they

180

sat, silently waiting their turn. Those who did speak conversed in low tones, as in a church. All waited expectantly for the man at the door to say: "Next two rows."

Lendrum chanced a quiet remark to a man on his right who seemed better dressed than the average.

"When's it all going to end?" he asked. It was a question that thousands like him were asking that year, and the answer was always the same.

"Nobody seems to know," the man replied quietly. He looked at Lendrum with puzzled eyes and then blurted out a brief confession: "I kept going as long as I could but now there's no jobs to be had anymore. It's getting worse. When I first came here, there wasn't the crowd there is now. Something ought to be done about getting money in circulation again. Your first time here?"

Lendrum nodded.

"Oh, you needn't worry about that. We're all alike."

All alike! Lendrum murmured to himself. There they all were, sitting with bowed shoulders on the backless benches – business executives, labourers, mechanics, artisans, housewives, salesmen, accountants, clerks, and tramps – all social and industrial rank gone, everybody reduced to the primary level of want, equality established by need.

"The Government ought to do something," somebody else said, breaking the silence. Lendrum had heard that line before and would hear it again. Yet he also knew that if anyone in this anonymous crowd were to stand up and denounce the system he would promptly be called a Red and ejected.

"Next two rows," the doorman called.

Two minutes later Lendrum's group passed through the doorway and found themselves in an inner courtyard. Lendrum noticed a rough booth labelled "Exchanges" and assumed it was for those who wished to substitute sago for salmon or rolled oats for rice. At the far end of the courtyard, in another large room, long lines of young women sat at tables and desks with thousands of cards stacked in front of them and placards marked with letters of the alphabet strung on wires above them. He went to the table marked by an L and after a few minutes managed to get the girl's attention. He gave her his name and address and the names and ages of his wife and two daughters.

"Get a declaration that you have no liquor permit and register at Lombard Street," the girl told him. "Do this before you come back next week. Please stand back until your name is called."

Lendrum joined the crowd – all standing, waiting to be called. A man ahead of him left empty-handed. "The inspector says you're not entitled to relief," the girl told him. "You made a three-dollar purchase on your liquor permit the day before he called."

Then, from the far end of the room, he heard not his name but his address. He was given some white squares of paper and a ticket the size of a cash register receipt.

"What about coal?" he asked.

"The inspector says you don't need any right away."

He made his way, coal-less, back through the labyrinth of rooms to the first waiting room.

"How do you work this?" he asked the ticket taker.

"Keep those" – indicating vouchers for milk, butter, and bread. "I'll take this ticket; now get your parcels there. Large," he told his assistant, and in twenty seconds, Lendrum's arms were filled from the various piles.

He carried this armful for half a mile to the office of a friend where he'd left his club bag, wondering all the time how many passersby recognized the parcels and asked themselves how it could be that a well-dressed man should get so far down on his luck. At home, he showed his wife the vouchers.

"What will the milkman say?" she asked in dismay.

But the milkman was used to it. "Nothing to be ashamed of, going on relief," he told her, and he showed her a sheaf of similar vouchers from her district. "I never let on," he explained.

By the time the baker and the grocer had received their vouchers, the Lendrum family had begun to feel like old hands. Mrs. Lendrum stopped blushing and accepted her lot.

"Who gives a darn anyway," she said to her husband.

2

Death by All across the country, families like the Lendrums were facing
Depression similar crises and undergoing the difficult and often searing experience of applying for public charity. It mattered little to those on relief that the major banks were again announcing that the

worst was over and that there was "a definite increase in business activity," to quote the Bank of Nova Scotia newsletter. That was no comfort to those who were forced to cut short a promising career, a high school or university education, or a chance to marry and raise a family.

The national marriage rate decreased annually in the early years of the Depression – from 77,000 in 1929 to 62,000 in 1932. Marrying was a hazardous business for those with no resources; the sight of a teenaged couple with a child was unusual enough to cause heads to turn, as Main Johnson discovered in the summer of 1933. Johnson, the editor of the Toronto *Star Weekly*, was hurrying down Yonge Street one hot, dusty noon hour when he was stopped in his tracks by an unaccustomed scene. Coming along the street, his hat tilted back on his head, was a telegraph messenger boy. Beside him walked a slim girl in a pink frock, brown hair blowing about her face. On the boy's shoulders was a baby. Johnson felt tears in his eyes as he watched them pass. He saw others stop and look back at the three happy children, oblivious to the glum faces around them. He went on to his luncheon appointment but couldn't get the picture out of his mind.

That afternoon, Johnson called in his best feature writer, Gregory Clark, and assigned him to find the couple and write about them. "Why do they look so happy?" he asked Clark. "Happiness isn't so plentiful nowadays. Yet here are two children, already launched on the adventures of life, in a stormy time like this, and if I ever saw joy, I saw it on Yonge Street at noon today."

Clark found the couple through the telegraph company. The *Star Weekly*, then a full-size broadsheet, devoted the entire front page of its general section to a story and pictures about Clara and Harry Watson, who had met at a soda fountain when he was unemployed and she was an eight-dollar-a-week clerk at Simpson's. They had married on impulse after Harry was hired as a messenger boy at three cents a message. She was seventeen; he was eighteen. They had no savings. The wedding supper was an ice cream soda at a Yonge Street fountain. Their first home, which Clark described as "their home of joy," consisted of a ten-dollar-a-month flat on Dupont Street. When the baby came, Clara had to quit her job.

In his feature story, Clark made much of the couple's courage in marrying: "Perhaps only two in a million would take the risk

183

of doing what those two have done. They have never had a quarrel. They have the same sweet, honest attitude toward life. They are happy. Hard working. Devoted. But it is not for the children we have told their story. It is for the older folk. The ones who come at life so practically and methodically, as if life were a cold pool, and they were prowling timidly or cautiously about its edge.

"He is a telegraph messenger.

"She is still a girl . . .

"And where they walk, the sun shines."

The *Star Weekly* did not follow up the story it called "a living testimony that marriage is not the hopeless adventure a great many people believe it to be." Nor is it probable that it would have published the sequel. For the sun did not shine for long on Clara and Harry Watson. They were so poor they were forced to move seven times, seeking cheaper and cheaper accommodation. Eighteen months after the story appeared, the constant worry about meeting the rent and the stress of scrimping for cheap food killed the marriage. They could not afford to live together and so agreed to part. He went back to his mother, and she, with a great sense of relief, returned to the home of the widowed grandmother who had raised her. Eventually they were divorced. She married again when times were better and raised three more children but could never forget that first failed attempt. "Another time, another place," she has said, "it would have been nice."

Though the Watsons' marriage failed, they both survived the Depression. But there were those who did not survive - victims of what might be called death by Depression.

Humiliation killed a seasonal farm worker in Cabri, Saskatchewan, in January. At the age of forty-six, living on the charity of relatives, broke, and with no visible means of support, Gannett Bissett found himself charged with vagrancy and sentenced to thirty days in the Regina jail. The shame was too much for him to bear. When he was released he went back to Cabri and shot himself with a .22 rifle.

Racism killed an aged Chinese in Saskatoon in March. When Orientals were no longer allowed to collect even the meagre rations doled out to other citizens on relief, sixty were reduced to scrabbling in back alleys for bones, offal, and kitchen refuse. When one old man was found dead of malnutrition, the local authorities hastily approved a paltry daily allowance of about a

184

pound of pork and rice per man – just barely enough to keep them alive.

Bureaucratic rigidity killed a Polish Canadian in Montreal the same month. In a building on Dominique Street, a crippled tenant was being ousted from his bed by bailiffs seizing his furniture for unpaid rent. An angry crowd of neighbours gathered and vainly tried to stop the eviction. As the police arrived to restore order, another tenant, Nick Zynchuk, tried to enter the building to retrieve two suitcases from his own flat. As he mounted the steps to the front door, a policeman shot him in the back and killed him. The policeman was acquitted of murder because, the judge said, a "riot" was in progress at the time.

Despondency killed four little children in the Quebec town of Ste Perpétue. Their father, Lucien Gerard, in despair over the loss of his farm, took a hammer and battered in their heads as they slept.

But of all the stark tales that illuminate the bitterness of those years, none rends the heart more than the tragedy of Ted Bates, of Glidden, Saskatchewan, and his wife, Rose.

Glidden was a tiny community some one hundred and twenty miles southwest of Saskatoon. Ted Bates was the village butcher – a big, jolly man, outgoing and cheerful, the kind who makes friends wherever he goes. In the words of G.V. Couper, the secretary-treasurer of the village, "he didn't have an enemy in the world."

Ted and Rose were in their early forties and both were English immigrants. Ted Bates had come out in 1914, lured by the propaganda campaign that depicted Western Canada as a farmers' paradise. He farmed for two years, moved to Glidden, and then decided to return to his original trade of butcher. In 1921, he met and married Rose Slatter, a quiet, slender Englishwoman, who had recently arrived from the old country. Three years later she bore him a son, Jack. In 1933, he was nine years old, a plump and cheerful boy, "the sunshine of their home," in the words of a village official. They called him the Nipper. As one friend was to remark, "I never saw a mother more devoted to a son in my life."

The Depression wrecked the Bateses' life. The butcher shop failed; even the cheapest meat was a luxury in Saskatchewan in those years. Bates sold his store in the spring of 1932 for $450. Like so many others who fled the drought-ridden prairies, the family moved west to Vancouver. Ted Bates opened a store in the suburb of Marpole, but that failed, too. The money that he had been promised for the sale of his store in Glidden did not materialize. The family was destitute, and Rose, always high strung, was now close to a breakdown from worry, her frail and anemic body reduced to a gaunt 105 pounds.

To Ted Bates the idea of living on public charity was shameful. But he had no option and at last was forced to apply for relief. At that point he came up against the complexities of the social welfare system of the thirties.

Direct relief was doled out by the municipalities, which were forced to put up a third of the total cost, the provincial and federal governments contributing the other two-thirds. Thus the municipalities set the rules. Vancouver, already jammed with newcomers escaping the arid plains, wasn't prepared to advance help to anyone it considered a johnny-come-lately. Ted Bates was told that he and his family did not fulfil the residence requirements. They would have to establish domicile in Vancouver by a year's residence or else go back home to get relief.

The Bateses were now caught in the trap that snared thousands of Canadians in the thirties. They had moved once, hoping to better themselves. Instead they had been rendered immobile by the times. They couldn't get help in British Columbia. They didn't have the cash to return to Saskatchewan.

The Salvation Army stepped in and offered them one-way tickets to Saskatoon, but they could not face the idea of returning to Glidden and applying for relief there. The whole neighbourhood would quickly learn that they had failed in Vancouver and been shipped home as charity cases. "I can't go back, Slim," Rose Bates told an acquaintance, Slim Babcock. "I would rather kill myself than go back to Glidden." Rose seemed to be a woman in a stupor, and her husband was no better. Babcock described him in Great War terms: "He looked like a man blown up by a shell, buried, and blown up again."

The family decided to accept train fare from the Salvation Army in the hope that they would be able to get relief either in Saskatoon or somewhere else in the province – anywhere but Glidden. That was a forlorn hope. When they applied for relief in Saskatoon on Friday, December 1, 1933, the authorities told them they'd have to go back to their home town. That was the rule.

Since there was no train to Glidden until Monday, they were given vouchers for a room at the Western Hotel for the weekend and two meals a day at the Ovido Restaurant.

At this point, Ted and Rose Bates, two middle-aged people with a nine-year-old son and no future, came to a terrible decision: they would kill themselves and their boy rather than accept charity in their home community. There followed a grisly discussion about the method. Rose Bates suggested cyanide. But Ted convinced her that carbon monoxide from the exhaust of a car would be simpler and just as effective. Rose pawned her jewellery for ten dollars, and with that sum they rented a 1929 Chevrolet coach at Allen's Service Station and bought a small amount of gas. On Monday morning they set off, apparently for Glidden.

At the little town of Perdue on the way to Biggar, they stopped to converse with a local barber. Bates was looking for an empty building. "A man's got to do something," he said cryptically. They drove on to the Avalon district and almost out of gas, bought two or three quarts from a local farmer, John Lee, who invited them to dinner. Later they parked their car near the drive shed of the Avalon district school. They turned the windows up, kept the motor running, attached a tube to the exhaust, and as young Jack in the rear seat innocently devoured two of the Big Little Books that were so popular with children of his age (*Chester Gump at Silver Creek Ranch* and *Mickey Mouse, the Mail Pilot*) they sat quietly in the front seat and waited for death.

It did not come for Rose and Ted Bates. They woke at dawn, groggy and physically ill from the effects of the gas, but alive. By the bitterest of ironies, their own poverty had saved them. Because they had not been able to afford enough gasoline for the car, the motor had died during the night. But not before their son had succumbed. There he lay in the back seat – the Nipper, his body already stiff and cold, the two Big Little Books beside him.

They had killed their own son! That knowledge fuelled their need to end their own lives. Rose pleaded with her husband to get the big butcher knife, the tool of his trade, out of his luggage and stab her to death. He shrank from that: unless he stabbed her cleanly he would cause excruciating pain. He decided, first, to knock her unconscious with the automobile crank. In spite of hitting her repeatedly, he did not succeed. The carbon monoxide had done part of its work; he was too weak to be effective. Now

187

he made a feeble attempt to kill her with the knife, but when he tried to plunge it into her heart, her winter clothes softened the blow. She begged for death, asked him to cut her throat. He pulled out a pen knife, severed the muscle on the right side of her neck, but missed the carotid artery by a fraction of an inch. With blood flowing down her clothing, she asked for razor blades. The couple then tried to sever the arteries in their wrists, but that was not possible either. Weak from loss of blood and the effects of the gas, they sat and waited for death.

Again, it did not come. Some neighbours had noticed the car in the schoolyard and assumed that the family, unable to find accommodation, had decided to stay in the car for the night with the engine running to keep out the December cold. Others thought there might be bank robbers in the car – a not farfetched possibility in those days – and so were afraid to approach it. At last somebody called the police, who discovered the pair lying half-conscious in a welter of their own blood with the corpse of their son in the back seat.

Rose and Ted Bates were taken to the hospital at Biggar. Both recovered; both were charged with the murder of their boy. Now the village of Glidden rallied round. The entire community turned up at a mass meeting, postponed for a day so that farmers from the outlying districts, blocked by snowdrifts, could attend. The meeting raised a fund to pay for Jack Bates's funeral and to underwrite legal fees for the coming trial.

The family's former neighbours in Glidden understood their dilemma – why they refused to accept local charity even at the cost of their own lives. It is this stiff-backed sense of pride that comes through again and again in the stories of those who were forced by circumstances to accept relief. It belies the attitude that in those days was typical of men of the Bennett calibre – and, indeed, is still alive in some quarters – who believed that the dole would weaken human initiative and produce a generation of sloths feeding from the public trough. Canada failed the Bates family as it failed thousands of others who were perfectly willing to pay their way but couldn't because of conditions over which they had no control.

The mass meeting in Glidden drafted a resolution declaring its firm conviction that the Bateses' tragedy was "a direct result of the Depression" and urging the Dominion government to take

188

full responsibility for relief so that those who were forced to move from one community to another wouldn't have to starve. It was ignored by Ottawa.

Meanwhile, an inquest was held at Biggar. A coroner's jury was asked by the Crown counsel to fix blame for Jack Bates's death – presumably on his parents. But the jury pointedly ignored the request. And when the case came to trial, one hundred days after the tragedy, another jury returned a verdict of not guilty, to general applause.

The hot light of publicity that had been focused on Ted and Rose Bates for all that time was finally extinguished. They returned to Glidden and obscurity. Ted Bates died at Rosetown on December 14, 1954. Rose Bates went back to England. They had no more children.

3

Most survivors of the Depression living today were children or *Childhood* teenagers in 1933. They weren't part of the labour force, however, *memories* and they had no personal experience of unemployment. Most were in school, and a remarkable number didn't realize there *was* a depression because they had no other period with which to compare it.

Memories of hunger and humiliation still linger in the minds of those who were shaped by the times – hunger because there was never quite enough for growing children to eat, humiliation because of the hand-me-downs or relief clothing that they were forced to wear to school. Charles Templeton, who became a media star, would never forget the feeling of an empty stomach on those days when the larder was empty. Templeton was sixteen in 1933, living with his mother and three siblings in Parkdale, a Toronto suburb. The family existed on groceries obtained with relief vouchers, but the mother couldn't make these stretch for more than six days. On the seventh they existed by drinking water to help dull the pangs.

Mike Bevan, who was thirteen that year, would always remember roaming the prairie south of Calgary, trying to fill up on wild strawberries, chokecherries, bear berries, Saskatoon berries, and even Russian olive. In the winter when there was no

189

wild fruit, the emptiness was worse, for there were no second helpings in his household. They did not go on relief until his father, a proud man, finally gave in to his mother's entreaties. She threatened to leave him unless he applied for the dole.

For Lara Rapson, who was five in 1933, a treat consisted of bread with lard and sugar. When things grew worse, Lara and her mother and three sisters had "bread and point" – meaning you could always point to where the butter and jam were supposed to be. Their luncheon sandwiches were filled with nothing more than ketchup or mustard, and the Rapson kids pretended to their classmates that they actually preferred these to beef or cheese. When the health teacher talked about good nutrition and asked each child what she'd eaten for breakfast that morning, Lara told another white lie: she simply announced that she'd eaten every-thing on the list of nourishing foods the teacher produced. She knew that the teacher suspected she was lying, but at least she saved face.

Lara's father, a Toronto printer, was out of work the entire decade. Because the family could never afford new clothes for Lara, her mother made over garments that the neighbours' chil-dren had discarded. Her most mortifying experience – the one that stood out in her mind above all others – was the day when she sat in church wearing a made-over rose-coloured coat with a matching wide-brimmed hat, knowing that just three rows be-hind sat the girl who had worn that very outfit the year before.

New shoes were a luxury that few lower-class families could afford. Eileen Palmer, who was thirteen and lived in Toronto's Cabbagetown, always remembered her single pair of shoes, which, when they started to wear out, were layered with card-board to make them last. That was a common experience in the thirties. More than one family made cardboard insoles from Turret cigarette boxes. The Palmer family wasn't on relief, but life was still precarious. Eileen's father worked for the gas com-pany, and they barely existed from week to week on his meagre pay. She would never forget the day when he was laid off for two weeks because somebody had spotted his truck outside a coffee shop. She was devastated. There was no food in the house – only what his fellow employees brought him. Christmas was coming, and when Eileen mentioned the family situation in church, St. Bartholomew's sent a Christmas packet. That infuriated her fa-

190

ther. He didn't want to take charity; besides, he said, the gas company would frown on it. That Christmas, Eileen Palmer's stocking contained nothing more than an orange and a quarter. Yet for Eileen Palmer, the Depression was not an unmixed horror. Her father had a job – one of only four breadwinners that did on their block of twelve houses. As she has said, "In those days it didn't matter how little you had, someone else had less."

Thousands of other young children were only vaguely aware of the Depression. Some were shielded from it by their parents or their own naïveté. Eva Lauzon, who was eight in 1933 and lived on Albermarle Street in Toronto, was told later in life by her father that he and her mother had made a conscious decision never to discuss money before their eleven children. Even though he had a job working for Canadian Pacific, it wasn't easy to bring up such a large family. Young Eva grew up believing that only rich people used toothpaste; she and her siblings used baking soda and salt. Nor could she afford to have her skates sharpened; indeed, she came to believe that skate sharpening was effete – or at least that's how she rationalized it.

Donald Radford of Palgrave, Ontario, was another child who had no idea there was a depression because his parents made a point of never mentioning it. He didn't know that the company his father worked for had gone bankrupt or that the family had been granted a moratorium on rent payments. He didn't know they couldn't afford to pay the instalments on the parlour piano or that the piano company had let them keep it because "there's a Depression on and we couldn't sell it to anyone else." He would always remember the Hallowe'en when his friends called for him and his mother insisted he finish his supper before joining them. Supper consisted of a bowl of pea soup; it was years before he learned it was the only food in the house. Yet for Donald Radford, as for so many other Depression children, the thirties were a wonderful decade – "an exciting time to be alive." The gift of a fifteen-cent Dinky Toy or a second-hand tricycle at Christmas was for him sheer heaven.

For every child scarred by the Depression there was another to whom the period was a veritable idyll. These were the ones whose fathers had jobs and, therefore, a measure of stability. One was Robert H. Thompson, who, after retiring, moved to Victoria, B.C., and decided to set down for his children and grandchildren

191

his remarkably sunny memories of growing up in Saskatoon in the thirties. He did, of course, remember the symbols of the decade – the jobless men who jumped off the freight at the end of Main before it crossed the railway bridge, where the police were waiting. They wandered up the back lanes, knocking on doors, asking for food and odd jobs. His mother got more than her share because on a fence behind their house somebody had chalked a sign that she was always good for a sandwich. Bob knew that his brother, who was thirteen years older than he, could find only part-time work – no more than two or three days a month – and that his brother's close friend, a graduate engineer, was reduced to delivering groceries. All the same, young Bob Thompson, who was just ten years old in 1933 and who lived in a big house owned by his grandfather, a lumber dealer, clearly had a wonderful time in a decade that is historically grim.

The ravages that were visited on the prairies in those years had little meaning for small, active boys. The grasshoppers came in clouds, devastating the fields, but to Bob Thompson they made wonderful bait to catch trout. The dust came, too, dark as night, thick as fog – so dense you didn't dare venture out of doors. It settled heavily on the furniture, driving housewives to delirium, but oh! the fun of writing your name with your finger or drawing a funny face on the dining-room table.

Saskatoon lay on the northern edge of the drought area. The long, lazy summers were remarkably hot and dry, but lazy for small boys only – desperate, for farmers praying for rain. Thompson, oblivious of the desolation on the farmland to the south, had a wonderful time picking pinchberries and salmon berries with George Johnson, wheeling down the sidewalks on rollerskates, toasting marshmallows on the river bank, carving whistles out of green willow, and rolling barrel hoops made of lathing. He never forgot the aroma of popcorn, hot from a two-wheeled cart, and all the inventive games of childhood that required no admission price: "Red Light," "I Spy," and "Simon Says."

Children and adults made their own fun in those days. On Broadway, Bob and the other kids would sit for hours in Storey's blacksmith shop, watching the smith straighten tires and sharpen discs. Then, when Tony, the fruit man, arrived with his horse-drawn wagon, they'd wangle a small slice of watermelon or a bunch of grapes. More often they would hang around Mylrea's

192

Garage on Broadway, watching the owner working on the new automobiles – Model A Fords, of course, but also the occasional conversation piece: a Whippet or a Star, an Essex or an Overland. The car was very much a pleasure vehicle in 1933. More sophisticated entertainment had yet to replace the Sunday drive.

Children's pastimes were simpler. George Johnson was the most popular kid in the neighbourhood because he owned the only magic lantern. Fifty years later, Bob Thompson could still recall the excitement of the picture shows in the Johnson basement – black-and-white slides of popular cartoon characters projected on a bed sheet. The walkie-talkie was more than a generation away, but the kids communicated, or tried to, by making telephones out of two tin cans and a fifteen-foot length of string.

There was a rage for stilts, made from six-foot two-by-fours. The footrests were blocks nailed thirty inches from the base, but some kids became so proficient they raised the height to four feet, which meant they had to mount the stilts from a fence or a porch.

Toys were also less sophisticated then, and being made of wood or metal instead of plastic, they lasted longer. Big items included a popgun with a cork on a string, steel cap pistols, and, of course, the ubiquitous Meccano set that made every boy an engineer. If you could scrape up a dime you could go to the Daylight Theatre – the cheapest of three in Saskatoon – and watch an entire show, which included a sixteen-part serial (John Wayne in *The Shadow of the Eagles* or Buster Crabbe in *Captain Gallant of the Foreign Legion*). Bob Thompson made it to the Daylight on a Saturday afternoon by taking the quarter his mother gave him for a haircut, sneaking into the student shop at Mohler's Barber School for a fifteen-cent cropping, and saving the extra dime for the movie.

When the Chautauqua travelling tent show came through there was cheap entertainment for all, mixed with culture. And there were medicine shows. To Bob Thompson the most amazing performance was given by an Indian "chief" who burned the palm of his hand with a white-hot iron and then applied a miracle snake oil remedy that appeared to cure it and sold for only a dollar a bottle.

A dollar was a great deal of money in 1933, almost as much as a week's pay to some people. Even a cent went a long way. At Turner's Drug Store and Soda Fountain a penny would buy a set

193

of paraffin wax false teeth, a licorice pipe, a package of sugar-flavoured powder that you sucked through a straw, or a flat packet of bubble gum with a hockey card inside featuring a photograph of an NHL star. Because soda pop cost a nickel, a good many people made their own – ginger beer, root beer, or birch beer from a package bought at Stewart's Drug Store.

Cigarettes were cheap, too, and rendered even cheaper because tobacco companies were offering free gifts to steady customers. If a small boy could find an accommodating sixteen-year-old, he could talk him into buying a five-cent package of Turrets or British Consols, choosing a smoke shop whose owner was just getting by and was prepared to overlook the fact that the purchaser's chin wasn't much higher than the counter. Bob and his friends prized the Turrets because each package contained miniature reproductions of playing cards that could be collected to make up poker hands that were good for gifts. Just about everyone he knew collected and traded Turret cards; it was one of the great fads of the thirties.

Most children in Saskatchewan didn't grow up in the larger centres, as Bob Thompson did. The majority lived on farms, like Doris Dillabaugh, whose father had two hundred acres at Skull Creek. Her family could not be said to have lived in luxury – they had no electricity, running water, or telephone – but compared to thousands of others they were well off in a single-storey frame farmhouse with four bedrooms. They lit kerosene lamps to read by at night and pumped water from a cistern in the basement for washing and from a well for drinking. In Doris's words, "We lived in that house for eight years and thought it was great because everyone else lived the same way."

They didn't have a car and there was no such thing as a school bus. Doris rode to the one-room prairie schoolhouse on her own horse, Skunk, and those days were among her happiest memories.

As was true with the city kids, the fickleness of nature that disheartened so many adults had the opposite effect on farm youngsters. Doris and her friends snared marauding gophers for a bounty of one cent a tail and gazed with fascination on the grasshoppers, which could eat a strip of wheat to its roots in a couple of hours, "stopping when they got to the summer fallow and turning around for another feast."

194

In the summer they made canoes out of pea pods and floated them in the horse trough, or searched through the hopper of the combine for green kernels of wheat that made excellent chewing gum, or hunted for the fruit of the small cacti that grew wild on the prairie, or built a raft and pushed it around a slough with poles. In the winter they skated on a community rink made by flooding a boarded-up square of land near the creek. They dug tunnels in the fifteen-foot drifts or made snow forts. Since the roads were never ploughed, they travelled everywhere by sleigh, their feet kept warm by flatirons, heated on the kitchen stove and wrapped in rags.

In the farm kitchen, the wood stove burned all day. Doris would never forget the simmering kettle of soup made from buttermilk, brown sugar, and butter. Her mother baked six loaves of bread a day from their own grain, ground and sacked at the elevator. They did all their Christmas shopping through Simpson's mail-order catalogue, and "when the box arrived it was almost as exciting as Santa's visit."

The family made it through the Depression because they had their own eggs and poultry and could slaughter the occasional pig or cow. Prairie farmers on relief received shipments of Ontario apples and cabbages and Nova Scotia salt cod and herring. The cod, after the salt was soaked out, was served creamed, baked, or fried, but few could abide the odour of the herring, which the small boys used to bait their traplines for weasels and the occasional coyote.

When Doris grew to womanhood she met and married a city boy from Saskatoon. His name, of course, was Bob Thompson. By the time they had children of their own the Depression was behind them, but those days would never be forgotten.

"You had to be tough to be a farmer," Doris would tell her children. "The hours were long, the days were hot, the work was demanding. And it was always a gamble. Grasshoppers, hail, drought, frost and rain at the wrong time were your enemies. You were never sure until the grain was in the elevator."

Nevertheless for her, as for her future husband, the Depression years were golden ones. "I am quite sure that a kid growing up in the city had more to do and more places to go than we did on the farm," she told them. "But I can tell you that I wouldn't have traded all of your candy stores, your movie houses, your parades or your sports events for my 'Skunk.' Unless you've owned your own horse as a youngster to ride to school, you'll never know what you've missed."

4

Making The newspapers in the Depression occupied a position that they
headlines have since lost to television and radio. For most Canadians they were the major source of news. Radio news was sketchy; only a minority could afford a newsmagazine; and the newsreels seemed to be concerned mainly with bathing-beauty contests. But the newspapers told Canadians what was going on in their own country and in the world. They were cheap – never more than a nickel and in some cases only two or three cents. They were complete: a big story, such as a court case or a parliamentary debate, was covered almost verbatim and ran to several columns – sometimes several pages – of remarkably small type. Even the smaller cities boasted two newspapers locked in frantic competition; Vancouver had three, Toronto and Halifax four. They ran to as many as five editions, the front pages changing almost hourly as the news poured in.

The daily press shaped the conventional wisdom of the times. Behind the "objective" copy that reporters were trained to write were certain inherent assumptions: that the Royal Family was sacrosanct, that there was no substitute for the free enterprise system, that the Christian religion was the best of all possible faiths, that without the work ethic the country would sink into sloth, that the male was the dominant member of the species, and that a woman's place was in the home. In the last months of the twenties, it was the press that had soothed investors into believing stocks would continue to rise. In the first years of the Depression, it was the press that pretended hard times were a temporary aberration.

By 1933, the newspapers were presenting their readers with a daily load of gloom. In addition to the regular diet of suicides, kidnappings, bank robberies, and murders that has always been grist to the presses, there were tales that hit closer to home: pay cuts, labour disputes, and hunger marches. Stories of global unrest also dominated the front pages: bank failures in the United States, the rise of fascism in Europe, and the Japanese atrocities in China.

No wonder, then, that editors yearned for lighter fare. It explains why, in those days, the comic strip was king. The major dailies hid their front pages on the weekend by wrapping their entire editions in the comic section. Rival broadsheets vied in proclaiming that they had more strips than the opposition. "72 COMICS!" the Toronto *Telegram* trumpeted on its cover – a happier line than the ones that predicted a national railway strike or reported on Adolf Hitler's accession to power.

Newspaper readers were ripe for tales of adventure – anything to take their minds off their troubles – and in May they got just that. Once again, like a rocket piercing the murk, a new kind of journalistic presence burst from the front pages, wafting Canadians to faraway places with strange-sounding names, where bizarre rituals and unspeakable practices transported them, if only briefly, from the realities of the times.

The Toronto *Star*'s Gordon Sinclair was off once more, this time on a voyage to the south seas – to New Guinea, which he described, with lip-smacking relish, as the "home of the fiercest and most treacherous people living today. An unknown, unexplored, and unmapped jungle hell where bone-crushing savages live as they lived in the stone age with neither clothes nor tools nor laws nor fear. Where wives come by conquest and seizure; where men are slaves and cannibals. Where tribal warfare, black magic and sacrificial rites reap a grim harvest of human skulls...."

What newspaper could resist the lure of Sinclair's heated prose? He had already made his name during a tour of India in 1932, with tales of tom-toms, nautch girls, black scorpions, and vipers. Rival publications in most cities now scrambled to buy syndication rights to the newest Sinclair adventures. The stories, which arrived in Canada two months after he wrote them (there were as yet no Pan American Clippers to speed them across the Pacific), were made to order for the times.

The Depression made Sinclair a national figure. His gaudy copy was read by millions. The books that he produced from his adventures were phenomenal best-sellers. He peered cockily from the front pages in his jaunty pith helmet and breeches, his broken nose giving his features a slightly battered and therefore exciting look. He arrived at the right time, in the right place, and on the right paper. The Toronto *Star*, with its legendary expense accounts and its aggressive coverage, had no intention of losing its position as the country's largest English-speaking daily. Sinclair was given his head.

Travel to foreign lands was slow, difficult, and expensive. The occasional student was able to work his way to Europe on a cattle boat – Hugh MacLennan, the future novelist, was one – but most people, sunk in the abyss of the Depression, could scarcely scrape up streetcar fare. Movies like *Flying Down to Rio* and *King Kong* and popular songs such as "The Isle of Capri" had provided a touch of the exotic in a drab world. But Sinclair provided Escape from the humdrum, day after day.

"I'll tell you nothing of trade, commerce or the profound yammerings which go to make up a modern business world," he wrote, undoubtedly to the relief of his readers. "But I'm going to learn how they stuff those skulls. I'm going to hunt the cuscuss. I'm going to sleep among the vampire bats where you have to wear your shoes to save your blood. I'll give you the low down on slavery and the weird rites of the longhouse. I hope to get where few whites have been before. . . ."

That must have been a welcome contrast to a typically gloomy news story that appeared that same day from Quebec City: "Evicted from his home because he was unable to pay rent, Arthur Drouin, 80, was obliged to live in a dilapidated shed with his sick wife until last night because he could not get near district relief officers to plead his case. It took physical injury to have his case brought to the attention of civic officials, the injuries coming as a result of being trampled on by a crowd of younger men when he tried to get near the relief office in city hall."

When front-page headlines reported on the destitution and near starvation of settlers sent to Northern Ontario, Sinclair enthralled his readers with a tale of "two million gaudy butterflies . . . drowned in the Pacific . . . as a monsoon boomed seaward from Papua and swept them helplessly into an enraged ocean."

On May 9, the *Star*'s readers could wallow in a whole series of disturbing headlines: "DREAD OF BEING DEPORTED DRIVES LAD ACROSS CANADA"; "GANDHI GROWS WEAK IN 2ND DAY OF FAST"; "TWO EXECUTED BY AXE IN PRUSSIA"; "KIDNAP THREATS BRING YOUTH, 19, FOUR YEAR TERM"; "COMPROMISE FAILED UPON DIS-

198

ARMAMENT." But no Depression headline could compete with the ones that Sinclair was making:

MISSIONARY RISKS DEATH BY
PLUNGE IN BLOOD RED LAKE
TO CHALLENGE VOODOO MYTH

Or his florid account of his arrival in New Guinea: "Tribal tom-toms throbbed through New Guinea's damp hills today and hundreds of savage eyes stared from behind giant jungle ferns as our sea-going coffee grinder loaded deep with gold miners, airplanes, cows, dynamite and one lone thrill-seeker slipped inside the great coral reef which spreadeagles the island. . . . "

A few days later, Canadians learned that one of Sinclair's colleagues, Pierre Van Paassen, had run afoul of the Hitler regime and that the *Star* had been banned in Germany. In spite of the Depression, it was becoming harder and harder to ignore the stories from abroad – and harder to get at the truth.

The spill-over from the new Europe also made domestic news. Canadian fascist parties were on the march, singing anti-Jewish songs in the Beaches area of Toronto, raising the swastika in that city's Willowdale Park, and provoking wild scenes that in one case involved ten thousand people. In Montreal in September, fifteen hundred fascists tried to break up an anti-clerical rally, and in Winnipeg, two days later, the Nationalist Party of Canada announced its formation to fight communism "tooth and nail" and to abolish all provinces in favour of a central government. The party soon showed its true colours by adopting the Hitler brown-shirt uniform, complete with swastika, and the Nazi salute.

Franklin D. Roosevelt was also making headlines, having launched his first term as U.S. president with an energy and imagination that contrasted with the retrograde policies of both R.B. Bennett and Mackenzie King. The parsimonious King was outraged at the amount of money being spent in Canada on relief – "an orgy of public expenditure," he called it, charging that the Tories were "running wild with the taxes of the people." King forced Bennett to limit the amount to be spent on direct relief to twenty million, except in cases of emergency. Bennett used that concession to sneak the "peace, order and good government" clause back into the relief act. It passed because nobody wanted to be seen opposing direct relief. Thus, the immigration department was again able to "shovel out" undesirables without resorting to formal legal procedure.

Bennett's brother-in-law William Herridge, Canada's minister to Washington, was enthusiastic about Roosevelt's innovations. He urged Bennett to start a public works program that might tie in with the reciprocal trade agreement the Prime Minister favoured. Bennett declined. When a Toronto sociologist urged that the government follow Roosevelt's lead and establish a board of economic stabilization, he got a blunt rebuff. Bennett wanted no part of that; Canada, he declared, was "not going to try to keep up with the Jones'," a phrase that hints at the Prime Minister's contempt for major spending, even when the future of the country was at stake. It was more important to balance the budget.

Bennett had seen a high-tariff policy as the economic salvation of the country. Mackenzie King, on the other hand, believed that Bennett's tariff increases would strangle trade. Both were looking back to an earlier era. The new Liberal policy announced that spring included reducing the cost of government and – as always! – balancing the budget. If trade barriers were reduced, the Liberals believed, the resultant profits would make up for the federal cheese-paring. Price fixing was to end; the Combines Investigation Act was to be rigorously enforced; the Criminal Code was to be strengthened to deal with monopolies. For these worthy goals they were suggesting band-aid remedies. There were other, vaguer pledges. To "revive" industry in order to provide jobs was one. Another was to form a national non-partisan commission to administer all federal monies with the co-operation of the provinces and municipalities. The most sensible promises were enactment of a system of unemployment insurance and establishment of a central bank to control credit.

Both political leaders were still taking their cues from Great Britain rather than from the United States. Indeed, it remained hard for Canadians to think of themselves as citizens of the Commonwealth and not the Empire, especially when Bennett reintroduced the practice of conferring titles on the famous or well-to-do. When Noel Coward's motion picture *Cavalcade* came to Canada it was promoted as "The Motion Picture Industry's Salute to the Great British Empire." The general attitude towards Americans remained faintly snobbish, as Bennett's "keeping up

200

with the Jones'" remark suggests – a hint there of the vulgar, free-spending *nouveau riche*. (Bennett, a poor Maritime boy who inherited a fortune, didn't think of himself in those terms.) Thus Franklin Roosevelt's vigorous attempts to deal with the Depression, especially through the National Recovery Act, were viewed with suspicion and even horror by a section of the Canadian establishment.

"I dread the thought of what may come out of the U.S. experiment," King wrote in his diary in September. "I am beginning to think Roosevelt is a little like Bennett in his outlook, methods, etc." Coming from someone who had that year categorized the Prime Minister as "a dog of a man . . . a brute in his instincts," that was strong stuff, especially from one who would later revel in his role as a confidant of the American president. A month later King was confiding to his diary: "I am beginning thoroughly to dislike the man [Roosevelt] as a dictator whose policies are absolutely wrong – amateurish, half-baked & downright mistaken."

What King feared was "the mad desire to bring about state control & interference beyond bounds." It made him shudder, he wrote; and he shuddered again that month when Raymond Moley, a member of the Roosevelt "brains trust," outlined the NRA program to a conference on Canadian Banking and Money Policy. King noted that Moley's speech made his "blood run cold."

In his years in Opposition, the former prime minister had more time on his hands to indulge in his fascination with the occult. This did *not* make headlines. In fact, no whisper of King's encounters with the supernatural ever reached the public. These were gentler times. The press was discreetly incurious about the private lives of public men. The Prime Minister's excursions into the spirit world undoubtedly served a very real need. He was a lonely bachelor whose closest friend was probably his little dog, Pat, on whom he lavished all the care and concern usually reserved for small children. When Pat was ill, King was despondent; when he rallied, King was delirious with joy. There is a charming, if somewhat saccharine, description in his diary of the two of them, man and dog, kneeling together, hand in paw, at the side of the bed, heads bowed, saying their goodnight prayers. Did the dog actually pray, paws on coverlet? King apparently believed he did.

Joy Esberey in her psychological biography of King has written of his constant need for reassurance. He sought the security of his "loved ones," the dear departed who spoke to him through the mouths of his mediums, who now included Mrs. Etta Wriedt of Detroit. A woman of international reputation, at least in spiritualist circles, she visited him several times during his years in Opposition. "The more I see of her the greater my admiration for her is," he wrote, "a quite exceptional type of unselfish, high minded person, managing alone in the world with wonderful energy and independence."

No doubt she was. Perhaps she really believed she was talking to the shades of his relatives and friends, even when the prophecies they made were dead wrong. Indeed, most of the time the voices that issued from her lips merely served to confirm King's own views, prejudices, and purposes.

By the end of the year, King and his closest human friend, the ever available Joan Patteson, found they were able to talk to the spirit world without the intervention of a medium, first through the rather awkward method of the ouija board, which answered either yes or no to previously posed questions or laboriously spelled out messages from the Beyond. Later they took up the practice of "table rapping," seated at a table with hands touching, while the table rapped out answers to questions.

King first encountered this phenomenon at the home of Dr. Arthur Doughty, the Dominion Archivist. It was, he wrote later, "an amazing evening." He did not know, of course, that the table-rapping craze had been hatched as a hoax by two teenaged sisters in Rochester, New York, in 1848. The sisters' secret was simple: they had double-jointed toes that cracked out convincing messages underneath the table. But King, who had received communications via the table from his mother, father, brother, and sisters, was totally convinced that "there can be no shadow of doubt of their genuineness."

Apart from his dog and the ghosts of his loved ones, King preferred the company of women. He was obviously heterosexual and made no secret, at least to his diary, that he enjoyed the sight of pretty girls in bathing costumes. After walking with friends along the beach of a lake in Manitoba one hot July afternoon, he commented approvingly on the spectacle. "Saw ladies in bathing – naked legs – am beginning to see beauty & truth in bare limbs

& to overcome prejudice re covering up what Nature & God has given us."

He was an enthusiastic member of the audience at the Minto Follies, an ice show given each year in Ottawa. "A wonderful exhibition like the old Greek days," he wrote. "There was no attempt to disguise bare legs. In that particular the exhibition was perfect. One wonders if we do not make a mistake in concealing natural beauty & help to create wrong ideas by so doing. I feel that it has been so in my life. . . . I am beginning to change my views in favour of the young people of today in some respects. . . . "

The following day his diary returns to that theme. "Thinking of last night's performance, I see more & more clearly what I have sacrificed in not having married long ago & having children growing up around me . . . someone helping me in my home & entertaining etc & others 'keeping me young' & interested in young and new ideas."

But then another, contrary thought crossed his mind – a typical vacillation, for King could not consider, let alone pursue, any plan, personal or political, without chewing it around the edges, like a dog worrying a bone. "Still," he wrote, "there might have been with that cares and anxieties and expenses which would have made public life impossible." It did not appear to occur to him that other men in public life – his great hero, Laurier, was one – had managed to cope with cares, anxieties, expenses, and even mistresses. But King, in private life, as in public, was notoriously close with a dollar.

He could easily have married. He was highly eligible and there were plenty of suitable women who would have jumped at the chance. One of these was his old friend Julia Grant, a president's granddaughter. Her marriage, to Prince Cautacuzene, an Italian nobleman, was breaking up, and she had leaped enthusiastically the previous year into a correspondence with the bachelor of Kingsmere. She was a stylish and articulate woman who had published two books on aristocratic life in pre-war Russia and Austria. For a time they exchanged letters or telegrams almost daily. (In one, King asked her, a little wistfully, if it were true that there were places in Paris where women danced in the nude.)

At King's suggestion, the princess paid a visit to his favourite medium in Detroit. The accommodating Mrs. Wriedt produced King's mother, whereupon, so the princess told King, the voice from the void put the seal of approval on their relationship. Thus challenged, King managed to conjure up, unaided, a confused vision of his own. In it his mother appeared with a somewhat different message. "She was making clear to me," he decided, "that carnal love was wrong, that it separated one from the divine & spiritual, and that what I have been experiencing was that."

The correspondence petered out and virtually ended at the close of the year when King wrote to warn the princess to expect few if any letters in the future because "it is necessary to concentrate all thought & energy & strength on public affairs from now on." Though the two remained friends (the princess was divorced the following year) there was no hint of a closer relationship. The ghost of King's sainted mother – or at least his interpretation of what that ghost signified – had triumphed once more. But then, the mother's boy clearly wanted it that way.

5

The Regina Manifesto In mid-July, 131 delegates and some one hundred visitors arrived in Regina to attend the first convention of the newly formed Co-operative Commonwealth Federation, whose name indicates a certain confusion of purpose. It was a movement, certainly, but was it a political party? Not quite. It was still a loose coalition of the Left, and although its central ideology would be socialism, the men and women who marched under that banner represented a remarkable spectrum of political thought. Had the two capitalist parties – Liberals and Conservatives – decided to unite at a similar convention, the differences could have been no more pronounced.

The farmers had a deep suspicion of the kind of state control that the socialists wanted to impose. The United Farmers of Alberta and their brother organizations in Manitoba and Ontario were no more than liberal reformers. On the far left, in British Columbia, was the Socialist Party of Canada, tinged with Marxism. On the far right, in Ontario, were the non-communist trade unions. Saskatchewan had its own socialist party, the Farmer-Labour coalition, committed to the principles of British Labour, organized around M.J. Coldwell, who would be Woodsworth's successor. Edmonton had a "Canadian Labour Party." The Eastern-based League for Social Reconstruction also had a Fabian
204

counterpart on the West Coast, the Reconstruction Party of British Columbia, to balance the B.C. Marxists.

The mucilage that held this uneasy amalgam together was the common agreement that the economic machinery was out of kilter, that the free enterprise system had failed, and that capitalism was no longer working for the people. In the interests of radical reform, these disparate groups were prepared to unite to change the existing economic, social, and political system. J.S. Woodsworth, who stood above the fray, would be the binding force. Without him, it's hard to see how the CCF could have come into being so quickly or how the Regina Manifesto could have been accepted by everybody.

The delegates came to Regina by passenger train and bus, some by boxcar, a few on foot, and others by Bennett buggy, the broken-down, horse-drawn automobile that more than any other artifact symbolizes the drought-ravaged years of the Great Depression. Eugene Forsey and King Gordon drove in from Montreal by way of Chicago, there being no Trans-Canada Highway in those days. Frank Scott made his way by the same route in an old Franklin touring car. With Harry Cassidy and Frank Underhill, these three were to become known as the "brains trust" of the convention, a popular title filched from the Roosevelt administration by George Ferguson of the Winnipeg *Free Press* and tied to the LSR.

The title was accurate. At the very last moment, the procrastinating Underhill, scribbling away in his Muskoka cottage, had produced the historic document that came to be called the Regina Manifesto. Vetted by Cassidy, Scott, and the other members of the LSR, the four-thousand-word draft was read aloud to the assembly and then debated, clause by clause. According to Harold Laski, the guru of the British Labour Party, it was the best democratic-socialist manifesto ever produced.

The document dealt with every aspect of change for which the new movement proposed to work. "Such an appeal to the intelligence of the people," Frank Scott was to write, "has never before been attempted by any political party in this country. It is a venture in audacity that implies at least a profound faith in the attractiveness of the program itself."

To pilot such a document through the mishmash of social and political philosophies represented in Regina was an act of considerable finesse. But none could object to the ringing preamble, read out to the convention by its secretary, Norman Priestley, in a great booming voice:

"We aim to replace the present capitalist system with its inherent injustice and inhumanity by a social order from which the domination and exploitation of one class by another will be eliminated, in which economic planning will supersede unregulated private enterprise and competition, and in which genuine self-government based upon economic equality will be possible. . . . The new social order at which we aim is not one in which individuality will be crushed out by a system of regimentation. . . . What we seek is a proper collective organization of our economic resources such as will make possible a much greater degree of leisure and a much richer individual life for every citizen. . . . "

The fourteen points of the manifesto proposed a system of social planning, public ownership at every level of government, the public encouragement of co-operative institutions, the nationalization of all financial institutions and health services, a steeply graded taxation system to pay for it all, security of land tenure for farmers, a labour code for industrial workers, a complete system of social insurance, the abolition of the Senate, and a strengthening of federal power to allow Ottawa "to deal effectively with urgent economic problems which are essentially national in scope."

The thunderous applause that followed Priestley's reading of the first twelve points of the manifesto did not hide a determination on the part of some delegates to add to or subtract from it. Ernie Winch from British Columbia, in Eugene Forsey's description "a dear old soul, a rip-roaring Marxist but the gentlest of men," kept insisting with considerable force that a clause should be added to the manifesto supporting the idea of public nudism. That sent a chill down Forsey's spine. "Can you imagine the Winnipeg *Free Press* headline?" he asked Winch. "J.S. WOODSWORTH GOES NUDIST!"

"But," Winch kept saying, "I *admire* the human form." His colleagues persuaded him to curtail his enthusiasm, at least in public.

William Irvine of the United Farmers of Alberta arrived at the convention fresh from the beginnings of his province's honeymoon with the burgeoning Social Credit movement. He tried, vainly, to get some obeisance paid to that new if baffling philosophy in the manifesto. Other delegates stretched and pulled to put over their own points of view until, in Forsey's words, "the whole thing seemed on the verge of breaking up over and over again." The British Columbia contingent, "more Marxist than Marx," despised the communists because they weren't orthodox enough. The United Farmers of Ontario were terrified by the mildest socialist rhetoric. The word "party" was anathema to them. W.G. Good, who, with the formidable Agnes Macphail, represented the Ontario group, had already confided to Frank Scott his fear that the CCF would become a political party – which was, of course, the general plan. To the Progressives, also, again in Forsey's words, " 'party' was a dreadful, wicked, dirty word." To the high-minded left-wingers it smacked of the kind of sleazy, backroom, ward-heeling politics they so bitterly resented. "Movement" – now *there* was a word! It had the ring of a crusade – people marching, trumpets blowing, banners flying high. But "Federation" would do, for that was the new CCF – a federation of farmers and working men, trade unionists, small-l liberals, Marxists, socialists, and Fabian intellectuals.

They were by no means a cohesive group. They clung to their separate ideologies, suspicious of any attempt either to water down their radicalism or, conversely, to seduce them to extremes. The traditional East-West rivalry, which has plagued every political party since Confederation, was very much in evidence, as Scott and Forsey learned. They did their best to try to find out what the agricultural policy of the Saskatchewan Farmer-Labour party was, but that party's representative, George Williams, refused to tell them anything. "We were reminded that we were from the East," Forsey recalled. In Montreal, the Fabians had been regarded as something close to the Kremlin's right-hand men, but here "we were regarded as the personal representatives of the CPR, the Royal Bank of Canada and the Bank of Montreal." Williams simply kept repeating over and over again, defensively, that "nobody is going to take our socialism away from us."

There were also personal divisions. Agnes Macphail, Canada's only woman Member of Parliament, couldn't abide the gangling B.C. Marxist Angus MacInnis but admitted that there must be

207

some good in him, otherwise Grace Woodsworth, daughter of the founder, wouldn't have married him. For the feminists who were also out in force Macphail had nothing but contempt. When the women delegates to the convention held a luncheon in her honour, she swept in, swathed in an opera cloak, and declared, "All the time I've been in the House, I've never asked for anything on the grounds that I was a woman. If I didn't deserve something on my own merits, I didn't want it. This woman stuff makes me sick!" Off she stormed, leaving behind, as Forsey put it, "an infuriated mass of seething feminists."

The two most contentious debates revolved around the question of compensation for industries nationalized by the state and the argument over whether the movement's objectives could be achieved entirely through parliamentary democracy. The Marxists wanted to strike out all reference to constitutional practice. Ernest Winch sponsored a motion to delete the phrase "we do not believe in change by violence." The Marxists lost that one, but on the other argument they had more success. When the die-hard British Columbians tried to insist that the original owners should get nothing when society took back "what rightfully belonged to it," a committee was struck to try to effect a compromise during the lunch hour. The result, scribbled on the back of a cigarette package in a Regina restaurant, was a paragraph that declared: "We do not propose any policy of outright confiscation" but added that "the welfare of the community must take supremacy over the claims of private wealth . . . a C.C.F. government will not play the role of rescuing bankrupt private concerns for the benefit of promoters and of stock and bond holders."

The convention, pushed hard by the radicals, added one sentence to Underhill's original draft. "No CCF Government will rest content," it read, "until it has eradicated capitalism and put into operation the full programme of socialized planning which will lead to the establishment in Canada of the Co-operative Commonwealth."

It was that final piece of rhetoric that M.J. Coldwell described as "a millstone" around the party's neck. It suggested that the new federation was revolutionary rather than reformist in its goals – determined to abolish the capitalistic system, though not by the violence that the communists were said to advocate.

208

The title of the Regina *Star*'s editorial that week, "Destroying Democracy," suggests the virulence of the anti-CCF campaign that followed. R.B. Bennett had already set the tone for the establishment following the movement's formation in 1932, when he attacked it in public. "What do they offer you for dumping you in the mud?" he asked. "Socialism! Communism! Dictatorship!" It was at this point that Bennett made his ill-considered request to "every man and woman to put the iron heel of ruthlessness against a thing of that kind." The left wing, especially the communists, always took a delight in referring to him as "Iron Heel Bennett."

The CCF's strongest opponent was the Roman Catholic Church, which held that socialism and communism were, in the words of the Archbishop of Montreal, "subversive political theories," an attitude that effectively throttled the CCF in the province of Quebec. The church's hostility spilled over into the Protestant world when King Gordon lost his job as professor of Christian ethics at the United Theological College in Montreal. There is no doubt that the primary reason was his identification with the new party. On the Ontario hustings, the gentle Woodsworth was attacked as "a Russian red" and "a dangerous citizen."

In spite of this opposition, the CCF would within a year establish itself as an influential political movement. In 1933 it would become the official opposition in British Columbia and the following year in Saskatchewan, where it briefly clung to the old "Farmer-Labour" name. It would have a profound influence on the policies of the old-line parties, and it would, by its presence and its rhetoric, act as the conscience of the country and prepare the way for the Canadian welfare state in the post-war era.

It was a child of the times. It is hard to believe that there would ever have been an effective socialist party in Canada if there had been no Depression. And when the Depression began to fade from people's memories and the welfare state was a *fait accompli*, the CCF's star faded too. The socialist movement took power in Saskatchewan, British Columbia, and Manitoba, where memories of the Depression were longer and more bitter. But it could not capture the hidebound Atlantic provinces, the Tory strongholds of rural Ontario, or the Alberta hinterland where the people had opted for their own Messiah. Nor could it make headway in Quebec.

In the end, the party changed its name and moved closer to the mainstream of Canadian political life. To the dismay of a dwindling band of die-hards, it shook off the millstone of socialized planning that its founders had believed would eradicate capitalism in those brave, sad years when young men and women of high ideals and selfless purpose struggled to transform the society that had betrayed them.

6

Bible Alberta marched to a different beat. With Saskatchewan, it was
Bill the youngest of the provinces. Its settlers had been in the last of the immigrant waves to arrive during the pre-war boom. The percentage of Americans among them was far higher than that in Saskatchewan and Manitoba. The province was also farther away from the manufacturing centres of Central Canada, so that goods from the East were more expensive. In the prosperous days of the twenties, Albertans had bought farm equipment, radios, and furniture on the instalment plan. Now, as prices fell and crops failed, they were forced to return them.

Farm foreclosures and crop seizures had bred a deep suspicion – indeed, a hatred – of Eastern financial institutions, and with good reason. When the UFA government tried to adjust farm debts, it received no co-operation from the East. One trust company raised hackles when its representative told the Alberta legislature that "farmers must pay their debts at the interest contracted for." This callousness was not lost on those local officials who were forced to carry out instructions from the East. H.H. Drecinson, a bailiff in Northern Alberta, would never forget the shame and pity he felt when he had to evict one family from their shack. The farmer, his fragile wife, four children, and a bedridden grandmother were allowed no period of grace. The orders were to oust them immediately.

These scenes became commonplace in the grim winter of 1932–33, when the price of eggs dropped to a nickel a dozen, when the sale of a hog would return only two dollars, and beef went so cheap (six cents a pound) that farmers lost money paying the freight to ship cattle to market.

John F. Milner, who farmed near Lloydminster, found his situation becoming desperate. Ninety-five per cent of the farmers in his district were burdened with crushing debts to the banks, the mortgage and machinery companies, and even the local grocery store. Every week when he went to the post office he emerged with a fistful of bills, unopened. He drove the six miles home in his wagon and handed them to his wife "because she had more pluck than I had." Yet Milner felt lucky, compared to a neighbour, a sick and illiterate farmer whose only income came from selling eggs at *four* cents a dozen. His wife was forced to trudge six miles to town carrying twenty-four dozen eggs, for which she received ninety-six cents. That was all the family had to pay for the week's provisions.

Devices once considered essential vanished. In the Camrose district, where farm families were living on potatoes and skim milk, Patrick Ashby discovered that he had the only telephone left in the area. The phone company had removed all the others for non-payment of bills.

What bothered the farmers everywhere in Alberta was that they were living in poverty in the midst of plenty. There was, after all, a surfeit of groceries. A representative of Gault Brothers, the big Edmonton wholesaler, begged H.G. Hammell, a general merchant in Carstairs, to take eight thousand dollars' worth of stock off the company's hands. He promised Hammell that he could pay for it when he wished. But Hammell couldn't sell the twenty thousand dollars' worth of stock that he had optimistically piled up in his store. That started him thinking that something was wrong with the economic system. All over the province, thousands had come to the same conclusion.

A verse from a popular radical song of the thirties said it all:

> *Our domestic situation is certainly hard to*
> *   beat:*
> *We have to go round hungry 'cause we raise*
> *   too much to eat;*
> *We cannot ride our railroads 'cause we*
> *   haven't got the fare*
> *And we pile up stacks of clothing till we*
> *   haven't much to wear . . .*

Something was clearly very wrong when children had to go to the rural school barefoot and wear potato sacks for clothing. Breakfast became a luxury for those who could have a meal only on alternate mornings. Yet the magazines were full of advertisements for breakfast foods, ranging from Dr. Jackson's Roman Meal to Red River Cereal.

The times were ripe for a Messiah, and Alberta found one in the person of a schoolteacher named William Aberhart, without doubt the most electrifying political figure the country has ever produced. He did not look like a politician and he didn't act like one. In fact, he had no intention of being a politician or even, at that time, of starting a new party. He was a big bulky man with a decided paunch, a beak-like nose, thick lips, jowls, and drooping eyes, shielded by a pince-nez - like Bennett, a cartoonist's delight. He was a high school principal and, more important, he was a lay preacher whose religious fundamentalism was both bizarre and spooky.

He believed, of course, every single word in the King James Version of the Bible. "The Bible, the whole Bible and nothing but the Bible" was the way he put it. He also believed in Old Testament prophecy based on an understanding of secret codes that he and his followers thought lay behind the words. These prophecies, which seem so outlandish, were accepted by thousands in the drought-ridden farms of Southern Alberta, the Bible Belt of Canada. Bill Aberhart would adhere to them long after he became premier of the province - indeed, until the moment of his death.

He was a "Dispensationalist" who preached that world history was divided into seven periods of unequal length known as "dispensations." The world, he said, had reached the sixth dispensation and must prepare for the seventh, which was known as the Rapture. During the Rapture, so the Dispensationalists preached, every Christian would be spirited away from the earth, which would then be caught in the grip of a truly frightful anarchy known as the Tribulation. Without the presence of Christians, they believed, the world would, literally, go to Hell: train passengers would die in dreadful accidents when the Christian engineers vanished from the locomotives; patients would succumb in hospitals as Christian doctors and nurses were removed. With the Holy Spirit having made off with all the Raptured Christians, the

212

globe would be plunged into chaos. Japan and China would be locked in a mortal battle with the West. Finally a super-figure would emerge – the "anti-Christ," in the jargon of the sect. Armageddon would follow until Christ established his millennium. More was promised – much more – including a return engagement with Satan and a titanic battle that would see Satan thrust into a lake of fire, the world destroyed, and a new heaven and earth created.

Anyone who would believe all that would have no trouble with the kooky ideas of Major Clifford Hugh Douglas, a British war veteran and a vicious anti-Semite. His economic theories, which he called Social Credit, were being taken seriously by thousands who, drowning in a failed system, were eager to grasp at the lifeline of an alternative.

Aberhart was just the man to spread the Douglas philosophy among the wretched of Alberta. A farm boy from Ontario, the fourth of eight children, a successful educator and one-time athlete (football, basketball) with a Bachelor's degree by correspondence from Queen's, he had reached the age of fifty-five. It was not only that the time was ripe for any man who could promise to set the country free from debt and the moneyed interests; the new factor in politics – radio – had now come into its own.

Franklin Roosevelt had inaugurated a series of fireside radio chats that would help him sweep the country again in 1936. To an even greater degree than Roosevelt, Aberhart captured the new medium and made it his own. It was said that in any town, village, hamlet, or city you could catch an Aberhart broadcast without missing a word simply by walking along the street and hearing his vibrant voice leaking from every radio set on the block.

He had adopted radio when it was still in its infancy. In the early twenties he had decided to bring his interpretation of Bible prophecy to a wider audience among Alberta's scattered communities by opening a Bible school in Calgary. His ten-week courses led to the Calgary Prophetic Bible Institute, which, in November 1925, went on the air for the first time, broadcasting on CFCN, the "Voice of the Prairies." Standing on the rostrum of the Palace Theatre with microphones suspended above him, Aberhart launched into his topic: "Is the Bible Story of Creation Scientific?" (the answer, of course, was Yes!). From that moment, radio was his medium, and his voice – rich, sonorous, and confident – became the best known in Alberta. Three hundred and fifty thousand listeners habitually tuned in to his broadcasts.

The Depression did not hit home to Aberhart until the winter of 1931–32, when he began to receive letters from desperate farmers asking him to pray for them. Former students came seeking advice on how to deal with hard times. Some, he noted, were suffering from malnutrition. And then, to his horror, one of his Grade 12 graduates, reduced to wandering through the hobo jungles, killed himself. That one event politicized him.

He was ripe for any unorthodox political or economic theory, just as he had been ripe for religious prophecy. He found it in the eccentric ideas of Major Douglas, a reserve officer in the RAF. Aberhart became an instant convert, thanks to a little book, *Unemployment and War*, written by the actor Maurice Colbourne, who had tried to simplify the Douglas theory. A teacher handed Aberhart the Colbourne book during an exam-marking session in Edmonton. Aberhart devoured it overnight and told one of his teaching staff the following day, "I read the most fascinating book last night on Social Credit. It seems to me it has got a solution which could be applied."

Put simply (and it is not easy to put it simply), Douglas's theory was that the capitalistic system couldn't provide people with enough purchasing power to allow them to enjoy the fruits of their countrymen's labour. The total sum of the wages they received would always be less than the total costs of production because of additional expenses: profit margins, overhead, distribution, and credit charges. Thus, Douglas argued, there wasn't enough money in the community to buy all the goods and services being produced. In short, to quote the Social Credit slogan, there was "Poverty in the Midst of Plenty." To redress the balance, Douglas argued, the government must provide the additional funds – "social credit" – so that people could buy the goods and services the system was producing. Douglas did not explain where the public money would come from or how his system would cope with inflation.

The debt-ridden farmers of Alberta might not be able to understand Douglas's theory – it is doubtful if Aberhart himself understood it – but they could understand the paradox of poverty in the midst of plenty, for they saw it all around them. And when

214

Aberhart took up the Social Credit crusade with all the evangelistic fervour he had lavished on his prophetic sermons, they were hooked.

He published anonymously a booklet with a yellow cover, properly titled *The Douglas System of Economics*, that quickly became known as the Yellow Pamphlet. In it he suggested that every adult citizen be given a monthly credit in the form of non-negotiable certificates worth twenty dollars (later boosted to twenty-five). This credit would act as an economic safety net, allowing everybody the bare necessities of life: food, shelter, clothing. It was the concept of twenty-five dollars a month for everyone that caught the imagination of the people. Without Aberhart's promotion, Social Credit would have remained an obscure economic theory. Aberhart was to turn it into a movement that would, in name at least, dominate the political arena in the two most westerly provinces for decades to come.

In 1933 his only purpose was to influence the established government. As he wrote to his niece in July, "Some people tell me I should run for Premier of Alberta – ha! ha! I have no ambition along that line but the Radio Broadcast has made me well-known all over the Province."

It certainly had. As one railway employee put it, "he had a voice that made the pilot lights on your radio jump." To Maude McLean, a Calgary housewife, it seemed "as if God had picked Mr. Aberhart and then prepared an audience for him in Alberta first as a religious leader and [later] as leader of the Social Credit movement." Mrs. McLean was quite convinced that Aberhart's arrival in Alberta and his subsequent career in the province were "the fulfillment of a Divine Plan."

Professor John Irving, a University of Toronto psychologist who interviewed scores of Aberhart's supporters from those years, later wrote that "it is, perhaps, not surprising that the attributing to Aberhart the 'special grace' of 'a man of destiny' recurs in the interviews with the most ardent of his religious followers. For nearly a quarter of a century he had been widely known and enthusiastically accepted in certain quarters as 'the greatest student of Bible prophecy in the world.' Under these circumstances, some of his followers naturally found it easy, by a certain shift in the apocalyptic emphasis, to endow their leader with Messianic qualities."

215

Irving noted that many of his respondents referred to Aberhart as "Our Great Prophet," "Our Beloved Leader," "That Man of God," "The Last Hope of Mankind," or "That Heaven Sent Saviour" and that these were the most vocal proponents of the Social Credit movement. But Aberhart's appeal went far beyond religion. He was literally loved – the word is not too strong – by thousands, many of whom had no ties with the evangelical movement. As his right-hand man and eventual successor, the quiet-spoken Ernest Manning, remarked, "You either believed he was right and followed him wherever he led, or you had nothing to do with him." Among Aberhart's followers were two prominent Christian Scientists, Wilson and Harry Southam, members of the colourful newspaper family and publishers of the *Ottawa Citizen*.

As a platform speaker Aberhart had no rival. He would enter the hall to thunderous applause and walk slowly down the aisle, his progress impeded by well-wishers, talking to everybody who wanted to speak with him. Then, a mischievous grin on his face, he would mount the platform. As one farmer put it: "We felt he was the law – he was the only man who could give us a decent hope in the future – who could free us from the money barons of Eastern Canada. Who wouldn't gather around a man like that? Who wouldn't love him?" The fact that he was obviously sincere – disinterested as to personal gain or public office – enhanced his appeal.

His platform technique, honed in his years as a lay preacher, ranged through all the emotions. Tears ran down his cheeks when he discussed the plight of the poor. But he could also get his audience laughing. He'd pull a letter from his pocket, wave it at the crowd, and say, "Listen folks, the Bible Institute just got this letter from one of our opposition – a big banker who lives in Eastern Canada. This banker expresses deep sympathy for me in this letter. . . . He writes 'I understand Mr. Aberhart has lost his equilibrium completely, that he's left Mrs. Aberhart and is living in a shack up in the mountains.' " The audience would roar with laughter at that and Aberhart would have them captive.

As one farmer northeast of Calgary told Irving, "He appealed to us because he attacked the banks and mortgage companies really fierce. You should have heard the crowd applaud this part."

"Let's knock on the door of an imaginary home," Aberhart would say. "A dispossessed farmer's wife comes to the door. Let's

216

ask her some questions. 'How long have you lived here?' 'Twenty-five years.' 'Have you a car?' 'Oh, my, no. We ride in a wagon.' 'You have an electric refrigerator?' 'Oh, no, not even an ice box.' 'Would you like a car and a refrigerator?' 'I certainly would.' 'Have you been to Calgary lately?' 'Not for a year.' 'Would you like to go?' 'I certainly would and so would my children.' 'Would you be interested in a plan that would give you a car, a refrigerator and trips to the big city? Social Credit, without any cost to you individually, will give you all these.'"

As soon as he adopted Social Credit, Aberhart began to add economic theory to his Sunday broadcasts. He knew he would have to tone down his biblical prophecies if he was to enlarge his audience. One trick to prevent non-believers from turning off the radio was to weave the Social Credit philosophy into his religious demagoguery. If you were interested in one, you also got the other, but you had to hear the whole broadcast to get the full message.

His target was the United Farmers of Alberta, who had held power since 1921. A pale shadow of the grassroots movement that had once galvanized the province (and established an Alberta tradition of unorthodox political behaviour that would help to legitimize the Social Credit movement), the UFA began to feel the heat of Aberhart's attack. When people wrote to Aberhart asking what they could do, he urged them to "tell your legislature." One petition, signed by twelve thousand Social Credit adherents, urged the UFA government to implement Social Credit principles.

In spite of the fact that Douglas had denounced Aberhart's Yellow Pamphlet as "fallacious from start to finish" (or perhaps because of it), the government was contemplating bringing the major to Alberta to discuss his theories. Meanwhile, using techniques perfected in his Bible study days, Aberhart had formed the Douglas Social Credit League, whose central committee was directly responsible to the Calgary Prophetic Bible Institute, which Aberhart headed and dominated. The league immediately set about establishing study groups across the province, as the Bible Institute had once done.

Aberhart's technique in conscripting members of his flock was described in detail to John Irving by Mary McCulloch, a Calgary housewife and rooming-house keeper who had been attending

217

the Bible Institute for a year. In the fall of 1932, Aberhart asked those of his flock who were interested in Social Credit to raise their hands. These were asked to stay after the service. At that meeting, Aberhart asked one of his deacons to take names; Mrs. McCulloch's headed the list.

The following week, Aberhart called a meeting of the thirty followers whose names he had. They met weekly for several months at the institute while Aberhart explained Douglas's economic philosophy, or at least his version of it. As Mrs. McCulloch put it, "I was sure hit with the Social Credit bug. Aberhart boiled the books on it down so anybody could understand it. . . . He was a wonderful teacher. . . . I've never seen people study the way he made us."

One night Aberhart told them, "We'd better organize and get out and tell everybody in Calgary about Social Credit. Who will help?" Each person was assigned to a district, and again Mrs. McCulloch took the lead. She organized twelve study groups in the Victoria school district where she lived, bustling around to all her friends and neighbours and keeping in constant touch with them by telephone. Soon the crowds became so large that the houses in which they'd started could not hold them, and they were all forced to move as a single unit to the Labour Temple.

Mrs. McCulloch neglected her rooming house for Social Credit work. Her front room became an office, piled high with the movement's literature, which she sold all over her district. She ran such a formidable organization that she had no trouble garnering eight thousand signatures on a petition to the government. At the Calgary Stampede in July, each of Mrs. McCulloch's twelve groups rode in the parade in cars with their names on the side – to the applause of the onlookers. Ironically, R.B. Bennett led the procession and, she insisted, "could hardly believe his eyes when all our Social Credit cars rolled by."

There were dozens like Mary McCulloch, driven to proselytize through Aberhart's study groups. As she said, "We really took over the city. . . . I don't think we missed any street or block. . . . We were everywhere. Everybody wanted to get into a group and find out what it was all about."

In Calgary alone, there were eventually sixty-three Social Credit study groups. In the province as a whole there were sixteen hundred. Aberhart's trained speakers were everywhere, organizing and lecturing. Some devoted all their working hours to spreading the word – men such as A.B. Hickox, a chicken rancher east of Delburne, who quit his ranch to work without pay for the movement. Hickox made thirty-five speeches and organized the entire district between Red Deer and Rocky Mountain House, then plunged into a speaking tour of the Peace River area, making as many as five speeches a day over a five-month period. As a result he had "that whole country talking Social Credit." So eager were the crowds to hear him that one audience waited patiently until he arrived very late, long after midnight. As he put it, "people were simply mad for Social Credit."

And yet, as the year wound down, Social Credit was not a political party and didn't act like one. Aberhart was not a politician – at least not in the old-fashioned sense. His task as he saw it was to force the Social Credit philosophy on the established order. But control of the events that he had set in motion were now out of his hands. Bible Bill was about to have greatness thrust upon him.

1934

1

The usual New Year's fanfare heralding the end of hard times *The*
("LOW POINT OF DEPRESSION REACHED IN FEBRUARY LAST YEAR, *seditious*
SAYS OTTAWA EXPERT") was scarcely off the front pages before *A.E. Smith*
the Prime Minister found himself in hot water in Vancouver.

With eight thousand families on relief in that city and more
than forty thousand on the verge of financial collapse, Bennett,
queried by a reporter on the question of the Dominion's public
debt, was so incautious as to reply: "If you want to know who is
responsible for all this debt, look at yourself in the mirror when
you are shaving tomorrow. There are people who say let's spend
more money, well and good, but where is the money coming
from? Where is the spirit of our pioneers who tilled our soil and
worked in your forests? Did they go to the government whenever
they wanted anything? They did not ask governments to be a wet
nurse to every derelict."

In vain, the Prime Minister tried to backtrack and insist that
he had meant to say "every derelict industry." The Vancouver
Sun, in full voice, flayed Bennett for using "a cruel and contempt-
ible description to flaunt in the faces of men and women who are
looking for some plan or economy that will enable them to do
something and to whom the dole is a heart-breaking shame and
disgrace." The *Sun*, a populist newspaper owned by the brilliant
if erratic Robert Cromie, then put its finger on what was generat-
ing the growing criticism of the Bennett regime. The so-called
derelicts, it said, "have been betrayed by an economic system so
vehemently defended by Mr. Bennett, which has always sacrificed the human structure to the money structure."

The following month the Prime Minister was further embarrassed by a court case in Toronto that was the direct result of
another of his incomprehensible encounters with the radical wing
of the dissident Left. The Reverend A.E. Smith, the founder of the
Canadian Labor Defense League, a communist organization,
was charged with sedition. The evidence suggested – and a good
many people believed – that the charges were trumped up and the
court case was another attempt to silence Smith and his organization, which had been campaigning for the release of Tim Buck

223

from Kingston and for a royal commission to look into penitentiary conditions in Canada.

Smith had been able to gather an impressive 459,000 signatures on a petition demanding both an investigation into the attempted shooting of Buck and the repeal of Section 98 of the Criminal Code under which the eight Communists had been charged. In November 1933 he had brought a delegation to Ottawa to present the petition to Bennett. The Prime Minister was in his usual belligerent mood.

"There will be no investigation into the shooting," he told Smith. "There will be no repeal of Section 98. It is needed on the statute books. And finally" – in Smith's account he began to pound his desk – "there will be no release for these men. They will serve every last five minutes of their sentences. That's all there is to be said! Now get out!"

Smith was undoubtedly nonplussed the following year to learn that Bennett himself had gone to Kingston for a half-hour visit with Norman "Red" Ryan, the notorious bank robber known as the Canadian Jesse James, then being touted as a model prisoner. Ryan, who was allowed extra privileges at Kingston, conned almost everybody from the prison padre to the Toronto *Star* into believing that he had reformed. "I was greatly impressed by what he said to me," Bennett wrote to the Ryan family. "I can only say that his demeanour . . . and surroundings were calculated to stimulate him to renewed efforts of usefulness." Ryan was paroled after serving one of the shortest life terms on record (eleven and a half years). He immediately returned to his old ways, staging hold-ups by night while making speeches and giving sanctimonious press interviews by day on his "reform," until he was killed during an armed robbery of a liquor store.

In spite of Bennett's curt dismissal of Smith, the CLDL was a voice to be reckoned with. With the usual communist efficiency it had managed to sign up seventeen thousand paid members. Few were dyed-in-the-wool Marxists, but all wanted to contribute to the defence of those who they believed were being hounded for their opinions. The league had three hundred and fifty branches throughout Canada and, to this point, had distributed five million pieces of literature. It had organized demonstrations across the country protesting the imprisonment of the Communists and attacking Section 98.

224

The CCF remained officially lukewarm. Woodsworth and his followers wanted nothing to do with the Communists or any form of united front; therein, they were convinced, lay political suicide. But they found it difficult to prevent members of the rank and file, and even some of the CCF clubs, from joining forces with the socialists' traditional enemies.

To Bennett, the CLDL's campaign was a maddening development. He thought he had destroyed the Red monster by striking hard at the leadership. But the Communist party was hydra-headed. It was bitterly ironic that the very court case that he had used as a weapon against the dissidents was now being employed as a weapon against *him*. The imprisonment of Buck and his comrades under Section 98 had given the radical Left a cause for which to do battle and had won over thousands who had previously been neutral. As justice minister Hugh Guthrie admitted, even the churches were committed.

After his Ottawa encounter with Bennett, Smith immediately launched a new attack – a play entitled *Eight Men Speak*, performed in the Standard Theatre in Toronto in conjunction with the Progressive Arts Club. Home-grown drama was an oddity in Canada. Even the fledgling Little Theatre Movement generally performed British or American plays. But this play dealt with events close to home – the Communist trials, conditions at Kingston, the attempt to murder Tim Buck, and the bloody climax of the Estevan strike. It played to a full house and was so successful that a second performance was planned. Before the actors could reassemble, however, the Toronto Police Commission banned the play as "distasteful."

Bennett asked for a copy of the script. On January 2 his secretary, Alice Miller, wrote to the Minister of Internal Revenue that the Prime Minister "thinks . . . appropriate action should be taken through the Attorney-General of the province to protect society against these attacks. . . . " Bennett was convinced once again that dissidents must be muzzled, that "the time has come when we must no longer allow Smith and his followers to spread propaganda of gross misrepresentation, deluding the people who they exploit." He dragged out the familiar excuse that censors always use to justify their actions: "we should not permit liberty to degenerate into license [*sic*]."

Prodded by Ottawa, the attorney general was not long in act-

225

ing. The Strand Theatre on Spadina Avenue, which was planning to stage a second performance of the play, was told that if it did so it would lose its licence. The CLDL immediately sponsored a protest rally at Hygea Hall on January 17. Smith took to the platform to tell of the attempt to shoot Tim Buck and to describe his reception by Bennett. Then he charged the government with the attempted assassination of the Communist leader.

"Was this an accident?" Smith asked. "Was not the government of the day to be held responsible?"

In the audience that evening were three members of Police Chief Denny Draper's Red Squad trying to write down everything that was said. None of them knew shorthand; the best they could do was to scribble certain abbreviated words and phrases in their notebooks. Nonetheless they produced a verbatim account of Smith's speech, including these words: "I say deliberately that Bennett gave the order to shoot Buck in his cell in cold blood with intent to murder him." The order, Smith was said to have declared, had come from Bennett through Hugh Guthrie to the penitentiary warden.

Two weeks later, A.E. Smith opened his Toronto *Star* to find a front-page headline announcing that he had been charged with sedition "with the intention of spreading discontent, hatred and distrust of the government."

The charge was not popular. More and more, the Prime Minister of Canada – "Iron Heel Bennett" – was seen as a bully trampling on the rights of ordinary citizens. Smith, a one-time Methodist minister who had helped in early negotiations to form the United Church of Canada, had quit the ministry following the Winnipeg General Strike of 1919 to work for the cause of labour. A former member of the Manitoba legislature, he was respected for his obvious sincerity if not for his politics. To many Canadians Smith's opinions didn't sound seditious. Opposition politicians were always fomenting distrust of the government; what was wrong with "spreading discontent"?

As Smith himself declared at a rally on February 3, in which three thousand thronged to Massey Hall to hear him, "I am charged with sedition because I criticize our leaders. Why is Mitch Hepburn [the Liberal leader in Ontario] not so charged? Does he not seek to create disaffection against the government? I am charged because Bennett is in an unstable position. . . . "

226

The Toronto *Star* backed him up: "If a man slanders the Prime Minister he can be charged with slander. Why should he be charged with sedition which is in a wholly different category?"

Offers of legal aid poured in. E.J. McMurray, K.C., a Winnipeg lawyer who had once been Mackenzie King's Solicitor General, offered to come to Toronto to help with the defence. He was joined by Leo Gallagher, who had been banished from Germany after defending Marinus van der Lubbe, charged by the Nazis with causing the Reichstag fire. Gallagher's fees were underwritten by the International Labour Defense, whose secretary stated that no expense would be spared to defend Smith.

The trial itself bordered on the farcical. McMurray scored the first point by demanding that Tim Buck be brought from Kingston as a defence witness, a tactic that the Crown attorney, Peter White, protested vigorously but vainly. McMurray was able to make his case to the judge that Buck's testimony would show "that there did exist an error in the administration of justice in Canada, which the defendant was trying to alter by lawful means."

Now Bennett's attempts to use the big stick against his shrill opponents began to backfire. The last thing anybody wanted was to bring up the embarrassing business of the attempt to shoot Buck. An exercise in damage control was put into operation. Buck, who had been denied all news, was smuggled in irons from the penitentiary to the train at Kingston and then from the train to the Don Jail in Toronto, where he was isolated from all other prisoners. Only one guard was allowed access to him; his exercise periods were held separately from those of the others. Thus he was to be kept from learning how the trial was proceeding. But a friendly guard, angered by the implications of the Smith case, found a moment after supper to whisper to him through the bars: "You'll have to be very careful, Tim, they are out to get Mr. Smith and they won't let you have your say if they can help it. I've written down the words Smith used so you'll know what it is all about. I'm going to pass it through your ventilator. Promise you'll tear it up and put it down the can right away." He threw the note and a newspaper clipping through the small square opening above the door.

Buck, now in possession of the bare facts of the case, decided the best thing he could do was to ensure that Smith's statement

227

was verified. He must get across to the jury the fact that a deliberate attempt had been made to murder him. He knew the Crown would try to prevent him from speaking and so spent some time working out the shortest possible answers to the questions he might expect at the outset.

At last he was brought into the courtroom, wearing his heavy blue prison suit and looking colourless and weak from his long confinement. His presence gave the Communist party another chance to provoke headlines. Even as he began his testimony, four thousand people were holding a demonstration in Queen's Park.

McMurray turned to the witness and asked if he remembered October 20, 1932.

"I remember it very well," Buck replied.

"What particularly impressed it on your mind?"

"I was shot at . . . " Buck began, his words almost drowned out by the Crown attorney's objections. The objection was sustained, but the damage was done. McMurray had managed to widen the scope of the trial, to broaden its appeal, and to milk it for its propaganda value.

The only evidence the Crown could produce against Smith was the notebooks of two of the Red Squad members. Unable to write down Smith's words verbatim, the two policemen had expanded and transcribed them after leaving the hall. McMurray was able to show that the longhand in both notebooks was so suspiciously similar that it appeared to have been written by one hand. A parade of defence witnesses counteracted this flimsy testimony by swearing that Smith had not uttered the words attributed to him.

The public was soon aware that the Crown had no substantial case. The jury believed Smith when he denied he'd said what the Red Squad claimed. Undoubtedly they were also influenced by the defence's summing up: "If you punish Smith, then you are going back to the Spanish Inquisition. Certain reactionary forces will be pleased if Smith is taken away. But out over Canada today this case is attracting wide attention. This is a state trial. This is a political trial. I often wonder, gentlemen, whether jails are built for labour leaders. Smith's fate is being watched in B.C., in the shanties among the miners of Alberta, in Brandon where he la-

228

boured as a young man, all over among the poor and working people, among people of the universities all interested in the fate of this man."

The verdict was a foregone conclusion. The jury found Smith not guilty. A few months later, in spite of Bennett's threat, Tim Buck was paroled.

2

By 1934, the radio had replaced the piano as the central piece of furniture in the living room. The Stromberg Carlson upright in its two-toned cabinet of polished walnut, the Gothic mantel Philco in its hand-rubbed casing of rare Oriental woods, or the Victor Globe Trotter with its "modernistic design" (which we now call art deco) are familiar artifacts of the Depression years. More than the railways they stitched the country together; more than the movies they brought solace to the impoverished. Radios were expensive – even a reconditioned table model cost fifteen dollars or more – so that those without radios often gathered in the home of someone more fortunate than themselves. But once you owned a radio the programs were free, except for the annual two-dollar licence fee about which everybody complained. You could tune into the CRBC and listen to the sugary tones of Mart Kenney and His Western Gentlemen or the exclamatory voice of Foster Hewitt calling the Saturday night hockey game. If you had no decent Sunday clothes you could stay home on the Lord's Day and worship at the altar of the Stromberg Carlson.

It is impossible to overestimate the power of the radio in the Depression years. It is not too much to say that it helped save the sanity of the dispossessed. It allowed the world to enter the parlours of the nation, and it provided a sense of community to the drought-ravaged farms and lonely coastal backwaters. Canadians heard Jimmy McLarnin wrest the welterweight boxing title from Barney Ross on the radio. They learned of Hitler's massacre of Ernst Röhm's Brown Shirts the same way – as well as Max Baer's heavyweight victory over Primo Carnera, the deaths of Bonnie and Clyde and John Dillinger, the kidnapping of the London, Ontario, brewer, John Labatt, and the charges against the boot-

Radio politics

229

legging Bronfmans for evading customs duties – and all to the strains of "Blue Moon," "June in January," and "The Object of My Affection."

If Canadians got much of their news from the local stations, they got most of their entertainment from the three powerful broadcasting networks across the border, which tended to drown out their fledgling Canadian counterpart.

The Bennett government, pushed and prodded by Graham Spry's Canadian Radio League, had adopted the measures advocated by the Aird report on broadcasting. Canada now had its first real network, the Canadian Radio Broadcasting Commission, whose chairman, the bearded and bulky Hector Charlesworth, had lofty plans for the medium. Charlesworth was already talking about bringing the finest British programs to Canada, of broadcasting symphonic music from seven major centres, and of creating a "theatre of the air" in which the work of the world's finest playwrights would be heard – Shakespeare, of course, but also Canadian works drawn from the Little Theatre Movement. As for commercials, Charlesworth was against them. "The best of American programs are those in which advertising has no voice . . . " he said. "Advertising has hurt radio programs."

In spite of this, Canadians were far more likely to turn to one of the despised American commercial programs, all of them, from "The Lone Ranger" to "The Romance of Helen Trent," controlled by advertisers. The Americans had already seized the continental initiative, and in the end, Canada would be forced to opt for their commercial pattern rather than Charlesworth's dream of a BBC-type network. Thus was Canada further seduced into the American orbit.

With the exception of William Aberhart of Alberta, no Canadian politician had yet mastered the techniques of radio, as Franklin D. Roosevelt had with his famous fireside chats. Bennett's bombast was fine for a live mass audience but quite unsuitable for the intimacy of the living room. Mackenzie King's plodding, fusty style put people to sleep. Aberhart was the only politician in the country to adapt American broadcasting techniques to the Canadian arena.

"Charisma" was a foreign word in the thirties; it wasn't even in the standard college dictionaries. But there's no doubt that Aberhart was blessed with it, as Major Douglas, the high priest of

230

Social Credit, discovered in the spring of 1934. The UFA government of Premier J.E. Brownlee had decided to bring Douglas to the province to explain Social Credit, a move designed to discredit Aberhart, whose own ideas were at variance with the Douglas dogma.

Douglas arrived in Edmonton on April 5 and snubbed Aberhart at the railway station. But the following day, when he appeared before the legislature (which had already heard Aberhart) and attempted to outline his theories, was not for him a success.

Douglas was thinking in world terms. Something, he felt, was wrong with a monetary system controlled by a ruthless band of international financiers and bankers. By arbitrarily advancing or refusing credit they were preventing citizens of the world from taking advantage of modern technology that theoretically should be organized to relieve them of want. Any Alberta farmer in hock to Eastern bankers could sympathize with his indignation. Why should they control the credit system? Credit, said Douglas, was a public, not a private, resource, and the issuing or withholding of credit ought to be a state monopoly.

When Douglas was asked to lay out a specific program to deal with the ills of the Depression, however, he was vague and evasive. He did not agree with Aberhart that Social Credit could be introduced provincially. The federal government, he was convinced, would declare it unconstitutional (which is exactly what happened later). Under questioning, he implied that Social Credit might be introduced by a revolution if the financial crisis led the world into another war; the wicked band of bankers wouldn't give up their power unless they were forced to. Certainly there was a hint of incipient fascism in his distrust of the masses and his concept of an elitist government run by experts. Later, in Calgary, he told his listeners: "You must have control of the army, and the navy and air force." As Aberhart's biographers Elliott and Miller have pointed out, what he was advocating, in the long view, was a military coup against the bankers. That was all very well; no doubt many Albertans would have welcomed one. But it was scarcely a practical solution. Floating in his theoretical cloudland, Douglas clearly had no specific cure for the province's problems.

As the Brownlee government hoped, Douglas's appearance led to a breach with Aberhart. Douglas wanted the famous Yellow

231

Pamphlet withdrawn, or at the very least his name removed from it. That caused a dejected Aberhart to lament, after a fierce encounter with his hero, "Douglas told me I am all wrong."

But Brownlee had not reckoned on Aberhart's popular appeal. Douglas's appearance in the province had the opposite effect to that intended. The major, with his military bearing and his close-cropped moustache, certainly looked the part of a leader. Aberhart, plump, Buddha-like, and double-chinned, didn't. None of that mattered. Since few could really understand what Douglas was trying to say, his theories attracted few converts. But everybody understood Aberhart, the master of radio politics, when he broadcast about the irony of poverty in the midst of plenty. He had trained his disciples well. The UFA government in trying to discredit the new Messiah had actually strengthened his hand.

The Premier, meanwhile, was embroiled in a spicy seduction suit brought against him by a family friend, twenty-two-year-old Vivian MacMillan, and her father, the former mayor of Edson. The court case occupied the last week of June and was covered verbatim by the Edmonton newspapers, which provided their eager readers with dozens of columns of testimony.

And sensational testimony it was. According to Miss MacMillan, Brownlee, who had met her when she was sixteen, had talked her into coming to Edmonton and offered to be her guardian; he had got her a job in the legislature and had taken her into his home, where she became a close friend of his ailing wife and his two teenaged sons. That was substantially true. It was Vivian MacMillan's account of Brownlee's subsequent actions that provided the spice.

Miss MacMillan testified that the Premier had persuaded her to have sexual intercourse (the newspaper word was "intimacy") in his Studebaker touring car after explaining that he was dreadfully lonely and that he could not have normal relations with his wife. Sex, he had declared, would kill Mrs. Brownlee; by yielding to his advances, Vivian would be saving the life of the woman who had befriended her – or so she swore under oath. Much of her testimony came as a godsend to the headline writers. "He played with me as a cat plays with a mouse," she explained. And again – more headlines – "he seemed to have me under some kind of spell."

She was on the stand for as long as eight hours at a time and sometimes was reduced to tears, but no amount of cross-exami-

232

nation could shake her story. Indeed, she added some lip-smacking embellishments. In those frugal times, the home of Alberta's premier was modest and crowded. Brownlee shared a bedroom with his son Jack, a nervous sixteen-year-old. Mrs. Brownlee slept in another bedroom with the younger son, Alan, a sleepwalker. Vivian shared the maid's room. All these bedrooms were close to each other on the upper floor. Yet Brownlee, so Vivian swore, managed to make love to her in his own room in a bed just eighteen inches from that occupied by young Jack.

How was that possible without disturbing the family? Vivian had an answer. It was the Premier's habit, so she testified, to walk past her room and run a tap in the bathroom next to his wife's room, partly to cover the creaking of the hall floor and partly as a signal. The two would then negotiate the hallway back to Brownlee's room by adopting a sort of lock step - her feet on his - so that only one set of footfalls could be heard. Once and once only young Jack mumbled in his sleep. Brownlee turned on the light for a moment, quieted the boy, and then resumed his lovemaking.

When Vivian fell in love with a young medical student, Jack Caldwell, she tried to break off relations with the Premier, but, so she said, he would have none of it. She confessed her indiscretions to her then fiancé (the engagement had ended before the case came to court). Caldwell and Vivian's father then talked her into filing the suit. In those strait-laced, chauvinistic days, a father could also sue if his daughter was seduced, the inference being that he owned her and she had become damaged goods.

Brownlee flatly denied Vivian's story and his wife backed him up. To many, Vivian's tale of the lock-step journey down the hall and the coupling in the bedroom beside the slumbering youth had the ring of melodrama. The judge came down on Brownlee's side, the jury on Vivian's; it awarded her ten thousand dollars and her father an additional five thousand. "I very strongly disagree with you," said the judge, W.C. Ives, who was at the time Acting Chief Justice for the province. He dismissed the suit on the grounds that Vivian had come to Edmonton with her parents' approval and "that no illness had resulted from the seduction and [there was] no evidence that the ability of the daughter to render services was in any way interfered with." In short, whether or not Vivian had been seduced, she was not "damaged" in the legal sense - for those days a remarkable pronouncement that aroused a storm of opposition.

This result was cold comfort to Brownlee, who resigned and left the political field on July 1, the day the trial ended. (The judge's decision to dismiss the case was later reversed by a higher court, and Vivian got her money.) The UFA, already in bad odour for its lacklustre leadership during the economic crisis, was now in disarray at the exact moment when a new movement and a new potential leader were on the rise.

Irritated by the almost universal attacks upon him in the daily press (only Harry Southam's *Ottawa Citizen* supported the concept of Social Credit), Aberhart that summer started his own weekly newspaper, the *Alberta Social Credit Chronicle*. That paper reported in August what the rest of the Alberta press was ignoring. Bible Bill had just completed another spectacular speaking tour, covering twenty-five hundred miles and delivering thirty-nine speeches to thirty thousand people.

In his radio broadcasts Aberhart was nothing if not ingenious. Announcing that a stranger from another planet was about to visit Alberta, he launched his hugely successful "Man from Mars" radio programs. These satirical playlets were the last dramatized political broadcasts to be heard in Canada. The law was changed shortly thereafter to make them illegal.

The Man from Mars, wandering perplexed through the province, quickly comes to the conclusion that the inmates have taken over the asylum. He meets a banker and is baffled. "I find that you are very rich in goods. In fact you have so much that you wantonly destroy your abundance. I am told that is necessary to keep up prices. But at the same time I find that many of your people are suffering from poverty and starvation. Even little children cry for food and clothing that your governments order destroyed. But their parents cannot buy the goods because they have no money. To get money they must work, but they cannot get work because you have invented wonderful machines to make your goods, so your people must starve in the midst of plenty. . . ."

Aberhart's banker was made to reply: "I am sorry that you have been influenced by the conditions of the idle loafers who are a blight to society. It's time we had another war and got rid of them." Those words hit home to the masses of Albertans, who had heard very similar sentiments expressed by the financiers and politicians who ran the country.

234

Network radio was in its infancy, but Aberhart had already put into practice techniques that were becoming familiar to the public. He knew better than to confine himself to long, boring political dissertations. Instead he adapted his style to that of the hottest new programs on the air – to soap operas like "Betty and Bob" or comic skits of the kind made popular by Joe Penner and Eddie Cantor. His style was remarked on by one correspondent whose letter he read aloud to his cast during the course of a broadcast, with this mock admonition, "Now, you helpers, listen to me. You must speak more natural after this. Don't use my tone of voice. Spruce up. Be your-selves. Here is a radio fan who declares that I'm taking all these parts myself. He says I'm like Amos and Andy."

He introduced characters such as Mr. Kant B. Dunn (who did animal imitations while getting across the Aberhart philosophy) and the Hon. Jerry Bluffem, leader of the Its Your Turn Next Party, attending a conference at the town of Never Get Anywhere.

The CCF, which was making inroads in both British Columbia and Saskatchewan that year, never was able to achieve the ex-traordinary steamroller success that Aberhart enjoyed in Alberta. The academics, labour leaders, and farmers who made up the new party either did not catch on to the appeal of the vulgar new medium or, if they did, could not or would not use it in the way Aberhart did. One simply cannot imagine J.S. Woodsworth or M.J. Coldwell stooping to these folksy, populist techniques. Graham Spry of the LSR brains trust, who had brought network radio to Canada, certainly never envisaged this kind of broadcast buffoonery. The federation was above that sort of thing.

Aberhart's mastery of the medium allowed him to trumpet the idea of what he called the Just Price (taken from Douglas), which by its name suggested that current prices were unjust. The reason was that the manufacturers (the Eastern manufacturers, of course!) took too much in excess profits as opposed to "legiti-mate" profits. Aberhart's idea was that the government would tax away these unjust profits and use the tax money to underwrite the twenty-five-dollar monthly dividend to which every adult citizen would be entitled. Like blood circulating through the human sys-tem, these dividends would release the stagnant credit that was smothering the system. "The Blood Stream of the State," Aber-hart called it.

The idea that every voter was entitled to twenty-five dollars – in credit, not in cash – galvanized the province and captured the imagination of the public. Everybody could understand a monthly stipend, and nobody cared that Aberhart had pulled that particular figure out of nowhere as an example, not a hard promise. As one farmer near Edmonton told John Irving, "I supported Social Credit because I was interested in getting more money, more purchasing power. That $25 a month appealed to me more than anything else. . . . There wasn't one of us farmers that wasn't after that $25. . . . We had got nothing from the UFA. We talked up Social Credit constantly among ourselves. 'By golly,' I said to my neighbours. 'We're going to get $25 a month from this new system that Honest Abe's going to introduce. Then we'll be able to buy things.' I counted on that $25 because I figured with our wonderful wealth there was no reason why the $25 couldn't be paid."

That was the paradox. Wealth was visible. Aberhart was promising to redistribute it. So was the CCF, but Aberhart was using language that every farmer and farmer's wife could understand. "Surely every citizen of Alberta should have enough common, ordinary horse-sense to know that there is no need to starve in a full hay paddock," he'd say. "Even a worm will not go hungry because the apple is too large. He invariably goes to the core of the matter and there raises his standard of living. We can if we will."

And he was still not considering a political career, at least not publicly. "These broadcasts," he told his listeners, "are conducted merely as an educational feature. . . . In no sense of the word do we wish to make it a political broadcast." The Douglas Social Credit League, he insisted, "is against party politics and holds no political affiliation." He added, however, that since its aim was to introduce Social Credit into the province, the league would back a candidate to support the cause in every constituency in the forthcoming election.

Although his stated purpose remained – to shake the UFA out of its complacency and force it to adopt Social Credit – he was moving closer day by day to the political arena. If the UFA refused to support the movement, there was an alternative, and Aberhart knew it. He wrote to his niece that Christmas, " . . . you may hear of me being Premier of Alberta." He was not anxious to

236

go into politics, he said, "but the people are urging me to do so." In the end, the people would get their way.

3

Job – that was the magic word in the thirties. The idea of the job *Harry* transcended all else. To have a job – *any* job – was the ultimate *Stevens's* aspiration. The country was divided between those who had jobs *moment* and those who had none. *Job* was the key to respectability. *Job* *in history* was the Open Sesame to status. *Job* made you a Somebody; it allowed you to hold your head high; it separated you from the shuffling mob of unemployed who were seen as members of a lower stratum. It didn't matter that they were the obvious victims of uncontrollable economic forces. The work ethic was still strong: there would always be a stigma attached to a man and many women who had no job.

Yet thousands of Canadians were paid such low wages and worked such long hours that they were living in a state close to slavery. In the Quebec shoe industry, for example, wage scales ranged from bare subsistence to outright exploitation. One particularly avaricious manufacturer paid his women workers $1.50 for a seventy-five-hour week – a pitiful two cents an hour. When he was eventually exposed and prosecuted for paying less than the legal minimum wage, the penalty was shockingly low. He escaped with a fine of ten dollars.

That was an extreme case, but there were scores of documented instances in which men and women worked more than fifty hours a week for five dollars or less. These came to light in the spring of 1934 as a result of the terrier-like dedication of Henry Herbert Stevens, the member for Kootenay East (B.C.), who was Minister of Trade and Commerce in the Bennett Cabinet. Since February, Stevens had cast himself in a new role – that of a shining knight, the people's champion, impaling the dragons of big business on the lance of his own special project, a parliamentary committee set up to investigate price spreads and mass buying.

From late February until the end of June the Canadian public was assaulted by a litany of horror as witness after witness appeared before the Stevens Committee, as it was called, to describe appalling working conditions and wage scales in a variety

237

of major Canadian enterprises. Time and again the eleven M.P.s who made up the committee registered shock and anger at the testimony, which covered a wide spectrum of Canadian industrial life from groceries to garments.

The last thing that Bennett wanted was a man like Harry Stevens poking his nose into the failings of the free-enterprise system. Certainly the committee was not his idea. It came about as the result of happenstance. In January, the Prime Minister had asked Stevens to fill in for him at the annual convention of the Retail Shoe Merchants and Shoe Manufacturers' Association to be held in Toronto in the middle of the month.

No doubt he expected the usual platitudes – words of encouragement to the shoe men, forecasts that the Depression would soon be over and business conditions on the mend, praise of the individual enterprise of small business. What he got from Harry Stevens was something quite different – a diatribe against big business, notably chain and department stores, for using their immense buying power as a stick to crush the small entrepreneur and bring about sweatshop conditions.

Stevens hadn't planned it that way. His original speech was prepared three days before the convention. But after listening to three delegations representing small business, he tore it up. At the last minute, working until three in the morning before taking the train to Toronto, Stevens wrote a new speech that brought him roars of applause and a standing ovation. With one stroke, the maverick Tory lit the fuse that touched off an exhaustive investigation into wages, profits, and conditions in the Depression workplace. It led in the end to Stevens's break with Bennett, brought about the formation of a new political party, and contributed to the downfall of the Conservatives in the election that followed.

At fifty-five, Harry Stevens was not a typical Conservative. In a later day he would have been called a Red Tory. He was the only small businessman in a Cabinet controlled by big businessmen. He was also an outsider, a Westerner, not part of the Eastern establishment. He had been, variously, a grocer, an accountant, and a broker. Elected to five successive terms in Vancouver, he had bounced back from defeat in 1930 to win a by-election in the Kootenays. In his photographs he looks passive and plump, peering benignly through his rimless spectacles, but he was anything
238

but passive. A grocer's son, born in England, he was a Methodist lay preacher and reformer. He had represented a middle-class district for almost twenty years and had a distaste for the corporate world.

"The Conservative party's prospects for victory would be greatly enhanced if the dollar stamp were less pronounced and if a man's personal wealth were less used as the yardstick to measure his value," he had written in 1929. The following year, with the Tories in office, he had the temerity to suggest to Bennett that a council made up of representatives from the political, education, labour, and industrial fields be established to cope with the unemployment situation. The Prime Minister squashed that idea. "Why talk such nonsense," he said. "Do you think I want a lot of long-haired professors telling me what to do? If I can't run this country, I will get out."

Stevens had established himself as a muckraker in 1926 when, in a two-hour speech to the House of Commons, he had helped unravel the customs scandal that almost brought the Liberals down. His *bêtes noires* included Sir Joseph Flavelle, the business magnate who had controlled the Robert Simpson Company, and J.S. McLean, the president of Canada Packers. Both men were clearly very much in Stevens's mind when he prepared his speech to the shoe manufacturers.

Lurking in the background was the powerful figure of Warren K. Cook, a wealthy Toronto clothing manufacturer with a social conscience. A big, handsome, self-made man, Cook had worked his way up through the rag trade with a line of quality merchandise that he sold to a number of independent outlets. He believed in paying his employees a fair wage (he never had a strike) and in producing well-cut suits using good cloth. As a result he found himself in a cut-throat struggle with his competitors who thrived on sweatshop conditions. He had no love for the department stores that would not take his lines, preferring to sell suits of poorer quality for as low as fifteen dollars. Cook's prices started at twenty-nine fifty.

Cook was convinced that the large concerns were using their massive buying power to cut prices and to squeeze out small businesses that could no longer compete. The previous year, in his role as president of the Canadian Association of Garment Manufacturers, he had launched an investigation of conditions in

239

the men's clothing industry and had chosen two prominent radicals – Harry Cassidy of the University of Toronto and Frank Scott of McGill – to undertake it. These two men supplied Cook with the ammunition to pass on to Stevens, who admonished his audience "to face the evils that have developed like a canker. I warn them that unless they are destroyed they will destroy the system." Stevens went on to hit the large meat-packing firms, whose mark-ups were breathtaking; the farmer was paid a cent and a half a pound for beef, for example, for which the consumer was charged nineteen cents. Stevens praised the small businessmen of Canada, of whom he was one, and declared that "it will be a sorry day for Canada when these independent citizen-businessmen are crushed out."

Stevens's audience loved it; the big Toronto department stores didn't. The speech, which was heard on the radio, elicited a howl of protest from Eaton's and Simpson's. "Don't let the tremendous weight of advertising in the public press muzzle you," Stevens had told his audience. Some newspapers, he said, "dare not publish these things or denounce them, because of the advertising office receipts that make it impossible for them to talk." The truth of that charge was evident the following morning when the *Globe* gave its front page not to Stevens's speech but to denials by both Eaton's and Simpson's.

The department stores took their case to the Prime Minister, who called Stevens into his office and told him to cease and desist. Stevens immediately offered his resignation. Bennett back-pedalled. He had been snowed under by a blizzard of letters supporting his maverick colleague. With an election coming up the following year it was no time to have any minister – especially *this* minister – causing a minor scandal, running around the country claiming that Big Business had muzzled him.

Bennett gave Stevens and Cook what they wanted – a special parliamentary committee with Stevens as chairman to investigate mass buying practices by chain and department stores and labour conditions in industry and the baking and meat-packing fields. The press called it "the most sweeping parliamentary probe into industrial conditions ever attempted in Canada," and so it was.

The final report of the committee and that of the royal commission that succeeded it together run to 9,278 pages of small type or well over three million words. They provide the most

240

comprehensive picture we have of working conditions and wage rates in Central Canada in the early thirties. The committee was forthright in its criticisms. Of conditions in the needle trades it had this to say: "We cannot, in frankness, refrain from stating that the labour and wage conditions . . . are such as to merit the most emphatic condemnation. They should not be tolerated in any state that claims to call itself civilized. . . . The statistics . . . have shown us that the worker in the clothing industry can expect neither comfort nor security; in many cases he can, indeed, expect hopeless poverty."

The food chains also came under bitter condemnation: "Hours of labour . . . are longer than any worker should be asked to endure. They commonly exceed 60 hours per week and in many stores often reach as high as 80 to 84. . . . There is no excuse whatever for conditions such as these."

Day after day a regiment of horrible examples was paraded before the committee. In the tobacco industry, for example, where profits were high and wages below the subsistence level, company executives were rewarded with unbelievably fat salaries and bonuses. The president of Imperial Tobacco earned $25,000 a year plus annual bonuses ranging from $32,000 to $61,000. The company's twenty-four executives received an average of $15,000 a year. Yet the average weekly earnings of the tobacco worker were less than $11 for a 44.7-hour week. No wonder that Imperial was able to show an annual net profit of just under six million dollars.

The tobacco companies were obviously using the Depression as an excuse to cut wages. In one of the factories, hourly rates shrank by 24 per cent between 1931 and 1933. The president of Macdonald Tobacco, however, managed to scrape by on a mere $260,000 in salary and bonuses, still leaving the company an undivided profit of $594,432.

The five-and-dime stores – Woolworth's, Kresge's, Metropolitan – kept their employees on a tight leash by staggering hours and using part-time clerks. The women were kept on call, never knowing when they would be offered work and unable to look for other jobs. In the Metropolitan chain, these women clerks averaged a miserable $4.30 a week – less, in fact, than the value of relief payments in Toronto.

The excuse the five-and-dime executives gave for low wages was their inability to pay more, "much as they desired to." Yet one chain in Montreal declared an 80-per-cent stock dividend, while Woolworth's in 1932 showed a net profit of $1,800,000, every cent of which went back to head office in New York. That same year, thousands of Woolworth's Canadian employees were hit with a 10-per-cent wage reduction.

In those days, the minimum wage laws applied only to women. As a result, women lost out because so many employers preferred to hire men or boys at a lower rate. In Toronto, the National Picture Frame Company fired seventeen of its female employees and replaced them with men at rates as low as ten cents an hour.

The authorities neglected to enforce laws defining the legal work week for fear more discharged employees would be eligible for relief. The Ontario Factory Act, which dated back to 1884, called for a ten-hour working day and a sixty-hour work week. Yet even this antiquated piece of legislation, "a relic of the dark ages of industrialism," to quote Harry Cassidy, was ignored. In Toronto, at one Red Indian service station the work week was sixty-four hours, the pay a mere $5.55. A worse example came from the restaurant trade. A restaurant on Spadina Avenue paid its kitchen workers and waitresses wages as low as $6.25 for a work week that ran as high as *one hundred* hours.

In Quebec, the Minimum Wage Act was also contravened. Quebec employers were allowed occasional exemptions, and as the Depression deepened these exemptions increased dramatically – from only 94 in 1931 to 1,067 by 1933. Of the thirty-one establishments studied by Harry Cassidy for Warren K. Cook, twenty-four violated the act anyway. In all these shops more than 95 per cent of the women employees were receiving wages below standard. None dared complain for fear of being fired.

Wages in Toronto were low enough to give the committee members pause. A messenger boy at the famous engraving firm of Rapid Grip and Batten, for instance, was paid five dollars for a fifty-five-hour week. Yet this sum seems princely compared with the miserly sums doled out in the needle trades in French Canada. Cassidy shocked the committee with a series of examples, including the story of a nineteen-year-old girl in Ste Rose who earned two dollars for a fifty-five-hour week.

In effect, he said, bargain hunters in Toronto were living off the avails of sweated labour. "The suits we wear, many of them, have been made in sweatshops under disgraceful conditions," Cassidy reported. Then, in a dramatic flourish he produced sixteen weekly pay envelopes received by a woman working in a Toronto shop. Printed on each envelope was a pious admonition by the bank, preaching that thrift leads to financial independence:

> *Think of tomorrow*
> *Divide your pay in two*
> *Take what you need to live*
> *Put the balance in safety.*

Cassidy quietly pointed out that the weekly pay amounts in each envelope ranged between four and eight dollars.

Warren K. Cook appeared before the Stevens committee on March 8 to ride his particular hobby-horse. "Retailers were driven to desperation," he said, by a price-cutting war between Eaton's and Simpson's in the winter of 1932–33. Both stores were selling suits made in Montreal under sweatshop conditions. In most cases, the Toronto retailers simply ordered suits from a contractor in Quebec. He cut the cloth and then subcontracted the piecework to families in rural areas, who worked in their homes for a pittance. Again the committee heard evidence of exploitation.

Four women, with their husbands helping at night, managed together to turn out between two and a half and three dozen pairs of men's pants in a day. For this they were paid sixty cents a dozen, but five cents of that was deducted for thread. In short, each woman was earning little more than forty cents a day.

There were worse examples. A woman and her daughter managed to turn out a dozen boys' short pants in a day. For all that work the pair was paid a total of twenty-five cents. The middlemen made as much as the farm women, who toiled far into the night with needle and thread. One Montreal contractor subcontracted men's pants at eighty cents a dozen. The subcontractor turned the job over to rural housewives who received forty cents a dozen; the subcontractor pocketed the rest.

Under such conditions, Simpson's was able to pay as little as $13 for a man's suit and sell it for $16.95 – a price no other retailer except Eaton's could match – advertising that "Only Simpson's Could Produce a Sale Like This." That wasn't exactly true, since Simpson's was trying to catch up with Eaton's, which was already announcing unbelievable bargains. This predatory price cutting resulted in a 10-per-cent wage cut across the board

243

in all union shops in Toronto. Cook told the committee that "these two alleged bargains meant a reduction in wages to at least ten thousand people. As a result of these two special sales the standard of living of everybody engaged in the clothing business – whether as employers, employees or distributors, was definitely lowered and their purchasing power reduced."

In June it became the turn for scrutiny of the department stores, who had enjoyed continuing profits while cutting salaries and vacation time. Eaton's employees, for example, had already lost their annual paid vacations and seven of nine statutory holidays. The store's 25,000 employees were averaging a mere $970 in annual wages – well below the poverty line – while the company's forty directors averaged an annual $35,000. Stevens said he could not justify in his mind Simpson's "handsome mark-up . . . over 100 percent – yet women are working for $10 and $11 a week."

Cook's earlier evidence that the Toronto department stores were encouraging sweatshop conditions in Quebec was confirmed by a Clarkson, Gordon study. Among its examples was that of a Quebec shoe company that paid its employees wages averaging 12.9 cents an hour. It revealed that 70 per cent of this sweated product was purchased by department stores.

By this time Stevens was the man of the hour in Canada. His committee had given the Canadian public a series of lessons in the workings of the free-enterprise system. It had dominated the news since its first sitting. Both Eaton's and Simpson's had scrambled to increase their employees' wages. The tobacco firms had signed a three-year contract offering the farmers a guaranteed price. Two Montreal companies that had evaded the Quebec minimum wage laws paid four thousand dollars in compensation to their employees.

Letters of commendation poured into Stevens's office in Ottawa, many suggesting that he become the next leader of the Conservative party. That did not seem unlikely. It was rumoured that Bennett intended to quit before the next election and accept a British peerage (over the dead body of Neville Chamberlain, one might add).

But Parliament prorogued early in July, and that meant the committee would have to be dissolved. This was, of course, unthinkable. There was more to do, more evidence to be heard. Stevens hadn't even finished with the pesky department stores! He persuaded Bennett to allow the work to continue by turning the committee into a royal commission, again with himself as chairman. Bennett agreed. The new sessions were planned for the following autumn, but as it turned out, Harry Stevens – impulsive Harry, intrepid Harry, rash, imprudent Harry – would not be chairing it. The defender of small business was riding for a fall, and by the time the sessions resumed, the lance that had skewered the titans of industry would be bent, if not broken, and Harry Stevens's future clouded and obscure.

4

To John Diefenbaker, a budding but as yet unsuccessful Saskatchewan politician, "travelling south from the park land into the northern rim of the Palliser Triangle was like moving from the Garden of Eden to the Dead Sea." By the summer of 1934 the drought had transformed the southern sections of the three prairie provinces into a bleak Gobi, in which forty thousand families and half a million head of livestock struggled for survival. For them there was no escape from the hot dry winds, the black blizzards of dust, or the plagues of grasshoppers that chewed up every living piece of vegetation in their path. *The year of the locust*

Because of the warm weather, the grasshoppers hatched in May, almost two weeks earlier than usual and more thickly than ever before – more thickly even than in the dreadful summer of 1933, when they had destroyed all the coarse grain in Saskatchewan. They arrived when the stalks were still short, so that they were able to gobble up the new shoots quickly, and then, with their hunger still unsatisfied, move on, executing twenty-foot jumps on their springboard legs.

There were so many grasshoppers that there was not room enough for all of them on the ground at the same time. And they ate *everything*. Their mandibles were strong enough to strip the bark from the trees. They devoured lace curtains hung out to dry on clotheslines. One man claimed they even ate the rawhide laces in his boots. They invaded cities, covering the streets so that, it was said, to walk down the sidewalk in Regina was like trampling on a million peanut shells.

They could strip an entire farm in a day, blotting out the sky in their millions, their wings flashing in the sun. The stories of their numbers are awesome. One flight, trapped by a cold wind over Lake Winnipeg, fell into the water, drowned, and was washed ashore in the millions. Their bodies covered a twenty-mile strip of beach to a depth of several feet.

The farmers, however, had learned the lessons of the previous year and were ready to do battle. They fought the grasshoppers with a witch's brew of bran, sawdust, and sodium arsenate, and they did it on a well-organized scale, "easily the greatest thing of its kind ever seen in Canada," in the words of James Gray.

In Alberta, 15,000 farmers picked up 15,000 tons of the poisoned bait from eighty-nine mixing stations and spread it on their fields. In Saskatchewan, 1,097 emergency committees were organized and enough bait was mixed to cover twenty-two million acres. In this way two-fifths of the grain crop in the Palliser Triangle was saved from the insects.

Alas, there wasn't much of a grain crop to save. In some areas there was no crop at all. The drought, which had been moving north year by year from the southern United States, now struck with merciless fury. In Nebraska (where they kept statistics) the temperature soared to 110°F, breaking all records, while the humidity stood at a barely perceptible 3 per cent. In Canada (where they didn't keep statistics), it was certainly the hottest year prairie residents had known. The Winnipeg *Free Press*'s diligent Cora Hind, travelling southwest of Regina through the drought area on the last Sunday in May, described it as "absolutely the hottest and dirtiest day I have ever been on the road in more than 30 years of crop inspection." Hind wrote that from "Cadillac to Kincaid is a wilderness plain and simple, so far as the eye can reach on each side of the highway. Even Russian thistle seems, for a time at least, to have given up the struggle. Clouds of sharp sand strike you in the face while billows like the waves of the sea rolled on either side."

To Konrad Istrati, who farmed south of Moose Jaw, 1934 was the year that brought "the morale of the farmers down to rock bottom." No one had expected the drought to last this long. Surely this year the rains would return! But they didn't. Except for a three-inch fall in June, the summer was dry. A wry parody of "Beulah Land" made the rounds:

246

Oh, prairie land, great prairie land
Upon your burning soil I stand,
I look away across the plains
And wonder why it never rains.

The hot winds, travelling at speeds as high as fifty miles an hour, lashed at the soil. Filling the ditches and sloughs, covering fences, burying telephone poles for three-quarters of their height, the blowing soil, now fine as talcum, drifted across land newly abandoned by destitute farmers, covered the good loam, and smothered the newly seeded crops they had left behind. That was the year in which the prairie ritual of the summer agricultural fair had to be abandoned. How can you have an exhibition if there is nothing to exhibit?

There was no escape from the dust – the insidious, all-pervasive dust – that crept ghostlike into the tightest houses, seeping through cracks in doors or window frames or down chimneys until everything – furniture, carpets, bedspreads, window sills – was covered in a spectral mantle of grey powder. Konrad Istrati remembered an east-southeast wind that dimmed the sun for three days and covered a railway crossing and fence to within two inches of the top. When the wind changed, the great dunes shifted back to the opposite side of the crossing. In these "black blizzards," farmers had to quit their fields because "conditions weren't fit for man, beast or tractor." Starving cattle ate dirt and died from mudballs in their stomachs. And still the rain did not come.

But the hail did. In mid-July a series of hailstorms lashed the three prairie provinces, causing ten million dollars' worth of damage. Thousands of acres of wheat were shredded. Granaries were blown down, barns wrecked, horses killed. Thousands of turkeys, chickens, waterfowl, and rabbits were battered to death. Windows were shattered and telephone lines crushed as the winds whipped up to one hundred miles an hour. In one ninety-mile stretch between Stettler and Carstairs, Alberta, the hailstones lay in an eight-inch-thick solid belt before they melted.

Under such blows of nature, repeated year after year, men and women were broken. Isabel Brown was one of these. The Browns had endured a series of crop failures at their farm near Strathmore before they finally gave up in March and moved farther

247

north, to the vicinity of Camrose in the fertile belt. But it was too late for Mrs. Brown. By the time she made the candy for her six children she was clearly demented. The ingredients were cocoa, sugar, and a heavy dose of strychnine. Five didn't like the taste and mercifully rejected it after a nibble or two. But the littlest, Kenneth, ate his. "I've just poisoned all the children," Isabel Brown told her husband, Charles, when he came home a short time later. Then she locked herself in her bedroom. A doctor was called, and the five older children were successfully treated; but Kenneth was already in convulsions. "You'd better come out and say goodbye to Kenneth, he's dying," somebody called to Mrs. Brown. Silence. Then a rifle shot. A few minutes after his mother's body was found, Kenneth Brown was also dead – twin victims of those terrible times.

It seemed as if all the furies had descended upon the pioneers of the southern prairies. Most of them had come out in the years before the war, lured by the siren call of free land – from the smoky industrial cities of England, from the American midwest, from the steppes of southeastern Europe. They had struggled through the sod hut era, broken the impossibly tough ground, doggedly worked the land, improving their lot year by year until the rolling country was transformed by substantial homes and prosperous farms. In a single generation they had changed the face of the plains and provided a legacy for their sons and daughters, only to see that legacy wiped out. Everything they had struggled for had been turned to dust. By 1934, thousands like the Browns were ready to abandon all that they had worked for. In the Depression years, a quarter of a million people simply packed up and left the sullen desert of the triangle.

Etha Munro's family was one of these. Her father lost his farm, first to the winds, then to the creditors. They lived for a time on relief handouts – dried beans, flour, dried apples, occasionally made tolerable by gifts from Eastern Canada (Etha would always remember the thrill of delight when they received a quart jar of preserved cherries). Etha's clothes were made from flour sacks, and she would never forget one "frock" on which the words "Quaker Flour" were faintly but indelibly stencilled. How she hated that dress! Her mother scrubbed it and dyed it, but the telltale trademark in its familiar circle never vanished.

248

By that time, the neighbours were all talking of a new promised land far away across the north – Peace River, Meadow Lake, Carrot River. Finally, in 1934, Etha's parents decided that they, too, would pack up. They had lived in the same place since 1909. Now they were fleeing with no particular destination in mind – just north to some place better. They loaded what they could take onto wagons. Etha's brother, on horseback, drove the cattle, and the dog, Towser, scampered behind.

They drove north through the desert, the road in places so badly drifted with sand and dirt they were forced to detour. Etha would always remember the sight of men working in a cemetery where the headstones had been completely covered, trying to remove the drifting soil. At last their trek ended somewhere between Biggar and North Battleford. "That country looked good to us, in fact almost like heaven after what we had left." It was, of course, not the end of hard times. But it was a new beginning.

Like Etha Munro's family, almost everybody in the drought country was on relief or in debt. What was there to stay for? Few could pay their taxes, which were often five years in arrears, even though municipalities were offering discounts as high as 20 per cent to those who did pay up. Schools were closing because there was no money to buy coal to heat the rooms or pay the teachers, or because the children had neither shoes nor clothing to wear to class. It was estimated that it would take thirty million dollars to bring clothing needs up to pre-Depression standards.

With the schools half empty, who was there to support education? In one district there were only seven ratepayers; the rest had fled, like the Munros. The teachers themselves were on relief, their payments in arrears even though their salaries had been cut in half. The municipality gave them IOUs, but they couldn't get cash or credit for these, even at a 50-per-cent discount. As one rural inspector reported that year, "teachers, although they have struggled on without complaint, are beginning to show the effects of the fight in their morale, in their attitude and general outlook on life." It was the same with the doctors: those who stayed often worked for nothing. But only those people who were seriously ill sought medical aid. It was no surprise when, after the Depression ended, Saskatchewan was the first jurisdiction on the continent to establish universal medicare.

Yet the drought was the great untold story of the early Depression years, especially in the East. The Toronto *Star* could send Gordon Sinclair to New Guinea, but it made no attempt to send a reporter through the Canadian dust bowl. In mid-September, however, two prairie newspapermen, D.B. MacRae, editor of the Regina *Leader-Post*, and R.M. Scott, assistant agricultural editor of the Winnipeg *Free Press*, following in Cora Hind's footsteps, set out to make a thorough study of drought conditions in Saskatchewan and Manitoba. They travelled for two thousand miles, and their findings, published in a series of fourteen articles in the Sifton newspapers and reprinted in the East, left no doubt of the severity of conditions in the southern parts of both provinces.

A Chinese restaurant owner in Fillmore, Saskatchewan, summed it all up in two sentences: "No crop, no garden, no oats, no potatoes, no feed. Nothing of everything." That was no exaggeration. Districts such as Shaunavon where farms had once produced forty bushels of wheat to the acre now produced ten. Others – Loomis was one – produced as little as two. In some districts, 95 per cent of the population was on relief; there were even areas where it was 100 per cent. Southeast of Assiniboia, in an area known as "no crop country," the two reporters found a district where every man but one was on relief. They wanted to know the reason for the exception. "I guess he's had no luck yet," came the sardonic reply.

At Big Beaver and Buffalo Gap, close to the U.S. border, even the kitchen gardens had failed. One man told the pair that his children had tasted no vegetables except potatoes for two years; and there were places where even potatoes didn't grow. Clothing was so old it was literally falling apart. One farmer talked wryly of the "patching of old clothes with clothes already patched only to find the garment has given way somewhere else." In a small-town hotel the towels were so thin that one reporter put his nose through one while trying to dry his face. Everything, in fact, from farm equipment to kitchen utensils, was wearing out and could not be replaced. No new farm machinery had been purchased for at least four years. Tractors had been repaired to the point where they ceased to work. Horse collars wore out, and those that survived were too large for horses grown thin on a diet of Russian thistle. Teakettles had long since been replaced by lard pails. Sheets of cardboard made do for broken windows. Two young

250

girls had a single dress to wear to school on alternate days; the other stayed home.

When MacRae and Scott visited Tribune, thirty miles south of Weyburn, they found a semi-ghost town. Once it was a substantial community, the centre of a prosperous farming district. Its shops were now vacant, the windows nailed shut, the people gone, and scarcely a scrap of crop was to be found. "Russian thistle," they wrote, "blankets the whole country like a quilt."

By autumn the drought country was faced with the overwhelming problem of keeping the livestock over the winter. In autumn, thousands of animals would have to be sold at rock-bottom prices, but there was no help for that. Yet some cattle would be needed over the winter for milk and some horses for farm labour. One municipality with 320 farm families figured it would have to retain two thousand milk cows and twenty-seven hundred horses; three thousand head of cattle would have to be sold. The federal government and the railways, belatedly aware of the dimensions of the problem, offered to split the cost with the municipalities of shipping livestock out of the drought area.

Fodder would have to be imported – a superhuman task, since each municipality would require something close to ten thousand tons to tide it over until spring. Some districts, such as Alameda and Oxbow, sent crews grubstaked by the province north to seek out fodder. Since each man could bale little more than one hundred tons a week, a winter's hard work was needed to find, bale, and ship south enough straw to feed the stock left behind. By mixing the straw with crushed Russian thistle and a little crushed wheat, the farmers hoped to stretch out their meagre supply of grain.

By the time they arrived, Scott and MacRae found few farmers planning to "skip out," to use the common phrase, simply because there was no place left for them to go. The earlier emigrants from the dust bowl had taken all the good land available as far north as the Peace River. Indeed, notices were posted warning people to stay out of Manitoba and Alberta. No relief would be made available to migrants.

Those who stayed still retained that quality of optimism that is the hallmark of the pioneer. Without it, the West would never have been settled. The two reporters ran across it again and again in their travels. Good times, the people said (echoing the politi-

251

cians), were just around the corner. As one farmer put it, "We're bent but not broken." The land was good; the soil was rich; it had produced excellent crops in the past; it would do it again. All that was needed was rain – and that would come. Surely, people said, they had reached the nadir of the drought cycle. This was the worst year yet; things could only improve.

But 1934 was not the worst year. The men in their tattered overalls, the women and children in their flour-sack dresses, surviving on potatoes and dried grains, their throats as parched as the grey land around them – these last holdouts could not know that there was a worse year to come, and it was still three years away.

5

Pep, There are certain manic spectacles that at their moment in his-
ginger, tory attract the enthusiasm and even the applause of the public
and and yet, in later years, take on the trappings of high comedy. In
Mitch retrospect, the pageantry that briefly excited the city of Toronto on August 27, 1934, falls into that category. On that morning, a jostling crowd of eight thousand jammed Varsity Stadium to witness an unlikely event.

Varsity Stadium had been transformed into a used-car lot! There they were for all to see, lined up at the end of the gridiron – eighty-seven fancy automobiles, all polished to a high gloss, ready to be knocked down to the highest bidder. Here was the very cream of the auto makers' art: Packard limousines, Chevrolet coupés, Buick touring cars, Dodge sedans, Cadillacs, Fords, and Studebakers, some almost brand-new, others with as many as 200,000 miles on their odometers, most equipped with one or other – or all – of the mechanical gimmicks of the times: "turret tops," "free wheeling," "knee action."

These were, of course, not ordinary second-hand cars. The users had been Cabinet ministers and senior civil servants in the now discredited provincial Conservative government. The new Liberal premier, Mitchell Hepburn, was keeping an election promise and selling them all off by auction.

Hepburn had promised the taxpayers that they would no longer have to pay through the nose to watch Conservative lackeys riding around in upholstered limousines. "If we are elected," he had told a cheering crowd in Midland in May, "we are going to line up all the limousines at Queen's Park and sell them to the highest bidder." It was a seductive pledge and an easy one to fulfil (though some of Hepburn's opponents wondered aloud if the Premier and his Cabinet colleagues intended to ride around Queen's Park on bicycles).

Now, on an unseasonably cool August morning, the crowd was shoving its way into the stadium to see Mitch Hepburn make good on his promise – some to seek bargains in used cars but most to take part in what the irrepressible Gordon Sinclair called "a combination three-ring circus, medicine show and deputation of protest."

That last phrase told the story. Hepburn, the young onion farmer from Elgin County, had chosen the cheapest and most flamboyant way of telling his Depression-ridden flock that he would countenance no lavish spending at a time when thousands were on the dole. He would not only sell the cars, he would fire the lieutenant-governor and close his official residence at Chorley Park. That might offend the blue bloods, but to the man on the street, the idea of a minor functionary living lavishly on the taxpayers' money in a miniature castle while laying cornerstones or attending garden parties had a whiff of the British class system about it. "There will be no more Lieutenant-Governors in this Province until we get out of the present period of Depression," Hepburn had shouted on the hustings, and again the crowd cheered.

The crowd at Varsity Stadium was impatient. Long before the announced start of the auction, thousands began clamouring for it to begin. Hundreds, fearful of missing a bargain, crowded the runways, overflowed onto the playing field, and swarmed around the auctioneers' truck, where the veteran Tommy Ryan stood, immaculate in white kid gloves and tan topcoat.

"You're all going to be put off the field, boys," Ryan warned. "You might as well get seats in the grandstand now while you've got the chance."

"Who are you?" demanded an elderly Torontonian, hanging on to his spot.

"Oh, I'm nobody," said Ryan, laughing.

The retort that followed suggested the strength of Hepburn's populism and the disenchantment with George Henry's Depression government. "That's just it. You don't run this province. The people of Ontario run this province now."

At last, Ryan's superior arrived in the person of the leather-lunged T. Merritt Moore of Aylmer, a personal friend of the new premier. Moore took off his hat and waved to the crowd as Ryan introduced him.

"Gentlemen," said Moore, ignoring the distaff side, "I am speaking on behalf of the people of the province of Ontario. I want you people to co-operate in making this the most unique [*sic*] auction sale that has ever been held." By now the crowd was cheering itself hoarse, drowning out Moore's further words.

"Sell the cars!" the people screamed, as Moore tried to launch into a political speech.

Moore continued to try to speak. Again the crowd drowned him out, and Moore finally gave in and signalled for the first automobile. It rolled slowly up the field, nosing its shiny way through the mob and onto a specially built ramp in front of the stands: George Henry's seven-thousand-dollar Packard, glittering with chrome.

The crowd went wild as Moore shouted: "This is the outstanding car in the province of Ontario. You will be proud to tell your grandchildren you bought the first government car sold at public auction – the car of Premier Henry."

"Ex-Premier!" shouted several members of the crowd, as the bidding got under way.

Schwartz the Wrecker was outbid by J.E. Montgomery of Mount Dennis, who paid fifteen hundred dollars for the Henry car. The terms were strictly cash – 25 per cent down, the rest in ten days (a finance company had already set up shop in the stadium). Some people tried to proffer cheques as the auction progressed and were turned away, angry. When Tommy Ryan tried to explain that this was an auction and not a fire sale he was roundly booed.

Car after car went quickly under the hammer, the limousines of the eleven Cabinet ministers first – some at bargain prices (a Buick listed at $1,400 went for $1,000) and some at inflated rates (a Studebaker valued at $100 sold for $255). In the end the government realized about $34,000 from the sale, but the publicity was worth far more than that to the cherubic, blue-eyed young

254

man who had galvanized the province with his oratory during the election campaign and was now firmly in charge in Ontario.

Hepburn's election that summer completed the Conservative rout at the provincial level and in Ottawa must have been seen as a portent of things to come in the federal arena. The Depression had doomed the hidebound Tory governments. In British Columbia the year before, a newly energized Liberal party had swept into power under another florid populist, T. Dufferin Pattullo. In Saskatchewan, James Gardiner, the tough little farmer whom everybody called Jimmy, had vaulted back into the premiership he had lost in 1929. That victory, coming on the same night as Hepburn's, meant that there wasn't a Tory government in any Canadian province west of the Maritimes.

Hepburn was just thirty-seven when he roared into office with the greatest Liberal majority in history, defeating a government that had previously boasted the greatest *Conservative* majority in history. That spectacular switch in political loyalties underlined the obvious truth that the voters wanted someone to do something about the Depression. Hepburn had promised just that, but he would have to do more than conduct a frivolous used-car sale in a football stadium. He had been rocketed into office by a desperate populace seeking a saviour and a spokesman. Now he would have to deliver.

He was a farmer turned politician who had followed in the footsteps of his father, another farmer turned politician. Hepburn Senior had been forced to withdraw from a 1906 by-election over some murky charges of personal scandal that drove him first to St. Paul, Minnesota, and then to Winnipeg before the family returned to Ontario. Young Mitch was only ten at the time. At sixteen he quit school to become a bank clerk and at nineteen he went to work on the farm of his grandfather, the bulk of whose $150,000 estate he inherited in 1922 – a legacy equal to more than one million dollars today.

By 1925, the wealthy young man was up to his elbows in politics, known as the best stump speaker in Elgin West riding, which elected him its federal Liberal member the following year. It is a tribute to his platform abilities that he managed to become the first Liberal to win that seat in thirty years. In the 1930 election he increased his majority eightfold and was judged a comer.

Mackenzie King did not care much for him, and when the brash newcomer took a shot at the provincial leadership in the fall of 1930, the strait-laced federal leader was very much opposed. Hepburn ran with a fast, hard-drinking crowd, and that was certainly not King's kind of crowd. But Hepburn won, and in his acceptance speech he set the tone of his regime: "I go forward as Ontario leader filled with optimism. I know I am going to succeed. . . . I'll supply the pep and ginger and you people hold the brakes. And we will never stop until we get to Queen's Park."

By the time the election was called in 1934, Hepburn was ready with the pep and ginger. "It's good politics," he had said, somewhat cynically, "to give a hand to the majority." The majority at that point was composed of those who had been felled by the Depression. "Get this fact," Hepburn told the voters. "We are in this thing because of the little fellow, the workman who isn't working anymore, the farmer who is struggling against unbelievable odds. I've seen these people, talked to them, you can't credit their situation. We're in this thing because of them and for them." And then, borrowing the Rooseveltian phrase that had caught the imagination of the continent: "There is going to be a new deal in this province."

It is doubtful that without the Depression as a spur Hepburn would have swept the province as he did. The good, grey voters of Ontario were not in the habit of falling for flashy leaders. But the times favoured Hepburn, and George Henry – as good and grey a politician as ever held office in Queen's Park – was no match for the dynamic young man with a face like a polished apple who inflamed the voters and managed by verbal gymnastics to make the Henry regime seem responsible for the hard times. It's probable that without the Hepburn glitter, without the pep and ginger, the Liberal party might not even have won a majority. All across the Far West, it was plain that the public had become fed up with stiff, hidebound, do-nothing politicians. Like Pattullo, Aberhart, Gardiner, and eventually Maurice Duplessis in Quebec, Hepburn was the antithesis of that image.

In Ottawa, as the returns poured in, a private farce was being enacted. Mackenzie King should have been overjoyed at the Liberal sweep in Ontario. Instead he felt "an anguish of mind and heart" – not over Hepburn, whom he had come to accept, and not because of the Liberal victory, which every Grit in the country was hailing as a forecast of great things to come. No; King's anguish of heart came because he felt he had been betrayed by the ghost of Wilfrid Laurier. That fickle shade had predicted, quite wrongly as it now turned out, that Hepburn would not gain a majority and would, indeed, lose his seat.

The ghost of the great Laurier *wrong* about an election? How could it be? King was hurt and baffled. He tried to puzzle it out in his diary. Clearly, Laurier "had not the knowledge evidently required and had seen only so much of the whole," he reasoned. He was not recording any feeling of disloyalty to the spectre of his hero; he was quite convinced that it was the voice of Laurier that had spoken to him across the void. Still, it was puzzling.

At last King came to rationalize this egregious error as fervent and faithful Christians rationalize the sudden, inexplicable death of a young child. "I felt it was all for a purpose, that behind this disappointment . . . there was some great good which I would soon see, that God was helping me to get a clearer vision of His laws and ways and purposes, that it was all to help me in an understanding of psychic phenomena, and spiritual realities."

Yet it continued to prey on his mind. He phoned his congratulations to Hepburn but remained "sick at heart," fearing that Laurier's ghostly failure might sow the seeds of doubt in his own mind. But then he rallied, feeling "that my faith was strong if not stronger than ever, that behind all this seeming shattering of our belief lay the understanding of a larger & truer belief, & a greater revelation of Reality."

King came to the conclusion that the vagrant spirits with whom he held intercourse were "still earthbound to some degree," that their vision might be limited and not wholly to be trusted. Perhaps, too, he told himself, Laurier's lapse was meant to teach him that God alone could reveal truths that related to the future. With the matter off his mind, the exhausted Liberal leader went to bed.

Hepburn, of course, had no qualms about anything. Totally confident and self-assured, he plunged into a series of highly visible "reforms." Every civil servant appointed since the previous October was fired, causing both consternation and chaos at Queen's Park. Cabinet ministers' salaries were cut by two thousand dollars. Work was stopped on the new Ontario Hydro building in Toronto (but only temporarily). The provincial display at the Canadian National Exhibition was cancelled. Chorley Park was closed, as promised, but Hepburn found that constitutionally it was not possible to rid himself of its occupant. Ontario House in London was also closed and a variety of boards and commissions were either abolished or amalgamated. Every game warden in the province was dismissed, not to mention 183 beekeepers, an intriguing piece of cheese-paring that undoubtedly caught the public's fancy. That fall Hepburn turned up on the hustings to work for the federal Liberals in five by-elections, helping his party to a net gain of two.

By this time he was close to exhaustion. The job of being premier was far more exacting than he had thought. Political leadership took more out of a man than onion farming, especially if the man had had only two years of high school and very little administrative experience. It was stimulating to be a maverick; it was quite another thing to run a province the size of Ontario in the midst of an economic crisis.

Mackenzie King's advice to Hepburn was to conserve his energies and avoid all social engagements. He might as well have counselled him to join a Trappist monastery. Instead, the gregarious premier bought himself some light clothing and with a couple of his supporters left the chill winds of Ontario for a midwinter cruise among the sunny islands of the Caribbean. For a couple of weeks the province could run without him.

6

The With the first sittings of the new Royal Commission on Price
Pang Spreads scheduled for October 30, its putative chairman was in
of a deep political trouble. Harry Stevens had given his name to the
Wolf earlier parliamentary committee. He was supposed to head its
successor and complete his work. But he had made a political blunder, and there was no way he could shake off that stigma.

It all stemmed from a speech that the impulsive minister had made just before the session broke up in June. His audience was the Conservative Study Club, whose members were undoubtedly eager to see the man being touted as their future leader in action. It was an informal occasion; Stevens spoke without notes, but a secretary took down his words verbatim. These included an at-
258

tack on the Robert Simpson Company and Sir Joseph Flavelle, Stevens's old enemy, who had at one time been the department store's chief stockholder.

Stevens claimed that Flavelle and his associates, after a refinancing in 1928, had stripped the company of ten million dollars, leaving it heavily mortgaged. As a consequence of this higher overhead, he said, Simpson's was forced to pressure its suppliers to sell for less, thus creating some of the sweatshop conditions that had been revealed by his inquiry.

That August the roof fell in on Stevens. His words, supposedly off the record and certainly off the cuff, had been printed in pamphlet form, of which three thousand copies were distributed. The Toronto *Star* and *Ottawa Citizen* (neither of them Tory organs) published excerpts. The Winnipeg *Free Press* published the pamphlet in full, frustrating R.B. Bennett's attempts to suppress it. C.L. Burton, president of Simpson's, threatened to sue Stevens for libel.

Stevens had broken an unwritten rule. He had revealed some of the committee's findings before its report was published. In the five federal by-elections that took place in Ontario that September, the Stevens pamphlet became an issue. Mackenzie King lambasted the minister for not quitting the Cabinet and fighting for his principles. "But no," said King, "Mr. Stevens is going to be chairman of the Commission." The Tories lost four of the by-elections, prompting the Montreal *Gazette* to question Stevens's role in the campaign.

With his twenty-three-year-old daughter, Sylvia, seriously ill in Montreal, Stevens was now the focus of a Cabinet attack led by two St. James Street spokesmen, C.H. Cahan and Sir George Perley. Cahan, the corporate lawyer, had an axe to grind in attacking Stevens, for his client was Sir Charles Gordon, head of the Dominion Textile Company, and the Stevens inquiry had certainly blackened that industry.

Now Cahan demanded that Stevens publicly apologize to Flavelle, and not without reason, for Stevens, in his attack, had some of his facts wrong. Among other things, Simpson's mark-up on goods had not increased since 1929; in fact, it had slightly declined. Nor had Flavelle siphoned off the profits in quite the unprincipled way Stevens had implied. Apologize or resign! Cahan insisted. With his daughter close to death, Harry Stevens, the giant-killer, resigned not only from the Cabinet but also from the chairmanship of the royal commission.

He continued, however, to dominate the inquiry, whose new chairman was a lawyer and a strong Tory, William Walker Kennedy, M.P. for Winnipeg South Centre. Stevens also carried his cause to the people in a series of speeches demanding government action on his committee's findings. The Tory party now seemed split down the middle, with the Liberal papers gleefully supporting Stevens and the Conservative press upholding Bennett.

Cahan continued to twist the knife, sneering at "political and social propagandists, blind leaders of the blind." Everybody knew who *that* meant. The Montreal lawyer kept insisting that the federal government was not equipped to regulate industry and went on to pooh-pooh reports of hunger, malnutrition, and starvation. In a remarkable statement in Montreal on November 27, Cahan claimed that he had seen many depressions when people were reduced to eating porridge and oatmeal scones and the boys and girls of those times had grown up just as healthy as they were doing under the higher standards of the present. "This Depression will go like the mist before the summer sun," said Cahan.

Stevens countered, on December 3, by announcing that he intended to press in Parliament for a federal trade and industries commission with "unprecedented powers" and that he would also urge that the Combines Investigation Act be toughened up. By now he was being widely touted as the successor to Bennett, who was considering retirement. Bennett promptly changed his mind, and there is little doubt that the wave of support for Stevens spurred that decision. Two days later, the Prime Minister headed off his erstwhile opponent by announcing that he would lead the Conservative party in the next election. More, he promised that the royal commission would continue its work, that his government would shortly introduce unemployment insurance, and that it would "come more and more to regulate business."

These were remarkable proposals for Bennett to make. They suggested a change of political direction, a move away from the right wing, dominated by men like Cahan, toward the centre or – dared one suggest it? – to the left.

What had caused this startling about-face by a man whose political philosophy had to this moment been as inflexible and unyielding as the banded gneisses of the Precambrian shield? The new and unaccustomed mantle that the Prime Minister was preparing to don was woven from a skein of threads that had come together by the end of 1934. There was, of course, the prices inquiry with its startling testimony. There was the presence of a new party of the Left, prepared to fight the coming election in as many constituencies as it could enter. There were the Liberal sweeps in three provinces, the threat of Social Credit in a fourth, the federal by-elections, and the example of Roosevelt's experiments in the United States, which had so excited William Herridge, Canadian minister to Washington. All these were factors.

One would like to believe, too, that Bennett himself had been softened in his outlook, that his best instincts had come forward as the result of the mountain of mail he was receiving – pleading letters, many of them agonizing, written from the depths by victims of the Depression whose awkward, ungrammatical, and often painful prose attested to the authenticity of their plight.

One cannot discount the power of these letters, which the Prime Minister had been receiving and reading for more than four years. The cumulative effect of these cries from the heart, like the constant drip-drip of a leaky tap, must have had some influence on the rigid mind-set of the man at the top. Being Bennett, he read them all personally and replied to many. Clearly, they troubled his conscience, for he often responded by enclosing a two-dollar or a five-dollar bill or, as in the case of Mrs. Thomas Hodgins of Perdue, Saskatchewan, ordering from Eaton's a set of high-grade, heavyweight Wolsey underwear for an ailing husband. "I have patched & darned his old underware [*sic*] for the last two years, but they are completely done now," Mrs. Hodgins wrote; "if you cant do this, I really dont know what to do. . . . We seem to be shut out from the world altogether we have no telephone Radio or newspaper."

Taken together the letters to Bennett provide a unique picture of the abject conditions in Canada in the early thirties. No other account of those desperate days, either scholarly or journalistic, can compare with the words of the victims, written not through the haze of hindsight but at the very moments of their despair.

Here is W.P.P. Hamel, a painter and decorator from Sherbrooke, Quebec, signing himself a "disheartened man" (out of work for six months, unable to pay his rent), explaining to his Prime Minister that the municipality has refused him relief: "Today I whent to get 3$ to keep us for a week and Mr. Valcourt of the City Office said I couldn't get it because someone said we had a radio: We have never had a radio: He send Mr. Lesseau from the City Office to search our home from top to bottom bedrooms and bathroom under and over: Then he says he don't have to give us help if he dont want to: I ask you Sir 'who was this money given to and what for'? is it for a man to crawl on his hands and knees to get a loaf for his family? I ask you Sir how do you think we live on $3 a week and can't get that because people make up a lie: What sort of a country have we . . . ?"

The reeve of one Alberta community enclosed a letter from Charles O'Brien, a Great War veteran, who announced that he was withdrawing his eight-year-old boy from school because "he is not getting enough nourishment to permit of his being able to study, and furthermore we have no soap to wash him or ourselves, or any of our clothes." O'Brien bitterly recalled an earlier promise by Bennett, who had pledged that "no man who has served his country in the war should want for food, shelter or fuel."

"We have done all we can to be decent, honorable, and to raise our family to be a credit to the country but what's the use," wrote Louise Elliott, a despairing farm wife in Milton, Ontario. " . . . today, if it were to save my life, I could not find one cent in the place. We own a note at the Bank for $150, and one would imagine from the fuss that is made over it, that it was $150,000. The worry of all these things is driving me mad."

Elsie Sproule of Oil Springs, Ontario, asked Bennett for money to help her father, John Thomas Sproule, Conservative member for Lambton East and the son of a former Speaker of the House. Sproule had lost so much money he couldn't keep up the interest on his bank loan. "I fear the worry is too great for him to bear," she wrote, "and I am afraid of him committing suicide." She asked for fifty thousand dollars. Bennett didn't send it, but he did send three dollars to Ruby Schultz, a little girl in Leney, Saskatchewan, who asked him to write to Santa Claus "and tell him I was a good girl all the time. . . . Daddy has no money to give Santa for my little brother and me and we can't hang our stockings up. . . . "

262

More than one correspondent threw back at Bennett his careless pledge that the government would see to it that no one in Canada would starve. "You stated that there would be no one starve in Canada," Clarence Ferguson of Winnipeg reminded him. "I presume you mean not starve overnight but slowly, our family amongst thousands of others are doing the same slowly and slowly. Possibly you have never felt the Pang of a Wolf. Well become a Father have children then have them come to you asking for a slice of bread between meals and have to tell them to wait. Wait until five of humanity's humans sleep all in one room no larger than nine feet square with one window in it. . . . "

Adam Armeny, who had been farming in Alberta for thirty years, wrote that he was "frantic with despair." He had been forced to come to Calgary to get hospital treatment for his wife, who was suffering from cancer, but because the couple didn't have a year's residence, he was turned down for relief. It took "courage of the bravest kind to ask for relief," he told Bennett. "I have been humiliated and sent from pillar to post, just as if I were a criminal or something."

Mrs. J.C. Bishop described how her family existed in a two-room shack in Tisdale, Saskatchewan. "Just enough room for two beds & the house is cold theres two inches of Ice freezes on the water in the house cold nights we are shivering in bed at night we have no mattresses on our beds only gunny Sacks & not enough blankets on our beds. Mr. Bishop has no underwear no top shirt no Socks only rags on his feet no trousers only overauls & they are done for, boots are near don my Self I have no house dresses & no wash tub. . . . there are times we live on potatoes for days at a time . . . I don't see how much longer it can last . . . there are a good meny people the same in this town I am five months pregnant & haven't even felt life yet to my baby & its I feel quite sure from lack of food. there has been many babys died in this town from neglect. . . . "

"I hear you are going to destroy some thousands of tons of wheat to get rid of it; while my family & stock are starving to death," J.L. Sullivan wrote from Leoville, Saskatchewan, on March 31, 1934. "There is lots of wheat and other things here but I have no money to buy them with. . . . We have kept off relief as long as we had a cent to buy food or a rag of clothes that would hang together. To date we have had $45.35 for food to feed ten of

263

us from Dec. 1st on until now and I did relief bridge work to about that amount. . . . But when I asked for a greater food allowance I was told that many were doing with much less as well as one insult upon another added thereto by the local relief officer. . . . We have to live ten of us in a cold one roomed shack. . . . We haven't even a mattress or even a tick just simply have to sleep on a bit of straw and nearly every night we have to almost freeze because we haven't bed clothes . . . the whole family have some kind of rash and running sores & I cannot take them to a Dr. as I have not the price to pay the Dr. or to buy the things that he would order. Also my wife has become badly ruptured and I cannot have anything done about it. . . . "

Of all the letters that Bennett received, perhaps the most touching came from a young woman named Jean McLean, for it illustrates how the cycle of unemployment was compounded for many young people by poor nourishment or lack of clothing. It became more and more difficult for any job seeker to be thought of as employable when her dress was shabby and her constitution weak from lack of food.

Jean McLean worked as a stenographer-bookkeeper for a firm in Essex County, Ontario. When it folded in 1934, she went to Hamilton looking for work and found none. As she told Bennett, " . . . my clothing became very shabby. . . . Many prospective employers just glanced at my attire and shook their heads and more times than I care to mention I was turned away without a trial. I began to cut down on my food and I obtained a poor, but respectable room at $1 per week. First I ate three very light meals a day; then two and then one. During the past two weeks I have eaten only toast and drunk a cup of tea every other day. In the past fortnight I have lost 20 pounds and the result of this deprivation is that I am so very nervous that I could never stand a test with one, two or three hundred girls. Through this very nervousness I was ruled out of a class yesterday. Today I went to an office for an examination and the examiner just looked me over and said: 'I am afraid Miss, you are so awfully shabby I could never have you in my office.'

"I was so worried and frightened that I replied somewhat angrily: 'Do you think clothes can be picked up in the streets?'

" 'Well,' he replied, with aggravating insolence, 'lots of girls find them there these days.'

264

"Mr. Bennett, that almost broke my heart. Above everything else I have been very particular about my friends and since moving here I have never gone out in the evening, I know no one here personally and the loneliness is hard to bear, but, oh, sir, the thought of starvation is driving me mad! . . .

"Day after day I pass a delicatessen and the food in the window looks oh, so good! So tempting and I'm so hungry!

"Yes, I am very hungry and the stamp that carries this letter to you will represent the last three cents I have in the world yet before I will stoop to dishonour my family, my character or my God, I will drown myself in the Lake. . . . "

There is no evidence that Bennett replied; and yet the hardest heart could not remain unaffected by these anguished pleas. Nor could Bennett escape the rueful reminders from some of his correspondents that they had voted for him in the belief that he could solve the country's economic problems. "Mr. Bennett, it was my vote that helped to put you where you are now," G.J. Steeves of Campbellton, New Brunswick, reminded him. "Is there anything you can do for me?" A crippled sixty-year-old, Steeves was the sole support of a family of five, unable to get help from a Maritime municipality as destitute as himself. How could the Prime Minister not have felt a sense of helplessness? What could he really do for this man with a crippled leg and a missing hand? What could he do for the Sherriff family of Montreal, who were being thrown out of their lodgings because the landlord refused to rent to the unemployed? Fred Sherriff's two daughters had been under a doctor's care for a year and a half. The doctor told him they needed better food. But how could they afford better food with the miserable dole offered by the city of Montreal?

Bennett had ridden into power believing he could solve the country's problems by adopting new trade and tariff policies. It hadn't worked, and in spite of his stubbornness, he was being forced to admit it. For more than four years he had tried to massage the body politic with his own brand of unction. Yet however optimistic his forecasts, he had been driven to retreat, step by step, from his personal and political philosophy. He had said he would never countenance the dole, but the dole had long since arrived. He had said that no one would starve, but here before him in the wobbly handwriting of ordinary Canadians was

265

all the evidence needed that people *were* starving. He had sworn that his government would never establish a system of unemployment insurance, yet here he was in the dying days of 1934 promising that very thing.

The Prime Minister could not entirely escape the importunings of his brother-in-law Bill Herridge, who was also conspiring to soften the Bennett line. Herridge, a son of the parsonage, outlined his own philosophy in the presence of both Bennett and Mackenzie King when he told the Ottawa Canadian Club on December 16: "... if we looked more to spiritual leadership and less to capitalistic leadership; if we made business less our religion and religion more our business; if we proclaimed by deeds the eternal truths of the Christian faith, we might find that this system did not work so badly after all."

Like Stevens, Herridge was what would today be called a Red Tory, though no Tory in the thirties would have wanted the dreadful adjective "Red" applied to his political philosophy. Stevens himself was not in Ottawa to listen to Herridge's message. He was at his daughter's side in Montreal. When she died on December 21, friends and foes of every political stripe extended their sympathy – with one exception. Harry Stevens did not hear from Richard Bedford Bennett. The Prime Minister was done with Stevens. Determined at last to make an about-turn in his political program, he was far too busy to concern himself with the personal agony of an old and increasingly bitter rival. Within a few days, without any prior consultation, he would drop the first of several bombshells on his unsuspecting Cabinet colleagues.

7

Slave By the end of the year, it ought to have been clear to those in
camps power that General McNaughton's much-vaunted relief camp program had become a political liability. McNaughton knew it but wouldn't admit it, though his own statistics suggested that the plan was in a shambles. For one ten-month period, between June 1933 and March 1934, the Department of National Defence reported no fewer than fifty-seven disturbances in the 120-odd camps across the country.

266

In the months that followed the situation became more tense. Complaints and mutinies grew to the point where, in defiance of every democratic principle, the government actually considered confining the troublemakers to barbed-wire enclosures in isolated regions. Anybody who refused to take a job or refused to work at a relief camp could be sentenced to as much as sixty days' hard labour at these "Camps of Discipline."

Although the plan was never carried out, an order-in-council designed to establish such camps had actually been drawn up the previous year under the "peace, order and good government" clause in the Relief Act. As was so often the case in that turbulent decade, ordinary British justice was dispensed with. The only evidence needed to imprison an "agitator" would be a certificate from the relief camp commander. Inmates were to be locked in separate cells and forbidden to speak a word for at least fourteen days – in short, solitary confinement without trial. The camps would be expressly designed to cow malcontents by harsh discipline. In McNaughton's words, "no man who serves a term in such a camp will want to enter it again."

Fortunately for the reputation of the country, the idea was abandoned as politically dangerous. Had it been carried out, Canada would have had the dubious distinction of being the only nation in the democratic world to initiate a penal system that differed only in degree from that being employed in Nazi Germany.

The reality was that the camps were prisons. Any man who left could never again get relief. Thus, unless he could find a job (and who could find a job in those lonely wilderness outposts?) he had no real choice. Either he stayed in camp or he starved.

The Prime Minister had seriously considered closing down the relief camps in the spring for political reasons; in many constituencies they represented an electoral bloc that could upset the political balance. More than one politician had warned him that there were enough anti-government votes in some camps to defeat a Conservative candidate in a federal or provincial by-election. Either close the camps and scatter the inmates or increase the daily allowance; otherwise, the Tories faced defeat.

Peter Heenan, Minister of Labour in King's government, appeared at the Petawawa camp during the Ontario by-elections and talked about "slave labour" – a reference to the daily allowance of twenty cents. The local M.P., Ira Cotnam, warned Bennett that the potential voters in the camp represented political defeat. In the words of the editor of the Pembroke *Standard-Observer*, Heenan's remarks were "just the same as putting a match to a keg of gunpowder." The term "slave camps" was already being used to telling effect by the Relief Camp Workers' Union, a communist-front organization. This reference by a mainstream politician gave it greater respectability.

Somehow Bennett was never able to sense the political implications of his twenty-cent-a-day policy. He and General McNaughton believed that the government was being munificent, feeding, clothing, and sheltering thousands of men and, in addition, giving them pocket money to buy "luxuries."

"You apparently do not understand the purpose of the camps," he wrote to Cotnam. "They are just what their name indicates – relief camps; and any man can leave without notice should he desire to take up other employment. . . . It is too bad there are those who talk about the paying of wages. It is merely a little pocket money for those who are on relief. . . . "

Cotnam, of course, understood very well that the general public, not to mention the camp inmates, would never grasp the fine distinction that Bennett insisted on making. It didn't matter whether the twenty-cent allowance was called pocket money or wages: it was an insult.

Andy McNaughton, however, could not bear to see his pet scheme abandoned. The Chief of the General Staff made no bones about the real reason for the camps – or at least the reason he gave to Bennett, knowing, perhaps, that it would clinch his argument to retain them. The program was designed to forestall the revolution that the Prime Minister feared by getting thousands of restless young men out of the cities and isolating them in remote areas. "If these had not been dispersed," the General told Bennett, "it is hardly conceivable that we would have escaped without having recourse to the military forces to suppress disorder." In reality, McNaughton had only shifted the potential disorder from the cities to the camps, and the day was rapidly coming when military force, or at least quasi-military force, would be called in to quell it. But Bennett, whose fear of revolution was palpable, was convinced. He backed up his chief of staff.

The Ontario electoral problem was still unsolved. The authorities did their best, disfranchising as many relief camp workers as possible by shifting them from one constituency to another so that they could not meet the residence requirements for voting. But the by-elections were lost anyway.

Meanwhile, in British Columbia, where the majority of the relief camps had been located, trouble was brewing. The Relief Camp Workers' Union was well organized. Scores of men were already quitting the camps and pouring into Vancouver, negating McNaughton's purpose of keeping them out of the cities. Both the mayor and the premier wired their alarm to Ottawa. McNaughton's solution was to use the vagrancy laws to hit the malcontents with longer and tougher prison terms, but that wasn't feasible. There weren't enough jails, let alone enough money, to accommodate the burgeoning army of homeless men. Bennett, as usual, refused to take responsibility for the growing crisis – that was the province's problem, he kept saying.

It was clear that the general public, especially in the West, was sympathetic to the cause of the relief camp workers. Organized labour was up in arms because the men were put to work for far less than union wages. The business community was appalled because of the inefficiency of the system. Since the tasks given the men were largely make-work, designed only to keep them as busy as possible – building a road from nowhere to nowhere in one instance – productivity dropped below 50 per cent. Labour-saving machinery was discarded to produce more hours of labour. The men toiled with picks, shovels, and wheelbarrows while, in some places, earth moving devices stood idly by.

Under these conditions, nobody worked very hard unless driven to it. Scores found ways of avoiding anything but the minimum of effort. One of these was "Steve" Brodie, whose life had been saved when he almost slipped off a boxcar on a cold Saskatchewan night in 1932. Brodie, a natural rebel, "refused to take part in any of this silly digging of holes." He not only avoided work himself – hiding in the latrines for hours – but he also found ways to get others out of work. On one occasion when the foreman wasn't looking, Brodie started a bridge game on the job. The army caught on to him and put him to work as a waiter in the mess hall. Brodie then buckled down because "you were working for the men and not for some ridiculous engineer at five dollars a month."

The fact that the camps were operated by the army was another sore point with a public that had been conditioned by the excesses of the Great War to distrust the military. Certainly, the army operated the camps with Scrooge-like parsimony. Strict economy was the order of the day. The budget for rations was set at between nineteen and twenty-two cents per man per day, providing a monotonous diet that was only barely adequate for men supposedly doing hard labour. The men ate their meals from chipped enamelware, a breeding place for bacteria. They received no special rations at Christmas. Clothing was mostly army issue; some shirts purchased during the Great War were now threadbare. All the men were dressed alike, as convicts were, and thus could be easily spotted if they deserted. No towels were provided. Laundry facilities were primitive. There was little medical aid and no provision was made for recreation – no radios, no musical instruments, no sports equipment, no books, magazines, or newspapers. If the men wanted to play baseball, they had to provide their own bats and balls. Those who wanted to play chess or checkers were obliged to carve their own pieces.

Yet these were not the main causes of complaint. The very reason for the camps – getting the jobless as far away from the cities as possible – militated against their success. The relief camp workers felt isolated – far from their families and, perhaps even more important, far from the company of women. These were mostly virile young men in their twenties who had reached a period in their lives when, under favourable conditions, they would have been fashioning their places in the world and preparing for marriage. Now that was denied them. They could not even vote in the coming federal election. The law now said that they could vote only in their home constituencies; Bennett had effectively disfranchised them.

It is true that they would also have been isolated if they had worked in the lumber camps and mining camps of the northwest. But there was a difference. The lumber workers were well paid, the end of their period of employment fixed. They could save money or send it home. At season's end they could go back to the cities. But for the relief camp workers there were no such incentives; there was no future, not even the chance to look for a job because the real jobs were far off in the cities and farmland. The "slave camps" were just that – camps of hopelessness and futility.

The men at the top didn't understand this, but one newspaper-man did. Bob Bouchette, the immensely popular columnist for the Vancouver *Sun*, was an iconoclast who, when covering heavyweight boxing matches, made it his business to interview the loser while his colleagues were crowding round the champion. His publisher, Robert Cromie, used to slip him five dollars from time to time to attack his own editorials. In February 1934, the *Sun* dispatched Bouchette to investigate the camps. His six-part series, a refreshing contrast to the usual newspaper puffery, helped form public opinion in British Columbia and confounded the authorities, who scrambled to find some way of counteracting the effect.

"There is no future to which these men are looking forward," Bouchette wrote. "That is why their faces are so wooden. That is why, as you drive by them on the road, they stare at you with an expression half sullen, half detached.

"They consider themselves outcasts from society with no part in the normal activities of men. . . . The expression on [their] . . . faces is, to me, a little terrible to behold. I can see no conceivable justification for a system which creates the feeling manifesting itself in that expression."

Then Bouchette touched on a topic that, in those puritanical days, no other journalist had discussed – the absence of sex. He quoted a doctor who regularly visited the camps: "You will notice that most of the trouble in the camps is from the young men. Much of it is due to the neurotic conditions arising from their manner of life. They are on edge and ready for any sort of action. . . . It is not the actual sex deprivation that produces this neurosis. It is the fact that the men feel that they are cut off from any association with women. . . . If they knew they would return to ordinary activity and the enjoyment of ordinary rights and privileges in six months to a year, it would not be so harmful. But they can see no end ahead."

Although the camps seethed with discontent, it was a brave man who dared to protest, for under army rules all complaints had to be made individually and through channels. King's Regulations made that clear: "Appeals for redress by means of any documentation bearing the signature of more than one complainant, or by orga-nized committees combining to make a complaint are strictly for-bidden"; and again: "the Department will not countenance any steps to bring accusations before any tribunal of public opinion, either by speeches, or letters or letters inserted in the newspapers. .... Such a proceeding is a glaring violation of the rules and shows a contempt for properly constituted authority."

The actual result of these rules was to *provoke* contempt for authority by bottling up grievances that might easily have evaporated if the men had been able to blow off steam. They were, after all, civilians – not military recruits who had signed up voluntarily, knowing what the rules were. Yet though still civilians they were no longer free to form their own associations or to air their grievances publicly.

Bill Gilbey found that out after he entered a relief camp at Winterburn, Alberta, north of Edmonton. He was chilled to the bone in a tent and angered to discover that he and his friends were allowed only forty minutes to enjoy a cup of tea in the warmth of the dining hall. He made the mistake of remarking to some of the men in his tent that something ought to be done about it. Word got back to the major in charge, who the following morning told Gilbey to pack his belongings. He put him in a truck, drove him to Edmonton, and dumped him at the corner of Jasper Avenue and 97th Street. You're not supposed to complain, he told Gilbey.

The authorities persisted in the fiction that the camps were totally voluntary. Bennett kept reassuring his growing army of critics that "anyone can leave without notice." He could not get it into his head that anyone who did leave would be jailed for vagrancy if caught. Worse, he would be blacklisted, so that if he tried to return to any camp the authorities would immediately expel him. It is a measure of the discontent in the camps that by the end of 1934 the blacklist ran to thousands.

The miracle is that in spite of these restrictive conditions the Relief Camp Workers' Union managed to organize all the British Columbia camps by the autumn of 1934. The organizers, who were blacklisted, simply changed their names and addresses and, thus disguised, moved from camp to camp. On arrival they were careful never to address an old acquaintance by name. Instead, they'd sidle up to him and whisper, "What name are you using here?" Some men had fifty or more names.

Steve Brodie simply picked names out of the Vancouver telephone book. Gerry Tellier called himself Gerry Winters; his

272

brother, Lucien, took the name of Lou Summers. They lived in hope that they might be arrested together, at which time they planned to announce: "We're Summers and Winters and we're brothers."

The glue that held this underground together was the union paper, the *Relief Camp Worker*, published in Vancouver and smuggled into the camps. The authorities made a practice of rifling through the incoming mail looking for the paper. If it was found it meant instant dismissal and blacklisting for the subscriber. But the *Worker* still got through. Sometimes it arrived in an innocent-looking envelope bearing the name of a prominent Vancouver businessman. Sometimes it was sneaked in by new arrivals.

In 1934, largely due to the efforts of the union, there were one hundred disturbances, strikes, and riots in the British Columbia camps. Twenty-seven of these occurred in December as the union prepared for a general walkout, which was to have its climax in a major demonstration in Vancouver.

To combat the rising power of the union, the police resorted to extra-legal methods. It was their practice to raid the camps late at night to pick up "agitators." At Moran's Camp, halfway between Spence's Bridge and Kamloops, fifteen policemen arrived, bundled all five members of the union executive into a truck, and dropped them on a lonely road in the middle of the wilderness. As one of the men, John Cawston, later pointed out, they were neither arrested nor charged: "If we were guilty of no crime or misdemeanour, it was a pure case of intimidation by kidnapping."

The rising chorus of complaints, many from prominent citizens in British Columbia, had little effect on Bennett. If Vancouver was crowded with vagrants who had left the camps, that was a problem for the provincial and city authorities. At the end of October the union had made its plans for a general strike in all the British Columbia camps. A delegation led by Matt Shaw of Saskatchewan - a major figure in the disturbances that followed - travelled to Victoria to see the Premier, T. Dufferin Pattullo, who had been swept into power on the slogan "Work and Wages." The union wanted work and wages but at trade union rates. It also demanded an end to the blacklist and the right to vote. And it wanted the army out. Pattullo passed the buck right back to Ottawa but did offer enough scrip to allow the members of the delegation to eat at Salvation Army hostels.

By mid-December hundreds of men from the camps were walking the streets of Vancouver, depending on handouts from sympathetic citizens. "This kind of thing cannot continue here without grave results," Pattullo wired to Bennett. He asked for "a tribunal to deal with alleged grievances" and a "generous program of public works." By this time the Prime Minister was inundated with telegrams and resolutions from British Columbians of every walk of life demanding an investigation into conditions in the camps and urging that the blacklist be abandoned. The Prime Minister heard from several federal M.P.s, from the Vancouver Council of Social Agencies, from the Vancouver City Council, and, indirectly, from General Victor Odlum, a Vancouver newspaper proprietor, who added to the chorus with a long "Dear Andy" letter to his old comrade-in-arms McNaughton. A "prompt committee of investigation would steady public opinion," Odlum wrote. The mayor, Louis D. Taylor, followed with another telegram on Christmas Eve, again urging a commission of inquiry, adding that "personally I feel the men have grounds for complaint."

To this unprecedented storm of protest the Prime Minister remained singularly obdurate. He wasn't going to let a bunch of Reds push him around! His telegrams to Pattullo read like the patient admonitions of a college professor trying to explain for the umpteenth time a perfectly sensible course of action to a remarkably dull student.

"No investigation is necessary," he wired on December 28, "for press and citizens have been invited to visit these camps ever since they have been established. . . . The so-called black list included the names of those who have been told to leave the camps because their further presence involved the destruction of the very camps which have been established for the benefit of those who are the victims of propaganda."

And again: "No powers of compulsion are exercised and discipline is maintained only for the purpose of preserving the orderly conduct of the camps."

At one point Bennett made the irritating suggestion that Pattullo visit the camps himself and return to reassure the public that everything was fine and thus "correct the effect of subversive propaganda." That invitation, which seemed to be extended to all citizens, was not as wide open as it looked. McNaughton made it clear that citizens *might* be given permission to visit one or two camps "provided that they went in the capacity of individuals and not as a corporate or collective body and it should be made clear that no permission was being given for them to visit the camps as a committee of investigation." They could look, but they could not listen to anybody except the camp authorities because the relief camp workers weren't allowed to complain to anybody but their immediate superior.

In short, the government had no intention of launching any investigation into the camps. The official line was that nothing was wrong, that, in Bennett's words, repeated over and over again, "a proper system has been arranged for hearing and correcting any grievances which individuals may feel they have and that this is being done sympathetically by officers in charge" and "except for disturbances directly traceable [to] activities [of] subversive organizations there have been no troubles or serious complaints."

Few British Columbians swallowed that hokum. Bennett may have believed it; he was sometimes a prisoner of his own self-deception. What he failed to recognize was that the young men in the camps, in spite of their isolation, were part of a larger circle. They had parents, relatives, and friends, and most of them could write letters. The voters of Canada didn't need Bennett's public statements or even the press to form their opinion of the relief camps. They listened to their own sons.

The government's failure stands out in sharp relief when compared with a similar and much more successful experiment south of the border. Why did the relief camps leave such a bad taste in the mouths of Canadians when the Civilian Conservation Corps in the United States was greeted with such enthusiasm? On the face of it, they were very similar. Yet one was a flop, the other a success. Why?

One reason – perhaps the chief one – had to do with perception. Although the Canadian government tried to make it appear that the relief camps were part of a plan to save the youth of the country from the disease of idleness, the real reason was to save the country from its youth – to get the single jobless out of the way and prevent revolution. Fear, not sympathy, was the main catalyst, and that worked its way down to the lowest levels. The government feared the young people and the young people feared the government: they knew that if they stepped out of line to complain they would be thrown back onto the streets to starve.

The American attitude was just the opposite. In keeping with that country's great traditions, the American government under Franklin D. Roosevelt saw the CCC as a crusade, in much the same way that a later president would visualize the Peace Corps. The Canadians built roads and military installations. The young Americans – the cut-off age was twenty-five – were put to work in the national parks, planting trees, saving forests, building dams, protecting the environment. No one complains about drudgery when working for a cause, and Roosevelt, with his interest in conservation and his innate sense of public relations, made it one. It was, as somebody has said, "the practical fulfillment of William James's idea of providing a moral equivalent for war."

In the American camps, work was seen as a means to an end. The purpose of the CCC was clearly defined in idealistic terms – saving the nation's natural heritage. In the Canadian camps, work was seen as an end in itself. Young men must work, no matter how meaningless, poorly planned, or stupid that work might be.

Harold Dew, a well-educated relief camp worker, described one job at his camp in central British Columbia. A portion of the road on the edge of a deep lake had fallen in. Every day, camp workers transferred loads of rock, by hand, to the outer edge of the road, attempting to fill in the gap. But every day the pile tumbled down into the lake and the road remained as before. "No one seems to worry," Dew wrote. "The appearance of this spot is at the end of a month's labor as at the beginning. But the number of men sent out on the grade each day has been duly recorded and all is well. It would be a joke if it were not tragic that men should spend themselves day after day to so little purpose."

Neither Bennett nor McNaughton or anybody else in power saw any farther than their own noses when contemplating the *purpose* of the Canadian camps. They were seen merely as holding units, nothing more. Roosevelt's vision was broader. The comparative generosity of the Americans stood out in sharp contrast to the Calvinistic Canadian attitude, which held that people on public charity must never be allowed to think they were getting something for nothing. There must be no frills, no "luxuries."
276

The defence department, in an internal memo, actually boasted that "not one cent of public money has been spent . . . on reading material and recreational equipment." The Americans in the CCC were paid a dollar a day, not twenty cents. Between twenty and twenty-five dollars a month was saved for their families so that the wage earners could feel a sense of worth and dignity. They worked a thirty-hour week and were given the weekends off besides compassionate leave with pay. The American government provided movies, entertainment, playing fields, radios, and sports equipment – and beer was available in the camp canteens. The term in the CCC was limited to six months. For many young Americans, the experience of the CCC was one of the high points of their youth. For the men north of the border, their confinement in relief camps was the nadir.

It is perhaps unfair to call up national stereotypes to explain such differences, but the temptation is there – to contrast the open-handed and open-hearted Yankees with their stiff-necked and parsimonious northern neighbours. In this instance, as in some others in that dark decade, we do not come off very well.

The government could have eased the situation at any time by being more generous and following the American lead. It must be remembered that the Communist party, which was blamed almost entirely for the trouble in the Canadian camps, was just as strong and as well organized in the United States as it was in Canada and had the additional advantage of being legal. But the Communists failed to get a foothold in the CCC because conditions there were not conducive to revolution or exploitation. With Ottawa stonewalling and as many as fourteen hundred crowding into Vancouver at the end of 1934, begging for food on the streets, any sensible politician would have smelled trouble. But the Prime Minister of Canada, obsessed as always with the idea of bringing peace, order, and what he considered good government to his country, paid no attention. In the election to come, that would be his undoing.

1935

1

Nineteen thirty-five was the watershed year of the Depression. It *Bennett's* marked a political divide: Mackenzie King's Liberals took power *New Deal* as R.B. Bennett's Conservatives faded into the background. It was also an economic turning point: at last Canada got the badly needed central bank that would eventually enable the federal government to exercise stabilizing control over the economy. There were other beginnings and endings. This was the last full year of the reign of George V, whose Silver Jubilee was celebrated by a chain of bonfires blazing from Victoria to Charlottetown. It was also the last year in office for Lord Bessborough, the aristocratically stuffy governor general, soon to be replaced by a commoner, the Scottish adventure and thriller writer John Buchan. But a commoner could not yet represent the King, and so Buchan would become an instant peer before taking up his viceregal duties as Lord Tweedsmuir.

Some of the worst excesses of the Depression were about to end. The infamous Section 98 of the Criminal Code would be invoked for the last time. And 1935 was the last year of the relief camps, which had become a symbol of the government's lack of concern for the unemployed. By spring, the rebellious spirit bred in the so-called slave camps would explode into a full-scale revolt that would keep the West in turmoil until July.

With his term of office coming to its legal end – he had waited almost to the last hour before considering an election – R.B. Bennett realized he must do something spectacular if he were to remain in office. But few of his colleagues knew just *how* spectacular until the second day of the New Year, when he launched into a series of five half-hour broadcasts that confounded and bewildered the nation.

His opponents (and, indeed, some of his supporters) talked of a deathbed repentance – meaning a political deathbed – and as it turned out, they weren't far wrong. Others were reminded of the sudden conversion of Saul of Tarsus on the road to Damascus. Certainly, Bennett's broadcasts were a revelation to members of his own Cabinet, none of whom had expected anything of the sort. He had not so much as whispered to anyone, except his brother-in-law William Herridge, that he intended to perform a

281

political right about-turn (or, more properly, a left about-turn) and offer Canadians a New Deal patterned after that of Franklin D. Roosevelt.

The five broadcasts were carried by a network of thirty-eight stations between January 2 and January 11, and the air time was paid for by Bennett himself. In them, the Prime Minister hurled a series of thunderbolts that excited some, shocked others, and surprised all. One wonders why; clues to his intentions had been apparent the previous month.

The sonorous voice that spoke to Canadians in the first broadcast was Bennett's, but the words were largely those of Bill Herridge, whose Washington legation served as an open house to the architects and engineers of the Roosevelt New Deal. Since 1933, the enthusiastic Herridge had been bombarding the Prime Minister with letters and memoranda urging that he strike out in a new political direction:

"The policy of *laissez-faire* must, for the time being at least, be abandoned. . . ." [September 13, 1933]

"The New Deal is a sort of Pandora's Box from which . . . the president has pulled the N.R.A. . . . We need a Pandora's Box . . . the national heart . . . will incline with profound fervour to the right sort of lead. That you alone can give. . . ." [April 12, 1934]

" . . . old-fashioned Toryism is dead . . . we must keep on the move until we find the answer to the question: 'What's wrong with Canada!' This is your job and no one can take your place. It is indeed a trust!" [June 22, 1934]

The gregarious Bill Herridge occupied a special place in the Conservative party. He had been Bennett's lawyer, adviser, and speech writer before his appointment to Washington in 1931. That year the bond with the Prime Minister was strengthened when he married Bennett's sister Mildred, his closest friend and confidante. No others could speak to the Prime Minister as passionately or as personally as he. The previous June he had urged Bennett to stay on as leader. "Canada is broken and the people are lost," he had told him. "Would you let a people in trouble forsake you? Would you forsake them? . . . You alone can save the day for Canada. . . ."

Herridge's eloquence, and his flattery, had their effect on Bennett. He was backed by Bennett's chief secretary, Rod Finlayson, who helped write the last three broadcasts at Herridge's cottage
282

on Harrington Lake. But the first two were almost pure Herridge; Finlayson, apparently, wasn't party to them, nor did he realize the scope of the opening broadcast. The script lifted ideas and even wording from Herridge's memoranda of the previous year. Indeed, there was more than a suspicion that Bennett hadn't studied Herridge's text very carefully. The Montreal *Gazette*, which could not have been expected to applaud his words, commented that he "appeared to be imperfectly familiar" with parts of it. He became nervous toward the middle, stumbling, fumbling, and racing through the speech with uncharacteristic sloppiness.

Typically, Bennett himself made the decision to introduce his New Deal, as it came to be called, on the radio and not in Parliament. He made all the arrangements personally and told no one. For once the usual ballyhoo wasn't needed to entice listeners. By the time the fifth broadcast went on the air it was estimated that eight million Canadians – virtually all the country's adults – were tuned in.

Here is Bennett in full voice in the first broadcast:

"The old order has gone. It will not return. . . . Your prosperity demands corrections in the old system. . . .

"In my mind reform means government intervention. It means government control and regulation. It means the end of *laissez-faire*. . . . There can be no permanent recovery without reform. I raise the issue squarely. I nail the flag of progress to the masthead. I summon the power of the state to its support. . . .

"Free competition and the open market place, as they were known in the old days, have lost their place in the system and the only substitute for them . . . is government regulation and control.

" . . . in all times, faults in the system have been seized upon by the unscrupulous and greedy as vantage points in their battle for self-advancement. And we will be dealing with the matter in a thorough and practical way if we remove these faults, so as to put a final stop to the unfair practices which they made possible. . . . "

Was this really Richard Bedford Bennett speaking? For years he had been announcing that the Depression was receding, that it was practically over, that his government had solved the country's economic problems. As a Tory opposed to state interference, he had again and again shrugged off all federal responsibility for helping the unemployed. Now here he was broadcasting almost a *mea culpa* to the nation, turning his back on the free-enterprise system, embracing with open arms those very principles of state intervention that his big-business supporters decried and, by inference, taking a swipe at some of them as "unscrupulous and greedy." No wonder that Angus MacInnis, in jest, suggested that he join the CCF immediately.

If Herridge's influence was predominant in that opening broadcast, there was also a whiff of Harry Stevens in Bennett's condemnation of "unfair practices." And there was more to come in the days that followed. Bennett was promising not only a contributory unemployment insurance plan but also a remodelling of the old-age pension scheme; health, accident, and sickness insurance; amended income tax laws to correct inequality in the distribution of wealth; minimum wage laws; laws limiting hours of work; and more legislation to help the farmers. Many of these proposals might be beyond the purview of the federal government, but Bennett glossed over that difficulty.

Only two years earlier, Bennett had declared that "we must maintain an export business . . . and therefore we could not by the very nature of things reduce hours of labour and increase pay. . . . " Now here he was, telling the country, "I believe there should be a uniform minimum wage and a uniform maximum working week. I hold the view that if we are to have equality of social and political conditions throughout the land, we must have equality of economic conditions as well." Harry Stevens might be out of the Cabinet, but his influence lingered on.

It all seems mild enough today, but what Bennett was advocating came very close to what both Tim Buck and J.S. Woodsworth had been urging in the early thirties, to the sneers of the Tories. It almost seemed that Bennett had appropriated communist rhetoric when he castigated "selfish men . . . whose mounting bankrolls loom larger than your happiness, corporations without souls and without virtue."

"These . . . will whisper against us. They will call us radicals. They will say that this is the first step on the road to socialism," Bennett thundered. "We fear them not. . . . "

This was too much for his Secretary of State, the Hon. Charles Hazlitt Cahan, who angrily wrote out his resignation and tore it up only after a group of prominent Montreal businessmen urged him to stay in the Cabinet to fight the Bennett program ("Fight it all you can, C.H., but whatever you do don't leave the cabinet").

284

For Bennett was already pledging that he would wipe out "corporate evils" by abolishing, among other things, the right to issue shares at no par value.

Although the *Gazette* tried to pretend that the public was "shocked and startled" by the broadcasts, the general attitude was favourable. The Cabinet, however, was split, and the Premier of Quebec, Louis-Alexandre Taschereau, wanted no part of Bennett's proposals, many of which infringed on provincial sovereignty. Mackenzie King, who had been advocating many of the same measures, was enraged because he was convinced that Bennett had filched his ideas from *Industry and Humanity*, his dense 1918 tome. "It is plagiarism of the most obvious kind," King wrote indignantly in his diary after the first broadcast, "with the most nauseating self sufficiency & egotism . . . the effrontery of it all – the downright hypocrisy – when I think of his money – the money that he is paying for the broadcasts no doubt – having been made largely from the life blood of women, some in the graves, of Eddy Mffg. Co – & his talking of standards in industry – humanitarianism & the like fills me with indignation too great for utterance."

It is hard to picture the impatient and impulsive Bennett wading through King's opus, but the former prime minister, who was convinced he had written an imperishable classic, was equally convinced that his opponent had purposely stolen his stuff. The more he brooded over it, the angrier he grew: " . . . this theft of my ideas . . . this effort to appropriate ideas, plans, etc – It is the most gigantic plagiarism and steal of another man's aim, work etc & those of a political party that I believe has been made at any time anywhere, by one man. This is 'the strange thing' that is to try me [a reference to a prophetic vision], the theft of my life's work & endeavour by Bennett to make his own."

Bennett's broadcasts, of course, constituted his election platform. He knew that under the constitution he must go to the country no later than October. He had seized on Herridge's advice as a means to embarrass the Liberals, and on the face of it, his strategy seemed brilliant. How could they oppose his New Deal, which embraced so many of their own stated principles? If they did find a way to oppose it – and Bennett hoped they would – he would call a snap election, make the New Deal a campaign issue, and sweep the country. He had presented the Opposition with an apparently hopeless dilemma. As R.J. Manion put it, "If

King backs Bennett he is merely trailing, and if he abuses him, he's a reactionary. I really think Bennett has scooped him rather badly."

But Bennett was up against the wiliest politician in Canada. Mackenzie King's original plan had been to oppose *any* Conservative legislation, fight it all the way in Parliament, and hope to force an election. On January 15, however, he heard Bennett declare, during the course of an address broadcast from Montreal, that his promised reforms would be laid out in the Speech from the Throne. King immediately changed his strategy. To his delight, the details of Bennett's New Deal could be debated in the House. Bennett, as usual, had plunged hastily – even recklessly – into his reform plan without drafting the legislation. That would come after he had won the election.

Now King prepared to call his opponent's bluff. Instead of opposing the New Deal, he would offer sweet co-operation and urge that specific legislation be placed before the current session so that it might be debated and passed. His attitude, King decided, would be "that not only of willingness but anxiety to join with him in getting a reform programme completed before any appeal to the electorate, [and] Bennett's bubble will be pretty effectively pricked. He will be like a flattened tire. . . . "

The throne speech was everything King hoped for. He immediately called in eight senior Liberal politicians (all former Cabinet ministers), told them his plan, and swore them to secrecy. "We must not hand over our tactics to the enemy," he warned.

Then, on January 21, he pounced. His was the only Opposition reply to the speech. In it he suggested that Bennett's apparent change of heart was offered only as a means of grabbing votes, a view that was beginning to dawn on the electorate. He praised his own party's record on social legislation and compared it with that of the Tories. Then he sprang his surprise. He would not move the usual no-confidence motion. His party would offer no amendments. He wanted Bennett to get on with it so the House could debate each proposal on its merits.

Bennett, caught by surprise, was furious. King had outwitted him and his own impetuosity had trapped him. The government had drafted only one bill, that for unemployment insurance. The others would have to be rushed to completion. And the Price Spreads Commission had not yet brought down its report. He was

286

able to present only six bills before illness put him out of action. Long before that, a majority of the electorate had come to accept King's suggestion that Bennett's election promises in 1935 were worth no more than those he had made in 1930.

Yet the long-term effect of Bennett's proposals cannot be discounted. His legislation may have been hastily drafted and some of it unconstitutional, but the impact of his words remained. Here was the leading Conservative, the spokesman for the Right, the self-made millionaire, rejecting *laissez-faire* and opting for the much despised principle of government intervention on a scale not known before. Bennett made that philosophy respectable. Bit by bit it came to be adopted, provincially and federally. Within a generation, the principles that R.B. Bennett enunciated in his famous series of broadcasts would be commonly held by all but the most moss-backed of Canadians.

2

On January 15, 1935, four days after Bennett's final New Deal broadcast, the Royal Commission on Price Spreads, which had been sitting for much of the winter, again turned its attention to the needle trades in the province of Quebec. Its real target, however, was the T. Eaton Company of Toronto, which was buying much of its merchandise from sweated labour in Victoriaville. Four young women, none of whom spoke English, appeared before the commission that month to describe, through an interpreter, the appalling conditions in the factories of the two largest garment manufacturers in that community, Fashion Craft and Rubins Brothers. *Speed-up at Eaton's*

Eleanor Hamel, a twenty-five-year-old seamstress, testified that she had gone to work at the age of thirteen – an example of child labour that smacked of the nineteenth century. It was, of course, illegal. The minimum age was sixteen, but nobody, it seemed, paid any attention to the law. The minimum wage was ten dollars a week, but nobody paid any attention to that, either. Miss Hamel made seven dollars a week at Rubins, and when she asked for ten she was denied it. The foreman jollied her along and when she threatened to go to Fashion Craft told her she would be blacklisted in the community. It was well known that anyone who quit one firm could get no work elsewhere.

Another seamstress, twenty-three-year-old Berthe Nolin, was paid six dollars for an official fifty-five-hour week (including five hours on Saturday). Actually, she worked much longer. Her work day began at 7 a.m. and was supposed to end at 6 p.m., with an hour for lunch. But she often worked until 10:20 p.m., although the foreman punched her time card out at 6:15 to maintain the fiction that the company was obeying the fifty-five-hour law. Because of these long evening hours, Berthe Nolin and her fellow workers often went without supper. The Minimum Wage Board winked at this and similar infractions. Its vice-chairman, Eugene Richard, was the owner of Fashion Craft.

The women who testified before the commission were unemployed as the result of a strike for better wages and shorter hours. It had lasted only four days. At the first hint of trouble the companies called in strikebreakers and the mayor ordered the fire department to turn its hoses on the picket line. Fourteen provincial policemen arrived and, according to Berthe Nolin, ordered the strikers to go back to work. But Miss Nolin and some fifty others weren't taken back. The strikebreakers had their jobs.

The commission then turned its attention to the T. Eaton Company, concentrating on its Factory F-8 in Toronto, where garments such as women's blouses and dresses and men's trousers were turned out on a piecework basis. Here the Depression had a devastating effect. In the first four years piecework rates were cut by more than half. By 1933, a seamstress who had once made $3.60 producing a dozen voile dresses was making only $1.75.

These drastic reductions presented Eaton's with a problem. Under the Ontario Minimum Wage Act, the company was required to pay its own women employees at least $12.50 a week. In 1929 the seamstresses had had no trouble earning that amount. But the cuts made it difficult for many and impossible for some to come up to the minimum wage. Eaton's was required to pay the difference between what the women actually earned and what the law required. To save money, the company instituted a speed-up system to force its employees up to the minimum – a practice that reduced some of them to a state of nervous exhaustion.

It had not been easy for the commission to persuade witnesses to outline Eaton's employment practices. The previous spring, one of the Stevens committee investigators had interviewed Winnifred Harding, a pieceworker in the factory. As soon as the foreman learned of this, he fired her for being "a poor producer." But Miss Harding was a determined young woman. Her production was no poorer than that of many of her colleagues who kept their jobs, and she didn't intend to be pushed around by the country's leading department store.

Off she went to Queen's Park to confront the attorney general himself. That forced an investigation. After two meetings with an official from the Department of Labour, Eaton's agreed to find another job for Miss Harding – but in a different division.

Again, the women who testified before the commission in Toronto – as in Victoriaville – had lost their jobs because of union activity. From thirty-eight who had been fired the previous July the commission selected several witnesses. All told of being bullied, threatened, and nagged to speed up their work so that they would produce enough goods to earn the minimum wage, saving Eaton's the cost of making up the difference.

"We were badgered, harassed, and worried," Annie Wells testified. "You were told to work and work so hard at these cheaper rates . . . and you were threatened if you didn't make $12.50 you would be fired. You felt insecure with your job." Mrs. Wells was a veteran employee. She had worked for Eaton's for eighteen years sewing skirts, blouses, and dresses and later as an instructor, training new girls. Eaton's high-powered counsel, R.L. Kellock, K.C. (a future Supreme Court Justice), couldn't shake her testimony. "You had to sit at your machine from a quarter to eight until twenty minutes to one and go as hard as you could," she told him. "You had no time to get up and have a drink of water or powder your nose or look at anybody, you just went on working. And, of course, they expected you to make and make more than you really could."

Mrs. Wells's daughter, Winnifred, another long-time employee, told the commissioners that she was so tired at night she couldn't eat her supper. Before the Depression, she had been supplied with a stool while examining dresses. In those days "you could sit down for a few minutes and kind of ease off the tension." But after 1933, when the stools were removed, no examiner was allowed even that brief rest. Miss Wells was on her feet the whole day, so tired that she dreaded getting on the streetcar when she

289

went home "because if I sat down I could not get up again, my knees and my legs would be so stiff." Yet her take-home pay was less than half what it had been in 1929.

Miss Wells swore that Carrie Cuthbert, the woman who worked beside her, suffered a nervous breakdown as the result of the speed-up. It kept her off work for two months – a perilous situation that everybody dreaded in those days when seamstresses lived from week to week fearful of being sent home for failing to make the quota. This actually happened to Winnifred Wells when she was found to be seventy-five cents short of the minimum wage. Her supervisor told her to stay home, without pay, and not to return until she was sent for. When Miss Wells accosted a foreman to demand an explanation, he told her the company was trying out a new system: every time a girl fell behind in her work, she would be laid off for a week.

"I asked him how I was going to live. I said to him: 'If I come back at the end of the week and I fall down again on my money, what is going to happen then?' He said: 'You will go home again the second week.' I . . . asked him how he thought a girl was going to live if she was going to be sent home every time she fell down on her money. He said it did not matter to him, none of his business, and got very angry about it."

Lilian Johnson's forelady was horrified when she found that Lilian was $3.60 short of the $12.50 at the end of the week. Some late orders had come in, so she kept Lilian on in the hope that she could make up the difference. "She said to me: 'Now you will have to work like the devil. . . . ' So I worked on it, and she told the girls, none of them to speak to me, and I did not look up from my machine from that work until I went home. . . . I was so all in and I worked so hard that when I went home I did not bother about my supper. I just laid on the bed with my clothes on, and there I stayed all night."

The threat of being fired was always present. Jean Chambers, a veteran of ten years with Eaton's, told of being nudged in the back while she worked and ordered to go faster. A large chart at the forewoman's desk showed how far each girl was behind in her quota. "You had better hurry up, speed up, because you are going to be fired, you are not going to be kept on if you cannot make it," the forewoman warned.

Nervous tension brought some employees close to tears. "You

290

had to work so hard, you were driven so fast that it just became impossible to make $12.50 and you were a nervous wreck," Kate Nolan testified. " . . . It almost drove me insane. . . . I went into hysterics several times, and I had to go to the hospital and the nurse said, 'What is the matter? You girls are always coming here.' "

The evidence made it clear that the T. Eaton Company had purposely chosen to evade the spirit of the Minimum Wage Act, if not the letter. Under the Act, the company wasn't required to pay the minimum wage to part-time workers, handicapped workers, or apprentices. The law allowed Eaton's to pay these people – up to a maximum of 20 per cent of the workforce – only for the piecework they did. The provision wasn't meant, of course, to apply to regular employees, but Eaton's lumped all its workers together and refused to pay the minimum wage to the lowest 20 per cent. Eaton's saved money because the faster workers in the top 80 per cent required a smaller bonus to make up the difference between what they earned and the minimum wage to which they were entitled. Eaton's refused to increase its piecework prices because it was cheaper to pay a small number of bonuses to the faster workers than it was to raise the rates for everyone.

Many of these practices had come to a sudden end after the formation of the Stevens committee was announced in February 1934. Eaton's quietly stopped laying off the poorest producers and threatening them with unemployment. By that March, the company had also decided to place all its women employees under the Minimum Wage Act and raise the piecework rates.

But it had no intention of letting the women organize a union. Nonetheless, some of them formed a committee in the factory and joined the International Ladies' Garment Workers' Union. Then, on July 11, 1934, a new and more intricate dress pattern was introduced, one that required fifteen separate operations to make. Twenty-eight union members stopped work that afternoon on the grounds that the dress was so complicated no seamstress could earn the minimum wage producing it. They asked permission to consult their union headquarters on Spadina Avenue before resuming work. Eaton's gave them permission to leave the building but warned them they must be back at work before 5:30 that afternoon. It proved impossible for them to walk to the union office and back before the deadline. The following morning, Eaton's locked them out.

Had the company been less hasty in its actions, had the women not lost their jobs in such a brutal fashion, the commission would not have had their testimony and the company's treatment of its piecework employees in the early Depression years might never have come to light. But the record is there, to be quoted and requoted and to haunt the T. Eaton Company down through the years. Today, a work stoppage at Eaton's and a subsequent lock-out could not be kept from the media. In 1934, the women did attempt to distribute handbills and carry sandwich boards to publicize their grievances, but the press paid no attention. Not a word of the trouble appeared in any of the four Toronto dailies, all of which treated both Eaton's and Simpson's as sacrosanct because of their pages of advertising.

This was a story perfect for the age of television: young women being exploited by a powerful corporation, carrying placards and picketing the biggest store in town. But in those days, even radio (which was less beholden than the papers to department store advertising) didn't have the facilities to cover this kind of news. No reporter ventured out into the streets with a microphone. Tape recording hadn't been invented. The tough, probing interview belonged to the future. And so the story went unreported until the following January, when the commission heard it from some of the union members, and even then newspaper readers in Toronto had to look hard to find it.

The Toronto papers handled the testimony very gingerly. On the day that Annie Wells and Jean Chambers testified, the *Star*'s front-page headline reassured its readers: "EATON F-8 PLANT PAID FAIR WAGE AUDITOR REVEALS." The story failed to make it clear that Eaton's had not changed its policies until after hearings were announced. That day the paper carried three and a half pages of Eaton's advertisements. Throughout the session, the *Star* gave far more prominence to Eaton's side of the story than to that of its employees: "HOUNDING DID NOT EXIST EATON OFFICIAL TESTIFIES"; "FACTORY WAGES ARE FAIR EATON ESTIMATOR INSISTS."

The *Star* at least put its coverage on the front page. The other three newspapers rarely did. Again, Eaton's got kid-glove treatment. Of nine stories in the *Telegram* between January 16 and 23, only one headlined testimony from an ex-employee; the others

292

favoured Eaton's. The *Mail and Empire* ran six stories; the Eaton's position was headlined in all but one. The *Globe* was fairer to the employees' testimony but went out of its way to mollify the store by printing a bold-face introduction to its opening report, quoting an Eaton official as saying, "We have every assurance of the loyal understanding of the vast majority of our employees during the difficult depression period."

The local coverage of the testimony contrasts sharply with that of the Winnipeg *Free Press*, which treated the Toronto story as a major scandal: "SAYS DRIVING IN FACTORIES MADE WRECKS OF GIRLS"; "SAYS FACTORY GIRLS DRIVEN NEARLY INSANE"; "TELLS PROBE MINIMUM WAGE ACT BROKEN"; "TELLS PROBE OF WORKING BY STOP WATCHES."

By the time the commission completed its hearings, Harry Stevens was again the man of the hour. He had continued to dominate the inquiry. When the hearings ended in February, he lobbied the other ten members of the commission to prepare the toughest report possible and also urged the general public to force acceptance of its recommendations. He took to the platform and to the microphone to hammer home his ideas and was not above leaking the recommendations to the press. In a nationwide broadcast, sponsored by the Canadian Federation of Youth, Stevens urged "common sense amendments to existing laws and then a fearless law enforcement." The law as it stood, he said, had "holes big enough for millionaires to crawl through and company laws that permitted the fleecing of the public on the one hand and the sweatshops on the other."

The Stevens-for-Party-Leader movement was growing, endorsed by Stevens's old sponsor, Warren K. Cook, and others who recognized that the country was in the mood for reform. One wing of the Conservative party thought that the former minister of Trade and Commerce was just the man to seize the opportunity and lead the party to victory. Indeed, though the chance of hanging on to power was slim, the two leading Tories – Bennett with his New Deal and Stevens with his reputation as a dragon-slayer – might have pulled it off if they had worked in tandem, with the support of a united party. But that was clearly impossible. The right wing of the party, led by Stevens's old adversary the white-goateed Cahan (known to some colleagues as "Dino," for "Dinosaur"), was bitterly opposed. Stevens himself at that point

293

had no desire for the leadership. And Bennett adamantly refused all attempts at reconciliation with a man he saw as his rival. Besides, after the effort of proposing his New Deal, the Prime Minister seemed to have run out of steam. Confined to his suite in the Chateau Laurier between February 27 and April 18 with first a respiratory infection and later a heart attack, he seemed like a forgotten hero sulking in his tent. "The colour has faded for the reform picture," Herridge wrote to Manion in March. "The promise of performance is gone." In fact, Bennett longed for retirement but clung stubbornly to power only to prevent Stevens from taking over.

The ideological rupture could not be concealed from the public – not with the Opposition leader goading both Cahan and Stevens almost daily in the House. On April 12, the machiavellian King got what he wanted – a major blow-up between the two men following the tabling of the report of the Price Spreads Commission. (Indeed, the scenes the report provoked in Parliament all but overshadowed its recommendations.) King had manoeuvred Stevens into defending, once again, the pamphlet that had resulted from his speech to the Conservative Study Club the previous year – the one that had led to his resignation as chairman of the commission. That opened old wounds and brought a tough rejoinder from "Dino" Cahan. But it was not Cahan the members cheered; it was Stevens.

The report, which contained five hundred pages of recommendations alone, was then the most important and exhaustive study of economic and social problems ever made by an official body in Canada. Its chief recommendation, which called for a federal trade and industry commission with wide powers of law enforcement, heralded the growing involvement of government in private business.

Other recommendations included a tightening and tough enforcement of the Combines Investigation Act, the regulation of industrial monopolies, the prohibition of unfair business practices, and more protection for investors and consumers. The report represented a victory for the Retail Merchants Association, which had enlisted Stevens in its fight with the big merchandisers and now saw its long struggle for retail price maintenance and the banning of loss-leader selling reflected in the commission's recommendations.

294

The government quickly established a three-man commission to oversee enforcement of the Combines Investigation Act and to prevent cut-throat competition among retailers. Within two years, Ontario, the most heavily industrialized province, accepted the principle, at least, of a minimum wage for men – only a tiny step forward, since the practice wasn't effected until 1963. The recommendations of the Royal Commission on Price Spreads were accepted piecemeal or sometimes not at all. But its lasting effect has been incalculable. It helped convince ordinary Canadians that business enterprise could never again be entirely unfettered and that the state had not only a role but also a duty in regulation of the marketplace. That, too, was a form of revolution, as influential in its own way as the one advocated by the radical Left. The irony is that it was initiated by the one party to whom state control of any kind was anathema.

It was also Harry Stevens's monument. When his successor in the Department of Trade and Commerce, R.B. Hanson, tabled the report in the House, it was Stevens, only a private member, and not W.W. Kennedy, the commission chairman, who leaped to his feet to move its adoption, another breach of the unwritten rules quite in keeping with Stevens's style. By this time, the Stevens-for-Party-Leader campaign was beginning to be overshadowed by the Stevens-for-Leader-of-a-New-Party campaign. Stevens, the closest thing to a knight in shining armour that the Conservative party could muster, was about to tilt his lance at the Prime Minister himself.

3

The purblindness of Andy McNaughton and R.B. Bennett on the *The tin* matter of the unemployment relief camps passes all comprehen- *canners* sion. Throughout that winter, in the face of overwhelming evidence to the contrary, they had continued to insist that all was well and that the camps were fulfilling their promise.

Duff Pattullo, British Columbia's premier, and Gerald McGeer, Vancouver's ebullient new mayor, deluged Ottawa with lengthy telegrams and letters that became increasingly peevish – as, indeed, were the replies from the ailing, reclusive prime minister and his deputy, Sir George Perley. Over and over again, Pattullo and McGeer urged a full-scale investigation of the camps plus a federal program of public works to give real jobs to the camp workers. Over and over again, Bennett and his deputy continued to insist that there was nothing wrong and that the Premier himself should visit the camps to "reassure" a public that was clearly on the side of the workers.

With seven hundred former camp workers congregated in Vancouver, British Columbia was demanding help from Ottawa. But Bennett insisted that it was the province's responsibility under the constitution to maintain law and order. McNaughton's solution was simple – and also simple-minded. Jail them all as vagrants, he urged.

By March, after three months of resisting the appeals of the province, the city, prominent citizens, and various organizations, Bennett realized he could no longer ignore their demands for a commission of inquiry. But again he dawdled and, typically, blamed someone else. On March 6 he wrote a testy letter to his Minister of National Defence, Grote Stirling, charging "a complete failure on the part of the Department to properly discharge its duties" regarding the relief camps. He wanted an immediate report, he said, because it was now clear that a royal commission or a parliamentary committee would be needed to reassure the public about the camps. The following day the Prime Minister suffered his heart seizure. Incredibly, a month elapsed before a commission went to work, and by then the relief camp workers, organized by the Communist party, were on the move.

On March 9, sixty delegates from the various camps in British Columbia and Alberta met secretly in an old store in Kamloops to plan a massive walk-out the following month. Most were members of the communist-controlled Relief Camp Workers' Union. The parent body, the Workers' Unity League, which had organized the two-day meeting, sent only one representative, its district organizer, Arthur Herbert Evans, but he was the one who counted. Although he kept quietly in the background, he was the guiding force behind the conference and the events that followed.

Evans is one of the great figures thrown up by the Depression – a dedicated communist, a brilliant organizer and stump speaker, "persistent and forceful," in the words of a royal commission that heard his testimony later that year in Regina. But it also described him as "suspicious and intolerant of anyone who does not

296

agree with him" and "reckless and indifferent as to the truth of his utterances."

Ron Liversedge, the chief chronicler of the events that followed, knew Evans well. He was so dedicated to communism, Liversedge recalled, "that he was like the absent-minded professor. Nothing outside the working class struggle held any interest for him. [He] had experienced police clubs and prison, and to him it was just a nuisance, in that it took him away from his work."

Evans was long and lean – his nickname was Slim – with red-brown hair parted soberly in the middle. His strongest feature was a square, pugnacious jaw. He habitually wore overalls and his face, in his photographs at least, was dominated by a scowl: his eyes burn out of the newspaper cuts as if to challenge the viewer.

He might have been created by Steinbeck or Dos Passos, for he was a member of that vanished breed, the itinerant labour organizer. In 1935, at the age of forty-two, he had a long history of left-wing radicalism behind him. He had known and worked with some of the mythic figures of the radical Left – men like Big Bill Haywood and Joe Hill. He walked with a limp sustained when two machine-gun bullets struck his leg during the bloody miners' strike in Ludlow, Colorado – the same one that brought Macken-zie King into the embrace of the Rockefeller family.

Evans's father was an English house-painter, his mother an Irish housemaid; both had been enticed to Toronto, where Evans was born, during the pre-war immigration boom. Young Arthur quit school at thirteen and eventually became a union carpenter. Five years in the United States, working on and off for the Industrial Workers of the World – the doomed "Wobblies" – moulded and shaped his radicalism. In 1912 he was jailed for his part in a free-speech demonstration on a Kansas City street corner, a role that involved nothing more than reading the Declaration of Independence. When he returned to Canada, he became an organizer for another lost cause, the One Big Union, which lost its battle with the United Mine Workers of America. He was a rebel through and through, within the union movement as well as outside it. Blacklisted for a year by the UMWA, he returned to that fold as a business agent for the Drumheller local, only to find himself in trouble with the international headquarters in the United States for calling a strike. When the Americans refused to issue strike pay, Evans supported the strikers' families by using funds that were supposed to go to the international. The parent union brought suit against him for "conversion" of funds, and, in 1924, Evans was sentenced to three years in the Prince Albert penitentiary.

It was this sentence that enabled his opponents, from the Prime Minister down, to label Evans as a thief and an embezzler. These were unfair epithets. Evans had long since rejected the opportunity for an easy life in favour of the Cause. Theft for his own purposes was not in his character. He was, in fact, so popular and the sentence was considered so unfair that eighty-seven hundred miners signed a petition successfully demanding his release. Nine months after entering prison he was out again.

Having joined the Communist Party of Canada in 1926, Evans became district organizer for British Columbia of the National Unemployed Workers' Association, whose hunger marches and demonstrations were a feature of the Depression years on the West Coast. He shortly moved to the same post with the parent body, the Workers' Unity League, and also helped to organize the breakaway Mine Workers' Union of Canada in Princeton, B.C. He played a prominent part in the strike that followed – a strike so bitter that Princeton businessmen organized a branch of the Ku Klux Klan to burn a fiery cross of warning to the strikers on a nearby hillside. Evans was arrested under Section 98 of the Criminal Code. In September 1933, he was sentenced to a year in prison and held without bail pending his appeal, which he lost on March 4, 1934. In a vicious ruling, the B.C. appeal court refused to subtract the extra time from his original sentence. Evans, with time off for good behaviour, was released on December 4, 1934, having spent sixteen months behind bars.

While Evans was in jail, his home in Vancouver was seized in a mortgage foreclosure and his family forced onto relief. That in no way dampened his revolutionary ardour. When he was released, he plunged back into organizing. Now three months later, he was in Kamloops, quietly planning tactics for the Relief Camp Workers' Union.

Evans outlined his plans. The union would call a walk-out for April 4, three days after payday so the men would have a little money in their pockets. It was not technically a strike. The workers would simply leave camp and go straight to Vancouver. That would require considerable organization. Food would have to be squirreled away. Clothing must be repaired or replaced. Exit routes and transportation would have to be planned and billets provided in Vancouver – in churches, ethnic halls, and union headquarters. And recalcitrants – or at least some of them – would have to be dragooned into joining the walk-out.

The meeting made its objectives clear. Briefly, the men wanted "work and wages" – Pattullo's election slogan – fifty cents an hour for unskilled labour, union rates for the rest. They demanded a thirty-hour week, better first-aid equipment in the camps, the end of blacklisting and military control, democratically elected camp committees, the federal franchise, non-contributory unemployment insurance, and the repeal of Section 98 and the vagrancy laws. In the turbulent months that followed, these demands were heard again and again.

There was as yet no hint of any tribunal to look into the camps. McNaughton was still toying with the idea of camps of discipline, and even went so far as to ask whether a Doukhobor detention camp might be available. The General was so far removed from reality that he thought public opinion might be favourable to these draconian measures if the situation worsened. In fact, the public was solidly behind the camp workers, as were Vancouver's two afternoon papers. Had the leaders been placed in isolation behind barbed wire without benefit of a trial, a most unholy row would have ensued.

Duff Pattullo was frustrated to the point of fury. For almost four months he had been vainly warning Ottawa that the men would riot if their needs were not met. Pattullo was, of course, a lifelong Liberal nagging a Tory government, but he was more than that – a disciple of Roosevelt attempting to give his province what came to be called a "little New Deal." One of the several populist leaders who emerged during the Depression, he believed that "no person in British Columbia should be allowed to want for food, clothing and shelter through inability to obtain employment."

Pattullo was an Ontario Grit turned B.C. booster by way of the northern frontier. In his youth he had been an editor of the Galt *Reformer*. He had gone to the Yukon in 1898 during the gold rush as part of a government delegation. He stayed on as gold commissioner and then moved to British Columbia, where he served as mayor of Prince Rupert before entering provincial politics. At sixty-two he was big and beefy, with pink jowls, blue eyes, and silver hair. The frontier had given him a boldness, even a recklessness, that the voters of British Columbia found refreshing after the caution of the Tolmie regime. "Work and wages" had touched a chord, and that was what he was now demanding from Ottawa.

"I have tried in all my correspondence to use temperate language," he told Sir George Perley, the acting prime minister, on March 25, "but the situation is getting so serious that I must convey to you in the strongest possible terms that some form of permanent solution must be found. . . . " To Pattullo, the government's failure to come to grips with the situation was "incomprehensible." If there was a riot and bloodshed, he said two days later, Ottawa would be to blame.

McNaughton was unmoved. Why was he being so stubborn? For it was the General who was calling the shots. Not only was he drafting Perley's responses but he had also persuaded Bennett the previous year, against the Prime Minister's political instincts, to keep the camps going. Now even General Ernest Ashton, the District Officer Commanding in British Columbia, having reported that a general walk-out was planned for April 4, went so far as to say that he, personally, would not object to a public inquiry. But McNaughton continued to insist that nothing of the sort was necessary, that nothing was wrong, and that the men would be happy and contented if it were not for a handful of professional agitators.

In this attitude, McNaughton was a product of his class and of his time. For most of the Depression, politicians, businessmen, army leaders, and police had tried to pretend that "agitators" (the RCMP word) were at the root of the nation's troubles. Get rid of them, Commissioner MacBrien had said, and the problem will go away. Jail them as vagrants, McNaughton had advised, or put them in cells behind barbed wire; that was how the army handled malcontents. But Bennett had jailed the Communist leadership without noticeable effect. At that very moment, Tim Buck, newly released from Kingston, was on his way to address a mass meeting of the unemployed in Vancouver.

McNaughton was acting like a typical Colonel Blimp, and that was odd because in the Great War he had been anything but Blimpish. His meteoric rise was due to his flexible mind, his

300

imagination, his eagerness to test new ideas that the Blimps in the British army had rejected. His unorthodox approach to gunnery had helped win the Battle of Vimy Ridge.

But now, at forty-eight, the shaggy general seemed incapable of seeing past his nose. Why? The simplest answer is probably closest to the truth. The relief camps were his baby. He had planned them, organized them, and, as at Vimy, basked in the warm enthusiasm they had originally inspired. He could not allow them to fail. Failure, after all, was not an admired word in the military lexicon.

Having risen to the peak of his profession, the General was not used to having his plans or his orders questioned. He had been a good soldier but was, as future events would demonstrate, a poor politician. On March 28, just one day after the last stonewalling letter had gone off to Pattullo, the Cabinet did a sudden about-face, caved in to British Columbia's demands, and at last ordered a royal commission of investigation into the relief camps.

The commission, headed by a retired provincial Supreme Court justice, W.A. MacDonald, was seen as little more than a last-ditch attempt to defuse a dangerous situation. Ernest "Smoky" Cumber, secretary of the Relief Camp Workers' Union, who appeared before the commission on April 4, categorized it as "only a stop-gap." Its terms of reference were narrow; it was empowered only to investigate conditions in the camps based on individual complaints. It had no power to deal with the union's demands.

By the time the commission held its first hearing, the walk-out that it was supposed to prevent had begun. Very little had been left to chance by the organizers. To keep the men from being apprehended before they could stage the walk-out, work crews were organized to cut telephone lines and fell trees across key roads. Others smuggled tents from the camp stores, dragged them into the bush, and cut them up to make knapsacks. Some piled logs and ties near the rail lines, ready to stop freights so that the waiting men could climb aboard.

Some walked, some hitchhiked, some rode the boxcars, some even arrived in Vancouver by water. James "Red" Walsh, who had chaired the organization meeting in Kamloops the month before, trudged and thumbed his way from camp to camp, inspiring the men to follow him. By the time he reached Princeton, hundreds were tramping along behind him, four abreast, military style. Walsh set up pickets around the taverns and brothels to keep his followers in check and arranged for food for 450 men until the first freight train arrived.

Similar scenes were enacted across the province as the union leaders routed out their members. At Half Moon Bay on April 3, the men walked out a day early in order to board the only boat for Vancouver. So did the group at Squamish – sixty strong – who were warned that the police were ready to pounce. Sixty-four men from a camp near Nelson weren't so fortunate. They were hauled off a westbound freight, charged with trespassing, and thrown into jail, to become the last contingent to reach Vancouver.

By mid-April, a human torrent was pouring into Vancouver, crowding the trains so thickly that, in the words of Robert "Doc" Savage, who brought a contingent from Spence's Bridge, "the freight was like a hill with ants on it – you couldn't have stuck another man on it."

Arthur Evans met each group as it arrived. He and the other leaders of the walk-out faced a superhuman task: they had fifteen hundred men on their hands, all broke, all requiring food and shelter. They had to maintain morale, prevent violence, and weld a ragged mob into a disciplined force capable of undertaking a series of carefully planned demonstrations.

What followed was a miracle of organization. It was also a wrenching example of the waste of human talent during the Depression years. A group of young men with minimal education was about to demonstrate a capacity for the kind of leadership and organizational ability that any industrial corporation – not to mention army or government – would prize. To have kept that many young, restless, hungry, and embittered men in a seaport one week without untoward incident would have been remarkable. To have kept them under strict discipline for the best part of two months and *then* to have moved this miniature army all the way to Regina was a feat that passes comprehension. Yet it was done without violence or bloodshed and with only one minor clash until the government moved in and, with unbelievable ineptness, precipitated a historic riot.

The basic building block of Arthur Evans's awesome organization was a "bunkhouse" group of a dozen men. Willis Shaparla

302

was one of those who were asked to form such a unit. He was told to choose men whom he knew personally and who knew each other. That tight commitment made it difficult for police informers to infiltrate the organization.

The bunkhouse groups were organized into four divisions of about four hundred men each, all originally from the same geographical area. Each division had its own headquarters in Vancouver's East End. A chairman handled administration, a captain or marshal discipline, a secretary-treasurer finance. A finance committee distributed two fifteen-cent tickets a day good for meals in one of the Chinese restaurants in the area, and also bed tickets, good for a flop in one of the labour temples, boarding houses, or cheap hotels commandeered for the purpose. Men with relatives or friends in the city were urged to bunk in private homes.

There were also a food committee, a publicity committee, a "bumming" committee to organize the "tin canners" who solicited funds on street corners, and a card committee that made sure each man carried a strike card with his individual number, his unit number, and his divisional number. The divisions met daily, receiving reports from the various committees and assessing the success or failure of that day's demonstration. The chairmanship rotated among those who had shown promise during camp days.

This key leadership was almost entirely Communist. An exception was Steve Brodie, who was regularly elected chairman of No. 3 Division. Brodie was too independent to join the party, at least at that juncture. Indeed, he tended to scoff at the orthodox members, who he felt spent far too much time talking and too little acting. His hero was Evans, a man, Brodie said, "who didn't want to save the world. He just wanted to do something about the unemployed in Canada."

Above the four divisions in the pyramid were an eight-man strike committee that made the major tactical decisions, a publicity committee headed by Matt Shaw, a brilliant twenty-one-year-old orator from Saskatchewan whose real name was John Surdia, and an action committee. The last was an amalgam of camp workers and delegates from forty-two local organizations, many of them non-communist, and ranging all the way from the streetcar workers' union and the CCF to the remarkable Mothers' Council, which included women of every political stripe. It was

303

the mothers who began to use the tellingly effective phrase "our boys," which established the strikers as something far removed from vagrants or bums.

At the pinnacle of the organization stood the Strategy Committee of half a dozen men, headed by Slim Evans. This was the ultimate governing body, the one that decided policy in the events that followed. Its task was daunting. It had to raise enough money to feed and house the strikers. It had to maintain the pressure on Ottawa. It had to devise a series of ingenious but peaceful demonstrations that would keep the strike on the front pages. Above all, it had to maintain good relations with the general public, which was at that time overwhelmingly on the side of the strikers.

Gerald Grattan McGeer, mayor of Vancouver, was in a quandary. He could not – *would* not – appropriate as much as a nickel from the city's nearly empty coffers to feed the men. A one-time boilermaker, he had just turned forty-seven and was reaching the peak of a career that would carry him to the House of Commons, the Senate, and eventually back again to the art-deco city hall he was then planning to construct some distance from the city centre. He had a florid Irish face with a bulbous Irish nose, and a gift of the blarney to go with it. His eccentric ideas on monetary policy attracted few converts, but as an activist mayor he was popular. He wanted the strikers out of his city and back in the camps until the situation could be resolved by Ottawa. He wanted it done as quickly as possible, and he wanted them all out – agitators, union leaders, and deadbeats, *everyone*, blacklisted or not. Only when the city was clear of them, safe from the possibility of riot and bloodshed, could their future be decided.

In this the mayor was supported by Judge MacDonald of the royal commission but not by General Ashton, who felt (no doubt correctly) that such action would only lead to more trouble and another walk-out. Besides, as Ashton said, "strikers would claim they have forced abolition of blacklist." This admission that there *was* a blacklist – which everybody from the Prime Minister down had denied – and that its abolition would cause the military and the government to lose face, scarcely spoke well for future negotiations.

In mid-April, with hundreds of unemployed men holding snake parades through the larger department stores, the federal government agreed to round up the strikers, weed out agitators, give all the men a medical inspection, and return them to the camps. That response angered McGeer. Not only would the red tape keep the men in Vancouver for several more days but it would also force the city to pay their room and board while they were being processed.

Now the elegant James Howden MacBrien arrived in town to support the McGeer plan, warning that "serious trouble may arise unless dealt with promptly." This interference by the head of a civilian police force infuriated McNaughton, who resented the RCMP commissioner's "giving out a lot of half baked ideas." He ordered Ashton to tell MacBrien bluntly and firmly that there would be no change in the government's policy. At that MacBrien hit the roof and said he had every right to tender advice.

"Tell him the government is very upset with him," McNaughton wired to Ashton.

"He spoke as if he didn't give a damn," Ashton reported.

"He is in for serious trouble," McNaughton replied, darkly.

He did not elaborate, but the idea of the Chief of the General Staff delivering a verbal spanking to the Commissioner of the RCMP is an entertaining one. MacBrien, a former CGS himself, had once been McNaughton's superior; no doubt that had something to do with the charade. Certainly McNaughton felt himself totally in charge, especially with Bennett out of the picture. Having recovered from his heart attack, the Prime Minister had gone off to London, refusing, a bit shakily, to miss the celebration of George V's Jubilee. McNaughton continued to draft most of the stonewalling replies that Perley was sending to McGeer and Pattullo.

Yet in spite of the General's firm stand, there *was* a change in government policy. Late in the afternoon of April 19, he and Perley decided to set aside the medical examinations in the interests of getting the men out of Vancouver. This tactic didn't work. The majority stayed, some through pressure, others out of conviction or bitterness. As Ashton himself reported, the widespread feeling in Vancouver was that the camp system had lasted too long. Something else was wanted, such as "work with wages on construction."

In retrospect, that seems obvious. On one side was a pool of young men, physically fit and eager to work. On the other was a variety of building projects that had been postponed because of

305

the Depression but would have to be undertaken sooner or later. Why not take the plunge now? Prices and wages had never been lower, and the government could save the small fortune it was spending on the camps. As McGeer pointed out, "there are now twenty million dollars worth of public works crying to be done in Vancouver," while in the vicinity "it is estimated that there are at least two hundred million dollars . . . [worth] waiting to be undertaken." He was convinced that there was enough work to "completely eliminate at least seventy-five percent of our unemployment troubles and pave the way for a restoration of prosperity."

But the government refused to borrow from the future to pay for public works. It would have no truck with J.M. Keynes's mad scheme of deficit financing. Even though the day was only four years away when the nation would be paying tens of thousands of men and women a minimum of $1.30 a day plus board and lodging, to have suggested that it could be done in 1935 was akin to suggesting revolution. The budget must be balanced!

Meanwhile, Vancouver was settling in for six more weeks of demonstrations, rallies, mass meetings, tag days, picnics, and parades. The strikers lived on a day-to-day basis. Evans's first rally on April 9 had collected an immediate fourteen hundred dollars, enough to feed and house his followers for no more than three days. By April 13, with money running out, he organized a city-wide tag day that saw men with tin cans standing at every major intersection, asking for contributions.

The Strategy Committee had applied for permission for the event three days in advance to leave time for reorganization in case the city council turned it down – as it did. That was a tactical error on the city's part. The strikers tagged anyway.

Operations were controlled from a central headquarters in the Holden Building on East Hastings Street, where every key intersection was marked on large maps. From there the tin-can teams were sent out on four-hour shifts. Other teams picked up the full cans and replaced them with empties while women volunteers kept track of the incoming funds on blackboards. Flying squads stood by to replace tin canners who were arrested.

The tin canners covered an enormous territory, from Point Grey to New Westminster. In the latter city, the police chief began making arrests only to find that the men he apprehended

306

were quickly replaced by others. "I'll have no bums tagging in this town," the chief declared.

"Oh yes you will, chief," replied the head of the flying squad. "There's a hundred men on the way. How many hundreds can you accommodate in here, chief?"

The police were defeated. "Turn every damned one out," the chief ordered the jailer, and the tagging continued.

Late that afternoon, the girls counting the nickels and dimes reported that the four-thousand-dollar mark had been passed.

"Comrades," said Evans, "that's a lot of dough. We must have protection. . . . We could be held up."

With a straight face, he called the Vancouver chief of police, Col. W.W. Foster, and asked for police protection. A short time later two stolid constables arrived and stood guard over the money as it continued to come in.

"Moscow gold!" cried Evans to the police. "Moscow gold!"

By the end of the day some fifty-five hundred dollars had been collected and stored safely in the police vault until the banks opened. The tag money could be stretched to maintain the strike for another ten days.

The following week was quiet, marked only by peaceful demonstrations, parades through the Vancouver department stores, and on April 19 a mass rally of ten thousand in the Vancouver Arena. Evans wanted no trouble that would turn public opinion against the walk-out, especially on the eve of Easter. But trouble of some sort was probably inevitable, and it came on April 23 in the Hudson's Bay Company store at the corner of Granville and Georgia.

Some fourteen hundred men, marching four abreast, packed solidly together, arms linked, weaving from side to side of the street in a "snake parade" that was designed to prevent a police attack, moved west along Hastings, passing Woodward's and Spencer's department stores, both of which, alerted by the police, had closed their doors. The parade turned south on Granville, reached Georgia, and encircled the Hotel Vancouver. Here No. 1 Division detached itself and entered the white-columned Hudson's Bay store.

The men snake-paraded through the aisles as customers and clerks scattered to the mezzanine. Malcolm McLeod, hoisted on his comrades' shoulders, made a short speech listing the strikers' demands and telling the others to hold their positions and occupy the store until those demands were met. A fifteen-minute stand-off followed.

Then the deputy chief, Albert Gundy, arrived to try to move them out. Twenty men started to leave. "Hold fast, boys!" the others shouted. When the police tried to take strikers by the arm and lead them out, the men responded by overturning the counters. A glass display case toppled with a crash. Others followed until the aisles were littered with everything from shoes to candy. Before the division finally left the store and formed up on Seymour Street, five thousand dollars' worth of damage had been done and Evans's careful attempts to avoid trouble were shattered. Three policemen were sent to hospital with fractured skulls, one constable was permanently crippled, two strikers were in jail, and more would follow.

The strikers marched north to Victory Square on Hastings Street, attempting to overturn a police car on the way. Jamming the entire square, they squatted on the turf in front of the cenotaph. In a dense ring around the perimeter were two hundred RCMP, many on horseback. Hundreds of Vancouver citizens added to the mêlée. Climbing up on the cenotaph were the strike leaders, including both Evans and the eloquent Matt Shaw, and Harold Winch, the lean, intense CCF member of the legislature for East Vancouver and son of Ernest, a CCF founder.

The gathering named a delegation of twelve strikers, led by young Shaw, to meet with the mayor, whose temporary office was also in the nearby Holden Building. They wanted the city to pay for their food and shelter, but McGeer was having none of that. He told the delegation brusquely that Vancouver was bankrupt, that he could do nothing for the strikers, and that he didn't intend to take orders from anybody.

The members of the delegation left empty-handed, only to be arrested for vagrancy as they stepped out of the building.* A police cordon was thrown around them to hold them until the van arrived to take them to jail. Only Matt Shaw, who had left his camp earlier that year and was living in Vancouver, was

*The building has since been renamed the Tellier Tower after Lucien Tellier, one of the delegation.

able to show that he had means of support. He returned alone to bring to an angry crowd at Victory Square the news of what had happened.

A few minutes later, the mayor himself arrived – "Jesus Jeremiah McGeer," as Evans called him – and for the first time since 1912 the Riot Act was read in Vancouver. At that, the divisions formed up and returned to their respective halls.

The mayor went on radio to lambaste the Conservative government, the Communist party, and the CCF for turning the city into a battleground. The men in the camps, he said, "were also assured that the general strike in Vancouver would be the commencement of a revolution that would . . . change our system of government into one of communist authority and soviet power." At the same time, Matt Shaw's organization blanketed the town with twenty-five thousand copies of a pamphlet attacking and caricaturing McGeer. The strikers sold them for a nickel apiece, keeping a penny for themselves to buy tobacco. The vagrancy charges against the eleven members of the mayoral delegation were quietly dropped.

Stalemate. McGeer continued to demand action from Ottawa and to blame its policy of inaction for the riot. The government continued to insist that maintaining law and order was a provincial responsibility: " . . . the Dominion cannot under our constitution intervene," Perley replied. But the Dominion could act, if it really wished to, as the events leading up to the riot in Regina in July were to prove.

The strikers still had the public on their side, as even McGeer admitted. The Parent-Teachers' Federation, the Lord's Day Alliance, and three of the larger United churches all backed them. The CCF, led by its women members, organized the most impressive parade Vancouver had ever seen, complete with floats and pipe band. By the time it reached Stanley Park, 14,000 spectators were on hand to greet it. On May Day another parade of 7,500 marchers was led by 900 high school students. On Mother's Day, 300 members of the Mothers' Council led 1,400 strikers to Stanley Park and formed a gigantic heart to encircle them.

But when McGeer again urged Ottawa to provide work for the idle men, Perley made the astonishing reply that "a work and wages policy . . . might result in retarding the gradual but steady revival of business."

By May 18, the strikers were again running out of funds, and Evans realized that a new kind of demonstration was needed to maintain momentum. People could easily become bored with the old tactics; something different was required. He hit upon the idea of occupying a public building, and the best choice was the public library and museum at the corner of Hastings and Main in the heart of the East End.

In order to achieve surprise, the planners kept the rank and file in the dark. Two divisions were dispatched to Woodward's and Spencer's department stores as a diversion, while No. 3 Division marched from the Ukrainian Labour Temple to the library. Only when they had entered the front door and climbed the spiral staircase to the museum on the top floor did the strikers understand what was planned.

Evans had chosen well, for the building was ideally suited for a siege. The museum was all alcoves and angles, its corners crowded with exhibits and artifacts. The sole staircase that led to it was so narrow and twisting that only one man could negotiate it at a time. The entrance could be closed with a sliding steel grill. It would be difficult to dislodge the strikers, and Colonel Foster, the police chief, had no immediate intention of trying. Foster was the direct opposite of Toronto's Denny Draper in temperament. A Great War hero too, with a long militia service, his policy in Vancouver that turbulent spring was one of dignity and restraint. The strikers, for their part, were scrupulous about maintaining discipline and preventing damage.

The men were hungry. They'd had only one meal that day. But as Ron Liversedge, the secretary-treasurer of the division, put it, there was "a spirit of exhilaration that could be felt" the moment they entered the building. A phone in the museum was used to alert and inform as many people as possible about the sit-in.

Now the other divisions started to march toward the library. Willis Shaparla, as chairman of the divisional maintenance committee, was allowed to climb to the roof and from there witnessed a spectacle that was denied the others – a snake parade filling Hastings Street, weaving its way east and stretching back for blocks, the men singing "Hold the Fort for We Are Coming."

Remarkably, the library stayed open. E.S. Robinson, the librarian, remained on duty until he closed the building at four. One

310

student, cramming for exams and oblivious to the action around him, emerged bewildered into the arms of the police.

By now, a large and good-humoured crowd had gathered, blocking traffic. The strikers hoisted a banner bearing the slogan they had chanted throughout the strike: WHEN DO WE EAT? The division's food committee began lowering baskets that were quickly filled. Bake shops for blocks around sent pies, pastries, and bread. Delicatessens and cafés swelled the contributions. The nearby White Lunch sent gallons of coffee in big milk cans. People in the crowd sent up cigarettes, candies, and chocolates – so much that some strikers, unused to quantities of food, complained of headaches. Thereupon somebody sent up half a dozen bottles of aspirin.

The object of the sit-in, again, was to secure relief supplies for the camp workers. The accommodating police chief offered to find the mayor. He located him at last at the Vancouver Yacht Club and urged him to work out some sort of settlement. McGeer agreed to feed and house the camp workers over the weekend at a cost to the city of eighteen hundred dollars. At that news, the strikers vacated the museum, to the cheers of the crowd. It was their first clear victory since the walk-out had begun.

McGeer sent another predictable wire to Bennett (who was back from England) demanding federal aid and received the same maddening answer: the responsibility lay with the province. "It was only at the request of the Provinces that the Dominion undertook the care of single homeless men in camps," Bennett argued. That wasn't true. It was done at the suggestion of Major-General Andrew McNaughton.

But the impasse in Vancouver could not long continue, and both sides knew it. "We are drifting on here, Mr. Bennett, through no fault of our own, to an explosion," the *Province* warned. With the longshoremen threatening a waterfront strike in June, a citizens' league made up of local business leaders and backed by the shipping federation offered to expose "the Communist menace." Lyle Telford of the CCF had already gone on the air to denounce Evans and the other strike leaders who, he claimed, wanted "to do something dangerous in the name of strike action."

It was growing more difficult for Evans to hold his hungry band together. Money was running out and, as public opinion began to change, harder to come by. On May 30, in a mass meeting at the Avenue Theatre, Evans asked the strikers: "Do you want the strike to continue?" The vote was 620 in favour, 270 against. The figures suggest that the strikers' ranks were thinning. A good many had, in fact, refused to vote, but an estimated two to three hundred had already left town. Obviously a new tactic had to be devised, and quickly.

There are conflicting accounts as to who first got the idea of moving everybody on freight trains to Ottawa to confront the Prime Minister. Evans always insisted that he brought the idea up at the Avenue Theatre, but Ron Liversedge, who was also there, claimed the idea came independently from the floor. However that may be, "the sheer effrontery of the motion startled the meeting."

It also startled the Communist party, whose leadership in Toronto did their best to stop the trek to Ottawa. Joseph Salsberg, a leading party member, and Tim Buck tried to reach Evans again and again by long-distance phone, without success. Salsberg was certain that Evans was purposely evading him. The British Columbia members of the party were thought of as "leftists," a whimsical designation for any member of a radical organization. But in the view of the conservatives, the crazy British Columbians were always on the verge of doing something foolish and dangerous. Back east the trek was considered just that – a piece of japery that could do no good and might do a great deal of harm by turning public opinion further against the party. But there was no help for it. The trek could not now be stopped, and the party would have to back it to the limit.

And so the On-to-Ottawa trek was born, with the starting day set for June 3. As Willis Shaparla said, "There wasn't a man who didn't think we could do it. After all, we were all experienced in riding the boxcars. Suddenly there was a new level of struggle. It was as if everything we had done up to that point, was preparing for the Trek."

4

On to What followed was truly remarkable – one of those historic inci-
Ottawa dents that illuminate the times and serve as a symbol for future generations. The march on Ottawa was the high point of the

Depression, and for many it was the high point of their lives. One of these was Shaparla, whose long career encompassed a series of adventures including the D-Day landing and the buzz-bombing of Amsterdam. But nothing in Shaparla's life matched the excitement, the *élan*, the heady exhilaration of the great trek. Half a century later, he had his own personal business cards made to mark its fiftieth anniversary. They carried the slogan "On to Ottawa."

From Evans's point of view, the trek did not begin a moment too soon. The men were beginning to stagnate. Two meals a day were scarcely enough for active youths in their twenties. Hundreds had roamed the streets of Vancouver far into the night so that they might sleep through breakfast time and spend their fifteen-cent meal tickets on lunch and dinner. They were hungry men, but hungrier for action; and now they had found it. They had a goal – Ottawa. Few believed they would reach it, but all were certain they would accomplish *something*. They were taking their cause beyond the mountains. They were going national.

The authorities were glad to see them go. The last thing Gerry McGeer wanted was the presence of a thousand bitter and angry men when the longshoremen struck, as they did on June 4, the day after most of the trekkers left town. There would be no police clashes before the trains pulled out. Evans and his committee had worked hard to organize the move, cutting the four divisions to three and dropping many of the committees. While Evans led an advance party of twenty men to prepare the way, a final picnic was held in Vancouver's great forested park, where the citizens, sprawling on the grass, shared family hampers with the men who were about to bid the city goodbye.

Just after ten on the night of June 3, the three divisions marched to the waterfront where the eastbound freight was waiting. A crowd of two thousand was on hand to see them off, many bringing parcels of food (the Mothers' Council had prepared hundreds of sandwiches). The men lined up beside the cars, waiting for Jack Cosgrove, a lanky Great War veteran, to give the signal to board.

They swung up almost as one man – after all, they'd all done it before – twenty-four to a car, their captains on the alert for unfamiliar faces. Once again the sound of "Hold the Fort" echoed through the night as the train lurched and got under way.

The crowd cheered. A small knot of police lined the right of way, making notes. As the train gathered speed the onlookers waved flashlights and blankets. A second contingent would leave on June 4 to join the vanguard at Kamloops. The On-to-Ottawa trek had begun.

The strikers clung to the tops of the boxcars, bracing themselves as the train swung around the bends. At Port Coquitlam, a few miles from Vancouver, the provincial police opened up four empty cars and allowed one hundred and fifty trekkers to climb down and jam inside.

When the freight pulled into Kamloops, every man held his place until Cosgrove, as marshal, gave the order to detrain. There was a rush to the North Thompson River to clean the grime from hands and faces. Although the mayor had refused to allow a tag day, the trekkers canvassed every house and business for food, then bedded down in empty boxcars on the sidings or under the trees at Riverdale Park, three or four to a blanket. They were joined by two young sisters, Yvonne O'Brien, aged nineteen, and Catherine, twenty-two, clad in mackinaws and slacks.

On to Revelstoke, fourteen hundred strong, for a one-hour wait. A few trekkers rushed to nearby restaurants for coffee and sandwiches, and here two drunks broke some crockery. They were expelled immediately and a money order for five dollars was sent to the café to pay for the damage.

On to Golden, where the trekkers got a pleasant surprise. In an auto park a mile from the tracks, long trestle tables loaded with dishes and piles of bread had been laid out. Washboilers bubbling with stew hung suspended over a dozen fires. An elderly woman, standing over a bathtub and stirring its contents with a long ladle, shouted a cheery "Good morning, boys!" The trekkers could see dumplings as big as footballs floating in the lamb stew. "Line up the boys, there," she cried, "and give them a hot meal!"

This was Mrs. M.E. Sorley, a Communist party organizer who had received Evans's telegram to be prepared to feed a thousand men. With the help of the ladies' auxiliary of the Unemployed Workers' Association and the local CCF, she had canvassed farms for miles around, while Evans had sent for eight hundred loaves of bread, four cords of wood, and every washboiler in town. The stew, in Evans's words, "would go down in [the] history of Golden and Canada."

314

Reluctantly, Evans returned to Vancouver on orders from the Workers' Unity League. His place was taken by George Black, a member of the action committee. The Glasgow-born Black had been in Canada for ten years and had worked for various power and construction companies in Saskatchewan before coming to British Columbia. He had been on relief since 1932 but was medically unfit for the relief camps. His service in the Brigade of Scots Guards had given him a commanding presence, a level head, and a strong sense of organization.

After sweeping the park clean, the trekkers boarded the 7 a.m. freight heading for the dreaded spiral tunnels. At Field, two RCMP constables warned the men to put wet handkerchiefs over their noses and mouths to protect themselves from the smoke in the tunnels. For the next half-hour, as the train lumbered through the bowels of the mountains, some were close to panic. They'd been used to travelling in warm empty boxcars; now, clinging unprotected to the roofs, they entered a dark, ice-cold world filled with stifling smoke – yellow, acrid, and gritty. One youth collapsed, and it took the Red Cross contingent attached to his division several minutes to bring him round. At last, the train emerged into the clear, clean air of the Rockies, and the trekkers breathed freely once more. At the Alberta border, twenty-four British Columbia provincial policemen waved and cheered them on.

At Calgary, the leadership realized, the trekkers would need time off to rest and wash clothes. Finding food was not the only problem; bandages, iodine, aspirin, soap, and other essentials were also needed. The trekkers leaped from the boxcars at the west end of the city and marched to the Exhibition Grounds as Calgarians crowded their housetops to cheer and wave. The mayor, however, refused any relief. He passed the buck to the province, which passed it right back. When the city refused to permit a tag day, the trekkers held one anyway and raised fourteen hundred dollars.

Meanwhile, the leadership decided to take direct action. Five hundred men snake-paraded through the centre of town and encircled the city hall while sympathetic onlookers tossed down coins from upper-storey windows. "Relief! Relief! Relief!" the trekkers chanted, and the citizens, now jamming the streets, took up the cry. Eighty men, led by George Black and Gerry Winters, entered the city relief office and held the chairman of the Alberta

Relief Commission, A.A. MacKenzie, prisoner. A two-hour wrangle followed. MacKenzie, who considered that he was facing "a dangerous revolutionary army," tried to insist that relief was for Albertans only. In the end he was forced to knuckle under and in a telegram to Edmonton, dictated by the strikers, asked the provincial government's approval for temporary aid. Edmonton authorized him to issue two fifteen-cent meal tickets a day to each man until the trek left Calgary after the weekend.

Meanwhile, Gerry Winters's brother, Lou Summers, had wired from Edmonton that three hundred more relief camp workers were on their way to join the trek. A fourth division had to be created to handle the newcomers from the north. A sprinkling of old-timers gave lectures on the history and purpose of the trek while the usual snake parades, band concerts, and picnics kept the town in a state of excitement. The Calgarians, who were clearly on the side of the men, donated canned goods, clothing, loaves of bread, and even sides of beef in response to Matt Shaw's appeal for supplies.

Ottawa had no intention of stopping the trek in R.B. Bennett's constituency, but the movement had to be halted before it could mushroom further. Bennett had argued that complaints from camp workers had come from only one province – British Columbia – and had resulted from the work of a handful of unscrupulous agitators. Now, however, with relief workers from Winnipeg, the Lakehead, and Toronto clamouring to join the cause, a halt would have to be ordered before Manitoba was reached. The obvious place was Regina, the headquarters of the Royal Canadian Mounted Police. Bennett's plan to bring the trek to an end would need the co-operation of both railway companies.

In Calgary, however, the CPR was co-operating with the trekkers. The company told George Black the exact time the morning freight would leave town. The superintendent of traffic explained the best way to load the men to escape injury and detailed some of his employees to lend a hand. He assured Black that there would be plenty of time to board everybody and "a few minutes here and there would not be missed." The city police were equally accommodating, guiding the men to their positions in the yard at six o'clock Monday morning.

In spite of the hour, a large crowd turned up to chat with the trekkers as they lounged on the grass, knapsacks at hand, waiting

316

for the train to be made up. An anxious mother threaded her way through the crowd seeking her son, trying to persuade him to stay behind; nobody could find him. A well-dressed youth appeared with a suit of clean overalls and a sweater for his brother. One man rushed up at the last moment to announce he'd walked forty miles to join the trek. A small boy proudly announced that his father was joining up. "I have twelve brothers and sisters at home," he explained, "and daddy hasn't been able to get a job for over a year." As the train prepared to leave, a group of Calgary women arrived with twenty-four hundred sandwiches and a side of beef to feed the trekkers on the next leg of the journey. Another group of fifty women offered to accompany the trek to provide solace for the men – an intriguing suggestion that had to be rejected.

Railway police held the crowd back as the various divisions swung aboard on Cosgrove's signal, packing the roofs of fifty boxcars. As marshal of the trek, Cosgrove had maintained an iron discipline. Like so many of the leaders, he had survived the Great War, having joined the army at fourteen and served the entire four years at the front except for a brief absence to recover from wounds received at the Somme. Now he ordered the unit captains and their deputies, standing at each end of their allotted boxcars, to check each man's strike card to make sure that no strangers tried to infiltrate. That done, he climbed aboard the tender behind the locomotive, waved to his grey-haired mother standing in the crowd, and they were off.

A late spring storm lay ahead. For fifty miles the freight chugged on through sheets of cold, driving rain. The men clung to the catwalks, wet to the skin, huddling together for warmth. At Medicine Hat, the advance party had washboilers full of hot coffee to warm up the shivering crowd, which included the two O'Brien sisters, who stepped off the train "looking like drowned rats" and were not heard of again.

The trekkers slept that night in Athletic Park on the outskirts of town. Steve Brodie, helping to keep the fires going, suddenly spotted a dark figure emerging from the shadows at the park entrance. "Well," somebody announced, "here's Arthur." Evans had persuaded the WUL to let him return.

To Brodie, Evans seemed "absolutely bone weary, almost staggering from tiredness and weakness. Because of the fire burning

317

in him all the time, he never had an ounce of fat on him and this night he looked like a living skeleton." Evans's face was black with soot, his eyes red from cinders and fatigue.

"Steve, for God's sake give me a cup of that coffee, please," he said. He had spent hours trying to outmanoeuvre the RCMP, who he was convinced were intent on stopping him from going east. Brodie was never sure whether Evans had really spotted Mountie spies: "Time after time in Arthur's life he saw policemen who weren't there." But it was also true, as Brodie said, that "they hounded that man unmercifully." A study of the RCMP's own records shows that every time he had made a public appearance an undercover man was on hand to take down everything he said.

At Swift Current, Matt Shaw tried to get the city to put up $250 in exchange for a promise that the trekkers would bypass the town. The mayor refused to submit to this blackmail – the town was bankrupt, anyway – but did issue meal tickets for local restaurants. The freight obligingly waited for fifteen minutes to allow the men to be fed.

At Moose Jaw a rumour spread that if the men weren't given food they'd smash up the town. Local policemen and members of the Junior Board of Trade, who pitched in to act as waiters in three Chinese restaurants, were flabbergasted to observe the iron discipline under which the trekkers operated. Steve Brodie thought the spectacle hilarious – a minister, a school teacher, and a storekeeper crying out: "Okay, send in 10 more men, we've got these tables cleaned." Again, the CPR was requested to hold the train until the men were finished. "They fell over backward to assure us we weren't going to go hungry," Brodie remembered. "They had been fed so long on their own propaganda that they believed it. . . . "

By this time the word was out. The government had no intention of allowing the trek to continue past Regina. In the words of justice minister Hugh Guthrie, the trekkers were "a distinct menace to peace, order and good government" – the sturdy phrase that served to mask so much repression in the thirties.

But to carry out his intentions, the Prime Minister was forced to make another about-turn and ignore all his earlier attempts to evade responsibility for the problem. For months, Bennett and his deputy had been telling Duff Pattullo that the maintenance of law and order was up to the province. As late as June 11, he had told John Bracken, the Premier of Manitoba, that his hands were tied

318

in the matter of the trek. Colonel S.T. Wood, the assistant commissioner of the RCMP in Regina, had been specifically warned that he could not act unless requested to do so by the attorney general of the province. The RCMP in Saskatchewan, having been contracted out as provincial police, were not under federal jurisdiction. Now, to reverse himself, Bennett would have to invoke the Railway Act, which would return the RCMP in Saskatchewan to federal government control. But before he could make this move, Bennett had to receive requests for protection from both the CPR and the CNR. Of course he got what he wanted. The presidents of both railways suddenly came to the conclusion that the trekkers were trespassing on company property. For the best part of a fortnight, the CPR had been leaning over backward to accommodate them. Now, the general manager, W.A. Mather, in a hasty letter to James Garfield Gardiner, Saskatchewan's Liberal premier, had decided that they threatened to become a menace. The same day, Colonel Wood received instructions from Ottawa to patrol both the railway yards and the trains to prevent the trek from continuing.

Gardiner, who had bounced back into power the previous year, was furious. Highly partisan by nature, he had no love for the Bennett government. He was short (five feet, four inches), barrel-chested, and tough. He had worked as a labourer, a farmer, and a schoolteacher, perfecting his oratory by remaining after classes to address empty desks. Since 1914 he'd been a hard-nosed politician and a champion of prairie interests.

The last thing he wanted was fifteen hundred or more jobless men – angry, now – dumped on his doorstep with no place to go. He shot off a blunt wire to Mather pointing out that the trekkers could scarcely be called trespassers since the CPR had supplied cars for their use. He added that they'd done nothing in his province to warrant police action. But they didn't belong in his province, Gardiner said: move them out.

Gardiner was even angrier at Bennett's high-handed methods. The attorney general of Saskatchewan hadn't asked for help, as Bennett had always insisted he must before Ottawa could move. The RCMP was paid by the province and was supposed to take orders from the province. Yet here was Bennett issuing orders to the RCMP. As of June 12, the province of Saskatchewan lost control of its police force.

319

The trekkers, now two thousand strong, reached Regina on June 14, eleven days after the first lot left Vancouver. The province had already agreed to allow them to bed down in the Exhibition Grounds and to give each man two meal tickets a day. Here, too, the citizens were heavily on the side of the newcomers. A hastily formed Citizens' Emergency Committee, incorporating a dozen organizations from the CCF to the Ministerial Association, pledged "to make the stay for the boys as comfortable and pleasant as possible. . . ."

The trek was scheduled to leave Regina on the evening of Monday, June 19. Mass rallies, picnics, and the arrival of another three hundred men from the camp at Dundurn had raised morale. Ottawa wanted to prevent a potentially dangerous confrontation with the police at the rail yards, especially with both citizens and strikers in their present mood. Besides, Bennett's plan was to delay – to keep the trekkers in Regina long enough to cool them down. A series of stalling tactics would, he hoped, tire everybody out until the movement collapsed.

To that end, he sent two Cabinet ministers to Regina to "negotiate" with Evans and his committee. R.J. Manion, Minister of Railways, and Robert Weir, Minister of Agriculture, arrived on Monday morning, and a long wrangle followed in the basement of the Saskatchewan Hotel. The two ministers found Evans and his associates far more tractable than Premier Gardiner, whose attitude "was very ugly and not very helpful." Gardiner poohpoohed the idea of a revolution. It wasn't the first march on Ottawa, he told Manion: a thousand Saskatchewan farmers had invaded the capital in 1910 and three thousand in 1922, and there'd been no revolution. If the men boarded the train that night and a riot ensued, he would call out the local police and arrest both the RCMP and the trekkers, since, in his view, both would be equally guilty.

When Evans presented the trekkers' demands, all of which had been publicized over the past six months, Manion insisted with a straight face that he'd never heard of them before. Since he could not let the trek proceed, he made a counter offer. If Evans would head a delegation to Ottawa to present those demands to Bennett, the federal government would provide the army of men with three meals a day – at twenty cents, not fifteen – while they waited in Regina for the outcome of the meeting.

320

Evans knew at once that he'd been outmanoeuvred. He could not reject the offer. The press and the public would turn on him, for he had been demanding just such a meeting for months. But the delay would be demoralizing. When he put the proposition to a volatile mass meeting that afternoon, the trekkers damned the offer as a ruse; there was no possibility that Bennett would meet those demands. But they knew they had no choice but to accept. That evening eight thousand people gathered outside the Saskatchewan Hotel while the negotiators ironed out the final details. The trek was temporarily sidetracked, to the relief of Colonel Wood of the RCMP, who did not yet have enough men in Regina to prevent two thousand trekkers from forcing their way aboard a train.

The eight delegates selected to go to Ottawa (the group included Evans, Savage, Walsh, and Cosgrove) left on June 18, travelling first class – "on the cushions," to use the current phrase. Red Walsh noted with astonishment that the dining-car waiter laid three sets of cutlery before them. In the Ottawa hotel where the delegation stayed, he saw his first bathtub in five years.

They met with Bennett and Perley on June 22 in a room so small that Doc Savage (who took his nickname from a popular magazine) likened it to a janitor's closet. A curtain was drawn over one corner and Savage always maintained he could see a pair of Mountie boots sticking out from under it.

The scene that followed resembled an old and oft-remembered play of which everybody has memorized the script. Bennett's New Deal did not include any negotiating with men he considered to be dangerous revolutionaries. Evans again outlined the trekkers' demands. Bennett shot them all down. "Work and wages," he declared, were beyond the capacity of the country. Food and shelter at the camps were adequate; there was no compulsion to join and no discipline. The daily twenty cents wasn't a wage, it was a gift. The real problem was agitators "representing ... Communism, which we will stamp out in this country." He hit out at the strike leadership: "You have not shown much anxiety to get work. ... What you want is this adventure in the hope that the organization which you are promoting in Canada may be able to overawe the government and break down the forces that represent law and order."

Shortly after that an acrimonious exchange took place between Bennett and Evans.

"I come from Alberta," Bennett said. "I remember when you embezzled the funds of your union and were sent to the penitentiary."

To that Evans angrily replied, "You are a liar!" He had been charged with converting funds, not embezzling them. "I used the funds for hungry people, instead of sending them to Indianapolis to a bunch of pot-bellied business agents," Evans said. As for Bennett, he declared in a burst of anger, he wasn't fit to run a Hottentot village.

The meeting was a waste of time, for neither side budged an inch. The delegation left Ottawa on June 23, making a series of platform speeches before reaching Regina on the twenty-sixth. There Evans learned that Ottawa intended to open a temporary camp at Lumsden, Saskatchewan, to house the trekkers until they went back to the camps or to their homes.

Evans now realized that the strike of the relief camp workers, which had begun on April 4, was virtually at an end. They had, in fact, come much farther than anyone had expected, but that did not lessen the disappointment. He put on a bold face when he addressed an enthusiastic meeting of citizens that evening. If the strikers couldn't go by rail, he announced, the trek would continue by road. He appealed to people with vehicles to come forward to take the men to Winnipeg. This was sheer bravado. The Trans-Canada Highway was not completed. The farthest east any motorcade could get would be Kenora, near the Manitoba-Ontario border.

But Ottawa had no intention of letting the trek move on by any method, even if that meant bending the law. Two days before, Colonel Wood had received a telephoned command from his superior, MacBrien, that all motor cars, buses, or trucks carrying relief camp trekkers east were to be stopped by the police and the drivers and passengers arrested. If worst came to worst, the government would proclaim a national emergency.

This was a remarkable order. Ordinary citizens were to be denied the use of the King's Highways. There were no legal grounds for it, although MacBrien, as an excuse, used the "peace, order and good government" clause in the Relief Act to justify the action.

322

Wood told Gardiner that the directive had been approved by order-in-council. That wasn't true. There never was such an order; in fact, the Cabinet couldn't pass one while the House was in session. A web of confusion was now woven around the police instructions. T.C. Davis, the province's attorney general, was led to believe that the non-existent order prevented the citizens from rendering assistance of any kind to the trekkers. Wood, apparently, believed this himself, for he told the Regina *Leader-Post* that anyone in Regina or its neighbourhood who assisted the trekkers was liable to prosecution – and that included offering food and shelter.

None of this was correct; but it was believed, and it killed any chance for Evans's demonstration convoy on the twenty-seventh. On that afternoon, when the motorcade was supposed to move the strikers east, only one truck and two automobiles turned up. The sad little contingent set off bravely toward the Manitoba border, led by Reverend Samuel B. East, a tall, lithe, and energetic United Church minister, like Woodsworth a follower of the Social Gospel. East was popular with his congregation but was looked on with some distaste by the church hierarchy because of his pronounced left-wing views. Communism, the sixty-two-year-old minister had once declared, was "one divine, far-off event, towards which all creation moves."

East was a leading member of the Citizens' Emergency Committee. The night before he had been a principal speaker at the trekkers' rally. "Bennett," he had cried in his best pulpit voice, "wants to be [the] Mussolini of Canada. Shall we let him?" Now, with the crowd's enthusiastic "No!" echoing in his ears, he was off to do his bit for the cause. "We're heading east with East" was his slogan. In less than an hour, he found himself in jail.

The tiny convoy, followed at a discreet distance by some five hundred cars crammed with onlookers, encountered a cordon of steel-helmeted police barring its way on the outskirts of town. In vain, East produced a permit from the highways department, giving him the right to use trucks on the roads. Another hundred police arrived, scooped up everybody in the convoy, and rushed them to RCMP headquarters. East was never charged and was released later that night. The others were held under the all-purpose Section 98 of the Criminal Code that was the only legislation the police could properly use.

Events were now moving towards a climax. In Winnipeg, fifteen hundred relief camp workers announced their own trek to Ottawa. In Regina, the men refused to go to the government's camp at Lumsden, believing it was a concentration camp where anything could happen to them. Their funds were low; there was only enough money left to feed the men one meal. Donations had dried up because the citizens had been misled into believing they would be arrested if they helped the trekkers. Evans himself was searching for a face-saving solution that would allow the men to return to their camps or their homes with some semblance of honour.

R.B. Bennett, however, was in a state of panic. Manion had warned him that "this Communistic crowd . . . are determined to stir up what would be practically a revolution." Strong measures, he insisted, would be needed to curb it. "Somehow the leaders should be got at and if possible got out of the position of leading these unemployed."

Bennett took that advice. On June 28, Colonel Wood received his orders. The government wanted the strike leaders arrested – urgently. Once again that handiest of all sections of the Criminal Code, No. 98, was to be invoked. Under it, all trekkers could be considered Communists and thus subject to arrest.

Wood was in an unenviable position. As head of the provincial police force in Saskatchewan, he was used to taking his instructions from the provincial attorney general and also having the benefit of his advice. Now, at this moment of crisis, he no longer had the opportunity to consult with the civil authority. Ottawa had taken that away and was calling the shots by remote control – the long-distance telephone from the capital, hundreds of miles removed from the scene of the trouble.

Wood did not have enough local evidence to charge anybody, and said so. As far as he was concerned, the trek leaders had done nothing while in Saskatchewan to warrant arrest. Ottawa replied that John Leopold, the man who had fingered Tim Buck and his comrades, would be arriving post-haste on July 1. (In fact, not one of the trekkers was ever found guilty under Section 98.)

Meanwhile, Evans was still trying to achieve peace with honour. On July 1, he approached C.P. Burgess, the local representative of the federal Department of Labour, to suggest that the trekkers be allowed to disband and return voluntarily to their camps or their homes. He also asked for amnesty for everybody

324

but himself. The federal government, having fought the trekkers to a standstill, now had a chance to cool the situation and, in victory, to be magnanimous. But Evans's plan was rejected. Ottawa insisted that everybody go to the Lumsden camp to be processed before going back to Regina to board the trains.

It was Monday, July 1, the Dominion Day holiday, the end of a long weekend. Communication with Ottawa had been maddeningly slow. Now the trekkers tried to reach Premier Gardiner. He was finally located at his farm outside Regina and persuaded to come back into town for a meeting. Again Evans was trying to get permission for his organization to handle the dispersal. Failing that he would have preferred to have the Saskatchewan government oversee the task rather than federal authorities. He also attempted one more meeting with Burgess and Wood. That was unproductive. Burgess refused to meet with Gardiner. Wood claimed that Evans was trying to get his men back to Vancouver to join the longshoremen's strike.

The holiday conspired to frustrate the most obvious of solutions. Gardiner did not reach his office until four that afternoon and, with most of his colleagues still out of town, scheduled a Cabinet meeting for eight. Those members of the Cabinet who could be reached were still gathering for the meeting – Attorney General Davis had not yet arrived – when the news came just after eight o'clock that a riot had broken out in Market Square.

5

Barring the Winnipeg General Strike of 1919, the Regina Riot of July 1, 1935, is probably the best-known civilian disturbance in Canadian history. But unlike the Winnipeg strike, which had a purpose and a meaning, the events in Regina's Market Square that evening had neither objective nor reason. *The Regina Riot*

The riot shouldn't have happened, didn't have to happen, and almost didn't happen. It was fuelled by fear, suspicion, stubbornness, pride, and, at the end, implacable fury.

The federal government under R.B. Bennett must bear the greatest share of blame. Bennett's pathological fear of bloody revolution provoked, in the end, bloody violence. Ottawa's stubborn insistence on running affairs in Regina at long distance and its equally stubborn refusal to make any concessions to Evans contributed. The trekkers' innate suspicions of the Lumsden camp and Evans's insistence on saving face by pretending that a victory of sorts had been achieved didn't help. And finally, there was the effect of the holiday weekend, which slowed down negotiations until they were outdistanced by the rush of events. Had Jimmy Gardiner been in his office that Monday, had the members of his Cabinet been at their desks, a solution would almost certainly have been found and the trek peacefully disbanded, for Gardiner did not share Bennett's unyielding antagonism to Evans and his followers.

One can only sympathize with Colonel Wood, the veteran Mountie, who was under continual pressure from Ottawa to arrest the leadership of the trek immediately. Although Evans and his colleagues could have been apprehended at any time or place in Regina, Wood wanted to move when he could take them all at once and without inciting an uproar among the trekkers. But Ottawa insisted they be arrested without delay.

Wood was surprised to find that the two government lawyers charged with preparing indictments against seven trek leaders had warrants ready for serving by the time he got back to his headquarters at five o'clock after his meeting with Evans and the trek leaders. He still doubted that there was enough evidence to justify issuing warrants, and as it turned out he was right. Nonetheless, he did not dare wait. In short, the RCMP, a supposedly independent police force, was bowing to political pressure. Equally incredible was Wood's failure to disclose his intentions to the Saskatchewan government. Later, he claimed he did not know that Evans was meeting with the Premier to suggest a way out of the impasse. As it was, neither Gardiner nor his attorney general had any intimation of what was about to happen.

The question was, where and when should the men be arrested? Certainly not at the Exhibition Grounds, surrounded by their followers. But a mass rally was planned that evening at Market Square, where several speakers were to make a final plea for funds. According to the plan, the police would go to the Unity Centre, the trek headquarters on the edge of the square, and try to make the arrests there. If their quarry wasn't present – and at seven o'clock that night the police found no one – the move would be made at the rally.

326

This was a dangerous decision. Regina's chief constable, Martin Bruton, who sat in on the strategy session with the Mounties, clearly had his doubts. Was it really advisable to try to take men into custody at a packed outdoor meeting? he asked. Bruton registered his disapproval, but after pointing out the seriousness of the move went no further. Wood apparently thought he had no choice.

The assistant commissioner would testify to the commission that later investigated the riot that he did not expect trouble. But he acted as if he did. The arrests would be made by a flying squad of RCMP and city plainclothesmen. Three big moving vans loaded with one hundred steel-helmeted Mounties would be stationed on three sides of the square. Twenty-nine uniformed city police armed with lead-tipped batons and sawed-off baseball bats would be hidden in the police garage on the south side. A troop of mounted RCMP officers would also be positioned to the south at Twelfth and Osler.

If Wood didn't expect trouble, why this overkill? Several interesting points emerged later. The police, it turned out, had no idea of how many of the wanted men would be present at the rally. Actually, only two – Evans and Black – were on hand. The crowd was largely civilian; most of the trekkers were elsewhere, watching a baseball game. Of the fifteen hundred people in the square, well over a thousand were curious spectators, enjoying the end of a holiday weekend – citizens such as John Cheers, who was on his way to see a movie but stopped off "because the wife had never seen these strikers in a body before and she said she would like to see the boys."

The policemen at the scene were badly confused about the tactics to be followed. Wood wanted all the police to be held back and not used unless the arresting officers (in plainclothes) ran into trouble. But Chief Bruton and also Inspector Duncan McDougall of the city police believed they were to rush the meeting as soon as a signal whistle was blown, whether the plainclothes detail needed them or not. That is what happened and that is what caused the violence that followed.

Until the whistle blew, the scene in the square was peaceful, with many of the spectators seated in rows of chairs around the speakers' platform. Gerry Winters, representing the trekkers, and John Toothill, on behalf of the Citizens' Emergency Committee, appealed for funds over a hastily contrived loud-speaker system. Evans, seated on the platform, was handed a note reporting that the square was surrounded by Mounties. Evans gave the note to George Black, the chairman, who asked if he should tell the spectators. Evans said no: "This is a peaceful meeting and if you announce it you're liable to cause a certain amount of unrest." Looking over the heads of the crowd, he could see the moving vans stationed on the perimeter of the square but couldn't be sure who was in them.

Steve Brodie, standing at the south end of the square facing the platform, also saw the vans. The night was so sultry that the rear doors were slightly open for ventilation, and Brodie could see the familiar yellow stripes on the blue breeches of those within. "Look what is here!" he said to Johnny Dean, a member of his division. "I can smell trouble."

At that moment the doors were opened another foot and the two men could see that the police were wearing steel helmets. "If there's no trouble," said Johnny Dean, "then they're going to bring it."

Even as he spoke, there came the shrill sound of a police whistle. Immediately a wave of city police, dressed in blue, burst from the rear of the police garage and tore into the crowd, swinging their batons above their heads. Evans tried to leave the platform but was knocked off his feet. The plainclothes squad seized him and Black, frog-marched them to a truck on Halifax Street, and took them at once to the city police station. Wood's elaborate preparations to arrest seven trek leaders had resulted in the capture of only two.

The moment the whistle blew, the steel-helmeted Mounted Police, who were supposed to be held in reserve, poured from the big vans and waded into the crowd.

In less than a minute, the scene in Market Square was transformed into a confused mêlée marked by scenes of unmitigated savagery. The people in the square, who had no idea what was happening and saw the police coming toward them, batons raised, began to flee in panic. The first impression Willis Shaparla had was of a terrible roar; his instant reaction was that the square had been hit by an earthquake. He could not associate the sound with human beings. Nor could he identify the source, for he was being pushed and shoved by those around him trying to

328

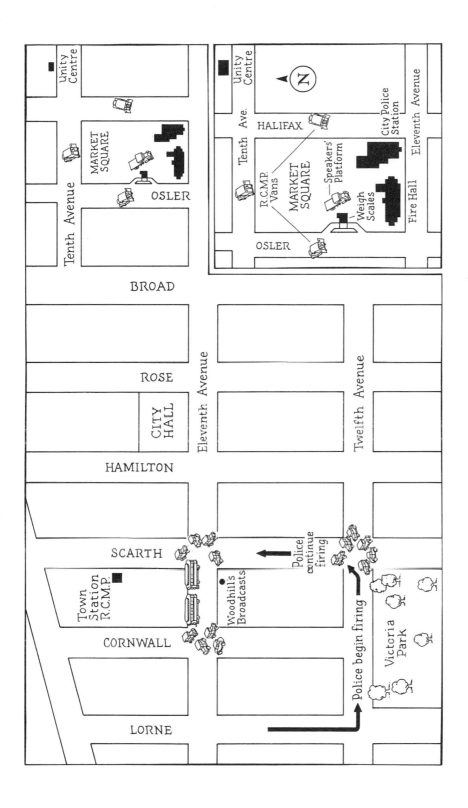

escape. Then he caught a glimpse of blue uniforms and realized what was going on. As he said later, "that was the most fearful moment of my life."

Few, if any, of the people in the square realized that the police attack was to support the plainclothesmen arresting Evans and Black. Most thought that both the city police and the RCMP were attacking them. That wasn't surprising. Jacob Brunner, a mechanic who ran a repair shop near the square, was twenty-five yards from the platform when he saw the police rushing toward him, swinging their batons "as though they were out to fight a bunch of wild Indians." The spectacle inspired fear, panic, and more violence. John McCarthy's first impression was of a stampede. The people rushing toward him "seemed to be mad." McCarthy, who lived at the nearby Regina Hotel, thought the wild animals had escaped from a travelling circus that was visiting the city. Looking into the crowd, he "never saw such fear depicted on human beings as on those faces."

If the testimony later sworn to by a score or more of witnesses is to be believed, the police laid about them with a will, swinging batons at anybody who got in their way and even striking people who had fallen on the ground. The police flatly denied it.

Certainly, the scene was so confused that only a trained observer could have remembered exactly what he or she saw. The citizens fled in disarray. Men who got in the way of the police were shoved aside. Women stumbled and were trampled. Baby carriages were knocked over. Hundreds who tried to get away from the city police ran directly into the three-pronged onslaught of the RCMP. There seemed to be no escape. Enraged, the crowd began to pick up stones, bricks, and pieces of wood to fling at the police, who responded with their clubs and batons. With the city's treasury empty, the sidewalks that bordered the square had been allowed to crumble, and now trekkers and citizens tore off pieces of concrete the size of softballs and hurled them at the police. The mob, after ebbing out of the square, surged back again, pushing the uniformed men before it, bent on revenge. When the police tossed tear-gas bombs into the crowd, people caught them and threw them back.

The rage of the trekkers, which communicated itself to the others in the crowd, is understandable. For three months they had been under strict discipline. Except for the brief skirmish in the
330

Hudson's Bay store in Vancouver, they had held themselves in and bottled up their feelings in order to maintain public support. Now their protest had failed; they no longer needed the public. They were convinced that the police were deliberately attacking them, and they struck back.

The chief victim was a city plainclothes detective, Charles Millar, a Great War casualty with a metal plate in his head. Millar was one of the reserves inside the police garage, but when the riot began he rushed out onto the square to his death, beaten to the ground with a length of cordwood wielded by one or more unidentified men. Although Evans would make capital out of this savage attack, claiming that Millar was killed by the police, the charge was hardly credible coming from someone who had already been hustled away when the tragedy occurred.

But were the police entirely innocent of unprovoked assault? A good many Regina citizens, who might be considered more objective than either the police or the trekkers, later swore to what they saw in the square when the riot began. Could they all have been wrong?

William Curtis, a garage man who had lived in Regina for fifteen years, was knocked down and trampled as the police advanced. As he struggled to get up he saw an old man on his knees. A Mountie ran over, so Curtis swore, and whacked at the man until somebody came and pulled the victim away. Christina Metcalfe testified to a similar experience. As she tried to flee from the square she swore she saw three RCMP and a city policeman beating a striker. "Murder!" she screamed just before she was struck in the knee by a block of wood swung by another policeman. She was lame for two weeks.

Jacob Brunner saw policemen "pounding a man all over." He went up to one of the policemen, whom he knew – Sergeant Tommy Logan – and cried out: "What are you doing here, are you trying to kill him? . . . Why don't you shoot him and be done with it? . . . Why do you keep pounding him?" Logan looked at him in a dazed manner, as if to say, "Who are you? What are you talking about?" The beaten man could no longer walk and had to be dragged to the police station.

Though much of the evidence is flimsy and some confused, though much of the supposed brutality reported to the commission might have been accidental, caused by the crowd pushing,

331

shoving, and trampling on each other, the account of this last incident has the ring of truth. The policeman is named and the description of his reaction sounds authentic. Police, citizens, and trekkers alike were all dazed by the fury of the attack and the response to it.

The battle was by no means one-sided. One angry group forced two Mounties against a wall at the corner of Osler and Tenth, battering them with fists and sticks. As one fell to the sidewalk, William Reader, a clerk, waded in, pleading with the crowd not to kill him. For his pains he got a blow in the chest from a piece of automobile spring wielded by an elderly citizen. But the crowd left the policeman alone.

Steve Fustas would never forget that Dominion Day because he thought he had lost his young daughter that night. He had taken her to Market Square with his wife and their baby-in-arms out of curiosity. What else was there to do in Regina on a summer night? Fustas was a barber by profession but a labourer by happenstance; people cut their own hair in those days to save money. He reached the speakers' platform just as Toothill was addressing the crowd. He lifted the little girl onto the platform. His wife kept the baby in her arms and gratefully accepted a chair. Suddenly, he heard her call out, "Steve, here is the police!"

"What police?" he asked.

"Look up!" she told him. He turned toward the police garage and saw the blue-uniformed men bearing down, waving their clubs and shouting, "Clear up the Market Square and get out of here! Get out!" Terrified, he ran twenty-five yards, only to hear his wife, somewhere in the mob, cry out, "Steve, we've lost our girl!" In his panic, he had left her on the platform.

He tried to struggle back with the baby, forcing his way toward the platform through a struggling mass of people. He asked a Mountie for help and was rebuffed. "I haven't time," the policeman told him.

He heard somebody say that a girl had been killed in the crush, and at that he began to cry, thinking it might be his own child. He clung to the Mountie's arm, pleading for help. The policeman took a swing at somebody behind him and Fustas thought he was the intended victim. "I'm a father!" he cried. The Mountie said he wasn't after him.

332

Fustas headed northeast. Looking down the row of seats he saw a man holding onto a club, his face, shirt, and hands covered in blood. He shouted to the crowd that the man needed attention; an ambulance arrived and picked him up. To the east he saw another man standing by a telephone pole, a Mountie on each side clubbing him on the head. People around him were hurling missiles and a policeman was throwing them back.

When the Mounties began to throw tear-gas bombs into the crowd, Fustas thought of his baby: "This is poison!" He ran through the fumes towards Osler Street, his hand over the infant's mouth to protect him. At the corner of Osler and Eleventh, a group of Mounted Police trotted down the sidewalk, clubbing people who got in their way. At this point, Fustas came upon his wife and discovered, to his great relief, that she had found their missing daughter.

The police managed to clear the square just before nine that evening, and the riot moved along Tenth and Eleventh avenues, evolving into a series of skirmishes in the alleys and laneways that ran off the main streets. The crowd surged onto Eleventh, the southern border of the square, and moved west along both Eleventh and Twelfth for several blocks as far as the intersections of Scarth, Cornwall, and Lorne, where the main battles took place. A troop of RCMP on horseback moved west along Eleventh past the city hall swinging their batons, riding over the civic lawns and flower beds, and clubbing the demonstrators who were pelting them with rocks and pieces of concrete, wood, and iron. From the rooftops, others were pitching debris down on the police.

Wilfred Woodhill, a reporter with station CJRM, had a spectacular view of the fray. The station was located in the Saskatchewan Life Building at the corner of Eleventh and Cornwall. Woodhill with two colleagues had shinnied up an adjoining telephone pole to the roof of the one-storey annex, carrying microphones and amplifiers, to watch the action. They had expected trouble and were now prepared to report on it.

Woodhill began his broadcast just after the police cleared the square. He could see a mob of perhaps one hundred and fifty rioters, armed with rocks, pouring along Eleventh as far as Cornwall and driving a dozen policemen into the shelter of the buildings. On they came, past his vantage point for another block, smashing windows as they went, until they reached the intersection at Lorne. The police retreated south on Lorne as the crowd surged back again as far as Scarth. Woodhill heard one man shout, "Hey, there's a good one!" pointing to Willson's stationery store on Eleventh. A barrage of rocks followed, breaking every window in the store.

Woodhill's listeners could hear the sound of the glass breaking. They could also hear Woodhill commenting on the remarkable restraint of the police, who while trying to defend themselves were taking the brunt of the crowd's attack. (Woodhill later testified that he had at no time seen a policeman raise a club to a striker.) His remarks about police restraint, blaring from store radios, enraged the mob. A man was sent to climb the telephone pole to tell Woodhill that such words would not be tolerated. The radio station, however, had posted a picket with a lead pipe at the top of the pole, who warned the intruder off.

By 10:10 that night, the scene had become one of incredible confusion. The crowd dragged half a dozen parked cars into the centre of the intersection at Eleventh and Cornwall to try to prevent the advance of the blue-clad city police, who had circled around from Lorne. Some of the cars were badly battered, their windshields cracked or broken. Traffic was at a standstill. A single streetcar had managed to run the gauntlet of a hail of rocks at Eleventh and Cornwall, but others were stalled. One was used as protection against the mounted RCMP troop, which was tossing tear-gas bombs to try to disperse the mob. "Come on, you yellow-legged sons of bitches," one man cried as he hurled rocks at the Mounties. Woodhill heard somebody shout, "They've got the machine-guns out!" Then he saw a man stagger and fall, apparently wounded, and try to creep under a stalled streetcar. A policeman seized him and dragged him out again.

At this point, the very climax of the riot, an incomprehensible event occurred - incomprehensible, at least, to a modern broadcaster. Woodhill received a direct order from his superior to kill the broadcast. At that moment, the scene below was one that any reporter today would give a month's salary to be able to broadcast live: the sounds of hundreds of windows being smashed, of men and women shouting and cursing, of horses screaming as they fell, and, most chilling of all, the crack of pistol shots (there were no machine-guns), the groans of the wounded, and the sirens of the ambulances.

But the height of the action was not heard or described on the radio. Woodhill obediently packed up his equipment, slithered down the telephone pole, and returned to the station. His later explanation would baffle a modern reporter: "We did not figure that it was the thing for broadcast purposes." The time was coming when no station would be governed by the sensitivities of its listeners. But radio was young then, and its listeners had yet to hear the sounds of war – bombs exploding, machine-guns stuttering, and reporters of the Murrow breed describing burning cities from the rooftops.

Meanwhile, the city police under Inspector Duncan McDougall, having come south on Lorne to Twelfth, after skirmishing with the crowd moved east toward Scarth. There, a mob of three hundred pelted them with rocks. McDougall's eighteen men were forced back as the crowd advanced. The inspector ordered his outnumbered men to unbutton their holsters, draw their .38 revolvers, and fire over the heads of their attackers.

It took a second volley to disperse them. In all, the police fired some twenty-five shots. McDougall and his men reached the intersection, moved around a small barricade of cars, wheeled left, and headed north on Scarth Street towards Eleventh. Now they found themselves caught in a crossfire of rocks hurled by a group protected by one stalled streetcar and some men coming up behind them along Scarth. McDougall, who had sent a runner for more ammunition, again ordered his men to fire. He saw a citizen stagger, fall, and try to crawl under the streetcar, shouting that he was wounded. This was the same man Woodhill had seen just as he ended his broadcast. McDougall and a constable pulled him free, called for an ambulance, and sent him to hospital.

At about the same time, Jim Cross, a summer bachelor, was walking home on Scarth from a friend's place. Just before he reached Eleventh, he heard the whine of a bullet above the almost deafening sound of screaming people and shattering glass. The bullet struck a steel lamp-post beside him and ricocheted. Then he felt "a terrific impact, like being kicked by a mule"; the bullet had hit him in the abdomen.

335

"You're the luckiest man in Regina tonight," the doctor told Cross when he finally reached the hospital. "If that bullet had moved over another half inch you'd never have known what hit you." The flattened bullet had gone directly through Cross's abdominal cavity without injuring any of his vital organs, to emerge one inch from his spinal cord. But Jim Cross couldn't sleep that night, for he was worried about his job. In those stark days there was no sick leave, pay for days off, unemployment or hospitalization insurance, or crime compensation. His boss came the following day with a bouquet of flowers and a blunt message: "If you've had anything to do with supporting these strikers, you'll be out of a job." The police also turned up to deny that they'd fired the shot that almost killed him. But ten days later when he left the hospital, he found his bill had mysteriously been paid.

No policemen were wounded by gunfire, although thirty-nine members of the RCMP were so badly injured they were sent to hospital. There is no evidence that the trekkers had firearms. Twelve of these, however, plus five Regina citizens, were hospitalized with gunshot wounds that night. All but one had been shot during the mêlée at Eleventh and Scarth at 10:10 p.m. Joseph Rothecker was one. He had come out of the King's Hotel beer parlour on Eleventh to buy a paper when a bullet struck him in the neck. His wife, Mary, would never forget the scene in the hospital when she was called to his bedside. She knew the building well because her husband worked there as an orderly. Now, she said, "I never saw the corridors so full of blood." The place was filled with the wounded, some, like her husband, seriously hurt, others only slightly (half were discharged the next day). Rothecker suffered partial paralysis from his wound and was unable to go back to work for a year. When he tried to take legal action against the police, his lawyer told him that no one could sue the Crown.

The police station, too, was jammed. Instead of the mere seven men the police were originally seeking, one hundred had been arrested. Most were swiftly released without being charged. Of the twenty-two who eventually came to trial, eight were sent to jail on charges stemming from the riot. All charges under Section 98, under which the seven arrests were to have been made, had to be dropped for lack of evidence.

After the fusillade of pistol shots at Scarth and Eleventh, the riot had begun to wind down. Small skirmishes continued, how-

336

ever, and the police patrolled the streets until midnight. By then the trekkers were back at the Exhibition Grounds, surrounded by a tight police cordon that confined them without food or smokes until well into the afternoon of July 2.

These tactics infuriated Jimmy Gardiner, who was convinced the police wanted to starve the men into submission and force them to go to the Lumsden camp. "This will end in a worse riot than last night," he told Bennett in an angry telegram. The Premier was convinced he could have arranged to disperse the trekkers peacefully. Now he demanded that the government abandon the plans for the Lumsden camp and allow the province to take over. Bennett grudgingly agreed, and Evans had the face-saving formula he had been willing to settle for before the trouble began.

After a hiatus of three weeks, the Saskatchewan government again found itself in control of its police force. The men at the Exhibition Grounds were fed immediately. Gardiner and Attorney General Davis worked round the clock arranging for an orderly withdrawal from Regina. Bennett had one small consolation: the responsibility was no longer on his shoulders. When frantic telegrams reached him from Victoria and Vancouver demanding that no trekkers be sent back to the coast, he fobbed them off on Jimmy Gardiner.

On July 5, the trekkers, now reduced to fourteen hundred, marched in good order to board CPR and CNR trains to the West, to their homes, or back to the camps. Fred Griffin of the Toronto *Star* was reminded of similar scenes in 1914 and 1915 when other young men in khaki boarded trains to go off to war. "Nowhere in Canada is there a body of youth with such a definite will and purpose as these," he wrote. " . . . They have lighted a flame that no amount of repression is going to put out."

There were other attempts to march on Ottawa that summer, but only one succeeded. Three hundred trekkers sponsored by the National Unemployment Council set out to walk from Toronto to the capital on July 17. It took them twenty-two days. They managed a brief meeting with Bennett, who dismissed them in fifteen minutes after telling them they wanted to embarrass the government.

By an odd coincidence, Andrew McNaughton retired as CGS on the very day of the Regina Riot. The relief camps would no longer have him as an advocate. Their days were numbered, anyway. Mackenzie King would make their abolition a plank in his election platform (together with a pledge to drop Section 98 from the Criminal Code) and carry out his promise after he was elected. On June 30, 1936, the camps were closed forever. By then Spain was under siege, and a good number of those who had taken part in the great On-to-Ottawa trek were preparing to set off secretly to face more bullets.

Saskatchewan appointed an official commission of three judges to look into the riot. It called 359 witnesses ranging from Premier Gardiner to Matt Shaw. It was clearly biased from the outset since it dismissed the testimony of all the trekkers and residents who swore they had witnessed or encountered police brutality and accepted that of the policemen who insisted that in every case they were acting in self-defence. The commission's eight-thousand-page report, issued in April 1936, defies credibility. It wholly exonerated the police and blamed Evans and his followers for the riot. It admitted official responsibility only in mildly questioning Ottawa's ill-advised attempt to exercise control from a distance.

The lawyers who acted for the trekkers at the commission hearings disagreed with the conclusion. One of these was Emmett Hall, a future Justice of the Supreme Court and one of Canada's most distinguished jurists. Fifty years later, Hall, recalling the events of those days, stated his continuing belief that "this was a police-provoked encounter." Hall said, "I never had any reason to change my opinion on that. There is no doubt that the direction to what was done . . . had to come from Ottawa." Without that interference, he said emphatically, "there wouldn't have been any riot."

6

Changing There has never been anything in Canada remotely like the Al-
the guard berta election campaign of 1935. Since those days Canadians have become used to more sophisticated hoopla on the hustings. But Bible Bill Aberhart's march to victory, accompanied as it was by the kind of high-jinks usually associated with old-fashioned medicine shows, has had no counterpart.

The big meeting that took place in the Edmonton Exhibition Grounds that summer was part picnic, part religious rally, part political kick-off, and part vaudeville show. There were singing and dancing, cakes and lemonade, and races for the children. As Aberhart came forward, to the cheers of the crowd, the band struck up one of his favourite hymns, "Tell Me the Old, Old Story." First, however, two very agile eighteen-year-old girls, clad in what were then known as scanties, did a buck-and-wing to enormous applause, followed by a throbbing baritone who sang "Old Man River," and then six more girls in tights who performed an energetic tap dance that brought the crowd to its feet.

These were only curtain-raisers for the main event, which was a horse race on the oval track in front of the stadium, with Aberhart himself as the announcer. Out pranced the four steeds with their jockeys, each wearing a label for one of the four competing political parties – United Farmers, Liberals, Conservatives, and Social Credit (significantly, the CCF wasn't represented). As the barrier was sprung, three horses bunched up in the lead, leaving the Social Credit horse a poor fourth. No one, however, had any doubt about the outcome as Aberhart, in his stentorian voice, calling the race and following the progress of the Social Credit jockey's strategy, suggested how the faithful should mark their second choice under the province's system of proportional representation.

The Social Credit campaign had everything – religion, scandal, dirty tricks. Aberhart flatly refused to allow any of his people to debate the principles of Social Credit; instead, he urged his followers to take him on faith. They were told not to read or to listen to criticisms of the movement. As a result, the *Calgary Herald* suffered a major circulation loss while another anti-Social Credit newspaper went out of business entirely.

It was a dirty campaign. Opposition speakers were booed off the stage or drowned out by the honking of dozens of horns outside the meeting halls. There were complaints of cars smeared with red paint, of tires slashed, of sugar and sand put into gas tanks. Although Social Credit theory was the main issue of the campaign, Aberhart's opponents raised it at their peril. His mesmerized followers refused to listen to any arguments while his candidates declined to debate the subject with anybody, publicly or privately.

Aberhart shamelessly used his radio broadcasts to make political hay. He got the air time at a cheap rate; after all, he controlled

339

the mortgage on the station. The UFA was infuriated, but there was little they could do about it. By this time Bible Bill had a radio following of more than three hundred thousand – more listeners than tuned in to Jack Benny's Sunday night half-hour. Aberhart linked his opponents to the traitorous Judas and lashed out at "fornicators, grafters, and reprobates," a not-very-veiled dig at the discomfited ex-premier, Brownlee, and others of his Cabinet, including the Minister of Public Works, O.L. McPherson, who had been involved in a messy and well-publicized divorce case. "Are you going to let this man cross-examine me?" Aberhart cried when McPherson dared to ask a question at a political rally. The crowd shouted McPherson down.

As recently as January Aberhart was undecided about contesting the election. If the UFA had agreed then to embrace Social Credit principles, he would have rested content. But the UFA at its January convention decisively rejected the proposal, though offering the balm of Major Douglas's advice. The major arrived in May as a "consultant," but that wasn't good enough for Aberhart. At its April convention the Social Credit League (Douglas's name had long since been dropped) had already decided to contest the election.

For an hour the delegates debated the method of choosing candidates. Aberhart sat silent throughout the discussion and then, in a one-minute speech, settled the question. *He*, as leader, would control the selection of all candidates. "If you're not going to let me have any say in the choice of my supporters," he said, "you will not have me as your leader." And that was that.

But he declined to be a candidate himself. He didn't want his opponents to throw all their resources into one constituency in an attempt to beat him. After the election was won, he would be premier and a seat would be found for him – not much of a problem, since every candidate was under his thumb and almost every seat in the province could be assumed to be a safe seat.

The party – no longer a "movement" – issued a new pamphlet with a blue cover and sold 60,000 at twenty-five cents apiece. A warning inside stated that the text was "not a detailed plan for the government of Alberta." In fact, Aberhart had no explicit plan except to give everybody who supported him twenty-five dollars a month. In spite of their falling-out, he still expected Major Douglas to come up with the details. The monthly credit –
340

it would not be in cash – would go to every adult who had lived for at least one year in the province and who, on application, acknowledged Social Credit principles.

The newspapers were unanimously opposed and so was much of the business community. That, however, helped the party rather than hindered it. In July, a group of business leaders formed the Economic Safety League to attack Social Credit, an example of overkill that drove more Albertans into Aberhart's camp. Neither the press nor big business was popular in Alberta in 1935.

Aberhart stumped the province tirelessly, making as many as four speeches a day. There was no way for the UFA to combat the mass hysteria he evoked. Few bothered to heed the full-page advertisement of the Calgary Board of Trade, which prophesied that Social Credit would bring "great suffering from which the Province will not recover for many years." The people had already endured great suffering. How could things get worse? At a meeting in Wetaskiwin at which the UFA leader spoke, a young farmer made the point graphically. "I sell a steer for hardly enough to pay the freight," he reminded the crowd. "Now would you tell me what I have got to lose by trying Social Credit, whether I believe in it or not?" The audience cheered.

By mid-August seers were predicting a Social Credit sweep, but no one expected the landslide that was revealed when the votes were counted on August 22. The Social Credit party took fifty-six of the legislature's sixty-three seats, the Liberals five, the Conservatives two. The United Farmers of Alberta received a death blow; not a member of that party was elected, and several of its candidates lost their deposits. Social Credit would win the next eight elections and under Aberhart and his successor, Ernest Manning, govern the province virtually unopposed for thirty-six years.

The dust had not yet settled in Alberta before the federal campaign got under way. It had really begun in January with Bennett's New Deal broadcasts. But Bennett had been out of action for much of the interval. He had waited longer than any previous prime minister to hold an election, stretching his term to its legal limit. The voters would go to the polls on October 14, and to most observers the result was a foregone conclusion. The smashing victory of the Liberals in New Brunswick, followed by another in Prince Edward Island in August, brought to six the number of Conservative governments that had been successively overthrown during the Depression. The only speculation revolved around the size of the prospective Liberal sweep.

Bennett's government was assailed by a host of problems, not all of its own making. The drought on the southern prairies showed no signs of abating. An outbreak of stem rust, the worst since 1916, lowered prospects of a crop even further. The failure of the relief camps and the resulting explosion in Regina had dealt government support a heavy blow. Bennett's name was being used as an epithet. To his fury, people joked not only about Bennett buggies but also about Bennett boroughs – shacktowns for the jobless in the urban centres – and Bennett barnyards, abandoned prairie farms. Worst of all, the party was badly split.

The split came out into the open when Harry Stevens bolted the Conservatives. The move was not unexpected. A group of Tories had already been boosting Stevens as a replacement for Bennett. Another group of prominent Montreal businessmen wanted a "National Party" with Stevens at its head. But Stevens wanted nothing to do with the very business interests he'd been attacking. Warren K. Cook, the spokesman for small retail businesses, was another matter. With Cook's backing and financial support, Stevens on July 7 announced a new reform party "to re-establish Canada's industrial, economic and social life to the benefit of the great majority." It was to be called the Reconstruction Party.

Stevens's defection embittered Bennett. "One man has crucified the party – Stevens," he told a friend in Calgary. His own Cabinet was in disarray. One minister had died; eight others had declined to run; Bennett himself, dogged by illness, was operating at half-steam. Nonetheless, as he told a Tory banquet in June, "I'll die in harness rather than quit now." That delighted Mackenzie King, who thought him the best possible adversary, considering the times. "He is the man the people rightly wish to defeat," King wrote. "He has been making enemies for himself, as I thought he would, from the day he assumed office, and if he goes through the campaign he will get one of the worst defeats any political leader ever sustained."

King had no use for Bennett. His diary is peppered with epithets, some of which – "blatherskite" is one – have slipped out of common usage. Bennett, King wrote, was "unctuous," "boor-
342

ish," a man of "low cunning and hypocrisy," "the Great I Am," "a dog of a man – a brute in his instincts," "a Pharisee of Pharisees," and so on. The accommodating Mrs. Wriedt, to King's obvious satisfaction, told him that Bennett was "like a snake in the grass in his Cabinet – he was not to be trusted." All the same, King could not help indicating his delight on those rare occasions when Bennett deigned to notice him.

The two were miles apart in personality and political savvy. Where Bennett was bombastic, King was bland. Where Bennett was blunt, King was devious. Where Bennett was loud and rude, King was soft and fawning. Where Bennett was outspoken, King was fuzzy. Where Bennett was direct, King was circuitous. Bennett used a cleaver against his enemies; King used a stiletto. Bennett never understood the art of the possible; King thrived on it. In short, King was a politician; Bennett was not.

King, who always disliked making election promises, was wise enough to realize he need make none this time. The Depression, not the Liberal party, would finish off the Tories. He confined himself to some vague statements about restoring parliamentary democracy, getting rid of government bureaucracy, and saving the nation from dictatorship. He managed to suggest that other parties had something in common with Hitler, Stalin, and Mussolini (who at that time was invading Ethiopia). Wasn't it obvious that Canada was becoming "a second Italy, a second Germany, a second Russia"? he asked. His pledge to get rid of the relief camps and the hated Section 98 formed part of that attack.

The Conservatives responded with another of those meaningless slogans that political parties seem to love: STAND BY CANADA – A CHANCE FOR YOUTH – VOTE BENNETT. The Liberals pounced on that, and with reason. The Tories, who had inaugurated the so-called slave camps and brutally stopped the protest of youth in Regina, were now talking about giving youth a *chance*? And how could they believe that the word "Bennett" was better than "Conservative" when it came to attracting votes? The Liberal slogan was more telling. It was KING OR CHAOS.

When the results were tabulated on October 14, the Liberal sweep was even greater than expected. King's party had captured 173 seats; the Conservatives were reduced to 40. Stevens's party failed to get off the ground; only its leader retained his seat. The big surprises were the good showing of the Social Credit party

343

with seventeen seats, all but two from Alberta, and the poor showing of the CCF, with only seven of its candidates elected.

Had Stevens stayed in the party and Bennett resigned, perhaps in his favour, the results would have been dramatically different. Stevens's defection had badly crippled the Tories. In forty-eight ridings, Ernest Watkins has pointed out, the total of Conservative and Reconstruction votes would have been enough to defeat the Liberal candidates. That would have given Mackenzie King a total of 125 seats in the House to a combined Opposition of 123 – an uneasy margin. Almost equally damaging was the impact on the CCF, which would certainly have gained more seats if independent voters had had one fewer option to the old-line parties. Stevens's party actually got slightly *more* of the total vote than the CCF.

The Liberal victory was no landslide, except in seats. The party barely increased its strength in total votes. Its gains in French Canada were matched by heavy losses in the West. As usual, the voters weren't voting for either of the old parties; they were voting against the Conservatives, whose strength dropped to three-fifths of what it had been in 1930.

When King and Bennett met the following day for an "intimate and friendly" discussion, the talk turned to Stevens. Both men were fervent in their condemnation of him. "You have no idea of the kind of man he is," Bennett said bitterly. He quoted Richard McBride, a former premier of British Columbia, who had once told him: "Do not trust that man Stevens; he will betray you. Stevens has no background whatever, and no principles." By which, of course, the self-made millionaire and the courtly, polished ex-premier understood that Stevens, the small businessman, didn't belong to their class and didn't adhere to *their* principles.

King was appalled at Bennett's appearance. "He has taken off much weight, and, particularly from his face – the bones . . . are quite visible, with just the skin drawn over them. His lower lip and jaw protruded a great deal, and all the time he spoke his mouth, at the corner, was filled with saliva, as though he had been using his jaws to the utmost. It was the look of a man who had become almost an animal in his fight."

In politics, perception is often more important than accomplishment. Bennett's unfortunate personality – his bullying, his

344

bluster, his public intransigence, and his handling of radical dissent – obscured his successes. The Canadian Radio Broadcasting Commission, the Bank of Canada, the Farmers' Credit Arrangements Act to help debt-ridden farmers, and the Prairie Farm Rehabilitation Administration to tackle the drought were among the solid achievements of the Conservatives' term in office. Bennett also paved the way for both unemployment insurance and a national health scheme, although his attempts in this direction were annulled by the decisions of the Privy Council.

Such progressive measures would have been unthinkable in the decade before Bennett took office. In a sense, he was forced into them by the times. Nonetheless, there is irony in the fact that Bennett, the big businessman leading a party dominated by other big businessmen, should preside over the dawn of a new attitude toward the relationship between government and the private sector. Until the Depression, the Bennetts of Canada had believed with absolute faith that the government had no business involving itself with economic or social issues. By the time Bennett left office, that concept was as dead as the passenger pigeon.

He carried on as Opposition leader until 1938, when he was replaced by Manion. That same year, he left Canada forever to spend the remainder of his days in England. Tommy Douglas was one of the little group of three who saw him off at the train station. As Douglas remarked, "the man who had been fawned [on] and flattered by all the politicians for years was completely ignored." Bennett told Douglas that he left Canada betrayed by his friends and deserted by his party. When he died more than a decade later, the leader who had presided over the five most turbulent years in Canada's domestic history was close to being Canada's forgotten man, remembered for the Bennett buggy and not much else. The *Canadian Encyclopedia* devotes sixty-three lines to Richard Bedford Bennett. Tommy Douglas, deservedly, gets far more.

1936

1

After more than six years of Depression, Canadians were no longer in a mood to be pushed around. Several incidents in Ontario in 1936 made that clear. In the farming hamlet of St. Charles, east of Sudbury, forty-five starving men attacked a district relief officer who had refused them food vouchers and shut him up in a room without anything to eat. When he brought a charge of assault against one of his tormenters, the magistrate let the accused go, remarking that "his destitution justified his action." In Blind River, a crowd of angry women threatened to strip two relief officials naked and ship them back to Toronto. "Give us enough to keep our children. That's all we want," they told the mayor at a mass meeting. At Stamford, near Niagara Falls, a crowd of more than one hundred, protesting relief cuts, imprisoned eight municipal officials in the town office. In the Toronto suburb of Etobicoke, the reeve received similar treatment; it was hours before he was set free.

State of the nation

The people were angry because of the authorities' grudging attitude toward relief payments. That was partly Mackenzie King's doing. Like Bennett he was obsessed with the dogma of the balanced budget – if not in 1936, then in the succeeding year. He raised the sales tax and the corporation tax slightly, but not the income tax; and because he, too, was convinced that Ottawa's money was being spent recklessly, he reduced grants-in-aid to the provinces by 25 per cent.

As a result, the country grew tense and testy as the lower levels of government responded to the cuts. Quebec decided to scrap the dole and force all relief recipients to work for their meagre allowance. The Ontario government began to fire its married women workers and replace them with spinsters. The mayor of North Bay, forced to remove eighteen hundred men from the relief roles, gave them permission to beg on the streets. This lack of compassion toward the jobless was further demonstrated by the mayor of Fort Erie, who suggested that all male applicants for relief be sterilized.

In the opening moments of the New Year, the new prime minister, as was his habit, had knelt in prayer "for all the loved ones in earth and in heaven, and to be of service to the poor and needy,

349

to my country and to the cause of peace." Service to the poor and needy did not, however, involve a plunge into the chilly seas of deficit financing. Brave words and fanciful public relations efforts, such as Winnipeg's "Business Is Better" campaign, did not reduce the number of jobless in Canada. At the beginning of the year there were still 1,300,000 Canadians on relief. That number would increase by at least 8 per cent before the year was out.

King was more interested in saving money than he was in creating jobs. In the United States, the Roosevelt administration was spending eleven billion dollars on the Works Progress Administration, which not only built dams, bridges, parks, and airports but also subsidized writers, artists, ballet dancers, and actors. To King, this was unbridled extravagance, and it horrified him. He was convinced that Canada's problems were caused by a similar prodigal attitude on the part of the provinces and municipalities. To solve that, he fell back on a traditional Canadian solution: he set up a commission. The National Employment Commission would co-operate with the provinces to secure efficiency in the dispensing of relief and thus save money. Its secondary task would be to recommend new employment programs. But the cautious Prime Minister made certain that its role would be strictly advisory. It would have no real power to create work for the unemployed.

As always, Mackenzie King felt himself to be teetering on the edge of exhaustion, "so weary and fatigued I could give it all up." But he soldiered on, dragging himself to his bed "disheartened and very lonely" and also bemused by his own situation, so "strange to possess great power (nominally) and in one's self to be so helpless."

The country seemed to be at a standstill that spring. It needed an infusion of new blood to help shake it from its lethargy, but that was not forthcoming. In 1930, it had welcomed 163,000 immigrants; now the annual flow had dried up to a trickle of 11,000. Mackenzie King might consider himself a leader capable of solving global problems – he told his friend Joan Patteson that June that he believed he had saved the world from war on more than one occasion – but the evidence suggests that the world paid Canada little heed. A minor player in international politics, it was seen by many as a cultural backwater. John Goss, the noted British singer, came to Canada in February and announced that

350

the country had the worst radio broadcasting system in the world. J.B. Priestley, the noted British novelist, arrived in May and declared that there was no literature in Canada worth speaking about. As usual the country was exporting much of its best talent, including Edna Mae Durbin, a fourteen-year-old girl from Winnipeg. As Deanna Durbin, singer and movie star, she would save Hollywood's Universal Pictures single-handedly from bankruptcy.

In spite of this cultural apathy there were hints that Canadians were gaining a sense of community. The Canadian Radio Broadcasting Commission was reorganized as a corporation – the CBC. Based partly on the British model, partly on the American, it would within a decade make Goss's peevish remarks obsolete. Clarence Decatur Howe, Mackenzie King's minister in the new Department of Transport, was hard at work on a plan for a national airline that would allow Canadians to travel coast to coast in a mere eighteen hours. The new Bank of Canada was issuing its own paper money, which King insisted carry bilingual wording despite the objections of Bennett, who thought that decision was "fraught with the greatest danger to harmony between races in other parts of Canada."

Bilingual currency, however, could not be any more divisive than the despised Section 98, which King struck from the Criminal Code that spring, or the relief camps, which he caused to be closed at the end of June. It was by no means a permanent solution to the transient problem. Although half the relief camp workers – some ten thousand – went to work for the railways at better rates of pay, with the government footing the bill, these jobs were only seasonal. And the farm placement scheme, also designed to absorb transients, was a year away.

An Imperial era was ending. In late January the life of George V drew "peacefully to its close," in the words of the Royal Physician, who was not above giving his dying sovereign a little nudge toward the grave. Now the new king reigned. "His subjects in every country in the British Commonwealth know that he will acquit himself with great distinction," John Dafoe wrote in the *Free Press* – brave words that he, in common with other editors, would have preferred to forget before the year was out. Rudyard Kipling, who wasn't poet laureate but acted as if he were, preceded George V to his tomb by a few days. King made no public comment; Kipling, in his view, was "a Tory imperialist [who] has never shown particular friendship towards myself or meant much to Canada. . . . It does not seem to me . . . [that] Canada has any particular tribute to pay."

King's aversion to Kipling was in keeping with his own nationalism. In the midst of the worst economic crisis in its history the country was slowly becoming disjoined from the British connection, with its colonial overtones. King's suspicion of titled governors general, who, he felt, were always trying to upstage him, also applied to the newest occupant of Rideau Hall. One might have expected John Buchan, a popular novelist, to be more accommodating than the blue bloods who had preceded him, but as First Baron Tweedsmuir he was, in the Prime Minister's view at least, decidedly stand-offish.

At the end of March, King tackled Tweedsmuir about his attitude and an embarrassing conversation took place. King asked if somebody had been telling the Governor General to beware of him. Why, at a recent Canadian Club dinner, with Bennett, of all people, present, had His Excellency made no reference to King as prime minister? And why had he delivered a eulogy of Lord Byng – whose treatment of King's position in the constitutional wrangle was still a sensitive topic after ten years? Surely, Tweedsmuir must have known that he was reviving an old controversy and striking at King personally! Or so King thought.

The Prime Minister complained that he didn't feel at home with Tweedsmuir as he had with the others; and that was odd, he felt, because the two had known each other for twenty years. Why, just that evening, at a reception, the Governor General had snubbed him, giving him nothing more than a formal shake of the hand before passing him on to Lady Tweedsmuir "and leaving me to straggle in as a schoolboy." King wondered why on informal occasions the Governor General and he could not be on first-name terms; yet even in private Buchan addressed him formally as "Prime Minister." This hypersensitivity was typical of King. He might be irked by the colonial connection; he might be distressed by ostentation; but he loved to bask in the friendship of the great and near-great – a Franklin Roosevelt, a John D. Rockefeller, Jr., a Ramsay MacDonald, or a member of the British nobility.

352

Buchan tried to make amends, but it didn't work. At a vice-regal dinner during Roosevelt's visit to Quebec at the end of July, King found himself seated at His Excellency's right but with a vacant chair at *his* right. That meant he had nobody to talk to half the time. The vice-regal staff apparently hadn't thought to bring someone else in. "It is this treating of one as a secondary consideration – when P.M. of the country that I do not like," he wrote.

He found it almost impossible either to talk to Tweedsmuir on a man-to-man basis or to write to him "as fully as I would have liked to be able to. I don't feel free enough to be natural; or that he is enough of a stranger to be formal." King at last decided to stop using "J.B." as a salutation and go back to "Governor General," but he did sign one last letter, wistfully, with "Rex," the name that only his oldest and most intimate friends used.

As the prime minister of an independent nation in the Commonwealth, in no way subordinate to Great Britain, King was, of course, feeling his position. It was not the first time he had been nettled by what he considered a patronizing attitude on the part of British nobility, and he was in the process of drawing Canada gracefully out from under the long imperial shadow. But Buchan was newly minted as a noble and still a commoner at heart. Why didn't he bend a little? Was it because, as a new peer, he was too conscious of his position? There is a simpler and more obvious explanation: the sophisticated novelist-viceroy had little in common with his fusty prime minister. He simply couldn't warm to him.

King was faced with more serious problems than imagined vice-regal snubs. The province of Alberta was technically bankrupt. Aberhart had asked for a two million-dollar loan the previous December; King cut it to one million. He and the Minister of Finance, Charles Dunning, wanted to establish a loan council that would allow the poorer provinces to borrow money more cheaply because the loans would be guaranteed by the federal government. But there was a string attached: each province must prove that it really needed the money. That was too much for William Aberhart, who balked at this attempt to extend Ottawa's control over provincial finances. King felt he had no choice but to let the province default on its maturing debentures, as it did on April 1 and again later in the year.

As the new premier of a depressed province, Aberhart was having a bumpy ride. There was as yet no sign that the voters would get their promised twenty-five dollars a month. Indeed, he had at one point referred to that election promise as "a figure of speech." And he had broken with Major Douglas, who said, quite correctly, that Aberhart's version of Social Credit was not *his* version. Douglas, for one thing, had never mentioned twenty-five dollars a month. But what *was* Aberhart's version? He had relied on Douglas to come to Alberta to put his Social Credit theory into effect. Now it appeared that neither Douglas, who thought in global terms, nor Aberhart, who thought in provincial terms, had *any* specific plan.

The new premier was sure the press was out to get him. The *Calgary Herald* hired its first staff cartoonist, Stewart Cameron (late of the Walt Disney studios), whose job was to caricature Aberhart and his program. The Premier hinted more than once that he would have to control the press. Meanwhile the Alberta Social Credit League bought the other Calgary daily, the *Albertan*, getting its radio station, CJCJ, into the bargain. Station CFCN, over which Aberhart had broadcast and on which he still held a mortgage, was told to stop reporting news adverse to the government. To its credit, it refused to be muzzled.

About the same time, Aberhart reassured his followers that the Rapture, in which the world would be deserted by Christians, was still a long way off. The second coming of Christ would not occur until after 1943, he told an audience in Edmonton.

On April 23, Aberhart moved to introduce a form of what he considered Social Credit. The government, he said, would issue scrip known as Prosperity Certificates in place of money. To keep the scrip valid, the holder would have to place a one-cent stamp on the back of each certificate every week. Aberhart hoped that this tax would keep the notes circulating.

It didn't work. People found they couldn't use "funny money" to pay fines or taxes or make purchases in government liquor stores. The banks wouldn't cash scrip. Some Cabinet ministers even balked at being paid with it. The Prosperity Certificates failed to bring prosperity.

To still the clamour for the monthly twenty-five-dollar dividend, Aberhart in August introduced a registration program for Albertans who, he promised, would start receiving the bonus

354

some time in 1937. The regulations laid bare the authoritarian nature of the Social Credit government. To receive Alberta Credit, a citizen would have to register, pledge allegiance to the government, and make a declaration of all assets and liabilities and a statement of other personal information. Nor could anyone be absent from the province for more than a month without permission of the local manager of one of the new State Credit Houses that the government was creating. These houses were designed to process all financial transactions within Alberta; they were, in effect, state banks. People rushed to sign up, either through fear of government retaliation or because they expected to get their twenty-five dollars at once. One man brought his wife all the way back from Detroit to sign. But an Edmonton bookstore owner named Surry refused, even though his MLA told him he'd lose his business. Instead he launched a "League of Freedom" to attack the whole idea.

2

The reforms that Aberhart introduced in Alberta in 1936 had *The weather* little to do with Social Credit philosophy. They were forced on *as enemy* him by the deepening drought. He increased the minimum wage, bolstered crop insurance and unemployment relief, created a moratorium on debt collection and land seizures, and reorganized the school system, including a much-needed consolidation of school districts. But he could not make it rain.

Saskatchewan was still the hardest hit of the prairie provinces; it had no choice but to cancel $75 million in debts and taxes owed by the citizens in 1936. The unprecedented dry spell forced the federal government to abandon all hope of balancing the budget. Conditions were now so appalling that Ottawa had to promise 100 per cent federal aid to the drought-stricken regions of the southern prairies.

The winter had been terrible, the coldest on record. From early January until the end of February there was no break in the constant cold. Temperatures dropped below minus forty degrees Fahrenheit and stayed there. City streets were deserted; traffic came to a halt. Blizzards buried railways and disrupted train schedules. Farm families lived in their stove-heated kitchens.

Every sideroad between Winnipeg and the Rockies was blocked by snowdrifts. In Saskatchewan, the average temperature was a startling twenty-five below, Fahrenheit. Brandon went nine days with the thermometer registering more than forty degrees below zero. In the ranch country of Alberta thousands of head of cattle perished in the cold as farmers were immobilized. In the schools, where heating systems had long ago broken down from neglect, makeshift stoves were fashioned out of oil drums. Teachers struggled through the drifts before dawn each morning hoping to kindle fires that might make their schoolhouses habitable by noon; on the coldest days some students missed their class work while trying to keep them fuelled.

Fred Williams, in his book *The Fifth Horseman*, described the scene in one Saskatchewan schoolhouse that winter: "When nine o'clock came, the half-frozen pupils would stand around the contraption, stamping their feet on the board floor until circulation was restored. Frozen mitts and snowshoes were placed in a circle around the heater and left there until it was time to go home; no attempt was made to throw snowballs or play outside games at recess. Life was a grim reality for the children of the 'thirties' – mitts, overshoes and warm clothing could only be obtained on relief orders once a year."

Ontario was affected almost as badly as the West. On a frigid morning at the end of January, in a two-storey house in Lindsay warmed only by a small oil heater, an old-age pensioner named Ella MacMurchy came downstairs to find her eighty-two-year-old sister, May, lying on the cold kitchen floor. "I think May is not so well this morning," she remarked to the milkman. He quickly discovered that May was dead.

On the prairies, there was no relief from the weather. The winter, which had been the coldest in history, was followed by a summer that was the hottest. Two-thirds of the western grain lands were withered by drought, producing the smallest harvest since 1919. Each day was hotter than the last. Right across the southern plains temperatures rose to ninety degrees, and then kept climbing.

Saskatchewan suffered for six straight weeks; in all that period there were only three days in which the thermometer dropped below 90°F. In many areas it was worse. Willow Creek endured thirteen days of 100-degree weather in July. On July 11, the tem-

356

perature reached 108° in Winnipeg, 110° in Brandon. It was almost as bad in Toronto, where the temperature reached 105° for three consecutive days.

James Gray, in *The Winter Years*, described the stifling Winnipeg heat. It felt, he wrote, "as if someone had left all the furnace doors open and the blowers on." In July, Gray, at that time a reporter for the Winnipeg *Free Press*, travelled with Robert M. Scott, the paper's agricultural writer, from Winnipeg to Regina and back again. The pair headed down the Souris River valley – now bone dry from the drought – and watched the dust clouds forming ahead. Soon "the sun vanished in an amber haze [and] the sharp dust particles ricocheted off the windshield." The visibility dropped to a few feet. They crawled blindly along the extreme right shoulder of the gravel road and then, suddenly, they were out of it. The blowing soil stopped "as if on command." A few miles farther on, they encountered it again; that was the pattern – alternate stretches of dark and light.

In this bleak wasteland, money was almost unknown – large bills, certainly. When Scott gave a Saskatchewan garageman a ten-dollar bill to pay for gas and oil and for cleaning out a radiator choked with dust, he was asked if he had something smaller, explaining that "it's awfully hard to spend anything out of a ten-dollar bill around here these days."

They stopped at a farmhouse west of Forget (a harshly significant name) – clothes sticking to their bodies, blisters on their feet from the heat of the floorboards – hoping to get a glass of cool buttermilk. It was a typical Saskatchewan spread – small, unpainted house, combination horse- and cattle-barn, chickenhouse, huddle of sheds, blown-over privy. And it was all empty. Though the door was unlocked, the house was still completely furnished, a Canada's Pride range and a Hoosier cabinet in the kitchen, a Quebec heater in one bedroom, and two large beds with their mattresses. Although every crevice had been stuffed with newspaper, floors and furniture within were covered with dust; a long drift, two inches deep, had crept in from a crack under the kitchen door. A cast-iron pump stood halfway between house and barn, but its mechanism was rusted and immovable.

They drove off, passing two or three more abandoned farms. Had the entire country been abandoned? Gray wondered. At last they came upon a working farm and accepted a glass of water from

357

the farm wife, Ellen Simpson. Why, they wanted to know, would a family walk away from a farmhouse and leave the doors open?

"Well, why not, for goodness sake?" Ellen Simpson replied. "Who'd steal anything around here? And, anyway, what is there that anybody has left now that's worth stealing?" Besides, she added, another family, fleeing from the dust bowl, might need shelter for the night on their way to better land.

By midsummer in southern Saskatchewan, most streams and rivers were dry, the cows had stopped giving milk, wild life vanished, the grain elevators stood empty, and even the potato crop failed. There was so little business that the railways reduced their daily schedules to once or twice a week.

The best farmers could not cope with the elements. Robert Miller, one of the few in the area not dependent on government relief, had a towering reputation. Years before he had picked a piece of high tableland near the Cypress Hills, where the soil was good and he knew he could catch every vagrant rainstorm. He used the most modern machinery and was known as one of the best farmers in the province – painstaking, thrifty, scientific. But now no rain came. In 1936 Miller planted two thousand acres with seed grain in a carefully prepared seed bed – and didn't reap a single bushel.

That summer, the Canadian Red Cross sent its Regina representative on a tour of the worst of the Saskatchewan drought area. He was shaken by what he found. On a farm near Consul he came upon a family – typical of many others – who hadn't been able to repair any household buildings since 1928. They couldn't afford laths or tar-paper to fix the roof or cribbing for the well, which had buckled and given out. As a result they had no decent drinking water. When the crops withered in the early summer, the farmer and his pregnant wife tended an acre and a half of potatoes, planted in a low place to capture any rain that fell. But no rain fell. The very weeds died. For all their work that summer, the family harvested a single sack of potatoes.

Near Shaunavon, the same man came upon a family with nine children, all dressed in gunny sacks. One child had died, and such was the despair among the siblings that one had to be watched carefully to prevent him from taking his own life. "Imagine a child of twelve years contemplating or attempting suicide," the Red Cross man wrote in his report.

358

In another desolate region, he encountered a widow, surrounded by seven black-eyed children, trying to break ground for a chicken coop, "attacking the stubborn prairie soil with a crowbar so heavy it would have daunted many a man." Her fourteen-year-old daughter, wearing a dress with the label of the Lake of the Woods Milling Company, was helping with an axe; the younger children plied rakes and hoes. The family lived in a three-room house, the holes in its broken windows stuffed with Russian thistle. The kitchen utensils were all gone; the only remaining pail was full of holes. They had tried to raise turkeys, but these had become thin and scrawny because the grass had withered. The only feed left was Russian thistle. "I can save some of them for Thanksgiving," she explained, "and the poor kids will be able to have a good dinner on that day but it is going to take all my time to have any left for Christmas." She hoped that the new hen house might protect the birds from the marauding coyotes, who were carrying them off one at a time.

"The spirit of this family was unbeatable," her visitor reported, "and it was affected neither by hardship, famine nor depression. It is such people that build a country."

At Bone Creek, a family of eleven was crammed into a one-room shack. The children used newspapers as mattresses and sheets and slept in the gunny-sack clothing they wore during the day. The parents were sick and the children suffered from "the apathy of despair." In the winter, even with a big fire in the stove, drinking water froze in the pail.

Another shack housed a father, mother, and eighteen children, ranging in age from two to eighteen. There wasn't a mattress in the house, daylight could be seen through the cracks in the roof, and the broken window panes hadn't been replaced. "It is almost incredible to think," the Red Cross worker reported, "that, in the Dominion of Canada, the father of a family finds it impossible to obtain work or earn sufficient money to replace a broken window pane. Nevertheless, it is a condition that actually exists."

Under such conditions, professional entertainment was out of the question. Mart Kenney, who was just starting out leading the dance band that would become famous as the Western Gentlemen, delightedly accepted an engagement at a small-town hall south of Calgary. Admission was fifty cents. The band arrived, wearing new uniforms, and waited and waited and waited, but

359

not a soul turned up. At ten, four people finally arrived – the only ones who could afford the price.

Political entertainment, however, was free and people made the most of it. Tommy Douglas remembered that for the politician "it was an ideal time because you could have a political meeting in every schoolhouse. People came! It was the cheapest entertainment in town." Douglas found that they would argue politics until one or two o'clock in the morning.

He sent out copies of Hansard, the verbatim record of the House of Commons debates, and was astonished to find that his constituents gobbled it up. "Who would read *Hansard* if they could get anything else to read?" he asked himself. "It was wonderful because when opposition speakers would come in, some farmer who looked as though he didn't even know one political party from another would get up in the question period and say, 'You said so and so, didn't you?' The fellow would say, 'Yes.' He'd get it out of his overalls pocket and say, 'Now on page 3347 of *Hansard* for February the 9th, this is what Mr. So and So said. . . .'" After a while, Douglas recalled, political speakers stayed out of the drought constituencies because so many farmers, with nothing else to read, had been devouring the Commons debates.

Douglas also paid tribute to the spirit of a deprived people who still managed to see some humour in their situation. One day, driving out to Weyburn, he saw ahead a patch of clouds hanging over the community. He thought, "They're getting a rain. That's marvellous." When he reached town, he came upon a group of men playing horseshoes. Stepping over to one, Andy Prentiss, he asked, "Hello, Andy, did you get any rain out of those clouds?"

"Well," Prentiss replied, "five drops." Then he added, "You know Bill Sykes south of town? Well, one of those drops hit him on the head, knocked him unconscious. We had to throw three pails of dust on him to bring him to."

"You can't beat courage like that," said Tommy Douglas.

3

Le Chef, *the Church, and the Reds* The Depression changed the political face of Canada. By 1936 eight out of nine provincial governments had fallen, to be replaced, except for those of Alberta and Quebec, by new-broom

Liberal administrations. Only John Bracken's United Farmers, in Manitoba, survived.

Quebec's turn came on August 17. In June, after sixteen years in office at the head of the entrenched Liberal party, Premier Louis-Alexandre Taschereau had resigned in a cloud of scandal and had been succeeded by the relatively colourless Joseph-Adélard Godbout. But the moribund Liberals, who had coasted along in power for nearly forty years, could not withstand the onslaught of the new Union Nationale under Maurice Duplessis. Godbout suffered personal defeat as the UN piled up seventy-six seats to its opponents' fourteen.

Duplessis ran and won on a reform ticket, but then, every politician in Canada who aspired to office claimed to be a reformer. Like Hepburn in Ontario, Duplessis only *talked* reform. As his background suggested, and as events were to prove, he was a Conservative *bleu* marching under a different banner. He had entered politics as a Conservative; that was the family tradition. His father had been a Tory member of the Quebec legislature from 1886 to 1900, and his birthplace, Trois-Rivières, was a bulwark of conservatism, both political and religious. Duplessis had represented it since 1927, one of a corporal's guard of Tories swamped in a vast army of Liberals.

By 1934, with reform everywhere in the air, a group of dissident Liberals under Paul Gouin, son of a former premier, had decided to form a new party called Action Libérale Nationale. It drew its support from farmers' groups and credit and labour unions. Too weak to fight the entrenched Liberals on its own, it formed an alliance with Duplessis's Conservatives, each group agreeing to take a share of the constituencies and to refrain from poaching on the other's territory. This uneasy alliance bore the unwieldy name of Union Nationale Duplessis-Gouin.

But not for long. The "morganatic marriage," as Taschereau dubbed it, lasted through the provincial election of November 1935, which saw the new party rocket to within six seats of the ruling Liberals. But it soon became Duplessis's party. Leading an invigorated opposition, he forced a series of hearings by the Public Accounts Committee, which had not met in eight years. As the chief inquisitor he laid bare a history of Liberal patronage, graft, and rascality that outraged the province. Taschereau, who, it was revealed, had forty-six relatives on the provincial payroll, was forced out. Gouin declined to run in the election that followed and faded into the background. The Union Nationale no longer needed to bear Duplessis's name. He was *Le Chef* - a stocky, conservatively dressed politician whose chief distinguishing feature was a prominent nose that, like Aberhart's double chin and Bennett's wing collar, proved a cartoonist's delight.

He had promised a series of reforms, but he made good on very few. The UN was simply the Conservative party under a new name. Duplessis's main attack was not on the trusts, which he had promised to smite, but on all those he considered to be communists. These included anybody who appeared to be left of centre, including, of course, the CCF. In this crusade against the supposed forces of evil, he had the backing and the encouragement of the ultramontane Roman Catholic Church.

The Spanish Civil War broke out in July. The Quebec clergy and the Quebec press were almost unanimously on the side of General Francisco Franco, leader of the insurgents who were attempting to overthrow the communist-supported Popular Front government.

This attitude was thrown into sharp focus when, on October 23, three delegates from the Spanish government arrived in Montreal under the auspices of the Committee for Medical Aid to Spain. These were Marcelino Domingo, a former education minister, Isabella de Polencia, who had been Spain's delegate to the League of Nations, and Father Luis Sarasola, a Franciscan priest. None was a Communist. Their purpose was to raise money and to present the Loyalist cause to Canadians. They had spoken without incident in Toronto, Hamilton, and Ottawa. But in Montreal they ran up against the hostility of the church.

Father Sarasola was already under papal indictment for taking sides in a political struggle. Translated, that meant taking the Loyalist side, since many priests were working for Franco without being censured. On the morning of his arrival, the church denounced the Franciscan in the press. A small force of students from the University of Montreal paraded to the city hall and squatted in the Hall of Honour until the acting mayor appeared to announce that the meeting the Spanish committee had planned to hold in the Mount Royal Arena that evening would not take place. "We will not allow Communism to take root here," he declared as the students cheered.

362

The student protest had been carefully organized by the church, as Eugene Forsey discovered. "Former students of mine have in their possession one of the notes sent round ordering youths to meet at the headquarters of the Jeunesse Ouvrière Catholique and 'bring their canes,' " he told C.H. Cahan.

The controversy was racial as well as religious. When the delegates turned up at McGill at the invitation of the university's Social Problems Club, several hundred French-speaking students from the University of Montreal invaded the campus to protest. They were dispersed by English-speaking McGill students.

With the police preventing anyone from entering the Mount Royal Arena, Frank Scott, one of the sponsors of that meeting, tried to secure Victoria Hall, which, being in Westmount, didn't come under the jurisdiction of the Montreal force. He was told that all the space in the hall had been rented for that night. Later he learned that the main auditorium was dark all evening.

That left the Mount Royal Hotel in downtown Montreal. A group of about a hundred people crammed into a small salon in an informal meeting with the delegates. Dr. Norman Bethune, who was about to leave for Spain, pointed out that the cancelled meeting at the arena was to have raised money for vaccines and serums for use against preventable disease. As a result of its cancellation, he said, thousands of children would die. "I would never have believed that a meeting of this sort could have been stopped in Montreal," he said.

Even as he spoke a body of students was marching through the streets crying "A bas les Communistes!" and, even more sinister, "A bas les Juifs!" ("Down with the Jews!") They poured into Westmount, found that the meeting at Victoria Hall had also been cancelled, and then advanced on the hotel. At 9:15 a worried management closed the salon doors, turned off the lights in the middle of Señora de Polencia's speech, and dispersed the group. For the rest of the evening hundreds of student demonstrators marched through the streets with little police interference, even though the parade, lacking the necessary permit, was illegal. The demonstration had strong anti-Semitic overtones. Six hundred camped outside the offices of the Jewish *Daily Eagle* until they were dispersed; others smashed windows in Jewish-owned stores. About this minor version of Germany's *Kristallnacht* the press had no comment.

What Montreal was witnessing were the early stirrings of overt nationalist sentiment in Quebec. The Jews and the communists were "outsiders" who seemed to threaten traditional French-Canadian values. This fear of the stranger – the "foreigner," the "outside agitator" – was not confined to French Canada. It was part of the Canadian pattern and had been since the days of the immigration boom, when the entrenched Anglo-Celtic community had vented its wrath on the immigrant Slavs. It manifested itself especially in periods of stress – war or depression – and was used cynically to hold on to power by various privileged groups, ranging from the Estevan coal operators to the Premier of Ontario and his cronies. The Communist party was well aware of this prejudice, especially as so much of its membership came from the ethnic communities, notably the Finnish and Ukrainian. It tried desperately to promote British- and Canadian-born members to positions of high-profile leadership.

On the day following the aborted meeting, Frank Scott charged, " . . . democracy is in a precarious position if a sane and considered statement for a lawful government is prevented from being given in a British colony by threats of violence from irresponsible elements." Duplessis, however, saw it differently: he publicly praised the students for their attacks on communism.

By 1936, hundreds of young French Canadians had been recruited into the small but burgeoning fascist movement of Adrien Arcand, a fanatical anti-Semite, who had links with international fascism and with Hitler's Nazis. He was also editor of the tabloid *L'Illustration nouvelle*, the semi-official organ of Duplessis's Union Nationale.

Fascism appealed to the growing nationalism of young Quebec. At a mass meeting in Maisonneuve the previous March, speaker after speaker had attacked the Spanish Popular Front, charging that it was controlled by Russians and Jews. Arcand's purpose was similar – to equate the Jews with the "Godless communists" as interlopers who wanted to take over the province. In his public pronouncements, he advocated stripping them of all civil and political rights and packing them off to the shores of Hudson Bay. During the 1935 election campaign he had been the Conservative party's political director in the province; now, in his new editorial position, he was in the Duplessis camp. Because of his political connections, Arcand played down his anti-Semitism in *L'Illustration nouvelle*. It was enough for him that he could follow the lead of Pius XI and Cardinal Villeneuve in attacking the Reds.

Two days after the demonstrations in Montreal, a mass rally of ten thousand persons celebrating the Feast of Christ the King in Quebec City heard Villeneuve condemn communism and call for all Catholics to join in a crusade for its extermination. Those who had supported the Spanish government's cause were denounced and the Loyalists were attacked as "a group comprised of new barbarians who have covered the lands of Spain with desolation and blood."

On that same day, Norman Bethune was on the high seas, sailing for Madrid on a one-way ticket donated by the Committee to Aid Spanish Democracy. The impetus for Bethune's trip had come, not from the communists, but from Graham Spry of the CCF, the editor of the party's paper, *New Commonwealth*. Spry invented a "Spanish Hospital and Medical Aid Committee" in the hopes of raising money for a hospital in Spain. Bethune helped him turn the committee into a reality and then, with the assistance of a broad spectrum of organizations on the Left, to form the larger Committee to Aid Spanish Democracy. Bethune had already offered his services to the Canadian Red Cross, only to be told by the national commissioner that the organization was not raising a unit for service in Spain "and has not, I think, any intention whatever of doing so."

Typically, Bethune had made up his mind to go to Spain on short notice. A young Montreal architect, Hazen Sise, who followed him to the war, was later to describe him as "a person who had no inhibitions, no gap between thought and action." Sise recalled that once Bethune had thought about something and thought "that something was worthwhile doing, he would just go right out and do it. And he would leave a trail of annoyed bureaucrats and hurt feelings behind him." But, Sise added, the dedicated surgeon was also "literally the sort of person who could say 'Rise up and follow me' and you would follow him. He had that sort of authority about him."

Sise was one such disciple, a member of a prominent Montreal family who was prepared to give up a career to follow his hero.

365

Another was Henning Sorensen, a Danish-Canadian insurance agent whom Sise described as a "very sweet, dreamy character, very emotional: [whose] heart literally bled for the sufferings of the Spanish people." Sise wrote from Spain that both Bethune and Sorensen "are a little in love with death" but that "the essential rightness of their action seems to give them a sort of shining hallowed quality." Sorensen, for his part, wrote that Bethune "loved the smell of danger. . . . He needed that adrenalin in his system that comes from a dangerous situation. . . . "

In late November, Bethune and Sorenson flew from Madrid to Paris to arrange for medical supplies for the unit that Bethune was planning. Bethune went on to London to consult with haematologists on transfusion techniques, for he intended to transfuse blood directly on the battlefield. For that he would need a truck loaded with equipment – everything from a gasoline-operated refrigerator and sterilizing equipment to vacuum bottles, hurricane lamps, and gas masks.

But once again he ran into the same hands-off attitude to the Spanish war that had prevented the Canadian Red Cross from offering any aid. This time it was the Canadian government. Bethune would require 1,875 separate items for his transfusion unit. He didn't want to waste money paying duty at the border and so went to the French embassy to ask for a *laissez-passer*. The French agreed to grant permission if the Canadians would assure them that Bethune was a bona fide doctor engaged in humanitarian work. Ottawa refused to provide such assurance. Ernest Lapointe cabled to the Canadian High Commissioner, Vincent Massey, that "while Government has full sympathy of any efforts to relieve sufferers on either side of present Spanish conflict, it would not be possible in view of what appears to be the political complexion of this mission . . . to sponsor it by making a formal request such as indicated." That piece of bureaucratese, translated, meant that the government had no intention of helping a known Communist, even one who was trying to save lives.

Bethune, furious at this fence-sitting, paid the duty and went on to Spain to become an authentic Canadian hero, an expatriate citizen of a country hungry for heroes but still unappreciated in his native land. More than a quarter of a century would pass before more than a handful of his countrymen would recognize his name.

366

On October 21, in the same week in which the Spanish delegates *Birth control* arrived for their confrontation in Montreal, a landmark trial *on trial* opened in the little Ontario community of Eastview that variously shocked, titillated, angered, or scandalized Canadians. A young woman was haled into court on the charge of distributing birth control information and therefore breaking one of the many taboos – this one enshrined in the Criminal Code – that covered everything sexual from contraception to pregnancy, and from words like "intercourse" to jokes about pre-marital dalliance.

Under Canadian moral standards of the middle thirties, sex was held to be dirty and therefore not to be discussed in public, on the radio, or in the newspapers. William Aberhart had come up against the taboo in January when he told a joke in Calgary, in which he talked about the hard time he was being given by his critics.

"It brought to my mind," Aberhart said, "the story of the young lady in the maternity ward who was in agony. She asked the nurse if there was a young man in a brown suit and a brown fedora outside in the corridor.

"The nurse said, 'Yes, I saw one there when I came in.'

" 'Well,' said the girl, 'tell him that if this is anything like married life, the engagement is off.' "

That parable, inoffensive by almost any standards, got Aberhart into a heap of trouble. The Social Credit leader was assailed by complaints that he had told a "lewd" joke. Efforts were even made to take him off the air.

The Canadian Radio Broadcasting Commission had come under a similar attack in March, when, as the result of a contest, it broadcast two prize-winning songs, the lyrics of which included the phrases "Let's pet beneath the serviette" and "I can't dance 'cause I've got ants in my pants." They brought such a roar of disapproval that the commission bowed to the moralists, announced it would take all responsibility for the offending program, apologize to all who complained, and make sure that "the program conductor will be sternly reprimanded."

The commission's successor, the Canadian Broadcasting Corporation, even refused to allow a Toronto radio station, CFRB, to broadcast any reference to eugenic sterilization during an address sponsored by the Eugenics Society of Canada. As a result, the broadcast was cancelled.

"Lewd" performances in theatres were forbidden. In Montreal, where all performances had to be governed "by the dictates of propriety and refinement," the Board of Censorship explicitly defined a lewd performance as the appearance on the stage of "bare-legged females," "the wearing of one-piece union suits by women," or any dance that involved "suggestive or repulsive contractions of the human body."

Toronto was equally puritan. When the distinguished British actor Maurice Colbourne appeared at the Royal Alexandra Theatre in *Reunion in Vienna*, a Robert Sherwood play, the censors were in full cry. Thanks to the vigilance of Mrs. Henry Cody, wife of the president of the University of Toronto, the police forced a number of script changes. The word "bathroom" was deleted, an eight-second kiss was reduced to five seconds, the word "damn" was cut out, and a love scene was toned down. And when the wildly successful new picture magazine, *Life*, published a photographic essay on the birth of a baby that year, the issue was denied entry into Canada.

Such moralistic taboos helped to contribute to the woeful ignorance of many Canadians regarding the clinical details of sex, birth control, and conception. How else to explain the widely held belief that Oliva Dionne, the father of the famous quintuplets, must have sexual organs of enviable proportions? There were those who were not above taking a peek in the public washrooms when Dionne went on tour.

Any public reference to birth control was taboo. The law made it clear that "everyone is guilty of an indictable offense and liable to two years' imprisonment who knowingly, without lawful excuse or justification, offers to sell, advertises, publishes an advertisement of or has for sale or disposal any medicine, drug or article intended or represented as a means of preventing conception or causing abortion."

Until the Depression there was no organized birth control movement in Canada. But after 1930 it began to be obvious that ignorance of birth control methods was causing hardship among the poor, who couldn't afford large families. Deaths from illegal abortions, many self-induced, were on the rise – not only in relation to all maternal deaths but also in absolute numbers. And to some Canadians, another statistic was equally alarming: the lowest quarter of the population in terms of income produced half the nation's children.

One who was concerned by these figures was Alvin Ratz Kaufman, owner of the Kaufman Rubber Company in Kitchener, which made boots and rainwear (but not condoms). When Kaufman laid off a number of workers in December 1929, some of them protested that because they had the largest families they were the most in need of work. Kaufman, a harshly practical man, investigated and found that it was true: the least skilled employees had the most children. But if he kept them on and fired others, he'd quickly go broke.

"We must choose between birth control and revolution," Kaufman declared. "We are raising too large a percentage of the dependent class. . . ." That was, of course, an elitist attitude, though Kaufman probably didn't think in those terms. "If we breed from the bottom instead of the top we are courting disaster," he said. He offered to pay for sterilization of any of his employees who asked for it or to have them fitted with diaphragms. The overwhelming response astonished him.

Birth control became a crusade for Kaufman, who spent some fifty thousand dollars a year to study the problem, to open clinics, and to offer birth control information by mail. He was not alone. A pioneer clinic in Hamilton also began operating quietly and unobtrusively in 1932.

The birth control controversy of the thirties parallels, in many ways, the abortion controversy of a later era. The Protestant Left espoused birth control. The United Church endorsed it formally in 1936; the Anglicans remained tepid. The Roman Catholic Church was totally opposed, and its influence alone was strong enough to keep the prohibitory statute on the books. No public health nurse was allowed to discuss birth control methods with her patients. Doctors avoided the subject, which was, as Dr. Gordon Bates of the Social Hygiene Council once admitted, "a very controversial one." The council, Dr. Bates had declared, was "not at all interested in the birth control movement." Many physicians had only the crudest knowledge of contraceptive methods. After one live birth and one stillbirth, a woman in Tecumseh, Ontario, wrote to Dr. Marie Stopes, the pioneer birth control advocate in the United States: " . . . the Doctor attending advised us to avoid having more: promising to give us birth control knowledge. This he did not do, and I did not care to bring the subject up again."

Kaufman was critical of the medical profession. After setting up clinics in Windsor and Toronto, he discovered that "about 50% of the patients cannot be fitted with a pessary for various reasons, some of which apparently are no credit to the obstetricians." In the rural areas "doctors frequently are not available at all and more frequently do not know how to fit pessaries anyway and do not care."

Those doctors who favoured birth control were convinced that the diaphragm or pessary was the only sure way of preventing conception. But these devices were expensive and awkward to use. Women who really needed them wouldn't use them. Kaufman opted for "J. N. and C." – jelly, nozzles, and condoms. They might be less effective, but in the long run they would prevent more unwanted births because people would actually make use of them.

By 1936, Kaufman had in operation a coast-to-coast distribution system with more than a thousand supporting doctors and a network of social workers and nurses paid to interview women in the poorer working-class districts. They offered to mail free contraceptive kits to any woman who signed a form asking for one. His Parents Information Bureau in Kitchener had by then mailed out more than sixty thousand birth control packages.

One of Kaufman's part-time social workers was Dorothea Palmer, a plump twenty-seven-year-old who canvassed poor families in the predominantly French-Canadian community of Eastview, a suburb of Ottawa. The Roman Catholic Church was incensed at the idea of a Protestant woman knocking on the doors of its flock, asking mothers if they'd like birth control information. The church complained to the chief of police, and a shaken Miss Palmer one September afternoon found herself under arrest, charged with a criminal offence that could put her behind bars for two years. She was indignant. "A woman should be master of her own body," she told the arresting officers. "She should be the one to say if she should become a mother." Her words would be echoed in the great abortion controversy of the 1980s.

Kaufman hired a lawyer, F.W. Wegenast, to represent Miss Palmer. On the first day of the trial, the tiny Eastview courtroom, which held fewer than fifty persons, was jammed with Catholic
370

women. The following day, apparently under orders from their priest, they did not turn up.

The case was heard by Magistrate Lester H. Clayton rather than a jury. It lasted until December, produced 750,000 words of testimony and 400,000 more of argument, and heard from more than eighty witnesses.

The Crown opened by calling twenty-one Eastview housewives. Most were poor, on relief, and mothers of large families; all but one was a Catholic. These were the women whom Dorothea Palmer had visited. They turned out to be as effective for the defence as for the Crown, for their testimony made it clear that the accused hadn't tried to sell them anything or give them anything directly. She had simply told them what most didn't know: where to get birth control information.

The Crown prosecutor, Raoul Mercier, asked each witness in turn if she thought she'd done anything morally wrong in accepting the box that later arrived in the mail. Most said no. He asked each if she had changed her mind since that time. Again: no.

Mercier asked one witness, who had explained that Miss Palmer had offered information concerning contraceptives: "What did you tell her?" The answer didn't help his case. "I told her she came too late," the witness replied.

At that, the Crown dropped one charge against the defendant – that she had tried to sell contraceptives. Obviously, she hadn't. The magistrate dismissed a second charge: the devices she carried with her were clearly for demonstration, not distribution. That left a third charge to be tried – that she had unlawfully advertised, by means of a pamphlet, materials intended as a means of preventing conception.

There was an escape clause in the law that read that "no one shall be convicted . . . if he proves that the public good was served by the acts." The onus was on the defence to prove public good, and it produced a powerful parade of witnesses to bolster that argument. These ranged all the way from an officer of the Salvation Army to a rabbi.

Anna Weber, the first defence witness and director of Kaufman's bureau, was asked why the spread of birth control knowledge couldn't be left to the doctors. She replied forthrightly that doctors knew little about the subject, that women patients might owe them money and were ashamed to go to them or were often

371

too embarrassed to be examined by a man, and that mothers couldn't afford the carfare to get to the doctor's office or to pay someone to look after their children. "They will open their hearts to another woman, however," Miss Weber said. "That is why we send nurses around to visit them."

The doctors called as expert witnesses by the Crown proved the point when the defence, in cross-examination, forced the admission from the physicians that they knew very little about contraception. The subject wasn't even taught in medical school.

Two surprise witnesses for the defence caused a mild sensation and some levity. They arrived with twenty-three birth control devices, which they spread out on an exhibit table already crowded with Kaufman's packages. The pair had bought them without any trouble at a local drugstore simply by asking for "something to keep my girl from getting pregnant."

Some of the Protestant clergy who testified for Miss Palmer gave a rather lukewarm defence of birth control. Rev. T. Summerhayes, secretary to the Toronto Anglican Social Service Council, was as guarded as his own church, conceding only that birth control might be justified if a woman's health was in danger or the family was below the poverty line – again a foreshadowing of some arguments used in the abortion controversy. The Anglicans, indeed, seemed to be on both sides of the argument. The Crown's last rebuttal witness, Canon Arthur Whalley, a Church of England minister from Ottawa, said that if his own church ever favoured birth control, he would resign.

Rev. John Coburn of the United Church was forthright on the other side when he said that "every child had the right to come into the world wanted." Morris Zeidman of the Scott Mission in Toronto chided the Anglicans for their caution, declaring that "if they had to deal with the problem I have, on the ground, they would take a more practical view." The star witness for the defence, however, was Rev. Claris Edwin Silcox, general secretary of the Christian Social Council, editor of *Social Welfare* magazine, and a renowned expert on sexuality. Silcox was on the stand for thirteen hours, his testimony stretching over three days. So voluminous was the list of authorities from which he quoted at length that a weary magistrate told him to stop giving references; he would take his word for the sources, he said, in the interests of saving time.

372

Silcox declared that "the only alternative to birth control was the acceptance of communism or socialism." Like Kaufman he believed that the state couldn't afford the burden of so many poor people with such large families. He also thought that a change in the law would ease tensions between French- and English-speaking Canadians because of the widely held belief that the French were trying to outbreed the English. In all, Silcox listed fifteen gains for society if birth control were made legal. The most important, he believed, would be to reduce the incidence of marital breakup.

It was apparent from the testimony that the mainstream Protestant churches, especially the ones that followed the Social Gospel, had been changing their traditional attitude toward the sex act. They now agreed that in addition to its role in procreation, it could be seen as an expression of marital love. On the other hand, there was the Crown's suggestion that contraception threatened the traditional authority of the husband. What would happen, Mercier asked each witness, if there was a disagreement between husband and wife on whether to use contraceptives or have another child? Some witnesses were uneasy with the question. Canada was very much a male-oriented nation. In spite of Dorothea Palmer's contention that a woman should control her own body, the trial did not take a feminist tack.

In his summing up for the defence, Wegenast introduced a touchy subject: the French-English, Catholic-Protestant dichotomy. The charge had been laid, he insisted, because of Roman Catholic pressure. Eastview wasn't different from any other Canadian community; he had been able to show that contraceptives were as easily obtainable there as anywhere else. "If so, where is the line to be drawn - geographically or between family and family? My submission is the line, if any, is at the Ottawa river."

The Crown's argument dwelt on the same schism. Palmer had been arrested, Mercier said, "because she knew or ought to have known that these people in Eastview stood in such a special relationship to the Bishop of Rome that the knowledge of the use of contraceptives ought to be kept from them."

The trial ended on December 11. The magistrate did not issue his verdict until the following March, and it was for the defence. He pointed out that a quarter of the population of four thousand in Eastview was on relief and that the province had paid

$125,000 of the total annual bill of $130,000. "An examination of birth statistics reveals that the poorer classes are generally breeding large families. Several of the witnesses in this case had 9 or 10 children and were 30–35 years old, husbands on relief or on small salaries. What chance had these children to be properly fed, clothed and educated? They are a burden to the taxpayer. . . . They glut the competitive labour market." Although this was on a par with the contention of the mayor of Fort Erie that relief recipients ought to be sterilized, that argument – a Depression argument – won the case.

The Depression, then, wrought a change in social attitudes. In fact, it is problematical whether, in better times, Dorothea Palmer would have been acquitted of the crime with which she was charged. She herself did not benefit from the trial; quite the opposite: she was harassed by obscene phone calls and mail and shunned by friends and relatives. Female passersby slapped her face, and the husband of one of her clients tried to rape her to show "what it's like without birth control." Undaunted, the young woman replied with a knee to the groin. She did not stay in Kaufman's employ but went back to the obscurity she craved, operating a small bookstore in Eastview.

As the trial moved towards its climax, an equally sensational affair was making headlines – one that also drew the issue of birth control into sharp focus. The Millar Stork Derby ended on October 31.

Charlie Millar, an eccentric, self-made millionaire who hated pomposity, had died ten years before, leaving an equally eccentric will designed to prove his oft-stated contention that every man had his price. He left racetrack stock to ministers who railed against gambling, brewery shares to temperance advocates, and a handsome home in Jamaica to three men who hated each other.

But it was the final clause in the will that made his name a legend. All residue left after earlier bequests was to go to "the mother who since my death has given birth in Toronto to the greatest number of children under the Vital Statistics Act."

The will was so carefully drawn that it survived ten years of contention in the courts and an attempt by the Ontario government to break it on the grounds that it was "against public policy." By mid-October, half a dozen women had come forward to qualify for the Stork Derby prize. One was a young redhead

374

named Mae Clark, who, with ten children, seemed to be in the lead. But Mrs. Clark offended the sensibilities of the day; five of her children had been fathered by a man other than her husband. Millar's second cousins tried to break the will on the ground that the deceased was encouraging illegitimacy from the grave. The court ruled that he hadn't intended to include bastards in the Stork Derby, and so the race continued – but without Mae.

In the end, four Toronto mothers, each of whom had produced nine children, were judged winners and awarded $165,000 each, a sum equal to about half a million in 1990 figures. In order to avoid a long and costly court challenge, the winners voted to give $12,500 apiece to Mae Clark and to a Mrs. Martin Kenny, who had also borne ten children, some of them stillborn and others unregistered. The winners were all in poverty-stricken circumstances – one married to a clerk, another to a city employee, the third to a fireman, and the last to a jobless carpenter. All kept their heads, paid their debts, and spent their winnings wisely.

But what was Millar's purpose in drafting such a strange and, to many, unsavoury will? Col. John Bruce, one of his associates, who helped draw up the document, had the most plausible explanation. "Millar believed that a good deal of human misery and poverty resulted from uncontrolled childbearing, which in turn he blamed on the ban against birth control information. . . . [His] hope was that by turning the spotlight on unbridled breeding and making us a laughing stock before the world, he could shame the government into legalizing birth control."

Certainly, the combination of the Eastview trial and the Stork Derby (which Mitch Hepburn called "disgusting and revolting") helped change the public attitude toward contraception. Birth control devices became more easily available; the subject began to be discussed more openly. And though it would be more than two decades before the law itself was changed, the public would make up its mind long before: that nobody should be burdened, financially or otherwise, with unwanted children.

5

Like so many of his fellow Canadians, the Prime Minister of *Abdication* Canada was an isolationist. It would have taken a bolder, indeed a reckless, politician to have tried to prepare publicly for war. The appalling casualties of 1914–18, and the wave of anti-war literature that followed, had convinced both Canadians and Americans that they should stay out of European entanglements. "It is becoming apparent to all that Europe is a maelstrom of strife," King wrote in his diary in March after Hitler sent his troops into the demilitarized Rhineland, "and that we are being drawn into a situation that is none of our creation by our membership in the League of Nations." There was, of course, another reason for avoiding foreign entanglements: French Canada's attitude. One war had almost split the country; the next might finish it.

Hitler's moves in Europe did not trouble the Prime Minister. He thought, optimistically and also naïvely, that "Germany having breathing space anew, may help bring about a situation that will break down other barriers." Later that summer he mused about setting down "in writing as Hitler has in 'Mein Kampf' – a constructive policy for 'protecting our peace.'" Hitler's anti-Semitism caused some concern, but not much. On August 9 King wrote that the news "seemed to centre around European conditions, the hatred of the Jews. The association of the Jews with Russian Sovietism: the association of Roosevelt with Jewish influence, etc. etc. My own view is that there are good as well as bad Jews and it is wrong to indict a nation or a race. . . . "

As long, one might be tempted to add, as one didn't have to have them as neighbours. King made no secret in his diaries of his anti-Semitism. Once, while taking a stroll down Wilbrod Street (those were the days when a Canadian prime minister could walk about the city unaccompanied by either press or security guards), he had come upon a little old man struggling along the icy sidewalk by himself. King was afraid the man would fall on the slippery pavement and offered him his cane, but the old man refused. The two strolled along together, chatting, and King, out of curiosity, asked him about himself. He was seventy-eight, he said; he lived in the Sandy Hill district, had a furniture and clothing business on Rideau Street, and his name was Cohen. He told King that he had three sons and a daughter and had divided all his possessions among them.

King walked him to the steps of his house and, as he shook hands with him, told him who he was. Mr. Cohen smiled "in a most benevolent and surprised sort of way," removed his glasses, took a good look, shook hands again, and went up the stairs.

King was charmed by the little playlet in which he had been the leading actor. Quite obviously the old man had come from Russia as a penniless immigrant, made his mark, saved his money, amassed a fortune, acquired a large property, left his children established, and now was "quite satisfied to leave the world possessing nothing, having, meanwhile, gained more than he could have dreamt of." A real Canadian success story!

Now, King told himself, the old man would have something to tell his children – of how the Prime Minister of Canada had actually walked with him, arm in arm, offered him his cane, spoken of him as a neighbour, and taken him to his door, "all of which is illustrative of the opportunity of Canada as contrasted with the peasant life as it has been in Russia for generations."

But King felt it necessary to conclude these remarks with a less agreeable comment: "The only unfortunate part of the whole story is that the Jews have acquired a foothold of Sandy Hill, it will not be long before this part of Ottawa will become more or less possessed by them. I should not be surprised if, some time later, Laurier House was left as about the only residence not occupied by Jews in this part of the City."

In September, King set off for Europe, where he met a variety of statesmen and diplomats ranging from Maxim Litvinov, the Soviet commissar for foreign affairs, to Winston Churchill. Litvinov told him, presciently, that Hitler was unpredictable and not to be relied on – that he would go after Czechoslovakia and Austria before turning on the Soviet Union. Churchill told him that England had never been in greater danger and that within five years it might be a vassal state of Germany.

At Arras, King viewed the great Vimy memorial with mixed feelings. It was "exceedingly fine and impressive," but he felt it would have been more suitable as a monument to all the Allied forces, not just the Canadians. This massive, twin-spired structure seemed to him a bit out of proportion. It was, in fact, "the most pretentious war memorial in the world." King was not enamoured of pretension. He was more impressed with the restored trenches, which had been his own idea, and also by the fact that the battlefield was Canadian property, tended by Canada and not by the Imperial War Graves Commission. That was also his doing. He had wanted it kept "distinct from any Imperial association," an expression of his stubborn nationalism.

In England, Mackenzie King heard for the first time whispers of the affair between Edward VIII and Wallis Warfield Simpson, a scandal that had been kept from the British public by an accommodating press. He would be meeting the King himself and wondered what that encounter might bring. He had a feeling that Edward didn't care for him, that others had prejudiced the monarch against him. "It is strange that I have had no word from him thus far." Not so strange, however, in the light of Edward's near total preoccupation with the approaching crisis involving the woman he loved.

Certainly there were those who were doing their best to prejudice the Canadian prime minister against the King. Nearly a decade before, during Canada's Jubilee celebration, Stanley Baldwin had hinted at a weakness in the young Prince of Wales. The problem that concerned him, he told Mackenzie King at the time, was "what shld. be done if the Royal Family were to 'throw-up' a sort of George IV."

"Let your fertile mind work on that," Baldwin said pointedly. As King noted at the time, the British prime minister did not "feel too secure with the present heir to the throne."

Now the British establishment felt even less secure. King's ears were assailed by gossip about the monarch. At a house party at Stanstead Park, Lady Kipps, an elderly courtier, while praising the previous reign, complained that there was "no sense of security or stability." Another, Mrs. Arthur James, "a real character," spoke disparagingly of the new King's going to the Vimy reunion without a hat, his hair blowing about, and "looking very dirty."

"She says he likes to look dirty," King wrote, "has no sense of responsibility, is not normal." He came away with a feeling of great uncertainty about the state of the British throne.

The following day there was more talk of the sovereign's deficiencies: his disinclination to attend church, his indifference to his obligations, and his refusal to listen to counsel. Ramsay MacDonald, the former prime minister, added to the chorus. "My own mother," he told King, "would not have stood for some of the things that he is causing people to submit to." MacDonald criticized the monarch for visiting the mining districts of Wales and asking the miners to call him by his Christian names, David or

378

Albert. He had actually slapped them on the back and "has no regard whatever for the accepted standards of behaviour." These were strange sentiments to come from the man who had headed the first Labour government in British history.

But the real problem was the twice-divorced Wallis Simpson. The British press was maintaining a discreet silence, but the Americans were headlining the scandal. It could not long be kept from the British public.

Now a concerted attempt was made to get the Canadian prime minister to reason with the King. Nobody else, it appeared, dared to attempt this embarrassing and distasteful task. Geoffrey Dawson of *The Times* was one who urged Mackenzie King to bell the cat. But King wanted no part of it. "Quite clearly," he wrote, "all were trying to get me to pull their chestnuts out of the fire." It was a phrase he used more than once as the pressure increased. "In certain circles," he discovered, "there was greater concern over the King's alliance with Simpson than there was in the worsening situation in Europe."

He travelled to Chequers on October 23 to confer with the Prime Minister. Baldwin met him at the door and told him he had come as close to a breakdown as he ever expected. Later, in the library, he confided that he wished he could leave England, "get out of this land and never see it again." The strain of office had become unendurable, he said; no man could cope with it for long.

It was Baldwin's view that Mrs. Simpson's hold on Edward VIII wasn't so much sexual as motherly. "He was a man in some particulars, in others he was not yet grown up." It was clear, too, that Baldwin wanted his Canadian counterpart to speak to the sovereign. So did Major A.H.L. Hardinge, the royal secretary. "I hope you will impress on him . . . that the Canadian people feel it. . . . He will listen to you." King refused; it was a matter, he said, for the people of England.

"I can see others are trying to use me," he confided to his diary that night, " . . . but I don't intend to be drawn into anything unless the King himself brings the subject up."

But the monarch had no intention of doing anything of the sort. The following day, October 27, Mackenzie King presented himself at Buckingham Palace in his soft morning coat, silk hat, and Gladstone cufflinks. Following a ceremony that saw the installation of three new imperial privy councillors, Edward asked the

379

Canadian to stay behind for a few minutes. King thought he looked much better, less dissipated, more buoyant, his hair still thick and golden, his eyes bright and clear. Moments like these in the presence of the high and the mighty always produced in Mackenzie King a sense of awe and a kind of reverse humility – a wonder that *he* of all people should have risen to such heights. He could not help noticing the portrait of Queen Victoria immediately opposite and thinking "how stranger than fiction was the fact that I should be looking at this portrait while standing in the presence of her grandson, the present King, not only as one of his advisers but as a Prime Minister."

He was not given any opportunity, however, to tender any advice on the one matter that was about to consume the nation. The two men covered a range of subjects from the Vimy pilgrimage to Mitch Hepburn (who the King thought was a communist). They talked of war and peace. Edward said he intended to keep England out of war "at all costs," even ("Let me say this to you within these four walls") at the cost of giving up some of Britain's colonies – a revelation that, had he known it, would have disturbed Winston Churchill, then trying to rally a party of "King's men" to support the monarch.

They talked candidly, even intimately, but there was no mention of Edward's obsession with an American divorcée. The closest they came was when the Canadian prime minister, on taking his leave, told Edward that the whole future of the Empire depended upon him, that he, the monarch, had the power to save civilization, and that he must follow "what he knew in his heart was the right thing to do." That was laying it on a bit thick, and it caused Edward to draw back a little and in a shy sort of way murmur that Mackenzie King was saying too much. "No, sir," said the Prime Minister, "you are far too modest."

When he returned to Canada the pressure continued, this time from the Governor General, who said that Canada was the key to the situation; Edward would be influenced by the senior dominion. King told him, in effect, to keep out of it. By late November he was convinced that Edward intended to marry his paramour "regardless of consequences." Privately, he wasn't sure those consequences would be fatal "either to the Empire or world relationship which the English aristocracy in particular believe they will be." King's long suspicion – it amounted to disdain – of the

380

aristocracy comes through in the diary entry: "His action would be of submarining a lot of the false and rotten life of society, and in accord with a showdown on realities, such as the world is witnessing in its social revolutions of today. The King clearly is throwing in his lot with the masses, and will be prepared to defy the classes. It may be the saving of the Crown and of revolution. . . . "

But King wanted to make sure that if a crisis came Canada would not be blamed for it. The latest dispatches from London incensed him because they suggested that Canada was taking the lead in trying to resolve the matter. King immediately put a muzzle on Vincent Massey. He was not to represent the Canadian government or attend any conferences on the crisis. King himself would communicate directly with London, not through the High Commissioner: "By putting a spoke in that practice, I have secured communication direct and uncoloured by the atmosphere in Government circles in London." The British wanted King to cable directly to Edward, tendering his advice. That the Prime Minister refused to do.

But on December 8, with abdication almost certain, he changed his mind and decided that a letter sent directly to the King through the Governor General would at last be appropriate. Couched in sympathetic terms, it would stress the fact that Canada believed he should renounce Wallis Simpson and remain on the throne.

To his surprise, he found the Cabinet divided. J.L. Ilsley, the Minister of National Revenue, said he didn't want to grovel before a King who had acted in a worthless way and didn't deserve any expression of sympathy. Neither Dunning nor Lapointe, two of his senior ministers, favoured a compassionate message.

The Prime Minister, however, was "unwilling to have my worst enemy undergo the torture of mind and soul which the King must be suffering." It was their duty, he told his ministers, to save the Empire, if possible, from such a calamity as an abdication. Once again, Mackenzie King had shifted his position. What he had earlier seen as a possible "saving of the Crown" he now presented as a potential disaster. And he now found himself veering toward the King's side. He blamed "fashionable society" as much as he blamed Edward for the impasse.

The Cabinet reluctantly came round. The Prime Minister deleted a sentence linking the Cabinet's view with that of the country as a whole and struck out the final sentence, which referred to the rejoicing there would be if the King made the right decision. "Rejoicing," the Cabinet felt, was too strong a word. Even after sending the official letter, King continued to vacillate; in his diary he wrote that "the King's usefulness was pretty well gone now, and it would be better if he was off the throne."

The Prime Minister's purpose had been to make it clear that Canada was in no way responsible for the abdication and had, on the contrary, tried to save the monarch from such a step. As usual, King's reasoning was circuitous. He didn't want Canada on the record as not having tendered advice, but advice offered at an earlier stage might, he thought, have been seen as an effort to force abdication. On the *other* hand, "advice at the present time would make clear our desire to see the institution of the monarchy held in the regard and reverence to which it should be held."

For most of the fall, Canadians had been agog over the royal drama, which served as a focus to relieve the boredom of the Depression. They learned of it from their own press, which was not inhibited by any self-censorship, and also from the American newsmagazines, which gave the story elaborate coverage. Large numbers sympathized with the King, if not with the elegant divorcée who was clearly his mistress. They had idolized him in the twenties during his well-publicized tours of the country – a glamorous bachelor, indeed a true Prince Charming, with his flaxen hair and his ready smile. In a sense they felt he was one of them; after all, he had purchased a ranch in Alberta! He symbolized all the glitter of the twenties, but now, in a darker decade, even that glitter was fading. When he abdicated on December 11, the entire country went into a tailspin.

There were those who felt betrayed by their sovereign, as they had felt betrayed by their own leaders. Mackenzie King put it into words when he wrote in his diary: "If that is the kind of man he is, it is better he should not be longer on the Throne." It was inconceivably sad, King thought, that "a man who has the highest position any man could hold or has ever held, could fall into the deepest abyss – be so blinded by his lust as to lose all moral sense, and sense of what he owes . . . to the subjects all over the world. . . . "

Just before five that afternoon, the Prime Minister and his Cabinet had gathered to hear Edward's abdication speech, broadcast by short wave. Mackenzie King would always remember the scene: his ministers grouped in a semi-circle around the short-wave radio, he himself in the prime minister's chair, the oddly affecting voice distorted by distance. "As we listened to the King's voice, there were times when it seemed almost as though it were being given through a terrific storm, as if the elements were raging and blowing across sea and land; a more dramatic effect could not possibly have been arranged had it been deliberately planned."

As they left the room, King remarked that history would record that Edward had been in some sense a sacrificial lamb; that he had given his life, as others had in the past, that others might be saved; that the person who really sought the abdication was Mrs. Simpson. That was King's romanticism coming to the fore. History has not been so kind.

Meanwhile, he was faced with what was for him a daunting task. With the new king, George VI, on the throne, he would have to compose a message of congratulation. But what was he to say? He didn't want to employ the conventional clichés, which nobody believed. The material he'd been given by his staff he found sycophantic – not at all the right tone for the prime minister of an independent Commonwealth nation.

Desperate to find a proper opening for the message, he pored over books of prayers until his mind was "so weary I could not think of their words." Midnight arrived before he finally worked out a cable that satisfied him. He did not give it to a secretary but phoned the telegraph office himself to dictate it and, still unsure of the wording, apparently told the clerk to hold the message.

He prepared for bed, but after he had undressed it occurred to him that the words "Prime Minister" should be appended to his name. It was now 12:30; he picked up the telephone and ordered the change. Then he worried that he perhaps should have also added the phrase "of Canada" after that designation.

He tossed in his bed, unable to sleep. He called for his little dog, Pat, to comfort him. Finally, he concluded that he had used the wrong words to the monarch and padded out to the library, searching in vain for a copy of the original message. But in his secretary's office he came upon a file of material that had been prepared for him at the time of the old king's death. That gave him some clues.

Back in bed he continued to worry. He probably should have used the word "respect" instead of "devotion." And wasn't

383

"affection" a little too cosy? Something else would be preferable. He got out a book of synonyms and decided to replace it with "attachment."

It was now 4:30 a.m. The Prime Minister of Canada had spent more than eight hours trying to write a one-paragraph message of congratulation. He called the telegraph office again and began to work over the contents of the wire with the clerk on duty. He had used the word "Majesty" twice; once was quite enough. He replaced the second "Majesty" with the simple pronoun "you." He returned to bed and continued to worry. At five, he rose once more to revise the message. He took out "devotion," which he had applied to the Canadian people, and substituted "respect." He took out the adjective "loyal," which had defined "homage." He thought he had used the word "respectfully" once too often. He cut out the second one.

And thus, having made obeisance to his new sovereign without appearing to grovel, the Prime Minister of His Majesty's loyal but autonomous dominion toddled off to bed and tried his best to get a little sleep.

1937

1

Tourist travel in the Depression years was not for the impoverished. Why, then, were so many shabbily dressed men applying for passports and flocking to the steamship offices in suspiciously large numbers? A good many claimed they were going to the Paris Exposition; others said they planned to study art on the Left Bank. Yet they didn't act like artists and they certainly didn't look like tourists. Most appeared to be labouring men; many spoke with an accent so thick they were hard to understand; others had trouble finding a bank manager or a clergyman to sign their passport applications.

In fact, these young men were going to war. By mid-January Ottawa awoke to what was happening: an organized effort was under way to recruit volunteers to fight in Spain on the Loyalist side. By that time some six hundred Canadians were on their way or had already arrived.

On a per capita basis, Canada supplied more volunteers to the Spanish cause than any other country except France. The casualties were appalling. Of the 1,488 Canadians who fought on Spanish soil, 721 never returned. A few remained in Europe; the rest were killed.

Although the Spanish Civil War is now seen as the curtain-raiser to the world war that followed and was so viewed by many of those who volunteered, the governments of France, England, the United States, and Canada remained strictly neutral. France had closed the Spanish border the previous fall, which meant that the bulk of the men trying to get to the war were forced to slip surreptitiously over the windswept Pyrenees – a dangerous, nerve-racking, and exhausting journey.

By April, passports issued in Canada were being stamped "not valid for Spain." Under the provisions of the Foreign Enlistment Act, anybody who volunteered or anybody who helped a volunteer could be sent to prison for two years. It required ingenuity, careful organization, and, above all, money to move hundreds of men from the various cities across the water to France and then over the mountains to assembly points on the Spanish side of the border. This was a task that the Communist party, with its long experience in clandestine organization, was equipped to undertake.

The men who fought in Spain – most of them with the Mackenzie-Papineau Battalion in the International Brigade – were not all communists, but the great majority were certainly communist sympathizers. As one of them, Ron Liversedge, later wrote, "if there were any pure adventurers, they were a small minority. . . ." An extraordinary number, perhaps as many as half, were, like Liversedge, veterans of the B.C. relief camps.

Liversedge's reasons for volunteering were typical of many: "The life that I had led over the past five years as an active member of the unemployed organizations had made the decision for me. I think that the terrible life of the Canadian unemployed during the depression . . . the boxcars, the flop-houses, the demonstrations . . . police clubbing men, women, and even children unconscious on the city streets for asking for food, the twenty cents a day slave camps, the 'On to Ottawa trek,' all this had conditioned the men who volunteered to go to Spain to make the decision without much soul searching." Two prominent activists in the trek, Red Walsh and Lucien Tellier (better known as Lou Summers), both fought in Spain.

Bill Beeching joined the Communist party immediately after the Regina riot and volunteered for Spain after reading a pamphlet by Tim Buck predicting a world war if the Loyalist forces lost. Jack Lawson, who spent three days in a Regina jail for rioting and was then given a suspended sentence, set out for Spain as soon as the war began.

The motives of others were mixed. Ross Russell, a twenty-three-year-old assistant manager of a Woolworth's store in Montreal, began to realize there would be no further promotions for him in the organization because he was Jewish. Spain was in his mind, but it was a ringing address at the Mount Royal Arena by Norman Bethune, just back from the battlefield, that fired him up for action. Bethune's appeal was, for him, "the cherry on the sundae."

Mike Hyduk of Edmonton was fed up trying to make a living as cook and dishwasher in his brother's café, where a meal cost only fifteen cents. He attended a meeting sponsored by the Committee to Aid Spanish Democracy, was impressed by what he heard, and with fifteen others volunteered. "I figured I was doing the right thing," Hyduk said.

388

It is difficult now to conjure up the wide-eyed idealism of those years. Here were young men, buffeted by circumstances and embittered by neglect, prepared to lay down their lives for a cause. As one early volunteer, Marvin Penn of Winnipeg, put it, "the only thought in everybody's mind was to do a job. Nobody worried about themselves. Nobody give a darn that they were going to get killed." Jules Paivio of Sudbury was one of many who didn't expect to come back. Born into a family of left-wing Finnish immigrants, he went to Spain because "it was an opportunity for a real purpose in life. . . . I didn't have any notions it would be easy . . . that I would return whole."

The Canadian government and the Royal Canadian Mounted Police completely misunderstood the motivation of these dedicated young men. Both Commissioner MacBrien in Ottawa and Assistant Commissioner Wood in Regina believed that "these youths are being sent to Spain, largely for the sake of gaining experience in practical revolutionary work and will return to this country to form a nucleus of a trained corps." In fact, many who came back arrived just in time to volunteer to fight for their own country in the war against Hitler.

"Just what the hell are you guys going to get out of all this? That's what I want to know," a burly immigration officer said to Lionel Edwards at the U.S. border. Edwards, who had quit a job in Alberta to make the journey, didn't bother to reply. "Okay – on your way," said the officer, who seemed to know exactly where Edwards and his friends were going.

This was an odd war, a secret war, a war without recruiting posters or recruiting offices, without marching bands or waving flags, without any public call to arms or patriotic editorials in the press. It was also a devilishly hard war to reach; it was even hard to find out *how* to reach it. Nobody, including officials of the Communist party, was urging young men to enlist; quite the opposite. To volunteer to fight in Spain was rather like trying to locate somebody who knew how to get a bottle of bootleg gin.

Jules Paivio, having left his job at Eaton's in Sudbury, went to Montreal hoping to look up some Finnish friends who, he heard, knew some other Finns who had managed to enlist. When he got in touch with them, he was told he'd have to go back to Toronto. There the Young Communist League had been deputed to screen volunteers for Spain. Ross Russell, who lived in Montreal, also found it difficult to join. He approached Fred Rose, a prominent Communist and future M.P., who tried to talk him out of it; but Russell was determined and left, not for Toronto, but for Quebec City, where passage was arranged for him.

The Toronto office of the YCL, through which most of the volunteers received instructions and transportation, had its unofficial headquarters at the Seamen's Hall at 441 Queen Street West. It was run by Peter Hunter, just back from the University of Moscow, and Paul Phillips, a fluent linguist born in Bessarabia. They provided the new arrivals with a cover story, a second-hand suitcase and a new suit, if necessary (both from the Salvation Army), and a dollar a day for expenses while in the city. The party also set up a travel agency to arrange for steamship reservations and tickets to France. Once the volunteers had been screened to weed out any Trotskyites or police informers, they were shipped off to New York.

Money was always short. Many waited for months before funds could be found to move them out. Bill Beeching applied in Regina in January but did not receive money for a third-class ticket east until June. "The idea of leaving home to go to Toronto was a big deal, let alone going across the ocean," he was to recall. Beeching ate cheaply at the way points where you could buy a fried sausage for a nickel, a scoop of mashed potatoes for another nickel, and have the whole thing smothered with gravy for an extra penny.

In Toronto Beeching was introduced to a giant of a man who called himself Orton Wade – the same Orton Wade who had once saved himself from deportation by proving he was a Canadian citizen. Wade, whose real name was Herman Anderson, had been appointed leader of a small group that would take the train to Halifax to board a Cunard liner for France. Wade told his charges that discipline would be strict, all liquor would be banned, and they were to tell nobody where they were going.

Ron Liversedge, in Vancouver, had no difficulty finding someone who would help him get to Spain. He had been a prominent activist in the On-to-Ottawa trek and was already a member of the party. He knew that Tom Ewen, one of the eight men jailed in 1931 for communist activity, was in charge of screening volunteers. Ewen warned him that not all applicants would be accepted, but Liversedge passed with ease. It was only when he tried to apply for a passport that he ran into trouble. He needed somebody to sign the application – a clergyman, doctor, politician, or other professional who had known him for at least two years. One minister of the gospel who had been loud in his public protestation against fascism backed away, explaining that he didn't know him and it was against his principles to lie. "How about Dr. Telford?" he suggested.

Lyle Telford, a prominent member of the CCF, had signed so many applications that Liversedge was reluctant to approach him. Nonetheless, he had no choice.

"My God, not another one!" exclaimed Telford, a benign surgeon with rimless glasses and a shock of well-barbered white hair. "I've signed enough to get me locked up already."

"Oh, come on, Doc," said Liversedge. "In for a penny . . ." Telford signed.

Tom Ewen told Liversedge to pack his suitcase and wait for a call, which might come at any time. It came on May Day – a day of parades and celebration for the organized Left. Huge demonstrations called once again for work and wages, for better standards of relief, and now for aid to the Spanish Republic and an end to the non-intervention pact – the hands-off policy of the European democracies that made it difficult for their citizens to fight against Franco.

Liversedge marched in the parade to Stanley Park and was listening to band music when Ewen's son, Jim, tapped him on the shoulder and told him it was time to go. As the pair left the park they could hear the elder Ewen's voice, booming over the loudspeaker, exclaiming that "right at this moment [there] is a man leaving this rally on his way to Spain. . . ."

With the cheers of the crowd ringing in his ears, Liversedge headed for the nearest streetcar. Jim Ewen stopped him. "That would be fourteen cents for both of us," he explained. "There isn't any money for non-essentials." They walked three miles into town, ate a fifteen-cent meal at a Chinese restaurant, and then entered the CPR depot where Liversedge was given a day-coach ticket to Toronto and five dollars for expenses.

In Toronto, Paul Phillips told Liversedge that three dozen men were in town waiting to be organized into groups. Liversedge was put in charge of a group of fifteen, assigned to a boarding house, and told to report daily to Phillips. When the time came to leave, Phillips gave Liversedge three hundred dollars in cash and a small silk flag with which to identify himself when he met his anonymous contact in New York.

Liversedge's group arrived at the Pennsylvania Station the following morning and booked into the nearby YMCA. Liversedge took his little flag and met his contact, who sent him to an address in the warehouse district. Here a second contact man told him the group would be sailing aboard the SS *President Roosevelt* in five days. He gave Liversedge the steamboat tickets and, on the day before the sailing, a sum of money to be divided temporarily among the men when the ship docked at Le Havre – in case the French officials demanded proof that the new arrivals were solvent.

All the elaborate attempts at secrecy fooled nobody on the various vessels that took the volunteers across the Atlantic. Ships' crews, passengers, customs agents in France – all knew exactly what was going on. Eighty or ninety young men of limited means, all dressed in hand-me-down clothing and carrying battered suitcases, obviously weren't headed for the Paris Exposition. On the *Roosevelt*, Liversedge's group encountered a similar party of Italian Americans intent on joining the Garibaldi Battalion in Spain, where they would presumably be fighting their former compatriots on the Franco side.

On the night before the *Roosevelt* docked, the ship held the usual gala dinner with paper hats, extra beer, and plenty of singing and shouting. Liversedge remarked to one of the stewards that it had been a real bang-up affair. "Hell," came the reply, "the bunch on the last trip going to Spain nearly tore the dining saloon apart." Only then did Liversedge realize that everybody on board had known their destination.

Lionel Edwards, travelling earlier on the same ship, learned to his astonishment that an elderly Irish couple returning to their native land had kept to their cabin, "terribly frightened because they had been told that on the ship there were ninety-three raving Bolsheviks." It was some days before they ventured out, but in the end they agreed to have their picture taken with the Canadians.

By the time Bill Beeching's group arrived at Le Havre on the SS *Alona*, everybody knew who the Canadians were and most crowded around to wish them good luck. Big Orton Wade gave

392

each man thirty dollars to show the officials that they were solvent, then stood behind the barrier, in full view, as they handed it back. When Wade opened his own suitcase for inspection it was found to contain a bottle of gin, a pair of socks, and little else. In Beeching's description, the customs inspector's eyes "opened very big and he looked at him and he looked at Wade and he looked back at that and then he closed it and marked it with a piece of chalk."

Both the British and the American governments tried, through members of their embassies, to persuade the volunteers to go back home. Lionel Edwards and his group were met at Le Havre by two officials, one of whom said, "Gentlemen, we are authorized by our respective governments to fully pay for your return fare to your country and town or village. No questions asked and no prosecution. And further, the border to Spain is closed." There were no takers.

The Communists provided the train fare to Paris. On the train, a member of the French *sureté* pleaded with one group not to waste their lives going to Spain. They would, he said, be fighting for a lost cause. The volunteers, in a spirited discussion, told him he didn't know what he was talking about.

In Paris, the newcomers were sent to the headquarters of the International Committee for Volunteers, a three-storey building half a block long in the Rue Mathurin Moreau. There they were assigned hotel rooms, given money for meals, provided with new cover stories, and told to get rid of their identifying suitcases and all surplus clothing. That went to a special depot where it was sold for the cause or dispensed to wounded volunteers returning from Spain.

The following day the Canadians were taken to a big room where an instructor drilled each group thoroughly on the routes they were to take and the contacts they were to meet at each stage of their journey. Some of these instructions might have come from one of the E. Phillips Oppenheim spy novels popular at that time. Liversedge overheard one instructor outlining the course to be followed by a group of American volunteers: "When you reach Orleans, you will leave the train. On the platform will be a girl sitting on a bench close to the news-stand. She will be dressed in a black skirt, a red leather short jacket, a red beret, and she will have a poodle dog on a leash, and will be reading a magazine . . . and you will follow her at a distance, but always keeping her in sight. . . . "

Liversedge's group, which was taking a different route, received simpler instructions. A stranger was brought in and the Canadians were told to examine him closely from all sides and memorize his features so that they could pick him out in a crowd. He would be their contact when they reached Marseille.

The need for secrecy en route to the border towns was carefully stressed, but on the train south, Bill Beeching was amused to realize that every man was easily identifiable by the brown-paper parcel, tied with string, he carried in lieu of the discarded suitcase. In some French towns the citizens rushed out and greeted them with the upraised fist of the Popular Front. So much for secrecy.

Nonetheless, the cloak-and-dagger atmosphere intensified as they neared the border. Beeching's party, staying at a hotel in a town in the south of France, was told to use only yellow taxis – the driver would know where to go. On a certain day his party was to stand on a certain corner until a mysterious bus arrived. They were to climb aboard and, no matter what anybody said, maintain that they were tourists.

The bus took them to Perpignan at the foot of the Pyrenees. From this point they faced a dangerous and gruelling journey on foot over the mountains to Figueras in Spain. They were taken to an assembly point where they met their guides – veteran smugglers – stocky, sturdy men who wore berets and carried a stick and a blanket.

"This part is dangerous," Beeching's group was told. "There are border patrols, they have dogs, they have rifles and you are totally unarmed. . . . You will not smoke unless I tell you to smoke because smoke lays in the air. You'd better be careful and do what I tell you to do because you can be killed with a fall." Then their guide passed out pairs of rope-soled shoes, laced at the ankles, for the climb.

Ross Russell, the Woolworth's employee from Montreal, was held with a dozen others in a store in Perpignan for twenty-four hours, forbidden to go outside in daylight. At last they were herded out into the dark to find a long line of buses drawn up to take them to the assembly point. In spite of the supposed clandestine nature of their journey, the whole town, which had a communist mayor, turned out to see them off.

There seemed to be hundreds of volunteers at the assembly point, meeting their guides and talking in a dozen languages. They set off in single file, following the goat trail through the foothills, one guide leading, one in the middle, a third bringing up the rear. They walked for three hours at a fast pace without a break, for they had to be across the border before dawn. When the man ahead of Russell, a big blond French Basque, could no longer stand the pace, his smaller brother helped to drag him along.

This was the most arduous part of the journey. Jules Paivio crossed the mountains in a blizzard with some thirty others. In the high altitude, one obese volunteer found he couldn't breathe. Six of his friends tied themselves together and literally dragged him across. Milton Cohen, a young pharmacy graduate from the University of Montreal who crossed the Pyrenees in June, saw the man ahead of him collapse. A guide picked him up and carried him over his shoulder to the border. Not everyone made it: some men stumbled off the trails and fell into the ice-cold streams; others who sprained their ankles had to be hidden and left behind to be picked up on the guides' return journey.

Murray Saunders, a Canadian from Alberta, crossed the mountains with a single companion and no guide. The pair had somehow been missed when the various parties were taken from the barn in which they had been hiding. "Well," said Saunders, "we came here to go to Spain. . . . That's Spain in that direction and tonight we leave this barn and over we go." Off they went, blindly. After several hours they met a shepherd who pointed the way to Spain. Later, another shepherd appeared and led them on.

Saunders realized he was in Spain when he saw bullet scars on some of the buildings. Here the pair ran into a convoy of trucks. "Can you drive?" somebody asked him. Saunders replied that he'd been a chauffeur in Canada. "Well, get in and drive to Albacete," he was told, and that was how he rejoined his comrades.

For Bill Beeching the long mountain trek was an adventure: "You taxed your physical strength and your determination." For others it was an ordeal; the realization that the border had been

395

crossed came as a blessed relief. When Tommy Bailey, who was raised in the Palliser Triangle, reached the little shed where the Spanish border patrol was stationed, he looked down the slopes toward the green forests and meadows of ancient Ara and cried out, as only a boy from the dust bowl of Saskatchewan could. "Why," he said, remembering the sullen desert of dust and thistle that he had left behind, "why, it's like being in Heaven!"

2

Dead in the water Ron Liversedge's party did not reach Spain by way of the Pyrenees, and some of it, tragically, did not reach it at all. He and his fourteen men were dispatched by train to Marseille to board a ship for Barcelona. They travelled in three groups of five. At Marseille, Liversedge's group, following orders, left the station by the main entrance, ignored the line of taxis on the street, turned sharp left, and walked a block to a short street behind the station. There they spotted three cabs and, again following instructions, took the first one to No. 1 Thournabeau Street. They left the taxi and walked down the street to the Hotel Camard where, after a whispered password to the proprietor, they registered. The other two groups of five, having memorized their contact man's face in Paris, spotted him in the crowd and followed him at a short distance. When he entered a café, one group followed, ordered coffee, and waited to be collected. The contact left the café and led the other group to a second café, where, they, too, were collected.

Meanwhile, Liversedge and his party found the Hotel Camard crowded with volunteers from all over the world. There, another contact man gave each of them five francs, and they spent the next three days strolling about the city. Then still another contact arrived to lead them to their ship, the *Ciudad de Barcelona*, a Spanish coastal freighter that was to be their home for the next four days.

The ship was jammed with men, some of whom had already been on board for forty-eight hours. Liversedge and his group were led down a long, narrow passage, stuffy and smelling of bilge. When the police searched the ship, as they did periodically,

396

everybody was forced to crowd into a tiny space behind a bulk-head door until they left. The men were fed two meals daily of bread, fish, and wine, but they could not wash, shave, or go up onto the deck until the vessel sailed.

By embarkation day, May 28, two hundred and forty volunteers were crammed onto the ship, including ten other Canadians who had come down from Paris with Liversedge. At last, with darkness falling and the ship steaming out of port, they were allowed on deck. Liversedge now shared a first-class cabin with another Canadian, George Sarvas, and was able for the first time to wash. In the dining room, the volunteers were served octopus stew, a strange dish that Liversedge didn't care for. The day would come, however, when his thoughts would turn back longingly to that banquet.

He found it eerie to move around the crowded deck in the pitch dark, listening to a dozen languages. By that time he had located all fifteen of the original draft and found there were other Canadians on board. In the lounge that night, the volunteers staged an impromptu concert with songs in various tongues. The following morning they entered Spanish waters and Liversedge could see the coast three or four miles away. Above them an airplane dipped and circled. They shook their fists at the man in the cockpit: a Franco supporter? Barcelona was forty miles away; they were due to land about five that afternoon.

Liversedge went down below for a nap but had barely settled on his bunk when a tremendous explosion shook the ship. It seemed almost to leap out of the ocean before settling back with a shudder. The engines ceased to hum. The *Ciudad de Barcelona* was dead in the water.

He sprang from his bed, thinking a naval shell had landed on deck. In fact, the ship had been torpedoed by an Italian submarine. Sensing there was no time to lose, Liversedge didn't bother to dress. He stuffed a rubber tobacco pouch into his shirt behind his life jacket and bolted for the door in his underwear. Through a porthole on the stairway he could see the shoreline, a long way off and apparently tilted.

When he reached the deck, he saw that the ship's stern was already under water and she was listing to port, surrounded by a mass of floating wreckage – barrels, crates, cases, planking, canvas, even wooden bunks. He could see, bobbing in the midst of this flotsam, the heads of men who had been flung overboard and also floating bodies, surrounded by a widening stain of crimson.

A lifeboat hung over the ship's starboard side, its ropes tangled in the davits. Fifty men crowded into the boat while one hacked away at the lines with an axe, but it was so overloaded that when the lines snapped, it plunged into the ocean and went straight to the bottom.

Liversedge found that he could now step directly from the deck into the water. He started to swim away from the foundering freighter but could not help looking back, fascinated by the spectacle of the ship's last moments. There on the deck was a man he knew, Karl Francis, trying to pull himself over the ship's rail. Men struggling in the sea were yelling at him to drop, but Francis was frozen with shock; when the ship went down, he went down with it. No more than five minutes had elapsed since the torpedo struck.

A seaplane appeared, seeking the submarine, and dropped depth charges, which burst under water. The force of these explosions was such that, for a moment, Liversedge thought his legs were coming off. The plane landed and took as many survivors aboard as it could accommodate, then flew off, never to return.

As Liversedge floundered through the floating debris, he came upon a diminutive New Yorker, Syd Shostick, who was trying to hold up a two-hundred-pound Finn named Sankari. Liversedge took one side of the big man, gathered some planking together, and then with some canvas fashioned a makeshift raft and hauled Sankari aboard.

The torpedo had struck the vessel amidships and blown the engines right through the decks. Corpses, mutilated by the force of the explosion, floated around Liversedge as he swam about. Some men were drowning and he could hear them singing the "Internationale," the Communist anthem, as they sank beneath the water. In the distance he spotted some fishing boats, but these were separated from the survivors by a vast tangle of floating wreckage.

He came upon a man clinging to the edge of a wooden bunk. "How are you making out?" he shouted.

"Not so good," came the answer. Then the man turned around, saw Liversedge, and cried out, "Good Lord, are you here too?" It was a friend from Vancouver, Ellis Fromberg. Liversedge had had no idea he was on the ship. Fromberg was in a bad way from cramps in his arms, but Liversedge gathered enough floating lumber together to keep the two of them from sinking. It was two hours before the first of the fishing boats reached them, took them aboard, and deposited them on the beach in front of the little town of Malgrat. Liversedge was relieved to see that Shostick and Sankari had also been saved.

He and Fromberg were taken to a fisherman's cottage whose owner cut the clothes from their bodies and rubbed them down to restore circulation. A young girl arrived with a bottle of cognac, and that stopped Liversedge from shaking. The family provided both men with clothes and the girl took them to the town square, where the other survivors had gathered. There, Liversedge learned that three of the Canadians had been lost.

The bodies were laid out in the local church. That evening the townspeople came down, set up tables, and served an outdoor supper. The president of Catalonia, Luis Companys, made a speech of welcome. (In the Second World War, Companys would be executed by the Gestapo.)

Later that night, the survivors were put on the train to Barcelona, ready to be drilled for the battles that would follow. It would be almost two years before those Canadians who survived would return to their native land, and it would not be to a hero's welcome.

3

While the volunteers were making their way across the ocean and over the mountains to support the troubled Spanish government, trouble of another kind was brewing in Ontario. Mitch Hepburn was about to take on the dragon of the labour movement – John L. Lewis's Congress of Industrial Organizations. *Mitch Hepburn v. the CIO*

The struggle that took place in April was perhaps the most significant in Canadian labour history. At the time it seemed that the decision went to Hepburn: he fired two of his Cabinet stalwarts and won a landslide victory in the election that followed. But in the long term it was a defeat. The strike at the General Motors plant in Oshawa that spring saw the tacit acceptance in

Canada of the United Automobile Workers of America, and that heralded the entrenchment of industrial unionism, the very thing that Hepburn had fought to quell.

The peak of the Depression had passed in Central Canada – or so it seemed. In his "sunshine budget" in March, Hepburn lowered taxes and announced an unprecedented surplus of seven million dollars. Large corporations were beginning to post handsome gains. General Motors workers had taken five wage cuts over the Depression years. At the beginning of 1937, the company had announced a two-hundred-million-dollar profit, the greatest in its history. Yet it refused to raise wages. Instead, GM's Oshawa plant hired an American efficiency expert, who persuaded the company to speed up the assembly line.

Unions had not flourished in the Depression years; there were too many people eager to take jobs at any price. GM had no trouble keeping its plants free of labour organizers. Canadian workers could look with envy across the border where their counterparts had left the old American Federation of Labor to form the UAW under the CIO's banner. A series of sit-down strikes – a new weapon in the industrial struggle – had forced the American parent to recognize and negotiate with the union.

In Canada, however, wages were still going down and hours were longer. Some of the Oshawa workers formed a clandestine "Unity Group." On February 19, four days after the speed-up was introduced, three hundred assembly-line workers struck and asked the Detroit office of the UAW for support.

The new American union had little interest in organizing Canadian workers. It was too busy with its own problems. The only man available to help was a slight, dark-haired UAW organizer named Hugh Thompson. He agreed to come to Canada to look over the situation and report back. Thus the American union and its parent, the CIO, were dragged into the Canadian struggle in spite of themselves.

In the weeks that followed, Hepburn and his friend George McCullagh, publisher of the *Globe and Mail*, would portray Thompson as a dangerous, wild-eyed radical, a "foreign agitator" acting as the spearhead for the CIO's campaign to infiltrate and disrupt Canadian industry. He was nothing of the sort. A British subject born in Ireland, he had lived ten years in Canada before marrying an American. Hepburn did everything he could

400

to have him deported. Neither the federal government nor Hepburn's own Department of Labour could uncover a shred of evidence to eject him, yet Hepburn could never get it into his head that, as a British subject without a criminal record, Thompson had every right to cross the border.

To J.B. Highfield, GM's personnel manager in Oshawa, the mild-mannered Thompson was "a swine of an outsider," a convenient epithet, perhaps, but a strange one coming from a man whose American bosses were themselves outsiders. The American Federation of Labor, which organized craft unions, had operated for years in Canada without being castigated as "foreign." But the CIO was different. Its ultimate weapon, the sit-down strike – an attack on the age-old principle of private property – scandalized the business world. John L. Lewis, with his quivering jowls and Satanic brows, was depicted in the U.S. and Canadian newspapers as an ogre, tearing at the foundations of the American way of life. Although Thompson did not advocate use of the sit-down strike in Oshawa, Hepburn and his mentor, McCullagh, used the threat of it to terrify the public.

Thompson arrived in Oshawa on February 19 and persuaded the workers on the line to return to their jobs until a proper union could be formed. So deep was the feeling at GM that within a month, four thousand employees had joined the UAW, making the new Local 222 the largest in Canada. This in itself was a major victory. As Felix Lazarus wrote in the *Canadian Forum*, "the foremen and straw bosses . . . began treating the men like human beings. That was something new, and without precedent."

The union, however, couldn't find a meeting place. The owners of the hockey arena "didn't want their kind of an organization." The Department of National Defence stalled on renting the armouries. The board of education denied them the collegiate auditorium. That was too much for Thompson. When he threatened to hold an outdoor meeting at Oshawa's busiest intersection at high noon on a Saturday, the board gave in.

In March, Hepburn got the ammunition he needed when workers at the Holmes Foundry in Sarnia staged a bloody sit-down strike, the first in Canada. The factory was a sweatshop, where sanitary conditions were appalling, short circuits on the production line threatened men's lives, wages were low, speed-ups were common, and men were fired on whim. On March 2, seventy workers, many of them immigrants, sat down at their machines. A mob of infuriated Sarnia citizens, only a few of whom were plant workers, descended upon the foundry wielding crowbars, baseball bats, and steel pipes against the "foreigners." The police refused to interfere while heads and limbs were broken. No member of the mob was charged, but the strikers were arrested and convicted of trespassing. In the legislature, Hepburn declared, "... my sympathies are with those who fought the strikers." He went on to say that "those who participate in sit down strikes are trespassers. ... There will be no sit down strikes in Ontario. The Government is going to maintain law and order at all costs."

A few days later, the Premier, with the Oshawa situation in mind, attacked "professional agitators from the United States – [who] agitate and foment unrest in our industrial areas ... " and declared that he would "put down these sit down strikes with the full strength of the Provincial Police if necessary. ... "

Five years before, during a provincial by-election in West York, Hepburn had wooed the labour vote with his declaration, "I swing far to the left where even some Liberals will not follow me." In fact, he was a closet conservative, a typical product of the southern Ontario farming community that had always held the key to political success in the province. The new premier's closest cronies, confidants, and advisers were industrialists and mining men, such as J.P. Bickell of McIntyre-Porcupine, Jules Timmins of Hollinger, and Sir James Dunn of Algoma Steel. The most influential was George McCullagh, the young Toronto broker who had talked the wealthy prospector William H. Wright into bankrolling the *Globe and Mail*. These men were terrified that the CIO would organize the mines in Ontario and cut into their phenomenal profits. The previous year the province's gold mines, with production valued at eighty-three million dollars, had distributed twenty-nine million in dividends. Hepburn himself was slowly and unobtrusively becoming rich, thanks to McCullagh's advice and help. Earlier that year, as Hepburn's biographer, Neil McKenty, has recorded, when the Premier was away on holiday, McCullagh secretly bought him a block of stock in Hyslop Gold Mines that had doubled in value by the time he returned. In the fight with the CIO, McCullagh's newspaper was flagrantly partisan.

In Oshawa, General Motors was flatly refusing to deal with any "outside agitator" – Thompson – or to have anything to do

402

with the CIO. Thompson, whose object was to prevent a strike and get an agreement, quietly withdrew, leaving the negotiations to a Canadian auto worker named Charles Millard.

A series of talks in the first week of April suggested that a settlement was in the air. The men, who worked a forty-eight-hour week without extra pay for overtime, wanted a forty-hour week with time-and-a-half. The company was prepared to meet them halfway. On April 6, it agreed to negotiate the various union demands with Millard. It was apparent that a compromise was about to be reached.

But not if Mitch Hepburn had his way. The Premier had been following these events from Florida. Suddenly he cut short his vacation and on April 7 returned to Ontario, which, he told a fellow Liberal, was "just seething with labour troubles." The seething was all in the Premier's mind.

He was so determined to break the union that he even made an unprecedented phone call to the company's vice-president, George Chappell. He told Chappell that the government was backing GM and urged him to stand firm and refuse to recognize the CIO. As a result, General Motors reversed its stand and said it wouldn't negotiate with Millard while he represented an American union. For five days both Millard and Thompson, acting as an adviser behind the scenes, had desperately tried to avert a strike, urging a restive rank and file to postpone any action as long as negotiations continued. Now on April 8, with the talks at a standstill, Hepburn got the strike he wanted.

Late that evening, he called in a *Globe* reporter and, in a voice shaking with anger, indicated his real reason for opposing the union. "We know what these CIO agitators are up to," he said. "We are advised only a few hours ago that they are working their way into the lumber camps and pulp mills and our mines. Well, that has got to stop and we are going to stop it!"

For the duration of the strike, both Hepburn and the *Globe and Mail* did their best to suggest that the city of Oshawa faced anarchy and bloodshed. The union was determined not to provide any excuse for police repression. "It will be peaceful picketing and violence will not be tolerated," Hugh Thompson announced. Millard declared that no sit-down strike had ever been contemplated and that the strikers would leave the buildings. That was the last thing Hepburn wanted. He had been primed for a violent confrontation and, in spite of Thompson's announcement, tried to suggest that one was in the offing.

He wired to the federal justice minister, Ernest Lapointe, demanding that one hundred Mounted Police be dispatched to Oshawa at once because a "report just submitted to me indicates the situation becoming very acute and violence anticipated any minute also impairment of heating plants and fire protection services." That was sheer fantasy; Oshawa was remarkably quiet. "A city more peaceful . . . cannot be imagined," the Toronto *Star* reported. "It is neither grim nor gay but placidly ordinary, showing signs neither of industrial strife nor of holidaying workers." But Lapointe did as he was asked.

Hepburn put his provincial police on alert and announced that the men on strike would get no government relief, thus reneging on a promise made by David Croll, his own Minister of Labour. "The time for a showdown has come," the Premier announced. The strike was "the first open attempt on the part of Lewis and his CIO to assume the position of dominating and dictating to Canadian industry."

The mayor of Oshawa, Alex Hall, condemned Hepburn for his "irrational and impulsive action," but the majority of newspapers supported him, the important exceptions being the Toronto *Star* and the *Ottawa Citizen*. Hepburn's intemperate remarks bore such a resemblance to the editorials in the *Globe and Mail* that both of them might have been written by George McCullagh himself, and probably were.

On April 10, Homer Martin, the bespectacled president of the UAW, arrived in Oshawa. A Yale graduate and a former Baptist minister, Martin scarcely fitted the stereotype of the wild-eyed union agitator. Thousands of people lined the streets to cheer as his flag-draped convertible passed down the main street; Oshawa was clearly on the union side. In a fiery two-hour speech that evening that belied his meek manner, Martin castigated Hepburn as "a puppet of General Motors." But it was really Hepburn who, with McCullagh's help, was pulling the strings behind the scenes.

That same day, the federal Minister of Labour, Norman Rogers, had wired to Mayor Hall offering his services as a mediator, as Hall had requested. This infuriated Hepburn, who sent a telegram to Mackenzie King charging "treachery" and "unwar-

404

ranted interference." He could not resist adding that the action was "quite in common with the treatment this government has received from most of your ministers," a gratuitous slur that underlined the widening breach between the provincial and the federal Liberals.

King, who wanted to keep the federal government out of the controversy, was astounded by this insult and even more affronted when he learned that Hepburn had asked Lapointe for another hundred policemen because "the situation was becoming more intense." His indignation was justified; the Premier's own undercover agents had reported from Oshawa that "the strike is proceeding smoothly . . . with no threat of violence in sight." Nonetheless Hepburn, ignoring the mayor's invitation to see for himself how peaceful the city was, added a new dimension to the struggle when he told the press that "it appears that the Communists are anxious to take an active part in case of disturbance."

Mackenzie King prevented an over-eager Ernest Lapointe from dispatching more police to Oshawa. He was alarmed at the Premier's "deliberate effort to identify the Ontario government's action . . . with an effort to suppress Communism. . . . In this he has gone out of his way to raise a great issue in this Country, the frightful possibilities of which no one can foresee." Hepburn's actions, he feared, would "cut the Liberal party in two."

King put his finger on the crux of the matter. "The truth . . . is he is in the hands of McCullagh of the Globe and the Globe and McCullagh, in the hands of financial mining interests that want to crush the C.I.O. and their organization in Canada. The situation . . . has all the elements . . . that are to be found in the present appalling situation in Spain. Hepburn has become a Fascist leader and has sought to have labour in its struggle against organized capital put into the position of being under Communist direction and control. Action of the kind is little short of criminal."

With Lapointe reined in, Hepburn decided to get rid of the RCMP and form his own private army – a force that quickly became known as "Hepburn's Hussars," or, more irreverently, the "Sons of Mitches." He already had seventy-five provincial police at Queen's Park on constant alert, which meant lounging about playing cards or working out with dumbbells. Now he announced that he would add a minimum of two hundred volunteers to their ranks. It was necessary, he said, because he had received a secret report that the CIO was working "hand in glove" with international communism.

Students from the nearby University of Toronto rushed to Queen's Park to join the new force. Hepburn promised them OPP uniforms, military training, and – even more enticing – a generous twenty-five dollars a week. The Eglinton Hunt Club also responded with an offer of sixty horses, apparently in the belief that a cavalry charge might be needed to stem the revolution, while the 133rd Battalion of the Canadian Expeditionary Force volunteered to swell the ranks of the new army.

The government was now ready for armed conflict. Hepburn was already in touch with the Lake Erie Chemical Company of New Haven, Connecticut, which advertised that it could supply "everything in police equipment except the uniforms." It sent along a brochure that trumpeted the advantages of its Jumper-Repeater Instantaneous Gas Candle, complete with a photograph of milk strikers in Wisconsin being ineffectively gassed by an inferior rival product. The New Haven company emphasized that *its* gas candle was "far more effective because it exploded so quickly the mob couldn't throw it back at their pursuers." In Oshawa, meanwhile, the situation was so quiet that an American movie cameraman, unable to capture any scenes of violence, tried unsuccessfully to bribe two strikers to stage a mock battle to enliven his newsreel footage.

Hepburn demanded total loyalty from his followers. He wanted more than passive acquiescence in his policies; he wanted full-throated support. When he didn't get it from two of his most prominent Cabinet members, Attorney General Arthur Roebuck and Minister of Public Welfare, Municipal Affairs and Labour David Croll, he fired them on April 14. Both represented the left wing of the Liberal party and both were anathema to George McCullagh.

Croll had just returned from a southern holiday in the belief that the negotiations, under way when he departed, had proved fruitful. He was nettled to discover that his chief had not only forced a strike but had also scuttled his promise to provide relief for the strikers, and he was equally indignant at Hepburn's attempts to link the union with the communists.

406

He and Roebuck held their tongues in Cabinet, but that wasn't good enough for the Premier. "It is quite clear to me . . . " he wrote to Croll, "that you are not in accord with the policy of the Government in fighting the inroads of the Lewis organization and Communism in general. . . . Ontario is facing one of its greatest economic crises . . . there must be solidarity and unanimity within our ranks." Croll's famous reply made him a hero to the labour movement. His place, he told Hepburn, was "marching with the workers rather than riding with General Motors."

McCullagh's newspaper, meanwhile, continued to predict bloodshed and lawlessness in Oshawa while hailing Hepburn on its front page as "Canada's Man of the Hour." These front-page editorials, which appeared almost daily, were masterpieces of venom. The titles alone give an idea of their quality: "DOUBLE CROSSING TREACHERY . . ."; "LEWIS BANDITRY SPREADS . . ."; "FIGHTING LEWIS FASCISM." In McCullagh's editorial view, the workers were "dupes of self serving and self seeking union agitators" while the CIO was "a gigantic dictatorship scheme."

"Is there a red-blooded Canadian," the *Globe* asked on April 17, "whose anger does not boil over at the story of intrigue, duplicity, and double crossing, which has run through events of the past ten days in the motor city?" These were pure figments of George McCullagh's overheated imagination, but they would have their effect on the voters in the fall provincial election.

With Croll and Roebuck out of the picture, Hepburn announced that "there is no turning back now . . . this is a fight to the finish." The mines, he said, would be next; industry would be demoralized; stock prices would tumble.

Hepburn was prepared to use any pretext to keep the strike going. On April 17, he personally took over negotiations with Charles Millard and the union's lawyer, J.L. Cohen. The meeting was genial enough until Hepburn discovered that Cohen was using the phone in his private vault, apparently to report to Homer Martin. Hepburn flew into a rage. "What!" he cried, "another long distance call?" With that he broke off negotiations, charging that the local had double-crossed him and the union was being run by remote control. He strode back into his office, clapped his hat on his head, pushed his way through a crowd of reporters, and headed for the elevator.

Homer Martin, however, was quite prepared to allow the local to negotiate with GM without interference from or apparent connection with the CIO. He wanted a Canadian contract – one that would run concurrently with the GM contracts in the United States so that all could eventually be negotiated at the same time on both sides of the border. To achieve that he was content to keep the congress out of the picture.

Hepburn was ecstatic at what he called Martin's "surrender." He had been vindicated, he declared, in his attempts "to root communism out of the Canadian labour movement." Negotiations resumed at once and it looked as if the strike would be settled quickly. Then, inexplicably, Hepburn again broke them off.

He had learned from his informants in Oshawa that Martin's strategic withdrawal was causing dissension among the rank and file. Now he saw a chance to break the union and stave off the threat to the mining industry – a threat that concerned him more than any menace to the automobile industry. "Let me tell Lewis here and now," he said, "that he and his gang will never get their greedy paws on the mines of northern Ontario as long as I am prime minister." The financial world was sceptical. On April 19, gold shares plunged on the Toronto market.

The Oshawa local *was* in trouble. Homer Martin had promised financial support from the United States, but none came. The union's funds were almost gone; it could no longer afford to pay its own pickets. The strike would have to be settled quickly or the local would be destroyed. This was a closely guarded secret; neither the press and general public nor the Premier realized that the union was broke. Instead, Hugh Thompson announced that the UAW in Detroit had unanimously voted funds to keep the strike going. It had done nothing of the sort.

Both sides were now desperate to end the strike; only Hepburn was desperate to keep it going. The union was facing bankruptcy. GM wanted to get back to making cars before its rivals stole a march on it. Hepburn pleaded (in vain) by wire with the vacationing GM president, Colonel R.S. McLaughlin, to break off negotiations. But GM feared Ford and Chrysler more than it feared the union. All that Hepburn was able to achieve in the parley that followed on April 22 was to force a statement from Charles Millard and J.L. Cohen that they did not represent the CIO.

408

Hepburn exulted over this paper victory. "The CIO is repudiated," the *Globe and Mail* reported triumphantly. But even George McCullagh admitted that it was not a decisive win. The CIO was in Canada for good – in fact if not in name. The strike ended on April 23, fifteen days after it had begun, and both sides, as usual, claimed to have won. The union got wage increases and a seniority system and compromised on a forty-four-hour week – almost everything it wanted except official recognition for the CIO. But once the strike was settled, the workers on their own boldly passed a resolution affirming their local's alliance with both the United Automobile Workers union and the parent congress.

Industrial unionism had arrived in Canada in spite of Mitchell Hepburn. Ironically, the CIO's role in the strike had been very slight. It had been reluctant to enter Canada, it hadn't contributed a nickel in funds, it hadn't called a sympathy strike in the United States to support the Canadian workers, and the final settlement had been negotiated by Canadians without its help. By over-emphasizing the role of the CIO in the walk-out, Hepburn had managed to give it a status it wouldn't otherwise have enjoyed. As it was, the Oshawa strike opened the door for a massive CIO organizing campaign that changed the nature of Canadian labour.

The strike also demonstrated the extent to which Hepburn was a creature of the Ontario mining industry. The most extraordinary postscript to this extraordinary affair was George McCullagh's manipulation of the Premier after the strike ended. McCullagh, on behalf of the mining fraternity, actually proposed that Hepburn's Liberals, who held seventy-three seats in the legislature, form a coalition with Earl Rowe's Conservatives, numbering seventeen.

Only a strong and united government, McCullagh felt, could keep the CIO out of the mines, and Hepburn apparently agreed. He had already informed Herbert Bruce, the lieutenant-governor, that a coalition government might be in the offing. Then he visited Rowe and offered the startled Tory leader not only the premiership but also the chance to choose half the Cabinet. Rowe turned him down, an action that caused his second-in-command, George Drew, to resign in protest. "The time had come," Drew insisted, "to end the two-party system in Ontario since only a

409

strong government could destroy communism." Those words had a familiar ring. Democracy was on shaky ground in Ontario, as it was elsewhere in the world, where other voices were calling for strong one-party government to destroy the spectre that was haunting Europe.

Even though it posited the end of the Liberal party in Ontario, the plan appealed to Hepburn because it would, in his view, strike the CIO a death blow and be a slap in the face to his enemy, the Prime Minister. The Oshawa strike had widened a breach with Mackenzie King – and between the federal and provincial Liberals – that would not be healed until Hepburn left office. In short, the Premier of Ontario was prepared to circumvent the democratic political system in order to pursue a paranoid vendetta with all the power of an authoritarian state. And in this he had the enthusiastic backing of the financial giants of Bay Street. Fortunately, the Toronto *Star* got wind of the plan, and Hepburn was forced to deny it publicly. That ended the idea of coalition.

In spite of this, the small-c conservative voters, who formed the majority of the Ontario electorate, were solidly behind Hepburn in his anti-CIO, anti-communist campaign. His repeated declarations that he would never tolerate "CIO lawlessness" reassured them. They had read about industrial strife south of the border. Both Hepburn and the press had made the most of those incidents. The last thing the voters wanted was to see it explode in their peaceful province. Hepburn's public announcement, "I am a Reformer but I am not a Mackenzie King liberal any longer," reinforced their traditional suspicion of Ottawa.

In the fall election campaign, Hepburn stumped the province with what was, in effect, a law-and-order platform. As others had before him, he conjured up the spectre of revolution – always an effective vote-getter in a nation historically sensitive to the very thought of violent revolt. Hepburn explained that he had needed extra police at the time of the strike because he had "confidential reports that 15,000 Communists were ready to take part in any uprising whether it took place in Toronto or elsewhere." In short, not only Oshawa but the entire province had been threatened.

The Oshawa strike became one of the major issues in the campaign. With his attacks on the American labour body, Hepburn scored a stunning victory, retaining sixty-three seats to his opponents' twenty-three and keeping the northern Ontario min-

410

ing country safe for capitalism. It was, according to one American mining entrepreneur interviewed by the New York *Post*, the one spot on the continent "where if a union organizer is ordered out of the district by the company police or a piece of rock drops down a 1,000-foot shaft on his head, there isn't a damn thing he can do about it."

But it was a Pyrrhic triumph. By moving the provincial Liberal party to the right and away from its traditional source of support, Hepburn effectively destroyed it and, in the process, made room for the CCF's eventual move into the vacuum.

4

On the day the Oshawa strike ended, Mackenzie King left Ottawa to attend the Coronation of King George VI in London, to confer with Neville Chamberlain, the British prime minister, and to arrange a meeting with Adolf Hitler in Berlin.

The Prime Minister and the dictator

Accompanied by Joan and Godfroy Patteson, he sailed for England on the CPR's sleek *Empress of Australia*, occupying Suite 140, the finest on the ship – the one in which the former Prince of Wales had travelled on his visits to Canada. In spite of the presence of his closest friends, King felt an indescribable loneliness. "Some evil spirit seems to have entered into my house of rest & peace to destroy both," he wrote. The evil spirit, no doubt, was responsible for the incessant jazz music, which King couldn't abide and which seeped into his room from the ballroom, disturbing his sleep. He much preferred the motion pictures shown to the first-class passengers: *Rhodes – Builder of Empire* (though he found himself "in little sympathy with the Empire-making side of the performance"), and *A Tale of Two Cities*, with Ronald Colman, which he found "a marvellous movie – the unrest of the French Revolutionary Times. Like today in some respects."

At the Coronation in Westminster Abbey, his puritan sensibilities were offended by the costliness of the vestments worn by nobles and clergy. The heavy embroidery, he thought, contrasted unfavourably with the simple garments of the fishermen of Galilee; the spirit of Christ was being overlaid by the materialism of the times. "Indeed it was only too apparent that without wealth or

411

position, no one could gain admission to the Abbey service or a place there. A great contrast to the scenes of Christ's ministry on earth!"

In June, he attended a small private dinner party given by Neville Chamberlain for the Dominion prime ministers. Anthony Eden, the foreign secretary, was also present. When King told Chamberlain and Eden that he had seen Joachim von Ribbentrop, the German ambassador, and arranged a meeting with Hitler in Berlin, both men heartily approved. Germany, Chamberlain said, was more likely to listen to King than to anyone from Britain. Eden thought the Germans would look upon him as speaking not only for Canada but "also to some extent for the United States" and would be much impressed by what he had to say.

King was anxious to tell Hitler "of my desire of his continuing constructive work among Labour, and not permitting it to be outdone by destructive work." He intended to make it clear that Canadians would not stand for aggression and that if Germany became aggressive "she would find it impossible to hold back our country or any of the Dominions." A statement like that, Eden told him, would help more than all the dispatches in the world to preserve the peace in Europe.

Nonetheless, King was careful to inform the British politicians that Canada had no intention of being drawn into a European war unless Germany or some other country was the aggressor. That would be "like expecting us to jump into a bag of fighting cats." He was careful, also, to underscore the voluntary nature of any Canadian involvement. Even then, the Canadian prime minister foresaw that conscription might jeopardize Canadian unity.

He left the dinner with the feeling that the British were "wholeheartedly working for the peace of Europe and are likely to be wise and sane in their attitudes." For Chamberlain he had "the greatest admiration and the greatest confidence."

In Berlin, King met first with Britain's ambassador to Germany, Sir Nevile Henderson, who asked if he might accompany him to the interview with the German dictator. King resented the suggestion; he told Henderson that "you people in the Old Land never seem to get an understanding of the point of view of the Dominions, or what is best in their own interests, in relations with other countries." The last thing King wanted was to have the Germans believe that he was under the wing of the British and

412

that Canada couldn't handle her own international relations. Henderson immediately backed off.

The British ambassador was badly afflicted with the virus of appeasement. Austria, he explained to King, was largely German; Czechoslovakia had a large German minority; Germany had her need to expand, and if Britain tried to prevent her moving peacefully into those countries, it would be a great mistake. King, on his part, agreed that Britain should not act "as 'a dog in the manger' re: Germany's legitimate development."

Henderson believed England could learn a lot from Germany in the treatment of the masses. Nazism wasn't all wrong, he told King. The German people were happy and had a right to live under any system they wished. Henderson spoke of the League of Nations as "a horror"; collective security "was worse than meaningless, a real danger."

King's diary entries during his days in Germany are remarkable not for what they say but for what they *don't* say. In his scribbled musings King could be remarkably prickly. His references to the British, especially the aristocracy, as well as to some of his own countrymen, such as Vincent Massey, were often tinged with asperity or, as in the case of Bennett and some other political opponents, with real venom. And yet, in the twenty-eight pages that cover his four days in Berlin, in which he met and talked with Hitler, Göring, Neurath, and a host of minor Nazi officials, there is scarcely a suggestion of reproof, let alone disgust or anger at the totalitarian and viciously racist program that held the German people in its thrall. King not only accepted passively and without comment the patent nonsense that was spoon-fed to him but he also, apparently, believed much of it, while his personal assessment of the Nazi leadership bordered on the sycophantic.

King told the British ambassador that he wanted to speak with Hitler "about his work on behalf of the people." Henderson was enthusiastic. Hitler, he said, was really an idealist who had the people's welfare very much at heart. If King could make Hitler feel that he, a Canadian, had an understanding of the German people, it would go farther than anything else to improve relations with the Reich. King left with the conviction that he had done the right thing "in the interests of Canada and the Empire in coming to Berlin at this time."

Two days later, King met the German dictator. Hitler told him, "... my support comes from the people – the people don't want war." That impressed King very much – "a real note of humility" he wrote later. Hitler continued to emphasize that "you need have no fear of war at the instance of Germany. ... We know what a terrible thing war is, and not one of us want to see another war." This was pure hogwash; Germany that year was actively preparing for war. But Hitler, who had successfully tranquillized diplomats more worldly than King, covered his intentions with a thick varnish of sweet reason that impressed the gullible prime minister.

"Let us assume that a war came," the dictator mused. "What would it mean? Assuming that France were to get the victory [over Germany] ... what she would find would be that European civilization had been wiped out. But suppose we were to win the war? ... We would find exactly the same thing. We would have obliterated civilization of both countries, indeed of a greater part of Europe; all that would be left, would be anarchy. ... " The interview, scheduled for half an hour, went on for more than twice that length, with Hitler quietly explaining the aspirations of his people and the German government's sincere desire for peace. King was hoodwinked. When he thanked the dictator for giving him so much time, Hitler "smiled very pleasantly and indeed had a sort of appealing and an affectionate look in his eyes." King sized him up as "really one who truly loves his fellow men and his country, and would make any sacrifice for their good. That he feels himself to be a deliverer of his people from tyranny."

Hitler's personality charmed King as it charmed so many other visitors. "His face is much more prepossessing than his pictures would give the impression of. It is not that of a fiery over-strained nature, but of a calm, passive man, deeply and thoughtfully in earnest ... ; his eyes impressed me most of all. There was a liquid quality about them which indicates keen perception and profound sympathy. ... One could see particularly how humble folk would come to have a profound love for the man."

Ribbentrop's liaison man, Walter Hewel, an intimate of the Führer, filled King's head with a lot of twaddle about his master, duly reported in the diary. Hitler didn't want to be treated as a deity, Hewel said. "He dislikes any of them thinking of him as anything but a humble citizen who is trying to serve his coun-

414

try. . . . " He was deeply religious, Hewel insisted, believed strongly in God, and during his tenure more Christian congregations had been established in Germany than in many years preceding. The outside world had misrepresented his religious views; all he wanted to do was keep the blood of the people pure. "He is particularly strong on beauty, loves flowers," Hewel told King, "and will spend more of the money of the State on gardens and flowers than on most other things."

King accepted all this without comment and went on that afternoon to learn something about the "Strength Through Joy" youth movement. "I found all these young men very frank, very alert, clean looking, active minded, enthusiastic," he wrote. "There was a splendid order and efficiency about everything I saw." At the opera that night – Verdi's *A Masked Ball* – he was impressed by the fact that the people came from love of music rather than shallow social reasons. "Dress was conspicuous by its absence." Between acts he talked to a member of Hermann Göring's staff, who "spoke about secret forces at work to bring about better conditions after this period of stress and strain." The opera over, King returned to his hotel feeling that this, perhaps, had been the most significant day of his life.

He saw Nevile Henderson the next day and found that the British ambassador shared his impression of Hitler. Henderson complained that the English kept finding fault with him for stressing anything good about Nazism, and reiterated his belief that Germany should be allowed to expand by degrees without interference from England. "It seems to me particularly fortunate that Henderson is Ambassador at the present time," King commented.

King followed this with a call on the German foreign minister, Baron Konstantin von Neurath, who declared solemnly that "as long as I am at the Foreign Office, there will never be war on Germany's account." Neurath spoke of how the country had been "going to pieces" when Hitler took over. For much of that he blamed the Jews. "He said to me," King wrote, "that I would have loathed living in Berlin with the Jews, and the way in which they had increased their numbers in the City, and were taking possession of its more important part. He said there was no pleasure in going to a theatre which was filled with them. Many of them were very coarse and vulgar and assertive. They were getting control of all the business, the finance, and had really taken advantage of the necessity of the people. It was necessary to get them out, to have the German people really control their own City and affairs. He told me that I would have been surprised at the extent to which life and morals had become demoralized; that Hitler had set his face against all that kind of thing, and had tried to inspire desire for a good life in the minds of young people."

If King took exception to this racist diatribe there is no evidence of it in his diary. Indeed, the context suggests that he agreed with much of it. What Neurath was saying about Berlin wasn't very different from what King himself had written about the Jews taking over an Ottawa suburb. This, after all, was the man who didn't want Jews as neighbours and who was always disgusted by what he considered to be vulgarity and coarseness – epithets that anti-Semites all over the world, including Canada, were using to support their version of the Jewish stereotype.

The Nürnberg laws had been in existence for almost two years when King visited Berlin. Jews could no longer be German citizens, couldn't marry Aryans, and couldn't employ Aryan servants. By this time they had been so rigorously excluded from public or private employment that half of them had no means of livelihood. They were forced to wear an identifying Star of David that barred them from entering a grocery store, drugstore, bakery, or dairy. Nor could they get a night's lodging in a hotel. Taunting signs forbidding them entry were everywhere. King must have seen these or known of them.

Nonetheless he quoted his host's remarks without comment and proclaimed himself delighted by his charm and hospitality. After Neurath insisted that they be photographed together, King was pleased to receive a copy of the picture in a silver frame. This discussion was followed by a luncheon party that King judged "one of the pleasantest I have ever enjoyed. The whole environment was most attractive; no one could have been kinder than the host. I felt in von Neurath's attitude something of the same kind of paternal attitude that I have experienced with Sir William Mulock and some older men."

The entire German visit overawed King, who misread all the signs and portents in that doomed country. "I can honestly say it was as enjoyable, informative and ever inspiring as any visit I have had anywhere," he exclaimed. Everything about Germany

416

seems to have entranced him, including the appearance, manners, and outlook of the people, who appeared to him to be more like Canadians than were either the British or the French. What others feared in Germany, King was persuaded, was that German ideas of liberty and equality for the masses might spread out into their own lands! As for regimentation, though one didn't like it, "it is apparently the one way to make views prevail."

He could not believe that the German people would ever revert to a purely materialistic way of life; the country was undergoing a revolution, fuelled by idealism. "I have come away from Germany tremendously relieved. I believe there will not be war. . . . The one danger to all countries is the Press; through its misrepresentations and persistent propaganda, some incidents will arise which will occasion conflict."

When King blamed "the interests behind the press," he wasn't thinking of Goebbels's propaganda machine in Germany but the democratic press, including McCullagh's *Globe and Mail*, which, he believed, was behind Hepburn's public attacks on him. He had read of Hepburn's vitriolic outbursts only after arriving in England and was convinced that "the *Globe* has got him in its pocket." King thought the Liberal party might have to fight the *Globe* "and its capitalistic backers." He relished that idea: "To me it would be both an easy and an enjoyable battle to continue till the end of my life the fight for the rights of labour."

The matter came up again on the voyage back to Canada in July. King had a conversation with Sir James Dunn, a fellow passenger and a strong Hepburn supporter. Dunn remarked that McCullagh was "far too immature and inexperienced to handle a paper like the Globe" and added that he had been in touch with Lord Beaverbrook, the Canadian-born proprietor of the London *Daily Express*, presumably as a possible successor. "It is quite clear," King confided to his diary, "that all these financial pilots are getting together to wheel [*sic*] what influence they can, through the Press." The talk with Dunn was amiable enough, but, King added, "I put no trust, however, in these men."

The following night, as the liner made its way up the St. Lawrence, the Prime Minister had another of his visions. In it, a magnificent star appeared, so real and strong that it woke him. In his sleep he had heard a chorus of angels in the background singing music from the concluding act of *Faust*. "It was all rapturously beautiful. I have heard no music like it, & beheld no greater beauty. . . . It was a magnificent vision, a marvellous ending to this great journey, with its mission of peace from beginning to close. . . . "

King rose from his bed, picked up the picture of his mother that was never far from his side, and pressed it to his lips. Then, convinced that he had experienced a divine revelation, he kissed one of the roses in his bedside vase.

In Europe that summer, Hitler was busy cementing the Rome-Berlin Axis with Mussolini and preparing for war, if necessary, with both Austria and Czechoslovakia. That same year he opened at Buchenwald the first of the Nazi death camps.

5

The black blizzard On the morning of June 22, while Mackenzie King was planning his itinerary for Berlin, Annie Bailey, on a small prairie farm near Bengough, Saskatchewan, was pouring one last cup of coffee before starting to do her chores. It was not the kind of fresh, dewy morning she had been used to as a child. She found herself panting for air as the hot, amber light of the sun filtered down through the dust. In the pasture beyond the barn she could see one of the horses pawing through the drifting sand, trying vainly to uncover a blade of grass. But the only vegetation was the ubiquitous Russian thistle, the prickly, red-stemmed weed that thrived on arid conditions and branched profusely into a dome-shaped plant. It was piled ten feet high at the fence corners, held there by the weight of the sand that had blown across it and even crushed part of the wire fence itself.

The Baileys had come to the end of their resources. Their only hope was to find another home, a place to settle far from the clinging dust that had turned their world into a monochrome, like a grainy black-and-white movie. The dust lay everywhere in the fields, on the roads, and inside the unpainted buildings. There was no escape from it. It clogged your throat and nostrils, got into your hair, ground itself into your very skin. It turned lace curtains grey and settled in a thick blanket on the rusty farm machinery. The greens and golds of spring and fall, which had once delighted the prairie people, had long since been replaced by a
418

common drabness – mile upon mile of dun-coloured land in which no living thing, save for the everlasting thistle, moved or flourished. The animals and birds and the wild flowers that had been the prairies' glory had retreated to richer pastures. Now the Bailey family was fleeing with them.

Mrs. Bailey had just seen her husband, George, off on a three-day journey of exploration in northern Saskatchewan to seek a farm far away from the dry belt where they hoped to make a new beginning. Now she wished she had gone with him. She could see the wind blowing swirls of dust high above fields already cracked by the intense heat. In the distance, a whirlwind of alkali from a dry lake rose hundreds of feet in the air.

With the help of Bob, the fourteen-year-old hired hand, she fed the pigs, cleaned the stalls, and did the cream separating. Then she made breakfast, dressed her small baby, Elaine, and sent her young son, Reginald, off to the same one-room school she herself had attended years before. Then she returned to the ritual of cleaning the dust from the window sills and floors, knowing that it would be back again almost as soon as she'd finished. As she went about her work, she thought ahead to the evening and the radio programs she enjoyed so much. This was a special night – the night of the heavyweight boxing match between Joe Louis, the contender, and James J. Braddock, the champion. Her husband would want all the details.

The wind blew all that day – hot and dry. By five that afternoon it had reached gale proportions. Now, as she and the others sat down to supper, a strange silence fell across the farm.

The wind suddenly died. It was, she thought, as if somebody had thrown a switch and turned it off. An hour later, as she did the dishes, young Reginald ran into the house, crying, "Come quick, Mom, there's a big black cloud coming!"

She ran out behind him. There, on the horizon, loomed "the blackest, most terrifying cloud I had ever seen." It was racing toward them at top speed – a shapeless monster blotting out the sky. Panic rose within her. Here she was, a woman alone on the prairie – the nearest neighbour a mile away – with a small baby and two young boys. What could she do? Where could she go? At the rate the cloud was moving, and she could see its edges literally rolling along, it would engulf them before they reached the neighbours.

"Where's Bob?" she asked.

"Over there, fixing the pigpen."

"Go, tell him to come quick."

She shut the door, picked up the baby, shouted to the others to follow, and ran for the barn, which was dug into the side of the hill. The shadow of the great cloud followed close behind.

The cow stood by, waiting to be milked. She pushed the animal into the barn and shouted at the children, "Go back as far as you can! Get up on those sacks of feed and sit there!" She fastened the door shut and, still carrying Elaine, joined the others. "We're safe here," she told them, marvelling at the calm of her voice - a calmness she did not feel. The boys, oddly, asked no questions but sat silent and still on the sacks of grain.

By this time it was pitch dark in the barn, and she sensed that the cloud was directly overhead. She expected to be lifted up at any second and carried into the air, or to have the barn blown away around them.

She had no way of telling time, but when she thought it was safe, she groped her way to the door, opened it a crack, and peered out. It was like a vacuum outside, quiet and dark, but she could hear the milk pails and stools being hurled about. She went back to the others and told them it would soon be all over.

At last it grew light enough so that she could distinguish forms. Now she felt it safe enough to open the door onto what she would remember as "the strangest phenomenon I had ever witnessed." A cloaking silence enveloped her. The dust hung so thick in the air it was clearly visible. And everything - land, air, and sky - was a dull grey colour. The black cloud had been saturated with dust sucked up many miles away and carried along in a sort of vacuum, to be dropped along the route. The wind had been blowing at a high altitude and the sand in the cloud had cut out the sound. That was what caused the eerie silence.

She scooped up the baby, and she and the two boys headed for the house, sinking almost to their ankles into drifts of sand. Inside, the dust was too thick to sweep up with a broom. She had to use a shovel.

When she turned on the radio to listen to the fight - the one in which Joe Louis became heavyweight champion of the world - she got only static. It was still dark, even though the evening was young. She was afraid to go to bed in case another storm struck

420

and so sat by the kitchen window and then lay on the couch, fully clothed and awake.

What happened that day convinced the Baileys that they had to move out of the dry belt. When George Bailey got home, he reported that conditions were far better two hundred miles to the north. And so, in the third week of July, they pulled out.

It was not an easy leave-taking. Annie Bailey had lived all her life in the same area; the home she was born in stood only a mile away. When the neighbours came down to the station to see them off, somebody said, wistfully, "Maybe it will change now and rain." Annie looked at her husband with a question in her eyes, but he replied, bluntly, "If it does, we won't be here to see it." Nor were they.

The Baileys had stood it for longer than many of their fellow farmers. This was the eighth year of the drought and by far the worst. In 1937, the prairies suffered the greatest crop failure in their history. Saskatchewan was the hardest hit. It had produced 321,000 bushels of wheat in 1928; in 1937 its farmers were hard put to harvest 37,000 bushels. By fall, crop failures forced two-thirds of the province's rural population onto the relief rolls; 290 of its 302 municipalities were forced to seek government assistance.

The effects of the drought had been cumulative. Debt built up; farmers who borrowed money in 1930 found that, with unpaid interest, they owed 50 per cent more by 1937 – and had nothing to show for it. The dust piled up as the blowing top soil grew finer and looser. The grasshopper plagues grew worse as each hot, dry spring provided the ideal climate for the egg pods laid the previous fall to open and release a swarm. An average of one pod of thirty eggs per square foot meant that each acre could hatch more than a million grasshoppers. At one point on the road between Regina and Saskatoon automobile traffic came to a standstill because the radiators were plugged with thousands of dead insects.

But even the hoppers were hard put to find sustenance. In June and July, scarcely a drop of rain fell in the drought country. In the last week of June, Mackenzie King's barrel-chested agriculture minister, Jimmy Gardiner, the former premier of Saskatchewan, made a twenty-five-hundred-mile swing through the Palliser Triangle, accompanied by the Minister of Labour, Norman Rogers. In all that vast area they saw scarcely a blade of grass, a haystack, or a flash of green – only a bare patchwork of grey and brown.

The wells, cisterns, ponds, and even the medium-sized lakes were dry. Johnstone Lake, a twenty-mile stretch of water south-west of Moose Jaw, was a weedy slough. Wildfowl perished for lack of water. People were forced to buy water to drink at a nickel a pail. Max Braithwaite, who taught school there during the Depression, remembered that even in Vonda, Saskatchewan, outside the Triangle, his family was rationed to eight pails a week.

The wind that year was devastating, as Mrs. Bailey discovered. John Boak, farming near Meacham, Saskatchewan, found that so much of his neighbour's summer fallow had blown onto his fields that his crop was smothered. In many cases seeds failed to germinate. Traditionally, the province's average yield had been fifteen bushels to the acre. In 1937 it dropped to 2.6.

By 1937 the prairie farm debt had reached half a billion dollars. Half the telephones had been taken out and more than half the automobiles were abandoned or converted to Bennett buggies. Education was hard hit because municipal tax revenues had dropped from six million a year to a million and a half. The average annual salary for a male teacher dropped from $1,186 to $536; women were paid as little as $350 and weren't always able to collect the full amount. Some teachers virtually worked for nothing. So did the doctors. Many had long since stopped sending bills and were taking payment in kind. As Dr. John Scratch of Maymont, Saskatchewan, put it, "I pull their teeth and lance their boils and deliver their babies. They pay me what they can – a chicken here, a ham there." That year, some medical men on the prairie reported that they were beginning to see signs of scurvy. Relief vouchers could not be used to buy fruit or fresh vegetables.

The worst victims of hunger were the million and a half cattle. With the farmers forced to switch from growing wheat to raising livestock, the cattle population had exploded. A surplus of at least three hundred thousand would now have to be sold at bank-ruptcy prices to the meat-packing plants. Families on relief were allowed to keep no more than four or five head.

When it finally began to rain in late July, it was too late for any crop save Russian thistle, which suddenly blanketed the drab prairie with a mantle of green. The farmers managed to harvest well over one hundred thousand bushels of the plant to serve as subsistence fodder for the livestock.

The rain helped to settle some of the dust and to bring down temperatures that in some places had exceeded 110 degrees Fahrenheit. The downpour came as a blessed relief to everybody – or, to quote some wags, to *almost* everybody. There were those who claimed, with a straight face, that small babies who had never seen a rainstorm cried out in fright when the unaccustomed water dropped from the sky. It could even have been true.

6

In times of economic crisis, strong or demagogic leaders tend to emerge and to entrench themselves through extra-legal means. It happened not only in Europe during the Depression but also in other parts of the world – in the sovereign state of Louisiana in 1935, and in Brazil in 1937. It also happened in Canada. *Bypassing democracy*

In Alberta, William Aberhart tried to control the banks, the financial institutions, the police, and the press. In Quebec, Maurice Duplessis passed a law that gave him the power to suppress any opinion he might happen to dislike. Aberhart's legislation was quickly and properly squelched by Ottawa. The scandal is that the federal government allowed Duplessis a free hand.

Aberhart was in trouble with the voters and with members of his own party because he hadn't been able to keep his election promise to pay everybody twenty-five dollars a month. In fact, he hadn't the remotest idea of where the money would come from His own Social Credit philosophy didn't include a blueprint for the future. Instead, he had always expected to hire "experts" to tell him what to do. To search out these experts and to appease the insurgents in the party, he created the Social Credit Board and appointed to it five MLAs – all back-benchers. This was an extraordinary delegation of authority and a slap in the face to responsible government, for it bypassed the Cabinet. But Aberhart's ministers went along with it because they didn't want to be blamed if the scheme flopped. Here was another example of provincial efforts to subvert the democratic process during the

Depression – as outrageous, in its own way, as Hepburn's attempts to install one-party government in Ontario. In effect, a group of experts, not elected but appointed by a small, unrepresentative committee, was to end up running the province.

The acknowledged expert, of course, was Major Douglas, whose curious notions had launched Aberhart's political career. The dissident members of the caucus, who wanted Douglas's theories put into practice in Alberta, had been in touch with him for some months. Now the first task of the all-powerful Social Credit Board was to invite him back.

In spite of his break with the Premier, Douglas wasn't averse to returning. His position as moral leader of the movement was shaky. Douglas's supporters could not long have clung to a leader who continued to shun the only Social Credit government in the world. Douglas was not prepared to come immediately but he did agree to send two of his followers to Alberta. If their report was favourable, then he would take on the job of directing the Social Credit Board.

Aberhart's troubles were not over, however; the dissidents in the party still wanted him out. And he was under attack not only from the conventional newspapers but also from a new and more virulent weekly, the *Rebel*, whose editor was a Russian-born journalist and Calgary school teacher named J.J. Zubick. Zubick was not one to shilly-shally. In his first issue he called Aberhart a "dishonest, dishonourable, lying blaspheming charlatan, who insinuated himself to power by deception and misrepresentation, and is morally unfit to hold the office of premier. . . . " There was much more to come.

Douglas's two emissaries from Britain arrived that summer and went to work. One was a tire salesman named George Frederick Powell. The other was a Southampton insurance man, L.D. Byrne. On August 3, a special three-day session of the legislature accepted their recommendations and made them into law, which the Opposition, with some truth, called "Hitler legislation."

The purpose of the Credit of Alberta Regulation Bill was to give the province dictatorial powers over the banks. Every bank and all bank employees were to be licensed and all their activities put under the control of the Social Credit Board. A companion bill made it impossible for any bank or employee who was refused a licence to seek redress in the courts. And under the

424

Judicature Act Amendment Bill, the courts could not take action regarding the constitutionality of these or any other pieces of government legislation.

The federal Minister of Justice wasted no time in disallowing this astonishing legislation. He threw it out in just eleven days. That, apparently, was what the Douglasites wanted – a chance to paint Ottawa as the villain on the side of the hated Eastern banks. As Powell later admitted, "The disallowed Acts had been drawn up mainly to show the people of Alberta who were their *real* enemies, and in that respect they succeeded admirably." Douglas himself was jubilant. He instructed his visiting experts to get rid of the RCMP and form a provincial police force in its place. That move had already been initiated. Every member of the new force was required to be an enthusiastic Social Credit supporter.

All of this was more than the Alberta attorney general, John Hugill, could take. Hugill was a Calgary lawyer, a one-time partner of R.B. Bennett, and one of the few Social Creditors who was a member of the province's business and social elite. He quit, calling his former chief a "Teutonic dictator," and began work immediately on an exposé of the government. When Aberhart heard about that, he threatened Hugill's publisher, the Ryerson Press, with cancellation of all its textbook projects in the Alberta schools. The book was never published. Aberhart himself became attorney general, his only qualification being a correspondence course in law he'd taken ten years before.

The continued opposition in the press, especially Stewart Cameron's wicked cartoons in the *Herald* and Zubick's unrelenting vilification in the *Rebel*, was driving the Premier toward the most intemperate legislation of all – a ham-handed attempt to stifle the press.

The move was popular with the party. Aberhart's biographers quote from one of the Premier's September broadcasts in which he excited wild applause when he attacked the press as a "mouthpiece of the financiers [who] persist in publishing fantasies. . . . I feel certain," he cried, "that the citizens of Alberta will soon come to judgment that something should be done to curb the mad-dog operations of certain of the financial newspapers. . . . We license doctors, we license lawyers, and school-teachers and businessmen and auto drivers and hotel keepers for the protection of the public. Why shouldn't the newspapers be licensed also?"

425

There's no doubt that Aberhart's muddled logic made sense to his audience – and, indeed, to all of his supporters. Yet the implications were horrifying; and that became clear in the fall session when he carried out his implied threat and introduced the euphemistically titled Accurate News and Information Act. Simply put, he intended to muzzle the newspapers as surely as any European dictator. The new act would require newspapers to publish *any* statement made by the chairman of the all-powerful Social Credit Board to correct or amplify a news report on a government activity or policy. The newspapers could also be forced to reveal their sources of information as well as the name and address of anyone who wrote an editorial or news story. If a newspaper refused to comply with this law, it would be prohibited from publishing! Writers who resisted would be banned from any further publication. In addition, fines of up to a thousand dollars a day could be imposed on those who failed to comply. The press, understandably, mounted a massive campaign against the legislation.

Other bills introduced in this spate of legislation included one to tax the paid-up capital of the banks and another to put all "credit institutions" under the direction of the Social Credit Board. Aberhart refused to have these bills tested by the Supreme Court of Canada, whereupon the lieutenant-governor, John Campbell Bowen, refused to sign them, an unprecedented act that forced a test. The court eventually ruled all three bills unconstitutional. For their spirited fight against the Alberta government, the province's five daily and ninety weekly newspapers would be awarded the 1938 Pulitzer Prize for upholding the freedom of the press, the only instance in which the Pulitzer board of judges went outside the borders of the United States to honour enterprise in journalism.

In Quebec, Maurice Duplessis did not need to make laws to muzzle the press. In his extra-legal war on communism, he had the newspapers, both French and English, on his side. They didn't utter a peep of protest when, following the scrapping of the infamous Section 98 in 1936, Duplessis introduced, in 1937, the even more infamous Padlock Law.

The catalyst was the Spanish Civil War. With the exception of a few urban intellectuals and a handful of radicals, the Quebec populace was wholeheartedly and enthusiastically on the side of

426

the insurgent general, Francisco Franco. That was, after all, the Roman Catholic side, a side that accepted uncritically the Franco propaganda that the Loyalists were murdering priests and nuns and were intent on destroying the church in Spain in the name of "Godless Communism." In the Quebec press, the Loyalists were almost invariably referred to as *les rouges* and Loyalist military victories were often described as massacres. As one American observer reported, "Any active advocate of the Loyalist cause or of any social or intellectual or labor union activity which, by any stretch of the imagination can be linked with Russia, is, in short, in the habitant's mind, not far from being a potential priest-murderer, nun-ravisher and sacrament-defiler himself." It was not the Left that threatened violence in Quebec. The powerful Catholic lay organization the Knights of Columbus in Quebec City forewarned that if they could not prevent communist activities peacefully, they would resort to force.

It was in this atmosphere that Duplessis on March 16, at the suggestion of Cardinal Villeneuve, the Archbishop of Quebec, introduced an Act to Protect the Province against Communist Propaganda. This was the notorious Padlock Law. In introducing the bill in the lower house, the Quebec premier used the familiar word that Canadian politicians have so often employed when facing a supposed crisis: "We are trying to establish order in the province." Leon Casgrain, a Liberal from Rivière-du-Loup, provided an echo from the opposite side of the floor. "It is about time we re-established order," he said.

There was no doubt about the kind of disorder the Premier was trying to stifle. He was after Communist party members, who numbered fewer than one thousand in the province, and also the unwitting communists who, in his mind, were legion. To Duplessis, their very presence constituted "disorder."

It was an incredible piece of legislation. Under the new law anyone who allowed his domicile to be used to propagate communism or Bolshevism "by any means whatsoever" could have it padlocked for up to a year. This could be done at the whim of the attorney general, a Cabinet post Duplessis had reserved for himself. As attorney general he could not only padlock a building at his own sweet will, but he could also authorize the destruction of any literature – newspaper, pamphlet, magazine, circular – *anything* he thought carried communist or Bolshevik propaganda.

427

Those whose homes were padlocked under the act were considered guilty until they could prove their innocence.

The most sinister aspect of the new law was that it nowhere defined "Communism" or "Bolshevism." Duplessis insisted that wasn't necessary. "Communism can be felt," he said. "We shall understand by Communism what everybody understands by Communism. . . . *Any definition would prevent application of the law*" (emphasis added).

In introducing the Padlock Law, the Premier had taken a long stride toward fascism in Quebec, but few members seemed alarmed by its implications. There were no Patrick Henrys in the Legislative Assembly that day, no Voltaires. Anglophones as well as Francophones accepted this monstrous attack on civil rights without a murmur. The second and third readings of the bill passed without dissent in the space of half an hour. No one, it seemed, was troubled by the omission of a definition of communism. Quite the contrary; that was seen as an asset. The province's most distinguished historian, Sir Thomas Chapais, declared that he "didn't believe in restricting such an evil within a narrow compass." His colleagues in the Legislative Council, the upper house, agreed. What they were attacking wasn't really communism; it was the whole idea of allowing the airing of opinions in their province that ran counter to the accepted view of the religious and nationalist establishment. The Hon. Jacob Nicol put it bluntly when he said that if communism *was* to be defined, it should include all those "who daily vilify public men." The Hon. John Hall Kelly said he was happy to pass the bill without a definition of communism but saw no problem in finding one. Kelly's definition of communism was equally broad. It meant "those actions which sap the foundations of things dear to the province."

Communism never was defined in Quebec because the government didn't want to define it. In a revealing, indeed appalling, statement one Cabinet minister, T.J. Coonan, explained that the act had to be broad enough to cover "the many who are Communists without knowing it."

One might have expected the press, or at the very least the Anglophone press, to take up the cudgels against this unprecedented invasion of traditional legal safeguards. But the press was either silent or, as in the case of the Montreal *Gazette*, in favour of the new legislation. The *Gazette* insisted that communism was rampant in the province and was also spreading alarmingly. Those who criticized the Padlock Law on the grounds that it conspired against free speech, the paper declared, "cannot discriminate between the legitimate exercise of that right and its flagrant abuse." Or as Cardinal Villeneuve put it in August, freedom of speech was "not freedom to outrage our social conceptions, to insult our traditions, our principles and our religion."

The implications might have been seen as ludicrous had Duplessis not been so deadly serious. The *Canadian Forum* pointed out that if the section dealing with papers and pamphlets were strictly enforced, it would prevent circulation of the Bible ("And all that believed were together, and had all things common") or the works of the early Christian Fathers, not to mention those of Sir Thomas More and Charles Kingsley. Frank Scott, perhaps facetiously, told Dr. Cyril James, the principal of McGill, ". . . you have in your library works of Lenin and Stalin and Marx. . . . If they're going to be allowed to circulate . . . you're distributing works of Communism and Bolshevism. You're breaking the Padlock Act." A worried James phoned the Montreal chief of police, who told him, "We're not going to apply the law against McGill." That, as Scott said later, underlined the unfairness of a law that could be applied unevenly. It made clear the government's intention to decide whom to punish and whom to absolve.

The Act was not immediately enforced. All that summer and fall communist meetings were banned as the police took arbitrary action against anybody they considered subversive. But it was not until November 9 that Duplessis actually invoked the new law. At 8:30 that morning, one of the employees of *La Clarté*, a communist newspaper published in Montreal, arrived at the office to find the door smashed with an axe. Twenty-five provincial policemen were on the premises confiscating everything from pens and inkwells to cash and postage stamps.

The same day, three policemen went to the home of the editor, Jean Perron, seized his books, files, and correspondence, and padlocked the house for one year. The next day a bookstore and two printshops were padlocked and the houses of several known communists were raided. The police also entered the Jewish cultural centre, a meeting place for young immigrants, seized its

429

library, and destroyed all the books believed to be communist. One victim had great trouble preventing the police from seizing a copy of a book called *The Land of the Free* on the grounds that any book with such a title could refer only to Soviet Russia.

Perron immediately took his paper underground, a move that led to more high-handed measures. Some travellers arriving in Quebec City from Montreal were treated like smugglers from a foreign land as police rummaged through their baggage searching for copies of *La Clarté*. An atmosphere of repression now reigned in the province. The censors wouldn't allow the Oscar-winning film, *The Life of Emile Zola*, to be shown. And when a Baptist missionary group tried to distribute the Old Testament in Quebec City, they were prevented by the police from doing so – no reason given.

By the end of the year, Ottawa was flooded with demands from Quebec and across Canada that the Padlock Law be disallowed, as Aberhart's legislation had been. Frank Scott, Eugene Forsey, and others had formed the Canadian Civil Liberties Union the previous spring in Montreal. Under its aegis, no fewer than forty-five Quebec organizations, ranging from the Musicians' Union to the Montreal Ministerial Association, signed a petition demanding that the Act be struck from the books.

When a civil liberties delegation applied for a meeting with Mackenzie King to protest the federal government's lack of action, the Prime Minister refused to see them. It had taken just eleven days for his government to get rid of two pieces of unconstitutional legislation in the West, but Quebec was sacrosanct. Although Duplessis's law had by then been on the books for almost ten months, Ottawa showed not the slightest inclination to do anything about it. And the worst excesses under the Padlock Law were still to come.

430

1938

In the tenth year of the Great Depression, Canada reached a *A loss* turning point. This was the year in which the government of *of nerve* Mackenzie King moved hesitantly and reluctantly toward the Liberal welfare state. It was also the year in which – again hesitantly and reluctantly – it began to come to terms with John Maynard Keynes's radical concept of cyclical budgeting: spending more money in bad times and (one hoped) paying off the deficit in better times. The balanced budget, in short, was about to become a thing of the past. And 1938 was, happily, the year in which the rains came at last – not the frustrating dribble that had characterized the drought years but real, drenching downpours in May and June that soaked the fields and produced the biggest prairie wheat crop in a decade.

The rains came a year too late. The previous year's crop failure, which reduced Canada's chief export to a trickle, had a devastating effect on the economy. In 1936 and in the early months of 1937, the country had seemed to be recovering from eight dark years of slump. But by the fall of 1937 the slump returned – a recession in the midst of a depression – caused not only by the drought but also by a general failure of nerve in the business community, which found its earlier expectations crushed.

Suddenly, after a few brief months of optimism, the light at the end of the economic tunnel winked out. Because there seemed to be no future for the country, not many were prepared to undertake long-term investments. The drought apparently had no end, and unemployment had not been solved – it increased by 30 per cent over the winter of 1937–38. In October 1937, when company earnings failed to justify the rising stock prices, the New York market crashed once again.

It was a time of uncertainty and doubt, fear and foreboding. Labour disputes were on the rise; there had been more strikes and lockouts in 1937 than in any year since the early twenties. War and rumours of war had also conspired against any long-term investment. Fears of political upheaval and financial instability pervaded the business community.

Manufacturers who had built up large inventories because of the optimism of 1936 had been unloading them in 1937. Construction had been on the rise; now it dropped as provincial governments reduced their expenditures. The lower birthrate and the lack of immigration meant that fewer families were building houses. Canadians (and Americans too) were like bathers who hesitate to swim too far into an untested lake. Years of economic depression had made them cautious.

The Liberal government was totally unprepared for this alarming change. King, banking on recovery, had rushed to reduce federal grants-in-aid to the provinces under the Unemployment Assistance Act by a hefty 34 per cent. He was, in fact, pinching pennies with as much zeal as his predecessor. Like Bennett, he was absolutely convinced that the provinces were wasting relief money and, again like Bennett, he still held to the belief that a balanced budget was the key to economic stability. He didn't want to spend a nickel more on public works than he had to, and he wanted, if possible, to get Ottawa right out of the relief business. With times improving, he thought that burden ought to go back to the provinces and the municipalities.

Now, in January 1938, he was still reeling from a shock he had received a month earlier. His own political creation had stabbed him in the back! After the election he had invented the National Employment Commission to recommend ways of saving money on relief. Instead, he learned that the NEC was about to recommend that *more* money be spent and, even worse, that the federal government take over the entire responsibility for relief. That was something King and Bennett before him had passionately resisted.

The NEC's approach stemmed partly from the growing demand for a national scheme of unemployment insurance. Bennett had promised it; King had paid lip service to it. When recovery seemed certain he had gone so far as to poll the provinces on the subject. Six, including Ontario (but not Quebec), agreed to accept a national unemployment insurance plan.

Thus in recommending unemployment insurance, the commission was only reflecting the tenor of the briefs placed before it and the apparent acquiescence of the government itself. But it did not stop there. Since such a plan would help only those who had jobs that they might lose, it could not cushion the effects of the Depression on the vast army of unemployed who weren't covered.

434

It made sense, then, that if Ottawa were to be responsible for relief through unemployment insurance, it should take over *all* relief. It was that proposed recommendation, leaked to him by the one dissenting member of the commission, Mary Sutherland, a Westerner, that drove King into a fury. His whole idea had been to get out, cleanly, and let the provinces do the job.

In addition to Mrs. Sutherland, the seven-person commission was made up of three businessmen, one labour representative, and a widely respected economist, W.A. Mackintosh of Queen's University. Its chairman was the president of Canadian Industries Limited, Arthur Blaikie Purvis. Now this essentially small-c conservative group was proposing a radical departure from conventional policies – nothing short of the centralization of all relief.

King moved to head off this alarming turn of events. He called in labour minister Norman Rogers, who had set up the commission and appointed most of its members – but not the recalcitrant Mrs. Sutherland (who had been King's personal choice). He was infuriated to find that Rogers was enthusiastically behind the NEC's proposals. Mrs. Sutherland's tip-off had been the first knowledge King had that this apparently captive commission was departing from what he considered its mandate – to advise the government on how to stop provincial and municipal waste and thus save Ottawa millions.

King was convinced that he was being bamboozled by professors like Mackintosh and Rogers, another former Queen's man. "I am beginning to see the wisdom of not taking into the government, men who have not had some political training," he wrote, "however able they may be. The academic mind is not the best one to handle problems of Government." He sensed a conspiracy The two most powerful civil servants, W.C. Clark, Dunning's deputy minister in the finance department, and O.D. Skelton, Under-Secretary of State for External Affairs, both backed the NEC proposals. They, too, were Queen's University economists. "These University men," King told the Cabinet, ". . . thought they had more in the way of wisdom than the rest of us put together. . . . " Their appointment, as James Struthers, the historian of the welfare state, has pointed out, was "a turning-point in cabinet/civil servant relations." These members of "an emerging mandarinate . . . had no fear" – as King had – "of an activist social service state."

435

To King, the commission's betrayal was political dynamite. Yet he was caught up by his own rhetoric. Ever since his defeat by Bennett in 1930, he himself had been calling for a commission on national unemployment; all during his five years in Opposition it had been the cornerstone of his unemployment policy. Now, if the NEC stuck to its guns, its report, in King's view, would be a millstone around the Liberal party's neck. It would "defeat the Liberal Party entirely by attempting something its members will not adhere to for one moment."

Federal commissions are supposed to operate independently, without political interference. King considered this commission was *too* independent, and he intended to interfere. He bluntly told Rogers and Dunning that the report must be rewritten and toned down before its release. Purvis, however, had resisted this unconscionable meddling. He was already peeved because the government had ignored the commission during its hearings. Worse, it had declined to take any action on the recommendations made public in an interim report released the previous August. Now Purvis was refusing to budge. King tried to split the commission, bringing pressure to bear on some of the weaker members. That tactic didn't work. The best he could hope for was the minority report promised by the obliging Mrs. Sutherland, who drafted it with his advice and help. Her point – and King's – was that the only way to keep relief costs from spiralling was to maintain responsibility at the grass-roots level. If faced with bankruptcy, the municipalities would think twice about being overgenerous with relief.

The Prime Minister sought refuge in delay, using another tried-and-true Canadian tactic. The report would have to be translated; that would hold it up until after the opening of Parliament, when the spotlight was off the Hill. He had one other stratagem. The Royal Commission on Dominion-Provincial Relations had been established the previous fall under Newton Wesley Rowell, the Chief Justice of Ontario, and was already holding hearings. King, through Rogers, managed to persuade the stubborn Purvis to see Rowell and discuss whether his report might conflict with the findings of the royal commission. Purvis did as he was asked and King got what he wanted – more delay.

But he was still angry with Purvis, whose action in signing the report against his advice he compared "to the action of Hitler in

436

invading and possessing Austria." It revealed, King wrote, a lack of political sense. In a telling insight into his own political philosophy King noted that "in politics, one cannot reach one's goal by a straight line. Account has to be taken of the rivers and mountains and other obstacles that have to be crossed on the journey."

With the report finally translated, Rogers rose in the House to bury it, explaining that because the whole matter of unemployment was bound up with some larger questions, the implementation of the report would be postponed until the Rowell Commission brought down its own recommendations. King had two years of breathing space.

Meanwhile, conditions in the country had grown worse. Unemployment was increasing and the hoped-for upswing in the economy, which had caused an optimistic prime minister to consider implementing unemployment insurance, hadn't occurred. Now King wished he hadn't got into the subject. He managed to scrap his plans, using the convenient excuse that three provincial premiers – Duplessis, Aberhart, and A.A. Dysart of New Brunswick – had yet to agree to unemployment insurance. He could, of course, have bulled it through, whipping up public pressure to change the minds of the minority, but he had no intention of doing that. Although unemployment insurance had become an acceptable idea, it would not go into effect until 1940.

King still clung to conventional economic theories. He had cut funds for relief, expecting better times, but he had no plans to restore the cuts now that the times were growing worse. Rogers tried to justify this in a remarkably convoluted explanation that larger grants were not necessarily the solution; they might, he said, "tend to aggravate the situation."

The government's new policy reflected the old belief that the unemployed really didn't want to work and wouldn't work if relief payments were raised enough to equal the minimum wage. Ottawa made it clear that any aid advanced to the head of a family or to an individual must always be less than the normal earnings of an unskilled labourer in the same district. With a callousness that evoked the Bennett years, the King government had placed a ceiling on the dole designed to reduce further the living standard of the jobless. Small wonder that it could not escape the rumblings at the constituency level, especially from British Columbia, where hundreds of men, released earlier than usual from the

437

provincial government's forestry camps and again unemployed, were already tin-canning in the streets of Vancouver. This was a direct result of the cut in federal funding, and it called up bitter memories of 1935.

In the United States, Franklin Roosevelt had launched a billion-dollar war on the recession through a program of emergency public works. King thought Roosevelt had gone too far, but his Cabinet, with the exception of Dunning, was clamouring for similar action in Canada. In April, King was forced to put Rogers in charge of a Cabinet subcommittee to recommend federal relief projects.

A month later, in a proposal that shocked the Prime Minister, Rogers declared no attempt should be made to balance the budget and tabled the subcommittee's recommendation that an additional seventy-five million dollars be spent at once on relief works.

A nasty struggle followed in the Cabinet, with the conservative Dunning and the Keynesian Rogers both threatening to resign. In the end both men were mollified by a compromise that whittled the sum down to forty million. It was to be spent on a national program of conservation and development, much of which had already been recommended in the final report of the NEC.

Like it or not, Ottawa was finally being forced to take on some national responsibilities. Two bills, designed that spring to revive the flagging construction industry, nudged the country forward on its path toward centralization. The Municipal Improvements Assistance Act offered loans for public works directly to the municipalities without going through the provinces, a procedure that both King and Bennett had said was impossible. The National Housing Act made low-interest loans available to the municipalities for low-cost housing, again bypassing the provinces.

Dunning admitted that the federal government was edging into a field it had not previously occupied, while King, in a rueful diary entry, noted that nations everywhere were moving "in the direction of the extension of State authority and enterprise." He feared that "Canada will not be able to resist the pressure of the tide. . . . The most we can do," King wrote, "is to hope to go only sufficiently far with it as to prevent the power of Government passing to those who would go much farther. . . ."

438

It was, in fact, happening just across the Ottawa River. In a different context, the Quebec government had already gone a long way towards imposing the authority of the state on those who disagreed with it. But King, for all his concerns about the authority of the state, was not prepared to interfere.

2

By May 10, 1938, the attorney general's department in Quebec was able to announce that it had ordered 124 raids under the Padlock Law and seized 521 "Communist" books. Yet no one was arrested or charged with any offence. As the Canadian Civil Liberties Union pointed out, "twice every three days, for six months, the provincial police have carried out execution without judgment, dispossession without due process of law; twenty times a month they have trampled on liberties as old as the Magna Carta." *Trampling on the Magna Carta*

Duplessis defended the Act, comparing it to "the British law which enables authorities to put handcuffs on undesirable subjects and dangerous persons." Under the British law, of course, such people, no matter how undesirable, were given their day in court. But the Premier had his entire Cabinet behind him, including the English-speaking members, one of whom, Gilbert Layton, praised the law as "one of the best pieces of legislation ever passed in the province."

The Duplessis government operated through fear. In most cases it wasn't necessary to go through the motions of padlocking a home or a place of business. The *threat* of being padlocked, or even the fear of being padlocked, was enough to cause the owners of public halls to close their doors to progressive or left-wing groups protesting the loss of civil liberties in the province.

Those who publicly opposed the law found themselves in danger of being labelled communists. The CCLU had trouble organizing any kind of protest because the owners of meeting halls refused to rent them out. When the Reverend R.B.Y. Scott of the United Theological College asked permission to hold a members' meeting of the CCLU at the Montreal High School, the assistant superintendent of the Protestant School Board refused on the grounds that the school might be padlocked. Scott asked him if that wasn't tantamount to making any discussion of civil liberties synonymous with communism. The answer was yes.

From time to time in Canada, the advocacy of civil liberties has been equated with communism – generally by cranks and extremists. But in Quebec it was quasi-official government policy, as Frank Beare of the Presbyterian College in Montreal discovered. Shortly after the school board's turn-down Beare wrote to the attorney general's office asking for assurance that it was not the province's intention to apply the Padlock Law against the CCLU. Deputy Attorney General Edouard Asselin replied, " . . . we are sorry to state that your request cannot be granted." The union found its efforts frustrated on every hand as the intimidation continued. Frank Leone found that out when he attended a meeting of the CCLU as the delegate from an Italian cultural organization. The very next day his home was raided and his entire library seized.

Where books were concerned, the police cast a wide net. During 1938 they seized works by Spinoza, George Eliot, and Aldous Huxley as well as a Gaelic Bible, the *Canadian Forum*, and a variety of American periodicals, including such mainstream publications as *Coronet, Pic*, and *Look*, not to mention the magazine section of the Vancouver *Daily Province*. All were identified as carrying "communist propaganda."

One Montrealer, James Gauld, lost his car because of the Padlock Law. He was sitting in the car when he was picked up by the police, taken to headquarters, photographed and fingerprinted, and then told there was no charge against him; he was listed, euphemistically, as a "visitor." His car was seized because he was using it to transport copies of the Toronto communist paper the *Clarion*. When the automobile was not returned, he tried to sue the chief of the Quebec Provincial Police but was told by the Superior Court that his only recourse was to take action against the provincial government by petition of right. Since the government itself would have had to consent to be sued – as it must under the law – the wretched Gauld found himself at a dead end. And automobiles weren't even listed under the Act as subject to seizure – only documents.

Any suggestion of a Russian connection was enough to cause a building to be padlocked. Early in February, the Maxim Gorky
440

Club was locked up. The club, with fifty branches in Canada, was devoted to educational, social, and cultural subjects. In Montreal, it engaged in dramatic performances and the education of children of Russian origin. The police damned it as Bolshevik after finding a picture of Stalin in one of the schoolbooks. The CCLU pointed out that similar pictures appeared in history texts across Canada, including the Grade 10 text of the neighbouring West Hill High School, which showed Lenin addressing the Red Army. The police did not padlock the West Hill building.

At one point the police and their political masters tried to attack communism by expunging the word from the Quebec lexicon. That touched off a day of comic opera at the Montreal High School, where the Montreal Youth Council was about to stage its annual Model Legislature. The provincial police descended on May 7 and told the council that the building would be padlocked unless they were guaranteed that no one would utter the words "communism" or "communist" during the proceedings. The council agreed, and for the rest of the day the delegates from the Young Communist League were solemnly described – and indeed so described themselves – as the representatives of "an unmentionable organization."

The Padlock Law brought forth a storm of protest from church, educational, and labour organizations across the country, but the federal government still stubbornly refused to take the kind of action it had adopted so swiftly in the case of Alberta. On July 6, Ernest Lapointe publicly announced he was not disposed, as Minister of Justice, to recommend either disallowance of the Act or a reference to the Supreme Court to determine its constitutionality.

The previous day the justice minister had justified his stand to the Cabinet by some devious legalese. Mackenzie King, to whom national unity was more important than civil liberties, went along with his Quebec lieutenant; the last thing he wanted was a split along racial and national lines. He appeared to be as confused as his colleagues over Lapointe's reasoning. "The recommendation," he wrote in his diary, "was rather lengthier than was necessary. Part of it seemed to justify the legislation itself rather than the question of whether it was properly disallowed, the line of justification being that Communism did not assert violence, as one of its methods, and, therefore, in making Communism a crime by the Province, it was not invading the Federal Criminal

Law jurisdiction which would permit propagation of communistic doctrines in other Provinces. Lapointe used the Oxford Dictionary definition. I sent for Palgrave's Dictionary of Political Economy. Found it too held the view that violence was not a necessary feature of communistic theories or teaching. . . ."

No one, including the Prime Minister, seemed to understand that Lapointe's hair-splitting amounted to a political about-turn in the common attitude toward the Red Menace. If communism didn't assert violence, why had eight men been jailed and scores more unmercifully harassed because the government feared violence from them? And why, if violence was not asserted, were buildings being padlocked without due process of law in Quebec? Lapointe, of course, represented the right wing of the Liberal party as well as its powerful Quebec wing. As the *Canadian Forum* shrewdly pointed out, it was not really communism that was disturbing the Quebec establishment. The real danger was anti-clericalism.

King must have been grateful for Lapointe's casuistry. It allowed him to salve his conscience and neatly dodge a Liberal split. He was convinced that disallowance would bring about a Quebec election that Duplessis would win, and "this would mean another great division in Canada." Thus he was prepared to accept "what really should not in the name of Liberalism, be tolerated for one moment." It was, he told himself, "a wise decision . . . but it is not a decision which does credit to Liberal thought, at a time when Liberalism is being crushed in other parts of the world."

This foot-dragging over the Padlock Law produced a sharp retort from the Canadian Civil Liberties Union, which found it "utterly disgusting . . . that the Government of Canada, so eager to respond to the pleas of bankers and mortgage-holders in the case of Alberta, openly and callously disavows responsibility in the case of a Quebec Statute which merely tears Magna Carta to shreds."

Lapointe had also stated that the constitutionality of the law could be more conveniently tested in a concrete case rather than by the submission of an abstract to the Supreme Court. "This means," the union pointed out, "that any victim of this legislation who is too poor to pay the costs of an action which might end only in the Privy Council, must suffer in silence until the Attorney General is foolish enough to proceed against someone of greater wealth. . . . "

The invasions of private property and the seizure of books continued that summer. The most sinister feature of these seizures was the secrecy in which they were shrouded, apparently to avoid arousing public indignation. The procedure taken against people who had not been accused of any offence, let alone convicted, was, in the CCLU's words, "that of a military dictatorship, which cannot exist without an efficient and deadly secret police, against which the courts can give no protection."

The actions went beyond seizure. Some destitute families in Montreal were refused relief for no other reason than that the authorities disliked their political views. One man who had joined a demonstration against the Italian and German intervention in the Spanish Civil War was arrested, fined twenty-five dollars, and cut off relief. Another was told bluntly that his relief would be cancelled "because of [his] non-conformist political views." A third was told he was an "undesirable individual" who engaged in illegal political activities and so was not eligible for public support.

The most notorious application of the Padlock Law came in July in Quebec City. Police arrived at the home of François-Xavier Lessard, nestled beneath the steep St. Sauveur cliff, and gave his wife and two children twenty-four hours to leave the house. The following day, when Lessard, a forty-year-old carpenter, was at work, they turned up at noon, padlocked the building, and turned Mrs. Lessard, seven-year-old Edouardine, and ten-year-old Cédard out into the street.

Lessard, hewing to the outdated belief that a Quebecker's home was his castle, decided to fight back. He proposed to break the padlock and re-enter his own domicile, not an easy job with two policemen in a car parked directly outside the house. Two of his friends engaged the officers in conversation while Lessard and Joseph Drouin hacked away at the lock. When the police tried to leave the squad car to stop them, they found that Lessard's friends had wired the door handles shut.

It was a Pyrrhic victory. Drouin and Lessard were charged with "wilfully violating a Provincial Law" - the Padlock Law - and "conspiring to interfere with a police officer." They were not, however, tried on the first count, thus denying their defence coun-

443

sel, R.K. Calder, K.C., of the CCLU (who took the case without fee), the opportunity to argue the unconstitutionality of the Act.

In spite of that restriction on the defence, the judge not only admitted but also commended to the special attention of the jury some "evidence" from the so-called communist literature seized in Lessard's home. What that had to do with a case involving conspiracy to obstruct a police officer no one was able to say. But the prosecution did its best to appeal to every form of local prejudice, including the curious as well as irrelevant statement that Lenin's advocacy of equality between the sexes was "an insult to French-Canadian motherhood."

Both men were found guilty and subjected to savage sentences. Lessard was given two years in penitentiary, Drouin a year in jail. When the Supreme Court upheld their convictions, the province cut off relief to Lessard's wife and children because of his "ideology."

The raids did not let up. Late in the year, the Duplessis attack on civil liberties entered a new phase, apparently designed to make it impossible for persons the police declared to be radicals to find shelter in their native province. In late December, during the Yuletide holidays, Quebec Provincial Police descended in pairs on some dozen Montreal dwellings, threatening to padlock the premises unless the owners evicted certain tenants.

In several cases the police enforced a deadline. On December 20, for example, a Provincial Police inspector named Beauregard visited Nathan Dubrinksky, a tailor, at his home on Laval Avenue and told him that he must evict his tenant, one D. Ship, by January 4, 1939, or have his premises padlocked. Three days later, the same inspector and another officer visited an unemployed tailor named Louis Fineberg, also on Laval Avenue, and ordered him to turn his son-in-law, Muni Taub, into the street. The eviction must be carried out by January 8, Fineberg was warned, or the premises would be padlocked.

The Canadian Civil Liberties Union persuaded Taub and his father-in-law to test the validity of the Padlock Law in civil court. Fineberg would ask Taub to leave; Taub would refuse. Fineberg would then sue Taub for cancellation of the lease and for $285 in damages on the ground that Taub was using the premises for the propagation of communism. Taub's defence, conducted by Calder of the CCLU, would be that the Padlock

444

Law was unconstitutional and therefore Fineberg's action was unfounded. The Quebec Superior Court, however, upheld the law, and Taub lost his case.

The Taubs, however, did not move out. The police threats were just that – attempts to scare people into taking action that the authorities themselves were reluctant to take. The Duplessis government was wary of test cases. None of the threatened premises was ever padlocked.

Although the police seized close to 140,000 papers, reviews, books, pamphlets, circulars, buttons, and badges (and once a child's doll and a pair of trousers), the total number of buildings padlocked in 1938 amounted to no more than ten. No one was charged or arrested under the Act so that none of the victims had the opportunity to defend themselves in open court – a fact that Duplessis and his police used to boast of brazenly as proof of their clemency.

The year was scarcely over before the Premier, in an address to the Montreal Canadian Club, openly challenged anyone to point to one abuse committed under the Act. The CCLU had for more than twelve months been pointing to dozens of abuses, but that was lost on both the Premier and the press. "What do we do when there is smallpox?" Duplessis asked his listeners. "We quarantine a person or a house where there is an epidemic and nobody kicks. . . . Communism is something affecting the heart and the brain. Don't you think that house should be quarantined too? . . . We don't arrest the man; we padlock the house; we keep the liberty of the man. . . ."

Duplessis claimed that the government had had "positive proof that the danger was real and imminent." Now, he said, the danger was over. Quebec had been the one province to "show the light and be the bulwark of law and order and common sense."

For those words he earned the plaudits of the English-language press. The Montreal *Gazette* rushed to congratulate the Premier on the success of his padlock campaign. "Quebec does not want Communism," it declared. "The Quebec government will not tolerate it." The *Montreal Star* described Duplessis's defence of the act as "a logical, forceful, and in more ways than one, an unanswerable argument. . . . We . . . accept – and the public of Quebec will do so with genuine relief and satisfaction – the Premier's declaration that the danger is now over. He attributes this to the application of the Padlock Law, and he is in the best position . . . to know the actual facts. . . . The citizens of Quebec will feel the safer in the knowledge that the Premier is as resolute as ever to fight against such a danger with all the energy and vigilance at his command."

Duplessis's war on the bogey of communism had its parallel in Hepburn's war on the bogey of the CIO. The two powerful premiers had a good deal in common and had, indeed, formed a loose alliance against the federal Liberal government in general and Mackenzie King in particular. Both were bon vivants who enjoyed hard drink, loose women, and lively parties. Both knew how to invent a scapegoat (godless radical; outside agitator) whom they could set up as a dangerous threat to society. Both had presented themselves as reformers; each had ended up in the pocket of the business establishment.

Hepburn's highly publicized war against the CIO had not squelched the American union group any more than Duplessis's trumpeted victory over the forces of evil in Quebec had wiped out communism. At the time of the passage of the Padlock Law, one of the leading red-baiters in the province, Father Bryan, had estimated there were nine hundred Communists in the city of Montreal. More than a year later, Eugene Forsey wrote in the *Canadian Forum* that "reliable information now indicates . . . there are several hundred more Communists in Montreal than there were in 1937."

But whether Duplessis's campaign was successful or not, the Act remained on the books. Nor did the threats and seizures cease just because the Premier had proclaimed victory.

3

Bloody By May, British Columbia was ripe for another explosion. Mac-
Sunday kenzie King had lit the fuse when he reduced grants-in-aid to the provinces by a third and then stubbornly refused to restore the cuts after the recession hit. It was this parsimony that led to the famous post office sit-down in late May and the events of Bloody Sunday in Vancouver on June 19.

When the federal government closed the relief camps in 1936, it had instituted a program of farm placement in which single

446

men were to be paid five dollars a month for agricultural labour. That was no more than the so-called "slave camps" paid, but for the government – if not for the men – there was an advantage. The transients were not only out of the cities, they were also isolated from one another. It would be almost impossible to organize them as Slim Evans had done in 1935.

The farm employment scheme ended with each harvest, after which the men were left to fend for themselves. The government justified this callous policy by pretending that they could exist all winter on their summer savings. That was patently absurd. Thousands began to move west – to Alberta, in the vain hope of getting Aberhart's promised dividend, and to British Columbia, where the provincial forestry camps were paying more than three times as much as the farm placement scheme. Ottawa paid half the cost of these camps (also set up in the fall of 1936 to replace the maligned relief camps). British Columbia had to shoulder the rest. With more and more transients reaching the coast, the cost soared. In 1938, the number of non-residents in the B.C. camps had increased by 50 per cent over 1937.

The province couldn't afford to keep them open alone. Faced with the federal cuts, the B.C. government closed them six weeks early, in April. Premier Pattullo cut all single men off relief and, as a result, hundreds of destitute men gravitated to the city of Vancouver. There they were organized by the Communist-led Single Unemployed Protective Association and its ally, the Relief Project Workers' Union, with headquarters on Cordova Street near Vancouver's skid row. Once again the city was faced with the spectacle of ragged men with tin cans begging for money on the street corners.

As before, the single unemployed were organized into four divisions, each division further divided into bunkhouse units of ten with the usual subcommittees. The leader of No. 1 Division, the so-called "youth division," was Steve Brodie, a veteran of both the On-to-Ottawa trek and the Regina Riot. He was now twenty-six, a medium-sized man with aquiline features, still very much a maverick. His father had been a blacksmith and lay preacher in Scotland; both his parents had died in 1919 of influenza. Brodie had come to Canada in 1925, one of a shipload of orphans sponsored by the Salvation Army. He worked on prairie farms until the Depression and then joined the army of boxcar

447

cowboys until he was shunted into the relief camps. The Regina Riot turned him into a Communist.

Brodie had lost a job at Bridge River that spring for union activity. Now in Vancouver with his division, begging on the streets, he felt a sense of frustration. He was too independent to be a good Communist. He didn't agree with his party's policy of continuing the tin-canning, which he found demeaning. And he didn't have much sympathy with those hidebound members of the party who sat around mouthing Marxist jargon – all talk and no action. It was ironic. The so-called wild-eyed radicals who led the party were, in their own way, as cautious as the politicians. As Brodie put it, "the image of Communist plots and rioting were [sic] only the product of wishful thinking on the part of the federal and provincial governments. That would have been the excuse for iron heel tactics which they were only too willing to invoke. And far from inciting the men, Communist Party organizers warned against provoking confrontation."

What Brodie wanted *was* confrontation – the kind his hero, Arthur Evans, had provoked three years before, to the dismay of Tim Buck and Joseph Salsberg. Brodie wanted to shake up the Vancouver business community to the point where it would pressure Ottawa to do something for the single unemployed. Some new strategy was required, and Brodie soon hit on one.

Long before the sit-in became the recognized weapon of American civil rights movements it had been used by the Relief Camp Workers when they occupied the Vancouver Public Library and Museum in 1935. Brodie had been chairman of a division during that brief but effective tactic. Now he realized that this was the way to strike at all three levels of government as well as the private sector. In one sudden move, he and his followers would occupy the federal post office, the city-owned art gallery, and one of the hotels. Then they would demand that the police arrest them for trespassing.

Brodie first paced off the distance to all three buildings, timing the length of each walk so that they could be invaded simultaneously. He chose the Hotel Georgia rather than the larger Hotel Vancouver because it was easier to enter. On May 19, he called a meeting of his division and told the men: "You've been howling for action and I think I have got something now." But first, he needed their support. Brodie always made sure that these meet-
448

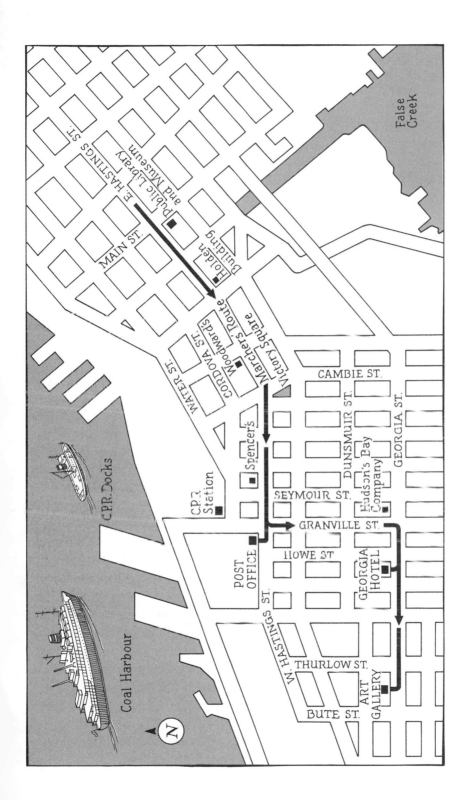

ings were scrupulously democratic, with parliamentary procedure followed to the letter. He asked for a vote of confidence and got one. "Go get 'em, Steve!" the men shouted, cheering and stamping.

Brodie, with the agreement of his division, wanted to create a four-man action committee composed of himself and the three other divisional leaders. Only in that way could he ensure tight security. But he had to argue with the other three until four in the morning before they agreed to his plan. After he brought them round, he wasted no time. Zero hour would be at two that afternoon.

He had already laid the groundwork by staging random marches about the city so that people would become used to long lines of men moving through the streets. The men, starting from four different halls in the East End, were not privy to Brodie's plan. They thought they were marching to Stanley Park. Only when his division reached the corner of Granville and Hastings did they realize that their objective was the newly redecorated federal post office with its granite façade, its copper dormer roof, and its English tower.

By two o'clock on the afternoon of May 20, seven hundred men were inside the post office. The police sergeant on the corner immediately called for help from the Granville and Georgia intersection, three blocks away. That left Georgia Street wide open for the two other divisions to march on the hotel and art gallery. At 2:15, three hundred men were crowded into the cramped lobby of the Hotel Georgia. Five minutes later, two hundred more poured into the art gallery, four blocks farther along Georgia. A fourth division acted as a decoy, marching aimlessly about town, confusing the authorities and allowing Brodie time to consolidate his position.

The post office closed for five minutes while Brodie polled his followers. Were they willing to stay until arrested? They gave him a unanimous yes. Nobody realized that the siege would last thirty days. For all that period the post office would keep regular hours, customers would come and go, and clerks would transact business while the jobless men hugged the edges of the L-shaped lobby. Brazenly, Brodie had tweaked the noses of the federal police force, whose headquarters were, in effect, part of the same building.

At eight that evening, Vancouver's police chief, Col. W.W. Foster, arrived to confer with the strikers. He had done so three

450

years before when the museum was occupied, and now he showed the same reasonable attitude that had distinguished his actions then. He congratulated the men, praised their discipline, applauded their behaviour, and declared that the incident would certainly have its effect on the authorities. Then he asked them to go home.

Brodie had the answer to that. "If we had homes," he said, "we would not be here."

Then he issued a challenge that he would continue to use for the month that followed. If his comrades were breaking the law, he said, the police must arrest them. Brodie knew, of course, that the authorities had no intention of maintaining some twelve hundred men in jail; that would cost even more than relief. Foster left after arranging for toilet facilities at the CPR depot a block away. The men slept that night on the marble floors of the post office and art gallery and the more comfortable carpets of the hotel.

The next day, as Brodie had foreseen, there was a chorus of protests to Ottawa from a variety of civic and political leaders. But there was no action. The government expected that the strikers would soon tire of the sit-in and leave the buildings of their own accord. That didn't happen at the post office and art gallery. At the Georgia, the men were well behaved, keeping the passageways clear for guests. The manager refused to call the police; nobody wanted a forcible eviction that might cost thousands in damage. On May 21, city aldermen distributed five hundred dollars from their own salaries to the hotel strikers. To Brodie's disgust, the strikers quickly evacuated the hotel. Most of the others held fast; the number at the post office dwindled by no more than a hundred over the month.

The men in the post office kept the doors and wickets clear. So did the occupants of the art gallery, which, however, was forced to close, thus denying the citizens the spectacle of poorly dressed men, with toes protruding from their socks, snoring in the shadow of marble busts and beneath the gilded frames of painted landscapes.

The public and the press were solidly on the side of the strikers. On the first night, five thousand people gathered outside the besieged buildings bringing sandwiches, tins of food, and cash. Employees of the Melrose Café near the post office sent over a constant supply of coffee. As the days dragged on, the odour of

451

unwashed socks and feet began to permeate the lobby. Two nearby clubs soon offered free shower facilities for the post office occupants.

Brodie was hard put to prevent the sit-in collapsing from boredom. On May 24, he held a sports rally to celebrate Victoria Day, organizing events such as peanut races that could be held in a small space. Gifts continued to pour in: bedrolls and blankets, free towels from a linen company, bread from a bakery, five hundred pairs of socks from a department store, tobacco from ordinary citizens.

Brodie let his men leave the building in small groups to take free meals offered by nearby restaurants or to attend services in churches that invited them. Musicians turned up to swell the impromptu banjo and mouth-organ concerts that helped keep up the men's spirits. In the art gallery, some of the men took up painting. Brodie, who habitually wore a bright orange sweater for instant identification, held regular press conferences and launched a weekly newspaper, the *Sitdowners' Gazette*, that sold for as much as five dollars a copy.

In the public's view, Ottawa was the villain that had disinherited the transients, but the city and province were blamed, too. Mayor George Miller, a plumpish and easy-going man, was roundly booed and hissed at a church hall when he tried to justify the city's refusal to come to the aid of the men. Pattullo's old pledge of "work and wages" returned to haunt him, but he held his ground and insisted there would be no relief for out-of-province transients. "We are not going to yield," he said. "If we give in it will not be a matter of a thousand or fifteen hundred men but five to ten thousand men." Pattullo was again trying to use the demonstration to force Ottawa to launch a program of public works in British Columbia. It hadn't worked with Bennett in 1935; it would not work with King.

The city of Vancouver was caught in a dilemma. Sooner or later the men would have to be evicted, but how? Brodie, who had never expected the sit-in to last so long, kept asking that everyone be arrested. Although the city refused to take that course, the situation was becoming more and more maddening. How could two public buildings be emptied without any arrests and without causing a political backlash and, perhaps, considerable damage?

A solution was finally provided by the chief sanitary officer, who said he feared an outbreak of meningitis and warned also that the appearance of even a single case of smallpox, diphtheria, or scarlet fever would be cause to quarantine both buildings. That provided the excuse the authorities were seeking. As Mackenzie King put it, the government had acted with patience and forbearance, but now something had to be done if the sit-downers were becoming a menace to public health. They were also, in King's private view, "a bad lot. They do not want work. They want trouble." Trouble, of course, was what William Lyon Mackenzie had sought a hundred years earlier, but not his grandson.

The eviction was planned for five o'clock on Sunday morning, June 19, a time when, it was hoped, there would be few witnesses on the streets. At three that morning some fifty members of the RCMP – the entire force in Vancouver – assembled at their Point Grey barracks to be addressed by Col. Cecil Henry Hill. A big man with a bristling moustache, the colonel had once trained the famous Musical Ride. Now he told his men that he had instructions to clear the post office. The city police would handle the art gallery.

At almost the same moment, Brodie was shaken awake from his mattress on the post office floor and told he was wanted on the telephone at the Melrose Café. "Is that you, Steve?" said the voice at the other end. Brodie grunted an affirmative. "Any hour now," said the voice, and the line went dead.

Brodie returned to the post office and told the pickets to wake him at the first sign of anything unusual. Ninety minutes ticked by. Then he was awakened again. "It's getting pretty busy," he was told. "There are cops on every corner."

These were city police. Brodie always insisted they were drunk. "Those who had not been called in from a Saturday night booze party were passing around mickeys at a great rate, evidently trying to catch up to those already drunk. Laughing and poking each other's ribs with their billies, they seemed to be anticipating their job with great relish." Brodie told the others that the police reminded him of children trying to set fire to the family cat.

Then Brodie heard something else: the measured *clip-clop, clip-clop* of horses approaching from the west. The Mounted

Police were coming on very slowly, and Brodie realized they meant business.

He herded the pickets inside. They woke the section leaders, who woke the sections. Brodie, fanatically meticulous as always about the trappings of democracy, called a meeting and asked for and got the usual vote of confidence. His tactics, he said, would remain unchanged. When ordered to leave the building, he would ask the police to put him and his followers under arrest.

Somebody asked what they should do if the police used tear gas. Brodie, seated on a window sill, pointed to a small cloud in the morning sky, touched by the pink of dawn. "Between the outside of that window and that little cloud," he reminded them, "there is an estimated four hundred miles of fresh air. The best antidote for tear gas is fresh air."

Out of the corner of his eye he could see Colonel Hill and two others entering quietly by the side door on Hastings Street. "There is no necessity for violence," he told the men in a loud voice, so Hill could hear. "I hope it will not come to that."

Walking beside Hill was Detective Sergeant Robert S.S. Wilson, the only Mounted Policeman in Vancouver trained in the use of tear gas. In his white haversack he had three small regulation gas bombs and five larger ones, new to the force. These were the Lake Erie Jumpers, the type offered to Mitch Hepburn during the CIO trouble in Ontario the previous year. They could not be picked up and tossed back at the police because the perforations in the tops made them too hot to handle. Timers could be set to make them go off consecutively, when they would explode and jump ten feet into the air half a dozen times before the gas supply was exhausted.

Outside the post office, the Mounted Police took up positions, twenty at the Granville Street door, twenty at the door off Hastings. Hill ordered both doors opened, barred the press from entry, climbed up on a counter, and addressed the men: "We are a federal police force and we have our instructions from Ottawa. After a month of vacillating, the federal government has instructed us to put you out. . . . " Pattullo would later claim credit for breaking up the sit-in, but Hill's remarks made it clear where the orders came from.

Almost at this very moment, by a peculiar irony, the Prime Minister was breakfasting at the General Brock Hotel in Niagara

454

Falls, having spent the previous day nearby visiting the newly restored home of his rebel grandfather. King was irked that Mackenzie was being represented to school children "as a rebel, traitor, etc." The true presentation of his character, he thought, "would be in the form of martyrdom, etc."

Now Hill was telling a group of modern rebels, and perhaps martyrs, "We would not put you out if we were not ordered to do so. But we have no alternative." They could go peacefully, but if they resisted somebody would get hurt.

To which Brodie replied, " . . . we will submit to arrest if we have broken any law. If we are an unlawful assembly, we are now your prisoners. We await your orders."

At this point, the police could have arrested all the men, booked them at the station, released them on their own recognizance, and later dropped all charges. But Hill told Brodie, "I have no orders about arrest."

Brodie insisted on convening another meeting. He told his followers that anyone who wanted to leave was free to do so. Nobody budged. "You have six hundred prisoners," he shouted at Hill. "What are your instructions?"

"You men are being stupid and ill-advised," Hill responded. "I think you should over-ride the decision of your leader because in a further five minutes force will be used."

These words were greeted with catcalls. Brodie walked over to a city police inspector named Grundy and asked, "Do I have your word that if the men step out orderly on the sidewalk that you'll arrest them and march them wherever they will be held until they can see a magistrate or a judge?"

"I have no instructions about arrest," Grundy replied. "I'm here to see that you keep moving when you hit the street."

Sergeant Wilson, standing on a counter, held up a Lake Erie Jumper for the crowd to see. He noted that many of the men were already reaching for various articles either to use as weapons or, more likely, to smash the windows to let in fresh air.

The RCMP were all inside the building now. A hush fell over the crowd. Nobody moved. Wilson couldn't help thinking that the scene resembled a still picture taken from a movie. The only sound came from the drip-drip of men urinating into their handkerchiefs to cover their faces when the gas attack came. To Wilson, the five-minute interval seemed like hours.

455

At last he leaned over to Hill. "Shall I throw it, sir?"

"Yes."

Wilson had never thrown a gas bomb at human beings before, but he'd had plenty of training in Regina following the riot. He pulled the pin, counted to three, then flung the bomb at the feet of the crowd.

In an instant, to quote Wilson, "all hell broke loose." He heard a single reverberating crash as every window in the building was shattered. The strikers had torn bars from the clerks' wickets to use as clubs and even heaved two old iron bedsteads through the windows. Objects of every kind were flying about – glass shards, iron bolts, rocks. It was exactly 5 a.m.

As the glass cascaded down, the RCMP formed a double row, ten abreast, across the lobby to drive the men from the building. A second gauntlet of city police waited outside. The police denied, as the police always do, that excessive force was used, but the press photographs that day made it clear that riot whips "designed to smash heads and break them open" (Brodie's phrase) were used to deadly effect. Of forty-two men hospitalized after the fracas, only five were policemen – all city constables.

Scores more were treated at the Ukrainian Labour Temple, where Dr. Zoltan Wirshafter rendered first aid. Maurice Rush, secretary of the B.C. Young Communist League, wrote that "the scene at the Ukrainian Hall was one that I will never forget. The grass outside and every available bit of space inside were covered with injured and gassed men. Blankets and bandages, collected earlier for medical aid for China, were rushed to the hall. Members of the YCL and other organizations tended the wounded and set up a kitchen to feed the men."

One of the strikers hospitalized was a former militia sergeant, Arthur Redseth, who slipped on the floor during the mêlée. As police and strikers battled over him, friends tried to help him to his feet and were whipped with police batons for their trouble. At last Redseth's friend, known as Little Mike to distinguish him from Big Mike, another Serbian, came to his rescue. Little Mike dragged Arthur Redseth through a gauntlet of club-swinging policemen. By then Redseth was in terrible shape, with one eye out of its socket. When Little Mike called to a policeman in the middle of Hastings and asked for an ambulance, he got a billy

456

across his face. He half dragged, half carried his friend nine blocks to Main Street, where a passerby picked them up and drove them to hospital.

Little Mike needed five stitches in his jaw. Redseth lost his eye – and for him that was tragic. All his life he had wanted to be a soldier. Now that ambition was shattered. When war came he tried to join the army and later the merchant marine and was refused by both because of his injury. He never recovered from what would always be known as Bloody Sunday. He became despondent, and in 1942 he shot himself. Little Mike was killed that same year at Dieppe. He was twenty-three years old.

The post office was evacuated in just ten minutes. Brodie was one of the last to be driven from the building. Easily identified by his orange sweater, he was the main target of the police attack. He kept his head protected from a rain of blows by the RCMP until he became numb. Unable to see because his head was down, he stumbled to the door, where the city police were waiting for him. They seized him by the heels and dragged him away bodily, his head banging on the stone steps.

Brodie went down three times before the onslaughts and would always remember those terrifying moments. "They got me out in the gutter and it got to the point that there were so many doing it they couldn't all hit my head so they hit me where they could. There comes a time when you don't feel it anymore. It seemed to me that I was watching somebody else. I was almost casually waiting for them to finish it. I was out, and then back, and then passed out again and then back. The same feeling you get when you smoke grass except that's not painful. I was simply numb. . . . "

It's probable that Brodie was saved from critical injury and possibly death by the presence of a photographer from the Vancouver *Daily Province*. He himself was certain that the police intended to murder him. Photographs taken that morning support that suspicion. There he stands, arms protecting his head, while a plainclothesman flails away with a rubber hose.

Some of Brodie's followers, seeing him lying insensible on the pavement, ran the gauntlet of police clubs, picked up their leader, and carried him across the street to one of their own first-aid men.

"Get an ambulance for Brodie!" one of them called.

"Get your own ambulance," the police retorted.

A private car pulled up and offered to take Brodie to the hospital.

"Don't take a chance, fellow," Brodie moaned.

But G.F. Johnson, who was heading off on a fishing trip when he reached the scene, took a chance. He helped hoist Brodie into his car as a sergeant and a constable advanced upon him. "Get out of here before I cut your heads off," the sergeant shouted.

In spite of the strategy to clear the post office at a time when few citizens would be present as witnesses, hundreds of onlookers had already turned up before the police entered the building. The crowd was enraged at the spectacle of hundreds of men, blinded by gas, frantic and screaming as they erupted into a hail of swinging clubs and whips.

In the Melrose Café, the waitresses were in tears as they watched men who had become their friends being pursued and beaten by the police. Some members of the crowd became actively involved in the fracas and were themselves injured. Innocent bystanders were not spared. Margaret Rickett, a visitor from Victoria, had left her suitcase in a nearby drugstore while she bought a return ticket at the CPR dock. When she tried to cross the street to get it, she suffered a stinging blow on the shoulder from a policeman's whip.

The intersection was packed with a struggling mass of policemen, strikers, and bystanders. The crowd followed the fleeing men down Cordova Street past Spencer's and Woodward's department stores. An orgy of destruction followed, as the enraged men vented their fury and frustration on the plate-glass windows. When the mob reached Cambie Street, one group swept east on Hastings, smashing windows as they went; the other moved south to attack the Imperial Bank and the B.C. Chamber of Mines. In a few minutes they did thirty thousand dollars' worth of damage.

The evacuation of the art gallery took place at the same time but without violence, except for the use of tear gas. Harold Winch, the CCF member of the legislature who had acted as a liaison between the city and the unemployed during the 1935 disturbances, had been effectively kidnapped by Chief Foster and driven aimlessly about town in a squad car until the zero hour. His task was to prevent the destruction of the gallery's collection of paintings and sculpture. Winch managed to persuade the sit-

458

ins to leave quietly. Many brought along the paintings they had worked on during their stay.

Brodie's reaction was one of contempt. To him, Winch, soon to be the party's leader in British Columbia, was nothing more than an "assistant chief of police." Brodie said that if he'd been in charge at the gallery, he'd have smashed everything in it. "That was the point . . . a million bucks in paintings and we were worth nothing."

The march from the gallery to the East End became a march of protest, with hundreds of citizens walking with the men and scores of cars following them. That afternoon, ten thousand people crowded the Powell Street Grounds for a rally to support the cause of the unemployed. The crowd cheered as speakers demanded Pattullo's resignation. Thousands then headed for the police station but were restrained by Winch, who climbed a telephone pole overlooking the crowd to calm it down. Thousands more gathered that night to cheer a delegation of one hundred who left by the midnight boat to take their case to the legislature in Victoria.

They got a cool reception from the Premier. "There comes a time," Pattullo said, "when too much sympathy can be shown the men. That time has come in Vancouver." Transients could not look to the province for any more help. If they all went home, Pattullo indicated, there would be no unemployment crisis in British Columbia.

Once again there was an exchange of testy telegrams between Victoria and Ottawa. Pattullo and King seemed to be following an old script from 1935 and the days of R.B. Bennett. Pattullo warned the Prime Minister that revolution was imminent and that "your government must accept responsibility for this transient problem." King had no intention of doing that. His argument was Bennett's: that relief was a provincial responsibility. The province was to blame for the trouble because it had cut off relief for single men. Pattullo's request for a public works program could not be met in 1938 any more than it could have been in 1934 or 1935. If a group of single men got special treatment, then what about married men, what about the heads of families, what about minors, what about war veterans?

Thus the sit-in ended with no resolution. No one was ever arrested for taking part in it. Twenty-two men were charged with wilful damage in the destruction that followed the eviction. Of these, seven were found guilty and given short sentences. However, the King government agreed to pay the cost of relief for all non-resident transients in the province, pending their return home or until they found work. That was no solution at all, and the public knew it. Unemployment was again rising. There was no work in British Columbia and little work elsewhere.

Bloody Sunday marked the beginning of the end of Duff Pattullo's political career. In the 1941 election, the Liberal party lost its majority and was forced into a coalition with the Conservatives to ward off the rising threat of the CCF. That spelled finish for both the old-line parties in the province. After the 1941 débâcle Pattullo himself was rejected by his own followers.

Ironically, Steve Brodie suffered a similar fate. He was too radical and too independent for the Communists and left the party shortly after his release from hospital with a permanent eye injury. When war came he was one of the first to try to enlist, but like Arthur Redseth he was rejected because of his eye. That was a loss to the country and to the forces. Brodie ended up in the merchant marine, but he would have made a wonderful sergeant-major.

4

The Nazi connection On July 4, a fortnight after the end of the sit-in in Vancouver, Adrien Arcand, the Quebec fascist leader, called a mass meeting at Toronto's Massey Hall to organize a coalition of fascist groups in Canada. These included Arcand's own National Socialist Christian Party, William Whittaker's Winnipeg-based Canadian Nationalist Party, and Joseph C. Farr's Toronto-based Nationalist Party. John Ross Taylor's Canadian Union of Fascists was not included; Farr had managed to push Taylor aside.

The new organization would bear the euphemistic title of National Unity Party. That must have been a source of frustration to Mackenzie King, who had planned to make those very words a Liberal slogan in the next election. The party retained the blue shirt by which Arcand's followers had been identified but exchanged the swastika on the armband for a new emblem – a flaming torch. Hitler's belligerence in Europe had made the crooked cross unfashionable in Canada.

460

The scenes on Shuter Street that night were more reminiscent of Berlin than of Toronto. A double line of eighty-five blue-shirted "Legionnaires" scrutinized each ticketholder who entered the hall and ejected half a dozen people whose credentials were suspect. Arcand and his henchmen preferred to speak only to the converted, and in that effort they had the full co-operation of Chief Denny Draper's finest.

The communists had been harassed for more than a decade by the Toronto police and denied the use of public halls for meetings and rallies. But the fascists asked for and got police protection not only at Massey Hall but also at the Hotel Isabella on Sherbourne Street, where the Montreal contingent was staying. An RCMP undercover agent at the meeting reported to his superiors that one of Arcand's lieutenants had met with the head of detectives in Toronto "and insured complete cooperation" between the fascists and the police.

That co-operation did not extend to the activities of another group of several hundred anti-fascists (a code name for communists) who organized a street corner protest a block away at Yonge and Albert. As the chief speaker, William Krehm, mounted a portable stand to address the group, a covey of young women whipped off their coats to reveal white sweaters bearing anti-fascist slogans. The police arrived and surrounded the speakers, who began shouting, "Down with Fascism!" and "Down with the brutal police; they are Fascist tools!"

More of Draper's troops arrived on horseback, forcing their steeds into the middle of the crowd. One woman was struck on the head and knocked to the sidewalk. A newspaper reporter who went to her aid was himself knocked down by a passing horse. Part of the crowd fled into a nearby store; others ran down Yonge Street. For the rest of the evening the police patrolled Shuter Street, keeping the crowd moving and away from Massey Hall.

Inside the hall, Joseph Farr, the stocky Toronto fascist, was haranguing the crowd and referring to Toronto as a "Jew-dominated city." Farr was followed by C.S. Thomas, a lanky fascist from Vancouver. High in the balcony a woman heckler shouted, "Get out of here!" to the speaker. She was immediately ejected by bouncers, some of whom carried lengths of rubber hose filled with lead. The woman tripped on the stairs and was dragged the

461

rest of the way by the hem of her dress. One or two other hecklers were also speedily ejected.

At last the main speaker strode onto the stage. Adrien Arcand looked the part – lean, dark, and intense, with flashing black eyes, a thin moustache, and a supple body. A forest of Nazi salutes sprouted as the crowd shouted, "Hail the King! Hail Arcand and the Party!" Arcand spoke fiercely for the best part of two hours in excellent English. His speeches rarely varied. Like those of his predecessors on the platform, this one was a diatribe against the Jews and a vicious attack on the idea of democracy.

According to Arcand's garbled version of history, democracy was the child of Freemasonry, which had been invented by the Jews following the French Revolution. The Jews had spread the system to all countries of the world with the aid of Napoleon Bonaparte. But democracy had become "a rotten apple," kept alive and financed by world Jewry.

In Arcand's skewed vision, every major politician was either a Jew or in the control of Jews – a belief that would have baffled those Jewish refugees from Hitler who were trying vainly to convince Canadian politicians to let them into Canada. But Arcand saw Jews in power everywhere. In his speech, he reached new heights of implausibility when he claimed that Generalissimo Chiang Kai-shek of China was actually a London Jew named Cohen.

In the Duke of Wellington's phrase, anybody who would believe that would believe anything. Many did not believe it; the audience had dwindled by several hundred before Arcand finished his marathon address. The die-hards were the products of the Depression described by R.E. Mercer, Assistant Superintendent of the RCMP in Toronto, in an earlier report to Ottawa. "This type of propaganda," Mercer wrote, "will appeal to a certain class – disgruntled small storekeepers, business men and others who have been finding it hard to make a living in recent years." Mercer added that it was this aspect of the fascist program that was finding a sympathetic hearing among many people "who do not agree with the aims of the party in other respects."

Outside Massey Hall, the Toronto police prevented any further anti-fascist outburst. Once the meeting was over, as the RCMP undercover man reported, "the various delegates left the hall in groups with the full co-operation of the police, who were very

462

considerate and kind to see that nothing happened to anyone. . . . Police kept constant guard near the Isabella Hotel."

Such police protection was not required in Arcand's own city, Montreal, where he already had the tacit support of the Duplessis government. It was his organization, after all, that had pressed for a provincial law to replace Section 98 of the Criminal Code and had praised the Premier when he introduced the Padlock Law a year earlier. Indeed, the notion of padlocking the premises of *La Clarté* had actually been discussed at a meeting of Nazi leaders two days before it took place.

Arcand had no trouble addressing the McGill University Social Problems Club in February 1938. But Tim Buck, who was also scheduled to speak, was barred at the last minute because the Students' Council feared the McGill Union would be padlocked if the Communist leader turned up.

Not only was the Duplessis government too busy chasing communists to worry about fascists but also Arcand was one of their own – a toiler in the vineyards of the Union Nationale, the editor of its quasi-official newspaper. His vicious anti-Semitism found fertile ground in a province that was the home of 60,000 of Canada's 156,000 Jews. Though many were native born, they would always be aliens to Quebeckers, who tended to think of them as "surrogate Englishmen," in the words of Lita-Rose Betcherman, who has made a study of fascism in Canada during the Depression. The anglophone industrialists who ran the province might be too strong to attack, but the Jews, who competed at the level of the French-Canadian businessmen, could be vilified without fear of retaliation.

Arcand distributed his hate literature without interference. No police raid seized copies of his thirty-two-page pamphlet, *The Key to the Mystery*, one of the most venomous anti-Jewish documents ever published. It was distributed by mail and also from door to door free of charge, although it was supposed to sell for fifty cents in Toronto and ten cents in Montreal. Copies went to prominent members of the Toronto police force as well as to civic officials, police officers, and leading citizens in the larger centres throughout Ontario.

Arcand's publication *Le Fascist canadien* was one of nineteen newspapers in Quebec that existed solely to propagate racial hatred, and that group does not include legitimate dailies such as

463

Le Devoir, the organ of Quebec intellectuals, which, under Georges Pelletier, was intensely anti-Semitic (Pelletier advocated that all Jews be expelled from the countries of their birth and be forced to live in Palestine). That notorious anti-Semitic forgery the *Protocols of the Learned Elders of Zion* also received wide distribution. In August, a journal of the Roman Catholic Church, *La Semaine religieuse*, published the discredited work as literal fact. Even more disturbing, a widely read francophone daily, *L'Action catholique*, reprinted it.

Most of Arcand's hate literature came directly from Germany. In 1938 Canada was flooded with more than four hundred kinds of anti-Semitic leaflets, most published in the interests of the German Nazis.

In addition to Arcand's new united front and several smaller fascist groups in Toronto and western Canada, four German-speaking organizations, financed and organized by the German government, were operating in Canada. The Deutscher Bund, with branches in all the principal cities, was supervised by the German consul general in Montreal. The bund maintained schools in Toronto, Montreal, Winnipeg, and Kitchener. Here children were taught the German language and the glories of the Hitler regime. The bund's weekly newspaper, *Deutsche Zeitung*, published in Winnipeg, was violently anti-Semitic. It existed for the sole purpose of fostering Nazi propaganda.

The NSDAP, or Nazi party, along with the Arbeits Front constituted the inner circle of the German Nazi movement in Canada. The latter was restricted entirely to Aryans who were not Canadian citizens. Its members were pledged to propagate Nazi theories "by word and deed."

The German Unity League was a union of all the Nazi organizations, with branches in most provinces. It was formed for the purpose of arranging the annual German Days in order to gain control of other non-political organizations and disseminate Nazi propaganda. In 1937, the league managed to secure the Minister of Trade and Commerce and M.P. for Waterloo North, the Hon. William Daum Euler, as guest speaker at a Nazi mass meeting during Kitchener's German Days. Euler agreed with other speakers who deprecated stories and articles critical of Germany, "which instead of healing sores [tend] to keep up hatreds." The minister declared that he sometimes thought that the publication

464

of such propaganda should be made a criminal offence for newspapers. In a town whose citizens had strong German ties, Euler was a good catch for the league.

Arcand was at some pains to deny any connection with the German Nazis, but a mass of documentary evidence makes it clear that he was in constant and intimate touch with Berlin. The German diplomatic community also tried to pretend that it had nothing to do with the pro-Nazi and anti-Semitic literature pouring into the country. Erich Windels, the German consul general in Ottawa, who was a master at getting pro-German publicity into the press, explicitly denied that his country was carrying on any pro-fascist or anti-Semitic propaganda in Canada, either directly or indirectly. "Any German who takes part in anti-Semitism is not acting in the limits prescribed by German laws for emigrants," Windels announced, suavely. That, of course, was pure rubbish.

Windels turned his considerable charm on the gullible Mackenzie King while complaining, among other things, that the American picture magazine *Peek* had been allowed into Canada after carrying a caricature of Hitler. The magazine was not banned (although another magazine, *Ken*, was stopped at the border the following year for carrying a caricature of George VI and the Queen), but King soothed the German as best he could by inviting him and his wife to Kingsmere, along with another Nazi couple.

"A most enjoyable evening" followed. King felt he had managed to cheer up the Germans, who "had felt lonely and depressed at times," no doubt because other more sensitive Canadians had shrunk from entertaining Hitler's minions. Before the evening was over the Prime Minister of Canada and Hitler's resident stooge and propagandist were singing songs together. King was delighted. "I could not help dwelling on the significance of the little gathering," he wrote. "It showed what was possible if only good-will could exist between people of different nationalities rather than ill-will." Windels and the others could not have been pleasanter, he thought.

There's little doubt that the Nazis' efforts in Canada, aided and abetted by Arcand and his ilk, were having an effect. Anti-Semitism was increasing, especially in Ontario and Quebec. Some insurance companies were treating Jews as bad business risks, for no other reason than their race. Entire residential subdivisions

465

were closed to Jews, to say nothing of the "restricted" summer resorts where the appalling expression "No Jews or dogs allowed" was making its appearance on public signs. A Jewish tennis team found it was no longer welcome in the Toronto Tennis League, while the St. Andrew's Golf Club changed its policy and banned all Jews – citing pressure from the membership.

During the CIO battle a year earlier, the *Globe and Mail* had gone so far as to identify Jews with the CIO and communism. "The indications are that a large percentage and probably a majority of Communists are Jews," the paper said. In fact, as the Committee on Gentile-Jewish Relations revealed, only 3 per cent of the party's membership was Jewish.

In a remarkable display of verbal gymnastics, Arcand managed to link the Jews with both communism *and* capitalism. "The Jew is everywhere," he declared. "He has seized control of our gold, our pulp, our press. He controls our government." The Big Lie was believed by many Canadians, but the truth was different. So violent was discrimination against Jews across the country that there wasn't a single one on the board of any Canadian bank, mortgage company, utility company, railway, or shipping firm. As for controlling the government, those members of the Jewish community who attempted to ease immigration restrictions would soon discover just how impotent they were. Jews did, however, make a convenient target for Canadians struggling blindly to find a scapegoat for their own misery. Arcand blamed them for causing the Depression. He promised, if elected, to disfranchise them all, revoke their citizenship, and expel them from Canada.

But as Hitler's star rose in Europe, Arcand's began to fall in English-speaking Canada. The invasion of Austria in the spring and the Munich crisis in the fall made Nazism repugnant to most Canadians.

Arcand's tactics in Ontario differed from those he used in Quebec. Among anglophones he portrayed himself as a British loyalist whose party would fight for "our King, our God and our Country." His Toronto meetings were marked by the singing of the National Anthem and cries of Long Live the King! In Quebec, however, Arcand's rhetoric was that of an extreme French-Canadian nationalist. Here he was able to appeal to the anti-war sentiment of French Canadians, who had a horror of becoming

466

involved in another European conflict. Why should they go to war "for rotten democracy," Arcand asked in fiery speeches that received hearty ovations across the province.

His was only one of several voices encouraging the sickly weed of independence and finding a sympathetic hearing among those Quebeckers who blamed their Depression ills on the economic dominance of a "foreign" minority. Even though he would be interned and discredited during the war that followed, the fascist leader's shrill tones would echo down the corridors of future decades to mingle with those of others calling for a new and distinct Quebec.

5

In 1938, John Murray Gibbon, a prominent Canadian literary *Keeping out* figure, popularized the phrase "Canadian mosaic" in a book *the Jews* with that title. The implication was that Canada had developed along lines different from those of the American melting-pot. Yet at the time, the concept of a series of closely knit ethnic communities fostered by the Canadian experience was largely a myth. It is true that government policy had brought tens of thousands of Slavic peasants to the Canadian West, but these people had little power. The real power lay with the WASPS of Central Canada and the Catholic hierarchy of Quebec, neither of which wanted any diluting of the traditional racial mix.

Canada was very much a British nation, pledged to maintain "British justice" and "British ideals." The Anglo-Saxons and Anglo-Celts of Ontario didn't want an alien strain polluting the purity of the line any more than the Quebec nationalists did. Although there were no pogroms in Canada, Jews were beyond the pale, as they had been in much of Europe. Now, facing the greatest pogrom of all, Jews from Central Europe were hammering at Ottawa's doors. But nobody in the government wanted to let them in.

It is a profound understatement to say that the Canadian government was lukewarm to the idea of Jewish refugees entering the country. As Irving Abella and Harold Troper have made clear in their remarkable book, *None Is Too Many*, the government didn't want *any* Jews to enter Canada.

467

The villain of the piece is Frederick Charles Blair, director of the Immigration Branch. Blair was the same man who, earlier in the decade, had engineered the deportation of twenty-five thousand people for economic and political reasons. A narrowminded bureaucrat who ran the department with little interference from Thomas Crerar, his minister, Blair was a man of strong religious views and a violent anti-Semite who despised all Jews. But it must be said that Blair worked in an atmosphere of anti-Semitism, which included the views of the Prime Minister himself. He had little trouble in convincing King and his Cabinet that Jewish refugees from Hitler should be kept out of the country.

All that year King kept telling his diary what a wonderful man Hitler was. "His desire for peace seemed to me to be important and significant and, I believe, true," he wrote on January 12. Similar sentiments followed: "I am quite sure he does not want to face war . . . " (February 4). "As I listened to the translation of his speech [he] stood out as *the* leader in Europe – a voice stronger than any other for order . . . " (February 20). "I believe the world will yet come to see a very great man – mystic in Hitler [who] will rank some day with Joan of Arc among the deliverers of his people . . . " (March 27).

He preferred Hitler to Tweedsmuir – the dictator "in his grey shirt, the absence of feathers, sword, etc.," the Governor General all "buttons and gold braid." On April 11, after the Austrian people voted to join the Reich, King wrote approvingly that "Hitler may well be a very proud man as he said he is today in relation to what he has done for his own class. . . . He has reason to feel that his achievements have been great indeed."

Like the vast majority of his countrymen, King viewed Chamberlain's backing down before Hitler at Munich with great relief. "Hitler," he wrote on September 14, following a particularly explosive speech by the German dictator, "has spoken out like a man. Exposed fearlessly some of the current hypocrisies." The dismemberment of Czechoslovakia he saw as a necessary manifestation of *realpolitik*. The Munich meeting, he believed, "is the most momentous meeting between two men that has ever been held in the history of the world." Chamberlain would "go down in history as one of the greatest men who ever lived."

King applauded the British prime minister's plan to separate Russia from its relationship with Britain and France – an act that

468

led to Stalin's pact with Hitler. "I cannot but believe," he wrote on September 20, "that Hitler has enough chivalry and sincerity of purpose to join with Chamberlain in seeking wholeheartedly to work out a plan for Europe as a whole which will begin to relieve all its nations of their armament burdens." King's perception was as clouded as it had been in February, when one of his visions had convinced him that his party would win a by-election in Argenteuil. The Liberal candidate lost badly and King was shaken. "I have never been deceived in a *vision*," he wrote, and mused that he should perhaps place less reliance on "visions, dreams and impressions." (He failed to take his own advice.)

But then, following the Munich crisis, the whole country was caught up in a dream of peace, a vision of a secure Europe – the wistful belief that Hitler, having got what he wanted at the expense of the Czechs, would have no further designs on other countries. Thus it would be unfair to single out the Prime Minister for his lack of insight.

King, however, appeared to believe that *he*, the Prime Minister of Canada and the grandson of a despised rebel, had actually been the catalyst that brought Chamberlain and Hitler together. He recalled that he had first introduced the British prime minister to the new German ambassador, Ribbentrop, during a reception at the House of Lords during the Coronation. The other guests stood back, "looking in a rather surprised way at the cordiality of the conversation the three of us were having." As a result, Ribbentrop had invited King to lunch and urged him to visit Hitler.

This placed King, in his own overblown view, at the very centre of the international stage, arm in arm with the British prime minister and the German dictator. "It is a remarkable fact," King wrote, "that beginning with a determination to see Von Ribbentrop the day of his arrival in London as Ambassador, from then on there have been links which have brought a closer relationship between the British and the German governments in which Chamberlain and I and Hitler have figured in a relationship that has been exceedingly significant."

On November 9 the dark and dreadful *Kristallnacht*, when the streets of every community in Germany and Austria were littered with broken glass from Jewish homes, shops, and factories, brought from King nothing more than a low moan. He did not mention Hitler in his diary, blaming German youth for the destruction, but he did admit that "the sorrows which the Jews have to bear . . . are almost beyond comprehension."

Abraham Heaps, the CCF member for Winnipeg North, who was Jewish, had just lost his wife, and this contributed to the Prime Minister's distress. He sat down with Heaps and the conversation turned to the subject of admitting Jewish refugees into Canada. "Something will have to be done," King told his diary that night. He repeated it the following day when he attended Mrs. Heaps's funeral in an Ottawa synagogue. But the emotion of the moment quickly passed, and nothing was ever done.

To the Prime Minister, national and party unity were far more important than the fate of thousands of European Jews. French Canada was solidly opposed to admission of any more Jews. The St. Jean Baptiste Society gathered 128,000 names on a petition opposing "all immigration and especially Jewish immigration." The Knights of Columbus, the Quebec press, and several of the *caisses populaires* were just as adamant. "Why allow in Jewish refugees?" *Le Devoir* asked. "The Jewish shopkeeper on St. Lawrence Boulevard does nothing to increase our natural resources." Quebec's Liberal M.P.s were unanimously opposed to Jewish immigration. One, H.E. Brunelle, told the House that the Jews caused "great difficulties" wherever they lived. More significant was the unyielding attitude of Ernest Lapointe, who led the opposition in Cabinet.

In English-speaking Canada, the most formidable public opposition to Jewish immigration came from the Canadian Corps Association, the powerful veterans' group, which sent a resolution to the Prime Minister opposing any weakening of immigration regulations that might "tend to make Canada a dumping ground for Europe." The CCA wanted all new Canadians to be predominantly British or at least capable of rapid assimilation. "Now is no time to bring in people who have nothing in common with us, who do not want to work in the open and who have no desire to come here other than to find a new home." This was a not-too-veiled attack on the Jews, who were stereotyped as people who didn't want to "work in the open," i.e., on the farms or in the forests and mines.

On the other hand, when the Canadian Jewish Congress held a national day of mourning on November 20, it attracted a broad spectrum of Gentile sympathizers in an attempt to convince the

470

government to allow Jewish refugees to immigrate. Meetings were held from Glace Bay to Victoria, with prominent speakers representing labour, the United Church, and local civic councils. Letters, telegrams, and petitions flooded the Prime Minister's office in what the *Globe and Mail* called an example of "the brotherhood of man asserting itself."

It did no good. Three days after the day of mourning, a powerful Jewish delegation from Toronto, Montreal, and Ottawa, led by Heaps and Sam Factor, the Liberal member for Spadina, met with King and Crerar. They announced that the Jewish community was prepared to care for any Jews admitted to Canada and asked that at least ten thousand be admitted. King shilly-shallied. He pointed out that unemployment was still high and that Canada must first take care of its own. He also had to consider "the avoidance of strife within our own country," not to mention the constituencies (meaning Quebec) "and the views of those who are supporting the government." Votes, in short, were more important than human lives.

King then shocked the delegation with the suggestion that *Kristallnacht* might be a blessing in disguise; international opinion, he said, was so outraged the Nazis would be afraid to molest the Jews further.

International opinion did not sway the Cabinet, though King, whose conscience was clearly bothered by his colleagues' intransigence, tried to bring the members around. On November 24 he asked his ministers "to try and view the refugee problem from the way in which this nation will be judged in years to come, if we do not play our part along with other democracies, in helping to meet one of humanity's direct needs." He pointed out that "we could not afford to lose the Liberal attitude . . . and that the time had come when, as a Government, we would have to perform acts that were expressive of what we believed to be the conscience of the nation, and not what might be, at the moment, politically most expedient." He got little response, "most of those present fearing the political consequences of any help to the Jews." Cabinet was prepared to find a home for the Jews somewhere else – in Africa, perhaps – but not in Canada.

By this time it was almost impossible for any Jewish refugee to leap the barrier that the Immigration Branch had erected against the Jews. At the beginning of the year, Jewish refugees were required to have capital of at least five thousand dollars on entering the country. By December the department was rejecting those who had twenty thousand or more. Just before Hitler seized Czechoslovakia, a group of Jewish farm families with a total capital of one million dollars begged for entry visas. They were bluntly denied entry. Blair and other officials of the department were convinced, without any evidence, that many refugees were faking their assets in order to gain admission.

In Europe, where time was of the essence for anybody fleeing the Nazis, the very word "Jew" on an application form was enough to cause immediate rejection by Canadian officials. Abella and Troper quote the case of Zita Plaut, who had managed to escape from Vienna to the Netherlands with her husband. In 1938 she applied for a visa to bring the couple and the rest of her family still in Germany to Canada. She told the Canadian official that the family had fifty thousand dollars in foreign currency. "Wonderful," he said, and handed her a form. She filled it out and signed it. "Oh," he said, "their name is Rappaport? They are Jewish? I'm sorry, we have no visas." And he tore up the document as she watched.

King had not since November pressed the matter of Jewish immigration on his colleagues, but Crerar did. On December 1, he told the Cabinet that he was prepared to admit ten thousand Jewish refugees. King was nettled. Crerar had made the recommendation, he felt, "really without consideration of the matter." With the rest of the Cabinet totally opposed, the Prime Minister fell back on that old bulwark, the BNA Act. He would announce publicly that the matter couldn't be dealt with until the provinces were consulted. "As legislation respecting immigration is concurrent," the government would leave it up to each province as to whether they would accept Jewish immigrants. The general feeling in Cabinet was that they would all be unwilling.

To further appease Crerar, King suggested tossing a small bone to Canadian Jews who were still pressuring the government for bolder action, especially in the light of Australia's commitment to admit fifteen thousand Jewish refugees. Jews who had come to Canada as tourists, it was announced, would be allowed to stay, but no more would be admitted "lest it might foment anti-Semitic problems."

472

That was the bizarre argument used by Canada's High Commissioner to Britain, the patrician Vincent Massey, who danced on the periphery of Lord and Lady Astor's anti-Semitic, pro-German Cliveden set. Massey told King privately that a further influx of Jewish refugees would "naturally swell the already substantial Jewish population of larger cities" and help create "anti-Semitic feeling."

The High Commissioner had another, more devious solution. Why not appease those Canadians who wanted to help alleviate the refugee problem by taking in another type of refugee – Germans from the Sudetenland of Czechoslovakia who had incurred Hitler's wrath by not supporting him at the time of the Munich crisis? Massey made his prejudices clear when he told King that "these refugees are of a superior type to certain other categories of refugees who are engaging our attention." For one thing, they were Aryans.

And that is exactly what happened. A few days before Christmas the Cabinet agreed that more than three thousand Sudeten Germans could emigrate to western Canada "provided they came with the amount of capital now required for settlement purposes."

King's conscience was salved. Canada would humanely admit these Germans, who "had been sacrificed for the benefit of the world's peace of which we were the beneficiaries." As Massey explained, they were among "the numerous non-Jewish people who [found] life quite intolerable under the Nazi regime," while Norman Robertson, of External Affairs, stated that "men of their type and history should be a really valuable asset and acquisition to this country."

Of all the disparate groups of refugees in Europe, the victims from Sudetenland were the newest. The Jews, of course, were the oldest. But Canada had made it clear that, as a Canadian official would later say of Jewish immigrants, none was too many. With a scratch of the pen, Canada's most distinguished and powerful mandarins and statesmen pushed the Jews aside and put the Germans at the head of the queue.

1939

1

The country was tired.

In this, the last year of the Great Depression – but who could know that? – the people were weary and dispirited and their leaders worn out in mind and sometimes in body. (Mackenzie King, on New Year's afternoon, took to his bed for two and a half hours.)

One million Canadians were still on relief. Jobs remained hard to get, even though many who had them were overworked. Social workers had too many desperate cases, doctors too many indigent patients, teachers too many ragged students crammed into rundown classrooms.

Since 1930, the country had been living from hand to mouth. The government had shovelled nine hundred million dollars into direct-aid works and projects for unemployment relief and agricultural distress and had precious little to show for it. The number of people dependent on public funds was still rising, yet the nation's leaders seemed incapable of effective planning.

The Canadian Welfare Council described the prevailing mood in its annual report that January: "A weary country and a disillusioned people have been in a mood of drift." Under such conditions, charismatic leaders often emerge to short-cut democracy. It had happened elsewhere. Could it happen in Canada?

There were hints that it could, especially in the three provinces whose leaders had, with the enthusiastic approval of the voters, tried to subvert the democratic process.

In Alberta, William Aberhart showed his contempt by a long silence in the legislature, which he explained in one brutally frank sentence. "I can reach the public by radio," he said, "so why take up the time of the House?"

In Quebec, the administration of the Padlock Law reached new heights of imbecility when two Protestant missionaries were thrown out of a lumber camp near Dolbeau. The police invoked the Act (supposedly designed to suppress only Communist literature) to confiscate 570 Protestant publications – Bibles, dictionaries, tracts, hymnals, and gospels. Then they ordered the offenders out of town on the next train. No amount of official protest brought so much as a peep of acknowledgement from Premier

Duplessis, lending further credence to the *Canadian Forum*'s suggestion that the real fear in Quebec was not communism but anti-clericalism.

In Ontario, the hunger for direction in an apparently pilotless nation erupted briefly with the creation of that curious, if short-lived, movement known as the Leadership League. Canadians in moments of crisis have tended to demand "strong leadership." Now, tens of thousands made it clear that they were prepared to accept one-party rule in the interests of peace, order, and imaginative government.

The league was George McCullagh's personal baby. Its sudden success provides an insight into the psyche of the country that spring. In a series of five broadcasts over a loose network of radio stations, the publisher of the *Globe and Mail* managed to strike a chord. Though his simplistic approach to the nation's problems might seem half-baked to some, there were multitudes who hung on his every word. McCullagh had the advantages of a rich and charismatic voice and the enthusiastic backing of his own news-paper. But he was clearly unprepared for the response to his call for stronger leadership. Before he knew it he found himself at the head of a national movement that had all the earmarks of an incipient political party.

McCullagh was one of those self-made men who believe that governments can be run on the same business principles that work so well in the private sector. The so-called Boy Millionaire was just thirty-three years old, a cabinet-maker's son who had become a king-maker, a phenomenon in the business, publishing, and political world. Mitch Hepburn had been his creature. McCullagh, it was said, was not above prompting the Premier, *sotto voce*, from his listening-post in an adjoining washroom. "I make and unmake governments," McCullagh once boasted.

Tall and ruggedly handsome, the Boy Millionaire bristled and brimmed with an overweening confidence undiluted by false modesty. Some of his business rivals were still tittering over his declaration, during a 1936 testimonial dinner, that his merging of the *Globe* and the *Mail and Empire* was a "masterpiece."

Much was made of the fact (by McCullagh himself, among others) that he had started his publishing career at twenty-one as a subscription salesman for the *Globe* and that when he had quit, he told the current owner, William Gladstone Jaffray, "when I
478

next walk into this office, I'll be buying the paper out from under you." He had made good that boast in the depths of the Depression. No wonder, then, that he was convinced he could solve the Depression's ills.

Everybody agreed that he was a supersalesman. As a broker, he had flourished even after the 1929 crash. But his biggest act of salesmanship was to convince William Henry Wright, an unpretentious prospector, to let him handle his business affairs.

Wright was McCullagh's real ticket to success. He had struck it rich in northern Ontario not once but twice. His income from two of the richest gold mines in Canada – Wright Hargreaves and Lake Shore – was estimated at two million dollars a year. McCullagh, the business evangelist, soon found the key to his client's pocketbook. "Link arms with me in a crusade," he told the former house-painter in 1936. Wright bought him two newspapers for his crusade, and added a fancy art-deco headquarters on King Street.

The McCullagh charm that had seduced Wright was invoked in the 1937 Ontario election campaign in the Liberal cause. The publisher's radio personality was so powerful that a single broadcast brought in two thousand letters and fourteen thousand phone calls. But within a year his relationship with the Premier soured, partly because of Hepburn's new association with Duplessis and his public feud with Mackenzie King. Hepburn, McCullagh had once said, wasn't "fit to be premier of a pub."

McCullagh's musings on leadership began to obsess him after the Munich crisis in 1938. Both King and Robert Manion, Bennett's successor, seemed to him to be lukewarm in their attitude toward Britain. Nor, he thought, did either have any fresh ideas about how to cope with Canada's domestic problems. (The best King could do was to take some of the burden of relief off the shoulders of the municipalities.)

In the *Globe* that fall, McCullagh had called for "fresh leadership." By late December, after talking it over with his Bay Street friends, he had decided on a series of five intimate, "man-to-man" broadcasts, designed to arouse public consciousness. The publisher had two goals in mind, one vaguely high-minded – "to reject the clap-trap the politicians have preached for years" – the other coldly practical, "to extend the influence of the *Globe and Mail*."

The Canadian Broadcasting Corporation turned him down, touching off an unholy row in the *Globe* about free speech. But the CBC, stung perhaps by the virulence of the paper's attack, discreetly allowed McCullagh to establish his own network by shipping recordings of his broadcasts to thirty Canadian radio stations.

The broadcasts, heard on successive Sunday nights in January and February, had all the fervour of an evangelistic revival. Like so many would-be leaders before and since, the Boy Millionaire catered to the age-old yearning for a return to traditional values. In the words of his own paper, which awkwardly attempted an objective report, he "challenged the Canadian people to awaken fully to the national crisis with which he believes them to be confronted, and to turn back – before it is too late – from the borderline of defeatism, disillusionment and disaster toward which irresponsible government, inadequate leadership and individual apathy, he believes, are slowly but surely heading them."

McCullagh embellished his talk with a call for "rugged honesty, clear purpose, tireless energy and unswerving loyalty" to long-established principles. But, stripped of the platitudes, his first broadcast had only one proposal to advance, the time-tested appeal for a reduction in taxes and a curb on "wild government spending."

These were hardly novel suggestions, but in later broadcasts McCullagh demonstrated his disdain for the traditional political process, which he, like so many other businessmen, found ponderous and tiresome. He called for a "National Government" in which the Liberals and Conservatives would bury their differences and form a single party to deal with the problems of the Depression. "In all humility," he cried, "I beseech them not to paralyze the government by a bitter election contest when these problems are facing us."

That was reminiscent of Hepburn's earlier attempt, inspired by McCullagh, to form a one-party government in Ontario. But McCullagh now went farther. He called for the abolition of all provincial governments – "political misfits" in his words. These were "luxuries we cannot afford."

McCullagh had no other specific proposals. The rest was a mishmash of old bromides – a plea for a return to honesty and thrift, a denunciation of government patronage, a call for a "strong national purpose," an invocation to make Canada "a virile nation." And yet – such was the temper of the times – these vague and possibly dangerous proposals produced a flood of letters that must have surprised McCullagh himself.

He hadn't contemplated any kind of national organization when he began. Now it was thrust upon him. In his final broadcast on February 12, he announced the formation of the Leadership League "through which a persevering people, by co-operative effort, may guard the country against further incompetency in public affairs . . . and may, if ever the urgency arises – smash the present political set-up with the launching of a potential new party of power and propriety, independent thought and action."

The *Globe and Mail* each day published two forms, one a membership request, the other to be mailed to a Member of Parliament asking him or her "to forget party advantage and co-operate for the common good." The response was overwhelming. In the first week following McCullagh's final broadcast, forty-two thousand form letters swamped federal M.P.s, though one, J.A. Glen, claimed that a number were addressed and filled in by the same hand. By mid-March, the league had taken on a staff of twenty-six and moved out of the newspaper's office to larger quarters on Richmond Street.

If McCullagh had taken the time and trouble to work out a specific program, if his attention span had been longer and his health better (he was, apparently, a manic depressive and would one day commit suicide), the Leadership League might have prospered, as Social Credit had, as a political movement and perhaps a new party. Certainly the public was ready for some new ideas. The trouble was that McCullagh didn't have any, unless one counts his appeal for a single-party state.

At the same time, the Leadership League was costing money and provoking a backlash. The federal government responded through the Minister of National Revenue, J.L. Ilsley, who told a Toronto business lunch that McCullagh (whom he didn't name) "showed a contempt for our political institutions." The yearning for leadership, Ilsley pointed out, was part of the trend of events in Europe, where "lead me, Führer" and "lead me, Duce," had become the highest expressions of civic virtue.

Most major national dailies, especially McCullagh's Toronto rivals, either attacked the league or ignored it, many seeing it, in

481

the words of *Saturday Night,* as "a newspaper stunt." Only the smaller Ontario dailies were supportive.

But the *Globe and Mail* went all out, devoting its front page and all of its page 7 to the league's activities. It also provided speakers to spread the gospel for the forty or more local league clubs that met in churches, schools, legion halls, and theatres. The new movement seemed to be accelerating – certainly anybody reading the *Globe* would have thought so – its membership expanding and its network increasing. And then suddenly, no more than a month after he'd announced its formation, McCullagh bowed out.

In mid-March his paper announced that the league would no longer be his personal vehicle. It would be taken over by a body of public-spirited citizens led by Dr. Herbert Bruce, the former lieutenant-governor, and Sir Frederick Banting, the Nobel laureate who helped discover insulin. Under this impeccable stewardship, the league seemed destined for greater triumphs. Its membership had reached 125,000 (or so it was claimed), and a mass rally was planned for Maple Leaf Gardens. The *Globe* forecast that at least twenty thousand would jam the hockey arena.

Only ten thousand turned up. McCullagh, who was suffering from nervous exhaustion as a result of all this activity, made a spirited appeal for funds, but for once his oratory fell flat. The public, which had seemed to support the league by filling out newspaper ballots, failed to respond. The total contributions amounted to a piddling $300. McCullagh himself had spent $105,000 on the venture.

Suddenly it was over. The *Globe and Mail* announced on April 26 that it could no longer afford to acknowledge membership applications. McCullagh resigned from his own organization the following day. His brainchild had flared like a rocket and fizzled out in just four months. On June 26, when its offices closed forever, the Leadership League died from lack of leadership.

2

Back They returned that winter and spring, the men who had fought in
from Spain, wearing dead men's clothes – garments and uniforms
the stripped from the corpses that lay thickly on the battlefields. They
dead came in groups of steadily diminishing size, the halt, the lame,
482

the ill, and the disillusioned. Others would never return. A third of those who had enlisted would lie forever on that foreign field, their clothing gathered up to cover the living in that most frugal of wars.

The first contingent of 272 reached Halifax on February 3 aboard the CPR's *Duchess of Richmond*. Most were veterans of the Mackenzie-Papineau Battalion, which had been named with unconscious irony for the Prime Minister's rebel grandfather. Their crusade was over. The previous fall the Loyalist government, in a futile attempt to influence international public opinion, had withdrawn all foreign soldiers from the line. It had taken more than four months to get them out of the embattled peninsula.

They had travelled by barge, rail, and foot to the French border. They had been whisked across France to the channel ports in a sealed train, guarded by French detectives. They had crossed to England and finally sailed from Liverpool, homesick and fagged out. Hundreds of others were waiting in England and France, some in concentration camps, to return home.

The RCMP didn't want them and urged the government to deny them immigration status because they had been "engaged contrary to the policy of the Government in the Spanish War." The government was embarrassed by them but didn't care to encounter a worse embarrassment by barring them; after all, England and France had resisted taking such a drastic step. Nonetheless, Ottawa was taking no chances. An RCMP inspector was dispatched to France to make sure all were bona fide Canadians. After two years of battle, some of the foreign-born could no longer remember the details of their original entry into Canada. These the French herded unceremoniously into concentration camps until their admissibility could be confirmed.

There were no brass bands on the dock at Halifax, no triumphant parades, no politicians mouthing speeches of congratulation - only a small corps of newspapermen and a crowd of anonymous well-wishers. Led by their commander, Major Ed Cecil-Smith, a former Toronto newspaperman, the veterans shambled down the gangway in their cast-offs. One man was carried off on a stretcher. Fifty-five required medical attention. Thirty-three needed surgery. Lionel Edwards - Captain Edwards now - who had been badly wounded by shellfire on the Ebro was heading for Edmonton. He'd been one of the passengers on that earlier trip who had so terrified the Irish couple aboard the SS *President Roosevelt*. Tom Ewen's two boys, Bruce and Jim, had no idea where they were going. They had enlisted in Vancouver but had lost touch with their family.

Some veterans didn't want to talk to the press because they feared the publicity would make it hard for them to get jobs in Canada. Others were defiant. Fred Baxter put it bluntly: "I went to Spain to kill as many Fascists as possible; that's all the less to kill when they get here."

That was the underlying theme of those who spoke up on their return to Canada. Bill Beeching, who had served with the Lincoln Battalion, was determined to travel the country warning Canadians that the Spanish conflict was no more than a curtain raiser for a new world war. "It was shocking to us when we first came back," he would remember. "We were elated to be alive. We were ashamed we had lost the war. We felt we had let the Spanish people down. We felt sort of cowardly that we had been repatriated, although we were not responsible for it. . . . Everything felt strange. It seemed to me that the Canadian people weren't aware of what was taking place in the world. . . . "

The sense of disillusionment and defeat hung like a pall among the survivors. It was, as Samuel Abramson of Montreal recalled, "a bitter end to the dreams we had cherished. We were leaving Spain shattered and in chains." Barcelona had already fallen. Madrid would do so soon. Gregory Clark, the Toronto *Star*'s diminutive reporter, wrote that day that "their war stories have a gentle madness that reminds you of Don Quixote."

The veterans were rushed from the ship to a special nine-car train that would take them to Montreal. Their passage had been paid partly by the Spanish government and partly by the Friends of the Mackenzie-Papineau Battalion. In England, the Friends had approached Matthew Halton of the Toronto *Star* to help raise ten thousand dollars to underwrite some of the costs. Halton knew two wealthy Canadian residents he thought might contribute – R.B. Bennett and Garfield Weston, the biscuit king. He phoned both. Bennett turned him down. Weston offered five thousand dollars before Halton finished his pitch. (Tim Buck wrote in his memoirs that A.A. MacLeod, editor of the Communist paper the *Tribune*, went to London on the same mission and "was so persuasive that Bennett gave him $500" – a remarkable piece of persuasion indeed.)

It wasn't enough. The former soldiers agreed to sleep in unheated colonist cars to save money. There was no dining car; they subsisted on 1,650 sandwiches donated by Halifax women. Just before the train pulled out, William Foley of Toronto, wounded in the shoulder and hip, said a final goodbye to his friend Gerald Shea, who was heading for Cape Breton. Foley would never forget the day when Shea had carried him to safety under intense machine-gun fire. "It's like the closing of a book," he said sadly.

There would be no civic welcomes for the men who now crossed the country to their homes, although there were crowds at the train stations. The Montreal City Council refused to let the veterans hold a banquet in the Atwater Market because they were "Communists," and the CPR police tried to stop the ongoing passengers from parading in Windsor Station. They relented briefly at the last moment to permit a short passage down the concourse – but not into the street – before herding the men back on the train. At Toronto, there *was* a brass band to welcome them. Here somebody told the Ewen brothers that one of their sisters was in Toronto, living on Bedford Road. That was the end of the journey for them. In proletarian Winnipeg, four thousand cheered the returning men. There was bitter criticism for the mayor and the Premier, who had declined to join the welcoming party.

With war looming in Europe, the press was less hostile to the crumbling Loyalist cause. *Saturday Night* found it extraordinary that Canadian public opinion "should have passionately sympathized with Czechoslovakia and under the same situation be so generally cold to a Spanish government, which received the same aid against the same enemies and now seems likely to receive the same treatment from France and Britain."

Other groups of volunteers followed the first but were received by smaller crowds and muted cheers. Red Walsh, one of the leaders of the On-to-Ottawa trek, arrived aboard the *Duchess of Bedford*, suffering from a still open stomach wound. The ship's doctor had slapped a pad on it and told him, "That'll keep your guts in until you get to Vancouver."

Another straggler, Ron Liversedge, had been trapped in southern Spain and made his way to France by a circuitous route. Like most of his comrades, Liversedge was always hungry. During all his months in Spain he was tormented by a vision of sausages and wheatcakes. When he reached Vancouver and the White Lunch, he placed his order at last only to find he was too overcome with emotion to eat it.

At the end of April, at least seventy-six Canadians, most of them former prisoners of General Franco, were still trapped in France. Although they faced incarceration under dreadful conditions in French concentration camps, the Canadian government showed no inclination to bring them home. With the same callousness that had characterized all its decisions in the Depression years, the Immigration Branch simply abandoned them.

With the fall of Madrid in March, funds from the Spanish government had dried up. The Friends of the Mackenzie-Papineau Battalion had also exhausted their thin resources. On May 2, Hazen Sise, Bethune's former associate, pleaded with Crerar to help out. The situation of these veterans was desperate, he wrote; the French camps had been the subject of an international scandal. It would "cause considerable resentment in Canada, if these remaining volunteers were to be shut up in them, merely because money for transportation was lacking." After months as prisoners of war, "their physical condition is deplorable and it is doubtful if some of them could withstand further rigorous treatment." The Friends had borrowed four thousand dollars for ten days with little hope that it could be repaid. It would cost no more than one hundred dollars a man to bring them home. Could the Canadian government not help, Sise asked, either by relieving France of the burden of maintaining the volunteers or by making a grant to the International Red Cross or one of the international refugee committees?

Five days later, Sise got his answer. The government refused to consider the request. A similar request from a senior mandarin, Norman Robertson, first secretary at the Department of External Affairs, was also ignored.

The statistics of the Canadian contribution to the Spanish Civil War are fuzzy. Dr. James McCrorie, executive director of the Canadian Plains Research Centre, who has done considerable work on the subject, has estimated that of the 1,448 Canadians now known to have fought in Spain, 721 never returned home. Hazen Sise's estimates in his letter to Crerar differ slightly, but
486

they were compiled as of April 30, 1939. They are also more specific. Sise reported that of 1,239 Canadian volunteers of whom they then had record, 677 had returned home, 86 were still in France or Europe, 32 had been repatriated to other countries, and 444 were killed or missing.

This last is an appalling statistic. Even in the Great War, that most savage of modern conflicts, the casualties did not reach 36 per cent. Yet in spite of this, a great many veterans from Spain enlisted or tried to enlist when war came to Canada in September.

Here again, they were the victims of muddle and confusion and a lack of clear government policy about what to do with "Communists." Some were welcomed because of their military experience; some were given the cold shoulder. The first four veterans of the Mackenzie-Papineau Battalion to sign up were discharged four days later because of their record in Spain. A few weeks after that, the policy was revised and they enlisted again.

Jules Paivio, the Finnish Canadian from Sudbury, also had trouble enlisting. A section leader in Spain, he'd spent a year as a prisoner of war. But the army wouldn't take him until December 1942. On the other hand, Mike Olynuck, who had been a captain, was quickly welcomed into the Toronto Scottish because of his experience.

As Paivio discovered, the RCMP had a file on each man, which followed the Spanish volunteers wherever they went. Fred Kostyck of Winnipeg, who had been cited for bravery in Spain, tried to get a job in a munitions factory when war broke out. He was taken on, then fired after three weeks. When he asked why, he was told it was because he had seen action in Spain.

"I fought against fascism in Spain," Kostyck said. "Isn't this war against fascism?"

"There is no debate or argument," he was told. "Here is your discharge and out you go. If you want to cause any more trouble, you will be blacklisted and you won't even get a job."

A week later Kostyck was called up. When he went to the local barracks, he asked if the army was prepared to trust him.

"They couldn't trust me working in a cordite plant," he said, "but you'll trust me with a gun out in the field. Aren't you making a mistake?" But the army took him in, and Kostyck served his country overseas.

487

On the other hand, Bill Matthews, who had been an officer in Spain and had suffered wounds to the neck and shoulder, was turned down when he tried to join the tank corps in Calgary. He then tried the air force, where he was asked if he'd ever been in combat.

"Oh, yeah, in Spain," said Matthews.

"We're filled up," he was told.

"There's a war on," Matthews replied. "There'll be casualties. I'll put my application in."

It was no use. "We don't want you," he was told.

Matthews was furious. "Well," he said, "from now on if you want me you'll have to come and get me. I'll probably live a lot longer than you will." He walked out, hopped an eastbound freight, got a job in Toronto, and never did serve in the forces.

As he later said, "I'm very thankful I didn't, because the Calgary tank regiment was practically wiped out at Dieppe."

3

The royal tonic That spring, the country witnessed the greatest outpouring of enthusiasm and goodwill in its history. There had been royal tours before by princes of the realm, and there have been royal tours since, but never anything like this one. The Royal Tour of 1939 was unique – a month-long revel that came at the end of the darkest of all decades and seemed to wipe away, if only briefly, the memory and the misery of those mean-spirited years.

When, on May 15, the discarded German liner *Tirpitz*, rechristened *Empress of Australia*, reached Quebec City, it marked the first time a reigning British monarch had visited North America. George VI and his consort had insisted on coming by passenger liner because, with international tensions so high, the King did not want to take a warship out of service.

They came, it was said officially, at the invitation of the Prime Minister, who certainly took credit for initiating the tour. Mackenzie King had invited the royal pair directly during the Coronation visit in 1937. In the fall of 1938, with the Munich crisis behind it, the British government gave official approval. But there were other considerations. Canada would be chosen to greet the monarch not only because she was the senior Dominion but also because the British government saw, or thought it saw, disturbing signs of a spirit of independence and neutrality in certain sections of the country. Mackenzie King had a different reason: a coast-to-coast tour would help bind the nation together and give all Canadians a sense of national pride.

It was King, ever conscious of his position as the Prime Minister of a Commonwealth nation, who insisted on making all the important decisions and who fended off attempts to place the Governor General in the ceremonial forefront. The British – notably Sir Alexander Hardinge, the King's secretary – had wanted Tweedsmuir to greet the couple when they stepped off the ship at Quebec City. But the Prime Minister was having none of that. It would be seen, he said, as "a reversal to colonial status." Since His Excellency was, in effect, the King's stand-in, he would have no real function when his sovereign was on Canadian soil. As a result, Tweedsmuir was packed off on a fishing trip to the Gaspé, and Mackenzie King, as Prime Minister to the "King of Canada" (a new title), took over.

In fact, he scarcely left the royal couple's side for the entire tour. Every attempt was made to sideline him for their trip to Washington and New York, planned for June. But King would not be cast aside, he said, "like an old boot." A first-class spat was in the making before royalty so much as touched Canadian shores – King even appealed to Roosevelt – but the British finally backed down. They could not afford to offend the Commonwealth's senior statesman, who was starting to make warning signals through the Governor General. "You have already lost South Africa pretty well out of the Empire," he told Tweedsmuir, "have lost Ireland out of it; are rapidly losing Canada." That came dangerously close to a threat, and it worked. Mackenzie King was front and centre during the entire tour, a situation that was viewed with considerable pique in some circles, where he was accused of "hogging the royal couple."

The vast crowds straining their eyes in the morning sunshine along the banks of the St. Lawrence were treated to a few moments of old-world pageantry as the white Empress was nudged into the docks at Quebec City. Three hundred members of the international press scribbled furiously as the Prime Minister and his huge Quebec lieutenant, Ernest Lapointe, mounted the gangway, resplendent in gold-braided Windsor uniforms and ostrich-

489

plumed hats. Then the King and Queen appeared – he tanned and serious in the cocked hat and navy blue of an admiral, she radiant in lavender. Guns boomed; scarlet-coated Canadian Guardsmen in bearskin busbies presented arms with a single *slap*; and the crowd went wild. It was clear from this first glittering moment that a unique and historic event was in the making and that French Canada was eager to be part of it.

Only the Premier of Quebec seemed out of sorts. After receiving Their Majesties, he failed to appear at the luncheon given by the Canadian government, using the transparent excuse that he had to visit his sister, who had just arrived in town. In reality, he was piqued because he felt he had been allotted a seat too far from the royal couple. He turned up in good spirits as host at dinner that night after arranging for the Prime Minister to be seated, tit for tat, at the remote end of the head table.

The two political enemies found themselves thrown together on the journey to Montreal – a disagreeable experience for Mackenzie King, who found the Quebec premier "anything but a pleasant person," talking only of voters and power in "almost a childish and fanatical way."

The scenes that followed, however, wiped out that contretemps. Montreal, the worst-hit city during the Depression, now responded with the greatest crowds of the tour. More than a million people lined the twenty-three-mile route of the royal procession, shouting themselves hoarse and conveying the impression (not quite correct) of a united royalist Canada. That night, Camillien Houde, the popular mayor of Montreal – a man of vast belly, bald head, and huge, popping eyes – broke through protocol and had the King laughing uproariously for the first time.

That touch of informality set the tone for the rest of the tour. In Ottawa the couple took part in the first royal walkabout, leaving their car at the National War Memorial in Confederation Square to mingle with a crowd of sixty thousand. Lost even to the sight of their aides, they grasped the hands of veterans who cried out, "You don't need any bullet-proof glass here," and, significantly, "If Hitler could see this!"

Tom MacDonnell, who has written a lively and definitive account of the tour (*Daylight Upon Magic*), reports that "no other event in the entire tour had such an impact on Canadians as a whole or, for that matter, on the King and Queen themselves." The contrast between the royal pair moving freely among their subjects and the reviewing-stand remoteness of the European dictators was not lost on the international press, who wrote now of the new "common touch." From that moment, the King and Queen, invigorated by the experience, took advantage of every opportunity to break through the red tape of protocol and get closer to the people.

In spite of his disdain for the British aristocracy, the Prime Minister, like everyone else, was captivated by Their Majesties to the point of sycophancy. While showing them around Laurier House he found himself blurting out that he was prepared to lay his life at their feet "in helping to further great causes which they have at heart." The success of the tour was exceeding his wildest dreams. When the King, seated in the red Senate Chamber, gave royal assent to nine bills passed by the Canadian Parliament, the Prime Minister gushed that the event marked "the full flowering of our nationhood."

As the country's fervour increased, so did that of the Prime Minister. More than nationhood was in flower; universal peace was in bloom, thanks to the Canadian example – or so he thought. "I feel increasingly certain," King wrote, "that this visit of the King and Queen is going to be the dust in the balance which will save a European and, if so, a world war. The unity, which Canada is showing, will be reflected in Europe. It will help to arouse Germany to be conscious of what she will encounter if the entire British Empire should rise. . . . "

The Prime Minister's enthusiasm was dampened in Toronto, however, during the running of the King's Plate at Woodbine Racetrack. This was *the* social and sporting event of the year. For the first time, the King himself would be on hand to present the traditional purse of gold guineas to the owner of the winning horse. And who did that turn out to be? None other than the Prime Minister's old *bête noire*, George McCullagh! King immediately suspected a fix. The horse, Archworth, was the favourite. It had led the field by a good ten lengths. George VI himself had picked it to win. Nonetheless, King hinted darkly, "financial circumstances had accounted for it . . . something had been done to ensure McCullagh winning." King was convinced the wily

McCullagh had worked behind the scenes to try to prevent his travelling the country on the tour. How could such a man be allowed this moment of triumph?

Canada's own royalty, the Dionne quintuplets, arrived in Toronto on their own special train – a red-and-gold air-conditioned streamliner. Since 1934 they had been the source of the only really cheerful headlines. At Queen's Park they made more, spontaneously kissing the royal couple and holding up their dolls and stuffed animals for inspection. But there could be no photographs. NEA Service, which had the Quints under contract, refused to relinquish its rights to any pool photographer.

The official royal train steamed westward by CPR, "a symphony in blue and gold," to quote the press – a twelve-car luxury hotel on wheels. Now the true shape of Canada was revealed on the front pages of the nation – a long, narrow country, really, from a population point of view, hugging the international border. Here was the armoured barrier of the Canadian Shield, seven hundred miles of Precambrian rock, where Van Horne, the railway builder, had erected three dynamite factories to blast a line through the dripping scarps north of Superior. Beyond that lay three hundred miles of muskeg that had once swallowed whole locomotives, now bridged and drained, and beyond that the southern plains, stretching seemingly forever toward the mountain wall, recently drought-ravaged but green now with new shoots of wheat. The downpours seemed to soak the fields just ahead of the royal procession, and the farmers began calling their King "George the Rainmaker." The immensity of the land and its deceptive shape – the tiny pockets of population isolated by vast natural barriers – gave visitors and natives alike a new insight into the problems the country faced.

But one problem remained hidden. On the advice of S.J. Wood, now Commissioner of the RCMP, the government subsidized the provincial forestry camps until the end of the tour to forestall jobless protestors from demonstrating in the cities. Further, it invoked the Railway Act to keep the boxcars free of transients.

The western trip took on the character of a gigantic carnival, as each city vied with its rivals to mount an extraordinary variety of pageants, street dances, thrill rides, and Indian powwows that marked a return to enthusiasm after a decade of despair. The people were saying, "Look what we can do!" not just to the royal couple and to the international press but also to themselves.

There were the usual complaints, especially from politicians who had been snubbed in their efforts to see the royal couple and from private citizens who complained that there were too many politicians getting in the way. King himself was sensitive to the criticism that he was in attendance for the entire tour. After hob-nobbing with royalty for a fortnight, he ventured to bring up the matter with the Queen during the stopover at Banff, remarking that he had felt "somewhat embarrassed" at spending the entire period at Their Majesties' side. "It looked like pushing myself to the fore, yet I felt that unless some evidence of Dominion precedence existed, one of the main purposes of the trip would be gone." The Queen, who showed herself a mistress of diplomacy at every whistle-stop, told him exactly what he wanted to hear – that they had both thought all along he should come with them.

In later years, people would speak of the moment when "the Queen looked at me." It was always the Queen. She charmed the nation with her intense blue eyes and her stunning pastel dresses, including her favourite colour, which the press dubbed "Elizabeth blue." She looked at everybody, it seemed – at the acres of Boy Scouts, schoolchildren in middies, bemedalled veterans, feathered Indians, pigtailed girls in ethnic dress, and even, on one memorable occasion, a group of nudists waving from an island in the Gulf of Georgia. When her frailer husband – grey with fatigue at tour's end – began to lose interest, she nudged him to look too. She had developed a personal salutation that saved energy, a twirl of the hand that became her trademark.

Her spontaneous gestures contrasted with the stiff newsreel formality of her predecessor, Queen Mary, with her solemn features and formidable mien. One moving moment occurred during a brief stop in the Rockies when the Queen spied a three-year-old child crying bitterly because she could not see over the crowd. Elizabeth moved quickly, picked up the little girl, hugged her, and stanched her tears.

The tour seemed to give the Prime Minister a new lease on life. There were fifty-five journalists accompanying the royal train and scores more at the way points, and here he was, always in the spotlight, the first to jump off the car almost before it stopped to rush forward and introduce local dignitaries to their sovereign and his consort. The protestations of fatigue and exhaustion that had peppered his diaries vanished. By the end of the tour he was fairly bursting with good health, while the King and Queen were close to a breakdown.

King's new glow seemed a metaphor for the nation. A dispirited people had suddenly discovered a hidden source of energy. The realm was a-flutter with flags of every size (one man in Toronto sold two million that summer), with miles of bunting and dozens of triumphal arches, one of which, in East Angus, Quebec, had required a million cords of lumber. The tour could only help a faltering economy. There was a brisk business in items ranging from rented top hats to cardboard periscopes. Cadbury's, the chocolate people, devised a special medal; Seagram's distilled an expensive whiskey, Crown Royal.

The country was eager for a return to pomp and ceremony. In Vancouver, the new CCF mayor, Dr. Lyle Telford – the same man who had signed so many passport applications for the Spanish volunteers – decided for the first time to wear his purple robes and golden chain of office. Until this moment he had felt that they would appear too pretentious in a city overrun with jobless transients.

By the time the royal couple returned to Vancouver from a boat trip to Victoria and headed east again – this time on the tracks of the government-owned CNR – the most jaundiced American newspapermen were turning out such effusive prose that the editor of one anti-British publication thought his man was drunk. The side trip to Washington and New York, which many thought more important than the entire Canadian tour, produced an even greater gush of enthusiasm.

George VI and Franklin Roosevelt got along swimmingly, and Mackenzie King basked in their presence as the three sat around drinks in the drawing-room at Roosevelt's mother's Hyde Park estate and frankly discussed world affairs. "The King," wrote the Prime Minister, "indicated he would never wish to appoint Churchill to any office unless it was absolutely necessary in time of war. I confess I was glad to hear him say that because I think Churchill is one of the most dangerous men I have ever known." But King, who had once thought Roosevelt a dangerous man too, would soon be luxuriating in Churchill's shadow.

494

The Prime Minister was convinced that the British Embassy was snubbing him, but the diplomatic president made a point of including him in the talks and, in the diarist's words, "told the King repeatedly that he and I understood each other perfectly and worked together on all matters of mutual relationship." The British, including the King, had wanted Lord Halifax as Minister in Attendance, but Roosevelt said, "Mackenzie and I know each other so well I was most anxious he should come." Roosevelt had made much of the fact that he and King were on a first-name basis. Actually, the President was the only man in the world who called the Prime Minister "Mackenzie."

King himself was in a near delirium over this cosy relationship. The real significance of the side trip to the United States, however, was its salutary effect on the isolationist American press and public.

Following a much-publicized luncheon at which Roosevelt served hot dogs, the tour returned to Canada and moved east. As the train slipped out of Quebec, George VI summoned his Prime Minister to the royal carriage to tell him how much the tour had meant to him and the Queen. Then, as King recorded, he asked "if I thought he had grasped the new idea of kingship." The Prime Minister asked if he meant the "common touch with the people, the first hand interest in their affairs." The King replied, "Yes, no more high hat business, the kind of thing that my father and those of his day regarded as essential, as the correct attitude. That certain things could not be done."

There followed an intimate and touching revelation by the King. The press was continually saying that he knew little about affairs, he said – that he could not speak, "was merely filling a place." He turned to the Prime Minister. "You know how all of this started," he said. Then he explained, "When my father was alive, he filled an important place; was very much before the public. My brother was equally prominent before the public. I was kept in the background. My father used to tell me that I could never do anything because I could not speak."

Mackenzie King was moved by this cry from the heart from a man who had never been able to master a childhood stutter and was painfully conscious of it. But as the Prime Minister noted, during this tour the stutter had diminished as the King gained new confidence.

The crowds increased in size as the tour drew to a close. One hundred thousand people jammed Halifax, so many that some were forced to walk the streets all night, unable to find a bed. In the Nova Scotian Hotel, the King and Queen made their farewell speeches. The King trudged bravely through his, though he was close to exhaustion and it was noticed that his stutter had grown worse. The Queen told the Prime Minister that when her husband spoke it was all she could do to keep from crying. The King said he felt the same way when the Queen spoke.

The Governor General had finally been allowed to take part on this last day, June 15. As the couple made their farewells aboard the *Empress of Britain*, a little bit of political jockeying took place. The Prime Minister had expected to walk off the ship last in company with the Governor General. But Tweedsmuir wanted it on record that *he* had been the last to leave Their Majesties. A contest of wills followed as the two manoeuvred for position. King won handily, purposely falling behind the vice-regal party and triumphantly bringing up the rear.

With the sun shining brightly on its white prow, the *Empress of Britain* pulled out to sea, accompanied by an informal escort of British warships, Canadian destroyers, and the entire fishing fleet, including the famous *Bluenose*. The watchers on shore could see the King and Queen at the very top of the vessel, waving gallantly and, no doubt, more than a little wearily, for the last time. The Royal Tour was over. For a month it had suffused the nation in a golden glow that would be dissipated only by the darker shadows of the coming war.

4

War While the King of England was proceeding across his senior Dominion with his subjects' plaudits ringing in his ears, another, grimmer voyage was under way across the Atlantic. By a bitter coincidence, the luxury liner *St. Louis* left Hamburg just one day after the royal couple reached Canada and returned to Europe just one day after they arrived back in London. It carried 907 Jews who had lost everything at the hands of the Nazis and who had learned, to their despair, that no country in the New World would give them refuge.

496

They had left, full of hope, carrying entrance visas to Cuba, but at the last minute the Cuban government turned them down. They appealed to Uruguay, Paraguay, and Panama, but all their entreaties failed. Nobody wanted them. Their only hope was that the United States or Canada would take them in, but that was a forlorn expectation. The Americans sent a gunboat to prevent the ship from landing. Canada, as it always had, flatly turned down their request.

When Mackenzie King met Roosevelt in early June, the matter was dismissed in a few sentences. It wasn't Canada's problem, the Prime Minister indicated in his diary. The *St. Louis* and its frantic passengers steamed back to Europe. England finally agreed to take in 288 refugees. France and the Low Countries, soon to be overrun by Hitler's panzers, admitted others. Of the 907 Jews who left Germany in May, only 240 survived the war.

But the prospect of war seemed remote and failed to dampen the revelry that attended the royal entourage that spring. The whole idea of war was anathema to Canadians. There were no hawks in Parliament and few if any in the country – only doves. There were no peace marches in those days – no chanting students carrying banners, no street demonstrations urging an end to war, no massed protests. None were needed because the entire population was firmly convinced that war was folly and peace preferable – at any price.

The nation had breathed a collective sigh of relief after the Munich crisis. Even Hitler's unwarranted attack in March on what was left of Czechoslovakia had not changed the general isolationism of Canadians. The unprecedented slaughter of the Great War – twenty thousand soldiers blown to bits in a single day on the Somme – had convinced politicians and proletariat that war was unthinkable. A soldier's life in Canada was scarcely a glorious one. Some mothers even refused to let their sons join the Boy Scouts because they were opposed to the wearing of uniforms.

A succession of anti-war novels such as Remarque's *All Quiet on the Western Front* had bolstered that view. Beverley Nichols's best-selling *Cry Havoc!* – an attack on munitions makers – had convinced his readers that the "merchants of death," to use the common expression, were evil men. When it was suggested to Mackenzie King that more jobs could be created if the country started producing munitions, the Prime Minister was outraged. Apart from his own pacifism, he knew only too well that such a program couldn't be sold politically.

King blamed the Poles as much as Hitler for the war in Europe. Why had this insignificant people taken so long to reply to the Führer's ultimatum? Why hadn't they been prepared to meet his terms? The delay "had helped to infuriate Hitler" when everything seemed to be so close to a settlement. King was quite prepared to agree to let Germany have all its colonies back, if it meant peace.

King was convinced there was still good in Hitler, that his actions could be explained by understanding the two-sided character of Richard Wagner, whose "life and music represented the study of good and evil" – the Christ versus the anti-Christ. The pagan (evil) side of Hitler's Wagnerian personality, King thought, had won out over the Christian side, with its higher inspiration. "I feel very strongly that Hitler's whole conduct is to be explained by his belief in himself as a reincarnation of some mythical or other personage – Siegfried, most probably."

But there had been no doubt in King's mind for some time that if war came Canada would stand with Britain. At the same time, he and Lapointe maintained the public fiction that the government was seriously considering neutrality. When the Lord Chancellor of England, Lord Maugham, arrived in late August to open the Canadian National Exhibition, he told the Prime Minister he intended to state that he had "been pleased to have assurances that Canada would be at the side of Britain in the event of war." King was infuriated at that suggestion; it would, he said, do irreparable harm. The idea that Canada was acting at the instance of the old country, or that the government had made up its mind before Parliament was given a chance to decide on the nature of the commitment, shocked him. Maugham struck out the offending sentence but was undoubtedly mollified by King's private assurance that the Cabinet was solidly united behind the war.

"I could not help thinking how desperately stupid some Englishmen are in appreciating any attitude other than their own," King wrote. "The superior way some of them have of assuming to know everything fills one with both exasperation and dismay."

498

Britain and France declared war on Germany on September 3. King announced a special war session of Parliament for September 7 and told his council that until Parliament met "all our measures would be for the defence of Canada." To his annoyance, his own broadcast that evening was ignored by the Ottawa *Journal*, which reported both King George's speech and Chamberlain's. "Not a line to our country's position and part," King complained. "It is this aspect of Toryism that fills me with grief, dismay and contempt. Anything if it is the King of England, but no mention whatever of Canada's own noble part or the words of her P.M."

Canada's part, however, was more ambiguous than noble. King's war plans did not call for sending a single Canadian soldier to fight in Europe. When he discovered that the Department of National Defence was ordering supplies to establish encampments to train soldiers for overseas service, he cancelled those plans. King believed, or wanted to believe, that the country's contribution could be confined to sending supplies, munitions, and pilots to England. He was equally disturbed to learn that the defence department had been spending most of its time preparing for an expeditionary force, apparently with the connivance of Ian Mackenzie, the responsible minister. Canada was not yet committed to anything of the sort.

King's views did not vary greatly from the attitude expressed by the CCF in January of that year. At that time the party's national executive had announced that it could not support any overseas adventure. Canada's forces should be used only for the defence of her own territory. There's no doubt that the majority of the CCF felt the same way. Of all the parties, it was the most pacifist, the most committed to neutrality. But by early September, with war almost certain, a good many CCFers, like a good many Canadians, had a change of heart. The old country was in trouble; British values, British justice, British fair play were in danger. Could Canada really stand by and let the mother of nations succumb to the German bully? The more pragmatic members of the CCF leadership found themselves stuck with what increasingly seemed to be an unworkable and eventually unpopular policy.

Given its disparate origins – farmers, progressives, union men, Marxists, intellectuals, British Labourites, Canadian nationalists

- it was not surprising that the CCF should crack in several directions on what many considered to be a matter of conscience. Woodsworth had helped to keep this uneasy partnership glued together as long as it faced the common enemy of capitalism. But what exactly was the new enemy? Hitler? The merchants of death? Or war itself?

On September 6, the party's national council of twenty-eight together with fourteen M.P.s met in Ottawa in a heated and racking session that would occupy two full days. Under the Gothic windows of a long committee room in the main block on Parliament Hill, the widening differences in the CCF's approach to international affairs became painfully apparent. The party was badly divided. Its selfless leader left no doubt about his own position. James Shaver Woodsworth was totally, unequivocally, and irreversibly opposed to his country's going to war. From that rock-like stance no power could shake him. Stanley Knowles, also a confirmed pacifist, nourished like his leader on the Social Gospel, stood by him as did the Fabians, Frank Underhill and Frank Scott. The practical politicians – Abe Heaps and David Lewis were among them – saw the danger of opposing the inevitable and argued that the party must support the coming war.

Angus MacInnis, married to Woodsworth's daughter, supported intervention. In doing so he alienated his Marxist colleagues in British Columbia, who insisted that Canada should keep out of an "Imperialist War." The Nova Scotians were going so far as to demand conscription for overseas service, while most of the delegates from Manitoba were for non-participation. On the other hand, the Saskatchewan CCF leader, George Williams, was urging the party to support the war.

Woodsworth put the question squarely to the meeting when he moved that "this council refuses to discuss any measure that will put Canada into the war." The council skirmished around that and decided finally not to put the motion to a vote. Instead a committee of six was struck to frame a compromise.

The party statement, which was debated through the following day and far into the night even as Parliament was sitting in its special war session, was intended to paper over the fact that the party had no clear policy. It contained a motherhood clause that "the root causes of war lie deep in the nature of our present society" and went on to urge that civil liberties be guarded dur-

500

ing the coming hostilities, that the government extend economic aid to England and provide for home defence, but that no expeditionary force be sent across the water.

With six members forced to leave the meeting before a vote could be taken, the compromise passed fifteen to nine. To the dismay of the others, Woodsworth rose from his seat to say: "You all know, as I know, what this must mean. . . ." With that he resigned from the leadership and the party. That his followers could not countenance. He was persuaded to remain on the condition that he would speak for himself alone in Parliament and that M.J. Coldwell, the future party leader, would follow to deliver the CCF's shaky position.

For the CCF and for Parliament itself, this was an emotional moment. King had been closeted with Woodsworth for two hours, apparently in an attempt to change his mind. Now, during a lengthy speech, he turned to the CCF bench to remark that "there are few men in this Parliament for whom, in some particulars, I have greater respect than the leader of the Cooperative Commonwealth Federation. I admire him, in my heart, because time and again he has had the courage to say what lay on his conscience regardless of what the world might think of him. A man of that calibre is an ornament to any Parliament. . . ."

Those honeyed words did not affect Woodsworth's fighting form. With his wife and two sons looking down from the gallery, he rose in his place and launched into a speech that none who were there that day would ever forget.

There he stood, a frail figure, grown frailer during the grim years of the thirties when he had criss-crossed the country carrying the message of the movement. His mind, Coldwell had told King in confidence, was beginning to falter, but there was no hint of that now as he lambasted the Prime Minister, regretting in passing that he had to do so in spite of King's earlier flattery.

Woodsworth saw through King's obfuscations. The Prime Minister had carefully fudged the whole question of exactly what Canada's war effort would be. "We stand for the defence of Canada," he had declared. "We stand for the co-operation of this country on the side of Britain!"

What exactly did that mean? Woodsworth wanted to know. King had talked vaguely about standing with Great Britain to the last man, but he had also promised there would be no conscrip-

501

tion in Canada. Well, what did that mean? Was the country going to send an expeditionary force or wasn't it? King had carefully slipped round that issue.

"We do not know," Woodsworth pointed out, "whether or not wealth is to be conscripted. If we are to stand to the very last man in this country . . . wealth should be conscripted before men are conscripted."

He reminded the House that King himself had attacked the Bennett government for giving a "blank cheque" (King's words) for the relief of the unemployed. "But in the speech today we are asked to give a blank cheque to the government. So far the Prime Minister has not enlightened us in any detail as to what the policy of the government is to be."

As Woodsworth continued, a veil of silence fell across the House, for now he was speaking personally as the Conscience of Parliament. He had no intention of departing for an instant from a lifetime's conviction for the sake of popularity or political gain.

"I would ask: did the last war settle anything? I venture to say that it settled nothing; and the next war into which we are asked to enter, however big and bloody it may be, is not going to settle anything either. That is not the way in which settlements are brought about.

"While we are urged to fight for freedom and democracy, it should be remembered that war is the very negation of both. The victor may win; but if he does, it is by adopting the self-same tactics which he condemns in his enemy. . . . As one who has tried for a good many years to take a stand for the common people, personally I cannot give my consent to anything that will drag us into another war."

The common people! Coming from Woodsworth's lips the phrase did not sound hackneyed. All of his years here in the Commons he had fought for commoners – for the Communists (whom he loathed) driven to prison by an unspeakable law; for the single jobless banished to the slave camps; for the boxcar cowboys riding the freights, beaten by the police; for the helpless victims of the Padlock Law; for the hungry children, deprived of proper nutrition by an unheeding government; for the union organizers, the maverick clergymen, the dust-bowl housewives, and all the desperate men and women who wrote him letters or met

502

him in back-kitchens and on railway sidings in small towns and poured out their anguish and anger because they trusted him to bring their case before the bar of the House.

Absolute silence now, as he continued.

"I do not care whether you think me an impossible idealist or a dangerous crank. I am going to take my place beside the children . . . because it is only as we adopt new policies that this world will be at all a liveable place for our children who follow us. We laud the courage of those who go to the front; yes, I have boys of my own and I hope they are not cowards, but if any of those boys, not from cowardice but really through belief, is willing to take his stand on this matter and, if necessary, to face a concentration camp or a firing squad, I shall be more proud of that boy than if he enlisted for the war."

"Shame!" cried George Tustin, a Tory from Napanee. In the words of Woodsworth's daughter, that was no more than "a little stone that rolled away into the cavern of stillness where men sat alone with their thoughts." No one answered. A hush of respect still hung like a pall over the House as Woodsworth finished.

That speech marked the end of an era - not only for the CCF, which lost its innocence, but also for the nation. It was the last crusading speech of the decade, the speech of an "impossible idealist," and even as the speaker took his seat, the echoes of that decade reverberated through the House. Woodsworth stood as the human symbol of the best of the thirties. Now his long political career was ended. The other symbols of that bitter and violent era, in which the people were so badly served by their leaders, were also about to go. But the folk memories of the hunger marches, the bloody riots, the soup kitchens, the black blizzards, the Bennett buggies, the grasshoppers, the relief depots, the police truncheons, the sit-ins and lockouts, and all the populist Messiahs who promised so much and delivered so little - these would linger on in the subconscious of those who survived.

On that day, September 8, Parliament declared that a state of war existed between Canada and Nazi Germany. On that day, the Great Depression can be said to have ended. For war, which would bring mutilation and death, would also bring jobs. There would be jobs in the munitions plants and the shipyards for women who had been kept out of the workforce by the Depression. There would be jobs in the services for men who had once ridden the freights and begged for handouts. There would be jobs even for teenagers and old men. Suddenly a country that had been unable to provide work for a fifth of its people found work for all. The chronicle of the Great Depression is a catalogue of ironies, but that is the bitterest irony of all.

Afterword
The first convoy

December 10, 1939: a cold, raw Sunday in Halifax, the harbour a-bustle with wartime shipping. The five big luxury liners stand out in the soft mist, their former dazzle erased by the camouflage of war, their prows now as grey as the ocean itself.

Here is the *Empress of Britain*, the vessel that brought Baldwin and Chamberlain to Canada in 1932, in the days when R.B. Bennett believed a new trade agreement could solve the country's economic problems. Beside her rides the *Duchess of Bedford*, which had brought remnants of the Mackenzie-Papineau Battalion home. The *Empress of Australia*, which took Mackenzie King to the Coronation and brought George VI to Canada, forms part of the convoy as does the *Monarch of Bermuda*. And the oldest ship of all, the venerable four-stacker *Aquitania*, which had served as a troopship in the first war, is serving again in the second, reprieved from the scrap heap at the last moment.

Half of the Canadian First Division – seventy-five hundred men, including their new commander, Major-General Andrew McNaughton – is already on board. The other half is to follow in a second convoy a week later. The Depression is winding down as Canada girds up for war.

> *We must pause and consider before embark-*
> *ing on enterprises calling for the expenditure*
> *of large sums of money.*
> – R.B. Bennett, in 1931

Suddenly, the government was offering to pay a living wage to those who were willing to risk their lives for their country. What eighteen-year-old Fred LeBlanc was earning was scarcely a living wage; as a stock boy at Northern Electric in Montreal, he was paid five dollars a week. He joined up in the first week of September, but when he went home to Point St. Charles, his mother was aghast.

505

"You silly ass!" she said. "You're the only one in the family working." So she sent Fred's jobless twenty-two-year-old brother, Leon, to take Fred's place and claim the army pay. (Leon told the army his middle name was Fred.)

All during the Depression the LeBlanc family had existed mainly on relief. With Fred's weekly five dollars and Leon's army pay as a private in the 9th Field Ambulance ($1.30 a day, seven days a week) their total income would magically triple. Now Leon was aboard the *Aquitania*, leaving the Depression behind.

McNaughton had his headquarters on the same ship. Through the accident of war, men who had once lived under quasi-military conditions in McNaughton's relief camps found themselves again under his command. The government had once paid them twenty cents a day and treated them as bums. Now it was paying six and a half times as much and treating them as heroes.

When Robert Humphrey from Scarborough, Ontario, another First Division volunteer, got his first army cheque, he couldn't believe his eyes. He would, he said later, have liked to frame it, but he needed the money for his family. His father had been out of work for the whole of the Depression. His mother and one of his sisters were in hospital. He himself had worked only intermittently; as an office clerk, he was paid six dollars a week. Now he discovered that by joining the army – again as a clerk – he'd been handed a 50-per-cent raise by a government that once insisted it could pay for no more than subsistence.

Bob Humphrey was one of fifty-eight thousand Canadians who rushed to the colours in the month of September, 1939. Some joined for reasons of patriotism or duty, others to escape the boredom and despair of those days. Large numbers had no choice: relief officials were loath to give "handouts" to able-bodied men of military age. But many were attracted by the money and the security.

In addition to their daily $1.30, Humphrey, LeBlanc, and the others got free food and shelter, clothing, and medical and dental service (including free spectacles and false teeth if they needed them). The wives of their married friends received a separate sixty dollars a month and twelve dollars additional for each child. Nation-wide medicare and family allowances – the heritage of the Depression – were still in the future, but the armed services already had them.

506

*It is my firm conviction that any effort to
raise from the Canadian people by taxation
any sum in excess of $400 million is to put
upon them a strain they cannot bear.*
　　　　　　 - R.B. Bennett in opposition, 1936

The country found it *could* bear the strain. At the peak of the war effort, more than two million men and women were being supported by public money, as many as had been publicly supported at the height of the Depression.

But shipyard and munitions workers, and even office staff in the public service, were dealt with far more generously than those who had eked out their existence on relief. In Montreal, in 1933, a family of four received a weekly relief voucher worth just $4.58. In 1943, a single female junior in a government weather office was paid more than four times that amount.

King and Bennett had been convinced that Canada did not have the resources to initiate either a more generous policy of relief or pump-priming through a program of public works. Bennett had specifically told Arthur Evans, during their acrimonious encounter in 1935, that a policy of "work and wages" was beyond the capacity of the country. Wartime spending underscored the hollowness of that faint-hearted attitude. The country had had the resources and the capacity to harness them. What had been lacking was the kind of commitment that wartime conditions made more attractive politically.

The sudden infusion of public funds solved the unemployment problem. In the fall of 1939, the jobless rate had still exceeded 10 per cent. By the next fall it had dropped to the rock bottom figure of 4 per cent. The bidding for labour became so intense that the government was forced to put a ban on help-wanted ads.

Four hundred million dollars had seemed a terrifying amount to Bennett. But in 1943, when the men of the first contingent finally went into action, the Canadian government spent four and a half *billion* dollars on the war; and everybody was better off.

*The mad desire to bring about state control
and interference beyond all bounds makes
one shudder.*
　　　　　　 - Mackenzie King, commenting on
　　　　　　 　 Roosevelt's New Deal in 1933

507

Once war had come, Ottawa could no longer maintain the hands-off policies that were part of its Depression philosophy. The new Ministry of Munitions and Supply under C.D. Howe was about to make the government itself Big Business. Of the seventy-five hundred men who climbed the gangplanks of the troopships that December day at Halifax, singing "Roll Out the Barrel," at least half were raw recruits. Their equipment was shoddy, worn out, obsolete. The Lee-Enfield rifles had seen service in the last war; the old Lewis light machine-gun had yet to be replaced by the more efficient Bren. Some recruits were lucky enough to be issued with the new battledress. Others wore First War uniforms or their own trousers. Successive governments had been as niggardly with the armed forces as they had been with the unemployed.

Now the penny-pinching was at an end. That very Monday, December 11, the press announced that federal revenues were soaring because of the increase in wartime business. The turnaround had occurred in just three months. In that period the government itself had spent forty-eight million dollars on war supplies.

For the embarkees, the new attitude was symbolized by the gleaming silver and fresh linen on the tables in the cabin-class dining rooms where the ordinary soldiers ate. Here the meals and service were identical with those enjoyed by the privileged few who had been able to afford crossing the Atlantic in pre-war days. This time, however, the government was footing the bill and paying full fare. Young men who had never seen a fish knife now found themselves sitting down to seven-course meals served beneath crystal chandeliers.

When Leon LeBlanc took his seat in the *Aquitania*'s dining room and saw the menu, he felt like a millionaire. Fish for breakfast! Duck for dinner! "Oh boy," he thought, as white-jacketed waiters with napkins on their arms scurried to serve him, "this war's all right." Some of the men insisted on tipping their stewards, like old transatlantic hands.

There was no crowd on hand to see them off; no reporters gushed over the leavetaking. The convoy left under a blanket of wartime secrecy. On the morning of the tenth, a small ceremony took place in the *Aquitania*'s lounge. McNaughton spoke briefly. A farewell telegram from the Prime Minister declared: "The

508

hearts of the people of Canada are with you." Prayers were murmured, McNaughton's official flag (a white ensign with red maple leaves and gold fleurs-de-lis) was dedicated. Then, at noon, the leading liner, *Duchess of Bedford*, moved off from the jetty and the convoy got under way.

> *In stating last night that the additional outlay*
> *for relief and employment will come to some*
> *50 millions, I find that I was 25 millions short.*
> *This is an appalling sum. . . .*
> – Mackenzie King, in 1936

The week's voyage across the Atlantic cost the Canadian government more than two million dollars in fares alone. (The second convoy a week later would rack up a similar cost.) The big liners, steaming out of Halifax harbour at half-hour intervals into the calm Atlantic, were encircled by their escorts: four Canadian destroyers (two-thirds of the country's pitiful fleet of six) and four British warships, the battleship *Resolution*, aircraft carrier *Furious*, battle cruiser *Repulse*, and cruiser *Emerald*.

There was only one untoward incident. On the final night at sea, an American vessel, *Samaria*, blundered into the zigzagging convoy, striking *Furious* on her starboard side and *Aquitania* on her port. The only serious damage was done to McNaughton's spanking-new Buick staff car. Lashed to the forward deck, it was pierced by a flying davit from a smashed lifeboat.

The following morning, the troops crowding the decks could see the low, snow-covered hills of the Clydeside looming through a fine mist. The Canadian destroyer escort had long since returned to Halifax. Now a welcoming fleet of twelve British warships, including *Hood* and *Warspite*, took over.

A crowd of thousands rushed to the shore as the convoy approached. No one was sure what the ships were carrying (wartime censorship was thorough), but the spectators sensed it was something important. It was generally believed that there were British soldiers aboard, returning from France for Christmas leave. Dimly, in the distance, the spectators began to see hundreds of khaki-clad figures cramming the decks of the leading liner, *Aquitania*. The sound of voices carried above the cry of the gulls, but it wasn't until the vessel came near the quayside at Greenock that the people on shore realized what was happening.

The first voice heard was distinctly Canadian. "Hail, hail, the gang's all here," somebody called. "What the hell do we care now?"

With secrecy blown, a reporter for the *Daily Express* wrote that "a burst of laughter sent the inquisitive gulls shrieking and circling high. Then more solemnly, and with no false modesty, the voices invoked their anthem: 'O Canada! We stand on guard for thee.' "

> *I tried . . . to get the Party to see . . . how impossible it was to solve the problem [of unemployment] through Government action.*
> – Mackenzie King, in 1938

It would be almost six years before the survivors of that first contingent returned to their home and native land. Like everybody else in the division, Leon LeBlanc didn't see action until the summer of 1943; then, as a medical orderly, he saw too much. When his transport was torpedoed off the coast of Africa, he suffered burns to the chest and legs before taking part in the campaigns in Sicily and Italy (including the famous Christmas attack on Ortona) and later in the Netherlands during the 1944 Continental campaign.

He returned home in the summer of 1945 to a different kind of country. In spite of Mackenzie King's assurance, Big Government and the Welfare State had arrived. Everybody was working. Unemployment insurance was in place. A massive amount of public money was being spent on the kind of projects that Bennett and King had dismissed as impracticable and extravagant. Leon LeBlanc's eyes widened at the number of cars on the street. The people, he noted, "looked a lot more cheerful – not desperate like they were before."

Leon LeBlanc went to night school, learned the plumber's trade, and got a job without any trouble. When he married in 1946, he was earning twenty-five dollars a week. By then Wilfrid Laurier's words were again being invoked. To a new generation, this was indeed Canada's Century. The Bennett buggy was an artifact from the past, the soup kitchen a folk memory, the hobo jungle as obsolete as the village smithy. Instead of existing on the dole, Canadians were about to enjoy family allowances, workmen's compensation, and old age security – all legacies from that

510

dark and dismal decade when compassion was a luxury and deliverance an impossible dream.

It was over and done with – the Great Depression that had brought so much heartache and despair but had changed the political face of the nation. It had scarred an entire generation. Now it was history.

Author's Note

A great many books have been published covering various aspects of the Great Depression in Canada. We have had scholarly studies; economic, political, social, and oral histories; statistical analyses; personal memoirs and reminiscences; biographies; reports, theses, and learned papers. In addition, most of the more dramatic moments of the decade, ranging from the On-to-Ottawa trek to the adventures of volunteers in the Spanish Civil War, have been recounted by the participants.

Yet there has not been a narrative history of the Depression in all its manifestations, arranged chronologically from the summer of 1929 to the autumn of 1939. This I have attempted to provide, for it seems to me that the cumulative effect of a continuing narrative is devastating. In order to keep the story within the limits of a single volume, I have had to condense, or, in some cases, omit, certain incidents that some readers will miss. That was inevitable. And if I have enlarged on certain aspects of that dismal decade and neglected others, it is because this is a personal book to which I have brought my own enthusiasms and prejudices.

Wherever possible, I have gone to standard primary sources for the main thread of the narrative. These include reports of royal commissions and other public documents (some obtained under the Access to Information Act), personal papers, unpublished manuscripts, the daily press, and some fifty personal interviews.

In a task of this complexity, it has also been necessary to lean on the spadework of others. These are identified in the Bibliography, but I should like also to name a few of those whose researches I found especially rewarding. They are Irving Abella, William Beeching, Lita-Rose Betcherman, Michael Bliss, Lorne Brown, David R. Elliott, Doug Fetherling, James Gray, Victor Hoar, Michiel Horn, John Irving, Ron Liversedge, Tom MacDonnell, Neil McKenty, Iris Miller, Blair Neatby, Barbara Roberts, James Struthers, Harold Troper, and J.H. Wilbur.

Two major sources were the files of the Winnipeg *Free Press* for the whole of the decade and the Mackenzie King Diaries from 1926 to 1939.

Few books of this kind can be the work of one man. I again want to thank the team of dedicated people who strove behind the scenes to keep me on the rails. Most of the research material was ferreted out by my wonderfully perceptive research assistant, Barbara Sears, who has worked on so many of my previous books. My editor, Janice Tyrwhitt, a hard taskmistress, forced me to rewrite certain sections over and over again; to her I am eternally grateful. My copy editor, Janet Craig, caught scores – nay hundreds – of errors of fact, grammar, spelling, and common sense, saving me from future embarrassment. I am also grateful to my wife, Janet, for her careful reading of the proofs, and my agent, Elsa Franklin, especially for her sage advice on recasting the Afterword.

Ms. Sears and I also wish to thank all the people who were kind enough to share their memories with us (their names are in the Bibliography) for the efforts they went to in bringing this decade to life for us. In addition, we should like to thank the following:

- Iqbal Wagle, Joan Links, and Judy Young Chong at Microtext, Robarts Library, University of Toronto, for their efficient and cheerful help
- the staffs of the Metropolitan Toronto Reference Library, Ontario Archives, University of Toronto Archives, and National Archives of Canada (particularly Ann Goddard for directing us to the Frank Scott Papers); Margaret Hutchison at the Saskatchewan Archives Board; Lindsay Moir at the Glenbow Museum; Frank Glass at the Rosetown Archives
- Michel Richer, Access to Information and Privacy Co-ordinator, Canadian Security and Intelligence Service, for processing several requests
- Gillian Wadsworth Minifie and Dr. James McCrorie at the Canadian Plains Research Centre, for their help and hospitality while working at the Centre in Regina
- Mr. Leonard Norris, President, Mackenzie-Papineau Veterans, for permission to consult the Ronald Liversedge Memoir of the Spanish Civil War; and the University of British Columbia Library, Special Collections Division, for supplying us with a copy of the manuscript
- Barbara Roberts, for taking the time to help with leads, and
- Canadian Broadcasting Corporation Archives for permission to listen to their collection relating to the Spanish Civil War.

514

Sources

The following are the major sources only, in abbreviated form, for the individual chapters and sections. For details, refer to the Bibliography.

OVERVIEW Background and statistics from Neatby (*The Politics of Chaos*), Struthers (*No Fault of Their Own*), Horn (*The Great Depression*), Croft, and daily press. Swanston's story is told in Pitsula. Interviews with Lara Duffy and Verdun Clark.

1929. **One**: Details of Queen's Park riot from Toronto *Mail and Empire*, supplemented by John Morgan Gray and Betcherman (*The Little Band*). **Two**: Safarian, *Canadian Annual Review*, and daily press. **Three**: Galbraith and Frederick Lewis Allen (*Only Yesterday*); Fetherling; *Montreal Star*; Toronto *Star*; *Financial Post*; Manitoba *Free Press*. **Four**: The works of Strong-Boag; various articles in *Maclean's* and *Chatelaine*. Other details from daily press and *Canadian Annual Review*.

1930. **One**: King Diaries, Hansard (House of Commons Debates), and daily press. **Two**: Various biographies of King by Ferns and Ostry, Neatby, Esberey, Stacey, and Hutchison as well as King Diaries. **Three**: King Diaries and daily press on the campaign; Betcherman (*The Little Band*); Beeching and Clarke on communist persecution. **Four**: Beaverbrook; MacLean; Manion; Meighen; O'Leary; Thomas, for T.C. Douglas; and King Diaries. **Five**: Betcherman (*The Little Band*) on Buck's troubles. Details of Bennett's relief program from Struthers (*No Fault of Their Own*). Also Bennett Papers, King Diaries, and daily press.

1931. **One**: Bennett Papers for Robertson, together with Roddan and daily press. **Two**: Horn (*League for Social Reconstruction*); Frank Scott Papers; Djwa on Scott; Francis on Underhill; Hansard; and daily press. **Three**: RCMP file on Woodsworth (obtained from CSIS through Access to Information Act); Ontario Attorney General's file on communism; Bennett Papers; transcript of court proceedings against Buck *et al.* plus Betcherman (*The Little Band*); Buck (*Thirty Years*); A.E. Smith; Hunter; and Toronto press. **Four** and **Five**: MacEachern on Sydney; McNeil on Glace Bay; Royal Commission Proceedings on Estevan-Bienfait; RCMP correspondence (obtained from CSIS through Access to Information Act); interviews obtained by Saskatchewan Archives Board and Canadian Broadcasting Corporation; Esteven *Mercury*; Regina *Leader*; Abella (*On Strike*). **Six**: Ontario Attorney

General's files on Communist party; Toronto *Star*: *Mail and Empire*; Betcherman (*The Little Band*).

1932. **One**: Whitton's correspondence and reports, from Bennett Papers; Struthers; 1932 Report of Halifax Citizens' Committee on Housing (from 1931 Census). **Two**: Roberts, Drystek, Rasporich. **Three**: Personal interviews and unpublished manuscripts from Drouin, Mavis, Mitchell, Sherwin, Zacher, and others listed in Bibliography; McNaughton Papers; Swettenham. **Four**: Major newspapers; Beaverbrook; Horn (*League for Social Reconstruction*); MacInnis. **Five**: Ryan (*Tim Buck*); Beeching and Clarke; Withrow; *Report* of Royal Commission to Investigate the Penal System.

1933. **One**: Bennett Papers; Hansard; daily press. Lendrum told his story in *Maclean's*. **Two**: Personal interviews and daily press. Saskatoon *Star-Phoenix* for Bates. **Three**: Personal interviews and correspondence with nine major participants; Robert Thompson manuscript (soon to be published). **Four**: Sinclair's syndicated newspaper stories; King Diaries. **Five**: Djwa; Walter Young; daily press; interviews with several of the founders of the LSR, notably Eugene Forsey. **Six**: Irving, and the Irving Papers (where the subjects are identified by name); Elliott and Miller's definitive biography, *Bible Bill*.

1934. **One**: Bennett Papers; Toronto *Star*; A.E. Smith; Tim Buck (*Thirty Years*). **Two**: Irving; Elliott and Miller; Edmonton *Journal* for Brownlee trial. **Three** *Proceedings* of Special Committee on Price Spreads; background on Stevens from Wilbur. **Four**: James Gray (*Men Against the Desert*); Etha Munro's story in *Western Producer*; Brown and Scott's newspaper series in Winnipeg *Free Press*; Istrati. **Five**: King Diaries; Toronto *Star*; McKenty. **Six**: Bennett Papers; Grayson and Bliss (this excellent collection disguises the names; I have used the real ones). **Seven**: McNaughton Papers; Bennett Papers; Plains Research Centre's On to Ottawa Trek Conference; Bouchette in Vancouver *Sun*; Struthers (*No Fault of Their Own*): Swettenham.

1935. **One**: Daily press; Forster and Read; Wilbur (*The Bennett New Deal*); King Diaries. **Two**: *Proceedings and Evidence* of Royal Commission on Price Spreads; Toronto newspapers for January and February. **Three**: McNaughton Papers; Bennett Papers; Vancouver *Sun* and *Province*; Liversedge; Brown (*When Freedom Was Lost*); Swankey and Sheils; Cook (*Politics of Discontent*); Sean Griffin; interviews with Brodie and Salsberg. **Four**: Bennett Papers; daily papers; Brown; Howard; Liversedge; Sean Griffin. **Five**: Testimony before the Regina Riot Inquiry Commission; Bennett Papers; Hoar; Brown; Howard; interviews with Brodie,

Shaparla, Mary Rothecker. **Six**: Edmonton *Journal*; King Diaries; Elliott and Miller; Wilbur ("The Bennett Administration").

1936. **One**: Toronto *Star*; Elliott and Miller; King Diaries. **Two**: Toronto *Star*; James Gray (*Men Against the Desert*); Braithwaite; Williams; T.C. Douglas ("Highlights of the Dirty Thirties," mimeographed pamphlet); files of Canadian Red Cross at Saskatchewan Archives Board. **Three**: Woodsworth Papers; Sise Papers; Montreal *Gazette* and *Star*; Djwa; Hoar (*The Mackenzie-Papineau Battalion*); Conrad Black. **Four**: Toronto *Star*; Dodd; Stortz and Eaton; Reed; Stephenson; Claris Silcox in *Canadian Forum*, May 1937; Hutton on Millar will. **Five**: King Diaries.

1937. **One**: Transcript of proceedings of Mackenzie-Papineau Battalion Conference, Canadian Plains Research Centre; Beeching (*Canadian Volunteers*). **Two**: Liversedge (unpublished memoir). **Three**: Hepburn Papers; *Globe and Mail*, Toronto *Star*; Abella (*On Strike* and "The CIO"); McKenty. **Four**: King Diaries. **Five**: Bailey; Braithwaite; James Gray (*Men Against the Desert*). **Six**: Elliott and Miller; *Canadian Forum*; Montreal *Gazette* and *Star*; Bulletins of the Canadian Civil Liberties Association in Frank Scott Papers.

1938. **One**: King Diaries; Struthers (*No Fault of Their Own*); Chambers. **Two**: Scott Papers; *Canadian Forum*; Woodsworth in Hansard, Muni Taub interview; Montreal press. **Three**: My essay "Bloody Sunday in Vancouver" in *My Country*; Vancouver press; interviews with Brodie and Robert S.S. Wilson; Sean Griffin. **Four**: CSIS files; King Diaries; Toronto *Star*; Betcherman (*The Swastika and the Maple Leaf*). **Five**: Abella and Troper; King Diaries.

1939. **One**: Frank Scott Papers; my profile of McCullagh in *Maclean's*; Brian Young; King Diaries; *Globe and Mail*. **Two**: Gregory Clark in Toronto *Star*; transcript of proceedings of Mackenzie-Papineau Battalion Conference, Canadian Plains Research Centre; Hoar (*The Mackenzie-Papineau Battalion*); Beeching (*Canadian Volunteers*). **Three**: King Diaries; MacDonnell; daily newspapers. **Four**: McNaught; MacInnis; Walter Young; King Diaries; Hansard.

AFTERWORD. Statistics from Department of National Defence; daily press on business boom; interviews with Humphrey and LeBlanc; Swettenham.

Bibliography

Archival Sources

Canadian Broadcasting Corporation Archives
Interviews with Alex Chambers; Milton Cohen; Frank Hadesbeck; Mike Hyduk; Paddy McElligott; Zack McEwen; Henry Meyer; Leonard Norris; Jules Paivio; Marvin Penn; Frank Roden; Ross Russell; Joseph Salsburg.

Canadian Plains Research Centre, Regina
On to Ottawa Trek Conference, 1985. Tape recordings of proceedings.

Mackenzie-Papineau Battalion Conference, 1984. Transcripts of proceedings.

Canadian Security and Intelligence Service
Adrien Arcand files (not numbered)
Arthur Evans files, 175/P1072
Estevan riot, files HV7, 1–7
J.S. Woodsworth file (not numbered)
National Unity Party files (not numbered)

National Archives
R.B. Bennett Papers MG 26K
Joseph Frank Papers MG 31 H69, vol. 1
Ernest Lapointe Papers MG 27 III B10, vol. 28
William Lyon Mackenzie King Diaries, 1926–1939
Mackenzie-Papineau Battalion Papers MG 30 E173
A.G.L. McNaughton Papers MG 30 E133 Ser. II
Frank Scott Papers MG 30 D211
Hazen Sise Papers MG 30 D187
J.S. Woodsworth Papers MG 27 III C7

Ontario Archives
RG 3 Mitchell Hepburn Papers
RG 4 Attorney General's files, MS 367, reels 36–38, Communist Party of Canada

Saskatchewan Archives Board
Red Cross files, SHS 101
Regina Riot Inquiry Commission, Records.
Royal Commission on the Estevan-Bienfait Mining Dispute, 1931, record of proceedings.
Interviews with Howard Babcock; Pete Gembey; W.D.MacKay; Harry Nicholson.

Thomas Fisher Rare Book Library, University of Toronto
John Irving Papers

University of British Columbia Library
Liversedge, Ronald. "A Memoir of the Spanish Civil War" (unpublished paper).

University of Toronto Archives
Harry Cassidy Papers

Government Documents

Census, 1931.

House of Commons Debates [Hansard], 1929–1939, *passim.*

National Employment Commission, *Final Report.* Ottawa: King's Printer, 1938.

National Employment Commission, *Interim Report.* Ottawa: King's Printer, 1937.

Royal Commission on Dominion-Provincial Relations, *Report*, Books 1 & 2. Ottawa: 1940.

Royal Commission to Investigate the Penal System in Canada, *Report.* Ottawa: King's Printer, 1938.

Royal Commission on Price Spreads, *Minutes of Proceedings and Evidence.* Ottawa: King's Printer, 1935.

Royal Commission on Price Spreads, *Report.* Ottawa: King's Printer, 1937.

Special Committee on Price Spreads and Mass Buying, *Proceedings and Evidence.* Ottawa: King's Printer, 1934.

Newspapers

Calgary *Herald*, December 1929, July/August 1932
Edmonton *Journal,* June 1931
Financial Post, January, July-December 1929
Globe (Toronto), December 1929, January 1935
Globe and Mail (Toronto), March-April 1937, Jan.-March 1939
Halifax *Herald*, December 1929, January 1933
Le Patriote, March 1934
Mail and Empire (Toronto), 1929, 1931, July 1933
Mercury (Estevan), 1931, 1932
Montreal *Gazette*, January, September-December 1929
Regina *Leader*, January and December 1929
Regina *Leader-Post*, September-October 1931, December 1933, March 1934
Saskatoon *Star-Phoenix*, December 1933, March 1934
Toronto Daily Star, 1929–1939
Toronto *Evening Telegram*, July 1933, January 1935
Vancouver *Daily Province*, 1938
Vancouver *Sun*, December 1929
Manitoba, later Winnipeg *Free Press*, 1929–1939

520

Magazines

Canadian Annual Review, 1929, 1930
Canadian Forum, 1929–1939
Chatelaine, 1929–1935
Life, 18 July 1938
Maclean's, 1929–1935
Saturday Night, 1929

Personal Interviews

John Archer; Harry Auld; Edward and Ruth Barker; Robert Barr; William and Elsie Beeching; Mike Bevan; Gordon Bongard; George Bothwell; Steve Brodie; Humphrey Carver; Verdun Clark; John Clyne; William Cook; E.M. Culliton; Rosella Diduck; Robert Drouin; Lara Duffy; James Ealey; Eugene Forsey; Peter Frankham; Tom Gallagher; Wilfred Gardiner; William and Anne Gilbey; King Gordon; Gordon Hogarth; Ken John; Henry Kanis; Eloff Kellner; William Krehm; John Langille; Blanche Lovely; Donald McLay; Dan Magee; Ed Mirvish; W.O. Mitchell; Claire Morrison; Eileen Nye; Joe Parkinson; Glenn Petersen; J. Lyman Potts; Albert Reid; Mary Rothecker; Mitch Sago; Willis Shaparla; Matthew Shaw; Charles Sherwin; Irene Spry; Allan Stapelton; Kathleen Stratton; Muni Taub; Charles Templeton; Gilma Williams; Edna Wilson; Robert S. Wilson; Joe Zacher.

Unpublished Manuscripts

Ewen, Jean. "You Can't Buy it Back." 1974.

Friess, Lorna. "The Unionizing of the Estevan Coal-Miners." March 1976.

Irving, John Allan. "A Canadian Fabian, The Life and Work of Harry Cassidy." Unpublished thesis, University of Toronto.

John, Ken. Memoirs.

Joliffe, Kyle. "Penitentiary Medical Services, 1835–1983." Ottawa: Ministry of the Solicitor General of Canada, Secretariat. 1984.

LeFresne, G.M. "The Royal Twenty Centers: the Department of National Defence and Federal Unemployment Relief 1932–1936." Unpublished thesis, Royal Military College.

Liversedge, Ronald. "A Memoir of the Spanish Civil War," *see* University of British Columbia Library.

Mavis, Harry. "Vancouver to Halifax by Side-door Pullman."

Sherwin, Charles. "Boxcar Cowboy."

Thompson, Robert H. "Memories of Saskatoon in the 1930s."

Zacher, Joe. "The Rod-Riders of the Dirty and Hungry Thirties."

Published Sources

Abella, Irving. "The CIO, the Communist Party and the Formation of the Canadian Labour Congress 1936-1941," *Canadian Historical Association Papers*, 1969.

—— (ed). *On Strike: Six Key Labour Struggles in Canada 1919-1949*. Toronto: James Lorimer, 1975.

——, and Troper, Harold. *None Is Too Many: Canada and the Jews of Europe, 1933-1948*. Toronto: Lester & Orpen Dennys, 1982.

Allan, Ted, and Gordon, Sydney. *The Scalpel, the Sword: The Story of Dr. Norman Bethune*. Toronto: McClelland and Stewart, 1971 (reprint).

Allen, Frederick Lewis. *Only Yesterday*. New York: Harper & Brothers, 1957 (reprint).

——. *Since Yesterday*. New York: Bantam Books, 1939.

Allen, Ralph. *Ordeal by Fire: Canada 1910-1945*. Toronto: Doubleday, 1961.

Alway, Richard M.H. "Hepburn, King and the Rowell-Sirois Commission," *Canadian Historical Review* 48, no.2, 1967.

Anon. *Canadian Problems. . . .* Toronto: Oxford University Press, [1933].

Anon. "Experiences of a Depression Hobo," *Saskatchewan History* 22, 1969.

Anon. *Not Guilty! The Verdict of a Worker's Jury*. Toronto: Canadian Labour Defence League, [1932].

Avery, Donald H. "British-born 'Radicals' in North America, 1900-1941: The Case of Sam Scarlett," *Canadian Ethnic Studies* 10, no.2, 1978.

Bailey, A.W. "The Year We Moved," *Saskatchewan History* 20, 1967.

Beaverbrook, Lord. *Friends: Sixty Years of Intimate Personal Relations with Richard Bedford Bennett. . . .* Toronto: Heinemann, 1959.

Beeching, William C. *Canadian Volunteers Spain, 1936-1939*. Regina: Canadian Plains Research Centre, 1989.

——, and Clarke, Phyllis (eds.). *Yours in the Struggle: Reminiscences of Tim Buck*. Toronto: NC Press, 1977.

Berton, Pierre. *My Country*. Toronto: McClelland and Stewart, 1976.

——. "The Amazing Career of George McCullagh," *Maclean's*, 15 January 1949.

Betcherman, Lita-Rose. *The Little Band*. Ottawa: Deneau, 198[2].

——. *The Swastika and the Maple Leaf: Fascist Movements in Canada in the Thirties*. Toronto: Fitzhenry & Whiteside, c1975.

Black, Conrad. *Duplessis*. Toronto: McClelland and Stewart, 1977.

Black, H. "The Saskatchewan Plan," *Proceedings of the Fourth Biennial Meeting, Canadian Conference on Social Work*, 1934.

Bliss, Michael. *A Canadian Millionaire: The Life and Business Times of Sir Joseph Flavelle, Bart., 1858-1939*. Toronto: Macmillan of Canada, 1978.

———. *Northern Enterprise: Five Centuries of Canadian Business*. Toronto: McClelland and Stewart, 1987.

Braithwaite, Max. "The Year It Didn't Rain," *Maclean's*, 19 March 1958.

Britnell, G.E. "Saskatchewan, 1930-1935," *Canadian Journal of Economics and Political Science* 2, no.2, 1936.

———. *The Wheat Economy*. Toronto: University of Toronto Press, 1939.

Broadfoot, Barry. *Ten Lost Years, 1929-1939: Memories of Canadians Who Survived the Depression*. Toronto: Doubleday, 1973.

Brown, Lorne. "Unemployment Relief Camps in Saskatchewan, 1933-1936," *Saskatchewan History* 23, 1970.

———. *When Freedom Was Lost*. Montreal: Black Rose Books, 1987.

———, and Brown, Caroline. *An Unauthorized History of the RCMP*. Toronto: James Lorimer, 1973.

Buck, Tim. *An Indictment of Capitalism*. Toronto: Canadian Labor Defense League, [1932].

———. *Thirty Years, The Story of the Communist Movement in Canada, 1922-1952*. Toronto: Progress Books, [1952].

Caplan, Gerald L. "The Failure of Canadian Socialism: The Ontario Experience, 1932-45," *Canadian Historical Review* 44, no.2, 1963.

Cassidy, Harry. "Relief Works as a Remedy for Unemployment in the Light of Ontario Experience, 1930-1932," in *Papers and Proceedings of the Fourth Annual Meeting of the Canadian Political Science Association*, 1932.

———. *Unemployment and Relief in Ontario, 1929-1932*. Toronto: J.M. Dent & Sons, [1932].

———, Heakes, A.G, and Jackson, G.E. "The Extent of Unemployment in Canada 1929-1932," in *Papers and Proceedings of the Fourth Annual Meeting of the Canadian Political Science Association*, 1932.

Chakravarti, A.K. "Precipitation Deficiency Patterns in the Canadian Prairies 1921 to 1970," *Prairie Forum* 1, no.2, 1976.

Chambers, Edward J. "The 1937-8 Recession in Canada," *Canadian Journal of Economics and Political Science* 21, no.3, 1955.

Clark, S.D. "The Religious Sect in Canadian Politics," *American Journal of Sociology* 51, no.3, 1945.

Cochrane, Ken (ed.). *Towards a New Past. Volume III: An Oral History of Industrial Unrest in the Estevan Bienfait Coalfields*. Regina: Department of Culture and Youth, Government of Saskatchewan, 1975.

Cook, Ramsay (ed.). *The Politics of Discontent*. Toronto: University of Toronto Press, 1967.

———. *The Politics of John W. Dafoe and the* Free Press. Toronto: University of Toronto Press, 1963.

Croft, Frank. "How Did We Ever Get Through the Depression?" *Maclean's*, 9 April 1960.

Diefenbaker, John G. *One Canada: Memoirs of the Right Honourable John G. Diefenbaker, The Crusading Years, 1895-1956*. Toronto: Macmillan of Canada, 1975.

Djwa, Sandra. *The Politics of the Imagination: The Life of F.R. Scott*. Toronto: McClelland and Stewart, 1987.

Dodd, Dianne. "The Canadian Birth Control Movement on Trial, 1936-37," *Social History* 16, no.32, 1983.

———. "The Hamilton Birth Control Clinic of the 1930s," *Ontario History* 75, no.1, 1983.

Donnelly, Murray. *Dafoe of the Free Press*. Toronto: Macmillan of Canada, 1968.

Drystek, Henry. "The Simplest and Cheapest Mode of Dealing with Them, Deportation from Canada before World War II," *Histoire Sociale* 30, November 1982.

Eayrs, James. *In Defence of Canada: From the Great War to the Great Depression*. Toronto: University of Toronto Press, 1964.

———. "A Low Dishonest Decade: Aspects of Canadian External Policy, 1931-1939," in Keenleyside, Hugh (ed.), *The Growth of Canadian Policies in External Affairs*. Durham: Duke University Press, 1960.

Edwards, Frederick. "Fascism in Canada," *Maclean's*, 15 April 1938 and 1 May 1938.

Eggleston, Wilfrid. "What of the Drought Area?" *Dalhousie Review* 17, 1937-1938.

———. *While I Still Remember: A Personal Record*. Toronto: Ryerson Press, 1968.

Elliott, David R. "Antithetical Elements in William Aberhart's Theology and Political Ideology," *Canadian Historical Review* 59, no.1, 1978.

———, and Miller, Iris. *Bible Bill: A Biography of William Aberhart*. Edmonton: Reidmore Books, 1987.

Esberey, Joy. *Knight of the Holy Spirit: A Study of William Lyon Mackenzie King*. Toronto: University of Toronto Press, 1980.

524

Ewen, Jean. *China Nurse*. Toronto: McClelland and Stewart, 1981.

Ewen, Tom, *see* McEwen, Tom.

Ferguson, G.V. *John W. Dafoe*. Toronto: Ryerson Press, 1948.

Ferns, Henry, and Ostry, Bernard. *The Age of Mackenzie King*. Toronto: James Lorimer, 1976.

Fetherling, Doug. *Gold Diggers of 1929*. Toronto: Macmillan of Canada, 1979.

Finkel, Alvin. "Alberta Social Credit Reappraised: The Radical Character of the Early Social Credit Movement," *Prairie Forum* 11, no.1, 1986.

———. "Social Credit and the Unemployed," *Alberta History* 31, no.2, 1983.

———. *The Social Credit Phenomenon in Alberta*. Toronto: University of Toronto Press, 1989.

Forsey, Eugene. *Freedom and Order: Collected Essays*. Toronto: McClelland and Stewart, 1974.

Forster, Donald, and Read, Colin. "The Politics of Opportunism: The New Deal Broadcasts," *Canadian Historical Review* 60, no.3, 1979.

Francis, R.D., and Ganzevoort, H. (eds.). *The Dirty Thirties in Prairie Canada*. Vancouver: Tantalus Research Ltd., 1980.

Francis, R. Douglas. *Frank H. Underhill, Intellectual Provocateur*. Toronto: University of Toronto Press, 1986.

Galbraith, John Kenneth. *The Great Crash*. New York: Andre Deutsch, 1980.

Garner, Hugh. *One Damn Thing After Another*. Toronto: McGraw-Hill Ryerson, 1973.

George, Isabelle. "Back-to-the-land Settlement in the Moose Mountains in the 1930s," *Saskatchewan History* 33, 1980.

Gibbon, John Murray. *Canadian Mosaic: The Making of a Northern Nation*. Toronto: McClelland and Stewart, 1938.

Gordon, King. "King Gordon Remembers F.R. Scott," *Saturday Night*, July 1985.

Gray, James. *Men Against the Desert*. Saskatoon: Western Producer Prairie Books, 1967.

———. *The Winter Years: The Depression on the Prairies*. Toronto: Macmillan of Canada, 1966.

Gray, John. "The Day a Whole Generation Went Broke," *Maclean's*, 15 October 1954.

Gray, John Morgan. *Fun Tomorrow: Learning to be a Publisher and Much Else*. Toronto: Macmillan of Canada, 1978.

Grayson, L.M., and Bliss, Michael (eds.). *The Wretched of Canada*. Toronto: University of Toronto Press, 1971.

Griffin, Frederick. *Variety Show*. Toronto: Macmillan of Canada, 1936.

Griffin, Sean (ed.). *Fighting Heritage*. Vancouver: Tribune Publishing Co. Ltd. [1985].

Harkness, Ross. *J.E. Atkinson of the Star*. Toronto: University of Toronto Press, 1963.

Heaps, Leo. *The Rebel in the House: The Life and Times of A.A. Heaps, M.P.* Toronto: Fitzhenry & Whiteside, [1984].

Higley, Dahn D. *O.P.P.: The History of the Ontario Provincial Police*. Toronto: Queen's Printer, 1984.

Hoar, Victor (ed.). *The Great Depression*. Vancouver: Copp Clark, 1969.

——— . *The Mackenzie-Papineau Battalion: Canadian Participation in the Spanish Civil War*. Toronto: Copp Clark, [1969].

Horn, Michiel. "Free Speech within the Law," *Ontario History* 72, no.1, 1980.

——— . "The Great Depression of the 1930s in Canada," *Canadian Historical Association Booklet No. 39*, 1984.

——— . *The League for Social Reconstruction: Intellectual Origins of the Democratic Left in Canada, 1930–1942*. Toronto: University of Toronto Press, 1980.

——— (ed.). *The Dirty Thirties: Canadians in the Great Depression*. Toronto: Copp Clark, 1972.

Howard, Victor [Victor Hoar]. *We Were the Salt of the Earth*. Regina: Canadian Plains Research Centre, 1985.

Humphrey, John T. "Homes Are Not Castles," *Canadian Magazine* 91, March 1939.

Hunter, Peter. *Which Side Are You On, Boys: Life on the Canadian Left*. Toronto: Lugus Productions, 1988.

Hutchison, Bruce. *The Far Side of the Street*. Toronto: Macmillan of Canada, 1976.

——— . *The Incredible Canadian*. Toronto: Longmans, Green, 1952.

Hutton, E. "Charlie Millar's Million-Dollar Joke," *Maclean's*, 15 June 1952.

Imai, Shin. "Deportation in the Depression," *Queen's Law Journal* 7, no.1, 1981.

Irving, John. *The Social Credit Movement in Alberta*. Toronto: University of Toronto Press, 1959.

Istrati, Konrad C. *Virgin Sod*. Assiniboia: Konrad Istrati, 1986.

526

Jamieson, Stuart Marshall. *Times of Trouble: Labour Unrest and Industrial Conflict in Canada, 1900-1966*. Ottawa: Task Force on Labour Relations, 1968.

Johnson, L.P.V., and MacNutt, Ola J. *Aberhart of Alberta*. Edmonton: Co-op Press [1970].

Jones, David C. *Empire of Dust: Settling and Abandoning the Prairie Dry Belt*. Edmonton: University of Alberta Press, 1987.

————. "Fall of an Hon. Member," *Horizon Canada* 10, no.118, 1987.

Jones, Richard. "Duplessis and the Union Nationale Administration," *Canadian Historical Association Booklet No. 35*, Ottawa, 1983.

Kappele, A.P. "The Administrative Set-up for Local Welfare Services," *Proceedings of Canadian Conference on Social Work*, 1930.

Keate, Stuart. "Maurice the Magnificent," *Maclean's*, 1 September 1949.

Kesterton, W.H. *A History of Journalism in Canada*. Toronto: McClelland and Stewart, 1967.

King, Elizabeth. "The Experience of Some Canadian Cities from the Angle of the Private Agency," *Proceedings of Canadian Conference on Social Work*, 1930.

Lawton, Alma. "Relief Administration in Saskatoon during the Depression," *Saskatchewan History* 22, 1969.

Leach, James D. "The Workers Unity League and the Stratford Furniture Workers: The Anatomy of a Strike," *Ontario History* 60, no.2, 1968.

Lendrum, Arthur. "On Relief," *Maclean's*, 1 April 1933.

Lewis, David. *The Good Fight: Political Memoirs 1909-1958*. Toronto: Macmillan of Canada, 1981.

Lipset, Seymour Martin. *Agrarian Socialism: The Co-operative Commonwealth Federation in Saskatchewan*. Berkeley: University of California Press, 1959.

Liversedge, Ronald. *Recollections of the On to Ottawa Trek*, ed. by Victor Hoar. Carleton Library no.66. Toronto: McClelland and Stewart, c1973.

Logan, H.A. "Unemployment Insurance in Canada," *Papers and Proceedings of the Fourth Annual Meeting of the Canadian Political Science Association*. 1932.

McCready, Margaret. "Relief Diets," *Proceedings of Canadian Conference on Social Work*, 1934.

MacDonnell, Tom. *Daylight Upon Magic: The Royal Tour of Canada, 1939*. Toronto: Macmillan of Canada, 1989.

MacEachern, George. *George MacEachern: An Autobiography*. Sydney: University College of Cape Breton Press, 1987.

McEwen, Tom. *The Forge Glows Red*. Toronto: Progress Books, 1974.

——— . *He Wrote for Us*. Vancouver: Tribune Publishing Company, 1951.

MacGill, Helen Gregory. "The Difference in the Pay Envelope," *Social Welfare* 11, February 1929.

MacInnis, Grace. *J.S. Woodsworth: A Man to Remember*. Toronto: Macmillan of Canada, 1953.

McKenty, Neil. "Mitchell F. Hepburn and the Ontario Election of 1934," *Canadian Historical Review* 45, no.4, 1964.

——— . *Mitch Hepburn*. Toronto: McClelland and Stewart, 1967.

Mackenzie, J.B. "Section 98, Criminal Code and Freedom of Expression in Canada," *Queen's Law Journal* 1, no. 4, 1972.

McLaren, Angus, and McLaren, Arlene Tigar. *The Bedroom and the State: The Changing Practices and Politics of Contraception and Abortion in Canada, 1880-1980*. Toronto: McClelland and Stewart, 1986.

MacLean, Andrew D. *R.B. Bennett, Prime Minister of Canada*. Toronto: Excelsior Publishing Company, 1935.

McLeod, E.S. "Shadow over Canada," *The Nation*, 12 February 1938.

McNaught, Kenneth. *A Prophet in Politics: A Biography of J.S. Woodsworth*. Toronto: University of Toronto Press, 1959.

McNeil, Bill. *Voice of the Pioneer*. Toronto: Doubleday Canada, 1988.

——— , and Wolfe, Morris. *Signing On: The Birth of Radio in Canada*. Toronto: Doubleday, 1982.

Makahonuk, Glen. "The Saskatchewan Coal Strikes of 1932: A Study in Class Relations," *Prairie Forum* 9, no.1, 1984.

——— . "The Saskatoon Relief Camp Workers Riot of May 8, 1933: An Expression of Class Conflict," *Saskatchewan History* 37, 1984.

Manion, R.J. *Life Is an Adventure*. Toronto: Ryerson Press, [1936].

Martin, David. "Adrien Arcand, fascist," *The Nation*, 26 February 1938.

Marum, Andrew, and Parise, Frank. *Follies and Foibles: A View of 20th Century Fads*. New York: Facts on File Inc., 1984.

Meighen, Arthur. *Unrevised and Unrepented: Debating Speeches and Others*. Toronto: Clarke, Irwin, 1949.

Moon, Barbara. "Aberhart, the Man and the Shadow," *Maclean's*, 15 March 1953.

Morton, W.L. *Manitoba: A History*. Toronto: University of Toronto Press, 1957.

Munro, Etha. "They Say It Couldn't Happen Again . . . " *Western Producer*, 1 April 1976.

Neatby, H. Blair. *The Politics of Chaos: Canada in the Thirties*. Toronto: Macmillan of Canada, 1972.

———. "The Saskatchewan Relief Commission, 1931–34," *Saskatchewan History* 3, 1950.

———. *William Lyon Mackenzie King, 1924–1932: The Lonely Heights*. Toronto: University of Toronto Press, 1963.

———. *William Lyon Mackenzie King, 1932–1939: The Prism of Unity*. Toronto: University of Toronto Press, [1976].

Nish, Cameron (ed.). *Quebec in the Duplessis Era, 1935–1939: Dictatorship or Democracy?* Toronto: Copp Clark, 1970.

O'Leary, Grattan. *Recollections of People, Press and Politics*. Toronto: Macmillan of Canada, 1977.

Owram, Doug. "Economic Thought in the 1930s: The Prelude to Keynesianism," *Canadian Historical Review* 66, no. 3, 1985.

Parker, Keith A. "Arthur Evans, Western Radical," *Alberta History* 26, no. 2, 1978.

Peck, Mary Biggar. *Red Moon Over Spain: Canadian Media Reaction to the Spanish Civil War 1936–1939*. Ottawa: Steel Rail Publishing, 1988.

Petryshyn, J. "Class Conflict and Civil Liberties: The Origins and Activities of the Canadian Labour Defense League, 1925–1940," *Labour* 10, Autumn 1982.

———. "R.B. Bennett and the Communists: 1930–1935," *Journal of Canadian Studies* 9, no.4, 1974.

Pimlotte, Ralph. "Closing Relief Camps Sparks Riot," *Briarpatch*, January/February 1983.

———. "Life in Saskatoon During the Hard Times," *Briarpatch*, March 1983.

Pitsula, James C. *Let the Family Flourish: A History of the Family Service Bureau of Regina, 1913–1982*. Regina: Family Service Bureau, 1982.

Powell, T.D.J. "Northern Settlement, 1929–1935," *Saskatchewan History* 30, 1977.

Power, Chubby [Charles G.]. *A Party Politician: The Memoirs of Chubby Power*. Toronto: Macmillan of Canada, 1966.

Prang, Margaret. "The Origins of Public Broadcasting in Canada," *Canadian Historical Review* 46, no.1, 1965.

Purvis, Arthur B. "Obligations of Government Towards Social Security," *Child and Family Welfare* 13, no.3, 1937.

Quinn, H.F. "The Bogey of Fascism in Quebec," *Dalhousie Review* 18, no.3, 1938–39.

Rasporich, Anthony. "Tomo Cacic: Rebel Without a Country," *Canadian Ethnic Studies* 10, no.2, 1978.

Reed, James. *From Private Vice to Public Virtue: The Birth Control Movement and American Society Since 1830*. New York: Basic Books, 1978.

Reid, Escott. "The Canadian Election of 1935," *American Political Science Review* 30, 1936.

Repo, Satu. "Lakehead in the Thirties: A Labour Militant Remembers," *This Magazine* 13, no.3, 1979.

Roberts, Barbara. "Shovelling Out the Mutinous: Political Deportations from Canada before 1936," *Labour/Le Travail* 18, Fall 1986.

——— . *Whence They Came: Deportation from Canada, 1900-1935*. Ottawa: University of Ottawa Press, 1988.

Roberts, Leslie. "What Happened in Quebec," *Maclean's*, 1 December 1949.

Roddan, Andrew. *God in the Jungles*. Vancouver, [1931].

Russell, P.A. "The Co-operative Government's Response to the Depression, 1930-34," *Saskatchewan History* 3, 1950.

Ryan, Oscar. *Deported!* Toronto: Canadian Labour Defense League, 1932.

——— . *Eight Men Speak*. Toronto: Progressive Arts Clubs of Canada, n.d.

——— . *Tim Buck: A Conscience for Canada*. Toronto: Progress Books, 1975.

S. "Embryo Fascism in Quebec," *Foreign Affairs* 16, no.3, 1937-38.

Safarian, A.E. *The Canadian Economy in the Great Depression*. Toronto: McClelland and Stewart, 1970 (reprint).

Scarrow, Howard. *Canada Votes*. New Orleans: Hauser Press, 1962.

Schultz, Harold J. "Aberhart: The Organization Man," *Alberta Historical Review* 7, no.2, 1959.

——— . "The Social Credit Back-Benchers Revolt, 1937," *Canadian Historical Review* 41, no.1, 1960.

Scott, F.R. "Communists, Senators and All That," *Canadian Forum* 12, no.136, 1932.

——— . *A New Endeavour: Selected Political Essays, Letters and Addresses*. Toronto: University of Toronto Press, 1986.

——— . "The Trial of the Toronto Communists," *Queen's Quarterly* 39, August 1932.

Shachtman, Tom. *The Day America Crashed*. New York: G.P. Putnam's, 1979.

Sinclair, Gordon. *Will the Real Gordon Sinclair Please Stand Up*. Toronto: McClelland and Stewart, 1966.

530

Sinclair, Peter. "The Saskatchewan CCF: Ascent to Power and the Decline of Socialism," *Canadian Historical Review* 54, no.4, 1973.

Smith, A.E. *All My Life*. Toronto: Progress Books, 1949.

Smith, Janet Adam. *John Buchan: A Biography*. London: Rupert Hart-Davis, 1965.

Snow, Duart. "The Holmes Foundry Strike of March 1937: We'll Give Their Jobs to White Men!" *Ontario History* 69, no.1, 1977.

Spry, Graham. "The Origins of Public Broadcasting in Canada: A Comment," *Canadian Historical Review* 46, no.2, 1965.

Stacey, C.P. *Canada and the Age of Conflict: A History of Canadian External Policies, Vol. 2, 1921-1948, The Mackenzie King Era*. Toronto: University of Toronto Press, 1981.

——— . *A Very Double Life: The Private World of Mackenzie King*. Toronto: Macmillan of Canada, 1976.

Stephenson, Bill. "The Great Birth Control Trial," *Maclean's* 3 November 1957.

Stewart, Roderick. *Bethune*. Toronto: New Press, 1973.

Stewart, Sandy. *From Coast to Coast: A Personal History of Radio in Canada*. Toronto: CBC Enterprises, 1985.

Stortz, Gerald, with Eaton, Murray. "Pro Bono Publico: The Eastview Birth Control Trial," *Atlantis* 8, no.2, 1983.

Strong-Boag, Veronica. "The Girl of the New Day," *Labour* 4, no.4, 1979.

——— . *The New Day Recalled*. Toronto: Copp Clark Pitman, 1988.

——— . "Wages for Housework: Mothers' Allowance and the Beginnings of Social Security in Canada," *Journal of Canadian Studies* 14, no.1, 1979.

Struthers, James. *No Fault of Their Own: Unemployment and the Canadian Welfare State, 1914-1941*. Toronto: University of Toronto Press, 1983.

——— . "Prelude to Depression: The Federal Government and Unemployment, 1918-1929," *Canadian Historical Review* 58, no.3, 1977.

——— . "A Profession in Crisis: Charlotte Whitton and Canadian Social Work in the 1930s," *Canadian Historical Review* 62, no.2, 1981.

Stubbs, Roy St. George. *Prairie Portraits*. Toronto: McClelland and Stewart, 1954.

Swankey, Ben. "Reflections of a Communist: The 1935 Election," *Alberta History* 28, no. 4, 1980.

——— , and Sheils, Jean Evans. *"Work and Wages!" Semi-Documentary Account of the Life and Times of Arthur H. (Slim) Evans, 1890-1944*. Vancouver: Trade Union Research Bureau, 1977.

Swettenham, John. *McNaughton*. Toronto: Ryerson Press, 1968.

Thomas, Lewis H. (ed.). *The Making of a Socialist: The Recollections of T.C. Douglas*. Edmonton: University of Alberta Press, 1982.

Thompson, John Herd. "The Political Career of Ralph Webb," *Red River Valley Historian*, Summer 1976.

————, and Seager, Allen. *Canada 1922–1939: Decades of Discord*. Toronto: McClelland and Stewart, 1985.

Topping, C.W. *Canadian Penal Institutions*. Toronto: Ryerson Press, 1929.

Turner, Allan R. "How Saskatchewan Dealt with Her Dust Bowl," *Geographical Magazine* 28, no. 4, 1955.

Urquhart, M.C. *Historical Statistics of Canada*. Toronto: Macmillan of Canada, 1965.

Ward, Norman. "Hon. James Gardiner and the Liberal Party of Alberta, 1935–40," *Canadian Historical Review* 56, no.3, 1975.

Watkins, Ernest. *R.B. Bennett: A Biography*. Toronto: Kingswood House, 1963.

Watson, Louise. *She Never Was Afraid: The Biography of Annie Buller*. Toronto: Progress Books, 1976.

Weisbord, Merrily. *The Strangest Dream: Canadian Communists, the Spy Trials and the Cold War*. Toronto: Lester & Orpen Dennys, 1983.

Westin, Jeane. *Making Do: How Women Survived the '30s*. Chicago: Follett Publishing, 1976.

Wilbur, J.R.H. "The Bennett Administration 1930–1935," *Canadian Historical Association Booklet No. 24*, 1969.

———— (ed.). *The Bennett New Deal: Fraud or Portent?* Toronto: Copp Clark, 1968.

————. *H.H. Stevens, 1878–1973*. Toronto: University of Toronto Press, 1977.

————. "H.H. Stevens and R.B. Bennett, 1930–34," *Canadian Historical Review* 43, no.1, 1962.

————. "H.H. Stevens and the Reconstruction Party," *Canadian Historical Review* 45, no.1, 1964.

Williams, Fred C. *The Fifth Horseman*. Calgary: Pandarus Books, 1973.

Withrow, Oswald C.J. *Shackling the Transgressor*. Toronto: Thomas Nelson & Sons, 1933.

Young, Scott. *Gordon Sinclair: A Life ... And Then Some*. Toronto: Macmillan of Canada, 1987.

Young, Walter D. *The Anatomy of a Party: The National C.C.F., 1932–61*. Toronto: University of Toronto Press, 1969.

532

Index

534

535

538

540

Holden Building (Vancouver), 306, 308
Hollinger Mines, 402
Holmes Foundry, 401–2
Home Oil, 30
Hood (battleship), 509
Hoover, Herbert, quoted, 33–34
Hotel Camard (Marseille), 396
Hotel Georgia (Vancouver), 448, 450, 451
Hotel Isabella (Toronto), 461, 463
Hotel Vancouver, 26, 307, 448
Houck, Izzy, 89
Houde, Camillien, 490
House of Industry (Toronto), 179
Housing, 109–10, 131, 438
Howe, Clarence Decatur, 351, 508
Hudson's Bay Company (Vancouver store), 307–8, 331
Hugill, John, 425
Human rights, *see* Civil liberties and rights
Humphrey, Robert, 506
Humphrey family, 506
Hunter, Peter, 97, 98, 99, 390
Hutchison, Bruce, 15
Huxley, Aldous, 440
Hyde Park, 494
Hyduk, Mike, 388
Hydroelectric power, 26
Hyslop Gold Mines, 402

Ilsley, J.L., 381; quoted, 481
Immigration, 25, 26, 48, 77, 145, 350, 470, 472
Immigration Branch, 468, 471, 486
Imperial Conference (1930), 72
Imperial Economic Conference (1932), 136, 159–62, 163, 177
Imperial Oil, 30
Imperial Tobacco, 241
Imperial War Graves Commission, 377–78
Income tax, *see* Taxes
Independent Labour Party of Manitoba, 164
India, 58
Industrial Workers of the World (IWW), 297

Industry and Humanity, 59, 285
International Brigade, 388
International Committee for Volunteers, 393
International Labour Defense, 227
International Ladies' Garment Workers' Union, 291
International Nickel Co., 31, 34, 75
Investment, 23–24, 26, 29–30, 433; foreign, 52–53
Irvine, William, 206–7
Irving, John, 215–16, 217, 236
Isolationism, 375–76, 495, 497
Istrati, Konrad, 246, 247
Italy, 27, 51, 59, 510
Ives, W.C., 233

Jaffray, William Gladstone, 478–79
James, Mrs. Arthur, 378
James, Cyril, 429
Japan, 62, 126
Jeunesse Ouvrière Catholique, 363
Jews, 42, 58, 363, 364, 376, 415–16, 462, 463, 465–66, 467–68, 469–73, 496–97
Johnson, G.F., 458
Johnson, George, 192, 193
Johnson, Lilian, 290
Johnson, Main, 182
Johnstone Lake, Sask., 422
Judiciary Act Amendment Bill, 425
"Jungles," 83–84, 151, 152, 155–56, 510
Just Price, 235

Kamloops, B.C., 296, 298, 314
Kampf (newspaper), 42
Kamsack, Sask., 152
Kaufman, Alvin Ratz, 369–70, 373
Kaufman Rubber Co., 369
Keenleyside, Hugh, 62
Kellaway, Montagu, 22
Kellock, R.L., 289
Kelly, John Hall, 428
Ken (magazine), 465
Kennedy, William Walker, 260, 295
Kenney, Mart, 229, 359–60
Kenny, Mrs. Martin, 375
Keynes, John Maynard, 306, 433

544

547

548

551

553

and principles, 165–66; anti-Communist, 165, 225; missionery zeal, 166; and CCF, 205; attacked, 209; and radio, 235; and war, 500–503

Woodward's Department Store, 307, 310, 458

Woolworth's, 241–42, 388

Worker (newspaper), 86, 102, 121; quoted, 165

Workers' Economic Conference, 161

Workers' Party of Canada, 67

Workers' Unity League (WUL), 95, 99, 102, 111, 112, 121, 296, 298, 315

Workmen's compensation, 510

Works Progress Administration, 350

Work week, 100, 161, 242, 284

World War, First, *see* Wars

World War, Second, *see* Wars

World Youth Committee, 97

Wriedt, Mrs. Etta, 202, 203, 343

Wright, Mr. Justice, 124–25

Wright, William Henry, 402, 479

Wright Hargreaves Mine, 479

Wylie, Judge Edmund, 120

Yeigh, Frank, quoted, 43

Yellow Cab, 31

Yonge Street Mission, 50

Young Communist League, 95, 97, 121, 389–90, 456

Young Pioneers, 95

Yugoslavia, 144, 145

Yukon, 122, 299

Zacher, Joe (Vermilion Kid), 152–53

Zeidman, Morris, 372

Zubick, J.J., 424, 425

Zynchuk, Nick, 185

Arthur Evans

William Aberhart

Maurice

Norman Bethune